GREAT NECK LIBRARY

3 1266 21026 3661

D0850596

DISCARDED OR WITHDRAWN
GREAT NECK LIBRARY

STATION BRANCH LIBRARY

JUL 2 3 2013

GREAT NECK LIBRARY
GREAT NECK, NY 11023
(516) 466-8055
www.greatnecklibrary.org

■ United States Holocaust Memorial Museum
Center for Advanced Holocaust Studies

Documenting Life and Destruction
Holocaust Sources
in Context

SERIES EDITOR

Jürgen Matthäus

DOCUMENTING LIFE AND DESTRUCTION

HOLOCAUST SOURCES IN CONTEXT

This groundbreaking series provides a new perspective on history using first-hand accounts of the lives of those who suffered through the Holocaust, those who perpetrated it, and those who witnessed it as bystanders. The United States Holocaust Memorial Museum's Center for Advanced Holocaust Studies presents a wide range of documents from different archival holdings, expanding knowledge about the lives and fates of Holocaust victims and making those resources broadly available to the general public and scholarly communities for the first time.

BOOKS IN THE SERIES

A project of the

United States Holocaust Memorial Museum

SARA J. BLOOMFIELD
Director

Center for Advanced Holocaust Studies

PAUL A. SHAPIRO
Director

JÜRGEN MATTHÄUS
Director, Applied Research

under the auspices of the

Academic Committee
of the
United States Holocaust Memorial Council

ALVIN H. ROSENFELD, *Chair*

Doris L. Bergen	Peter Hayes	John T. Pawlikowski
Richard Breitman	Sara Horowitz	Harry Reicher
Christopher R. Browning	Steven T. Katz	Aron Rodrigue
David Engel	William S. Levine	George D. Schwab
Willard A. Fletcher	Deborah E. Lipstadt	Nechama Tec
Zvi Y. Gitelman	Michael R. Marrus	James E. Young

This publication has been made possible by
support from

The Conference on Jewish Material Claims
Against Germany

The William S. and Ina Levine Foundation

The Blum Family Foundation

and

Dr. Alfred Munzer and Mr. Joel Wind

The authors have worked to provide clear information about the provenance of each document and illustration included here. In some instances, particularly for journals and newspapers no longer in print, we have been unable to verify the existence or identity of any present copyright owners. If notified of any item inadvertently credited wrongly, we will include updated credit information in reprints of this work.

Documenting Life and Destruction
Holocaust Sources in Context

JEWISH RESPONSES TO PERSECUTION

Volume II
1938–1940

Alexandra Garbarini

with Emil Kerenji, Jan Lambertz, and Avinoam Patt

Advisory Committee:

Christopher R. Browning
David Engel
Sara Horowitz
Steven T. Katz
Aron Rodrigue
Alvin H. Rosenfeld
Nechama Tec

AltaMira Press
in association with the United States Holocaust Memorial Museum
2011

GREAT NECK LIBRARY

For USHMM:
Project Manager: Mel Hecker
Researcher: Ryan Farrell
Translators: Ania Drimer, Marcel Drimer, Gideon Frieder, Kathleen Luft, Margit Meissner, Isaac Nehama, Stephen Pallavicini, Michael Rosenbush, Hadar Sadeh, Stephen Scala, Samuel Schalkowsky, Veronika Szabó, Nicole Weismann, and Leah Wolfson.
Research Assistants and Interns: Brian Berman, Anna Borejsza-Wysocka, Ivana Bradaric, Barbara Czachorska Jones, Ulrike Ecker, Ilona Gerbakher, Diana Gergel, Anca Glont, Hannah Ewing, Rachel Heidmann, Rachel Jablon, Alexandra Karambelas, Melissa Kravetz, Anya Nowakowski, Romy Proschmann, Frédéric Vagneron, and Greg Wilkowski.

Published by AltaMira Press
A division of Rowman & Littlefield Publishers, Inc.
A wholly owned subsidary of The Rowman & Littlefield Publishing Group, Inc.
4501 Forbes Boulevard, Suite 200, Lanham, Maryland 20706
http://www.altamirapress.com

Estover Road, Plymouth PL6 7PY, United Kingdom

Copyright © 2011 by AltaMira Press

All rights reserved. No part of this book may be reproduced in any form or by any electronic or mechanical means, including information storage and retrieval systems, without written permission from the publisher, except by a reviewer who may quote passages in a review.

British Library Cataloguing in Publication Information Available
Library of Congress Cataloging-in-Publication Data

Garbarini, Alexandra, 1973–.
  Jewish Responses to Persecution, 1938–1940 / Alexandra Garbarini; with Emil Kerenji, Jan Lambertz, and Avinoam Patt.
    p. cm. — (Documenting life and destruction: Holocaust sources in context)
  Includes bibliographical references and index.
  ISBN 978-0-7591-2039-6 (cloth : alk. paper) — ISBN 978-0-7591-2041-9 (ebook)
  1. Jews—Germany—History—1938–1940. 2. Jews—Persecutions—Germany—History—20th Century. 3. Jews—Germany—Social conditions—20th century. 4. Germany—Ethnic relations—History—20th century. 5. Antisemitism—Germany—History—20th century. 6. Holocaust, Jewish (1938–1940)—Germany. I. Title.
  DS134.255.M38 2010
  940.53'18—dc22   20110471

♾™ The paper used in this publication meets the minimum requirements of American National Standard for Information Sciences—Permanence of Paper for Printed Library Materials, ANSI/NISO Z39.48-1992.

Printed in the United States of America

"I feel like I'm falling ever more deeply into the night, the black, hopeless night. Hopeless?! False! Day must come at some time after all, I will be able to breathe again the fresh air of daybreak and the happiness of love. Everything sleeps in the meantime."

— Lutek Orenbach, Tomaszów Mazowiecki, Generalgouvernement, to
Edith Blau, Minden, Germany, October 19, 1940 (see document 12–6)

The following documents are reprinted with permission:

Document 2-5 © Archiv der Israelitischen Kultusgemeinde Wien; Document 3-4 © Schocken Books, a division of Random House, Inc.; Document 4-3 © Oneworld Publications; Document 7-19 © Emil Dorian; Document 8-18 © Wayne State University Press; Document 10-3 © Am Oved Publishers Ltd. and Yad Vashem.

For further provenance information see document headers.

Front cover: (top row left to right) USHMMPA WS# 41033, courtesy of American Jewish Joint Distribution Committee; USHMMA, RG 15.079M, Żydowski Instytut Historyczny im. Emanuela Ringelbluma collection; USHMMPA WS# 31515, courtesy of Bildarchiv Preussischer Kulturbesitz; (bottom row left to right) USHMMPA WS# 86548A, courtesy of Samuel Soltz; USHMMPA WS# 23569, courtesy of Mary Catalina (Siegmund Sobel collection); USHMMPA WS# 99687, courtesy of Inge Engelhard Sadan.

CONTENTS

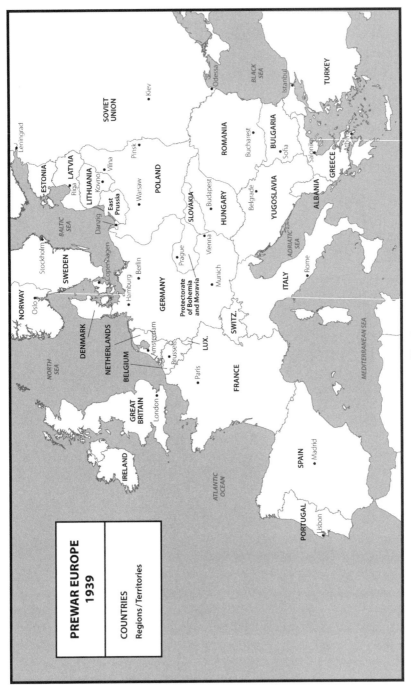

PREWAR EUROPE
1939

COUNTRIES
Regions/Territories

Map 1

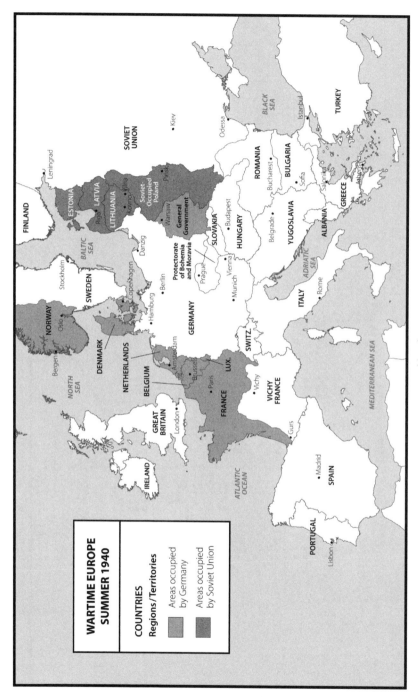

WARTIME EUROPE
SUMMER 1940

COUNTRIES
Regions/Territories

Areas occupied
by Germany

Areas occupied
by Soviet Union

Map 2

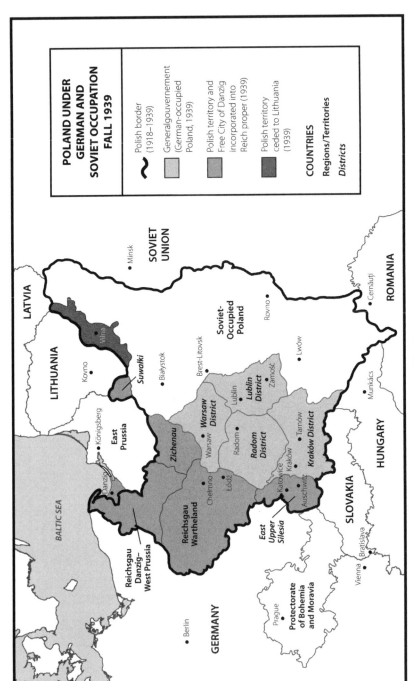

POLAND UNDER
GERMAN AND
SOVIET OCCUPATION
FALL 1939

Polish border
(1918–1939)

Generalgouvernement
(German-occupied
Poland, 1939)

Polish territory and
Free City of Danzig
incorporated into
Reich proper (1939)

Polish territory
ceded to Lithuania
(1939)

COUNTRIES

Regions/Territories

Districts

Map 3

READER'S GUIDE

FOR UNDERSTANDING the Holocaust, documents generated at the time of persecution have a special significance and expressiveness, particularly those stemming from the hands of victims rather than perpetrators.[1] This series attests to that fact. Such documents recover the agency and subjectivity of those too often seen merely as the objects of Nazi policy. In them emerges the diversity and individuality of millions of women, men, and children whom their tormentors tried to treat as faceless, undifferentiated "Jews." And they are evidence of the uncertainty, confusion, and disbelief of those confronted by measures and processes that until then had been unimaginable and only in retrospect have become an irremovable part of our mental landscape. The emphasis in the volumes of this series is on these contemporary witness statements, on sources created close to the events by those who, regardless of their self-identification, were discriminated against as Jews.

This series presents a selection of documents in the English language to which university teachers can turn for a firsthand sense of the breadth and diversity of Jewish responses to persecution in the years leading up to and during World War II. In so doing, it follows in the footsteps of earlier publications

---

1. For more on this series' rationale, the meanings of "Jewish responses," and the criteria for including sources, see Jürgen Matthäus and Mark Roseman, *Jewish Responses to Persecution,* vol. 1: *1933–1938* (Lanham, MD: AltaMira Press in association with the USHMM, 2010), xiii–xxi.

and complements recent source editions with different foci.[2] If the volumes in this series achieve nothing else, they will hopefully convey the sheer richness, vitality, and depth of Jewish witness records preserved in archives and libraries across the globe and stimulate interest in further research.

While the series makes no claim to comprehensiveness as far as the entire history of the Holocaust is concerned, it does integrate the selected documents within their broader context. Each volume is organized chronologically, while allowing for thematic clusters to feature key topics outside a rigid time line. Chapter introductions and analyses interweaving the reports, letters, diaries, photographs, and contemporary testimonies aim to deepen readers' understanding of the framework of antisemitic persecution, its central building blocks and impetus, and their impact on Jews' perceptions and actions. Annotations and a glossary round out the contents of each volume, offering useful suggestions for further study. We focus exclusively on sources of Jewish provenance, that is, on material produced by Jewish organizations and by Jewish men, women, or children inside and outside the countries dominated by Germany. We have tried to strike a balance between well-known, even iconic figures and those who have remained unknown in existing scholarship. Overall, we have opted for the latter. Indeed, our selection and contextualization of sources together aim at exploring new angles but also at reminding readers of the better-known aspects of the story. In trying to reconstruct Jewish agency for the period featured in this volume, we focus on broad questions of daily life and its diverse social, economic, cultural, and religious features. In so doing, we seek to contribute to an integrated history of the Holocaust, one that shifts the balance from the current prevalence of perpetrator studies to more victim-oriented research.[3]

---

2. Isaiah Trunk, *Jewish Responses to Nazi Persecution: Collective and Individual Behavior in Extremis* (New York: Stein & Day, 1979), presents the first English-language source compilation on the topic, but it has long been out of print. For different approaches to Jewish responses, see Philip Friedman, *Roads to Extinction: Essays on the Holocaust*, ed. Ada June Friedman (New York: Jewish Publication Society of America and the Conference on Jewish Social Studies, 1980); David G. Roskies, *The Literature of Destruction: Jewish Responses to Catastrophe* (Philadelphia: Jewish Publication Society, 1988); Monika Richarz, ed., *Jewish Life in Germany: Memoirs from Three Centuries* (Bloomington: Indiana University Press, 1991); Yehuda Bauer, *Jewish Reactions to the Holocaust* (Tel Aviv: MOD, 1989); Saul Friedländer, *Nazi Germany and the Jews* (New York: HarperCollins, 1997, 2007). The German-language source edition, *Die Verfolgung und Ermordung der europäischen Juden durch das nationalsozialistische Deutschland, 1933–1945* (Munich: Oldenbourg, 2008), aims at presenting a comprehensive compilation of documents on a broad range of Holocaust-related subjects with a heavy focus on perpetrators.

3. On the notion of writing an "integrated history" of the Holocaust and its importance as a corrective to the orientation toward studying perpetrators in most historical scholarship outside Israel, see Friedländer, *Nazi Germany*, vols. 1 and 2.

The documents included in this volume were originally written in a number of different languages. For foreign-language sources printed here in English, we have indicated in the document headers or in the footnotes whether we have produced our own translations or rely on translations drawn from other publications. The authors of this volume owe a great debt to a rich trove of postwar publications—monographs, edited diaries and collections of letters, specialized articles, survivor memoirs—as well as earlier document collections.[4] Where a reliable and accessible print version of a document already exists, we refer to it; more often, however, we provide our own translations in order to do justice to the original sources. Indeed, we have taken special care in the editorial process to avoid glossing over inconsistencies of logic in documents, which sometimes serves to simplify the story or adapts it to postwar interests. In a similar vein, we have made every effort to differentiate as clearly as possible between contemporary accounts (for instance, diaries) and postwar accounts (memoirs), although sometimes even the most assiduous research could not clarify the murky history of a particular archival collection.

Transliterations of text passages and words in non-Latin scripts follow established standards unless document authors have followed their own distinct formats. Many foreign-language terms used by commentators during the late 1930s and war years carry meanings that are difficult to capture in English. Sometimes they represent specific religious concepts or the peculiar, new—often racialized—bureaucratic terms of the Nazi state or wartime occupation regimes. Sometimes, however, they simply constitute the distinctive vocabularies of sentiment, identity, mood, and so forth that pertain to every language. The nuances of particular terms can be important for understanding both the rhetoric of public appeals and the language of private reflection. For this reason, in some cases we have indicated the difficulty of translation by adding the original word or phrase in brackets after the English version.

Geographical names also vary from language to language and changed repeatedly during the war years to reflect the shifting power constellations. Following the German annexation of Austria in 1938 and takeover of Czechoslovakia and Poland in 1939, Nazi planners and occupation officials renamed entire regions to conform to their visions of a new order in Europe.

---

4. Of particular value are, to name but a few, the studies by Raul Hilberg, *The Destruction of the European Jews,* 3rd. ed. (1961; New Haven, CT: Yale University Press, 2003); Isaiah Trunk, *Judenrat: The Jewish Councils in Eastern Europe under Nazi Occupation* (New York: Macmillan, 1972); Christopher R. Browning with contributions by Jürgen Matthäus, *The Origins of the Final Solution: The Evolution of Nazi Jewish Policy, September 1939–March 1942* (Lincoln and Jerusalem: University of Nebraska Press and Yad Vashem, 2004); and Friedländer, *Nazi Germany,* vols. 1 and 2.

Consequently, period-specific place names and geopolitical designations can be found in the documents as well as in the chapter texts. The index provides guidance on multiple or alternative spellings of these cities and regions. This volume also includes maps of prewar Europe, occupied Poland, and Europe in 1940 to orient readers in the basic geography of the period under discussion.

A number of names, events, concepts, and organizations appear in boldface throughout the volume when they are first mentioned in a chapter. This indicates that readers can find further information on that term in the glossary at the end of the volume. Using the rich resources of the United States Holocaust Memorial Museum's library and archives, we have attempted to track the ultimate fate of each author of a document through the war years. Some of this information appears in the glossary and some of it in footnotes to the original documents. Regrettably, we were unable to determine the wartime fate of every individual who makes an appearance in these pages.

The documents in this volume have been printed in a distinct format to set them apart from our commentary. We have tried to reproduce the original texts as faithfully as possible and worked to provide clear information about the provenance of each document. We have standardized emphases used by the authors of the documents by underlining them. In cases where we could not print a document in its entirety, we have marked any omitted text with ellipses ([. . .]).

Readers will find two other resources at the back of the volume to orient them in the complex events of this period. We have provided a basic chronology of important events that unfolded in the years covered by this volume. Our bibliography also offers the reader an opportunity to explore the topics and events touched on here in greater depth. In addition to the most important publications used in producing this volume, the bibliography presents suggestions for further reading.

Forthcoming volumes in the series:

Volume III: Jewish Responses to Persecution 1941–1942
Volume IV: Jewish Responses to Persecution 1942–1944
Volume V: Jewish Responses to Persecution 1944–1946

ABBREVIATIONS

(Bold indicates a Glossary term.)

AJJDC, the AJDC, JDC, the Joint	**American Jewish Joint Distribution Committee**
AJYB	*American Jewish Year Book*
BAB	German National Archive (Bundesarchiv), Berlin
CEKABE, Tze-ka-be	Central Organization of Societies for the Support of Noninterest Credit and Promotion of Productive Work
CENTOS	Central Office of the Union of Societies for Care of Orphans and Abandoned Children (Centrala Związku Towarzystw Opieki nad Sierotami i Dziećmi Opuszczonymi)
Centralverein	Central Association of German Citizens of the Jewish Faith (Centralverein deutscher Staatsbürger jüdischen Glaubens)
CSHJR	Center for the Study of the History of the Jews from Romania, Bucharest
Ezra	self-help organization in Kovno/Kaunas, Lithuania (Hebrew, "help," "aid")
FZGH	Research Institute for Contemporary History (Forschungsstelle für Zeitgeschichte), Hamburg
Gestapo	Secret State Police (Geheime Staatspolizei)

H&GS	*Holocaust and Genocide Studies*
HIAS	Hebrew Sheltering and Immigrant Aid Society
HICEM	Jewish aid organization, established in 1927 by merger of HIAS, JCA, and the United Committee for Jewish Emigration
Hilfsverein	Relief Association of German Jews (Hilfsverein der deutschen Juden)
ITS	International Tracing Service, Bad Arolsen, Germany (copy of records at USHMM)
JA	Jewish Agency, **Jewish Agency for Palestine**
JCA, ICA	Jewish Colonization Association
Joint	see AJJDC
JSS	**Jewish Social Self-Help** (Jüdische Soziale Selbsthilfe)
JTA	**Jewish Telegraphic Agency**
KK	**Coordinating Commission of Jewish Aid and Civic Societies** (Koordinir komisiye fun yidishe hilf- un sotsiale gezelshaftn)
LBINY	Leo Baeck Institute Archive, New York
LBIYB	*Leo Baeck Institute Yearbook*
NARA	U.S. National Archives and Records Administration
NKVD	People's Commissariat for Internal Affairs (Narodnyy komissariat vnutrennikh del)
NYPL	New York Public Library
OSE	Children's Relief Association (Œuvre de secours aux enfants)
POW	prisoner of war
PSAŁ	Polish State Archives (Przełożony Starszeństwa Żydów w Getcie Łódzkim)
Reichsvereinigung	Reich Association of Jews in Germany (**Reichsvereinigung der Juden in Deutschland**)
RELICO	Relief Committee for the War-Stricken Jewish Population
Ring.	see ŻIH Ring
RM	German currency (Reichsmark)
RSHA	Reich Security Main Office (**Reichssicherheitshauptamt**), Berlin
SA	Nazi Storm Troopers (Sturmabteilung)

SAM	Special Archive Moscow (Osobyi Archive; Rossiiskii gosudarstvennyi voennyi arkhiv, Russian State Military Archive)
SD	"intelligence service" of the Nazi Party (Sicherheitsdienst)
SS	Schutzstaffel
TOZ	Society for the Protection of the Health of the Jewish Population in Poland (Towarzystwo Ochrony Zdrowia Ludności Żydowskiej w Polsce)
Tze-ka-be	see CEKABE
USHMM	United States Holocaust Memorial Museum, Washington, DC
USHMMA	USHMM Archive
USHMMPA	USHMM Photo Archive
WJC	**World Jewish Congress**
WL	Wiener Library, London
YIVO	Jewish Scientific Institute, Institute for Jewish Research (Yidisher Visnshaftlekher Institut), Vilna, Lithuania, later New York
YVA	Yad Vashem Archive, Jerusalem
YVS	*Yad Vashem Studies*
ŻIH	Jewish Historical Institute (Żydowski Instytut Historyczny), Warsaw
ŻIH Ring.	Ringelblum Archive, Jewish Historical Institute, Warsaw

Volume Introduction
Jewish Life in Europe after Five Years of Nazi Rule

A "REPORT ON a Visit to Germany" marked "SECRET" and dated November 21–24, 1938, appears in the records preserved by the **Jewish Telegraphic Agency**, an international news service with offices in capital cities in Europe and the Americas. The anonymous writer offers an eyewitness account of the damage and violence unleashed on the Jewish population of the Third Reich less than two weeks earlier: "Overnight, German Jewry has been destroyed. The property of the Jews is being destroyed or confiscated, their synagogues burnt, their organizations closed, a considerable part of the adult male population sent to concentration and labour camps. [. . .] What happened on November 10th in Germany was a carefully and systematically planned and prepared pogrom of an extent hitherto unheard of in the history of the Jewish people." Yet, even possessing inside knowledge of the extent of the destruction suffered by German Jewry and expressing certainty about the impetus behind its perpetration, this writer could not determine its meaning for the future: "Is there a definite line of policy adopted by the German Government, in other words, is emigration or rather evacuation the real goal of all these persecutions? It is difficult to give to that question a definite and equivocal [*sic*] reply."[1] In the aftermath of this countrywide pogrom in the closing weeks of 1938, this Jewish official, like Jews throughout Germany, Europe, and the rest of the world, tried to discern the Nazi regime's goals in order to chart a future course of action.

---

1. "A Report on a Visit to Germany," November 21–24, 1938, USHMMA RG 11.001 M25 (SAM 674-1-109a), reel 106.

In our shared historical memory, the November pogrom of 1938 clearly demarcated a new phase in German anti-Jewish policy. That it came to be referred to widely by its own appellation, "*Kristallnacht*," and Jews and non-Jews in the twenty-first century continue to mount ceremonies annually to commemorate it underscores its significance in our postwar understanding of the history of the Holocaust.[2] From 1933 to 1938, we are taught, the Nazis gained and consolidated power. They suppressed potential forces of opposition, replaced preexisting social and professional associations with Nazi movements, organized a powerful propaganda machine that extended into all areas of cultural production, and launched an enormous military operation. And all along the way, they steadily began to stigmatize and isolate German Jews, in propaganda and in law. But "*Kristallnacht*," with its uncontained destruction, we imagine, marked an unmistakable move into violence. In retrospect, that violence plainly indicated the shift in how Jews would be treated under the Reich from that point forward. The glass broken that night, we are told, spoke loudly of Nazi intentions to break all bonds of humane obligation in their treatment of the Jews in their midst.

While we in the next century are inclined to interpret "*Kristallnacht*" as a clear indicator of the Nazi embrace of antisemitic violence that would henceforth define the Reich, at the time the events were read differently. From the perspective of contemporaries, there was but one certain conclusion to draw from November 9 to 10, 1938. As **Victor Klemperer** spelled out in a diary entry soon thereafter, for Jews in the Reich, "there is no longer any choice: We must leave."[3] Yet, even as German and Austrian Jews tried to find the swiftest route out of the country and suffered the financial, physical, and emotional toll of the destruction, neither they nor Jews outside the Reich saw the pogrom as foreshadowing a clear program of attack. They struggled to interpret the meaning of what they had experienced.

This book, like the other volumes in this series, *Jewish Responses to Persecution*, aims to illuminate that very challenge of interpretation. Looking back across decades, we of course think we know what each act of the Reich meant, how it laid the foundation in some way for the coming of the "Final Solution." In thinking that way, however, we project a false clarity and teleology onto the uncertain actions of Nazi policy makers who themselves could not

---

2. For a history of the appellation "*Kristallnacht*" and the events of early November 1938, see Alan E. Steinweis, *Kristallnacht 1938* (Cambridge, MA: Belknap Press, 2009).

3. Victor Klemperer, diary entry for December 3, 1938, in *I Will Bear Witness: A Diary of the Nazi Years, 1933–1941* (New York: Random House, 1998), 278.

have predicted where their efforts would lead. Even more, though, we erase the significance of the very vital and demanding task that Jews around the world were forced to undertake: trying to make sense of, trying to understand, trying to respond to what was happening. To set aside our assumptions that Jews should somehow have known what was coming and instead to pay heed to their words as they struggled to interpret the actions of the Reich is to conceive of Jews as historical agents. In so doing, this book offers a new account of the critical period from late 1938 to the end of 1940, when Europe descended into war and antisemitic persecution reached a stage that engulfed not only Jews in the Reich but also Jews living in countries across the European continent. By focusing squarely on the efforts Jews made both to grasp what was happening and to formulate responses, we attempt to suspend what we know about how this story ended and to open a window onto how Jews in the past experienced their plight.

Being attentive to contemporaneous Jewish perspectives has the potential to alter our conceptions of Holocaust history in several ways. First, it suggests alternative periodizations of the years from 1933 to 1946. Indeed, this volume's time frame—from the aftermath of "*Kristallnacht*" in late 1938 to the sealing off of the Warsaw ghetto in the final months of 1940—departs from the standard chronology that positions the start of World War II as a watershed. Contemporaries certainly perceived the German assault on Poland on September 1, 1939, as a dramatic caesura in world history. For Polish Jewish civilians, the war immediately rendered them vulnerable to brutal mistreatment and sometimes outright murder by German military and SS or by ethnic Germans who were formerly their neighbors. Furthermore, the start of the world war increased pressure on Jewish communities in other parts of Europe, especially in countries with strong antisemitic traditions. Nevertheless, in commencing the volume in late 1938, we seek to underscore the asynchronies of this history when written from the vantage point of Jewish communities in Europe and the world. As the chapters in this volume indicate, different time lines and different significant developments existed for different Jewish communities. Moreover, the pace of antisemitic persecution varied substantially. Two examples that connect the first volume of this series to the present one will suffice. For German Jews, the Nazis' coming to power in 1933 commenced the gradual tightening of the noose. By contrast, for Austrian Jews, the antisemitic acts accompanying the Nazi incorporation of Austria into the Reich in March 1938 hit them like a thunderclap. While the sources presented in this volume attest to a clear progression of persecution over the course of the months between "*Kristallnacht*" and the outbreak of war and during the first year and a half of the war, they also reflect vast differences in the timing of measures affecting Jewish communities, groups, and individuals within and beyond the German grasp. And most significantly from our perspective, avoiding a standard chronology reflects our efforts to think our way into the tenuous and confusing nature of Jews' situations as they struggled to respond to the deeds of their governments and fellow citizens.

Second, being attentive to the voices of Jewish men, women, and organizations from the period of late 1938 to 1940 has also compelled us to broaden the geographical scope of this second volume of the series. When the glass began to break on "*Kristallnacht*," the sound echoed around the globe. Even though Jews in Vienna and Berlin were struck more directly, Jews in Warsaw, London, Paris, New York, and Jerusalem all tried to make sense of the events and to formulate responses of some kind. In part they did so because they identified with the Jews of Germany. At the least, Jewish communities became more drawn into the refugee crisis that had predated "*Kristallnacht*" but now grew more acute as the numbers of Jews desperate to flee the Reich spiraled. As a result, Jews scattered across the world in locales as far from Europe as Shanghai and Latin America found their own situations in their respective countries rendered more vulnerable and their sense of connection to events in Nazi territory intensified. And as the reach of the Reich expanded so fantastically from 1938 through 1940, their vulnerability only grew. Indeed, the Jewish history of these years is best studied as a transnational history, for national frameworks alone cannot do justice to the complexity of interactions across borders by Jewish organizations and families in this period. This second volume, then, features Jewish voices from Germany and Austria, some of whom already appeared in the preceding volume. But it also extends beyond the Reich's beleaguered Jewish communities to feature the perspectives of native and refugee Jews in western and southeastern Europe and around the world.

At the same time, the geographic heart of this book rests in Poland. In 1939, Poland was home to the largest population of Jews in Europe outside the Soviet Union. As we will see, stigmatization, displacement, dispossession, and worse measures exacted a terrible toll on Polish Jews beginning with the military campaign and early phase of German rule. Half the chapters here will introduce Polish Jews who speak to us from the pages of diaries and letters, from clandestine reports and testimonies, from the correspondence of Jewish agencies and leaders, as well as in the visual language of photographs and other images produced at the time. Our decision to focus so heavily on Poland reflects our reading of contemporary sources that urgently drew attention to the plight of Polish Jewry. Well before German anti-Jewish policies turned genocidal, Polish Jews and Jewish onlookers described the extent of the destruction in Poland as having "no parallel" and as "the greatest tragedy in the entire history of Israel."[4] In hindsight, such assessments of what was befalling Jews in Poland in 1939 may strike us as having been astute, even premonitory. Yet, our aim in placing Poland at the center of this volume is not to suggest that people could and did imagine genocide looming, but rather to stress—as did contemporary commentators—the unprecedented nature of Nazi actions in Poland in the first two years of the war. Subsequent developments have tended to overshadow that historical reality.

Third and last, revisiting the history of these two years through the lens of Jewish sources foregrounds not only the range of Jewish responses to persecution but also the diversity of individuals and communities being lumped together by antisemitic policies as "Jews." This book—and indeed this series as a whole—eschews the notion of Jews as having been a unified group with a single destiny. Not even during the war, in places under German hegemony, did personal differences cease to matter. Age, gender, family situation, education, economic means, communal standing, ideological conviction, religious belief, national framework, and wartime situation influenced how people interpreted the meaning of German aggression for their lives and the lives of other Jews, as well as the possibilities they perceived for agency. As the foregoing list reflects, Jews' responses to their persecution were the outgrowth of modern Jewish history, which "came into play on different levels and in different settings," as much as they were the product of the Reich's policies.[5] These factors and the ways they shaped Jewish responses emerge in each chapter of this book, from individual attempts to flee the Reich in the early months of 1939, Poland in September 1939, or Belgium and northern France in May 1940, to the strategies people pursued to evade, protest, or mitigate the effects of the antisemitic laws and decrees introduced in many different countries in Europe as early as 1938 and intensifying with the extension of Germany's military domination of the continent in 1940.[6]

---

4. Chaim A. Kaplan, diary entry for March 10, 1940, in *Scroll of Agony: The Warsaw Diary of Chaim A. Kaplan*, ed. Abraham I. Katsh (Bloomington: Indiana University Press in association with the USHMM, 1999), 129; "Review of the Year 5700—Poland," *AJYB 5701* 42 (1940): 365.

5. Dan Michman, "Understanding the Jewish Dimension of the Holocaust," in *The Fate of the European Jews, 1939–1945: Continuity or Contingency?*, ed. Jonathan Frankel (New York: Oxford University Press, 1997), 228–31, 240.

6. For a lengthier discussion of the historical and theoretical considerations of using Jewish source materials to study the Holocaust, see Alexandra Garbarini, *Numbered Days: Diaries and the Holocaust* (New Haven, CT: Yale University Press, 2006), 3–11.

The chapters that follow reflect our effort to approach the study of the past from the perspective of Jewish historical actors. What was the spectrum of Jewish perceptions and actions under Nazi domination, and how did those affected directly or standing on the outside view the situation? What possibilities did Jews have at their disposal to influence their fates, and how did they make use of them? Not surprisingly, with experiences so diverse, the answers supplied by the documents often remain partial, varied, and inconclusive. Nevertheless, this volume's twelve chapters, divided into four parts, track the trajectory of German expansion and anti-Jewish policies chronologically, attesting to a clear progression of persecution over time and space. In addition, they reflect the vast differences in the responses of Jewish communities, groups, and individuals within and beyond the Germans' grasp, differences that resulted both from the unevenness of the Reich's policy toward Jews and Jews' own varied backgrounds, traditions, expectations, and life histories.

As discussed in Part I, a massive radicalization of Nazi anti-Jewish policies followed the Germany-wide pogrom of November 1938. We know today that the aim of those policies continued to be forced emigration, which heightened the already intense refugee crisis. Observers outside the Reich—a selection of whom, from Poland, Great Britain, France, the United States, and Holland, feature in chapter 1—harbored few doubts about the Nazis' determination to follow through with a "solution to the Jewish question" by pushing as many Jews as possible over the border. At the same time, Jewish writers interpreted the meaning of the violence directed at German and Austrian Jews in light of different historical, theological, and political frameworks, depending on their own orientations. Chapter 2 explores the aftermath of "*Kristallnacht*" from the perspective of Jews in the Reich. What had previously seemed to many German Jews a decision about emigration now became a matter of flight. Indeed, documentation generated after 1933, some of which appears in Volume I of this series, shows how German Jewish leaders grasped, within less than three years of Hitler's appointment to power, that Jewish life in Germany had no future. Running contrary to the stereotypical postwar image of a highly assimilated German Jewry unable or unwilling to understand what the Nazis were up to, Jewish organizations encouraged those who could to emigrate, and, indeed, half of the Reich's Jewish population did leave before the beginning of the war. Nevertheless, the trauma of having to relinquish their roots in and identification with Germany ran deep. They often carried that sensibility to their new places of residence. Lacking, however, was not German, Austrian, and, as of March 1939, Czech Jews' determination to leave German-controlled central Europe, but opportunities to do so. Germany's neighbors, as well as more distant countries, remained loathe to open their gates for more than a few select groups, such as famous artists and intellectuals, persons of wealth, relatives of their own citizens, and children who had to leave their parents behind in order to escape. For those who remained in the Reich, as depicted in chapter 3, local Jewish organizations, with the help of Jewish organizations abroad, provided support for a population confronting worsening poverty, marginalization, and stigmatization as the "enemy" of the "people's community." Individuals relied upon the social welfare furnished by organizations and also drew on other coping strategies, some personal and some communal, in their efforts to get through the indignities and hardships of everyday life.

Part II addresses some of the immediate consequences of the outbreak of war, focusing on the situation of Jews in Poland during and after the German invasion. September 1, 1939, marked first and foremost not the onset of a specific "war against the Jews" but rather the beginning of the war in Europe—indeed, as some historians see it, a "war of destruction" partly prefiguring the aggressiveness of the German attack on the Soviet Union in June 1941.[7] Already in the first week of its campaign, the **Wehrmacht** had occupied vast areas of Poland. The Polish army resisted fiercely, hoping for help from France and Great Britain after they declared war on Germany. Yet Poland found itself outmaneuvered and overwhelmed, especially after the Soviet Union—Germany's ally since August 23, 1939—crossed the border from the east on September 17, ostensibly to protect the Ukrainian and Belorussian populations of eastern Poland. Warsaw capitulated on September 28, 1939, and the fighting concluded in early October.[8]

The German military's swift advance had a massive impact on the civilian population, even where it did not target them directly. The Wehrmacht's onslaught affected the Jewish minority, with 3.5 million men, women, and children comprising roughly 10 percent of the overall population in 1939, in much the same manner as the rest of the Polish population. Yet, with the ideological image of the "Jewish enemy" much more firmly established in the German

---

7. See Alexander B. Rossino, *Hitler Strikes Poland: Blitzkrieg, Ideology, and Atrocity* (Lawrence: University Press of Kansas, 2003); Jochen Böhler, *Auftakt zum Vernichtungskrieg: Die Wehrmacht in Polen 1939* (Frankfurt am Main: Fischer Verlag, 2006); Klaus-Michael Mallmann and Bogdan Musial, eds., *Genesis des Genozids: Polen, 1939–1941* (Darmstadt: WBG, 2004).

8. See Gerhard L. Weinberg, *A World at Arms: A Global History of World War II* (Cambridge: Cambridge University Press, 1994), 48–64.

mind than the post-World War I goal of eliminating the "Polish problem," it was not surprising that executions carried out by German military and police units targeted a disproportionate number of Jews, mostly men of military age or prisoners of war.[9] Chapter 4 covers the issue of how Polish Jews perceived the first weeks of the war and related their experiences to those of their Polish non-Jewish compatriots. It details the varying degrees of confusion and disruption of daily life, most visibly expressed in the stream of women, men, and children attempting to escape from the war zone in a chaotic mass exodus. Overall, Jews took to the roads in larger proportion than Polish civilians; they were aware of Hitler's measures against German Jews and sensed that they had more to fear from the advancing army. As chapter 5 documents, heading east made sense to many Jews, initially because the Germans were advancing from the west and later because the area occupied by the Red Army seemed to offer the possibility of greater protection.

While escape became a mass phenomenon in the first stage of the war, many Jews in Poland lacked either the conviction that the uncertainty of refugee existence was preferable to life under German occupation or the means to leave their homes. The majority of Polish Jews thus remained in German-controlled territory. The late fall and early winter of 1940 exposed them to a new onslaught, no longer in the form of military operations but in the form of "Germanization" policies. Driven by ideas of race and space, the Nazi regime envisioned the revitalization of German national strength by a combination of territorial expansion into what they perceived as the uncivilized East and the improvement of the German people's imagined racial qualities through eugenics and other biopolitical means. Poland fell under Hitler's call for depopulation and resettlement. One part of the conquered territory, now called the **Generalgouvernement**, was turned into a dumping ground for Poles and Jews expelled from other parts of Poland that were being Germanized and incorpo-

---

9. According to Polish estimates, German bombs or artillery killed more than ten thousand civilians. Between early September and the end of October 1939 (the period in which the Wehrmacht was responsible before handing over authority to civilian agencies), more than sixteen thousand civilians were shot in mass executions. See Böhler, *Auftakt zum Vernichtungskrieg*, 241. By the end of 1939, German Security Police and local ethnic German auxiliaries had killed up to fifty thousand Polish citizens, with an estimated minimum of seven thousand Jews among them. See Rossino, *Hitler Strikes Poland*, 234.

rated into the Reich.[10] Even those Jews who were not subject to expulsion suffered the destruction of their livelihoods caused by the war's extensive material damage and the occupation authorities' rapid succession of measures aimed at exploiting Jews' labor and expropriating their property. The lack of sufficient material means to survive hit Jewish communities hard, particularly where they had lost their prewar leaders and faced a large influx of displaced Jews from other parts of Poland. Chapter 6 examines the efforts of beleaguered Jewish communities and relief organizations abroad—most notably the **American Jewish Joint Distribution Committee** (AJJDC or the Joint)—to accommodate these massive changes.

Jews outside Poland anxiously tracked news of the war and subsequent occupation. Part III shifts our attention from Poland to more than a dozen different countries across western, central, and southeastern Europe and beyond to North Africa, Palestine, and North America. In the fall of 1939, in sources as varied as newspapers, private diaries, and official memoranda, Jews abroad reflected on the situation in Poland with great fear for the fates of fellow Jews. They also harbored concerns about their own safety, be it in the Reich proper or in countries where Nazi-friendly regimes were trying to follow the German model in dealing with their own "Jewish question." Chapter 7 features the concerns Jews outside Poland articulated in these months and their initial responses to invasion in the spring and summer of 1940, when Germany expanded its military operations to northern and western Europe and the Soviet Union forced Romania to cede part of its territory. Shock reverberated throughout Europe as a result of the Wehrmacht's rapid victories over and occupation of Denmark and Norway, swiftly followed by the Netherlands, Belgium, and France in 1940. Great Britain remained the sole obstacle standing in the way of total German domination of Europe and Axis victory in the war. German goals, policies, and methods in the occupied parts of western Europe differed from the brutal subjugation of Poland. Yet, despite the more lenient form of German rule in its more recently acquired territories, it seemed that the stunning success of the Wehrmacht in the west had not only swept away armies and defenses but also seriously undermined the basic principles of democracy upon which the safety and well-being of Jewish minorities in these countries rested.

---

10. See Map 3, p. xiv. Hitler gave a speech to his generals shortly before the beginning of the war in which he expressed the wish that the parts of Poland under German rule would be "depopulated and settled by Germans" (from Hitler's speech to the Wehrmacht commanders, August 22, 1939, quoted from Rossino, *Hitler Strikes Poland*, 10).

As chapter 8 shows, Jews' freedom and equality had been rescinded in a host of European countries by the end of 1940. And as a result of Germany's winning campaign after campaign, more and more borders closed to Jews seeking refuge. The range of what Jews could do to help others was as limited as their own choices. With the proliferation of antisemitic laws and decrees, Jews in different national contexts sought answers to questions about the impetus behind these multifarious legislative assaults and where they might lead in the future. For example, if the new French regime in **Vichy** saw itself more as the protector of core French values than as the executor of German orders, what would this mean for upholding the achievements of the Enlightenment in general and the status of the Jews in particular? And beyond France, Jews in many different locales tried to determine whether more changes were in store and whether they would emanate from local pressures or from the demands of the Germans in their unrelenting, if uneven, pursuit of the "Jewish question." In view of all the disparate and confusing consequences of a war still uncertain in its outcome, Jews asked, was there any coherence or obvious trajectory to the events impacting on Jewish life in Europe in 1940 and beyond? Chapter 9 takes up the latter question in greater detail by focusing on different Jewish interpretations of one particular set of Nazi policies in the first year and a half of the war: deportations of Jews from the Reich itself to the Lublin district of Poland (in the fall of 1939 and then again in February and March 1940) and to the Unoccupied Zone of France (in October 1940). These deportations were widely reported by Jewish and non-Jewish newspapers around the world and became a specter in German, Austrian, and Czech Jews' appraisals of what the future held.

Compared to the situation outside Poland in 1940, affairs in the core area of Nazi Germanization appeared in a different, yet equally opaque light, as Part IV suggests. Since late 1939, German authorities had created ghettos as an interim solution to problems they faced, in many instances problems related to Germanization measures. In the delimited geographical and social space of the emerging ghettos, Jewish marginalization and expropriation took on new, more radical forms. As a result, urban and rural Jewish communities found themselves without the means to organize effective relief structures suitable to meet even the most basic needs of their constituents.[11]

Even with the benefit of hindsight and equipped with access to a wealth of German wartime sources, historians continue to debate the basic rationale for

---

11. Christopher R. Browning, introduction to *The United States Holocaust Memorial Museum Encyclopedia of Camps and Ghettos, 1933–1945*, vol. 2: *Ghettos in German-Occupied Eastern Europe*, ed. Martin Dean (Bloomington: Indiana University Press in association with the USHMM, 2011).

ghettoization. How much harder was it for Jews at the time to orient themselves in a rapidly changing environment, with their leaders excluded from the centers of decision making and anxiously preoccupied with providing the essentials for survival? To Jews in Poland with little else to rely on than their own experiences and those of other Jews in their immediate surroundings, the picture seemed fragmented, partial, and contradictory. To those with access to information from a variety of sources, like **Emanuel Ringelblum**'s Warsaw-based **Oyneg Shabes** archive or the **Jewish Agency** office in Geneva, German conduct may have seemed more calculable. Despite some inconsistencies, they discerned certain broader patterns like dislocation, concentration, and dispossession, even though the overarching goals of Nazi policy remained a matter of speculation.

To Polish Jews at the time, 1939 and 1940 marked a transition phase. The fluidity of Nazi policies in that period offered opportunities for Jews to shape, at least partly, what would happen next. Beginning in chapter 10, with its focus on uprooting, forced labor, and early economic initiatives in the ghettos, and continuing in chapter 11, with its focus on Jewish leadership, we see how Jews in emerging ghettos attempted by various means to influence their German rulers and also how the Jewish Councils, established at the Nazis' behest, worked to gain legitimacy within their communities. The documentation generated by Jewish organizations and individuals inside and outside the ghettos makes visible the element of improvisation and stopgap adjustment in their responses to German rule. Though the prospects were not promising and success was rare, the situation appeared bleak enough for leaders and activists to seek redress from German agencies on all levels, at times overstepping the narrow confines of the permissible and engaging in forms of evasion or resistance. Large, financially and politically powerful organizations such as the Joint could apply a degree of leverage on behalf of entire communities; local groups and initiatives tried to fill gaps in the overstretched relief network and cater to people's various material, health-related, spiritual, or educational needs. The sources included in these chapters provide a glimpse of Jews' determination to influence the course of events in very diverse ways, often outside of official channels. Yet, they also show the limits in terms of what was possible and what could be documented.

From the start of ghettoization, the official Jewish leadership faced internal challenges: some persons with clout or assets tried to improve their fate with little concern for the fate of others; intellectuals and others critical of the Jewish Councils saw them merely as a "tool of the Germans" and tried to provide alternative leadership in areas they saw as vital to the survival of the community; families and individuals in ghettos with no access to those in positions of power and nothing to offer as incentive pursued every avenue, legal or illicit, to make a living. The irrefutable fact that the Jewish Councils served as the executors of German orders impacted massively on their legitimacy. To this day, the irresolvable conflict built into the Jewish Councils in their dual function as tools of the Germans and caretakers of the ghetto inmates has dominated the way they are depicted in history. The documents presented here attest to the need to reserve moral judgment in view of the complexities, severity, and unpredictability characterizing the situations within which members of the Jewish Councils were operating—even at a time when the "Final Solution" as we know it had not yet been implemented. Chapter 12 concludes the volume with a variety of perspectives on what was in sight at the close of 1940, as Jews in different parts of Europe looked to the future and to the second year of war.

Like the previous and subsequent volumes in the series, this volume is based on the general assumption that events appear in a different light at the time they occur than they do in hindsight. It is difficult to maintain this focus, given the long shadow cast by later knowledge about the Holocaust. Yet, looking through the lens of Jewish documentation produced at the time gives rise to new insights. German anti-Jewish policy appeared to be contradictory, confused, and improvised. This vantage point thus provides an important corrective to the ex post facto interpretation of Nazi measures as a clear, structured, and well-planned sequence. For Jews documenting what was going on, "state policy" often took a very direct, personal form—as physical attacks or other measures immediately encroaching on their well-being or that of others—and at the same time looked highly intangible and inchoate, given the lack of clarity about the intent and root causes of anti-Jewish regulations. The documents presented here leave no illusion about the fact that scarcity, blatant inequality, and the threat of violence increasingly dominated communal life. But the lack of clarity about the future left open the hope that the war would come to an end before it had totally destroyed the basis of Jewish life in Europe.

This book draws on the help of far more individuals and institutions than we can acknowledge here. We are grateful to the Conference on Jewish Material Claims against Germany, the William S. and Ina Levine Foundation, and the Blum Family Foundation for their generous support and to the Dorot Foundation for funding summer research fellows involved in the project. Dr. Alfred Munzer provided vital material as well as linguistic help. Our research assistants Anna Borejsza-Wysocka, Ivana Bradaric, Anca Glont, Hannah Ewing, Rachel Jablon, and Melissa Kravetz handled our many demands professionally and in good spirit, as did our wonderful interns Brian Berman, Ulrike Ecker, Ilona Gerbakher, Diana Gergel, Rachel Heidmann, Alexandra Karambelas, Anya Nowakowski, Romy Proschmann, and Frédéric Vagneron. Ryan Farrell provided meticulous and critical assistance in the long editorial process; the closing of late-stage archival gaps we owe to Stephen Scala's expert knowledge. For their crucial help with translations and scholarly advice, we are indebted to Daniel Brewing, Diana Dumitru, Gershon Greenberg, Jolanta Kraemer, Peter Landé, Kathleen Luft, Jessica MacLeod, Maddalena Marinari, Beate Meyer, Iael Nidam-Orvieto, Veronika Szabó, and Leah Wolfson. Cristina Florea, Stephen Pallavicini, Hadar Sadeh, Benjamin Thorne, and Nicole Weismann helped with translations as well.

From among the many USHMM colleagues involved in the project in one way or another, we thank the staffs of the Museum's Library, Archives, and Photo Archives, the Art and Artifacts Section, and the Holocaust Survivors and Victims Resource Center; we are particularly indebted to Michlean Amir, Judith Cohen, Radu Ioanid, Henry Mayer, Teresa Pollin, and Susan Snyder for their guidance. Paul Shapiro, director of the Museum's Center for Advanced Holocaust Studies, provided support as well as stimulus throughout the work on this volume. We could not have finished the book without the patience, commitment, and hard work of Mel Hecker, the center's publications officer. Gwen Sherman and Wrenetta Richards played an important role in administrative matters. Again, we have been extremely fortunate to be able to rely on the life experience and wonderful help of museum survivor volunteers, especially Gideon Frieder, Margit Meissner, Isaac Nehama, Michael (Motl) Rosenbush, Samuel Schalkowsky, Marcel Drimer, and Ania Drimer. At Altamira Press we would like to thank Marissa Parks, Elaine McGarraugh, Jennifer Kelland, and Kim Lyons for their dedication to the project. We thank the members of the USHMM's Academic Committee for their ongoing support. Doris Bergen (Toronto), David Engel (New York), and Mark Roseman (Bloomington) took time from their busy schedules to provide vital feedback on different versions of the manuscript, for which we are extremely grateful. Last but not least, we thank our series editor, Jürgen Matthäus, for his unstinting support and thoughtful collaboration at every stage of research and writing.

Alexandra Garbarini, Emil Kerenji, Jan Lambertz, and Avinoam Patt
May 2011

PART I

FROM *"KRISTALLNACHT"* TO WAR

IN 1939, when Mally Dienemann reflected on the events of November 1938 that had triggered her and her husband's escape from Germany to Palestine, she wrote that "despite the many hours of despair, despite the many hours of the most bitter attacks and the loss of faith, somewhere in the depths of my soul an absolutely unshakeable faith remains, impervious to all the terrible things that have happened to people: though we cannot see it with our eyes, this must, must all have a meaning."[1] That year the number of Jews pondering what it meant to be persecuted by the Nazi regime grew exponentially as Germany moved from threatening military action to waging outright war.

More than five years of the Third Reich's anti-Jewish policy had produced a disillusioned if not desperate German Jewish minority, one that was numerically much reduced, socially marginalized, and economically shattered. The **Anschluss** of Austria had provided stimulus for even more radical measures to exclude, rob, and expel Jews. The wave of violence sweeping the Reich in November 1938 showed how committed the regime remained to its own ideological agenda. Reflecting on the pogrom's meaning just one day after the worst of the terror campaign ended in Breslau, **Willy Cohn** recorded in his diary,

---

1. Mally Dienemann, diary entry written ca. 1939, quoted from Jürgen Matthäus and Mark Roseman, *Jewish Responses to Persecution*, vol. 1: *1933–1938* (Lanham, MD: AltaMira Press in association with the USHMM, 2010), 376.

"I no longer believe in the rebuilding of Jewish life in Germany; I don't even consider it to be desirable."[2]

Jews who found no hope for life within the expanding German borders saw some glimmer of improvement on the distant horizon. Within European and overseas countries, awareness of the refugee crisis and acknowledgment of the Jewish plight grew, along with the perception that Hitler's Germany could not be contained in its aggressive drive. Indeed, the months between the aftermath of "*Kristallnacht*" and the beginning of war saw not only an upsurge in the refugee crisis but also an increased willingness by Great Britain, the Netherlands, and the United States to accommodate some groups of Jewish refugees, most notably children. Moreover, Jewish relief agencies began to play an important role in the lives of an increasing number of European Jews, dedicating tremendous energy and resources to helping refugees and prospective emigrants from the Reich.

By and large, however, Jews were left knocking at the doors of western democracies. As long as public opinion in most countries remained preoccupied with the impact of the world economic crisis, politicians showed little enthusiasm for challenging widespread prejudice against Jewish immigration. Furthermore, Nazi policy, although ostensibly aimed at pushing Jews out, created a crucial impediment to departure from the Reich by depriving people of all material means to start a new life elsewhere. The tightening of measures in Germany, aimed at stripping would-be emigrants of as many of their possessions as possible, neutralized any positive developments abroad. Worse still, for governments and right-wing movements in countries such as Poland, Romania, and Slovakia, where anti-Jewish prejudices had become firmly woven into the social and political fabric, the path of German anti-Jewish policy seemed to offer lessons for how to pursue the "Jewish question" at home. Once the war had started, the massive obstacles to emigration multiplied. The increase in the number of the uprooted hardly eliminated already existing maladies and created new difficulties for the individuals and organizations engulfed in the crisis.

---

2. Willy Cohn, diary entry for November 11, 1938, translated from Willy Cohn, *Kein Recht, Nirgends: Tagebuch vom Untergang des Breslauer Judentums, 1933–1941*, ed. Norbert Conrads (Cologne: Böhlau Verlag, 2007), 2:538.

CHAPTER 1

RESPONSES TO "*KRISTALLNACHT*" OUTSIDE OF GERMANY

THE ANTI-JEWISH pogrom unleashed throughout the Reich on November 9–10, 1938, shocked Jews all over Europe—indeed, around the world. The violence was extensive. Hundreds of German and Austrian Jews died as a result of murder, suicide, and longer-term consequences from the pogrom; some thirty thousand Jewish men were sent to concentration camps.[1] Many outside observers expressed concern for the victims and assured them of their solidarity. Not all displays of sympathy were as manifest as in the Netherlands, where the **World Jewish Congress** (WJC) reported a "complete change in Dutch public opinion toward emigrants, a reversal of government attitude, and a wave of goodwill never experienced before."[2] But in general, the global news coverage represented the event as barbaric and unimaginable, all the more so because of its setting, in the heart of Europe.

In Poland, the Jewish population witnessed "*Kristallnacht*" and its aftermath with fear and concern. After all, the brutality being inflicted on their neighbors was hardly contained by the German-Polish border. Indeed, from the perspective of Polish Jews, the November pogrom extended the breadth of a humanitarian crisis that had been unfolding since late October. At that

---

1. On "*Kristallnacht*," its origins, impact, and legacy, see Alan E. Steinweis, *Kristallnacht 1938* (Cambridge, MA: Belknap Press, 2009), and Martin Gilbert, *Kristallnacht: Prelude to Destruction* (New York: HarperCollins, 2006).

2. Confidential WJC report on Holland, January 12, 1939, USHMMA RG 11.001M, reel 108 (SAM 1190-1-334), fol. 184 (translated from German).

time, the Nazi regime had expelled about sixteen thousand Polish Jews from Germany, dumping them over the border in the Polish border town of Zbąszyń. As an act of protest against this mass expulsion, a seventeen-year-old whose parents and siblings numbered among the expellees, a young man named Herschel Grynszpan, assassinated a German diplomat in Paris. The Nazis pounced on the opportunity afforded by Grynszpan's act of political violence to terrorize the Reich's Jewish population. Nazi propaganda dressed up the November pogrom as uncontainable "popular outrage" in response to this episode of Jewish vigilantism.[3]

When Polish authorities refused to allow thousands of the expellees to enter Poland, Zbąszyń became an ad hoc refugee camp. Polish Jewish relief organizations quickly mobilized their resources on behalf of these new refugees. The Warsaw office of the **American Jewish Joint Distribution Committee** (AJJDC), as well as the Society for the Protection of the Health of the Jewish Population in Poland (Towarzystwo Ochrony Zdrowia Ludności Żydowskiej w Polsce, or **TOZ**) and the Central Office of the Union of Societies for Care of Orphans and Abandoned Children (Centrala Związku Towarzystw Opieki nad Sierotami i Dziećmi Opuszczonymi, or **CENTOS**), found themselves having to take responsibility for the relief effort. These organizations and others carried out fund-raising campaigns that were nothing short of remarkable to assist the men, women, and children stuck on the Polish border near Zbąszyń. The Central Refugee Committee, established in Warsaw at the behest of the AJJDC to coordinate relief efforts and to collect contributions, put together

---

3. Herschel Grynszpan (1921–1942?) was born in Hanover, Germany, the son of Polish Jewish immigrants Sendel and Rifka Grynszpan. In 1936 he left Germany; after briefly living with an uncle in Belgium, he entered France illegally and lived with his uncle and aunt, Abraham and Chawa Grynszpan, in Paris. In the summer of 1938, the French police ruled that Grynszpan had no grounds to stay in France; however, his Polish passport had expired, as had his permit to return to Germany. He remained in France illegally, and on the morning of November 7, Herschel Grynszpan walked into the German embassy in Paris and shot Ernst vom Rath, an embassy official on duty, to protest the recent German actions against Jews of Polish nationality in Germany. He was subsequently arrested and spent the remainder of his life imprisoned in France and Germany. He perished some time after September 1942. For a biography of Herschel Grynszpan, see Andy Marino, *Herschel: The Boy Who Started World War II* (Boston: Faber and Faber, 1997). On the number of expelled Polish Jews, see Saul Friedländer, *The Years of Persecution: Nazi Germany and the Jews, 1933–1939* (New York: HarperCollins, 1997), 267–68.

a campaign in four hundred locales in Poland.[4] To cite one example, in the eastern Polish town of Baranowicze, the Yiddish-language weekly newspaper *Baranovitsher Kurir* published articles throughout November and December, exhorting its readers to assist German Jewish refugees in the region. A piece on November 25, 1938, carried the headline "Brother Jews! Your Duty Is to Support the German Refugees!" and pleaded, "We appeal and we call to all in whom glimmers [*es glit*] a piece of a Jewish heart: Help with as much as you can and even more, Give—now is the time—more than it would seem to you that you can give."[5] In all, Polish Jews contributed 3.5 million złoty (US$700,000 in 1938 dollars) and donated mounds of blankets, clothing, and other supplies.[6]

ASSESSING THE DAMAGE

The AJJDC responded to the unfolding humanitarian tragedy at Zbąszyń promptly and with practical concerns in mind. Although it usually financed local projects implemented by local organizations, in this instance AJJDC activists from Warsaw **Emanuel Ringelblum** and **Yitzhak Giterman** soon arrived in Zbąszyń and organized the relief operation themselves. Ringelblum, on top of his work as an employee of the AJJDC, was a historian for the Warsaw branch of the Jewish Scientific Institute (Yidisher Visnshaftlekher Institut, or **YIVO**). In that dual capacity, Ringelblum combined his passion for Jewish folk culture with a commitment to improving the economic livelihoods of the eastern European Jewish masses. During World War II, Ringelblum would spearhead the creation of an underground archive in the Warsaw ghetto, known by the code name **Oyneg Shabes**.[7]

---

4. The AJJDC's activities on behalf of the Zbąszyń refugees are well-represented in the selection of documents reprinted in Henry Friedlander and Sybil Milton, eds., *Archives of the Holocaust: An International Collection of Selected Documents* (New York: Garland Publishing, 1995), 10:489–639. For an overview, see in particular the documents on 591–95.

5. *Baranovitsher Kurir*, November 25, 1938, 2.

6. Samuel D. Kassow, *Who Will Write Our History? Emanuel Ringelblum, the Warsaw Ghetto, and the Oyneg Shabes Archive* (Bloomington: Indiana University Press, 2007), 100; AJJDC Report, "German Deportees in Poland," April 2, 1939, facsimile reprinted in Friedlander and Milton, *Archives of the Holocaust*, 10:594–95.

7. Yehuda Bauer, *American Jewry and the Holocaust: The American Jewish Joint Distribution Committee, 1939–1945* (Detroit, MI: Wayne State University Press, 1981), 33. For a detailed account of the Zbąszyń episode and AJJDC's operation, as well as sample letters from refugees of the camp who lingered on until after the German invasion of Poland in September 1939, see Jerzy Tomaszewski, "Letters from Zbaszyn," *YVS* 19 (1988): 289–315.

Document 1–1: Letter by Emanuel Ringelblum, Środborów, Poland, to Raphael Mahler, New York City, December 6, 1938, Moreshet, Mordechai Anielevich Memorial Archive D.1.4927 (translated from Yiddish).[8]

Dear Raphael:

I am in Środborów now to rest. I worked in Zbąszyń for five weeks. Apart from Ginzberg,[9] I am among the few who managed to hold out there for a long time. Almost all the others broke down, sooner or later. I have neither the strength nor the patience to describe for you everything that happened in Zbąszyń. Anyway, I think there has never been so ferocious, so pitiless a deportation [*gerush*] of any Jewish community as this German deportation. I saw one woman who was taken from her home in Germany while she was still in her pajamas (this woman is now half-demented). I saw a paralyzed woman of over 50 who was taken from her house; afterwards she was carried all the way to the border in an armchair by young Jewish men. (She is in hospital to this day.) [. . .]

In the course of those five weeks, we (originally Giterman,[10] Ginzberg, and I, and after ten days I and Ginzberg, that is) set up a whole township with departments for supplies, hospitalization, carpentry workshops, tailors, shoemakers, books, a legal section, a migration department and our own post office (with 53 employees), a welfare office, a court of arbitration, an organizing committee, open and secret control services, a cleaning service, and widespread sanitation services, etc. In addition to 10–15 people from Poland, almost 500 refugees from Germany are employed in the sections I listed above. The most important thing is that this is not a situation where some give and some receive. The refugees look on us as brothers who have come to help them in a time of distress and tragedy. Almost all the responsible jobs are carried out by refugees. The

---

8. The letter is published in Hebrew translation in Raphael Mahler, "Mikhtavei E. Ringelblum mi-Zbonshin ve-al Zbonshin," *Yalkut Moreshet*, no. 2 (1964): 24–25. Raphael Mahler (1899–1977), historian from Nowy Sącz, trained at the University of Vienna and worked as a teacher in Jewish secondary schools in Poland. Mahler was a close associate of Ringelblum's; in the mid-1920s, the two had led a group of young Jewish historians called Yunge historiker. When Ringelblum wrote this letter, Mahler had already immigrated to New York, where he taught Jewish history until his move to Tel Aviv in 1950. See Israel Biderman, *Mayer Balaban: Historian of Polish Jewry* (New York: I. M. Biderman Book Committee, 1976), 275–84.

9. Shlomo Ginzberg was, like Ringelblum, a teacher in a Jewish secondary school; he most likely perished in the Warsaw ghetto.

10. For more on Yitzhak Giterman, see the glossary.

warmest and most friendly relations exist between us and the refugees. It is not the decaying [*farshimlt*] spirit of philanthropy, which might so easily have infiltrated into the work. For that reason all those in need of our aid enjoy receiving it. Nobody was humiliated. [. . .]

We have begun to develop cultural activities. The first thing we introduced was speaking Yiddish. It has become quite the fashion in the camp. We have organized classes in Polish, attended by about 200 persons, and other classes. There are several reading rooms, a library; the religious groups have set up a Talmud Torah [religious school]. There are concerts, and a choir is active. [. . .]

Zbąszyń has become a symbol for the defenselessness of the Jews of Poland. Jews were humiliated to the level of lepers, to third-class citizens, and as a result we are all visited by terrible tragedy. [. . .]

Please accept my warmest good wishes and kisses from
Emanuel

DOCUMENT 1–2: **Jewish expellees from Germany in the refugee camp in Zbąszyń, Poland, fall/winter 1938–1939, USHMMPA WS# 13547.**

Although the events were separated by a mere two weeks, the fates of German and Austrian Jews during *"Kristallnacht"* largely eclipsed the plight of

Polish-born Jews expelled from Germany. While the *New York Times* described the pogrom as an unprecedented episode of violence in modern German history, many Jewish commentators contextualized it differently, placing "*Kristallnacht*" within a long tradition of violence against Jews. The November 21, 1938, issue of the educational journal *Olami* (My World) published by the Zionist educational organization **Tarbut** in Warsaw, is a prime example of the latter tendency. *Olami's* numerous references to the "*Kristallnacht*" pogrom assimilated this anti-Jewish outrage into a Jewish historical narrative that identified persecution and victimization as central to Jewish experience. The cover page of the journal, which normally featured scenes from life in the Jewish settlement in Palestine, depicted the prophet Ezekiel in the valley of the bones, represented as a graveyard. The third page of this issue presented a report titled "Destruction of the Jews in Germany," while the back cover carried a photo of the Jewish refugees on the Polish border. The historical section of the journal detailed the April 1298 massacre of thousands of Jews in Bavaria, Franconia, and Austria and included lamentations composed in the Middle Ages following the massacres of Jewish communities during the Crusades. At the same time, and in tension with these other images and reports, the journal portrayed "*Kristallnacht*" as an unprecedented experience of violence in modern Jewish history.

DOCUMENT 1–3: **"The Destruction of the Jews in Germany,"** *Olami* (Warsaw) 7, no. 55 (November 21, 1938): 99, USHMMA Acc. 2003.300 Sztejnsznajd family collection (translated from Hebrew).

The Jewish People in the lands of their dispersion[11] were shocked by the terrible cry that arose in the days from the Valley of Tears on the banks of the Rhine River. Our flesh bristled upon hearing of the killing and loss,

---

11. "Dispersion" means exile from Israel.

about the murder, plunder, and ostracism that the Nazis inflicted on the Jews of Germany. For three consecutive days, on the 9th, 10th, and 11th of this month, the destroyers rampaged, and their bloodstained hand is still outstretched . . .

[. . .]

In these days of destruction, the rioters did not take pity on the babes of the house of [rabbinical] learning—the authorities issued an edict outlawing the teaching to the children of Israel of the holy book—the *Tanakh*[12]—that which is the lone candle shining a light for us in the lands of the Diaspora, our source of hope and comfort.

These cruel deeds have befouled the Nazi scent in the entire world. There is no enlightened person who will not protest against this evil, which has no comparison except to the Middle Ages.

In these days of destruction we have no comfort except for our renewed hope in a total redemption and our belief in the triumph of justice that will finally come. And our enemies should know, pray, that we will not be destroyed from under the heavens of God: the eternal strength of Israel will not be refuted![13]

Religious responses to "*Kristallnacht*" sounded a similar note. They, too, harkened back to the Crusades and contextualized Nazi anti-Jewish actions as a resurgence of a deep, violent streak in German history. Different, however, was the messianic meaning with which they invested recent events. If the Zionist readers of *Olami* looked to the establishment of a national home in Palestine as the longed-for "total redemption" from Nazi antisemitism, the Orthodox readers of another Polish Jewish educational journal, the eponymous publication of the Beys Ya'akov schools for girls, placed their hopes in an otherworldly redemption to bring an end to the worsening situation.[14]

Document 1–4, an article from *Beys Ya'akov*, presumably responded to "*Kristallnacht*," although that event is never directly mentioned. The lack of explicit references to this pogrom is characteristic of Orthodox writing on

---

12. This refers to the Hebrew Bible, the Old Testament.

13. *Netzach Israel lo yeshaker* comes from the biblical verse 1 Samuel 15:29.

14. The first Beys Ya'akov school was founded in Kraków in 1917. Its founder, Sarah Schenirer (1883–1935), was a daughter of a prominent Jewish religious teacher. In the interwar period, she created a network of Jewish Orthodox schools for girls. The Kraków school started with thirty students; by 1939, over thirty-five thousand girls were enrolled in about three hundred schools across Poland. See Lucy Dawidowicz, *The Golden Tradition: Jewish Life and Thought in Eastern Europe* (Syracuse, NY: Syracuse University Press, 1996), 206–7.

contemporary political events, which perceive the present as a manifestation of the "eternal."[15] Of particular significance in this article is the portrayal of German agency and the repetition of the word ***khurbn*** (or *churban*), Yiddish for "great destruction," to refer to the actions of the Nazis. Jews traditionally used *khurbn* to refer to the destruction of the First and Second Temples in Jerusalem in 586 BCE and 70 CE. Beginning in 1940, depending on their ideological orientation, Jewish writers began alternately referring to the mass killings of Jews as (*der driter*, or "the third") *khurbn* in Yiddish or *shoah* in Hebrew. The use of *khurbn* was thus unusual in this earlier period, though its interpretive stance was consistent with later usage. It clearly "located events directly in a succession of previous destructions, even as it suggested the divine scheme of sin and retribution that explained every *churban*."[16]

DOCUMENT 1–4: **"Before the Final Verdict," *Beys Ya'akov: A Literary Publication for School and Home* (Łódź, Warsaw, Kraków) (Kislev/November–December) TRZ"T (5699/1938): 152:1 (translated from Yiddish).**

A volcano has erupted in Europe, and it shakes the earth . . . The former country of culture, of civilization, of science and art, the former country of human beings, has been devoured by the murderous lava of evil [. . .] which has surged forth from all sides . . .[17]

To the great destruction [*khurbn*] of culture and civilization, the wild and murderous campaign of cruelty has returned to life. The thousand-year Germany with its murderous eyes [. . .] has raised its deadly head

---

15. Gershon Greenberg, "Kristallnacht: The American Ultra-Orthodox Jewish Theological Response," *American Religious Responses to Kristallnacht*, ed. Maria Mazzenga (New York: Palgrave Macmillan, 2009), 146. On the range of religious responses to the Holocaust, see Steven T. Katz, Shlomo Biderman, and Gershon Greenberg, eds., *Wrestling with God: Jewish Theological Responses during and after the Holocaust* (New York: Oxford University Press, 2007), and Esther Farbstein, *Hidden in Thunder: Perspectives on Faith, Halachah and Leadership during the Holocaust* (Jerusalem: Mossad Harav Kook, 2007).

16. James E. Young, *Writing and Rewriting the Holocaust: Narrative and the Consequences of Interpretation* (Bloomington: Indiana University Press, 1988), 86.

17. The invocation of the image of volcanic eruption is interesting in this context, as it prefigures the later treatment of the Holocaust in Jewish historiography, which has often relied on the image of the volcano. This image is problematic, for it "strips the victims of their particularity, frustrating efforts to explain why the encounter produced its devastating results." David Engel, *Historians of the Jews and the Holocaust* (Stanford, CA: Stanford University Press, 2010), 179–80.

from its dark hole, from its old, long-forgotten grave . . . [. . .] Amalek[18] now burns synagogues [*bote-kneyses*] and schools [*bote-medroshim*]. It had once burnt down the Temple, and Jerusalem had been reduced to ruins, but us, the eternal people of God, he has not been able to destroy. He destroyed Jerusalem, and in response we built Yavne. So must our answer be today, too! [. . .] We must build and support, with all our strength, our educational fortresses, use in the struggle our invincible weapon, our spirit, the spirit of the Torah, of justice and righteousness, the great weapon through which the evil empire will be eradicated from the earth! . . .

Deaf, listen and hear! Blind, open your eyes and see! A *khurbn* is taking place by force, death follows upon death, the last day of Evil is approaching the world! [. . .]

The Judge of the Universe is about to pass his ultimate verdict and reckon with evil and cruelty and vileness in the world before it comes to its dismal end!

References to theological and long-standing Jewish historical patterns of meaning were absent from analyses of "*Kristallnacht*" in secular Jewish publications. In *Aufbau*, a German-language weekly established in New York in 1934, German Jewish emigrés in the United States called for a collective response to recent events in Germany. The editorial in the December 1, 1938, issue sought to represent humanity as standing together with Jews in their time of need. Moreover, world Jewry's dignified silence and restraint in response to "*Kristallnacht*" demonstrated that it could rise above the callous and brutal attacks of the Nazis. At the same time, the editorial presented in document 1–5 is strikingly hesitant and conveys an overwhelming feeling of helplessness with its focus on "enlightenment" and the importance of correct behavior by Jews.[19]

---

18. Amalek, according to the Jewish tradition, was "the first enemy that Israel encountered after the crossing of the [Red Sea]" in their exodus from Egypt. Since biblical times, the term has been a metaphor for an archenemy of the Jews. See Samuel Abramsky, S. Sperling, and Elimelech Halevy, "Amalekites," in *Encyclopaedia Judaica*, ed. Fred Skolnick and Michael Berenbaum, 2nd ed. (Detroit, MI: Macmillan Reference USA, 2007), 2:28–29.

19. For the background on *Aufbau* debates about Jewish immigration and assimilation in the 1930s, see Jean Michel Palmier, *Weimar in Exile: The Antifascist Emigration in Europe and America* (London: Verso, 2006), 562–64.

Particularly notable is the absence of any reference to the need to lobby the U.S. government to increase immigration quotas for German and Austrian Jews.[20]

DOCUMENT 1–5: E. G. O.,[21] editorial, *Aufbau* (New York), December 1, 1938, 5 (translated from German).

I. Sorrowful but unbowed, we stand at the graves of our brothers and sisters who were killed in the past weeks, innocent victims of the madness that is on the rampage in Germany. [. . .] Though we cannot respond to the pleas of so many unfortunates at the same moment, we still can tell them with certainty that everyone in this country is united in working day and night to put a stop to the barbarity in central Europe and to help its victims.

II. "What is needed now is action rather than anger." These words from the *New York Times* can be regarded as the leitmotif, the dominant theme, of our approach. The discipline that enabled the Jews of the world to answer the ignoble attack by the strong on the weak with a silence that was more eloquent than words was fully in keeping with the order of the day. We have no grounds for despair: with a unanimity for which we waited long and anxiously, our brothers—that is, the representatives of the entire civilized world—have spoken out and voiced the opinion that it is not the Jews, but all mankind, that is being driven to the edge of the abyss by demented barbarians, and that anyone who is worthy of wearing a human face has a duty to stop the plundering, murdering mob. [. . .]

III. "The answer to barbarism has always been enlightenment." With these words, John W. Studebaker, the U.S. commissioner of education, passed sentence on the terror in the heart of Europe. The government of this country, headed by President Franklin D. Roosevelt, has made its position clear in both word and deed. We can follow it wholeheartedly in choosing education and enlightenment as a way to drive back this gravest of assaults on human culture. Each of us has his field of work before him. Besides emergency relief for our brothers on the other side of the ocean, the best weapons we can forge are purposeful reinvigoration of our own

---

20. On U.S. immigration policy during the 1930s, see Richard Breitman and Alan M. Kraut, *American Refugee Policy and European Jewry, 1933–1945* (Bloomington: Indiana University Press, 1987), 80–111.

21. The authors have been unable to identify this writer for the reigning German Jewish paper. "E. G. O." continued to write many editorials for *Aufbau* in 1939, the year that Manfred George became its new editor in chief.

existence, and cooperation and integration in the cultural activity of the American democracy. Precisely because we are Jews, it is our particular task to distinguish ourselves, even more than usual, through diligence, discipline, and decency, for hatred can be overcome only by rising above it to accomplish something positive. [. . .]

V. Desperate, immature Herschel Grynszpan has been selected as an opportunity and a victim by those who hold power in Germany. This poor man has been blamed in an attempt to turn his torment into the abominable celebration of a Sicilian Vespers massacre.[22] We must not forget that the victims of these acts are not only those against whom they are perpetrated but also those who perpetrate them. To make this clear, we invited a wide variety of groups to share their views with our readers in today's issue of *Aufbau*, in an effort to shed light both on the tragedy and on the road into the open. Especially at this time, we ask our readers now more than ever to put aside what separates us and respect the intentions and opinions of our fellow men; now more than ever, in these pages and in our weekly Saturday afternoon radio broadcasts, we will offer an arena for widely differing views and a broad forum for the free exchange of ideas, free art, and free action. For we must make our way through, must move beyond the antisemitic morass and the ruins of shattered lives into a better future. [. . .]

FORWARD ACTION

The British newspaper the ***Jewish Chronicle*** issued a bolder and more forceful call to action in the editorial it published one week after "*Kristallnacht*."[23] In an issue almost entirely dedicated to coverage of the "German pogrom," its editorial offered a sharp critique of the British and French policy of **appeasement**, taking "the world" to task for not responding earlier to Nazi "savagery."[24]

---

22. This is a reference to the 1282 insurrection of the Sicilian Vespers against Charles of Anjou. This insurrection of the locals against the French king led to the massacre of several thousand Sicilian Frenchmen over the first several weeks of the uprising.

23. For the history of the *Jewish Chronicle*, see David Cesarani, *The Jewish Chronicle and Anglo Jewry, 1841–1991* (New York: Cambridge University Press, 1994), esp. 158–92, dealing with the period of the Holocaust.

24. For an introduction to the historiographical debates surrounding appeasement in the 1930s and an argument in its defense, see James P. Levy, *Appeasement and Rearmament: Britain, 1936–1939* (Lanham, MD: Rowman & Littlefield, 2006).

Echoing **Willy Cohn**,[25] this editorialist concluded that there was no future for Jews in Germany and that emigration remained the only option. Yet, the piece also implicitly recognized the unlikelihood of rescuing all German Jews and thus made a case for giving priority to children and the expansion of the *Kindertransport* program.[26] In general, this editorial urged, a rescue plan would oblige British Jewry to make sacrifices, for the German Jewish population that used to play a leading role in supporting Jewish causes around the world no longer had the means even to support itself. The editorial thus called attention to the transformation in the balance of power then underway among Jews throughout the world.

The *Jewish Chronicle*'s historical framing of German anti-Jewish actions is reminiscent of the perspective taken by the Polish Jewish articles excerpted above. Unlike those pieces, however, it cited the recent history of German atrocities, namely the atrocities committed by Germany during World War I, which had played such a central role in British wartime and postwar accounts of that conflict.[27] Beyond an implicit reference to a transhistorical "German character"—that is, the resurgence of World War I's savage "Huns"—this editorial offered additional economic causes to explain why the Nazis had committed such widespread acts of violence.

DOCUMENT 1–6: "The German Pogrom," *Jewish Chronicle* **(London), November 18, 1938, 7.**

The savage pogrom which has disgraced the name of Germany in the eyes of civilisation has created something like consternation throughout practically the entire world. Yet it is only the culmination of a process which began five years ago with the accession to power of the most ruthless set of desperadoes that has ever seized the reins of a government. Through all those years a slow pogrom has been proceeding. But the pace was not hot enough. The extremists shouted "faster." And the criminal act of retaliation by a Polish Jewish boy, driven mad by the torturing of his parents, gave the long and impatiently awaited pretext for more speed.

---

25. See the introduction to Part I.

26. See Mark J. Harris and Deborah Oppenheimer, *Into the Arms of Strangers: Stories of the Kindertransport* (London: Bloomsbury, 2000).

27. On the history of German atrocities committed during World War I and postwar politics surrounding their memory, see John Horne and Alan Kramer, *German Atrocities, 1914: A History of Denial* (New Haven, CT: Yale University Press, 2001).

Had the world spoken out in the past five years, had it taken practical steps to arrest the extermination of the German Jewish community, had it made one determined stand for common humanity, this last final stage might have been averted. Instead, it folded its arms and did nothing; with the result that it is now confronted by the grim spectacle of savagery triumphant—to say nothing of the material difficulties which apathy has piled up for the nations. [. . .]

Why these ruffians who rule the German people should have chosen this moment, when British and French statesmen are strenuously seeking friendship with them, to show that they are the same old Huns who caused repulsion and horror by their methods in the Great War, it is for others to say. It is for these others, too, to decide whether a peace of "justice" and "understanding" is possible with such men.

One explanation of the inopportune choice of hour may probably be found in the increasing German financial straits. Eight months ago, the Nazis completed a census of all Jewish property above a trivial amount. This step was not taken out of mere idle curiosity. It was fully expected that it would be followed by a raid on Jewish belongings.[28] But a colourable pretext was lacking and this was provided by the Paris incident. Vengeance for a murdered German was conveniently made to cover not merely organised looting by Nazi gangsters, but wholesale plunder by the Nazi government in the shape of a fantastic levy on Jewish capital. It is just the squalid method of the common footpad—the highwayman in action but without a trace of the romance that clung to these one-time knights of the road who were at least daring enough to take risks, while the cowardly Nazis wreak their lust for plunder upon a tiny and wholly defenceless minority already broken by persecution. [. . .]

For German Jewry this calamity spells a virtual sentence of death. Their capital gone, their trading prohibited, the community cannot hope to survive on German soil. The new rules are the last tug of the hangman's rope—or nearly the last, for further punitive decrees are promised. In these tragic circumstances, unparalleled in modern times, the need for relief, some relief, of Jewish suffering is urgent and acute. What, one may

---

28. On Nazi economic decrees against Jews in the 1930s, see Martin Dean, *Robbing the Jews: The Confiscation of Jewish Property in the Holocaust, 1933–1945* (New York: Cambridge University Press in association with the USHMM, 2008), 17–171. On German Jewish expectations and responses to these regulations in early 1938, see Jürgen Matthäus and Mark Roseman, *Jewish Responses to Persecution*, vol. 1: *1933–1938* (Lanham, MD: AltaMira Press in association with the USHMM, 2010), 286–94.

fairly ask, are the great free nations prepared to do? They can be under no illusion as to what these events really signify. This degradation of government to the robber's level, by men who now dominate Europe; this invocation of the law of a "tooth for a tooth"—a law, incidentally, which Jews never interpreted literally, and which in any case applied only to the actual culprit and not to innocent masses of people: this cynical defiance of every decency of human governance, in the case, be it noted, of Catholics and Protestants as well as Jews—do these things mean nothing to other governments? [. . .] The apostles of appeasement must surely realise that while there is a Christian conscience in the democratic countries, the abominable treatment of the Jews in Germany is a major barrier in the policy which they are so eager to promote.

If only on these grounds, the Governments which seek German friendship must realise that somehow the Jews must be got out of Germany. If the Nazis are as anxious as they assert to be free of them, then they can be called upon not to put obstacles in the way of the Jewish flight. But exodus means the provision of havens, temporary and permanent. It means careful planning by sympathetic Governments, singly or, better still, in co-operation. It means the abandonment of sporadic and hasty improvisations which get us nowhere. Some weeks ago the urgency of comprehensive planning to meet the refugee problem was discussed in these columns and an outline scheme suggested.[29] It is obviously the duty of the Jews to prepare and elaborate some such plan with a view to securing Government co-operation. [. . .]

Above all, however, the Jews of this country have a duty of overwhelming imperiousness to their stricken brethren in Germany. They must bring succour to these poor people if the German Jewish Community are not to be left to die where they stand. Up till now the wealthier German Jews have helped their poor brethren actively with relief. Today they are beggared and themselves need help. The hospitals, the homes for the aged which they supported, cannot be kept open. Where are the inmates to turn? And it is not only immediate succour that is pressingly demanded, but money for the ultimate deliverance

---

29. On British immigration policy at the time, see Louise London, *Whitehall and the Jews, 1933–1948: British Immigration Policy, Jewish Refugees and the Holocaust* (New York: Cambridge University Press, 2000). Also see Cesarani, *The Jewish Chronicle*. On relief efforts organized by British Jews, see Amy Zahl Gottlieb, *Men of Vision: Anglo-Jewry's Aid to Victims of the Nazi Regime, 1933–1945* (London: Weidenfeld and Nicholson, 1998).

of our fellow Jews from the modern Haman.[30] Temporary camps for housing and retraining refugees will probably have to be formed. The children must be rescued as fast as possible and given a chance of life in Palestine, in accordance with the preference of the British Government. And then of course, will come the need for financing the permanent resettlement of the older refugees if places of refuge can be found.

All this demands giving on a heroic scale, and every Jew must brace himself for heavy sacrifice.

Since the murder that served as the pretext for the November pogrom had been committed on French soil and French authorities were preparing to put Herschel Grynszpan on trial, it is not surprising that this political assassination became a more central part of the discourse surrounding "*Kristallnacht*" in France.[31] In an article published in a monthly French **Sephardi** periodical, editor Ovadia Camhy empathized with Grynszpan's personal plight as a powerless refugee fearing for his parents' lives.[32] Like the *Jewish Chronicle* editorial writer, Camhy condemned democratic governments; yet, he took a less strident, more circumspect tone. He continued to praise France for its "generosity" in offering asylum to refugees, a reference to an earlier French tradition of welcoming those in flight from political persecution rather than the reality of French governmental policy in late 1938. The new government, headed by Édouard Daladier, had for several months been introducing decrees that dramatically restricted entry into France and threatened recent arrivals with expulsion. Just two days after "*Kristallnacht*," France created internment camps to detain refugees illegally residing in France, especially Spaniards and fighters from the International Brigades who had escaped from civil war and Gen. Francisco

---

30. The Book of Esther features Haman as the main persecutor of Persian Jews; the Jewish holiday Purim commemorates his defeat. See Bezalel Porten et al., "Haman," in *Encyclopaedia Judaica*, 8:293–94.

31. On the preparations for a Grynszpan trial, before the war and during, see Alan E. Steinweis, "The Trials of Herschel Grynszpan: Anti-Jewish Policy and German Propaganda, 1938–1942," *German Studies Review* 31 (2008): 471–88.

32. Ovadia Camhy (1888–1971?) was born in Hebron and worked as a journalist. Active in the foundation of the World Sephardi Federation in 1932, he served as long-time editor of the federation's journal in France, *Le Judaïsme Sephardi*. See Richard D. Barnett, ed., *The Sephardi Heritage* (London: Vallentine Mitchell, 1971), 1:638–39. On Camhy, see Neil Caplan, *Futile Diplomacy: Early Arab-Zionist Negotiation Attempts, 1913–1931* (London: Frank Cass, 1983), 1:104.

Franco's dictatorship.[33] Camhy issued a plea for a return to humanitarian policies toward asylum seekers.

DOCUMENT 1–7: Ovadia Camhy, "Under the Sign of Satan," *Le Judaïsme Séphardi* (Paris) 7, no. 66 (December 1938): 135, 140 (translated from French).

When the news broke that legation secretary vom Rath had been assassinated at the German Embassy in Paris by a 17-year-old Polish Jew, Herschel Grynszpan, we felt a deep mixture of fear and pity. We feared that such a crime would provoke reprisals in Germany against the Jews, and we felt a profound pity for the young diplomat, an innocent victim.

Certainly, Grynszpan's crime was not a villainous one. His motive was not robbery or any other dishonorable objective. It was an act of despair. When one is 17 and overwhelmed by the horror of persecutions inflicted on one's own race and one's own parents, one quickly loses one's balance and, faced with the inadequacy of the civilized world and the impunity of tyrants, becomes obsessed by the desire for vengeance, or by the desire to cause a scandal capable of overcoming the silence of the world and centering world opinion on collective crimes that have been left in the shadows for too long.

Despite that, we condemned as strongly as possible the ill-considered act of Grynszpan, all the more so as it was likely to cause difficulties for France in its relations with Germany: for a France that, in offering a generous hospitality to refugees from other countries, has the right to expect better behavior from them.

After the success of the assassination, what could we do but express our deepest sympathy? The affair was henceforth a matter for French justice, and it was appropriate to await its verdict.

If the Reich had any shame, it would have waited for this verdict. In civilized countries, a crime is adjudicated and punished. In civilized countries, the people, let alone the rabble, do not substitute themselves for justice. In civilized countries, only the person responsible is punished, and not the innocent.

But people in the Reich acted as they would have done in barbarian countries. [. . .]

---

33. On French refugee policy in the late 1930s, in particular in 1938, see Vicki Caron, "Prelude to Vichy: France and the Jewish Refugees in the Era of Appeasement," *Journal of Contemporary History* 20 (1985): 157–76.

The extreme cruelty of these measures and the desperate and inescapable situation of an entire community have roused the indignation of all the nations that have not yet been contaminated by the racist virus and that remain sensitive to human misery. [. . .]

Certainly, this general agreement on two continents to condemn the posture of a dictatorial Germany blinded by an implacable hatred is in itself a fine expression of human solidarity that gives us solace in such benighted times. But it is not only an expression. It is accompanied by steps aimed at ending the sufferings of Germany's Jews as they search for lands of asylum. [. . .]

The time has come to find an international solution to the alarming refugee problem. It must be understood that offering them aid alone is not enough. Aid that is distributed just for some period of time does not solve anything. They need to work, and work is forbidden to them! They need to live, and life is forbidden to them! The fate that often awaits refugees who leave the Nazi inferno is poverty in all its horror, accompanied by forcible repatriation or imprisonment.

The evil must be overcome at the root. We must combine all Jewish and Christian efforts to put *work* at the heart of all humanitarian aid to help the refugees.

Antisemitism posed more than a distant threat; in fact, its domestic dimension alarmed many native-born French Jews. The extent of their distress was most evident in a controversial interview given by Grand Rabbi of Paris Julien Weill to the conservative Parisian daily *Le Matin* ten days after "*Kristallnacht.*"[34] Weill sought to reassure the French public that French Jews did, in fact, support the Franco-British policy of appeasement. He strongly opposed any further assistance for German Jewish refugees, insisting that France had already discharged its responsibility toward them and that concern for refugees needed to be subordinated to larger diplomatic considerations.[35]

---

34. Born in Versailles, Julien Weill (1873–1950) became a rabbi in that city, like his father before him. He taught and published widely in the Jewish press before being appointed grand rabbi of Paris in 1933, succeeding his uncle in the post. He chose to remain in Paris during the occupation, conducting religious services and aiding the city's remaining Jews, including internees held in Drancy. Weill survived the war. See his *New York Times* obituary from April 26, 1950.

35. Vicki Caron, *Uneasy Asylum: France and the Jewish Refugee Crisis, 1933–1942* (Stanford, CA: Stanford University Press, 1999), 306.

Weill's remarks generated strong responses from moderate French-born and immigrant Jews. The Paris **Consistory** adopted a resolution at the end of November 1938 that ran directly counter to Weill's statements to *Le Matin*, stating that "it was a 'human duty [. . .] to assure every possibility of life to the unfortunate Jews. [. . .] The Paris Consistory will do everything possible [. . .] to ensure that this relief effort will be completely effective.'" Even the grand rabbi of France, Isaïe Schwartz, took a position contrary to that of Weill.[36]

Léon Blum, both the first Jew and the first Socialist to serve as prime minister of France (1936–1937), delivered perhaps the farthest-reaching and most penetrating response to Weill.[37] In his speech to the ninth annual meeting of the International League against Antisemitism (Ligue Internationale contre l'Antisémitisme, or LICA), Blum critiqued conservative French Jews who would turn their backs on refugees from Nazi Germany.[38] In order to enlist broader support for his position, he universalized the threat posed by Nazism, contending that Jews were hardly its sole victims. Blum's rhetorical strategy here echoed that of leftist antifascist movements in general and of the LICA in particular. Rather than narrowly focusing on the fate of Jews, Blum pitted the entire civilized world against Nazi Germany and reiterated his belief that humanity would resist the threat of barbarism.

DOCUMENT 1–8: **Speech by Léon Blum delivered at the banquet dinner at the ninth annual meeting of the International League against Antisemitism, November 26, 1938, Centre de documentation juive contemporaine, fonds LICA, CMXCVI/série I/3.2.2, dossier no. 42, 2–12 (translated from French).**

[. . .] We are witnessing phenomena that, I believe, we have not witnessed for fifteen centuries, since the collapse of the Roman Empire and the barbarian invasions.

---

36. Caron, *Uneasy Asylum*, 306–7. Isaïe Schwartz (1876–1952) was the grand rabbi of France (see document 8-2).

37. On Léon Blum, the Popular Front, and French politics in the 1930s, see Julian Jackson, *The Popular Front in France: Defending Democracy, 1934–38* (New York: Cambridge University Press, 1990).

38. The International League against Antisemitism (LICA) was founded in 1927 to provide public support for Sholom Schwartzbard (1886–1938). Schwartzbard was a Jewish anarchist who in 1926 in Paris assassinated Symon Petliura (1879–1926), a Ukrainian nationalist leader. After Schwartzbard's acquittal, the league ran campaigns against intolerance and xenophobia. During World War II, LICA helped Jews by hiding them, issuing fake IDs, or helping them flee to Switzerland. It has remained active since the war and eventually changed its name to the International League against Racism and Antisemitism (LICRA).

I myself have lived since my youth, and all of you have lived, and many generations before us have lived, with the idea that mankind was above all governed by the law of progress; that indeed mankind is progressing pretty steadily and that its scientific progress—thanks to the increasingly great, powerful, and definite influence of human reason on natural forces—[has marked its development], but that it is also marked by the development, by the blossoming, of a moral sense in man, of feelings of fraternity, solidarity, and equity.[39] [. . .]

And now everything seems to have been placed in question again, not only is humanity no longer advancing, but it seems that suddenly an inconceivable, an inexplicable, decline is being imposed on it. Not only has everything been called into question, but everything seems to have been destroyed, and humanity seems to be in retrograde motion, moving backward, appears to be reverting suddenly to epochs of which we have lost all trace in our memory, that we can hardly understand or imagine accurately anymore, back to times of idolatrous fanaticism, from which all human civilization must have slowly escaped.

Yes, that is it, that is the terrible spectacle; it is seeing, I repeat, what we never thought possible: civilization is going backward. It is of that that the Jewish people is the victim, it is of that that hundreds of thousands of Jews are victims. They are not the only victims, however; do not forget, never forget it: they are the most public victims, but they are not the only victims.

How could this have happened? How will this real mental conundrum be solved? [. . .]

And so, what is the cause of all this today? It is a dogma, it is a dogmatic theory, an alien dogma, the racial dogma, the dogma that confounds the nation with the existence of pure, homogeneous, unalloyed race and that wants to propound the idea and implement the practice of a specific difference between races, of a difference between superior races, created for rule and conquest, and inferior races, condemned and made for one knows too well what.

I do not want to go at length here, tonight, into a critique of racial theories. You know that if a pure and homogeneous race was necessary to make a nation, then there would not be a single nation in the world [lively applause]. [. . .]

---

39. The verb is missing in the French original.

In France, with all the efforts in the world we could not arrive at that odd idea of a racial hypothesis. We could not submit to the same criterion a man from Provence and a man from Brittany.

Nevertheless, whatever its worth may be, it is that racial theory that is at the origin, in it that one must see the cause, it is its development, full of all kinds of fanaticism, that has led to this human regression that we are witnessing today. [. . .]

But finally, my dear friends, whatever the causes—and I think I am providing you with the essentials right now—the spectacle is here before our eyes. In a big European country, in several countries of Europe, hundreds of thousands of Jews today are destined for, condemned to the most miserable and atrocious fate. Will they be able to leave their prison, even stripped bare? I do not know. I am not sure of this. I am not at all sure that racism is not determined to keep its serfs and hostages, regardless.

But finally, for those who have already left and for those who are going to leave, one must find a refuge.

I will say here everything I'm thinking, even if I must offend the feelings of other Jews, even if I dispute the words recently uttered or published by men who, at least from a religious point of view, may pass for representatives of the Jews [bravo! bravo! very sustained applause].

I could not imagine anything in the world as painful and as dishonorable as French Jews taking great care to close the doors of France today to Jewish refugees from other countries [prolonged applause]. Let them not imagine that they can preserve their tranquility, their security in this way. There is no example in history of security being acquired by cowardice [applause], not for peoples, not for social groups, not for individuals.

As for me, things lead me to an idea that you perhaps will find quite simple, quite rudimentary, but I can't imagine these things any differently: You are at home, at night, in the country. Several kilometers away, a natural disaster strikes, a natural catastrophe, either a fire or a flood. There are men, there are women, there are children, fleeing across the fields, half naked, trembling from the cold, threatened by hunger. Your house may already be full, that's possible, but when they knock on your door, you open it to them [bravo! bravo!], and you don't ask them for their identity papers, their police record, or their vaccination certificate [enthusiastic applause]. [. . .]

Naturally, these unfortunates will not be able to stay forever, of course. Naturally, solutions of a stable and lasting kind will have to be found; but after all, for now, until they find themselves a safer and more durable refuge elsewhere, how are you going to refuse them shelter for a night? [. . .]

I know what the difficulties are today. I repeat with passion that I hope the conference which will soon convene in London will finally succeed in finding common ground between two branches of the Semitic family, the Arabs and the Jews, and that immigration can start again on a larger scale and that it can even spread to other regions of Asia, whether it be to Transjordan, to certain regions of Syria, or to Iraq.

Perhaps this will not suffice and new lands will have to be found instead. Let us look for them, find them, but by really doing what great democratic states must do in order for new cities really to be opened, with all the higher possibilities of human life. May they find there, at least, something that looks like a new fatherland and not international concentration camps [prolonged applause]. [. . .]

I do not believe that the catastrophe of mankind is irreparable. I am sure that civilization will return to its path. An eclipse may be prolonged, yet that does not mean that it completely gets rid of the sun. What are we facing? In the end, to me, it seems that what is happening all depends on details specific to a certain country, explicable by their domestic history, one of the forms of mental delirium that more or less hit all mankind after World War I. [. . .]

Don't be surprised; there is no disproportion between the facts and the cause. Since the war, mankind has experienced strange illnesses, and this is one of them in many respects and the worst of them all. But mankind will recover; mankind will recover because it must go on living. So one must withstand the ordeal with confidence, bear it with courage, without selfishness, without snobbery, without fear, without shame. One must rid oneself of all petty forms—so degrading—of complaint. One must be worthy of oneself. One must be worthy of one's past and of one's origins. One must be calm and courageous. One must have confidence in the future of mankind.

For those who believed "the future of mankind" required divine guidance, the events of "*Kristallnacht*" inspired a liturgical response. The recitation in synagogue of a new prayer commemorating the pogrom in the German Reich and invoking God's power to protect the new refugees conveyed these congregants' sense of communal identity. It also connected this recent experience of persecution with others in Jewish history, as well as with a future in which the wish embedded in the prayer would be fulfilled. Such transhistorical interpretations commemorated historical events and rendered them meaningful in and through their linkage to earlier episodes of Jewish persecution and expulsion. In so doing, they reaffirmed that Jews continued to have faith in God and His covenant, even when they had been forced to undergo such trials.[40]

The prayer presented in document 1–9 was inserted into a Dutch prayer book following the *"Kristallnacht"* pogrom. Written in a traditional Hebrew liturgical style, it asks that God shield the Jewish people "from all destroyers and plagues" and have mercy on all "who confront misfortune or imprisonment." A copy of the prayer was saved by Ilse Lichtenstein (b. 1923), who along with her younger sister Inge joined a *Kindertransport* in 1939 that took them from Volkmarsen, Germany, to a camp in Bergen aan Zee in the Netherlands. In 1940, Ilse fled to the United States with her older brother. She settled there and later married a childhood friend and fellow refugee.

DOCUMENT 1–9: **Prayer inserted into a Dutch prayer book following the *"Kristallnacht"* pogrom of November 1938, USHMMA Acc. 2004.351 Ilse Lichtenstein Meyer collection (translated from Hebrew).**

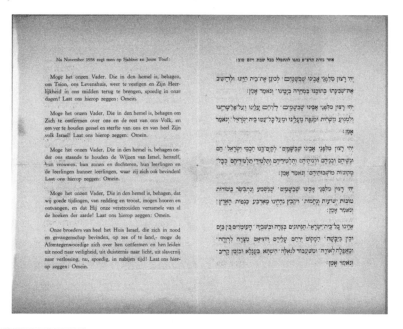

---

40. On the history of Jewish "Liturgy of Destruction," see David G. Roskies, *Against the Apocalypse: Responses to Catastrophe in Modern Jewish Culture* (Cambridge, MA: Harvard University Press, 1984), 15–53.

After *gzerat tartzat*,[41] the following prayer is recited on Shabbat and holidays:

May it be thy will, Our Father in Heaven, to establish our house of Life and to return in our midst the Divine Presence speedily in our day and let us say, Amen:

May it be thy will, Our Father in Heaven, to have mercy on us and on our refugees and to shield us and all the people of the house of Israel from all destroyers and plagues, and let us say, Amen:

May it be thy will, Our Father in Heaven, to support among us all of the wise men of Israel, they and their wives, sons, daughters, students, and the students of their students, in all their places of residence, and let us say, Amen:

May it be thy will, Our Father in Heaven, that we may hear good tidings of salvation and comfort and collect those who have been banished from the four corners of the earth, and let us say, Amen.

Inge's foster parents sent her home when it no longer appeared safe for her to remain in the Netherlands. Inge and their parents, Meinhard and Käthe Lichtenstein (née Frankenthal), were deported and killed, probably in Sobibór, in 1942.[42]

41. The "*Kristallnacht*" pogrom is referred to here as *gzerat tartzat*, meaning literally "the decree of 5699" (the year corresponding to 1938–1939 on the Jewish lunar calendar).
42. See *Gedenkbuch*, www.bundesarchiv.de/gedenkbuch (accessed March 3, 2011).

CHAPTER 2

FROM EMIGRATION TO FLIGHT

"LEAVING GERMANY or Austria cannot be termed emigration. It is
flight."[1] So wrote the unknown author of a report titled "Purgatory,"
which reached several Jewish organizations outside the Reich, in the wake of
the November pogrom. This declaration captured the transformation in the
scope and sense of urgency that emigration acquired in the months between
November 1938 and the outbreak of war.

ATTEMPTING TO GET OUT

Even before "*Kristallnacht*," 1938 had been a year of crisis. Austrian Jews and,
later, Czech Jews from the **Sudetenland** desperate to flee their new overlords
swelled the numbers of asylum seekers. By the end of the year, the stream of
emigrés from Germany and its newly acquired territories threatened to over-
whelm the willingness of European and non-European governments to take
them in.[2] Jews' desperation to get out of the Reich was so great that destination no longer mattered in the way it had in the early Nazi years. From
1933 to 1938, German Jews had asked themselves where they could build a

---

1. Anonymous report, "Purgatory: The Fate of the Jews in Germany and Austria by an
Eye Witness," 5, about the situation of the Jews mainly in Berlin and Vienna; see document
2–1.

2. For a review of interwar Jewish emigration from Germany, obstacles to emigration,
and the international refugee crisis of 1938–1939, see Michael R. Marrus, *The Unwanted:
European Refugees from the First World War through the Cold War* (1985; Philadelphia: Temple
University Press, 2002), 128–207, esp. 166–88.

better life in Germany or elsewhere. By 1939, few central European Jews continued to pose that question. As Max Goldstein declared in a column for the *Jüdisches Nachrichtenblatt Berlin* in August 1939, "There is surely no one nowadays who does not see clearly that we need to emigrate. No Jew remaining in Germany has failed to understand that two words hover prominently over every Jewish life: New Beginning! The will to emigrate is ubiquitous; the problem lies entirely in the fact that this will to leave cannot be put into practice, for the countries to which one might emigrate have almost all closed their doors to those who seek entry."[3] Central European Jews placed their hopes in building their lives elsewhere, anywhere outside of Germany. Their willingness to consider places previously out of the question is reflected in a letter from early 1939 by Georg Landauer, a **Jewish Agency** official: "Jews appear at travel agencies early in the morning, to stand in long lines and ask what kind of visas are available that day. [. . .] Great hopes were placed on Bolivia and San Domingo, but that ended in disappointment, and then Shanghai became the most sought-after destination."[4]

While the leaders of Western democracies failed to meet the humanitarian crisis sparked by the Nazi regime, many private organizations, mostly Jewish, attempted to mobilize resources to rescue Jews from the Reich. Could Jewish organizations and communities outside of Germany have done more? Historians examining Jewish political efforts in the United States, Great Britain, and France have concluded that Jewish leaders in 1938 and 1939 overwhelmingly did not turn their backs on their coreligionists suffering under Nazism. Their failure to rescue larger numbers of German, Austrian, and Czech Jews

---

3. Max Israel Goldstein, "Einwanderer, nicht Emigrant," *Jüdisches Nachrichtenblatt Berlin*, August 15, 1939, 3. Max Goldstein wrote extensively for the Vienna edition of the official Jewish community paper *Jüdisches Nachrichtenblatt* during 1939. Many of his contributions through the summer focused on emigration opportunities. His later fate remains unknown.

4. Letter from Georg Landauer (in German) to Arthur Ruppin, dated February 17, 1939, facsimile reprinted in *Archives of the Holocaust: An International Collection of Selected Documents*, ed. Henry Friedlander and Sybil Milton (New York: Garland Publishing, 1990), 3:94. Georg Landauer (1895–1954) was a World War I veteran who trained as a lawyer in Berlin and became a leading activist in Zionist and Jewish organizations in Germany during the 1920s and early 1930s. He headed the Palestine Office in Berlin from 1924 to 1925 and again from 1929 to 1933, when he also served as general secretary of Germany's Zionist Federation. After emigrating to Palestine in 1934 he worked with refugees for the Jewish Agency and helped found the Youth Aliyah movement in 1935. At the end of the war, Landauer focused on restitution issues, spending time in Munich to promote improved restitution legislation. He settled in New York in the year before his death. See Werner Röder and Herbert A. Strauss, eds., *Biographisches Handbuch der deutschsprachigen Emigration nach 1933*, vol. 1 (Munich: K. G. Saur, 1999), 413–14.

stemmed from their powerlessness in those countries where government leaders and popular opinion remained fiercely opposed to more liberal immigration laws.[5]

The report presented in document 2–1, which reached the Jewish Agency and the **World Jewish Congress** (WJC), reflects the widespread despair of German Jews in late 1938. In response, this author argued that all Jewish organizational efforts should be focused on rescue. As part of those efforts, it would be necessary to procure new sources of financing. The cost of emigration and resettlement had become ever more exorbitant during this period because of the numbers of people involved and new Nazi decrees that prevented emigrés from leaving Germany with their savings and financial assets.[6]

DOCUMENT 2–1: **An Eye Witness, "Purgatory: The Fate of the Jews in Germany and Austria," no date (ca. late 1938), USHMMA RG 11.001M.36, reel 107 (SAM 1190-1-334).**[7]

[. . .] EDUCATION. What cultural or educational activity can be carried on in such circumstances? After two visits to schools I stopped. Both the teachers and pupils had one appeal on their lips:—Save us! It can be easily imagined how lessons are carried on. [. . .]

There is one Jewish cafe open in Berlin. Anyone who wants to see what likely suicides look like should enter this cafe. The conversation of people sitting there revolves round two topics: how to obtain a passage to Shanghai or how to commit suicide. [. . .]

---

5. On American Jewish organizational responses to the refugee crisis of the 1930s, see Richard Breitman and Alan M. Kraut, *American Refugee Policy and European Jewry, 1933–1945* (Bloomington: Indiana University Press, 1987), 80–111; Yehuda Bauer, *My Brother's Keeper: A History of the American Jewish Joint Distribution Committee, 1929–1939* (Philadelphia: Jewish Publication Society of America, 1974), 138–79. On French Jewish responses to the refugee crisis in 1938–1939 and how they represented a reversal of previous antirefugee positions among French Jewish organizational leadership, see Vicki Caron, *Uneasy Asylum: France and the Jewish Refugee Crisis, 1933–1942* (Stanford, CA: Stanford University Press, 1999), 302. On Anglo-Jewry's rescue attempts following the November pogrom, see Pamela Shatzkes, *Holocaust and Rescue: Impotent or Indifferent? Anglo-Jewry, 1938–1945* (New York: Palgrave, 2002), 65–82.

6. Marrus, *The Unwanted*, 166–77, 182–83.

7. The report is also included in the Central Zionist Archives, Jerusalem, files of the Jewish Agency, Political Department, RG S25, File 9703; a facsimile is reprinted in Friedlander and Milton, *Archives of the Holocaust*, 3:85–91.

COMPOSITION OF AGES. [. . .]

World Jewry must exert all its efforts first of all to save the 250,000 Jews up to the age of 15. For the first 3 or 5 years, the question was to find a collective solution. America was absorbing 30,000 per annum. Negotiations are in progress with the Australian Government for the immigration of 15,000 Jews from Germany over a period of 3 years. Of the remainder Palestine should have taken the bulk. However, we were not given 5 years, not even 3. It is imperative to evacuate the Jews from Germany in the course of the coming year. If it is impossible to effectuate the emigration and absorption simultaneously, it will be essential to concentrate all the Jews from Germany up to the age of 50 in camps wherever possible, and to keep them there until they should be able to be absorbed. World Jewry must realise that no matter under what circumstances, it will be necessary shortly to maintain all the German Jews out of funds from abroad.[8] It were [sic] better to spend all those millions of pounds necessary for the maintenance of German Jewry in a more appropriate manner and thereby to put an end to the Jewish question in the Reich. If we shall bring before the Jewish world a daring yet fully worked out plan, we shall be able to arouse the generosity commensurate with the magnitude of the tragedy of German Jewry. [. . .]

PALESTINE THE ONLY RAY OF LIGHT. Just as it is difficult to describe the terrible havoc played among German Jewry, so it is impossible to express in words the importance of Palestine to them. It is the only ray of light in the darkness of destruction. The Palestine Office is a centre of hope. Jews, particularly in Vienna, come to this house to revive their spirit, and even such people come who have no hope to receive an immigration certificate. It is essential that we explore every avenue of refuge even if it be only for one single Jew.

---

8. This is likely a reference to the negotiations underway in mid-December 1938 between Hjalmar Schacht, head of the Reichsbank and former German economics minister, and George Rublee, the American head of the Intergovernmental Committee on (Political) Refugees, to allow some 150,000 German Jews and their dependents to leave Germany, financed by a massive loan from Jews outside Germany. See John Mendelsohn, ed., *Jewish Emigration, 1938–1940: Rublee Negotiations and the Intergovernmental Committee* (New York: Garland Publishing, 1982); Saul Friedländer, *The Years of Persecution: Nazi Germany and the Jews, 1933–1939* (New York: HarperCollins, 1997), 314–16. For more on the Intergovernmental Committee on (Political) Refugees, see the Glossary.

Although Palestine became the "only ray of light" for many central European Jews, even those who would not previously have considered themselves Zionist, immigration to Palestine under the British mandate government remained severely restricted.[9] The main reason was the British government's reluctance to further inflame Arab public opinion, which strongly opposed the large-scale Jewish colonization of Palestine. The so-called **White Paper**, published in the spring of 1939, formally codified this concern, with Britain pledging to tighten Jewish immigration in response to the Arab revolt that began in 1936. Rather than constituting a radical shift in British policy on Jewish immigration to Palestine, however, the White Paper in fact merely confirmed the restrictive government policy already in place: whereas 30,000 Jews immigrated to Palestine legally in 1936, according to official British figures, the number dropped to 10,500 in 1937. Despite the crisis unleashed upon Jews in the Reich and the fact that the *Yishuv*—the Jewish community in Palestine—had demonstrated considerable skill in organizing immigration, British authorities continued to severely restrict the number of newcomers in 1938 and 1939 (to 12,900 and 16,400, respectively).[10]

The deluge of desperate requests from prospective emigrés in response to events in 1938 forced Zionist leaders to debate whether they ought to rethink their missions and strategies of selection. Should selection criteria for immigration certificates to Palestine still favor applicants with a Zionist background? Should an organization such as **Youth Aliyah** redefine its mission to focus on philanthropy and rescue rather than education and realizing a particular vision

---

9. The British mandate, given to Britain by the **League of Nations** in 1923, authorized that country to rule the southern part of former Ottoman Syria. The formal purpose of the mandate was to administer parts of the collapsed Ottoman Empire until a political solution could be found. The territory was divided into Palestine (comprising today's Israel, the Gaza Strip, and the occupied West Bank), which remained under direct British rule with a seat in Jerusalem, and Transjordan (today's Jordan), an autonomous territory under the rule of the Hashemite dynasty. The British mandate in Palestine saw increasing rivalry and outright civil war between the Palestinian Arab and Jewish communities. On November 29, 1947, the UN General Assembly adopted a partition plan, dividing Palestine into Arab and Jewish states, with Jerusalem remaining under international control. The partition plan increased tensions between Palestinian Arab and Jewish communities, and on May 15, 1948, the British formally ended the mandate and withdrew from Palestine completely. On the previous day, the Jewish community had proclaimed an independent state of Israel. A war between Israel and neighboring states followed. See Tom Segev, *One Palestine, Complete: Jews and Arabs under the British Mandate* (New York: Henry Holt, 2000).

10. Marrus, *The Unwanted*, 184–85; Dina Porat, *The Blue and the Yellow Stars of David: The Zionist Leadership in Palestine and the Holocaust, 1939–1945* (Cambridge, MA: Harvard University Press, 1990), 12–14.

of the Jewish homeland? Depending on their ideological commitments and particular locations, different Zionist leaders took different positions on these issues.[11] More and more, Zionist officials tried to carve out a compromise position, as articulated in a letter from **Henrietta Szold**, head of the Jewish Agency's Social Services Department, to Kurt Goldmann in mid-August 1939: "Rescue as many as possible, but not at the expense of their education."[12]

DOCUMENT 2–2: **Henrietta Szold speaks to a group of Youth Aliyah immigrants from Austria at Kiryat Anavim, Palestine, October 1938, USHMMPA WS# 07146.**

Selective immigration for Palestine remained official *Yishuv* policy until 1942. The Youth Aliyah movement continued to screen applicants, rejecting around one-quarter during the first six months of 1939 for physical or

11. Brian Amkraut, *Between Home and Homeland: Youth Aliyah from Nazi Germany* (Tuscaloosa: University of Alabama Press, 2006), 100–1, 111.

12. Quoted in Amkraut, *Between Home*, 121. Kurt Goldmann formerly served as a regional leader for the Habonim youth group in Cologne and took over the organization in Berlin in mid-1938. His ultimate fate is unknown, but he may have managed to emigrate to Palestine himself at the beginning of 1940, changing his name to Reuven Golan. See Amkraut, *Between Home*, 97, 173n40; German "Minority Census," 1938–1939, USHMMA RG 14.013M.

psychological reasons. At the same time, Zionist leaders attempted to respond to the desperation of central European Jews and to the challenges posed by British immigration restrictions without sacrificing their pedagogical operations. Toward that end, Youth Aliyah established *hakhsharot* training centers in eight European countries outside of Germany. (These *hakhsharot* were unrelated to the training centers that the **Hehalutz** organization established in Poland during the 1930s for a "Zionist elite.") Zionist leaders hoped that such centers would be temporary outposts, offering a Zionist educational component until certificates materialized for Palestine.[13]

Document 2–3, an article that appeared in a Jewish newspaper on the eve of the Nazi invasion of Poland, provides a good illustration of the complexity of the Zionist position on emigration in this period. On the face of it, the article affirmed Zionists' dedication to the colonization of Palestine. It emphasized the ideological nature of the transformation of the immigrants and invited the "young Jews in Germany to take this first step" toward *aliyah* by enrolling in a *hakhsharah* program. In that sense, the article was no different from earlier Zionist calls throughout the Jewish press in Nazi Germany. The context had changed, however. After "*Kristallnacht*," the Jewish press in the Third Reich was abolished. The only Jewish publication allowed to continue after November 1938 was the *Jüdisches Nachrichtenblatt*, published first in Berlin, then from December 1938 also in Vienna and from November 1939 in Prague as well. Reading this article that appeared in a newspaper controlled by the Nazi regime thus invoked a very different set of associations for readers, despite the fact that its rhetoric projected continuity with earlier Zionist efforts. The idea of emigration to Palestine had once seemed like a peculiar choice for many people. Now they correctly viewed it as a critical means of rescue. And yet, ironically, even as the enrollment in a *hakhsharah* program with its promise of emigration seemed a serious option for many Jews—Zionist or not—it had become a virtually futile gesture. A more restrictive British policy and the increasing obstacles imposed on the Jews in the Third Reich itself had practically closed the door to *aliyah*. The article was thus divorced from the reality of its readers' situation.

DOCUMENT 2–3: "Jewish Youth to Palestine. New Registrants for *Hakhsharah*," *Jüdisches Nachrichtenblatt Wien*, **August 18, 1939, 1 (translated from German).**

The Vocational Preparation Department of the Palestine Office in Berlin offers this information:

---

13. Amkraut, *Between Home*, 110–20.

At this time, applications for placement in *hakhsharah* are being accepted on a large scale. Registration forms are to be sent to the Palestine Office in Berlin or to its branch offices and counseling centers in the Reich. Young people between the ages of 17 and 28 are eligible to apply. Initially, a short, accelerated home-country *hakhsharah* is required; upon satisfactory completion, it will be followed immediately by a *hakhsharah* abroad or by *aliyah*.

In most cases, emigration is merely going to a new country of residence; it is not an attempt to prepare for a fundamentally new life at the same time. Therefore, emigration in general means, first of all, only solving the nearest problem, not also making systematic preparation for the future.

Hakhsharah—"preparation"—however, has always entailed emigration and restructuring at the same time. Through *hakhsharah*, an emigrant first becomes an *oleh*, who "ascends" [makes *aliyah*] to a new life, whose purpose, meaning, and possibilities are clearly present in Palestine. That was always the advantage that the path of *hakhsharah* offered, in contrast to all other methods of mere emigration. Certainly, enthusiasm, a desire for integration, and willingness to make a complete change were always prerequisites for setting out on this path. These qualities to a great extent have been implanted and developed by *hakhsharah*. Even now, thousands of young Jews from Germany still are participating in *hakhsharah*, in their home country and also, most notably, in Denmark, Sweden, Holland, and England. No White Paper can prevent Jewish youths from preparing their road to Palestine; to the contrary, new groups of Jews from Germany are continually being called to take this path and prepare themselves in other countries to make *aliyah*. Nevertheless, it is necessary for the time being to select some from the many who are equipping themselves for that purpose, and such a selection is now taking place in Germany. Therefore, a short *hakhsharah* in their home country marks the start of their path.

The people who participated in *hakhsharah* in Germany late last year left Germany as early as April 1939, and of those who first became involved in *hakhsharah* since the beginning of the year, a great many have already followed those earlier groups. The last of them probably will go to a *hakhsharah* program in another country in the fall.

Thus, an opportunity to start on the *hakhsharah* path presents itself anew for many people, and a call is being issued to young Jews in Germany to take this first step. Young Jews are being asked to show that they still have enough strength to take the *chalutz* ["pioneer"] path and lay the foundations for a new life in Palestine.

If Palestine now appeared as a good place to live, it was not only because some Jews imagined it as their ancestral homeland or because a vibrant Jewish community existed there; most Jews who wanted to emigrate in 1939 were desperate to go anywhere, as long as it was out of the Nazis' reach. With no visas or other forms of documentation required for entry, the International Settlement in Shanghai thus became an unexpected refuge for Jews fleeing the Reich in the few months between November 1938 and the end of August 1939. During that period, Shanghai's Jewish population more than tripled. Yet, the "open city" did not remain open for long. A combination of new restrictions on entry introduced by the Japanese government and the difficulties in reaching Shanghai created by the outbreak of the war meant that the Jewish population stabilized at approximately seventeen thousand by the end of 1939.[14]

The Gerson family from Hamburg was dragged into the immigration wave to Shanghai and would also run up against the obstacles blocking Jews both from leaving the Reich and from gaining entry to Shanghai. Samuel Gerson had owned a kitchen wares shop in Hamburg for twenty-five years; Nazi anti-Jewish measures forced him out of business, beginning with damage incurred during the Nazi boycott of Jewish businesses of April 1, 1933. In 1937, one year after his shop closed, he declared personal bankruptcy. Thereafter, his son Theodor, who worked for a clothing firm, struggled to support the family.

Samuel Gerson's other son, Robert, set his hopes on fleeing Germany for Shanghai. Robert had lost his position as a baker's apprentice in 1938 when the bakery where he worked was forced to close. After he learned of his former boss's horrible experiences in a concentration camp following his arrest during "*Kristallnacht*," Robert decided to emigrate. His brother, Theodor, went with him. They left for Shanghai in March 1939, their transport financed in part by a loan from the Warburg Bank but mostly paid for with their savings. Samuel, his wife, Johanna, and their daughter, Edith, did not join them. The Gerson parents even tried to dissuade their sons from emigrating with the argument that Hitler would not remain in power much longer. Upon arriving in

---

14. Marrus, *The Unwanted*, 180–81. On the history of the Jewish community in Shanghai during the war, see David Kranzler, *Japanese, Nazis and Jews: The Jewish Refugee Community in Shanghai, 1938–1945* (Hoboken, NJ: KTAV Publishing House, 1988); see also Irene Eber, *Chinese and Jews: Encounters between Cultures* (London: Valentine Mitchell, 2008), 39–64.

Shanghai, Robert and Theodor could not find work and lived in a refugee home supported by the Red Cross and Jewish relief organizations.[15]

In the meantime, Samuel and Johanna decided that emigration was, in fact, the only option for German Jews. Yet, between the decision to leave and actual escape stood German bureaucracy, with its massive emigration hurdles. First, the Gersons applied for and received from the local finance office a Certificate of Nonobjection to Emigration, which was issued after they proved they had paid all the necessary taxes and fees. This certificate was only valid for a few months, in their case from the date of issue in May 1939 until the end of August 1939. Next, they applied for a certificate from the Reich Foreign Exchange Office, which was necessary in order to apply for a passport. This certificate required that a Jewish individual furnish the German authorities with documentation about property and debts. Samuel declared that he was essentially penniless and was being supported by his wife, a seamstress, and by proceeds from the sale of their household possessions. Then, on July 15, 1939, he applied to the Foreign Currency Office for permission for the three of them to take with them what remained of their personal belongings. An investigation into the Gerson family belongings, perhaps by customs officials (the particular agency responsible for this investigation is not clear from the documentation), found a problem with releasing the sewing machine in the Gerson family's possession, despite the fact that the Foreign Currency Office expert had approved its release along with the other declared items. Purchased by Johanna second-hand in January 1939, the sewing machine's monetary value was small, but it was nonetheless considered an "object of value" that could not leave the Reich. The difficulties that the Foreign Currency Office created for the Gersons show the degree of ill will directed toward emigrants and how German Jews tried to negotiate with Nazi authorities.

---

15. In 1947, Theodor Gerson emigrated to the United States, where he continued to build up his business as a stamp dealer. His brother Robert also settled in the United States after the war. Sybille Baumbach et al., eds., *"Wo Wurzeln waren . . . ": Juden in Hamburg-Eimsbüttel, 1933 bis 1945* (Hamburg: Dölling und Galitz, 1993), 109.

DOCUMENT 2–4: **Letter by Samuel Gerson, Hamburg, Germany, to the senior finance president, Hamburg Currency Office, August 14, 1939, in** *"Wo Wurzeln waren . . . ":* *Juden in Hamburg-Eimsbüttel, 1933 bis 1945,* **ed. Sybille Baumbach et al. (Hamburg: Dölling und Galitz, 1993), 106 (translated from German).**

Hamburg, August 14, 1939
Chief Financial Officer
Hamburg Foreign Currency Transactions Office
Attention: Mr. Schnak

I, the undersigned, politely request the release of the sewing machine surrendered in my list of items for emigration to Shanghai. By mistake, I gave the date as 1931, whereas the accompanying invoice shows that it was bought secondhand in 1939; this was a slip of the pen. In my ignorance, I also put down 75 marks for the machine; the retailer took our old machine with 15 marks in payment. Both errors were made with no intent to defraud, as I knew that the matter could be checked on by looking at the receipt, and I also stated that right away to the bailiff during the appraisal in my apartment.

I am a German Jew, a frontline soldier, with no criminal record, and I took part in the war against France. I am 57 years old. My father served in the military in 1866 and 1870/71. My two brothers and I all took part in the war.

I am a trained baker, also worked here as a journeyman, and for 25 years—until 1936—had a shop for household and kitchen utensils, located on the Eimsbütteler Chaussee.[16] I was forced to declare bankruptcy in 1936, but it was refused due to insufficient [remaining] assets. I sought a settlement, which was agreed to by every creditor but one, who had my property seized, and I had to close my business. As my sons did not earn enough, I was supported in part by welfare until early 1938, and until November 1938 my sons provided for my wife and me. My wife is a seamstress, and in November 1938 she received permission to practice her trade, as her sewing machine was more than 30 years old and no longer

---

16. Eimsbütteler Chaussee is a thoroughfare in Eimsbüttel, one of the residential areas of Hamburg in which Jews started settling after the removal of residential restrictions placed on the community until the end of the nineteenth century. Astrid Louven, "Juden in Eimsbüttel als gesellschaftliche Minderheit," in Baumbach et al., *"Wo Wurzeln waren . . . ,"* 16–19. For the demographic and economic situation of Hamburg's Jews in Nazi Germany, see Frank Bajohr, *"Aryanisation" in Hamburg: The Economic Exclusion of Jews and the Confiscation of Their Property in Nazi Germany* (New York: Berghahn Books, 2002), 104–9.

good for professional use. We wanted to buy a new one, but it was impossible to raise the money, as my wife earned just enough for us to live on. Now, when we sold many of our things, the first thing we did was buy a secondhand sewing machine, as my wife is forced to support me. The welfare doctor certified that I am unemployable and unfit for work because I suffer from chronic asthma and have had hernia surgery twice. It is impossible for me to pay any amount, as it seems that I am forced to go to the Welfare Office because my wife has no work at the moment. As my wife needs a decent machine for her trade, I would like to politely request once more that this machine be released to me, especially as it is not a new one, after all, but a secondhand one.

Sincerely yours,
Samuel Gerson
Paulinenallee 6

The Foreign Currency Office denied Samuel's request, refusing to permit the Gersons to take the sewing machine. Indeed, they had to return to the store in order to exchange the "new" machine for their former machine, which they were permitted to take with them. By that point, however, Japanese authorities had started requiring entry visas, and they did not receive one before their German Nonobjection to Emigration Certificate had expired. As a result, even though at the end of 1939 the Gerson sons successfully obtained entry permits for their parents and sister during their second attempt with Japanese authorities, Samuel, Johanna, and Edith were never able to use them.[17]

The Gerson family's experiences exemplify the novel aspects of emigration following the November pogrom. Jews now overwhelmingly favored flight, and the Nazi regime's official stance was that Jewish emigration constituted the "solution" to the Reich's "Jewish question." Toward that end, the regime shuttered almost all Jewish organizations and community offices and created a new compulsory organization for all Jews in Germany, the **Reichsvereinigung der Juden in Deutschland**, which had as its chief aim to accelerate Jewish emigra-

---

17. All three were deported on the first transport from Hamburg to the ghetto in Łódź on October 25, 1941. According to a non-Jewish uncle who received word of their fates, Samuel and his then pregnant daughter, Edith, were killed soon after arriving in Łódź. Johanna, the daughter of a furrier, sewed German uniforms until the end of 1944, when she was killed outside of Łódź (possibly in Chełmno). See www.bundesarchiv.de/gedenkbuch; Jürgen Sielemann and Paul Flamme, eds., *Hamburger jüdische Opfer des Nationalsozialismus: Gedenkbuch* (Hamburg: Staatsarchiv Hamburg, 1995); Yad Vashem, "Central Database of Shoah Victims' Names," www.yadvashem.org.

tion. The regime also set up its own body, the **Reichszentrale für Jüdische Auswanderung** (Reich Central Office for Jewish Emigration) in Berlin, whose sole purpose was "to remove the Jews from the country as quickly as possible," with priority given to getting rid of poor Jews. The Reichszentrale adopted the methods developed by **Adolf Eichmann** in Vienna to get rid of Austrian Jews after the *Anschluss*.[18] But the reality of emigrating was hardly more straightforward than it had been before the pogrom. Indeed, the steps necessary to secure exit certificates and entry visas were similar to the highly complicated prepogrom procedures, with the added disadvantage that competition for visas was now far worse. The flow chart below compiled by the Vienna Jewish Community in the fall of 1940 shows the many steps involved in a process euphemistically called "Jewish migration" (*jüdische Wanderung*).

18. Yehoyakim Cochavi, "'The Hostile Alliance': The Relationship between the Reichsvereinigung of Jews in Germany and the Regime," *YVS* 22 (1992): 241–43; Shaul Esh, "The Establishment of the 'Reichsvereinigung der Juden in Deutschland' and its Main Activities," *YVS* 7 (1968): 25.

DOCUMENT 2–5: Flowchart and map depicting "Jewish migration" from Germany, Austria, and the Protectorate, October 31, 1940, USHMMA RG 17.017M, IKG Vienna 447, film 1259, 58128 (A/W 2557,2).

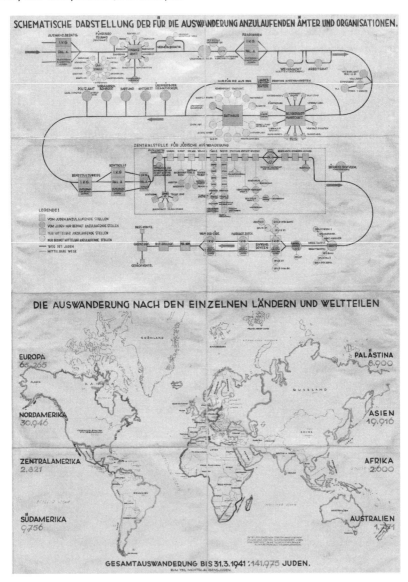

Older people like Samuel and Johanna Gerson usually had the hardest time securing visas to emigrate. By 1939 the German Jewish population was disproportionately elderly and destitute. The fact that their sons escaped but their daughter stayed behind was also typical of the gendered experience of emigration. Several factors, including the arrest of thousands of Jewish men during the November pogrom, along with the widespread belief that women—even Jewish women—would be spared direct violence, led many families to give priority to rescuing their sons and fathers.[19] This contrasted with attitudes from earlier in the 1930s, at which time women were more likely than men to push to emigrate.

Adults like the Gersons and the author of the letter in document 2–6, Amalie Malsch, found themselves in the position of being cut off from their adult children who had been able to leave Germany. Amalie and Paul Malsch, both in their fifties and living in Düsseldorf, were the parents of an only son, Wilhelm (Willy), who had left Germany in 1935 or 1936 at the age of twenty-two. The distance from loved ones abroad only compounded the "social death" that German Jews experienced as the objects of increasingly vigorous anti-Jewish policies. These parents felt lonely and even abandoned.[20]

DOCUMENT 2–6: **Letter by Amalie Malsch, Düsseldorf, Germany, to her son Willy, United States, April 4 through 7, 1939, USHMMA RG 10.086 Malsch family papers (translated from German).**

Tuesday
Düsseldorf, April 4, 1939
    My dear Willy! To date, I still haven't received any mail from you, although the *Bremen* came in yesterday. In the meantime, you've surely

---

19. For a gender analysis of emigration, see Marion A. Kaplan, *Between Dignity and Despair: Jewish Life in Nazi Germany* (New York: Oxford University Press, 1998), 138–44.

20. Paul Malsch (1885–1942), a sales manager for a leather goods manufacturer, lived with his wife, Amalie (née Samuel; 1889–1942), in Düsseldorf before he was taken into "protective custody" and sent to Dachau following the events of "*Kristallnacht*." The couple was deported to the Łódź ghetto in October 1941 and later murdered in Chełmno. Wilhelm Malsch (later William Ronald Malsh, 1913–1994), a Düsseldorf native, was sent out of Germany in late 1935 or early 1936, first to Britain and then to the United States (in early 1937). He initially lived with an uncle (Eugene Malsch) on Long Island. *USHMM ITS Collection Data Base Central Name Index*; Wolf Gruner, ed., *Die Verfolgung und Ermordung der europäischen Juden durch das nationalsozialistische Deutschland, 1933–1945*, vol. 1: *Deutsches Reich, 1933–1937* (Munich: Oldenbourg, 2008), 647; ship passenger list for January 27, 1937, NARA I.

gotten our last, detailed letter of March 30, sent via the *Europa*.[21] This morning we already got a reply from the Hilfsverein[22] in Stuttgart. You have copies of what we sent there, of course. Once again, the letter from the Hilfsverein is <u>very</u> sad for us. They write, among other things, that ["]Sponsorships No. 3 and 4 were filled out not by relatives but by friends. In that case, your sponsors, who are not related to you, are required to send the consulate a sworn statement, made before a notary, in which they state that they know you are hard of hearing and that they make their pledge in full awareness of that fact, and are prepared to vouch for you in times of health and illness, and also during times of unemployment or inability to work. Moreover (see attachment), they also would have to make a detailed explanation of why—as they are not related to you—they are taking on the obligation of sponsorship. We do not advise you to inform the consulate of your work-related plans, unless you can provide some evidence that it is your own independent venture. It is very regrettable that your case is being delayed, but we see no possibility of altering this in any way. The quota for the 1938/39 quota year is exhausted in April, and no more quota numbers are available, so that in the last two months of the old quota year, May and June, no letters of summons [to the U.S. Consulate in Stuttgart] for the German quota can be sent out. Your reservation, of course, will continue in force [and] once your paperwork is complete and approved by the consulate, nothing stands in the way of the issuance of a visa, presumably in July. We assume that your relatives and friends in the States will see to it that you are not in need during the period of the delay. Respectfully[."] Now you know the main content of the letter.

What are we going to do here, and what are we going to keep living on, we certainly don't have any idea what will happen now. Soon we'll be completely ruined, absolutely everything is going wrong for us, you know. Will we ever see each other again? Darling child, <u>that's my greatest sorrow,</u> there's no longer any ray of sunlight for us. Only the hope of seeing you again soon has kept us going thus far. Then there's also the concern that you write so little. We can't perish here, after all. <u>Can you tell me, please,</u>

---

21. The *Bremen* and *Europa* were transatlantic passenger ships owned by the German Norddeutscher Lloyd Line. Such ships also carried mail across the Atlantic. On the separation of parents from children and the importance that mail took on, see Alexandra Garbarini, *Numbered Days: Diaries and the Holocaust* (New Haven, CT: Yale University Press, 2006), 96–98, 101–4; Michael Geyer, "Virtue in Despair: A Family History from the Days of the Kindertransports," *History and Memory* 17 (2005): 323–65.

22. For more about the Hilfsverein der deutschen Juden, see the Glossary.

just what we should do and what is supposed to happen? Don't let us down, dear child. Papa doesn't know anything about this letter, I have to keep his spirits up, and my own heart is about to break from grief. I feel very sorry for poor, good Papa, with his ear. But you must continue to help us, whatever happens.

Wednesday, [April] 5. No mail came today either, yesterday I talked to Artur's mother, A. has already written again, you probably can't imagine how I feel whenever I hear how often other children write home. Papa has gone to [Vryna ?], so I'm taking the opportunity to write more again. Papa said just yesterday, if our only child doesn't even take time to write every Sunday, then I don't know what I still have to say, then I don't have any confidence either. Instead of him writing to us clearly and plainly what's going on with the sponsorships, we have to make guesses about everything here and month after month goes by, and on top of it all we're getting sick from sheer worry. Dear fellow, I've certainly written you enough about your failure to write, I'm completely tired out in general, soon I can't go on any more, I also have to cheer Papa up, and inside I'm on the point of collapse, not letting any of all this show outwardly is intolerable. What is to become of us, that's what I ask myself a hundred times a day. Once I start thinking about it, it's all over, sometimes I try to totally blank out my thoughts, but I simply can't manage to do so, and I keep on wondering what is to become of us, sometimes I imagine the worst. The rent also has to be paid on time, and we have to live too. Dear fellow, I beg you with all my heart as your mother, write and tell us what's going on with you, I've often written that something must not be right with you. Why do you always beat around the bush in your letters, I read a lot between the lines, you don't come out and say it. After all, you wrote regularly before you went to Chicago. You're 26 years old now, and you certainly know what you want. Papa will write you on his own about the Stuttgart letter on the other side of the page. So, now you know more or less everything that's going on with us here. I have to have at least one person in the world, after all, to whom I can pour out my heart at times, so don't take my words amiss, I'm too distraught. Sometimes I think you've already half forgotten us, I simply can't account for how you're acting. Up to now you haven't even asked us what we're living on.

Friday, April 7. Dear Papa has just sent you the original letter from the Hilfsverein. Yesterday he wrote to your work address. Today, again, there's no mail from you. I won't say another word about it now, enough certainly has been written on this topic. If you just don't have any time for us, then I have nothing more to say. I've reached the end, and I've complained to you long enough now. Let us know whether you've gotten all the letters. Later on, after this letter is mailed, I'll tell Papa that I wrote you on my own.

So for today, 1,000 hugs and kisses, stay well and healthy, your ever-loving

Mother

Also let us know whether you got the letter sent to you at work.

The feeling of abandonment was not unique to parents separated from their children. Thousands of Jewish youth and young adults remained in Germany in 1939, and in the midst of preparing for their own hoped-for departure, they regularly bade farewell to friends and acquaintances who had secured visas before they did. The letter in document 2–7, written over several weeks by the seventeen-year-old Susanne (Suse) Behr, expresses the range of emotions and frustrations of one teenage girl in Hamburg as she tried to cope with her daily existence and to help the adults in her life. Like all of Behr's letters to her friend Lilo in the United States, this one is ungrammatical but full of compelling detail about everything from emigration and the feeling of being trapped, Jewish leisure and vocational training for girls, the fate of relatives and friends, the banalities of daily life that affected teenagers, religious life, and more. She also described the departure of a ***Kindertransport***. The joint effort by German Jewish and foreign organizations made it possible for between eight and ten thousand children, albeit without their parents, to leave Nazi Germany and the annexed territories in 1938 and 1939.[23] In contrast to the largely celebratory mood accompanying the departure of earlier Youth Aliyah groups, *Kindertransporte* "could be a terribly wrenching experience, a considerable adventure, or both."[24] Behr lived in Hamburg until she was arrested by the **Gestapo** and deported to the Minsk ghetto on November 8, 1941. No records testify to the date and place of her death.

---

23. Marion A. Kaplan estimates that at least eighteen thousand children were sent out of Germany by their parents between 1934 and 1939. Between eight and ten thousand were sent to Britain in the aftermath of the November pogrom; the rest, both before and after "*Kristallnacht*," ended up in other European countries, Palestine, and the United States. Kaplan, *Between Dignity*, 116–17; Amkraut, *Between Home*, 113–14.

24. Kaplan, *Between Dignity*, 117.

DOCUMENT 2–7: **Letters by Susanne (Suse) Behr, Hamburg, Germany, to Lilo Rieder,[25] Philadelphia, February 27, 1939, and unspecified date (probably March 1939), USHMMA Acc. 2000.51 Liselotte Feinschil family papers (translated from German).**

[February 27, 1939]

Dear Lilo,

I received your dear letter and want to answer you quickly. Unfortunately, I'm still here and will probably remain here for the time being it is too awful there is no chance for me to get out my waiting number is 12000 it is not even close to my turn, you only get out when you have a guarantee and I don't have one, as we don't have any friends or rel[atives] in Engl[and] or Holland. [. . .] I'm bored from morning to night I do help at home but you know how that is, it gets worse here every day. [. . .]

Starting next week I'll go to the sewing class, I was already in the class there for a week and had to stop they make it so difficult you can't possibly imagine but I'll write you a little about it anyway there are 15 of us girls some not from here and older but it is nifty we have a lot of fun well you know how it is at school I'm not exactly skillful but I'll learn how to sew decently at last. [. . .] Also, I always go to the religious service it takes place in the community hall, and now there are movies here too going to a movie is very expensive not less than 90 Pfennig and you always need an identity card from the Kulturbund[26] which costs 1 Mark and is valid until September I saw the film "Lord Jeff" it was in English have you seen it? It was great at last a film that is not a love film. Next week "Hoheit tanzt incognito" is playing but it's for adults only I wouldn't have gone anyway. I can't imagine how you look with a perm I look fine with my puff I would be very glad to get the promised picture I don't know what you all look like anymore [. . . or] whether we will ever see each other again but I don't believe so until now everyone has still thought that something would happen but do you believe that? [. . .] now I will close again the letter has

---

25. After a delay due to illness, Liselotte (Lilo) Rieder (later Feinschil), born 1924, followed her parents and four siblings to the United States in July 1938, arriving with a dozen refugee children. Lilo's grandparents managed to emigrate the same year. Her father, a Czech native, had owned two shoe stores in Hamburg. See Baumbach et al., *"Wo Wurzeln waren"* 114–17.

26. For more on the **Jüdischer Kulturbund**, see the Glossary.

become far too long warmest regards from me to everyone and especially to you from your friend

Suse

P.S. I think you're naïve to ask me if I still play with dolls or do you still play with your human children all day. I have English 4 times a week at school which is very nice. [. . .] We don't have any butter, eggs, coffee, margarine or many other things here, nice isn't it? The Rosentals have already landed in America and we are envious of them. I will close once again

Suse

Dear Lilo,

   The letter should have been sent a long time ago but I've experienced some things again [. . .] recently a children's transport went to England again they all have a guarantee, they ate with us at school and then traveled on with the Manhattan. Lilo I started to cry, first there were at least 15 children aged 3 and 4 they cried so much that we cried along with them I was helping because I've been through all that often before I would have loved to go along even the teacher felt differently when she saw that they were all children from the Reich including a few little ones from Hamburg Lilo if you had seen the misery but no one can understand who hasn't seen it himself and it's just good that only a few see it every time I've already seen more than enough most of all I'd like to just get into the car with them sometime and go along you always have a feeling when a transport goes but nothing can be changed I'm going to stop now otherwise I'm afraid that the letter will be too heavy I'll include pictures but they are nothing special I'm taller than I look in the pictures and above all not so fat on the contrary I'm rather thin and am envied by many!!! [. . .] I've made many typos but I don't feel like correcting them though I really should my nail is broken from typing I hope you all are well

   Warmest regards to you all

Suse

Kindertransporte became ever more frequent in the months after November 1938. Among the thousands of children sent on such transports were Inge Engelhard (b. 1930) and her two siblings, Berta and Theo. After "*Kristallnacht*," their parents, Moshe and Rachel Engelhard, managed to put Berta and Theo on a *Kindertransport* and send them to Britain. Inge was put on a train that departed from Munich in July 1939, and she made it to Britain as well. Document 2–8 includes Inge's identification card issued by the British, permitting her entry into the country. With their children safe in Britain, the Engelhards managed to flee Germany to Yugoslavia; when Germany invaded Yugoslavia in 1941, they again managed to escape, this time to Rome, then eventually to Spain and Portugal, from which they reached Britain and reunited with their children in 1943.

DOCUMENT 2–8: *Kindertransport* identity document for Inge Engelhard issued by British authorities, spring 1939, USHMMPA WS# 99687.

The *Kindertransporte* stirred up a range of conflicted emotions in adults. As the author of document 2–9 (published in early January 1939 in the Berlin edition of the *Jüdisches Nachrichtenblatt*) noted, the language in use reflected this ambivalence. The new circumstances demanded a new vocabulary, words that sounded odd and ominous but at the same time promised hope and deliverance. It was almost as if a new language was needed—perhaps one along the lines of Suse Behr's ungrammatical writing—to capture the increasingly fractured link between the nightmares of everyday life and the hopes and aspirations of individual Jews.

DOCUMENT 2–9: Martha Wertheimer,[27] "Children Are Dispatched. Snapshots from a Jewish Orphanage," *Jüdisches Nachrichtenblatt Berlin*, January 5, 1939, 2 (translated from German).

Today we are all learning words, and not only English, Spanish, and Portuguese ones. Our daily life has become full of terms that sounded new and strange at first and by now go with the territory, just as packing crates and wood shavings are part of the supplies needed for moving. In this Jewish vocabulary book, a new word is added almost every week to the end of the list we've just memorized. *Affidavits, llamadas* ["calls"], *Unbedenklichkeitsbescheinigungen* ["certificates of unobjectionability"], and *Umzugslisten* ["moving lists"] have been at the top of the list for a long time now, and down at the bottom, barely a couple of weeks old, is the new word *Kinderverschickung* ["sending children away"].

It's not a fine word, but it is a fine and good thing. It originated as the shortest and most practical term for the opportunity to let Jewish children enjoy the hospitality of Holland, Belgium, France, and Switzerland, to relieve Jewish mothers of worry about the hungry little mouths and the placement of their children. Suddenly the word was there, in orphanages, in children's homes, and in the offices of Jewish communities. Today we no longer know who coined it. It has no official origin, and it is not quasi-official in nature. It is a new word in our vocabulary book and is no longer to be eradicated from our usage, from our understanding, or from our thoughts.

Kindertransporte were complex rescue operations that demanded focused and relentless work on the part of the Jewish organizations involved. These organizations had to compile the lists of children they were going to put on the transports and then navigate the various constraints and strict rules that stood in the path from plan to implementation: the British government demanded,

---

27. A journalist from Frankfurt am Main, Dr. Martha Wertheimer (1886–1943) wrote for an Offenbach newspaper in the 1920s and early 1930s until she was dismissed under the Nazi regime. Active in Jewish cultural and youth affairs after 1933 in Frankfurt and Berlin, she organized emigration schemes to transfer Jewish children to England. She continued writing articles on cultural and religious questions for the state-sanctioned Jewish community press until the spring of 1941. Unable to emigrate in time, she and her sister Lydia were deported to Łódź and did not return. See LBINY catalog; Hanno Loewy, ed., *Martha Wertheimer. In mich ist die grosse dunkle Ruhe gekommen* (Frankfurt am Main: Stadt Frankfurt am Main, 1992); Kaplan, *Between Dignity*, 138–39, 254n47.

for instance, that private citizens or organizations cover the costs of each child's stay in Britain (including education), as well as guarantee his or her eventual emigration from Britain.

Édouard and Germaine de Rothschild led one of these rescue operations.[28] They worked with the Comité Israélite pour les Enfants venant d'Allemagne et de l'Europe Centrale, providing shelter for Jewish children from Germany, Austria, and Czechoslovakia. Between March and April 1939, the committee housed and educated 131 children at the Rothschilds' Château de la Guette in Seine-et-Marne near Paris. Families unable to leave the Third Reich provided parental renunciations in order to allow their sons or daughters to leave for France.[29]

DOCUMENT 2–10: Document signed by the widow Miriam Goldfarb,[30] Berlin, Germany, April 24, 1939, giving custody of her thirteen-year-old son, Eryk, to the

---

28. Édouard de Rothschild (1868–1949) was a French financier and member of the prominent European Jewish family. In 1905 he married Germaine Alice Halphen (1884–1975). For their activities during the German occupation of France, see the following footnote.

29. The Comité Israélite pour les Enfants venant d'Allemagne et de l'Europe Centrale (Jewish Committee for Children Coming from Germany and Central Europe) was an organization that worked with **OSE** (see Glossary) to provide shelter to Jewish refugee children. From January to June 1939, between 300 and 400 Jewish children entered France and were put under the care of these two organizations, often in hostels such as the one owned by the Rothschilds; some 150 of the total number of children were placed with families. Judith Tydor Baumel, *Unfulfilled Promise: Rescue and Resettlement of Jewish Refugee Children in the United States, 1933–1945* (Juneau: Denali Press, 1990), 206. On the relief operation at the Château de la Guette, see *Les enfants de la guette: Souvenirs et documents, 1938–1945* (Paris: Centre de documentation juive contemporaine, 1999). On the Rothschilds' relief work, see Herbert R. Lottman, *The French Rothschilds: The Great Banking Dynasty through Two Turbulent Centuries* (New York: Crown, 1995), 138, 211–12. The children at Château de la Guette were evacuated elsewhere just before the Germans entered Paris.

30. Eryk (Eric) Goldfarb's mother also established a lunchroom for young Jewish immigrants in their home. His brother, Hermann (born in 1919), helped support the family as a cabinetmaker in a factory. Eryk attended a Jewish school and joined a Zionist youth group. The family scattered as the war approached: Eryk's sister, Sonja (born in 1920), went to England in early 1939. In June of that year, Hermann left for Shanghai, while Eryk left Berlin in July on a *Kindertransport* bound for France. In August their mother went to England with a permit to work as a domestic. Eryk passed through a number of children's homes in France during the war, assumed a false identity, and eventually went into hiding. In June 1944 he and a group of friends joined the French armed resistance. He survived the war and immigrated to Canada in July 1952 with his wife and children, joining his sister and mother there. Information comes from a donor file, USHMMA Acc. 2004.362.

Comité Israélite pour les Enfants venant d'Allemagne et de l'Europe Centrale (Jewish Committee for Children Originating from Germany and Central Europe) USHMMA Acc. 2004.362 Eric and Fee Goldfarb collection (translated from French).[31]

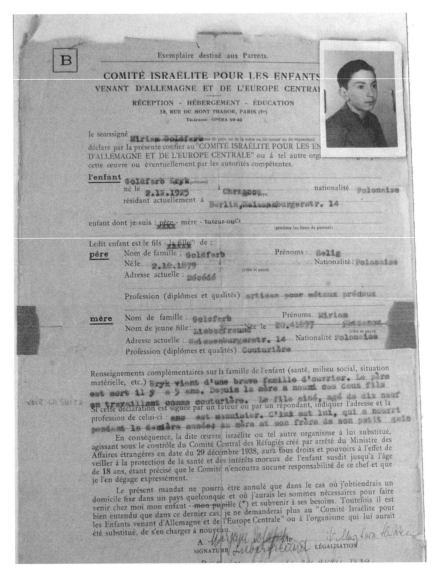

---

31. This form was printed; italicized text represents typed passages.

The undersigned *Miriam Goldfarb* hereby entrusts to the Comité Israélite pour les Enfants venant d'Allemagne et de l'Europe Centrale or to another such [text concealed by photo] this charity or if necessary to the appropriate authorities:

<u>the child</u> *Goldfarb Eryk*

born on *December 2, 1925* in *Chrzanów*, nationality *Polish*

currently residing in *Berlin, Weissenburgerstr. 14*

relationship of undersigned to child: *mother*

The aforesaid child is *the son* of:

<u>father</u> Surname: *Goldfarb*   Given names: *Selig*

    Born on *October 2, 1879*   Nationality: *Polish*

    Current address: *deceased*

    Profession (certificates/degrees and skills): *craftsman in precious metals*

    <u>mother</u> Surname: *Goldfarb*   Given names: *Miriam*

    Maiden name: *Lieberfreund* Born on   in *Chrzanów*
April 20, 1897

    Current address: *Weissenburgerstr. 14*   Nationality: *Polish*

    Profession: (certificates/degrees and skills): *dressmaker*

Additional information about the child's family (health, background, financial circumstances, etc.) *Eryk comes from a good working-class family. His father died when he was five. Since then his mother has supported her two sons by working as a dressmaker. The elder son, age 19, is a carpenter. It is he who has supported his mother and brother on his small salary for the past year.*

If this declaration is signed by a guardian or by a guarantor, indicate his/her profession and address: _____

Accordingly, the aforementioned Jewish charity or another such agency in its place, operating under the control of the Comité Central des Réfugiés, created by decree of the Minister of Foreign Affairs on December 29, 1938, will have full rights and powers for the purpose of watching over the health and moral interests of the aforesaid child until the age of 18 years, noting that the Comité will incur no responsibility on these grounds and that I expressly relieve it of such.

The present document cannot be declared void unless I obtain a fixed residence in some country and unless I have the necessary sums to send for my child and provide for his needs. However, it is understood that in the latter case I will not request the "Comité Israélite pour les Enfants venant d'Allemagne et de l'Europe Centrale," or the agency that takes its place, to take responsibility for him once more.

[Signed:] Mirjam Goldfarb Lieberfreund, Berlin, April 24, 1939
[Notarized, signature illegible]

TRYING TO SETTLE IN

The characterization of Jewish efforts to leave the Reich in this period as "flight" rather than strictly as "emigration" also encompasses the situation of Jews who got over the border but lacked official status on the other side. Indeed, some had even been expelled by German authorities, as were the refugees "marooned" in Zbąszyń. As a result, many Jews fleeing the Reich led transient existences. Many also found themselves back under Nazi authority as the Reich expanded its borders over the course of 1938 and 1939.

Jews fleeing the Sudetenland are a case in point. With Nazi Germany's annexation of this region of western Czechoslovakia in September 1938 as part of the **Munich agreement**, roughly 118,000 Jews were among the 200,000 people who were forced out or who escaped.[32] Most tried to resettle in what was left of Czechoslovakia, although its government did not automatically recognize all former Sudeten residents as citizens. Of course for those living in the Czech part of the country, citizenship made little difference when they fell back under the Nazi juggernaut six months later. Upon dismembering Czechoslovakia in March 1939, the Nazi occupiers quickly implemented the anti-Jewish measures they had put in place twelve months earlier in Austria. That "Austrian model" included setting up a Prague branch of Eichmann's Reichszentrale für jüdische Auswanderung to compel Jews to leave while expropriating their property and savings in the process.[33]

Arnold and Erna Stein and their two young daughters were among the Sudeten Jews who fled their home in Karlsbad (Karlovy Vary) upon the Nazi

---

32. On September 29, 1938, Britain and France signed the so-called Munich agreement with Hitler. Hoping to appease Nazi Germany's further expansionist demands and evade the war, Britain and France decided without consulting Czechoslovakia to cede a part of its territory populated by ethnic Germans (the Sudetenland) to Nazi Germany. Today, this agreement is widely seen as a shortsighted failure to check Hitler's aggression. For a discussion of the various aspects surrounding the Munich crisis, see Igor Lukes and Erik Goldstein, eds., *The Munich Crisis, 1938: Prelude to World War II* (London: Frank Cass, 1999).

33. For the aftermath of the Munich agreement and the history of the Holocaust in Czech lands, see Livia Rothkirchen, *The Jews of Bohemia and Moravia: Facing the Holocaust* (Lincoln and Jerusalem: University of Nebraska Press and Yad Vashem, 2005), 63–97.

annexation of that territory, losing everything as a result. Their experiences in flight were captured, in part, in an unusual diary kept jointly by Arnold and Erna. It was a "baby diary" they had commenced when their younger daughter, Gerda (Gerti), was born in June 1927. In sporadic entries addressed to Gerda, both parents wrote in the hope that she would retain a record of the big and small events in her young life.[34] Such a diary took on added significance when they were uprooted from their home and Gerda subsequently departed for England, in March 1939 at the age of eleven, to live in the care of an English professor as part of a *Kindertransport*. The diary entries from February and March 1939 describe the transient nature of their family's existence ever since leaving Karlsbad, their efforts to emigrate from Prague, and, failing that, their successful efforts to secure the future of at least one of their daughters.[35]

DOCUMENT 2–II: Arnold Stein, Prague, diary entries for February 18 and March 14, 1939, LBINY MM132 (translated from German).

Prague, February 18, 1939

Emigration and Jewish distress are two words that determine your fate and ours. We <u>had</u> to escape from Karlsbad, we were obliged to, although we did it voluntarily, despite being told 100 times by the kind locals that of course nothing would happen to us. Nonetheless, it was good that we fled in time. We left my business and the apartment behind. We brought Mama's knitting machine. Now we've been living here in Prague since the end of September [19]38. First with Aunt Trude and then with Serafine Novotna on Belskeho Street and since February 15 at 8 Nekazanka Street.—From our constant rushing and chasing from office to office, every week new regulations, with necessary documents etc., a chaos in which no one knows what he's doing and when it's all done the whole

---

34. For another example from this genre relating to a family from Bratislava, Slovakia, see Béla Weichherz, *In Her Father's Eyes: A Childhood Extinguished by the Holocaust*, ed. Daniel H. Magilow (New Brunswick, NJ: Rutgers University Press, 2008).

35. A child-rescue mission brought Gerda Stein (later Mayer) and nineteen other Jewish children by plane to England. She ultimately became an English-language poet. Her older sister (aged eighteen around 1939) was too old to qualify for a similar mission; see Muriel Emanuel and Vera Gissing, *Nicholas Winton and the Rescued Generation* (London: Vallentine Mitchell, 2002), 102. Gerda last heard from her father, Arnold Stein, in June 1940 from Lwów; he may have died in a Soviet camp near Moscow. Her mother, Erna Stein, died in Auschwitz; WL, finding aid, collection 578. No information on her aunt in Prague was found.

thing was a waste of time. In addition, running about to the consulates. I'm writing this because it indirectly concerns you, although you have almost nothing to do with all these things; still, it affects you. We put you in the Czech *Bürgerschule* after there was no longer any point in keeping you in the *Gymnasium*. After a week you were thrown out. The reason: no Czech school until now, and besides, you really don't know Czech. We then put you in the Czech Jewish *Volksschule*. But after it became clear to us that you couldn't stay there, you had 3 hours of English lessons daily and we took you out of the Jewish Czech school. Naturally, a year has been lost. But what is a lost year today, when decades of work melt away into nothingness.

We now have the possibility that an English professor will take you in. He's already applied to take you, and we hope it will happen. We have to emigrate, but where we'll go is not yet decided, as all countries are hermetically sealed against immigration. With you, getting launched in the new country would be almost impossible for us, so your acceptance is just as lucky for us as it is for you, as you will have the best education.

While I'm writing this entry, you're trying to draw, and not very successfully yet. Brush and drawing ink (?), simple wavy lines, spirals, etc. This is not up your alley. You only want "to paint something," not to practice monotonously, as with everything. [. . .] You're talented at everything but lack patience and diligence. You're more like me than your mother.

(c[ontinuation]) On March 14, [19]39, Gerda flew by plane to England. Mr. Chadwick, who took 20 children along, is taking Gerti into his home. God bless him and his family. Gerti, you're beginning a new life, good luck![36]

Among those who found themselves stranded were Jewish academics, not only from Germany but also from countries that adopted discriminatory measures of their own. The situation in these countries will be addressed in greater detail in chapter 8. For now, a letter from an Italian scientist banned from

---

36. An Oxford-educated schoolteacher from Dorset, Trevor Chadwick (1907?–1979) became involved with refugee child rescue in Prague at the end of 1938 and remained there into the following year. He served with the Royal Air Force Voluntary Reserve during the war until he was injured in 1943. Chadwick eventually settled in Oslo and worked in publishing. See Emanuel and Gissing, *Nicholas Winton and the Rescued Generation*, 91ff., 102–3, and Chadwick's account in Karen Gershon, ed., *We Came as Children: A Collective Autobiography* (New York: Harcourt, Brace & World, Inc., 1966), 22–24.

returning to her home country and resuming her career exemplifies some of the difficulties that academics faced trying to establish themselves abroad.[37]

DOCUMENT 2–12: **Letter by Gina Castelnuovo, Copenhagen, Denmark, to Emergency Committee in Aid of Displaced Foreign Scholars, New York City, April 8, 1939, NYPL MssCol 922, box 49, file 1.**

[. . .] During my stay in Amsterdam in summer, I learned that I had lost my position in Italy on account of my being a Jewess.[38] The same misfortune has arrived to my father [Guido Castelnuovo] as well as other members of my family, and it is impossible now to have another position in Italy.[39] At the end of my permission to stay in Amsterdam I had the chance to be called here, helped by Prof. Niels Bohr,[40] by the Marinbiologisk Lab. of Copenhagen to accomplish some researches, but when I arrived here, I heard from the police, it cannot possible [*sic*] be permitted to me a long permanence in this country and th[ere]fore that I am to leave Denmark at the 25th of May. Now I am very troubled, because it is impossible to find another position in all countries of Europe, because the

---

37. Gina Castelnuovo's letter found its way to the office of the Emergency Committee in Aid of Displaced Foreign Scholars at the Institute of International Education in New York City. Originally formed in 1933 to assist refugee professors who had lost their positions in German universities and institutions through antisemitic legislation, the committee gradually expanded its mission to help scholars facing political and anti-Jewish discrimination and peril in other European countries. The committee provided assistance for several hundred people, often placing them in temporary academic posts in the United States, although it lacked funds to provide substantial aid to more than a fraction of applicants. It disbanded in 1945. See NYPL, Manuscripts and Archives Division, MssCol 922; USHMMA RG 19.061M Records of the Emergency Committee in Aid of Displaced Foreign Scholars; Stephen Duggan and Betty Drury, *The Rescue of Science and Learning: The Story of the Emergency Committee in Aid of Displaced Foreign Scholars* (New York: Macmillan, 1948).

38. A biologist by training, Castelnuovo specialized in experimental endocrinology and hormone research and had been dropped from her post at a scientific institute in Rome.

39. Her father, a prominent mathematician at the University of Rome, survived the war and was asked to revive Italy's scientific institutions. He became a senator in 1949.

40. Niels Bohr (1885–1962) was a Danish physicist and a 1922 Nobel Prize winner for his groundbreaking work on atomic structure and quantum mechanics. In 1943 he escaped to Sweden and ultimately the United States. Though involved with the project that produced the first atomic bomb, he later advocated for the peaceful application of nuclear science and international agreements to resolve the problems arising from atomic weapons. See the website of the Nobel Organization at http://nobelprize.org/nobel_prizes/physics/laureates/1922/bohr-bio.html (accessed April 13, 2010).

different Governments don't give the permission of work to a foreigner and it cannot possibly be permitted to me to work in Italy. [. . .]

I am really very sorry to disturb you. But my position is now very critical and I am really very down-spirited because the difficulties of finding a position are really enormous. [. . .] I fully understand that it will be very difficult, especially as there are already many other foreigners to be helped. [. . .][41]

As was the case with Castelnuovo, even central European Jews who got out of the Reich confronted enormous new challenges. They suddenly found themselves in unfamiliar and even alien environments, living far below the standards that they had been used to at home and having to compete for jobs with local inhabitants who often showed little sympathy for their plight. Not only did they face the hardships brought about by the uncertainty of their situations, but some also struggled with the difficulties of adjusting to a society very different from that in their place of origin. Sometimes this unwanted change led to frustration and anger (as, for example, in the case of Tobias Farb, see document 2–14); at other times, however, people found ways to establish themselves in a foreign environment and to forge social bonds. Walter Jacobsberg, for example, worked as a German-English interpreter in Shanghai. He had fled to Shanghai with his father in 1939 from Stettin. In the course of his work helping German Jewish refugees with their paperwork before Chinese courts, he developed contacts with several Chinese interpreters. Although we know little about the names and fates of the Chinese with whom he worked, we can infer that the bonds of business and friendship were strong enough to have led them to decide to take a photograph together. Walter and his father emigrated to the United States in 1947.

---

41. It is unclear what the committee did for her apart from circulating her name a bit. Betty Drury, the committee's assistant administrator, wrote Gregory Pincus at Clark University on May 17, 1939, "There is unfortunately very little we can do for Dr. Castelnuovo beyond keeping her papers here on file in the hope that some suitable opportunity may come to our attention." The "List or Manifest of Alien Passengers for the United States Immigration Officer at Port of Arrival," July 13, 1939 (NARA I files), showed that Gina Castelnuovo, a thirty-one-year-old biologist, arrived in New York on the SS *Rex* from Naples. She held a series of posts during the war, including at a laboratory of the Museum of Natural History in New York and the Woman's Medical College in Philadelphia. After the war, she eventually returned to Italy and continued her professional work there.

DOCUMENT 2–13: **The family of a Chinese translator who worked with Walter Jacobsberg, Shanghai, China, ca. 1940, USHMMPA WS# 25771.**

The letter Tobias Farb wrote from Shanghai in April 1939, copies of which were circulated among Jewish relief workers in the United States, amply illustrates the hardships this Viennese refugee experienced in an unfamiliar and seemingly threatening environment. It also reflects a central European's preconceived notions about Chinese society and culture—prejudices probably amplified by hardship. The majority of the Jewish refugee population in Shanghai was supported by local and American relief organizations, in particular the **American Jewish Joint Distribution Committee** (AJJDC), since few economic opportunities existed in the city as a result of the ongoing Sino-Japanese conflict.[42]

---

42. Because this letter is a typed copy from the AJJDC files, typographic errors have been corrected here without being annotated.

DOCUMENT 2–14: **Letter by Tobias Farb,[43] Shanghai, China, to an unnamed recipient in the United States, April 28, 1939, facsimile reprinted in** *Archives of the Holocaust,* **ed. Henry Friedlander and Sybil Milton (New York: Garland Publishing, 1995), 10/1:316–18.**

My dear:

Since February 22nd I have been in Shanghai, and feel wretched. The first impression on arrival and the journey through the war shelled area to our camp was depressing beyond words. The conditions we are faced with, the surroundings, the deplorable economic circumstances and consequently the hopelessness of getting a job, the remoteness of the world the difficulties to get away from here some day and the dread of spreading diseases, these each in turn add to inexpressible despair and drive us, who had to go through inhuman hardships already to a complete breakdown. We keep ourselves upright as yet, as we are newcomers but are aware of sufferings on end to come.

Hope for a change for the better gives us strength to stick [with] it. I never thought my fate to take such a turn. I feel lonely and forlorn once it is true, while a war prisoner but no such distress, despair and despondency I never felt before. I somehow try to buck up but usually fail as I cannot believe in the future. There are moments sometimes—the strong will and an overpowering longing to get to wife and child again will, so I hope, keep me upright. It is not dependent on myself entirely though, I hope unto the almighty that my wife, my youngest brother who is to go to the United States too, and you my dear, who are lucky to be already there, will be able to help me. I am helpless here as are the thousands with me. Have I to give up hope to get reunited with my family again then my life has become useless.

We live here in the ravaged part of town called Hongken about 3/4 of an hour's journey to the International Concession. This part is under Japanese control and has the only advantage that a few Chinese only live here so that the air if one can speak of an air at all, is better and the dangers of disease lesser. But on the other hand to get into the International Concession where you have to go to find a job or post letters, is very

---

43. Tobias Farb (1898–1978), an Austrian Jew, left Vienna for Shanghai, arriving in early 1939. He survived the war there, while his wife, Erna (1897–1978), may have spent the duration in England. In March 1947, Farb left for the United States, where he rejoined his wife. Eventually they settled in California. *USHMM ITS Collection Data Base Central Name Index.* Information on their child is not available.

difficult. Either you have to walk a long way along dusty roads or fight with filthy Chinese for room in the bus. The town itself except for a few stately buildings leaves no deeper impression. It is teeming with Chinese who are fighting and spitting everywhere so that you fall sick at the sight of it. Everything is dull nothing to cheer you up. At the bank of a dirty river in the Dschunken, there are the slums, the major part of the population. Through the war there are nearly 1 1/2 million refugees and also the bad economic situation is caused by the war. With the European inhabitants the tendency for closing down is prevalent. The Chinese are cheap labor get miserable wages though they are skillful workers. Each office, banking house, workshop is flooded with them and have for us no chance whatsoever. On the one side economic depression and the other the impossibility to compete with the Chinese that is the situation we are faced with and this is to give you courage and hope. Some of our people try to set up in business but they can keep themselves as long only as the German refugees have a penny still to spend. What is to become of the others who are there already and those who are forced to come yet? For everyone endeavors to escape the hell of the Nazis no matter whatever fate has in store for him elsewhere. Are you lucky enough to get a job then you get a Kuli's [*sic*] pay so that you have not enough to buy food. Besides nobody cares to engage you where cheap labor is in abundance. There remains hope only to get away from here; even if there is a spark of it left in me. I shall put up with anything when still in Vienna Shanghai did not offer any promising outlook for me but I had no other possibility as I was compelled by the Nazi authorities to sign a paper saying to leave at a certain date, and what I find here is beyond any of my expectations. I must be glad after all that I did not take dear Erna and the child with me for then it would have come to a catastrophe on top of all I am to[o] worried about them because I did not hear anything from them. They were to depart on the 11/11 had everything ready already and till now I had not a single line has reached me. With all that you can imagine what ordeal I go through. The building where we are housed was a school formerly. There are 40 people in one room with 40 bunks, little room left to one individual as you can imagine. One cannot even unpack the suitcases, all the clothes are getting dusty and crumpled. If you need anything you must search your suitcase for it what happens to be a hundred times a day. Very little sanitary conveniences too. One washing basin for about 8–10 people food is monotonous there is only one dish without any change, there is also tea that is smelling of carbolic acid as the water has to be disinfected every other day, lunch and supper and you have to stand in queu[e]s. Pocket money there is none, underwear, postage and sundries you have to defray yourself.

How are you my dear I hope you are well which is somewhat a consolation to me for I know you will endeavor with whatever means you can to help me. Don't let dear Erna know what I am writing to you it would break her heart and she has to be brave for the child's sake.

I kiss you with all my love.

DOCUMENT 2–15: Jewish refugee women preparing vegetables in the refugee colony, Shanghai, China, undated (between 1939 and 1948), USHMMPA WS# 23569.

In countries where, unlike in Shanghai, established and sizable native Jewish populations existed, they were quite sensitive about the issue of central European refugees "blending into" the majority culture. They perceived the refugees' alien ways as impinging on their own situation, fearful that the increased visibility of Jews in the news and on the streets would aggravate anti-Jewish sentiment in their own countries. Yet, they also felt sympathy for and wanted to assist their persecuted coreligionists from central Europe. In western Europe, local Jewish populations had established committees to assist refugees as early as 1933, within months of the Nazis coming to power. In Britain, Belgium, and the Netherlands, the financial burden of accommodating, retraining, and resettling refugees fell to these Jewish organizations rather than to the government. With the worsening refugee crisis in 1938, the demands placed on these organizations grew exponentially. What was more, the difficulty of their position became all the more acute. They felt trapped between wanting to rescue Jewish refugees and to demonstrate their patriotism, not to come across as too narrow and "particularistic" in their concerns at a time of increasing international tension.[44] In 1939, the German Jewish Aid Committee in Britain (formerly the Jewish Refugees Committee) published bilingual guides in German and English with advice and information for newcomers to their country.

DOCUMENT 2–16: "While You Are in England: Helpful Information and Guidance for Every Refugee," pamphlet distributed in England by the German Jewish Aid Committee, 1939, USHMMA Acc. 2003.58.1 Joseph family papers.

THE TOLERANCE AND SYMPATHY
of Britain and the British Commonwealth

The traditional tolerance and sympathy of Britain and the British Commonwealth towards the Jews is something which every British Jew appreciates profoundly. On his part he does all in his power to express his loyalty to Britain and the British Commonwealth, in word and in deed, by personal service and by communal effort.

This loyalty comes first and foremost, and every Refugee should realise how deeply it is felt.

The Jewish Community in Britain will do its very utmost to welcome and maintain all Refugees, to educate their Children, to care for the Aged and the Sick—and to assist in every possible way in creating new homes for them overseas. A great many Christians, in all walks of life, have spontaneously associated themselves with this work. All that we ask from you in return is to carry out to your utmost the following

44. On the Netherlands, see Dan Michman, "The Committee for Jewish Refugees in Holland (1933–1940)," *YVS* 14 (1981): 205–32; Bob Moore, *Victims and Survivors: The Nazi Persecution of the Jews in the Netherlands, 1940–1945* (London: Arnold, 1997), 29–34. On Britain, see Shatzkes, *Holocaust and Rescue*, 26–27, 33–39. On Belgium, see the WJC untitled report on refugee assistance in Belgium, 1933–1938, USHMMA RG 11.001M36, reel 107, folder 289.

lines of conduct. <u>Regard them, please, as duties to which you are in honor bound</u>:

Spend your spare time immediately in learning the English language and its correct pronunciation.

Refrain from speaking German in the streets and in public conveyances and in public places such as restaurants. Talk halting English rather than fluent German—and <u>do not talk in a loud voice</u>. Do not read German newspapers in public.

Do not criticize any Government regulations, nor the way things are done over here. Do not speak of "how much better this or that is done in Germany." It may be true in some matters, but it weighs as nothing against the sympathy and freedom and liberty of England which are now given to you. Never forget that point.

<u>Do not join any political organization</u>, or take part in any political activities.

Do not make yourself conspicuous by speaking loudly, nor by your manner or dress. The Englishman greatly dislikes ostentation, <u>loudness of dress or manner</u>, or unconventionality of dress or manner. <u>The Englishman attaches very great importance to</u> modesty, under-statement in speech rather than over-statement, and quietness of dress and manner. He values good manners far more than he values the evidence of wealth. (You will find that he says "Thank you" for the slightest service—even for a penny bus ticket for which he has paid.)

Try to observe and follow the manners and customs and habits of this country, in social and business relations.

Do not spread the poison of "It's bound to come in your country." The British Jew greatly objects to the planting of this craven thought.

Above all, please realise that the Jewish community is relying on you—<u>on each and every one of you</u>—to uphold in this country the highest Jewish qualities, to maintain dignity, and to help and serve others.

* * *

If you are planning to make your permanent home overseas, regard this stay in England as a "mark time" period during which you are preparing yourself for your new life. Do not expect to be received immediately in English homes, because the Englishman takes some time before he opens his home wide to strangers.

Use your energies and your special skill to help those even more unhappy than yourself—the lonely Refugee Children, the Aged and the Sick, in your neighborhood.

Spread courage by word and deed.
There is a new and better future before you.
<u>Be loyal to England, your host.</u>

Native British Jews' concern for appearances and for the assimilation of German-speaking Jewish immigrants revealed their wider insecurity and fear of antisemitism. In other countries as well, negative stereotypes and a narrow range of opportunities for newcomers had a direct impact on the lives of those who had managed to escape persecution in the Reich; sometimes, however, people could beat the odds. Nathan (third from the right in the photograph in document 2–17) and Julius (Nathan's son, fourth from the left) Wolfinger were Jewish refugees from Austria, part of the extended Wolfinger-Spitzer family that managed to flee to La Paz, Bolivia, in 1939. Pooling their familial resources, the family survived and even prospered. Like Walter Jacobsberg's photograph from Shanghai (see document 2–13), the image in document 2–17 hints at the promises and challenges that Jewish refugees encountered as they worked to integrate themselves into new and unfamiliar environments.

DOCUMENT 2–17: **Austrian Jewish refugees and local workers, La Paz, Bolivia, ca. 1940, USHMMPA WS# 33977.**

Eduard Cohn's letter to the AJJDC, written in the spring of 1939, testifies to the obstacles that Paraguayan authorities erected in order to forestall Jewish immigration as well as to the wider phenomenon of Jewish families dispersed over different regions, countries, and sometimes continents.[45]

DOCUMENT 2–18: Letter by Eduard Cohn, Asunción, Paraguay, to AJJDC, New York, June 4, 1939, LBINY MF 488 (AJJDC case file).

Asuncion, June 4, 1939
Calle Oliva 226.

The American Jewish Joint Distribution Committee, Inc.
New York City.

Gentlemen:

I wish to thank you for your letter of March 27th, 1939, which I received in reply to my letter of February 25th. As I advised you already, my wife and my two children arrived in Montevideo [Uruguay] on April 21st, 1939.

In accordance with a new Paraguayan decree, all immigration documents for Asuncion have to be forwarded prior to embarkation from Montevideo, in order that their propriety may be ascertained. After that has been done also in the case of my wife and my children, another decree was passed, on the basis of which the amount of 1,500 Pesos oro, or 3,410 Argentinian Pesos, [equals] 800 U.S.A. Dollars. Of course, I have tried all in my power to have the validity of the immigration documents, once issued, upheld. However, in response to my intercession the Immigration Department advised me that Jews will not be permitted to immigrate. I have also contacted a lawyer who refused offhand to represent my interests, as immigration of the Jews was considered to be undesirable on the part of the military authorities. Thereupon, I got in touch with a lawyer whose name was given me by the Hamburg-Sued steamship agency. Although he was on friendly terms with the Chief of Immigration, he was

---

45. For an overview of Jewish emigration to Latin America during the Nazi years, see Judith Laikin Elkin, *Jews of the Latin American Republics* (Chapel Hill: University of North Carolina Press, 1980), 84–99. When the Cohn family was reunited or whether they remained in South America is unknown. The petitioner's parents in Berlin, Mr. and Mrs. Carl Cohn, also sought help in joining Eduard in Paraguay, but were still in Germany after the outbreak of war. See LBINY MF 488 (AJJDC case files).

unable to do anything for me. Negotiations to that effect have been conducted since April 21st, and it was only yesterday that I was notified that the immigration of my wife and my children would only be permitted on the basis of the above mentioned debarkation money.

In the awareness of the fact that my wife has no possibility to raise the said amount in Montevideo, a perfect strange city, and that my income as a worker on a mill will not enable me even in a few years to send her the required sum, we have to realize that we have to remain separated for the time being.

The main trouble is, however, that my wife and the children have nothing to live on. They cannot expect any assistance from the Sociedad de Proteccion a los Imigrantes Israelitas, as my wife advised me that they have no funds available for assistance. She has immediately accepted a household position and makes 15. Uruguayan Pesos per month, including dinner for the children, while my wife has to take care of her own breakfast and supper, and, in addition, has to pay the rent. The rent amounts to 24. Uruguayan Pesos, which makes it impossible for my wife to get along with the two children. The local Community does its best to alleviate the needs, but the funds are very limited, so that my wife can face the future only with a feeling of horror. Unfortunately, I don't possess anything, as I had to leave Germany immediately after my release from concentration camp.

On June 10th, my boy had his Barmizvah [sic], and I could neither be there, nor send him something.

I therefore appeal to you to assist my wife and my two children with some money. I did not turn to any other organization for help, and it is my sincere and only hope that you will make an exception. I am enclosing a telegram which I received from my wife, and you will kindly note therefrom what the situation is. I am giving you below the address of the place where my wife works and also her home address. I assure you that I have stated the entire truth and beg you to help my wife and our two children.

Very respectfully yours,
Eduard Cohn,

Home address of my wife
Margot Cohn,
Montevideo,
San Salvador 1767.

Employer's address
c/o Dr. Holz,
Pensionat, Montevideo.

Translation of Cable:
HAD DISCUSSION WITH CONSUL IMMIGRATION FAILS
BECAUSE OF LACKING DEPOSIT WHICH DESPITE
INTERVENTION REQUIRED stop ADJUSTMENT HERE
IMPOSSIBLE ALMOST PENNILESS TRY EVERYTHING
(NO SIGNATURE)

As the above documents lay bare, legal and financial restrictions in Europe and beyond, as well as political pressures, economic conditions, and social climates in which Jewish emigrants were clearly not welcome, made emigration from Germany in the aftermath of "*Kristallnacht*" a complicated and expensive undertaking, impossible to navigate without help from Jewish organizations. Many Jews who embarked on the uncertain path of emigration realized this and, like Eduard Cohn, appealed for aid from the few remaining bodies that could be expected to help. Ultimately, the burden of providing relief fell on the shoulders of individual Jewish organizations and communities, from rather sizeable ones with international reach—such as the AJJDC, the Jewish Agency, or Jewish political parties in the *Yishuv*, with their networks in central and eastern Europe and the United States—to local ones, such as the various Jewish communities across the globe. But Jewish communities and organizations outside the Reich were not equipped for as large-scale and coordinated a rescue effort as the Nazi peril demanded. Ironically, they lacked the very things that Nazi propaganda demonized them for conspiring to use to destroy Germany and assert "world domination": a centralized political leadership, political clout, and significant financial means.

The growing disproportion between Jews' urge to escape the Nazi grip and the lack of immigration opportunities fueled an illegal movement that had sprung up in the mid-1930s in Palestine, known among Zionists as **Aliyah Bet**. It was supported separately by the *Yishuv*'s mainstream Zionist leadership and the opposition Revisionist Zionist organization and aimed to bring as many Jews to Palestine as possible, despite the restrictions imposed by the British. The Nazis were aware of these activities, unofficially sanctioned them, and even maintained contact with the Zionists—the two camps being, in the words of Yehuda Bauer, "enemies with a common interest."[46] Because of the need for secrecy and the lack of resources, Jews in flight risked their lives

---

46. For an overview of *Aliyah Bet* and Nazi-Zionist contacts, see Yehuda Bauer, *Jews for Sale? Nazi-Jewish Negotiations, 1933–1945* (New Haven, CT: Yale University Press, 1994), 44–54. See also Francis R. Nicosia, *Zionism and Anti-Semitism in Nazi Germany* (New York: Cambridge University Press, 2008).

traveling on dangerously overcrowded and old ships from ports in Yugoslavia and Romania or down the Danube, trying to reach the shores of Palestine without detection. Some ships were at sea for weeks or even months because of the obstacles to landing safely. Most eventually did make it, but Jewish refugees then faced possible internment in British detention camps, some located as far away as Mauritius in the Indian Ocean. In all, an estimated 18,100 immigrants arrived to Palestine illegally, half from central Europe and most between 1938 and 1941.[47]

Outside the Jewish political networks, individual Jewish communities struggled to respond to the refugees' desperate need of assistance, trapped on unseaworthy ships in their ports. The president of the Salonika Jewish Community sought help from the **World Jewish Congress** (WJC).[48]

DOCUMENT 2–19: Letter by Leon Gattegno,[49] president of the Jewish community of Salonika, to the World Jewish Congress, Paris, June 7, 1939, USHMMA RG 11.001 M36, reel 107 (SAM 1190-1-299) (translated from French).

Dear Sirs:

We confirm our letter of May 12, 1939, and acknowledge receipt of your letter dated May 22, 1939.

The situation here is becoming more tragic every day, and we are literally overwhelmed and do not know how to relieve the immense misery spread out before us. The unfortunate 1,500 refugees on the ships *Agios*

---

47. Marrus, *The Unwanted*, 186; Dalia Ofer, *Escaping the Holocaust: Illegal Immigration to the Land of Israel, 1939–1944* (New York: Oxford University Press, 1990). For a description of the journey via the Danube through the Mediterranean Sea to Palestine after the beginning of the war, see also chapter 7 of this volume.

48. For a history of Jews in Greece in the interwar period, see Katherine E. Fleming, *Greece: A Jewish History* (Princeton, NJ: Princeton University Press, 2008), 91–109. For a history of the Holocaust and Nazi occupation in Greece, see Steven B. Bowman, *The Agony of Greek Jews, 1940–1945* (Stanford, CA: Stanford University Press, 2009); Mark Mazower, *Inside Hitler's Greece: The Experience of Occupation, 1941–1944* (New Haven, CT: Yale University Press, 1993).

49. Leon Gattegno (1863?–1943) was a Jewish secondary school principal and the president of the Jewish community of Salonika from 1938 to 1941. He had previously been elected, in 1915, to serve as a deputy in the Greek Assembly. In 1943 he was deported to Auschwitz, where he perished.

Nikolaos,[50] *Astir,*[51] and *Assimi*[52] are well on the way to being struck by an attack of collective insanity as a result of the despair that grips them, and this thought makes us shudder. Until now, and despite the lateness of the season for our regions, the weather has been exceedingly mild, but we see with real anguish that the period of great heat is coming. It will torture our coreligionists, who are taxed already, as they are forced to sleep in overheated and stinking ship holds and the slightest illness can provoke catastrophes.

The Jewish Communities of Athens and Salonika have made every sacrifice and every effort to help them, but the task is far beyond our means and is becoming a superhuman effort for us. Help is indispensable and needed immediately, and we beg you to tell us ways to further our effort to feed these unfortunate people, to prevent them from sinking into madness, and, above all, to find a definitive shelter as soon as possible.

It is impossible to prolong their stay on these miserable little boats, which are cramped and unhealthy, and where they are penned up like a herd of animals headed straight to the slaughterhouse.

We are coming to you to let out a cry of anguish and to make you aware that this desperate situation cannot, must not, continue. A remedy must be found before it is too late!

With our hearts broken by compassion for the dreadful spectacle before us, we nonetheless retain the hope that your organization will

---

50. The *Agios Nikolaos* set sail from Varna, Bulgaria, in June 1939 with 693 people on board. It arrived on July 3, 1939. It is not clear who organized the transport.

51. The *Astir* left Varna, Bulgaria, on March 6, 1939, with 699 people on board. This was an especially important transport, organized by the Revisionist Zionist Betar youth movement, with two hundred of its most important members from Poland along with a group of Danzig refugees. The British intercepted the boat on shore, brought it to Haifa, and then forced it to leave Palestine. On June 13, the passengers moved to a different boat and tried again, reaching Palestine two weeks later. Of the 724 passengers, 303 refugees were arrested.

52. The *Assimi* set sail from Constanța, Romania, on March 20, 1939, with 369 people on board. A total of 141 persons reached land in Palestine before the ship was captured by the British off the coast of Caesarea. Forced to set sail with the remaining passengers on board, it tried twice more to land before the passengers were transferred to a different ship, ninety miles away from the Palestinian coast. For a list of immigrant vessels with Jewish refugees during *Aliyah Bet*, consult annexes A and B in Ninian Stewart, *The Royal Navy and the Palestine Patrol* (London: Frank Cass, 2002), 183–95.

immediately do whatever is necessary to send financial assistance and to end this terrible martyrdom.

Please accept the assurances of our highest consideration.

The Secretary   The President
[illegible]   [signed] L. Gatteg

The tone of Gattegno's letter illustrates the desperate situation in which the refugees found themselves. Uncertainty about reaching their destination and a lack of basic supplies contributed to the extreme anxiety among the passengers to the point where, to outside observers, an eruption of "collective insanity" seemed imminent. In some cases, refugees took up a pen themselves and addressed the outside world in their own words. The *St. Louis*, a luxury liner owned by the German company HAPAG, set sail in May 1939 from Hamburg for Havana, Cuba, with 937 passengers on board. Most of the passengers were Jewish refugees who hoped to remain in Cuba while awaiting American visas. A sudden change in Cuban immigration laws, however, rendered invalid the "tourist letters" already in the passengers' possession. As a result, all but twenty-two refugees, whose papers were deemed in order, were denied entry into Havana. The U.S. government would not yield and grant asylum; the ship had no other choice but to return to Europe with virtually all of its original passengers. After strenuous negotiations carried out by the AJJDC, the Netherlands, France, Great Britain, and Belgium each accepted a portion of the refugees. They disembarked in mid-June, after having crossed the Atlantic twice.[53] The letter in document 2–20, written on board the *St. Louis* by one of the passengers, conveys a sense of the mood prevailing among passengers beset by a mixture of anxiety, cabin fever, hope, and anticipation while adrift in an unreal setting.

---

53. For the story of the *St. Louis*, see Sara A. Ogilvie and Scott Miller, *Refuge Denied: The St. Louis Passengers and the Holocaust* (Madison: University of Wisconsin Press, 2006); Breitman and Kraut, *American Refugee Policy and European Jewry*, 70–74.

DOCUMENT 2–20: Letter by Lici Dzialowski,[54] aboard the MS *St. Louis*, to Hella Slagter,[55] June 12, 1939, USHMMA Acc. 1997.36 Betty Troper Jaeger papers (translated from German).

40th parallel, north of the Azores
June 12, 1939

It's been several days since I wrote. But the events, or rather the non-events, really could put anyone off writing. This is true to the extent that one interprets "events" as positive events. Because enough negative things have happened.

We've made progress only in the voyage eastward, headed toward Europe, and have taken giant strides in that direction. I estimate that we've already covered easily 2/3 of the way from Havana back to Hamburg. Though only three days ago it was still frowned on as defeatism even to utter the word "Hamburg," the word is now being used quite openly among close acquaintances. Possibly it's just being identified.

For several days, on almost a daily basis, there have been general meetings in the big hall, in which the captain, too, usually takes part now, taking the most irreproachable attitude, which has to be acknowledged, given his especially delicate task. He manages to avoid giving offense at every possible point, while the entire ship is firmly convinced that he fully and completely discerns and represents our interests.

The possible period of time for a return to Havana or Dominica with sufficient fuel and food expired yesterday at noon, and now, in the best case, we will have to take on both in Europe before we can sail any farther.

Through the senior crew members and through the committee, we are in contact by cable with all the institutions and all the influential figures of the world from whom any help at all is to be expected. Meetings

---

54. Lici Dzialowski (née Grünthal; 1894–1984), was on the ship with her brothers and their families. Upon being returned to Europe, she and her second husband, Bruno Dzialowski (1884–1970), a former bank director in the Silesian town of Liegnitz, ended up in Rotterdam. They later managed to get to Palestine, survived the war, and were buried in Berlin's Weissensee cemetery. See Michael Hepp, ed., *Die Ausbürgerung deutscher Staatsangehörigen, 1933–45* (Munich: K. G. Saur, 1985), 1:260; USHMMA Acc. 1997.36 Betty Troper Jaeger collection.

55. Hella Slagter may have been Lici's sister-in-law, Helene Slagter (née Dzialowski; 1892–1945), in Rotterdam, who was sent first to the Westerbork camp and then to Bergen-Belsen, dying in the spring of 1945 after being liberated. Her son Mozes (1930–1944?) was also evidently killed in the Bergen-Belsen camp. See www.joodsmonument.nl (accessed March 3, 2011); *USHMM ITS Collection Data Base Central Name Index.*

and notices from the senior crew members and the committee alternate; we have the feeling that everything humanly possible is being done to bring this odyssey of a modern-day Flying Dutchman to a happy conclusion, but even today, when we are only four days from Hamburg, there is still no success, no result, to record.

The day before yesterday, a cable from WARBURG New York was made public, saying that he considers Cuba and Dominica impossible.[56] From that, everyone then drew the only possible conclusion. The Joint [AJJDC] in New York and its branch office in Havana provide no positive news of any kind, or even negative news. Its behavior is an absolute puzzle, but it can't be condemned outright until clarification is available. Negotiations are also under way with Woburn House in London and with HICEM in Paris.[57] There was a cable asking how many men, women, and children are on the ship, who has affidavits (about 75%), and who has permits for England. There is word of a projected temporary stay in England or France until the question of accommodating us all together or dispersed somewhere in the world has been resolved. People say that the *St. Louis* should continue to be chartered by one of the organizations so that we keep this floor, so essential to us, under our feet or that we should be reloaded in Southampton onto a foreign ship. The French Joint Committee cabled yesterday that a huge variety of schemes are in the works and that we'll get a cable within 36 hours notifying us of a result. And the ship continues its voyage eastward, at full steam, toward Europe. We've now come from the 22nd parallel to the 40th parallel and are heading sharply and unswervingly to the east. We know that the ship's course

---

56. Edward Warburg (1908–1992) was cochairman of AJJDC from 1939 to 1965, except for the period of his service in the U.S. Army during World War II. He was the son of Felix Warburg (1871–1937), one of the original founders of the Joint and, until his death, its undisputed leader. See Bauer, *My Brother's Keeper*, 251, and Yehuda Bauer, *American Jewry and the Holocaust: The American Jewish Joint Distribution Committee, 1939–1945* (Detroit, MI: Wayne State University Press, 1981), 22–23. At the time Dzialowski wrote her letter, in June 1939, the chairman of AJJDC was Paul Baerwald. This accounts for the fact that the author of the letter lists the organization's news separately from the Warburg cable; at that time, Warburg was still leading the AJJDC committee on refugee countries. Bauer, *My Brother's Keeper*, 251.

57. Woburn House was the London seat of a number of British Jewish organizations, including the headquarters of the Board of Deputies of British Jews, the central Jewish organization in Britain. For a history of the board of deputies, see Todd Endelman, *The Jews of Britain, 1656 to 2000* (Berkeley: University of California Press, 2002). For more on **HICEM**, a Paris-based international organization for Jewish refugees, see the Glossary.

does not lie within the captain's discretion but is determined solely by the Hapag shipping company.

We know what "east" can mean, and yet we refuse to believe it, we can't imagine that the fate of these still more than 900 people—up to 99% of whom were unemployed, penniless, and homeless in their home country—cannot be worked out. But we also know that our lot is the lot of all those back at home who must emigrate; we, on whose behalf the press, the radio, and the organizations and influential people of the world are exerting themselves, can't even be helped, we, who for more than 18 days, since our ship was turned away from Havana, actually have had no country where we can go, and who, were it not for the ownerless ocean, would have no place on earth. Today is our 31st day at sea, the 18th day since we knew that we had "certain landing difficulties" in Havana (this was the first indication). Readers, do you know what that means for nerves that unfortunately are not made of mooring ropes? And nevertheless, the attitude of everyone, with quite minuscule exceptions, is irreproachable and contrary to all expectation. If a stranger came on board, he wouldn't notice at first what's going on. But fortunately, people have kept their composure to a great extent.

At the same time, besides the common lot, there is still so much personal tragedy: the couples and families who have been separated, some on the ship, the others in Havana. Some members of these families had come to Havana from every corner of the world especially to meet their loved ones and in most cases had spent their last penny for that purpose. In addition, there were quite a few engaged couples in the same situation. How inhumane the Cuban government was: not even the widow of the man who died aboard ship and was buried at sea, whose son was in Havana after a cable to that effect, or the wife of the man who had jumped into the sea in Havana and was hospitalized there were allowed to stay there; they are continuing on this odyssey, just as we are. [. . .]

I've revised one of my opinions: in Havana, I thought that patience was required only in dealing with the Cuban authorities; apparently, however, it is also needed when dealing with all the rest of the world, whether it be the Joint, Woburn House, HICEM, the Hilfsverein,[58] Warburg, large shipping lines, or powerful people in world politics, the press, and film. What use are cables to us in our situation; let people work day and night and try everything humanly possible if they will, should we keep calm and

---

58. For more on the Hilfsverein, see the Glossary.

stay confident if nothing, and I mean nothing, positive happens and our course takes us farther and farther eastward? [. . .]

And with that I conclude my report today, which I'm writing in the open mezzanine during the morning concert again. So let's continue to wait, prepared for all eventualities, but prepared at any rate—that's the only thing that's important now.

The situation of Jewish refugees remained at a crisis level in the summer of 1939. As of that June, several thousand of the Jews expelled from Germany to Poland more than eight months before were still living in a no-man's-land as stateless persons and refugees. Their initial feelings of despair mixed with relief to be out of Nazi Germany had turned into simple despair as they continued to be denied entry into Poland or any other country. Sharing that status were other groups of Jews who had been forced out of their homes and pushed over the border from different regions of the former Czechoslovakia, Danzig, and Memel. These refugees were considered "marooned," a powerful image that captures the experience of entrapment, hopelessness, and abandonment repeated in many reports by Jewish relief organizations from the first six months of 1939.[59]

The threat of war further complicated the work of Jewish officials trying to assist Jewish refugees. Their reading of the political situation had an impact on the strategies they pursued. Officials working with the AJJDC and local refugee committees in Poland struggled with the dilemma of trying to apply pressure on different countries to absorb the refugees in Zbąszyń while simultaneously attempting to meet the pressing physical needs of the refugees. In a letter of July 1, 1939, **Morris Troper**, chairman of the European Executive Council of the AJJDC, expressed his frustration with the major powers and Poland over the lack of progress in resolving this particular offshoot of the global refugee crisis.

DOCUMENT 2–21: Letter by Morris Troper, Paris, to Joseph C. Hyman,[60] New York City, July 1, 1939, facsimile reprinted in *Archives of the Holocaust*, ed. Henry Friedlander and Sybil Milton (New York: Garland Publishing, 1995), 10/1:633–34.

[. . .] In the last few days further expulsions of small groups from Germany have occurred with the result that several hundred people are again living in No Man's Lands between the Polish and German borders. There have again

---

59. For example, see the "Interim Report on Refugee Problems in Poland," June 8, 1939, facsimile reprinted in Friedlander and Milton, *Archives of the Holocaust,* 10/1:600.

60. For more on **Joseph C. Hyman**, see the Glossary.

been stories of physical violence affecting even children and the aged. That the conscience of the world has not been shocked in proper proportion to the significance of what is happening is, I assume, due to the fact that these incidents are overshadowed by the present general political situation. This very week-end in fact appears to be a dangerous one, and it is in any event expected that in the course of the next few days, and certainly within weeks, Germany will deliver its ultimatum on Danzig [demanding the reincorporation of the "Free City" into the Reich]. The problem of the moment with respect to the border cases is whether or not to build barracks in these No Man's Lands. Again general considerations of relief and assistance are clouded by political issues, and we as a foreign organization must be careful in determining our course in this situation. The Polish Central Refugee Committee has itself not yet reached a decision and is holding daily meetings in which our representatives participate in order to resolve this question. I shall keep you informed as developments occur.

With kind regards, I am

Sincerely yours,
(signed) Morris C. Troper

P.S. Since dictating the foregoing I have had a telephone conversation with one of our Warsaw representatives. He informs me that the Central Refugee Committee has decided against the construction of barracks for refugees in the No Man's Lands on the grounds that these people are Polish citizens and as such are entitled to enter the country. However, they do intend to canvass the various organizations concerned with Jewish emigration for emigration opportunities for as many of these people as possible.

By the end of the summer of 1939, more than 350,000 Jews had emigrated, fled, or been expelled from Nazi territory. Of those who escaped the Nazis in the preceding months and years, according to Michael Marrus, "about 110,000 Jewish refugees were spread across Europe as the fighting began." The beginning of the war swelled the numbers of European Jews desperate to leave the European continent. It also made flight even more of a "complex gauntlet" of restrictions and rejections.[61] Nevertheless, many European Jews continued to try to find a way out, while all Jews in areas under German control struggled to find a way to live.

---

61. Marrus, *The Unwanted*, 203.

CHAPTER 3

FACING NEW FEAR AND VIOLENCE

A LTHOUGH TENS of thousands of Jews left Nazi central Europe in 1939, many more were forced to stay.[1] Those who remained behind, among them a disproportionate number of women and elderly, struggled to find a way to cope, practically and emotionally, with changes to their daily lives. They were subjected to further economic, social, and cultural restrictions that rendered most of them destitute and increasingly isolated.[2] Moreover, the Nazi regime intensified the violence directed against Jews, which in turn increased Jewish anxieties and fears about the future. This chapter examines the responses of those who stayed in Germany to the ominous developments of this period. What did they feel and how did they react?

So voluminous is Jewish documentation from late 1938 and 1939 on issues of emigration and refugees—including diaries, letters, official correspondence,

---

1. The number of Jewish emigrants who left the Altreich (old Reich)—Germany, with Austria excluded—in 1939 reached a record high of seventy-eight thousand. Marion Kaplan puts the number of racially defined Jews remaining in Germany in September 1939 at 185,000; Saul Friedländer cites the German census of May 1939, according to which 213,000 "full Jews" resided in the Altreich at the time the census was taken. In addition to this number, the Austrian *Anschluss* of the previous year brought, according to Friedländer, an additional 190,000 Jews into the Nazi realm, and the Nazi dismemberment of Czechoslovakia increased this number with a further 118,000 Jews. Marion A. Kaplan, *Between Dignity and Despair: Jewish Life in Nazi Germany* (New York: Oxford University Press, 1998), 132; Saul Friedländer, *Nazi Germany and the Jews:* (vol. 1) *The Years of Persecution, 1933–1939* (New York: HarperCollins, 1997), 241, 305, 316–17.

2. Kaplan, *Between Dignity*, 143; Friedländer, *Nazi Germany*, 1:317.

reports, and news articles produced within Germany and beyond its borders—that it can obscure other critical aspects of people's lives during this period. Nevertheless, the fact remains that more than half a million Jews continued to live under Nazi domination in 1938 and 1939, and that number would only grow as a consequence of Nazi Germany's seemingly unstoppable territorial expansion. Despite harsh political realities, daily life went on. Notwithstanding the obstacles to emigration, destroyed synagogues, and increasing restrictions on Jews' access to public spaces, the Jews who remained struggled to find a way to make do under Nazism.

In the spring of 1939, **Victor Klemperer** described in one of his diary entries how he and his wife coped. "[E]ven more than before, I try to bury myself. I think it is exactly the same for Eva. She tidies up, puts in order, weeds out, sews a lot, so as to be ready. But ready for what? There is no out for us."[3] Scholars such as Victor Klemperer and **Willy Cohn** tried to immerse themselves in their reading and writing. Cohn, like other observant Jews, continued to seek solace in religious tradition as well. Many people, among them teenager Suse Behr (first encountered in chapter 2), busied themselves with foreign-language and training courses and community work. But Klemperer's image of "burying" himself raises the question of how we should interpret such varied activities. Can we read these everyday activities as signs of hope, even acts of resistance? Or were they acts of mere survival, even escapism?[4]

SEEKING DIGNITY IN CULTURE AND RELIGION

Historical interpretations of Jewish cultural activities in this period emphasize their complex functions and meanings. The **Jüdischer Kulturbund** is a case in point. As one of a small handful of Jewish organizations that Nazi authorities did not abolish after "*Kristallnacht*," it clearly served the intentions of the regime. According to Saul Friedländer, the Kulturbund was "the first Jewish organization under the direct supervision of a Nazi overlord[;] it foreshadowed the Nazi ghetto, in which a pretense of internal autonomy camouflaged the total

---

3. Victor Klemperer, diary entry for April 7, 1939, in *I Will Bear Witness: A Diary of the Nazi Years, 1933–1941* (New York: Random House, 1998), 1:296.

4. To take the most extreme example, is it appropriate to interpret the numerous Jewish suicides during this same period as acts of resistance against Nazism or acts of despair when they were in fact triggered by a multitude of factors? On Jewish suicides during the Nazi years, see Christian Goeschel, *Suicide in Nazi Germany* (New York: Oxford University Press, 2009), 96–118.

subordination of an appointed Jewish leadership to the dictates of its masters."[5] Yet, as Friedländer also recognizes, the Kulturbund filled a vital psychological need within the Jewish community for entertainment and escape. Even with the drastic constraints on Jews' familial, social, cultural, religious, intellectual, and economic existences after the November pogrom, the Kulturbund continued to stage theatrical and musical productions—by Jewish performers, for Jewish audiences—in the months leading up to the outbreak of the war.[6]

Document 3–1 from the Berlin edition of the *Jüdisches Nachrichtenblatt* indicates that, to Jews in Germany at the time, the Kulturbund was more important because of what it preserved of the past than for what it might have prefigured. The author of the piece, well-known German Jewish journalist Leo Hirsch, argued for the ongoing importance of the Kulturbund in a time when emigration was the leading topic of the day. He called attention to the reality that Jews continued to reside in Nazi Germany. In that context, he framed culture as more than a form of escapism; to him, it was a spiritual and moral undertaking. The fact that he had to make such an argument in the first place, however, suggests that the Kulturbund was no longer able to satisfy the psychological needs of the Jewish community. Though the Kulturbund's mission remained unaltered, had the context perhaps changed sufficiently that its salutary effect had diminished? The *Jüdisches Nachrichtenblatt*, we should keep in mind, was controlled by the regime.

DOCUMENT 3–1: Leo Israel Hirsch, "What Matters Now! What You Need besides a Permit and a Ticket," *Jüdisches Nachrichtenblatt Berlin*, August 11, 1939, 10 (translated from German).

> For months there has been just one topic of conversation for us Jews here: emigration. Wherever you go, the word "affidavit" goes with you, the word "permit" greets you, and the word "passage" is on every tongue, again and again. [. . .] That is just the way it is and must be and will remain until our problem is solved. But none of us would deserve even an interim stay if the term "interim stay" actually occupied the entirety of our mechanisms of consciousness and emotion. Our reasoning power, our purpose in living, encompasses other notions as well. Here I am not

5. Friedländer, *Nazi Germany*, 1:66.

6. On debates within the Jewish press about "Jewish culture" in the Nazi years before "*Kristallnacht*," see Herbert Freeden, "Kultur 'nur für Juden': 'Kulturkampf' in der jüdischen Presse in Nazideutschland," in *Die Juden in Nationalsozialistischen Deutschland*, ed. Arnold Pauckerm with Sylvia Gilchrist and Barbara Suchy (Tübingen: J. C. B. Mohr, 1986), 259–71.

talking about the fact that each of us wants to live and must live, that the performance of a thousand individual daily tasks is necessary to make that possible, that we have to do all kinds of running around and errands and work to ensure that private life goes on.

General matters are what must be discussed here. Whether we can afford it or not, whether we get the ease of mind for it or not, we must see, we must hear, we must read, we need intellectual self-preservation, we need mental stimulation, we need a modicum of inner fulfillment, we need books, theater, music, art, instruction, film, conversation. We need all that in a worthy form, we need it as a collective experience, we cannot simply exclude centuries of our own development from our own lives. We cannot play dead mentally. Even if the form of our outward life is altered, even if we work hard, harder than we were accustomed to, or need to do the even harder work of doing nothing, living by sleeping, eating, and affidavits alone means that we are giving ourselves up for lost. We cannot get by without culture. [. . .]

How We See It

We must at some point be allowed to criticize our audience as well, with equal candor. Actually, we have two "audiences." One consists of our regular members, and the other . . . I will mention later. Our regular members, including many who have been with us from the outset and have gone through thick and thin with this institute of theirs despite all the difficulties of the past years, have indeed made the most important contribution to the preservation of the Kulturbund. We know that often enough, loyalty was difficult for many of them; we know that words of gratitude can be our only response to them. But the number of Jewish people here is declining, and emigration and the economic restructuring are contributing factors. We need new members, we need many more members. [. . .]

What Concerns Us

Our situation is such that we essentially need every Jew who lives here to be a member of the Jüdischer Kulturbund. [. . .] To preserve [the elements of culture] as long as there are still Jewish people who need this opportunity for inquiry and relaxation is not least of all a moral responsibility. Membership in this kind of Jewish community is also a moral responsibility that no one should shirk, even if we had enough members to sustain our existence.

It is the idea of the Jüdischer Kulturbund that we are working for and promoting. It is the idea of the Kulturbund to make art of all kinds productive through Jews and for Jews. It is this idea on behalf of which the Jewish community agreed to do promotion for us, and it has done so on a rewardingly extensive scale. It is this idea—that is, the commitment of Jews to art, to the intellect, and to creative discussion despite everything— that should be a hallmark of the "Day of the Jüdischer Kulturbund" on August 13. Think about this long and hard, and hesitate no longer.

The question of culture's function and meaning emerges in a different form in documents 3–2 and 3–3 from Willy Cohn's diary. Cohn was a faithful diarist from 1907 on. The fifty-eight notebooks he filled during the years he lived under the Third Reich comprise one of the most voluminous and detailed contemporaneous accounts by a Jewish writer of the intensification of Nazi anti-Jewish measures and their impact on Jewish daily life. The entries included in this chapter impart only a minuscule fraction of the detail and insight contained in his meticulous daily accounts. In addition to his diary, Cohn also continued to produce scholarship on a variety of topics and themes, particularly Jewish history, despite the impossibility of Jewish writers publishing their work in Nazi Germany after 1938.[7] Writing seemed to function as an escape for Cohn, as a way to process contemporary events, and as a means of overcoming isolation, especially when a window toward the West opened up in the form of an offer by a Dutch publisher. Cohn's experiences also attest to the fact that anti-Jewish decrees affected people unevenly, even in these months after "*Kristallnacht.*"

DOCUMENT 3–2: **Willy Cohn, diary entry for May 10, 1939, translated from** *Kein Recht, Nirgends: Tagebuch vom Untergang des Breslauer Judentums, 1933–1941*, **ed. Norbert Conrads (Cologne: Böhlau Verlag, 2007), 2:642).**

Breslau, Wednesday. Barbershop, read the newspaper there; thank G-d, things look more peaceful again. The regulatory statutes for the new law on Jewish tenants have appeared. To start with, landlords are supposed to report their Jewish tenants, to facilitate an overview of the [Jewish] community. For us, therefore, the law will have no immediate consequences.

Room 85/86, Foreign Exchange Office, about my book on the Sicilian fleet under the rule of Frederick II. Basically, treated nicely; it now is apparent that the officials always address me as Mr. Cohn, omitting

---

7. The Nazi regime permitted Jewish publishing houses to exist from 1933 to 1938 under strict control. See Volker Dahm, "Jüdische Verleger, 1933–1938," in Paucker, *Die Juden*, 273–82.

the [academic] title. Obviously there now exists a directive, because this happened not only at the Foreign Currency Transactions Office but also at the Reichsbank, where I was sent next. As for my business, the official first apologized for the long delay in my receipt of an answer, saying that there was so much to do; then I told him that the Germans also have a stake in the exporting of my book, because it would bring in Dutch guilders; he opined that it could give rise to foreign assets; I told him that I would be prepared to assign them unconditionally and that I have only a scholarly interest in this matter. I explained the same thing at the Reichsbank. There, they evidently called the Foreign Exchange Office next, and finally I was told that I would receive a decision in writing. As a Jew, you have the feeling that to begin with, you have to prove that you're a decent human being.

Cohn's experiences a few weeks earlier reveal additional consequences of the harsher antisemitic economic restrictions imposed in these months. Here we find an example of the myriad ways in which Nazi anti-Jewish measures impacted Jewish religious observance, even when those decrees and orders ostensibly had nothing to do with religion. Economic strain forced religiously observant Jews to break Jewish law. Cohn noted this and also commented on having to compromise his principles in a diary entry describing a visit he paid to the *Leihamt* (the government "pawnbroker" office) in Breslau and subsequently to a clothing store. Such indignities left him clinging to the increasingly faint hope of escaping from the Reich some day.[8]

DOCUMENT 3–3: Willy Cohn, diary entry for April 29, 1939, translated from *Kein Recht, Nirgends: Tagebuch vom Untergang des Breslauer Judentums, 1933–1941*, ed. Norbert Conrads (Cologne: Böhlau Verlag, 2007), 2:637.

We got the notice from the municipal pawn office about compensation for the valuables we brought in. As it had to be taken care of today, I rushed to the pawn office despite the Sabbath and received 102 Marks [Reichsmark] there; it's surely just a fraction of what they're worth, but

---

8. In order to forestall Jewish capital flight from Germany, especially through emigration, the Nazi regime ordered all Jews to hand over all valuables (primarily precious metals and jewelry) in February 1939. Jews were forced to sell their valuables at designated "purchasing posts" or "pawnbroker offices" for a fraction of their value. See Martin Dean, *Robbing the Jews: The Confiscation of Jewish Property in the Holocaust, 1933–1945* (New York: Cambridge University Press in association with the USHMM, 2008), 126–27, and Wolf Gruner, "The German Council of Municipalities (*Deutscher Gemeindetag*) and the Coordination of Anti-Jewish Local Politics in the Nazi State," in *H&GS* 13 (1999): 181–87.

even so, it's better than nothing at all. At my family's request, I immediately converted the sum into things for myself, a pair of shoes, two pairs of socks, and a suit with two pairs of trousers. I am indeed pretty scruffy and for many years have bought hardly anything at all for myself. I also don't care much about my external appearance, though in point of fact one should think somewhat better of oneself. And then I don't like going into these shops, where all the Jewish employees have been cut off. But nothing can be done about that now. It's best, of course, to invest the money in some clothing, to avoid having to purchase too much right away abroad.

Jews' flight from the Reich and the circumstances created by worsening Nazi persecution had a direct impact on Jewish religious life. In Breslau, for example, which had been the home of the third largest Jewish population in Germany, two-thirds of the city's Jewish population had emigrated by the end of 1939, burdening those who remained with more responsibilities for supporting religious congregations and upholding prescribed rituals and customs, as Willy Cohn detailed in his diary.[9] In a separate example from this period following the "*Kristallnacht*" pogrom, a new halakhic dilemma confronted observant families of those killed and cremated by the Nazis in German concentration camps. At the time it was German government practice to return the ashes of deceased Jewish prisoners to relatives. The bereaved families approached Rabbi Menahem Mendel Kirschbaum of Frankfurt am Main, a prominent Orthodox rabbi in Germany.[10] They requested rabbinic guidance concerning the proper procedures for mourning, burial, and memorial. Because Jewish law proscribes cremation, the cremated are generally not buried in Jewish cemeteries, and traditional mourning practices are not observed. For this reason, observant families were at a loss for how to care properly for their loved ones' ashes.

The burial procedures that Rabbi Kirschbaum formulated in the wake of "*Kristallnacht*" cleaved as faithfully as possible to Jewish traditional practices, both in terms of referencing scripture and in using a format generally referred

---

9. For example, see Willy Cohn, diary entry for April 29, 1939, in Cohn, *Kein Recht*, 2:637.

10. Menahem Mendel Kirschbaum (1895–1942) was born in Kraków, Poland, and in 1927 became the rabbi of Skała nad Zbruczem in eastern Galicia (today Skala-Podilska in Ukraine); the following year he was appointed *Av Bet Din* (head of the religious court) in Frankfurt am Main. In 1936 he became rabbi of the Orthodox community in Frankfurt but fled to Belgium on the eve of the war. Arrested by the **Gestapo** in September 1942, he was deported to Auschwitz, where he and his wife both died. Robert Kirschner, ed., *Rabbinic Responsa of the Holocaust Era* (New York: Schocken, 1985), 55; Michael Brocke and Julius Carlebach, eds., *Biographisches Handbuch der Rabbiner*, vol. 2: *Die Rabbiner im Deutschen Reich, 1871–1945* (Munich: K. G. Saur, 2009), 2/1:330.

to as the "responsum," or (based on the Hebrew plural) "queries and replies," for matters pertaining to religious life.[11] Kirschbaum's advice attempted to restore dignity to the deceased and to bring closure to the mourners. He communicated this responsum orally to his Frankfurt community's burial society in 1939 and subsequently committed it to writing, in a leaflet, for wider distribution.

DOCUMENT 3–4: **Responsum by Rabbi Menahem Mendel Kirschbaum, Kraków, Poland, 1939, recorded in** *Tsiyun le-Menahem*, **ed. Jehuda Rubinstein (New York: Research Institute of Religious Jewry, 1965), 361–65; translated from Hebrew and published in** *Rabbinic Responsa of the Holocaust Era*, **ed. Robert Kirschner (New York: Schocken, 1985), 56–61.**

<u>Regulations on how to proceed at this time with the ashes of the cremated (owing to our many sins)</u>

With God's help, Wednesday, Sabbath <u>Vayehi</u>, 5699 [4 January 1939], Frankfort-am-Main:

The guarding of ashes is not necessary.[12] [. . .]

When notification [of death] arrives from the gentile authorities, one is obligated to commence the seven-day mourning period immediately. (See Sh[ulhan] Ar[ukh] E[ven] h[a-Ezer] 17:5 which prohibits mourning as long as there is no testimony sufficient to permit [the wife] to remarry. This is explained in Sh[ulhan] Ar[ukh] Y[oreh] D[e'ah] 375:7: if one drowns in waters with [visible] boundaries, they count [the seven-day mourning period] from the time they give up the search [for the body]. [. . .])[13]

---

11. See Israel Ta-Shma, Shlomo Tal, and Menahem Slae, "Responsa," in *Encyclopaedia Judaica*, ed. Fred Skolnik and Michael Berenbaum, 2nd. ed. (Detroit, MI: Macmillan Reference USA, 2007), 17:228–39.

12. Robert Kirschner summarizes this provision as "The prohibition against leaving a corpse unattended from the moment of death until burial does not apply to the ashes of the deceased." Kirschner, *Rabbinic Responsa*, 55.

13. Again, as summarized by Kirschner, "The seven-day mourning period (*shivah*) commences upon notification of death, despite lack of certain proof of death and consequent apprehensions concerning remarriage." Kirschner, *Rabbinic Responsa*, 55. Shulhan Arukh (literally, "set table" in Hebrew) is a codification of Jewish law, or halacha, composed by rabbi Yosef Caro in the sixteenth century. It consists of four major parts: Orah Hayim, concerning the daily commandments, Shabbat, and holidays; Yoreh De'ah, concerning dietary laws, mourning, purity, and other subjects; Even ha-Ezer, concerning laws of marriage, divorce, and related issues; and Hoshen Mishpat, concerning civil and criminal law. See Louis Rabinowitz, "Shulhan Arukh," *Encyclopaedia Judaica*, 18:529–30.

The box of ashes should be placed upon a bier out of respect for the dead. (In our community this was the ruling of the illustrious Matteh Levi, in his letter to our community of 22 June 1893. If this should be done for those who did so [i.e., were cremated] willingly, how much more so should it be done for those [who were cremated against their will]. He also decided that two cremated bodies should not be buried together in a grave (cf. Sh[ulhan] Ar[ukh] Y[oreh] D[e'ah] 362) and that [the cremated body] should be given a grave like those given the other dead, without any discrimination or alteration. All the more so should these [cremated against their will] be given a proper grave. On whether there is an obligation to bury the ashes of the cremated, see my book [Menahem Meshiv], part 1, p. 204.)

[The ashes] should be buried in a coffin; when this is not possible, they should be buried in a small casket; and if this too is not possible, the ashes should be buried in the box they came in.

The box of ashes should be wrapped in a prayer shawl; also, burial shrouds should be placed inside (in order to strengthen the belief that the deceased is prepared to awaken and rise at the resurrection, and that he is not, God forbid, among the people of Titus and his followers who do not believe). [. . .]

When it is not possible to bury the ashes in a coffin but only in the box they came in as is, they should see to it that in any event the shrouds are inside the box and a small board or stone is placed on top so the shrouds will not be soiled.

On the day of burial, which in the majority of cases is after the seven-day mourning period and often after the thirty-day mourning period, [the mourners] should mourn the entire day.

When they rend [their garments] on the day of the news [of death], they need not rend on the day of burial. (Although according to Y[oreh] D[e'ah] 403:2 one who rends at the time of death also rends at the time of the gathering of bones, in our case there are no bones; furthermore, ashes do not defile. [. . .])

They should recite the funeral service and stand in the row [to console the mourners]. [. . .]

The meal of condolence is not necessary on that day [the day of interment]. [. . .] However, on the day of the news [of death], the meal of condolence should be conducted. [. . .]

On the day of burial one should lay *tefillin*, except if one heard [the news of death] on the day of burial in which case it is like the day of the news [of death, and consequently he may not lay *tefillin*].[14] [. . .]

The day of death is the date of the *yahrzeit* [annual commemoration of death].

All of the foregoing I explained in public on Thursday evening and Friday, 21 Shevat 5699 [10 February 1939] before the burial society of our community, so that they should know how to proceed according to our holy Torah in case of any misfortune that may occur.[15] May God destroy death forever.

To this I affix my signature today here in the community of Frankfort am Main, 5699 [1939].

Menahem Mendel Kirschbaum

<u>Av bet din and Rosh Yeshivah</u>
Frankfort-am-Main

Many Jews who strongly identified with being Jewish turned inward, drawing strength from Jewish tradition and faith in God in order to cope with the intensification of Nazi anti-Jewish policies. Focusing on one's own identity as a Jew and investing it with a sense of dignity did not insulate such individuals from the pain of persecution but did provide them with a coping strategy of sorts.

This coping strategy is apparent in a poem titled "Holiday Happiness" by Karl Rosenthal, a rabbi in Berlin's Reform congregation. He had also previously been a leader of the Centralverein deutscher Staatsbürger jüdischen Glaubens (Central Association of German Citizens of the Jewish Faith), the defense organization founded in the 1890s to resist antisemitism and promote Jewish assimilation and banned by the Nazis after "*Kristallnacht*." He had also served

---

14. Tefillin, or phylacteries, are a set of cubic, black-leather boxes on leather straps that observant Jewish men wear during the morning prayers on weekdays. Scrolls with verses from the Torah are contained in the boxes.

15. Kirschbaum composed the responsum on the date listed at the beginning of the document, January 4, 1939. However, because it was impossible to publish it in Nazi Germany, he sent it to his brother in Kraków, Poland, who had it published there. On February 10, 1939, in a public sermon to the members of the Hevra Kadisha (the Jewish burial society), Kirschbaum went over the rules set in the responsum and gave detailed explanations so that burial society members would know the exact procedure. Hirsch Jakob Zimmels, *The Echo of the Nazi Holocaust in Rabbinic Literature* (New York: KTAV Publishing House, 1977), 27–28.

as the president of a B'nai B'rith lodge and an active member of the association for German Jewish War Veterans.[16]

DOCUMENT 3–5: Dr. Karl Rosenthal, poem titled "Holiday Happiness," no date (ca. 1939), USHMMA RG 10.087 Karl Rosenthal family papers (translated from German).

Outside, the noisy day makes a din,
Outside, the brawl of the wicked rages,
Harsh words, harsher deeds,
Passions, poisonous envy.
Outside, the cry of the mob is shrill,
Outside, the world of illusion prances and swaggers,
The world of reality flees
Quietly away from the clamorous day.
What you carry in yourselves
Is all that gives life value,
What human deeds you accomplish
Are heeded by God alone.
To be a Jew—is painful,
To be a Jew—is happiness!
Proudly turn away from illusion,
Return to your true selves.
Let the world outside make a din;
You must stand firm in your own strength,
Joyfully create quiet happiness
That you bring into being daily for yourselves.
Then you will soon forget the brawl,
Pay no attention to scorn and derision,
Lead lives fit for human beings,
Know: one day our God will be victorious!

16. Dr. Karl Rosenthal (1889–1952) fled to England after securing his release from Sachsenhausen concentration camp in the wake of "*Kristallnacht*." One of his sons managed to emigrate to the United States, but another perished in Mauthausen concentration camp. His wife, Gertrude (Trudie), survived Bergen-Belsen concentration camp, and the couple reunited in 1945 in the United States, where Rosenthal served as a rabbi during his remaining years. See USHMMA RG 10.087M; LBINY catalog.

CZECHOSLOVAK JEWS CONFRONT NAZI OCCUPATION

The worsening political situation in Europe, in general, and Hitler's unchecked aggression and victorious advance in central Europe, in particular, tightened the vise on Jews. After the incorporation of the **Sudetenland** into the Reich in October 1938, a direct consequence of the **Munich agreement**, Hitler moved to dismember Czechoslovakia: under Nazi sponsorship, its eastern part— Slovakia—declared independence and seceded on March 14, 1939, while the German army marched into the western regions—Bohemia and Moravia—on the following day. Speaking from the Prague castle on March 16, Hitler proclaimed the **Protectorate of Bohemia and Moravia**. As had happened after the *Anschluss* of Austria and would happen again with every instance of German expansion, the German reach across the border brought more Jews into the Nazi realm—in this case either under direct Nazi control (in Bohemia and Moravia) or within the Nazi orbit (in Slovakia).

The Jewish community in Slovakia had already begun to suffer from a barrage of antisemitic laws, edicts, and decrees following the Munich agreement. These accelerated in intensity from March 1939 with Slovakia's proclamation of independence. The thrust of such measures was, first, to define what it meant to be a "Jew," largely borrowing the definitions laid out in the **Nuremberg Laws** and its supplementary decrees, and, second, to restrict Jewish economic activity in Slovakia. Jewish practitioners in a range of professions faced strict new quotas, Jews lost their posts in the military and civil service, and businesses and property were expropriated.[17] Meanwhile the Nazis unleashed open terror against the Jews in the Protectorate. They burned synagogues and other Jewish sites, they rounded up individuals—especially refugees from Germany—and sent them to concentration camps, and they confiscated property and introduced racial laws.[18]

The extent of the anti-Jewish measures against Slovak and Czech Jews, as well as glimpses of Jewish responses to those measures, emerges in a daily bulletin put out by the Paris office of the **Jewish Telegraphic Agency** (JTA).

---

17. For anti-Jewish measures in Slovakia in this period, see the detailed overview given in Ivan Kamenec, *On the Trail of Tragedy: The Holocaust in Slovakia* (Bratislava: Hajko & Hajková, 2007), 33–109. For a general overview of the period, see Stanislav Kirschbaum, *The History of Slovakia: The Struggle for Survival* (New York: St. Martin's Press, 1995), 185–204.

18. Livia Rothkirchen, *The Jews of Bohemia and Moravia: Facing the Holocaust* (Lincoln and Jerusalem: University of Nebraska Press and Yad Vashem, 2005), 98–110.

Comparing the persecution of Jews in Slovakia by the Hlinka Guard, the militia of the antisemitic right-wing Catholic nationalist Slovak People's Party, to the persecution in Austria by the Nazis after their takeover a year earlier, the JTA signaled how difficult things had become in a country that was not even formally under Nazi rule. What choices were available to Slovak Jews, and what did the future in Slovakia have in store for them?

DOCUMENT 3–6: Daily Information Bulletin issued by the Jewish Telegraphic Agency, April 4, 1939, USHMMA RG 11.001.M25, reel 106 (SAM 674-1-114) (translated from French).

Paris, April 3 [1939]. Reported from Bratislava:

The famous Slovak "Hlinka Guard" is presently engaged in an anti-Jewish campaign, the scale of which recalls that of the German Nazis in Austria just after the *Anschluss*. The word "pogrom" describes precisely what is currently happening in several cities in Slovakia: Jewish homes looted, Jews manhandled and ill treated. Thousands of Jews have been arrested by the "Hlinka Guard" and are being kept in "temporary" prisons, with cellars requisitioned for that purpose almost everywhere. In one case, almost 40 Jews were held in a cellar with no exit but a small door, and with no ventilation or light. The prisoners, several of whom were elderly, could not even lie down on the floor because of the lack of space.

No reason for these arrests was given. Most often, entire families are arrested. In certain places, only young people are being arrested; elsewhere it is elderly people who are taken away. It is impossible to communicate with the prisoners, and cases of their being released are rare.

In these circumstances it is not surprising that thousands of Slovak Jews are leaving their hometowns and trying to get to Prague, where they feel safer. They arrive there completely dispossessed, with no money or spare clothes. Others try to cross the border and take refuge in Poland, but are turned back by the Polish border guards. Those who succeed in entering Polish territory are forced back into Slovakia, but the Slovak authorities in turn refuse to admit them, and these unfortunates camp in the border zone between the two countries.

In the Slovak cities with a Czech majority, the situation is better; it is very bad where the German minority is sizable.

Jewish assets in banks, savings banks, and the post office are being sequestered. Jews are allowed to withdraw from their accounts up to one thousand crowns per week, if this money was paid in after March 15.

Jews are forbidden to leave Slovak territory. To obtain a travel permit, one must present a certificate of baptism. The anti-Jewish campaign in the newspapers is under the expert leadership of members of the National Socialist press service. The *Stürmer* is being distributed on the street.[19]

In the Protectorate of Bohemia-Moravia.

Paris, April 3 (J. T. A.)

Reported from Prague:

The "de-Judaization" of Bohemia-Moravia is continuing systematically. The head of the civil administration of the Protectorate has just announced a decree banning the sale and purchase of Jewish properties. Moreover, according to the new regulations, anyone leaving the territory of the Protectorate must first present a document attesting to his Aryan origin. These measures are intended to prevent the Jews from taking funds out of the country.

In addition, the Society of Café Owners has decided to put up notices in non-Jewish cafés prohibiting Jews from entering. Stores in Prague are putting in their display windows signs from the civil administration, attesting that the establishment is an Aryan one. Stores that lack this notice are empty for the most part.

In Brno a German woman got a divorce "because her husband was a Jew, she felt a profound aversion to him."

A special edition of the *Völkischer Beobachter*, the official organ of the German National Socialist Party, will soon be published in Prague.

In response to this government-sponsored persecution, Slovak Jewish communities banded together to create the Jewish Central Office (JCO) as their national representative body. In so doing, they took a step similar to Jews' efforts to reorganize their communities elsewhere. The majority of Slovak Jewish communal organizations across the country lent their support to the JCO. Only mainstream Orthodox communities, organized in the Central Office of Jewish Autonomous Orthodox Communities (COJAOC), chose not to be a part of

---

19. *Der Stürmer* was a violently antisemitic journal published in Nuremberg by prominent Nazi Party official Julius Streicher.

the association; other Orthodox communities—most notably, the "status quo" communities, which followed the Orthodox rite but were not affiliated with the COJAOC—supported the JCO. The JCO took charge of efforts to assist the unemployed and refugees, to represent Jewish interests before Slovak ministers, and to organize cultural activities that permitted Jewish youths and adults to gain a multifaceted Jewish education. It was abolished in 1940, together with all other Slovak Jewish institutions except the government-imposed Jewish Center.[20]

The diary entry in document 3–7, recorded by the Slovak rabbi of Nové Mesto and later Bratislava, Abraham Abba-Armin Frieder, describes one of the projects he instigated to cope with the new strains placed on Slovak Jewish communities in this period.[21] Rabbi Frieder was elected to the board of the JCO at its inception and spearheaded the creation of its cultural department. Later in the war, he became a central figure in the Slovak Jewish underground, particularly in its efforts to rescue Jews. He began to keep a diary in 1933, when he started his career as a rabbi. That diary expanded during the late 1930s and war years to include developments not only in his own community, but affecting all of Slovak Jewry as well as Jews of other nationalities who found themselves stranded in the country. In an entry from June 1939, he recorded a speech he had delivered to the Jewish community of Nové Mesto. He elaborated on how the Jewish concept of *tsedakah* (charity) guided his work in responding to the refugee crisis in Nové Mesto, where he had founded the Ohel David old-age home and soup kitchen. According to Rabbi Frieder, "In the first month of its existence, Ohel David served over 7,000 meals to the needy, free of charge."[22]

---

20. Gila Fatran, "The Struggle for Jewish Survival during the Holocaust," in *The Tragedy of the Jews of Slovakia*, ed. Wacław Długoborski et al. (Auschwitz and Banská Bystrica: Auschwitz-Birkenau State Museum and Museum of the Slovak National Uprising, 2002), 141; Kamenec, *On the Trail*, 36–38; Emanuel Frieder, *To Deliver Their Souls: The Struggle of a Young Rabbi during the Holocaust* (New York: Holocaust Library, 1991), 5, 33–35.

21. Abraham Armin Frieder (1911–1945) was born in an Orthodox family and became the rabbi in Nové Mesto nad Váhom (Neustadt an der Waag in German; Vágújhely in Hungarian) in Czechoslovakia in 1938. After the German occupation of Slovakia in 1944, he was taken to a labor camp, from which he managed to flee. He died immediately after the end of the war.

22. Frieder, *To Deliver Their Souls*, 37–38.

DOCUMENT 3–7: **Speech by Rabbi Abraham Abba-Armin Frieder to the Jewish community in Nové Mesto, Slovakia, on laying the foundation stone to the Ohel David House, June 9, 1939, YVA RG M5.192.46–47 (translated from German and Hebrew).**

<u>Brothers and Sisters!</u>

I praise You, for You have answered me, and have become my deliverance. [From Psalms 118:21; in Hebrew]

[In German:]

In such a solemn hour as this, in which all these ideas that constitute the essence of Judaism are to become reality, I find no phrase more apt to express all the emotions that hold sway over me than the words of the psalmist: I praise You, for You have answered me, and have become my deliverance.

A fateful hour for the Jews has come to pass. Hundreds of our brothers have had to leave their workplaces and their homes and have emigrated to their places of birth, or to other towns previously unfamiliar to them. To our town too, to Nové Mesto nad Váhom, have come nearly 100 such unfortunate brothers and sisters, uprooted from their existences, and bringing with them nothing but the clothes on their backs. We always have proved that the concept of *tsedakah* ["zdoko"] is not one of charity; we always have understood that we are merely the custodians of the assets entrusted to us by God, and as such *shomrim* ["custodians"], we must give money to those who have less than we do. Among us, *tsedakah* did not mean alms: instead, we interpreted *tsedakah* as compensatory justice, which for us meant that God's children who have less than we do must receive from us, in order to advance divine justice and thereby signify that we indeed are people who bear the image of God, who are imbued and permeated with the idea of practicing and advancing social justice.

Now, when I visited our poor emigrés and came, right at noontime, into a house where there were five small children and where the stove was still cold and nothing at all was being cooked yet, I heard a pretty 3-year-old child there crying to its mother, *Anyuka kérek kenyeret, éhes vagyok* ([Hungarian for:] "Mama, I want a little piece of bread, I'm hungry")[23] and the mother replied, "I can give you my heart, but no bread, because we don't have even a scrap in the house." And the mother cried because she couldn't give her frail, undernourished little children any bread, and

---

23. Like many Slovak Jews, Frieder spoke a host of languages used in the region of the former Austro-Hungarian Empire.

they had to go hungry, these five innocent children. Then I felt that we are the ones who are to blame. We give our children the best tidbits, and the other children, who just like us are beloved children of fond parents, have no bread to eat. I put myself in the place of my *Anyuka* ["mama"] and started to consider what impression it inevitably would make on me if my child were to ask for only *kenyeret*, a little piece of bread, and I couldn't give it to him, and then I decided to put an end to this misery. Nobody in this town must go hungry so long as anyone has food, and now we have to prove that we are Jews, not only by birth but by our actions. And I decided to bring an institution into being, to set up a place that provides care and shelter, with a public soup kitchen, where—as our exemplary presiding officer has so correctly said—there will be only one slogan: "All who are hungry, come and eat" [from Passover Haggadah, in Hebrew].

Many secular central European Jews were not guided by Jewish religious concepts. Much in keeping with Frieder's interpretation of *tsedakah* as "practicing and advancing social justice," they adhered to key elements of Enlightenment tradition and Jewish culture. Conversion could be regarded, paradoxically, as a familiar feature of Jewish encounters with the Enlightenment since the nineteenth century. Thus, if after the German dismemberment of Czechoslovakia some individuals resorted to baptism in the hope that it might ease their situation, they did not necessarily relinquish their own identities. Jews in Germany and Austria had learned that baptism did not work as a means of gaining exemption from Nazi racial laws. But Czech and Slovak Jews, lacking direct experience of Nazi racial laws before March 1939, still hoped that it might offer a means of escaping the injustice imposed by the state as well as the prejudices and suspicions held among the population (for example, which took the form of blaming Jews for the German occupation of the Sudetenland because of their historic connection with the German cultural sphere since the time of the Austro-Hungarian Empire). A German-language Czech newspaper reported on the incidence of "production-line baptisms": "All possible ways and religions are chosen," it claimed, "for those who want to emigrate or who are fearful of the future because they are Jews."[24] A letter written in the same period by a Czech Jewish employee of the **World Jewish Congress** (WJC) conveys the general atmosphere prior to the Nazi dismantlement of Czechoslovakia and his individual situation in the face of mounting antisemitism. As he tried to fathom

---

24. "Fabrication of Baptisms in Prague," *Express Prag*, January 9, 1939, 1–2 (translated from German).

the future of Jews in Czechoslovakia, he contemplated baptism and emigration in order to save himself and his family.

DOCUMENT 3–8: **Letter by Walter Schwartz, a WJC official in Brünn (Brno), Czechoslovakia,[25] to the WJC, Paris office, December 18, 1938, USHMMA RG 11.001. M36, reel 107 (SAM 1190-1-288) (translated from German).**

[. . .] By the way, in circles that are close to the German National Socialists, there is skepticism regarding the fate of the Czechoslovakian Jews. The other day I had a discussion with Dr. Brancsik, whom Dr. B[ermann] knows well, who strongly advised me as a friend to be baptized as a Protestant and to at least be an export firm [sic], because only these two circumstances could save me. He also said that the Jews here would suffer the fate of the Jews of the Third Reich, only more quickly and even more effectively!! And thus far these people have always given the right advice and known what was what!!! [. . .]

So this is the thought that takes shape: emigrate and don't wait until the big [emigration] flow comes. [. . .] I also can't wait until the entire CSR [Czechoslovak Republic] comes under the control of the Third Reich, and this will happen soon, very soon, it will take until February at the latest, and then will come the big war with Poland or the peaceful penetration of the CSR and Poland, which amounts to the same thing in the end.

Thus my fate rests with my friends in the WJC and with the connections that you have. [. . .]

As regards the situation of the Jews who stayed in the Sudetenland, they all must leave the region, some within five days, others within 30 days, and the last ones—such as my father, for example—by the end of January. All of them, without exception, were locked up after the Rath Affair,[26] again with the exception of the very old, such as my father, who is 80. You are aware, of course, that all the temples were burned down and that this is already beginning in Slovakia as well. [. . .]

Kind regards to all of you, and please send me news soon,

Sincerely,

[Signed:] Schwartz

---

25. Details about the correspondents or the fate of those mentioned in the letter are unknown.

26. This refers to the assassination of German diplomat Ernst vom Rath, which served as a pretext for "*Kristallnacht*" (see Glossary).

THE LIMITS OF JEWISH IDENTITY AND FUTURE EXPECTATIONS

In the Reich itself, the issue of conversion was being rendered moot by anti-Jewish measures that isolated the Jews further. On July 4, 1939, the Nazi regime passed the tenth supplementary decree to the Reich Citizenship Law and established a new central Jewish organization, the **Reichsvereinigung der Juden in Deutschland,** directly subordinated to the Reich minister of the interior.[27] The Reichsvereinigung had as its purpose, the decree stated, "the promotion of Jewish emigration." However, the organization was also responsible for "a Jewish school system" and "for Jewish welfare work"—in other words, for implementing the Nazis' idea of removing Jews from German society. Ominously, the decree mandated that "all Jews who are state subjects or are stateless and have their place of domicile or permanent residence within the territory of the Reich" were to become members of the Reichsvereinigung.[28] This last provision brought the issue of the fate of converts to the fore: even though they had been defined racially as Jews since 1935, "Christian non-Aryans" now found themselves forced into a "Jewish organization" by the state.

A memo on the meeting between Reichsvereinigung officials and sympathetic representatives of some Christian churches in Germany shows the attempts by Jewish leaders to negotiate the new situation and to find the best way of providing for the needs of the new Christian members of the organization.

---

27. Friedländer, *Nazi Germany,* 1:318. Effectively, this put **Reinhard Heydrich's** Security Police and SD in charge of the Reichsvereinigung, as the police were nominally part of the Reich interior administration.

28. Quoted from Karl A. Schleunes, *Legislating the Holocaust: The Bernhard Loesener Memoirs and Supporting Documents* (Boulder, CO: Westview Press, 2001), 167–69. On the Reichsvereinigung, see Beate Meyer, "Between Self-Assertion and Forced Collaboration: The Reich Association of Jews in Germany, 1939–1945," in *Jewish Life in Nazi Germany: Dilemmas and Responses,* ed. Francis R. Nicosia and David Scrase (New York: Berghahn Books, 2010), 149–69.

DOCUMENT 3–9: Memorandum by the Reichsvereinigung on a meeting held July 20, 1939, USHMMA RG 14.003M.01, BAB R 8150, 214–17 (translated from German).

File Memorandum
on the meeting on July 20, 1939
Present: from the Büro Pfarrer Grüber: Pastor Grüber[29]
Dr. Heinitz[30]
Dr. Kobrack [Kobrak][31]
Dr. Reissner [Reisner][32]

---

29. Heinrich Grüber (1891–1975) was a Berlin pastor who ran the so-called Grüber office, through which the Confessing Church—a splinter Protestant church that had emerged in Nazi Germany as a reaction to the nazification of the Protestant Church—channeled its aid to the "Christian non-Aryans." On the Grüber office, see Victoria J. Barnett, ed., *For the Soul of the People: Protestant Protest against Hitler* (New York: Oxford University Press, 1992), 144–46.

30. Former judge and Reich government official Paul Heinitz (1887–1942) worked for the office from 1938 to 1940, heading up the department for emigration. From 1941 to 1942, he performed similar work for the Reichsvereinigung and was killed in 1942. His brother, lawyer Günther Heinitz (1892–1943), also worked for Pastor Grüber's office from 1939 to 1940 before he was assigned to forced labor, deported, and murdered in Auschwitz. See Hartmut Ludwig, *An der Seite der Entrechteten und Schwachen: Zur Geschichte des "Büro Pfarrer Grüber" (1938 bis 1940) und der Ev. Hilfsstelle für ehemals Rasseverfolgte nach 1945* (Berlin: Logos, 2009), 73, 100–5.

31. Dr. Richard Kobrak (1890–1944), a lawyer and city official in Breslau and later in Berlin, was forced into retirement in 1935. Kobrak then began volunteering on behalf of "non-Aryan Christians"; in Grüber's office, he headed up the welfare department. Designated a Jew, he was deported to Theresienstadt in 1943 with his wife, Charlotte (née Stern; 1893–1944), and both were murdered in Auschwitz. See Aleksandar-Saša Vuletić, *Christen jüdischer Herkunft im Dritten Reich: Verfolgung und organisierte Selbsthilfe, 1933–1939* (Mainz: Philipp von Zabern, 1999), 229n321; Ludwig, *An der Seite*, 123–26; *USHMM ITS Collection Data Base Central Name Index*.

32. Pastor Dr. Erwin Reisner, a theologian-philosopher, ran the division for church and school affairs in the central Grüber office in Berlin. A former Austrian officer (who would have counted as a "*Mischling* of the 2nd degree"), he worked as an advisor for Christians of Jewish origin in Vienna until relocating to Berlin with his family after the Austrian *Anschluss*. See Eberhard Röhm and Jörg Thierfelder, *Juden, Christen, Deutsche, 1933–1945* (Stuttgart: Calwer, 1992–1995), 2/II:193, 224, 299n284, 309n422, and 3/I:106; Ludwig, *An der Seite*, 70n234, 72; Vuletić, *Christen jüdischer Herkunft*, 177n133.

	Superintendent Albert[z][33]
from the St. Raphaels-Verein:[34]	Father Dr. Grösser[35]
	Dr. Püschel[36]
from the Quaker Office:[37]	Frau Dr. Israel[38]
from the Reichsvereinigung:	**Dr. Hirsch**[39]

---

33. Martin Albertz (1882–1956), superintendent of the deanery in the Spandau district of Berlin and prominent member of the Confessing Church, assisted "Christians of Jewish descent" and was imprisoned during the war for his opposition to the Nazi regime along with other Confessing leaders and teachers. See Wolfgang Gerlach and Victoria Barnett, *And the Witnesses Were Silent: The Confessing Church and the Persecution of the Jews* (Lincoln: University of Nebraska Press, 2000), 81, 154–55, 158, 192; Vuletić, *Christen jüdischer Herkunft*, 198.

34. The St. Raphaelsverein was a Catholic society founded in 1871 to provide aid to German emigrés. Despite some compromises with Nazi racial thinking, the association helped "Christian non-Aryans" to emigrate. See Guenter Lewy, *The Catholic Church and Nazi Germany* (Boulder, CO: Da Capo Press, 2000), 282–83.

35. Pater Dr. Maximilian (Max Joseph) Größer (1887–1940) served as general secretary for the organization. He had been active in social work for prospective emigrants since the 1920s. The Gestapo imprisoned him several times in the late 1930s, but he continued his work until he died in 1940. See Manfred Hermanns, "Max Grösser," *Biographisch-Bibliographisches Kirchenlexikon* 31 (2010): 566–73; Ulrich von Hehl, et al., *Priester unter Hitlers Terror: Eine biographische und statistische Erhebung* (Paderborn, Germany: Ferdinand Schöningh, 1996), 2:1122.

36. Erich Püschel (1898–1984) worked from the early 1920s as head of the Reich Center for Children's Health and Welfare until he was forced out in 1934 on political grounds. He then served as an official with the Caritas organization in Berlin and emigration advisor for the St. Raphaelsverein beginning in early 1938. A POW for part of the war, he survived to serve again with the German Caritas organization in providing aid to expellees and refugees. See Jana Leichsenring, *Die Katholische Kirche und "ihre Juden": Das "Hilfswerk beim Bischöflichen Ordinariat Berlin," 1938–1945* (Berlin: Metropol, 2007), 79n10.

37. The American Friends Service Committee and the British Society of Friends had been active in aiding Jewish children since the 1930s; see Jürgen Matthäus and Mark Roseman, *Jewish Responses to Persecution*, vol. 1: *1933–1938* (Lanham, MD: AltaMira Press in association with the USHMM, 2010), 234–35.

38. Dr. Herta Israel (1893–1971) worked in the Berlin Quaker center and was seconded to Pastor Grüber's advisory center until she found refuge in Britain; Israel later emigrated to the United States. See J. E. Brenda Bailey, *A Quaker Couple in Nazi Germany: Leonhard Friedrich Survives Buchenwald* (York, United Kingdom: Sessions, 1994), 5, 82; U.S. Social Security online death index; German "Minority Census," 1938–1939, USHMMA RG 14.013M.

39. For more on Dr. Otto Hirsch, see the Glossary.

Dr. Cohn[40]

Dr. Eppstein[41]

Frau Fürst[42]

Dr. Lilienthal[43]

I. Registration of members

The registration of members who previously were not members of Jewish religious associations [*Kultusvereinigungen*], but on the basis of the tenth executive ordinance appended to the Reich's citizenship law are members of the Reichsvereinigung, is to be effected by first making an announcement in the news bulletin. Reprints of this announcement are to be made available to the three organizations so that they can be sent with an appropriate circular note to the group of people in question.

The registration deadline specified in the announcement of the Reichsvereinigung is to be observed. In the event that the registrations have not been made by that time, registration through the police Registration Offices is to be taken into consideration.

II. [deals with "Processing of emigration applications"]

III. Counseling of those who are not Jews by faith [*Nichtglaubensjuden*]

In amendment of the **Hilfsverein**'s[44] circular letter, we inform you that people who are not Jews by faith always are to be referred to the Christian relief organizations and that counseling by the Hilfsverein is to take place only on a fallback basis.

IV. Welfare work

Payment of welfare support is to be made only by the office of the Reichsvereinigung. In the case of welfare-related care proper, however, the offices of the Reichsvereinigung will enlist the Christian organizations (for example, for inquiries, home visits, etc.). All participating organizations are to inform their local or district offices that there is to be collaboration

---

40. Conrad Cohn (1901–1942?) was a former lawyer who oversaw much of the Reichsvereinigung's relief program and vocational training for prospective emigrés. Arrested in the summer of 1942, he died in a concentration camp. See Esriel Hildesheimer, *Jüdische Selbstverwaltung unter dem NS-Regime: Der Existenzkampf der Reichsvertretung und Reichsvereinigung der Juden in Deutschland* (Tübingen: Mohr, 1994), 109, 122, 134, 243; Ernst Lowenthal, ed., *Bewährung im Untergang: Ein Gedenkbuch* (Stuttgart: Deutsche Verlags-Anstalt, 1965), 36–37.

41. For more on **Dr. Paul Eppstein**, see the Glossary.

42. For more on **Paula Fürst**, see the Glossary.

43. For more on **Dr. Arthur Lilienthal**, see the Glossary.

44. For more on the Hilfsverein der deutschen Juden, see the Glossary.

in welfare-related care to that effect. It is to be left to the local and district offices to regulate, by agreement, the participation of the Christian organizations in the welfare work of the offices of the Reichsvereinigung. Central regulation in detail will take place only to the extent that difficulties should arise locally.

With regard to enclosed welfare work, the following is agreed upon:

a. In the Jewish hospitals, pastoral care by clergymen of the two Christian denominations will be made possible.

b. Plans call for establishing special old people's homes for Christian non-Aryans.

V. Schools

Where a sufficient number of Christian children are available, classes for the Christian children are to be established within the Jewish schools. Breslau, Hamburg, Cologne, and Frankfurt a. Main were tentatively named as places that come into consideration for this purpose. In Berlin, a Christian school with three or four grades comes into consideration. For the Christian schools or classes, curriculum guidelines are to be submitted to the Reichsvereinigung by the organizations in question.

To the extent that Christian children attend Jewish schools without separate classes for Christians, religious instruction will be provided for them.

Berlin, July 25, 1939

The issue of "mixed marriages" gained in urgency after "*Kristallnacht.*" Couples in "mixed marriages" and their children, the "***Mischlinge***," faced the danger of having to share the fates of other German Jews. The status of non-Jewish spouses also came to the fore: on which side of the divide between "Jew" and "Aryan" did "Aryan" spouses, particularly converts to Judaism, belong? In the face of ambiguous Nazi racial categories, people tried to protect themselves and their spouses through various means.

DOCUMENT 3–10: **Letter by Jakob Sieskind, Leipzig, Germany, to Rabbi Gustav Cohn, Leipzig, November 27, 1938, USHMMA RG 14.035M, reel 1 (translated from German).**

Leipzig, November 27, 1938

Esteemed Rabbi,

The terrible events of the last few weeks and the associated laws enacted by the government of the Reich have greatly heightened the severe anxiety I already feel about the future of my wife after my death. My wife converted to Judaism to ensure that any offspring of our marriage would be regarded as Jewish. Our marriage has been childless. To make the fate of my wife after my passing at least a bit easier, I myself advised her to withdraw from the Israelite Religious Congregation. I persuaded my wife, and thus I am herewith announcing her withdrawal, with her consent, which she indicates by her signature below.

I remain respectfully yours,

Dr. jur. Jakob Sieskind

Elise Sieskind née Pohl (February 3, 1876)

A letter of January 3, 1939, from an administrator of the Leipzig Jewish Religious Congregation to Elise Sieskind responded "that as a result of your request [. . .] you have ceased to be a member of our congregation."[45]

The status of "**Aryans**" and "Jews" in "mixed marriages" and their offspring continued to be the source of considerable wrangling among Nazi Party and

---

45. Dr. jur. Jakob Sieskind (1872–1943), a Leipzig lawyer and banker, was arrested for allegedly violating "war economy measures" and deported to Auschwitz in late 1942, where he died. The authors have found no evidence that his wife, Elise Sieskind (née Pohl; 1876–?), a convert to Judaism, was deported and killed during the war. Her name and that of her husband were recorded in the German census, supplement for Jews, in 1939, but she was listed as having no Jewish grandparents. See *Gedenkbuch*, available at www.bundesarchiv .de/gedenkbuch; Yad Vashem, "Central Database of Shoah Victims' Names," www.yad-vashem.org; Ellen Bertram, *Menschen ohne Grabstein: Die aus Leipzig deportierten und ermordeten Juden* (Leipzig: Passage, 2001), 216. Born in Stettin, Gustav Cohn (1881–1943) arrived in Leipzig in 1921 and served as a rabbi for the Reform Jewish *Israelitische Religionsgemeinde* until he was arrested during "*Kristallnacht*" in late 1938. Sent to the Buchenwald concentration camp, he was released after a short time and fled to Amsterdam with his wife, Elsbeth (née Wittkower; 1885–1943). Arrested and sent to Westerbork in 1942, they were subsequently deported to Auschwitz, where they were presumably killed. See Heike Kirchhof, ed., *Jüdisches Leben in Leipzig* (Leipzig: Passage-Verlag, 2006), 101; www.joodsmonument.nl (accessed March 3, 2011); *USHMM ITS Collection Data Base Central Name Index*.

state officials. In December 1938, Hermann Göring introduced a new legal distinction between "privileged" and "nonprivileged" "mixed marriages," which had implications for couples' place of residence and the racial status of their children. A Führer decree of April 30, 1939, further elaborated these measures. "Nonprivileged" couples and families—defined as those in which a "Jewish" man was married to an "Aryan" woman without children or with children who were registered with the Jewish community as of September 1935—were essentially defined as part of the "Jewish" side and could be forced to live in Jewish-owned houses with other Jewish tenants, referred to as "Jew houses." "Privileged" marriages—between an "Aryan" man and a "Jewish" woman with or without children or between a mixed couple with baptized children— remained part of the "Aryan" side and were not forced to move.[46]

The implications of these newly imposed categories for people's sense of self are often hard to uncover; however, they surely reached to the core of personal perceptions of status and identity. As an institution that both validated one's class position and allowed for social mobility, marriage was critical as a vehicle for social integration. The restrictions the Nazis imposed on marriage for Jews and their partners impacted massively on the internal and external dynamics of partnerships.[47] The diary of **Luise Solmitz**, an "Aryan" married to Fredy, a Jewish convert to Protestantism and decorated World War I officer, offers insight into one family's experiences. Luise and Fredy Solmitz were deemed partners in a "privileged mixed marriage" thanks to their "*Mischling*" daughter, Gisela. As the entries from Luise Solmitz's diary appearing in volume one of this source series testify, she struggled throughout the early years of Nazi rule to reconcile her conservative, German-nationalist outlook and complete lack of any affiliation with the Jewish community with the racial categorization thrust upon her family by the Nazi regime.[48] Most of all, she worried about the toll it was taking on her daughter. Gisela's "*Mischling*" status spared her from the worst antisemitic persecution, but her awareness of the predicament only deepened as she became more of a social pariah.

---

46. Friedländer, *Nazi Germany,* 1:289–91.

47. For a discussion of Jewish and "mixed" marriages and divorce in Nazi Germany in this period, see Kaplan, *Between Dignity,* 74–93.

48. Matthäus and Roseman, *Jewish Responses, documents* 2–1 (35–36), 6–7 (152), 7–1 (185–86), 7–6 (196), 10–14 (291), 11–8 (329–30), and 12–6 (352–53).

DOCUMENT 3–11: Luise Solmitz, Hamburg, Germany, diary entries for July 8 and 9, 1939, FZGH 11 S 11 (translated from German; stray punctuation in the original).

July 8, 1939

I'm worried about Gisela, she's grown gaunt, lean, doesn't eat, is act-ing peculiar. Bit by bit, the Nuremberg Laws weigh more heavily on her the older she gets.—Getting married has never been easier than now, and yet she's barred from it all, just how completely barred she doesn't even suspect. [. . .] Even Voges, the optimist, who wishes us so well, said "impossible," and Else said the same thing . . . "But even if—what man would take on all that?!" Gis asks. It's too bitter and incomprehensible, I keep thinking it's a bad, hideous dream that my child, who once was so cheerful, should be barred from finding happiness. Surrounded by other girls her age who are making plans for the future.

July 9, 1939

. . . How is it possible, how is it permitted, to spoil life for young, innocent, healthy human beings?! How can anyone have the heart to do that—regardless of all reasons of state.

Nazi racist marriage restrictions sometimes combined with long-standing gender relations that limited Jewish women's paths to self-realization. **Jenny Marx** from Mannheim, for example, was left with the responsibility for look-ing after and supporting her ailing parents after her younger brother, Max, emigrated to Palestine in 1933. The custom of giving women and daughters more responsibility for family care trumped Jenny's own desire to emigrate. Beyond this, the feeling that Jewish men faced greater danger and had greater opportunities meant that they were often sent abroad before their sisters or wives. With each passing month, Jenny's depression deepened as she contem-plated how hopeless her future was and compared it to the opportunities that she imagined existed outside Nazi Germany for starting a new life. She wrote to her brother on March 3, 1939,

It makes little sense to write to you about the same subject [her various efforts to emigrate] over and over, yet there is nothing else to write about. I am so tired of life, that I have often wished it would end. In your case it is quite different. You are held in esteem and you have a fantastic position, for which I congratulate you. You enjoy life. In my case all is finished. The tragedy with our parents, the long separation from you, everybody loaded down with sorrows, so the interest in life is not great.[49]

Only her engagement one month later to Siegmund Mayer—in her words, a "plain workman, baker, and confectioner"—brought renewed hope to the thirty-three-year-old woman. As the letter in document 3–12 and many others from this period indicate, her decision to marry Mayer was fraught because of how it conflicted with her earlier conceptions of marriage and because of its close causal and chronological correlation to Siegmund's concentration camp imprisonment. Indeed, her ambivalence was only compounded by the marriage of her brother during these same months to a woman who seemed to embody her abandoned ideal.

DOCUMENT 3–12: Letter by Jenny Marx, Mannheim, Germany, to Max Marx, Jerusalem, Palestine, April 21, 1939, private collection (translated from German).

Thanks for your and dear Ruth's [Max's fiancée] good wishes, also for the picture. I must compliment you on your choice, which is not bad at all. I had envisioned my sister-in-law very much like the picture, a good-looking, stylish woman, which should suit you well. Dear Max, I can't send you a picture of us yet, as Sigi's [Jenny's fiancé] hair needs to grow some more after his "big trip."[50] Please be patient for another month. With regard to our plans, there's nothing concrete yet to say. As you know, we rented one room, so now we only have the parents' room and the living room with my bed. It makes no sense to buy additional furniture for a few months. I intend to marry shortly before Sigi's departure, partly because he's supposed to take my luggage with him. [. . .] His request for my immigration will take from 1/2 to 3/4 year since I don't have any papers. Immigration there [to South Africa] is very difficult. I hope we'll be lucky. With regard to him personally, it can be said that he really is a very good craftsman, who can handle almost anything that you can think of. Unfortunately, when it comes to writing he gets a failing grade.

---

49. Letter by Jenny Marx, Mannheim, Germany, to Max Marx, Jerusalem, Palestine, March 3, 1939, private collection (translated from German).

50. This appears to be a reference to Siegmund Mayer's internment in a concentration camp. In earlier letters, Jenny Marx described Siegmund as "still 'away'" and indicated that she had had no word from him. Mayer was apparently arrested during the November pogrom and held in a camp for several months.

Don't hold that against him, I'll teach him everything as far as I can. Each person is different. Nothing is perfect. Our meeting is like a real novel. Man does not escape his destiny. I fought this tooth and nail. We were separated by his "trip" for four months and still have become much closer. You know my temperament, he suits me incredibly well. He is not like Ludwig Strauss [to whom Jenny was engaged in the early 1930s], an egoist of love, on the contrary, totally like me. He was married for more than three years, divorced. It's a pity that I can't describe all the details to you in person, a real tragedy. It's a miracle that he is still alive.

It's hard to comprehend what he has lived through, that a human being can endure so much. Especially because he's a little below my educational level, I'm doubly kind to him. I've changed a lot. I've begun an entirely new life, and I've made a clean break with all that's past. It is impossible to love all men at the same time, and maybe a little marriage of convenience can be as happy as an ideal one. I'm 10 years older than you, and I see the world through rather dark glasses. My life will be devoted to working together, love will play second fiddle. He's very nice to our parents, gets along better with Mother than with Father. He brings them whatever he can. He works as a brick mason at the cemetery at present for 70 pfennig per hour. Almost every day, he brings along a sack of wood so that we can have some heat. The in-laws send food, so the family is extremely nice. There isn't an errand that we don't do together, whether I'm buying myself shoes or going to the dressmaker, he comes along. When some correspondence has to be taken care of, I do it, so we need each other. We travel about every two weeks to his family and never come home empty-handed.

In a certain way I'm happy, since I no longer have to be by myself. Since I broke off the previous engagement nine years ago, none of my many friends has asked me to marry him. He was the only one. It's possible that I could have married later on, if I had emigrated, but I'm not waiting for that anymore. [. . .] My future father-in-law has been a shoe buyer in foreign countries for many years, his wife was the head cashier at the Schmoller department store. Both are really nice people. I'm doubly glad that we'll stay together after emigration, too. Max, I could write you much more today, but I still have some work to do. Alfons [their first cousin] in Amsterdam is also engaged. Please write him a note, Vechtstrasse 71, Amsterdam. They sent us matzoth for Passover. All the best for the future. Please remain true to me, as I am to you. A hearty kiss also for Ruth from all of us.

Jenny

Throughout the winter and spring, and especially during the summer of 1939, it became ever clearer that war was on the horizon. For this reason, Jews and non-Jews monitored Hitler's pronouncements closely. Jews within the Reich also listened carefully to Hitler's speeches for signs of what else he had in store for the Jewish population within Germany's borders. Thus, because of the amplification of antisemitic measures since the November pogrom and mounting tension in Europe, the speech he delivered on January 30, 1939—his annual speech in the Reichstag to mark the anniversary of his appointment as chancellor—took on more significance than usual.

The speech, on the occasion of the sixth anniversary of National Socialist rule in Germany, came at a critical moment for Hitler. On the one hand, Nazi Germany had managed to assert its domination of central Europe without much interference: it had annexed Austria and was practically given a free hand by the British and French at Munich to dismember Czechoslovakia. On the other hand, Hitler recognized that the allies might draw the line of **appeasement** at the German-Polish border.

In his speech, Hitler repeated the familiar anti-Jewish themes that filled many of his speeches. Harkening back to the failure of the **Évian Conference** to resolve the refugee crisis, the widespread condemnation of Germany in response to the events on "*Kristallnacht*," and the negotiations underway between Hermann Göring and the American chairman of the **Intergovernmental Committee on [Political] Refugees**, George Rublee, he also criticized the "whole democratic world" for its hypocrisy: it was "oozing sympathy for the poor tormented Jewish people but remains hard-hearted and obdurate when it comes to helping them."[51] Toward the end of this speech, however, he issued a threat and "prophesy" of a different character. He presaged, "If the international Jewish financiers in and outside Europe should succeed in plunging the nations once more into a world war, then the result will not be the Bolshevization of the earth, and thus the victory of Jewry, but the annihilation of the Jewish race in Europe!"[52]

Historians have long debated the meaning of Hitler's pronouncement. That it threatened the physical destruction of European Jewry seems fairly clear, especially in light of Hitler's preceding discussion in the speech of solving the "Jewish problem" by means of emigration and resettlement. But under what

---

51. Friedländer, *Nazi Germany*, 1:314–16.

52. "Extract from the Speech by Hitler, January 30, 1939," in *Documents on the Holocaust: Selected Sources on the Destruction of the Jews of Germany and Austria, Poland, and the Soviet Union*, ed. Yitzhak Arad, Israel Gutman, and Abraham Margaliot (Lincoln and Jerusalem: University of Nebraska Press and Yad Vashem, 1999), 132, 134–35.

circumstances would "annihilation" be carried out? What did Hitler have in mind when he contemplated "world war" as the necessary precondition for the "annihilation of the Jewish race"? The answer to these questions has implications for determining the origins of the "Final Solution" and, in particular, the timing of its implementation.[53]

Because of the significance accorded the speech by historians, it is particularly interesting to investigate how Jewish listeners responded to the speech at the time Hitler delivered it. Indeed, several of the diarists with whom we are already familiar included mention of the speech in their entries. In her brief reference to it, Luise Solmitz barely touched on the threat to Jewish existence, despite the drastic effect the anti-Jewish legislation of the preceding six years had had on her own and her husband's and daughter's lives: "Führer's speech in the Reichstag. Colonial demands . . . Streets deadly silent during the speech."[54] "Colonial demands" likely alluded to Hitler's insistence that Germany was entitled to the colonies it had lost at the end of World War I; in fact, Hitler linked Germany's economic difficulties to the issue of colonies.[55] Like Solmitz, Victor Klemperer did not attribute any particular significance to Hitler's most recent pronouncements, declaring in a diary entry of February 5, 1939, "Politically everything the same. Germany all-powerful, Spain will soon be finished. Campaign against the Jews further intensified. In his Reichstag

---

53. For three different interpretations, see Philippe Burrin, *Hitler and the Jews: The Genesis of the Holocaust* (London: Edward Arnold, 1994), 61–62; Christopher R. Browning with contributions by Jürgen Matthäus, *The Origins of the Final Solution: The Evolution of Nazi Jewish Policy, September 1939–March 1942* (Lincoln and Jerusalem: University of Nebraska Press and Yad Vashem, 2004), 321; and Hans Mommsen, "Hitler's Reichstag Speech of 30 January 1939," *History and Memory* 9, nos. 1–2 (fall 1997): 147–61.

54. Luise Solmitz, diary entry for January 30, 1939, FZGH 11 S 11 (translated from German).

55. There was, however, an important subtext to the "colonial demands" noted by Solmitz. Ever since the emergence of political antisemitism in Europe at the end of the nineteenth century—a continental European political movement that, unlike agents of traditional anti-Jewish prejudice, sought to "solve" the "Jewish question" in Europe by political means—African colonies figured as possible extra-European territories to which Jews would be expelled. These ideas resurfaced in the 1930s and were in wide circulation, especially in France, Poland, and Germany. For a brief overview of resettlement plans proposed by antisemites, see Dwork and van Pelt, *Flight from the Reich*, 102–3. That the questions of German colonial expansion and the "solution" of the "Jewish question" were intertwined in the Nazi mind can be surmised from Hitler's comment, on January 5, 1939, to Polish foreign minister Józef Beck, paraphrased by Friedländer: "Had the Western democracies had a better understanding of his [i.e., Hitler's] colonial aims, he would have allocated an African territory for the settlement of Jews." Friedländer, *Nazi Germany*, 1:310.

speech of January 30 Hitler once again turned all his enemies into Jews and threatened the annihilation of the Jews in Europe if they were to bring about war against Germany."[56]

Even outside the Reich, Hitler's speech and its murderous anti-Jewish rhetoric did not stir Jewish audiences. On the front page of the January 31, 1939, issue of the New York Yiddish daily, the **Forverts** (*Jewish Daily Forward*), the headline screamed, "HITLER THREATENS JEWS WITH EXTERMINATION IN THE EVENT OF WAR."[57] Yet, the rest of the headline and accompanying article focused on the menace of war and Hitler's professed allegiance to Italy and Japan. Similarly, the largest, Warsaw-based Yiddish daily, *Haynt*, covered Hitler's speech in several issues. On January 31, the first day after the speech, *Haynt* offered a brief summary of Hitler's main points, omitting the "prophecy" altogether.[58] Only on the following day did *Haynt* editors notify readers in a subtitle for the speech that "Hitler threaten[ed] Jews with annihilation."[59] And in the political analysis of the speech, reproduced below, the *Haynt* contributor (under the pseudonym "Itshele"[60]) concentrated on British **appeasement** of Hitler and other geopolitical implications rather than Hitler's open threats against the Jews. To contemporary observers, the speech did not sound out of the ordinary; they noted the vicious anti-Jewish rhetoric, but by then they had come to expect as much from Hitler.

DOCUMENT 3–13: Itshele, "After the Speech (a Political Letter)," *Haynt* (Warsaw), February 3, 1939, 3 (translated from Yiddish).

The satisfaction and naive enthusiasm with which the leader of the British government, the old Chamberlain, received and relished Hitler's speech was much more shocking and astonishing for us than the speech itself.

56. Victor Klemperer, diary entry for February 5, 1939, in *I Will Bear Witness*, 1:293.

57. *Forverts*, January 31, 1939, 1.

58. "Hitler's rede in raykhstag," *Haynt*, January 31, 1939, 1.

59. "Foler tekst fun Hitlersrede; Hitler droht di Yidn mit fernikhtung," *Haynt*, February 1, 1939, 2.

60. Itshele was one of the pen names of Moshe Yustman (1889–1942), a popular Warsaw journalist of the interwar period. As "Itshele" or as "B. Yushzan," Yustman wrote sharp feuilletons and perceptive political analysis for *Der Moment* until 1925 and thereafter for *Haynt*. When the war broke out, he managed to escape to Vilna and from there to Palestine. His wife and two daughters perished in the Warsaw ghetto. Yustman died of a heart attack in Palestine in 1942. See Chaim Finkelstein, *Haynt: A tsaytung bay Yidn, 1908–1939* (Tel Aviv, 1978), 146–51; David Flinker, Mordekhai Tsanin, and Shalom Rozenfeld, eds., *Di Yidishe prese vos iz geven* (Tel Aviv, 1975).

The substance of the three-and-half-hour-long speech can be summarized in a few sentences: The economic condition of Germany is very, very dismal. [. . .] The quiet economic war undertaken by England, and especially by America, whose purpose is to drive out German goods from the large world market, along with the strengthened boycott, has shattered Germany. German exports fall from day to day, and, should this continue, it simply threatens catastrophe. As a result of this, Germany demands two things: first, stop the economic shenanigans, open the markets to Germany, and give her the opportunity for greater exports of German goods. Second, return the colonies which were robbed from her by the Versailles treaty. The colonies are vital to her, without them she cannot exist. She must have colonies in order to derive from them the raw materials needed for her economy and, particularly, as a refuge for the human overflow of the narrow and overpopulated Germany.

And if not?

An answer to the "if not" was given in the speech in a very delicate manner, in just a few words, which said, "Germany hopes for a long-lasting peace and is determined to undertake energetic action to lead the country out of its economic difficulties and to receive its appropriate share in the distribution of the colonial wealth." [. . .]

And the next morning the old Chamberlain stood up in Parliament and savored Hitler's speech, almost applauding and clapping bravo and trying to show that the fascist dictators are both highly decent people whom one can fully trust.

The day following Hitler's speech President Roosevelt declared before the Military Commission of the American Senate that in case of war in Europe, America will come to the aid of England and France and will actually support them by supplying them with all needed war material. Should a war break out—Roosevelt said—then the borders of America will extend into France.

Unlike Jewish commentators writing about Hitler's speech in the period immediately after it was delivered, **Chaim Kaplan**, writing eight months later on the first day of World War II, seemed to regard Hitler's "prophecy" as of great consequence. A long-time resident of Warsaw, Kaplan dedicated long entries in his wartime diary to political analysis. In an entry dated September 1, 1939, he recalled the speech and related it to the fate of Polish Jews, should Poland be defeated: "Wherever Hitler's foot treads there is no hope for the Jewish people. Hitler, may his name be blotted out, threatened in one of his speeches that if war comes the Jews of Europe will be exterminated. The Jews comprehend and sense all that is in store for them wherever Hitler's armies make a temporary conquest."[61] Kaplan recalled the rhetorical linkage Hitler had drawn between world war and Jewish annihilation. Now, at the start of that long-dreaded war, those words in the speech took on new meaning, as they would again when historians looked back after the war to interpret the implementation of the "Final Solution" and the significance of Hitler's pronouncements.

---

61. Chaim A. Kaplan, *Scroll of Agony: The Warsaw Diary of Chaim A. Kaplan*, ed. Abraham I. Katsh (Bloomington: Indiana University Press in association with the USHMM, 1999), 20.

PART II

INVASION AND EARLY OCCUPATION OF POLAND

O N SEPTEMBER 1, 1939, Germany invaded Poland, initiating the global conflict that lasted for almost six years, referred to today as World War II. Germany's fall campaign against Poland was relatively short; the period between the beginning of the invasion and the final defeat of Poland spanned barely five weeks. Yet, this military operation marked a radical shift in German policy. The German aggression, with its modern military technology, novel strategy and tactics, aerial bombardment, and blurring of distinctions between the front and rear lines, as well as between combatants and civilians, provided a glimpse into the upcoming horrors of total war. It is estimated that over 150,000 Polish civilians lost their lives during this blitzkrieg. In addition, tens of thousands of former Polish government officials, military officers in hiding, landowners, clergy, and members of the intelligentsia were killed in targeted massacres carried out by German *Einsatzgruppen*, with some help from the regular **Wehrmacht** troops.[1] In the run-up to the attack on Poland, Nazi Germany had struck a deal

---

1. Scholars disagree about the number of Polish civilians executed during the Polish campaign. Alexander Rossino puts the conservative estimate at "no fewer than 16,000 . . . [by] early October," quoting Czesław Madajczyk, *Die Okkupationspolitik Nazideutschlands in Polen, 1939–1945* (Berlin: Akademie Verlag, 1987), 12. Werner Röhr, ed., *Europa unterm Hakenkreuz: Die faschistische Okkupationspolitik in Polen, 1939–1945* (Berlin: Deutscher Verlag der Wissenschaften, 1989), 80, estimates the number at twenty-seven thousand. Alexander B. Rossino, *Hitler Strikes Poland: Blitzkrieg, Ideology, and Atrocity* (Lawrence: University Press of Kansas, 2003), 86–87, 263n129. Christopher Browning quotes an estimate of fifty thousand executed Poles "by the end of 1939." Christopher R. Browning with

with its ideological enemy, the Soviet Union, which triggered the Red Army's occupation of eastern Poland on September 17, speeding up the Polish defeat and adding to the feeling of national humiliation. More importantly, however, the short Polish war allowed Hitler and the Nazis to test and implement parts of their broader vision of territorial expansion encapsulated in the slogans of "living space" (*Lebensraum*) and "Germanization," even if these concepts were still undifferentiated and hazy in their concrete meanings.[2]

Nazi occupation was not an "ordinary" takeover of enemy territory. Rather, underpinned by racialized notions of space characteristic of the Nazi ideology and radicalized by the massive application of force, this was the beginning of the violent and mammoth project of racial, spatial, and demographic reorganization of eastern Europe. To the Nazi mind, Poland presented a gateway to the future German "East," a pastoral realm uniquely suited for domination by German settlers. In this vision, little room remained for "racially inferior" Jewish and Slavic populations, especially for those ideologically and politically opposed to German dominance. To the Nazis, members of the Polish intelligentsia were "natural" targets for elimination, along with Jews, who had already been demonized by years of Nazi propaganda, and other groups deemed "undesirable." During the campaign and in its aftermath, members of the SS and other German occupation forces murdered tens of thousands of Poles—both non-Jewish and Jewish—whom they viewed as dangerous to the Nazi project of Germanization. In the words of Christopher Browning, a preeminent historian of the Holocaust, Poland became the "'laboratory' for Nazi experiments in racial

---

contributions by Jürgen Matthäus, *The Origins of the Final Solution: The Evolution of Nazi Jewish Policy, September 1939–March 1942* (Lincoln and Jerusalem: University of Nebraska Press and Yad Vashem, 2004), 35. This figure includes roughly seven thousand Jewish civilians; see Klaus-Michael Mallmann, Jochen Böhler, and Jürgen Matthäus, eds., *Einsatzgruppen in Polen: Darstellung und Dokumentation* (Darmstadt: Wissenschaftliche Buchgesellschaft, 2008), 88. Note that these estimates refer to Poles executed by the Germans; the number of total Polish casualties (defined as Polish citizens, thereby including Jews) in both German and Soviet zones in 1939 exceeds six hundred thousand; see Dieter Pohl, "War, Occupation, and Holocaust in Poland," in *The Historiography of the Holocaust*, ed. Dan Stone (New York: Palgrave MacMillan, 2004), 88–105, esp. 105.

2. For the history of racialist thought in Germany, its linkages to the German "mission" in eastern Europe, and the history of racist legislation in Nazi Germany, see Michael Burleigh and Wolfgang Wippermann, *The Racial State: Germany, 1933–1945* (New York: Cambridge University Press, 1991), 23–73.

imperialism."[3] Soviet-occupied eastern Poland became the setting for a different, comparatively more benign form of restructuring from above.

Two different zones emerged within the German-dominated Polish "laboratory" once the Wehrmacht had relinquished its authority in the fall of 1939. The western regions were annexed to the Reich, either as new administrative entities (Reichsgau Wartheland, or **Warthegau**; Reichsgau Danzig-West Prussia), or as additions to existing administrative units, such as East Upper Silesia, which included the cities of Katowice (German: Kattowitz) and Oświęcim (German: Auschwitz). These areas were earmarked to be "cleansed" of racially inferior stock in favor of Germans. Further east, on the fringe of direct German rule, central Poland became a German fiefdom called the **Generalgouvernement** under **Hans Frank** and his administrators. At the time of its creation, many in the Nazi leadership saw this region as a "dumping ground" for unwanted population groups in general and Jews in particular.[4] Until the German attack on the Soviet Union in June 1941, and through the convergence of a number of complex factors, these two large areas with a Jewish population of about 2 million became the pressure cooker within which Nazi anti-Jewish policy evolved in new, yet not predetermined directions.

Most Polish Jews realized that nothing good would come of the German occupation of their country. The plight of German Jews between 1933 and 1939 had made clear what Jews could expect under Hitler. For this reason, and despite their ambivalence toward life in Poland engendered by the complex history of Polish-Jewish relations through the preceding decades and even centuries, Jews were eager to defend Poland from German aggression.[5] For

---

3. Browning, *The Origins of the Final Solution*, 14, and for the importance of the Polish campaign to the evolution of Nazi policies, 12–35; also see Rossino, *Hitler Strikes Poland*.

4. See Browning, *The Origins of the Final Solution*, 36–44; also see Map 3, p. xiv.

5. From the early modern period until today, the history of Polish-Jewish relations has been complex and shifting, following the twists and turns of Polish history. For the early modern patterns of Polish-Jewish relations, see Murray J. Rosman, *The Lords' Jews: Magnate-Jewish Relations in the Polish-Lithuanian Commonwealth during the Eighteenth Century* (Cambridge, MA: Harvard University Press, 1990); for an analysis of the emergence of modern, exclusivist, antisemitic Polish nationalism in the nineteenth century, see Brian Porter, *When Nationalism Began to Hate: Imagining Modern Politics in Nineteenth-Century Poland* (New York: Oxford University Press, 2000); for relations between the Polish government-in-exile and the Jews during World War II, see David Engel, *In the Shadow of Auschwitz: The Polish Government-in-Exile and the Jews, 1939–1942* (Chapel Hill: University of North Carolina Press, 1987), and David Engel, *Facing a Holocaust: The Polish Government-in-Exile and the Jews, 1943–1945* (Chapel Hill: University of North Carolina Press, 1993). World

several weeks it seemed that Poles and Jews were united against a common enemy.[6] The Jewish experience of the initial phase of the war largely resembled that of the overall Polish population—yet already entailed some specific features emanating largely from Jews' prior experiences of persecution both in Poland and in Germany, Austria, and other Nazi-dominated areas.

With the beginning of the German attack, civilians fled, leaving the areas affected by the fighting or looking for shelter in cities hit by the Wehrmacht's military might. While most felt they were living through "historic days," few had the time, energy, and calm to write down their experiences immediately after events happened. September 1, 1939, disrupted diary keeping and letter writing the same way it transformed life in Poland in general. In addition, what did get written down often did not survive the war. In view of the highly unsettling effects of the first days of the war, it is not surprising that fewer sources generated by Jews in the immediate aftermath of the German attack have survived compared to those written after the events. As we will see, the fluidity of the situation and great uncertainties of the time dominated the work of Jewish organizations and the lives of Jews in German-occupied Poland. Even weeks or months of reflection rarely helped to arrange the pieces of the puzzle—what the future would hold—into a wholly coherent picture.

War II and the Holocaust understandably exacerbated this complicated relationship, which appeared obvious and worthy of analysis to contemporary keen observers as well. For a classic contemporary account written during the war and first published in 1974, see Emanuel Ringelblum, *Polish-Jewish Relations during the Second World War*, ed. Joseph Kermish and Shmuel Krakowski (Evanston, IL: Northwestern University Press, 1992).

6. For Polish-Jewish relations in the wake of the German invasion, see Engel, *In the Shadow of Auschwitz*, 46–50.

CHAPTER 4

INITIAL REACTIONS

JUST DAYS before German tanks rolled into Poland, the leaders of world Zionism convened the **Twenty-First Zionist Congress** in Geneva, Switzerland. In the concluding address delivered to the assembled delegates, **Chaim Weizmann**, president of the World Zionist Organization, warned that Europe would continue to be cloaked in "darkness" for the foreseeable future. Yet, he also expressed his ongoing faith that a better future lay ahead. In the meantime, with Europe in turmoil, few Jews would be in a position to build a Jewish state:

> There is darkness all around us, and we cannot see through the clouds. It is with a heavy heart that I take my leave. If, as I hope, we are spared in life and our work continues, who knows—perhaps a new light will shine upon us from the thick black gloom. [. . .] We shall meet again. We shall meet again in common labor for our land and people. [. . .] There are some things that cannot fail to come to pass, things without which the world cannot be imagined. The remnant shall work on, fight on, live on until the dawn of better days. Toward that dawn I greet you. May we meet again in peace.[1]

---

1. Quoted in Norman Rose, *Chaim Weizmann: A Biography* (New York: Penguin, 1986), 354. On Zionist reactions to the Holocaust, see Dina Porat, *The Blue and the Yellow Stars of David: The Zionist Leadership in Palestine and the Holocaust, 1939–1945* (Cambridge, MA: Harvard University Press, 1990).

On the eve of the war and during its first months, Jewish leaders in Poland had to make fateful decisions: should they stay and organize relief efforts? Or should they attempt to reach the safer shores of Palestine, the United States, or neighboring countries such as Lithuania and prepare for an uncertain postwar future alongside Weizmann and other Jewish leaders already living abroad?

The German invasion of Poland pressed the majority of Polish Jews to ponder similar choices about fleeing or staying put. Flight at this point did not mean starting anew in a faraway land out of Nazi reach; rather, it amounted to joining the masses of Poles, Jewish and non-Jewish, who took to the roads in the hope of avoiding direct experience of combat and Nazi dominion. By the same token, staying put rarely connoted high-minded communal responsibility. At the outset of the war, most Jews, like their Polish compatriots, put their own and their families' and friends' survival before consideration of any other sort of "response." Polish Jews soon discovered that they had few allies to rely on in their struggles. The ties of citizenship that imperfectly bound Jews and non-Jews together frayed under the intensity of the assault, especially in the aftermath of Poland's defeat.

The rapidity and radical nature of the changes brought about by the victorious **Wehrmacht** left little time for Jews to reflect on the causes and aims of German occupation policy. Not surprisingly, then, the relatively few people who did end up writing about the events as they unfolded concentrated on documenting their course. Very few conveyed their thoughts and reflections on the causes and goals of German occupation policy. For the most part, as the documents in this chapter show, they wrote accounts of upheaval and their initial experiences of the violations to their sense of human decency perpetrated by German occupiers.

THE INVASION OF POLAND

In the days between the conclusion of the Twenty-First Zionist Congress and the actual outbreak of war on September 1, 1939, Poles, Jewish and non-Jewish alike, tracked diplomatic developments anxiously. They harbored few illusions that the war could be averted. The increasing likelihood of armed conflict meant that everyone in the Polish population became focused on the present, as people attempted to secure their own families' safety and contribute to Poland's preparations for war.

Dawid Sierakowiak, a fifteen-year-old Jewish boy living in Łódź at the time of the German invasion, proved a particularly insightful chronicler of the events that unfolded around him.[2] Not long after he began keeping his diary in late June 1939, Sierakowiak observed the worsening tensions between Poland and Germany and the increasing likelihood of armed conflict. In the excerpts from his diary presented in document 4–1, Sierakowiak wrote about his puzzled reactions to the signing of the **Molotov-Ribbentrop Pact** and the tense anticipation that greeted the impending invasion. His entries from these final days of peace do not set Jews' experiences apart from those of Poles. Indeed, his only reference to Jews in particular signals that they were responding in a manner similar to Polish non-Jews. Sierakowiak conveyed the unity in action among all Polish citizens at the time, evident even in the language they used to talk about their German enemy.

DOCUMENT 4–1: **Dawid Sierakowiak, Łódź, Poland, diary entries for late August 1939, USHMMA RG 10.247 Dawid Sierakowiak diary collection (translated from Polish).[3]**

Tuesday, August 22. Łódź.

A terrifying, interesting, and strange piece of news. The Germans are concluding a 25-year nonaggression pact with the Soviets! What a turn of events. What a capitulation of Nazi ideology. The Soviets clearly do not want to get mixed up in European politics and want to secure their rear for a fight with Japan. Speaking of Japan: what do they think about this pact? The Germans probably won't be able to count on Japan's help any more. In any case, it's a pretty good propaganda trick for Germany. Who knows how the European situation will develop now? Chamberlain called the British parliament back from vacation and convened an extraordinary session.[4]

---

2. Dawid Sierakowiak was born in Łódź, Poland, in July 1924 to Majlech and Sura Sierakowiak and had a younger sister, Nadia. He attended a private Jewish *Gymnasium* in Łódź. Dawid's diary writing spanned the period from June 28, 1939, until April 15, 1943, a few months before he would have turned nineteen. He died on August 18, 1943, apparently of tuberculosis. A total of five notebooks from his diary survived the war. See *The Diary of Dawid Sierakowiak: Five Notebooks from the Łódź Ghetto*, ed. Alan Adelson (New York: Oxford University Press, 1996).

3. This is also printed in a differently worded translation in Sierakowiak, *The Diary of Dawid Sierakowiak*, 26ff.

4. Arthur Neville Chamberlain (1869–1940), British prime minister at the outbreak of World War II, was best known for his policy of appeasement of Nazi Germany (famously embodied by the 1938 **Munich agreement**). For more on **appeasement** and the Munich agreement, see the Glossary.

Wednesday, August 23. Łódź.

The situation is becoming worse. The pact is going into effect. Tension in the city is growing. People aren't talking about anything but the situation in Europe. Polish radio calmly provides information on everything and contributes to calm and stability in the country.

Thursday, August 24. Łódź.

Mobilization! We just don't know whether it's only scare tactics or not. In any case, nearly all age groups are being called up. A large number of our neighbors have gone. Although terrible farewell scenes are playing out on the city's streets, in our apartment block there is a heroic calm. The wives of those who have been called up calmly but relentlessly glower at the Germans and rush to sign up for the women's PW.[5] "Cut the Kraut's throat in the cradle," "Don't wait, thrash him now"—these are the sentiments of almost everyone nowadays. There isn't any sign of defeatism in the least. Our family is in a rough spot because we don't have any cash at all. What will happen—nobody knows. If we only had dough. And kill as many Krauts as you can. The streetcars are overflowing with conscripts. The loud singing of soldiers, often drunk, can be heard. In the afternoon, a prohibition on the sale of alcohol was posted. At dinnertime, father brought home six kilograms of flour. In the afternoon, Mrs. Heller wasn't allowed to buy any—rightly so. The food supply in Poland is sufficient. We also aren't buying any more for now. Those six kilograms will be used up quickly. They said on the radio that summer vacation will apparently be extended by a few days. Not a bad idea at all. It's so hot (in more ways than one) that no one wants to go to school. [. . .]

The requisitioning of horses and carts continues. All the schools have been given over to the military. Drunken conscripts (and they say there's no vodka?!) roam the streets and raise enthused cheers. An atmosphere of uncertainty grows stronger. The command of the OPLG[6] has already issued appropriate orders. I sleep lightly and at the ready. Mobilization has begun throughout Europe. France has called up 700,000 people. During an extraordinary session of the British parliament convened today, Chamberlain said that, with God as his witness, he has done everything to preserve peace in Europe, but the issue of checking German aggression has now become a matter of life and death for Europe. "And let those in whose hands lies the decision to start the bloody slaughter of nations

---

5. Polish: *przeszkolenie wojskowe* (military training).
6. Polish: *Obrona przeciwlotnicza i gazowa* (air and gas defense).

consider what they are doing before they send millions of human beings to their death." In response to Chamberlain's letter, Hitler said that eastern Europe should be under his control, that he will not abandon his vital interests, and that no other state should interfere with his interests.[7] England mobilized its entire Navy. [. . .]

Saturday, August 26. Łódź.
    A Polish-English alliance has also been signed. The die has been cast, and now the Germans have to make a decision. But they are not in a hurry. Hitler has postponed a speech and inspection that were announced for tomorrow in Tannenberg. Thus the state of unease is prolonged yet again. [. . .]
    Today I read President Kwapiński's appeal calling for volunteers to dig antiaircraft ditches.[8] I signed up immediately at the police station after gaining permission at home, as all my friends did, and tomorrow morning I'll go to work. There are tens of thousands of volunteers. The mass of registrations is not even hampered by a lack of tools. Jews old and young, women, Hasidim, like all citizens (except the Germans), are volunteering in droves. The damned Kraut will not pass! At the border, instances of German aggression that constitute clear acts of provocation are continually recorded.

Sunday, August 27. Łódź.
    Dad and I have been up since six digging (with shovels from the city administration). [. . .]

Wednesday, August 30. Łódź.
    General mobilization! All reservists up to 40 years of age are being called to arms. Father, although he is seven years older than the oldest drafted age group, is very nervous, as is Mother. [. . .]

Jews experienced the first weeks of the war in much the same way as their Polish neighbors did; the bombs did not discriminate. Jewish soldiers and volunteers joined in the struggle against Germany in September 1939.

---

7. For a good summary of Nazi Germany's interwar territorial expansion and road to war, see Wolfgang Benz, *A Concise History of the Third Reich* (Berkeley: University of California Press, 2007), 155–70.
    8. Jan Kwapiński (1885–1964) was the mayor of Łódź at the time of Sierakowiak's writing. During the invasion of Poland, he was arrested by the Soviet secret police (NKVD) but released in 1941, when he joined the London-based Polish government-in-exile.

In the Polish army, they fought on the battlefront; in the civilian brigades, they dug trenches in large cities. Many contemporary testimonies, including the diary of Dawid Sierakowiak excerpted in document 4–1, mention the prevailing sense of common destiny and even camaraderie shared by non-Jewish and Jewish Poles, engendered by the awareness of imminent danger of Nazi aggression. At least for a short time, Jews "volunteering in droves," in Sierakowiak's words, to dig trenches in order to defend Polish cities were a common sight.

DOCUMENT 4–2: Jewish Poles dig trenches in the city around the time of the German invasion, Warsaw, Poland, late August or early September 1939, USHMMPA WS# 41033.

After the outbreak of hostilities, however, many Polish families faced the dilemma of whether to leave or to stay. A series of events contributed to the uncertainty of the situation. The surprising Soviet annexation of Poland's eastern territories on September 17, followed by the German occupation of Warsaw on September 28 and the partitioning of the country by the two invading powers, led to massive confusion, as Jewish and non-Jewish individuals in flight seemingly traveled in circles. Some chose to flee to the east or the south with varying degrees of success.[9] Others left their homes only to find their path blocked or to decide that flight seemed far more dangerous than staying put. Miriam Wattenberg took notes that later became the basis for her published "diary-memoir"[10]; her early entries capture the confusion experienced by Jews who witnessed the invasion and participated in the short-lived defense of Poland. Like Sierakowiak, Wattenberg offers a teenager's perspective. Her family, however, belonged to a wealthier stratum of society, which colored her experience of the last days of peace and the first weeks of war when her family fled from their home in Łódź to the Polish capital city of Warsaw.

DOCUMENT 4–3: **Miriam Wattenberg, Warsaw, diary-memoir entry for October 10, 1939, in** *The Diary of Mary Berg: Growing Up in the Warsaw Ghetto* **(Oxford: Oneworld Publications, 2006), 1–2, 7–8.**

Today I am fifteen years old. I feel very old and lonely, although my family did all they could to make this day a real birthday. They even baked a

---

9. On September 6, 1939, Polish radio broadcast a call for all able-bodied men to leave Warsaw and regroup in the eastern part of the country; this, however, was understood to be a government sanction for mass flight. Samuel D. Kassow, *Who Will Write Our History? Emanuel Ringelblum, the Warsaw Ghetto, and the Oyneg Shabes Archive* (Bloomington: Indiana University Press, 2007), 104. On the confusion in Poland surrounding the joint attacks by Germany and the Soviet Union, see Gross, *Revolution from Abroad*, 17–18.

10. Miriam Wattenberg, aka Mary Berg (b. 1924), stayed with her parents—including her mother Lena, a U.S. citizen—and her sister Ann in Warsaw until January 1943, when she was transferred to the Vittel internment camp in France based on the family's citizenship. She left Europe for the United States in March 1944. Parts of her diary notes first appeared in print in 1944 in various journals. The diary was published in full in 1945 as Mary Berg, *Warsaw Ghetto: A Diary* (New York: L. B. Fischer, 1945). Susan Lee Pentlin has prepared a new edition, *The Diary of Mary Berg: Growing Up in the Warsaw Ghetto* (Oxford: Oneworld Publications, 2006). In the preface to the original edition, Samuel L. Shneiderman (1906–1996), who helped get the text published, explained that the book combines notes taken by Wattenberg during the war with later revisions made after the author came to the United States; the changes "clarify details that would otherwise have been unintelligible for American readers." In the new edition Susan Pentlin suggests designating the published work "a diary memoir" (*The Diary of Mary Berg*, xiii, xvi). Saul Friedländer, *Nazi Germany and the Jews*: (vol. 2) *The Years of Extermination: 1939–1945* (New York: HarperCollins, 2007), 157, cautions that "Berg's diary may well have been thoroughly reworked by the author and the publishers" and uses it sparingly. See also Alexandra Zapruder, ed., *Salvaged Pages: Young Writers' Diaries of the Holocaust* (New Haven, CT: Yale University Press, 2002), 444.

macaroon cake in my honor, which is a great luxury these days. My father ventured out into the street and returned with a bouquet of Alpine violets. When I saw it I could not help crying.

I have not written my diary for such a long time that I wonder if I shall ever catch up with all that has happened. This is a good moment to resume it. I spend most of my time at home. Everyone is afraid to go out. The Germans are here.

I can hardly believe that only six weeks ago my family and I were at the lovely health resort of Ciechocinek, enjoying a carefree vacation with thousands of other visitors. I had no idea then what was in store for us. I got the first inkling of our future fate on the night of August 29 when the raucous blare of giant loudspeakers announcing the latest news stopped the crowds of strollers in the streets. The word "war" was repeated in every sentence. Yet most people refused to believe that the danger was real, and the expression of alarm faded on their faces as the voice of the loudspeaker died away.

My father felt differently. He decided that we must return to our home in Łódź. In almost no time our valises stood packed and ready in the middle of the room. Little did we realize that this was only the beginning of several weeks of constant moving about from one place to another.

We caught the last train which took civilian passengers to Łódź. When we arrived we found the city in a state of confusion. A few days later it was the target of severe German bombardments. The telephone rang again and again. My father dashed from one mobilization office to another, receiving a different-colored slip of paper at each one. One day Uncle Abie, my mother's younger brother, rushed unexpectedly into our house to say goodbye before leaving for the front. He was ragged, grimy, and unshaven. [. . .]

We spent most of our time in the cellar of our house. When the word came that the Germans had broken through the Polish front lines and were nearing Łódź, panic seized the whole population. At eleven o'clock at night crowds began to stream out of the city in different directions. Less than a week after our arrival from Ciechocinek we packed our necessities and set out once more.

Up to the very gates of the city we were uncertain which direction we should take—toward Warsaw or Brzeziny?[11] Finally, along with most

11. A town in Poland, nineteen kilometers (twelve miles) east-northeast of Łódź, Brzeziny had a Jewish population of about 6,850 on the eve of World War II. Martin Dean, ed., *The United States Holocaust Memorial Museum Encyclopedia of Camps and Ghettos, 1933–1945*, vol. 2: *Ghettos in German-Occupied Eastern Europe* (Bloomington: Indiana University Press in association with the USHMM, 2011), 44–47.

of the other Jews of Łódź, we took the road to Warsaw. Later we learned that the refugees who followed the Polish armies retreating in the direction of Brzeziny had been massacred almost to a man by German planes [. . . After fleeing through Łowicz, Sochaczew, and Okęcie, Mary and her family reached Warsaw, where they endured the German siege until the end of September.]

On the last night of the siege [of Warsaw] we sat huddled in a corner of the restaurant below our house. [. . .] The grownups simply sat or lay motionless, with stony faces and vacant eyes. Hours went by. When daybreak came I was struck by the sudden stillness. My ears, accustomed to the crash of unceasing explosions, began to hum. It was the terrifying silence that precedes a great calamity, but I could not imagine anything worse than what we had already been through. Suddenly someone rushed into the cellar with the news that Warsaw had capitulated. No one stirred, but I noticed tears in the eyes of the grownups. I, too, felt them choking in my throat, but my eyes were dry. So all our sacrifices had been in vain. Twenty-seven days after the outbreak of the war, Warsaw, which had held out longer than any other city in Poland, had been forced to surrender.

In most cases, it was the bombing raids of the Luftwaffe that plagued Jewish and non-Jewish Poles alike at the start of the war. According to the estimates of the **American Jewish Joint Distribution Committee** (AJJDC) in Warsaw, twenty thousand Jews were killed in the first month of the war, with seven thousand Jews killed in Warsaw alone in September 1939.[12] Those Jewish casualties represent but a fraction of the overall casualties in Poland. The experience of the military campaign was so lethal and traumatic, as indicated by Wattenberg's reference to the air raid that killed almost all the refugees in flight to Brzeziny, that some Jews hoped for the attack to stop and for the occupation to begin. Memories of the "Great War" (World War I) prompted optimism in some circles, for perhaps German soldiers would at least be able to restore order

---

12. AJJDC Warsaw report about their work during the thirteen war months from September 1939 to October 1940, AJJDC Warsaw, USHMMA, Acc. 1999.A.0154, ŻIH 210/6. The report also counted 59,000 Jewish homes, factories, workshops, shops, and so forth, destroyed by the bombing and fires; the AJJDC estimated the number of destroyed Jewish homes in Poland at 6,850, including Warsaw, 1200; Warsaw district, 800; Lublin district, 2,200; Radom district, 1,400; and Kraków district, 650. For the history of AJJDC work in Europe during the Holocaust, see Yehuda Bauer, *American Jewry and the Holocaust: The American Jewish Joint Distribution Committee, 1939–1945* (Detroit, MI: Wayne State University Press, 1981).

to the chaos unleashed by the invasion.[13] The cruel and sadistic nature of the new German regime (so shockingly different from the one in power in 1914) became apparent soon after the occupation began and, in some cases, immediately upon the arrival of German troops.

In fact, Jewish experiences of the German occupation were so radically different from other waves of persecution and physical violence to which Jews in eastern Europe had been subjected in the past that, as the initial general chaos of the occupation gave way in the following months to ominous signs of systematic persecution, including murder, some Jews realized that they needed to document their experiences as a way to bear witness to this tragedy. Nobody could yet imagine total physical annihilation as the ultimate goal of the occupiers, and the Nazi leadership had certainly not yet made that decision. But the unchecked daily humiliation, physical violence, forced labor, and murder to which the Jews were subjected looked like an unprecedented situation that needed to be documented for future generations.

Already in the fall of 1939, the historian of Polish Jewry and AJJDC employee who had organized relief for the refugees in Zbąszyń in November 1938, **Emanuel Ringelblum**, assembled a group in Warsaw that made its mission the gathering of documentation about the persecution of the Jews. Under the code name **Oyneg Shabes** (the joy of Sabbath), Ringelblum and his colleagues started collecting, in Warsaw, testimonies of Jewish refugees from across Poland. They aimed to create an archive that would make possible the writing of future works of history on the persecution of the Jews in this terrible period. As the German plans changed, however, and assumed ever more radical and ultimately genocidal proportions over the years, the purpose and breadth of the archive changed as well. By the time of the liquidation of the Warsaw ghetto in 1943, the Oyneg Shabes archive had brought together numerous testimonies, diaries, essays, works of art, and other materials that bore witness to Jewish experiences of life and death in Warsaw and other Polish cities and towns.[14]

---

13. In the aftermath of World War I, a myth about the benevolent German occupation of eastern Europe emerged among the Jews in the region, a myth about a fundamentally decent German soldier who observed customs of war and did not harass civilians, especially not Jews. For a historical overview of the realities of Austro-German occupation of eastern Europe during World War I, see Mark von Hagen, *War in a European Borderland: Occupations and Occupation Plans in Galicia and Ukraine, 1914–1918* (Seattle: University of Washington Press, 2007).

14. For background on Emanuel Ringelblum and the Oyneg Shabes archive, see Kassow, *Who Will Write Our History?*

Ringelblum's was not the only documentation effort among the Jews in Poland and Lithuania; individuals elsewhere—Herman Kruk and Avrom Sutzkever in Vilna (Polish: Wilno; Lithuanian: Vilnius), a city briefly occupied by the Red Army in September 1939 before falling under Lithuanian control, Mordechai Tenenbaum in Białystok, **Chaim Rumkowski** in Łódź, to give a few well-known examples—organized collection efforts of a similar nature. However, a combination of factors, including the sheer number of documents and the comprehensiveness it sought to achieve, has made Ringelblum's undertaking the best known.

Testimonies from the Oyneg Shabes archive that document the early days of the occupation were recorded and collected slightly later, mostly in 1940 and 1941. These texts thus do not offer a strictly contemporaneous perspective on the events of the fall of 1939. Though retrospective, they were written during the war and, most importantly, before the implementation of the "Final Solution" in Poland, which altered Jewish perceptions of this early period of the war. The report presented in document 4–4 about the experiences of Jews in Kutno, a town approximately sixty kilometers north of Łódź (halfway between Łódź and Włocławek in German-annexed **Warthegau**), offers the perspective of some Polish Jews who hoped that German occupation might bring about the resumption of order. And it suggests how quickly direct experience of Nazi German antisemitic persecution dashed those hopes.

As was the case in hundreds of localities throughout Poland, many Jews in Kutno fled back and forth from the town, unsure of where to find refuge from the bombers overhead and the artillery advancing on the ground. Jews had dwelled in Kutno for centuries, and in December 1939, 7,709 lived there out of a total population of 27,761.[15] The city enjoyed a fair degree of prosperity, owing largely to its central location at the junction of several important rail lines. Unfortunately for the residents of Kutno, this central location also drew the attention of German bombers aiming to disrupt commerce and communication. The anonymous author of document 4–4's report describes the September 1939 bombardments, the start of the German occupation in mid-September, and the beginnings of oppressive measures and persecution directed at the Jewish residents. As the author suggests, the initial period following the invasion was chaotic. Residents' hopes that the German occupation would at least end the devastation of the invasion quickly gave way to new fears of what life would look like under the Nazis.

---

15. *USHMM Encyclopedia of Camps and Ghettos, 1933–1945*, 2:69–72, entry for Kutno.

DOCUMENT 4–4: **Testimony of an anonymous woman from Kutno, no date (ca. 1940), USHMMA RG 15.079M (ŻIH Ring. I/839), reel 39 (translated from Polish).**

[. . .] Kutno was bombed already on the morning of September 1. These were likely the first bombs of the war which, to use [H. G.] Wells's expression, "ignited the world."[16] The results were terrible: out of a group of recruits waiting for a train near the station, 120 were killed and 200 were wounded. The train never left—there was no one to be transported.

On September 2, it was the same thing, the only difference was that 80 were killed and a couple hundred wounded.

From then on, German planes visited us every day. It was always at the same time (6 a.m., noon, and 5 p.m.), three times a day and with such punctuality that it wouldn't be an overstatement to say that you could set your watch by their visits. They attacked various military targets on the outskirts of town (the train station, the military barracks, the airport), but not the town itself. Yet this practice didn't continue for long: at first, the center of town was bombed sporadically, but soon the bombings took on a mass character and claimed so many victims that people started to leave town.

Now a few words about my own experiences: on September 8, I, like many others, fled Kutno for Gostynin[17] because I presumed that the town, lacking military installations, would be much less at risk of getting bombed. It wasn't particularly safe to travel at the time: the German planes continuously circling above would swoop down over the road again and again and strafe the refugees with machine-gun fire. Because of this, we had to hide in the ditches on the side of the road, which didn't at all help to speed up our progress. Luckily, I made it to my destination. But after I found out that the front line kept getting closer, I decided to flee

---

16. Herbert George Wells (1866–1946) was a best-selling English author, famous for his science fiction novels. In *The War of the Worlds* (1898), the novel to which the quote in the document most likely refers, he describes the invasion and rampage of Martians in southern England. A writer trying to escape the devastation of the Martian invasion narrates the novel. *The War of the Worlds* was widely read and quite well known across Europe in the first half of the twentieth century and became part of popular culture, as this reference suggests. For the most recent edition, see Herbert George Wells, *The War of the Worlds* (London: Penguin, 2005).

17. This town is approximately twenty-five (fifteen miles) north of Kutno. In August 1939 it had roughly twenty-three hundred Jewish inhabitants. See *USHMM Encyclopedia of Camps and Ghettos, 1933–1945*, 2:54–55, entry for Gostynin.

all the way to Warsaw via Gąbin.[18] And I got stuck in that village: there were no means of transportation, and on top of that we were surrounded by Germans. [. . .] near a place called Holendry, a German settlement, a Polish lieutenant stopped us: "Gentlemen, you will witness the punishment of a local official who is a German spy." We didn't care much for this little performance, but we couldn't help it, we were dead tired. One of the soldiers showed us a dead body in a ditch. "This one has been already punished," he said with satisfaction. We didn't end up waiting long, a taxi arrived within a half hour with a few policemen and the accused, who was dressed in a boy scout's uniform. The investigation of the crime was simple, uncomplicated: since he did not admit his guilt in any of the accusations, he was given a good beating, and when that still didn't have any effect, one of the soldiers put a gun to his temple and pulled the trigger.

Around September 11, I returned to Kutno. The next day, the town was bombed in a crueler and more merciless fashion than ever before (there were no more antiaircraft defenses by this point). From among the Jews alone, 18 people were killed. Entire neighborhoods stood in flames, which were visible from a distance of even several dozen kilometers. Not only hospitals, but also synagogues, the *bethamidrasz*[19], and even private homes were literally bursting at the seams with the wounded, both soldiers and civilians, who lay about and died without medical attention, food, and medicine. But that was the last day that Kutno was bombed. The entire town breathed a sigh of relief and thanked God that they had survived. But too soon! One shouldn't give thanks to anyone, especially God, too soon: from September 11 to 16, artillery on the outskirts of town fired continuously. Imagine our situation: the town overflowing with refugees from Pomerania (about 4,000), which exacerbated the food shortages that already existed. It was impossible to get any food, because getting out of the basements, where everybody was hiding, meant endangering one's life. [. . .]

We all even prayed for the Germans to come so this hell would end. Madness! We didn't realize what we were wishing for! The future would show us soon enough.

---

18. Gąbin is located about sixty kilometers (thirty-seven miles) northwest of Łódź. On the eve of World War II, the Jewish population of Gąbin was 2,312 (*USHMM Encyclopedia of Camps and Ghettos, 1933–1945*, 2:52–54, entry for Gąbin).

19. *Bethamidrasz* is the Polish rendering of the Hebrew word meaning "house of study."

On the morning of September 16 the advance troops of the German army entered Kutno. It must be said that on the first day, but only on the first day, the Germans behaved beyond reproach. They gathered all the men, both Jews and Poles, in the center of town, and an officer gave a speech to us:

"Don't be afraid! We will not hurt you. Maintain order, obey our commands and, most importantly, surrender your weapons." This was the gist of his speech. To implement it, he ordered his men to immediately take from us everything that could be defined as "weapons," such as small knives, pocketknives, scissors, etc. They eagerly carried out his order.

A few days later, however, our new masters showed what they were capable of: they summoned all the men—this time only Jews—and locked them up in one of the churches. Although they released some a couple days later, the rest were deported to the village of Piątek for labor.[20] There, these unfortunate ones were beaten and tormented so cruelly that perhaps half of them came back very sick as a result of being overworked and beaten. Each of them had a number painted on his back with white paint.

---

20. The town of Piątek, thirty-eight kilometers (twenty-four miles) north of Łódź, had a prewar Jewish population of about thirteen hundred Jews. See *USHMM Encyclopedia of Camps and Ghettos, 1933–1945*, 2:92–93, entry for Piątek.

DOCUMENT 4–5: **Jews move their belongings to the Kutno ghetto, no date (ca. June 1940), USHMMPA WS# 18609.**

As in Kutno, fear and uncertainty about how to respond to the German threat gripped Jews and Poles in the town of Lipno.[21] Another testimony from the Oyneg Shabes archive about Jewish experiences outside Warsaw, this one recorded by an unidentified female resident of Lipno, adds layers of complexity to our understanding of Polish-Jewish relations during the first weeks of the war and the decision people faced about whether to flee or remain in their homes. Looking back on early September 1939, the author of this testimony suggests that she

---

21. Lipno is a town in Poland, some 150 kilometers (ninety-three miles) northwest of Warsaw. According to the 1921 census, the town's Jewish population stood at roughly twenty-five hundred. See "Lipno," in *The Encyclopedia of Jewish Life before and during the Holocaust*, ed. Shmuel Spector, (Jerusalem and New York: Yad Vashem and New York University Press, 2001), 2:735. Also, [Avotaynu Foundation], *Black Book of Localities Whose Jewish Population Was Exterminated by the Nazis* (Teaneck: Avotaynu, 1989), 198.

decided not to flee because she preferred the familiarity of home to the uncertainty of seeking refuge in a chaotic situation. As had been in the case in Kutno, she describes how Jews, while sharing many of their neighbors' experiences, were marked for special persecution. She also highlights the variety of responses among Poles to scenes of Jewish humiliation in a time of national disaster.

DOCUMENT 4–6: **Testimony by unknown woman from Lipno, recorded ca. 1940 in the Warsaw ghetto, USHMMA RG 15.079M (ŻIH Ring. I/854), reel 39 (translated from Polish).**

[. . .] On the day the war started—it was a Friday, an ill-fated day—everything changed, as though someone had covered the town with ashes. Everyone's face turned gray, with smiles fixed on their pale lips that instinctively, instead of speaking, began to whisper; various pieces of news spread like wild fire around town, creating confusion, panic. [. . .]

Every day brought something new. On Friday the first of September, enemy bombs fell on the town, on the railroad tracks in particular—an attempt to damage them so as to disrupt communication with Warsaw; there were no antiaircraft defenses whatsoever, people hid in basements and discussed what was going on. Polish forces moved in the direction of Pomerania. [. . .]

On Saturday the second of September, people from Pomerania began to flee with whatever and however they could, on wagons and crowded into trains, there were shortages of food and water too. Aid committees immediately sprang up, Polish and Jewish, antisemitism disappeared. Women ran through the streets with baskets as people threw bread, fruit, and tomatoes from windows and balconies and stores donated soda water, *kvass* [a beverage], etc. All of this was driven out to the station and distributed among the refugees regardless of religion. A great migration began; day and night, wagons were constantly in motion, cars sometimes flew by, everything was moving in the direction of Włocławek; Polish forces began to retreat in the night from Saturday to Sunday, the entire camp was returning, with thousands and thousands of people in tow. Fear of the enemy was becoming more and more widespread. The residents of Lipno, following the example of neighboring towns, also began to buy and to rent new wagons and horses and to pack things up to get ready to leave. One mother said to me: "I'm afraid, so I'm sending my daughters along with the camp, and when they leave I'll be calmer."

[. . .] people continued to travel through Lipno and the residents of Lipno were leaving too; my husband and I watched this with a heavy heart [. . .] our best and closest friends were leaving town. We, mainly my husband, decided to stay: "Let whatever is going to happen to me happen at home—I'm not moving until I'm forced to." It stayed like this until the following Friday; on September 8, X [the Germans][22] entered the town. After they took control, a whole series of orders and prohibitions was issued. One could only be on the street until 5 o'clock, Jews had to wear yellow ribbons, and when these markings proved too small, Jews were ordered to pin yellow sashes onto their backs and chests. Walking on the sidewalk was forbidden; [there was] an order to walk on the road, to bow. A despicable little Jew from a neighboring town conveyed all these orders. [The Germans] began to round up Jews to clean the streets and squares, and you had to see how the Aryan overseers stood laughing as the Jews of the town swept the streets.[23]

The Polish intelligentsia watched this with indignation and often spoke to the Jews, comforting them and advising them not to preoccupy themselves too much with what, according to them, was a temporary annoyance. All Aryan and Jewish organizations were disbanded.

THE ASSAULT ON JEWISH LIFE

For the more religious among Poland's Jews, the timing of the invasion, which coincided with the holiest time of the Jewish year, the Days of Awe, carried a meaning that transcended the sphere of history into the realm of theology. The Days of Awe of the new Jewish year 5700 fell on September 14 and 15, 1939 (Rosh Hashanah), and concluded on Yom Kippur, September 23, 1939. During the Days of Awe, sometimes known as Days of Repentance, observant Jews are enjoined to turn to introspection, to atone for their sins before God and other Jews, and ultimately to repent. Some religious observers of the invasion

---

22. Here, the author clearly crossed out what she had written and replaced it with an *X*. From the context, one can tell she meant to write "Germans" but decided against it. This occurs once more in the document later on, when she merely writes an *X* (without crossing out anything else).

23. Humiliation of and sadistic violence against the Jews in the first months of the occupation were ubiquitous phenomena. For a similar account from a non-Jewish physician, Dr. Zygmunt Klukowski of Szczebrzeszyn, that describes German treatment of Jews in nearly identical terms, see Friedländer, *Nazi Germany*, 2:29.

were thus even more inclined to comment on the events by putting them in a theological framework of meaning.

DOCUMENT 4–7: **Rabbi David Lifszyc (later Lifshitz) in front of Torah scrolls smuggled from German-occupied Suwałki to Kalvarija, Lithuania, 1940, USHMMPA WS# 35460.**

The religious landscape of Polish Jewry on the eve of the German invasion was diverse and in flux, a consequence of historical processes that belonged to the realms of both Jewish and broader European history. Hasidism had originally emerged as a radical Jewish movement in the eastern Polish borderlands amid the complex eastern European intellectual and political currents of the eighteenth century. Its success among large numbers of Jews provoked a range of religious and ideological responses from the traditionalists, who saw it as a challenge to the practices of rabbinic Judaism. In the early decades of the nineteenth century, the pitched rivalry softened to mostly peaceable coexistence. And with the increasing prominence in the Russian Empire of the mid-nineteenth century of *Maskilim*—the adherents of the Jewish Enlightenment movement Haskalah—and their subsequent sponsorship by tsarist authorities, Hasids and traditionalists developed a sense of common cause. By the eve of World War I, Orthodox Jews had banded together for political reasons in defense of a Jewish identity based on religious observance against the forces of secularization and acculturation in their various guises, including Zionism and **Bundism**. In the interwar years, the growing strength of Polonizing influences on Polish Jews, as well as of rival secular political parties, pushed Hasidism and other branches of Orthodoxy in Poland toward more rigid conservatism. In 1939 the ideological and religious landscape of Polish Jewry was riddled with fault lines that were not crossed easily.[24]

When Nazi Germany invaded Poland, one of the leading figures of Hasidic Jewry in Poland, **Rabbi Kalonymus Kalmish Shapira**, was in Warsaw. Unlike some other prominent Hasidic rebbes[25] at this time, Shapira refused to abandon his community and family and opted, instead of fleeing Poland, to tie his fate to that of his followers. Over the course of the war, the Piaseczner rebbe and founder of the Yeshivah Da'as Moshe became known as the rebbe of the Warsaw ghetto and won the respect of Jews from across the religious and ideological spectrum because of his fervent devotion to Judaism, his warmth, and his love of all Jews.

The sermons Shapira wrote between 1939 and 1942 provide a unique insight into the life and thought of Hasidic Jews in Poland. In particular, they offer an important overview of the range of concerns that preoccupied Shapira, from Nazi persecution and Jewish suffering to the Divine.[26] Shapira's sermon on Rosh Hashanah 5700 (September 14, 1939) focused on traditional themes of repentance, forgiveness, and the need to accept God's sovereignty. In Shapira's

---

24. For a short introduction to Hasidism and reactions, see Israel Bartal, *The Jews of Eastern Europe, 1772–1881* (Philadelphia: University of Pennsylvania Press, 2005), 47–57. For an authoritative overview of modern Jewish politics in eastern Europe, see Zvi Gitelman, ed., *The Emergence of Modern Jewish Politics: Bundism and Zionism in Eastern Europe* (Pittsburgh, PA: University of Pittsburgh Press, 2003), and on Polish Jewish politics during the interwar years, see Ezra Mendelsohn, *The Jews of East Central Europe between the World Wars* (Bloomington: Indiana University Press, 1987), 43–63, 68–83. See also the entries on "Hasidism" by David Assaf and "Haskalah" by Immanuel Etkes in *The YIVO Encyclopedia of Jews in Eastern Europe*, ed. Gershon David Hundert (New Haven, CT: Yale University Press, 2008), 1:659–70, 681–88.

25. In order to distinguish themselves from rabbis, who were tied to official educational and religious hierarchies, Hasidic teachers adopted the title of "rebbe," which connoted a leader of tight-knit groups of students independent from the structures of rabbinic Judaism.

26. Kalonymos Kalmish Shapira, *Sacred Fire: Torah from the Years of Fury, 1939–1942*, ed. Deborah Miller (Northvale, NJ: J. Aronson, 2000). On Rabbi Shapira and his writings, see Nehemia Polen, "Divine Weeping: Kalonymos Shapiro's Theology of Catastrophe in the Warsaw Ghetto," in *Modern Judaism* 7 (1987): 253–69.

theology, suffering and punishment could be understood as reinforcing the need to tremble in awe before God. He opened his sermon with a reference to two verses found in the liturgy recited before the blowing of the shofar on Rosh Hashanah: "In distress I called on the Lord; the Lord answered me and brought me relief" (Psalms 118:5) and "Hear my plea; Do not shut Your ear to my groan, to my cry!" (Lamentations 3:56). According to Rabbi Shapira, it was incumbent upon the Jews to seize the opportunity for *teshuvah* (repentance) during the Ten Days of Repentance between Rosh Hashanah and Yom Kippur and to return to God, for in liturgical time, this is the period of the year when God is particularly attuned to the cries of the Jewish people.

While Rabbi Shapira made no clear reference to the German invasion, anyone listening to him at the time would certainly have associated the cries and pleas of the Jewish people during these Days of Awe with the fearsome events that corresponded with the dawning of the new Jewish year 5700. The allusion to Lamentations, traditionally recited on the saddest day of the Jewish year, *Tisha B'Av* (the ninth day of *Av*, marking the destruction of the First and Second Temples in Jerusalem), similarly evoked a theme of devastation and destruction.

DOCUMENT 4–8: **Rosh Hashanah sermon of Rabbi Kalonymus Kalmish Shapira, September 14–15, 1939 (1 Tishrei 5700), USHMMA RG 15.079M (ŻIH Ring. II/370), reel 58 (translated from Hebrew).**[27]

[. . .] There is great need for us to arouse and excite our own fear of heaven during this period, because the fear itself is an acceptance of the yoke of God's sovereignty upon us. All the cries of the Jewish people heard in this period are a revelation of God's sovereignty upon us. Even those pleas and prayers in which we beseech God to take care of our physical needs are also a kind of revelation of His sovereignty and a praising of Him. God has revealed His majesty to us and we have accepted His sovereignty over us. We have returned to Him, and so we also ask of Him that He meet our needs. [. . .]

Now, it is also true that people repent each in his own way, all year round, and that every day we pray for our life, health and sustenance. Why then should Rosh Hashanah be considered so unique? What makes the day so easily distinguishable is the sounds associated with it—not only those of the shofar but also more generally the piercing sounds made by our voices of repentance and the poignancy of our pleas for sustenance.

---

27. This is also printed in a differently worded translation in Shapira, *Sacred Fire*, 3–9.

Soon after he wrote these words, personal disaster struck Rabbi Shapira as well: his son, who had recovered from a serious illness in the mid-1930s, died on September 29, 1939, from wounds suffered during the invasion, his daughter-in-law was killed on September 26 in a bombing near the Warsaw hospital, and his mother died on October 20. The rabbi's sense of personal loss was profound, but he channeled his work toward the spiritual support of his community. In the words of historian Esther Farbstein, his writings were an "extraordinary expression of faith at a time of personal distress, [and] reflect[ed] the depth of the faith that later emanated from him in the ghetto and shaped his sermons when all the Jews were suffering."[28]

When, during the first months of German occupation in Poland, the Nazis targeted Polish and Jewish elites for particularly harsh treatment,[29] Jewish men bearing telltale external markers of traditional religious observance, especially beards, were subjected to special forms of humiliation and torture. The testimony of another Jewish woman from Lipno describing her experiences on Yom Kippur, three weeks after the German invasion, highlights the manner in which the town rabbi was singled out for persecution and how terrorized the Jewish population of Lipno felt within days of the German occupation. She conveys how difficult it was to figure out which actions were permitted or forbidden by the new authorities, leaving Jews who wanted to observe the high holidays all the more vulnerable. Jews did not know if they would be allowed to pray on the holiest day of the year (whether in private, in groups, or individually, for the synagogue had already been boarded up) or whether their Polish Catholic neighbors would be able to intercede on their behalf with the occupiers.

The woman retelling the story also introduces an important element of the nature of the Jewish encounter with the Nazis in many different national contexts: the degree to which Jewish women in the early period of the war were called upon to interact with the German authorities in the belief that men were special targets for persecution.[30] This inversion of gender roles, though not

---

28. Esther Farbstein, *Hidden in Thunder: Perspectives on Faith, Halachah and Leadership during the Holocaust* (Jerusalem: Mossad Harav Kook, 2007), 481–83.

29. See Alexander B. Rossino, *Hitler Strikes Poland: Blitzkrieg, Ideology, and Atrocity* (Lawrence: University Press of Kansas, 2003), 58–87; Phillip T. Rutherford, *Prelude to the Final Solution: The Nazi Program for Deporting Ethnic Poles, 1939–1941* (Lawrence: University of Kansas Press, 2007); also see Richard C. Lukas, *The Forgotten Holocaust: The Poles under German Occupation, 1939–1944*, 2nd rev. ed. (New York: Hippocrene, 1997). For the debates about numbers of victims, see note 1 in the introduction to Part II.

30. Marion Kaplan also documents this phenomenon of role reversal between Jewish men and women in Germany in *Between Dignity and Despair: Jewish Life in Nazi Germany* (New York: Oxford University Press, 1998), 59–62.

unique to the Jews of Poland during the war, does demonstrate a remarkable bravery in this woman's encounter with German forces.

DOCUMENT 4–9: **Testimony by unknown woman from Lipno, recorded after 1939 in the Warsaw ghetto, USHMMA RG 15.079M (ŻIH Ring. I/974), reel 43 (translated from Polish).[31]**

Yom Kippur of 1939 fell on September 23, a Saturday. From the crack of dawn on September 22, there was already a heavy, oppressive atmosphere in town: at the crack of dawn a horrible roundup of men for forced labor took place. The G . . . [Gestapo][32] came to Rabbi C.'s home, and he was taken to work.[33] The rabbi's wife went to see the pastor, with whom the rabbi, as a fellow cleric, was on friendly terms. He solemnly swore to an arrangement whereby he promised to do everything within his power, and, indeed, he was seen going to see the *Landrat* [German regional administrator] without delay. He was received there and came back with the very good news that the rabbi would be excused from all work, that Jews would not be forced to work on Yom Kippur, and that group prayers would be allowed. This news served to lighten the oppressive atmosphere in the town, and the Jews exhaled a little; but it was all an illusion! As a result of this relaxation, I allowed myself to go out onto the street and made it to the rabbi's wife in order to calm her down a little. It was already the time when prayers should have been started, that is, shortly before "Kol Nidre."[34] As I sit with the rabbi's wife, she cries, very upset, I try to calm her down, the door opens and in comes the rabbi. His face was deathly green!! Covered in sweat, he sees me and yells: "I am lost, they specially abused me because I'm the rabbi, they ordered me to carry horse manure with my bare hands." The rabbi's wife immediately gives him hot water to wash up, I bid them farewell and go, bearing in my soul the image of someone tormented in this way—a sight that I'll never forget. The night passed calmly. The next day, Jews, believing the news they had been given, gathered in private homes for group prayers. The synagogue had already been boarded up for a few days, although prayers were still held there for

31. The change of verb tense between past and present is in the original text.

32. For more on the **Gestapo**, see the Glossary.

33. This probably refers to Rabbi Cuckerhorn; see *Sefer Lipno, Skepe, Lubicz ve-ha-sevivah* (Tel Aviv: Society of Former Residents of Lipno and Vicinity, 1988), 228.

34. This refers to a ritual declaration that precedes synagogue services on the eve of Yom Kippur.

the New Year. My husband didn't feel well and stayed home, he didn't even get out of bed. At around 11 o'clock we hear screams and yells, I walk quickly to the window and . . . again, there is an unforgettable sight before me: I see all the Jews running away in their socks, with prayer shawls and without, in skullcaps or with bare heads, rushing through the streets and chased by S.D.[35] Two acquaintances, Mr. P. and Mr. L., come to our home in a hurry to hide—they sit by the bed as though they came to visit someone who is ill. In the meantime, things on the street quieted down. These two men told us that X[36] and S.D. burst in everywhere where people were praying, beating them with whips and dispersing those who were gathered, who jumped out windows and saved themselves however they could by fleeing. It became quiet on the street, but no one had the nerve to come out because the risk of having an unpleasant encounter [with the Germans] was high. My husband stayed and got dressed; I told the men to lock themselves in the bedroom, to remove the key from the door, and to sit quietly. I also locked the second dining room and my husband put the key in his pocket. The two of us sat in the first room, which resembled a waiting room, likewise locked. Not finding anyone on the street, [the Germans] began to search in apartments. After some time, we heard loud knocking on the door and shouts of "*Aufmachen*" (open up). I slowly, calmly open the door; one comes in while the other stays on the steps to make sure that no one slips out: "*Gibt es hier keine Männer?*" (are there no men here?). I reply calmly: "*Nein, es gibt keine, nur wir zwei alte und niemand mehr*" (No, there are none, just us, two old people). "*Und was ist dort?*" (And what's over there?), he asks, pointing at the door to the

---

35. The SD, or Sicherheitsdienst (Security Service), was the intelligence service of the SS and the Nazi Party, which in late 1939 became integrated into the Reich Security Main Office (**Reichssicherheitshauptamt**) headed by Reinhard Heydrich. Like the Gestapo, the SD supplied an officer cadre and personnel who took part in the execution of anti-Jewish policy and the murder of the Jews in the territories occupied by Nazi Germany. The woman, whose testimony was recorded some time later in Warsaw, might have recognized the culprits by their uniform (SD badge on the left arm). For an overview of the history of the SD and its participation in genocide in Poland, see Klaus-Michael Mallmann, Jochen Böhler, and Jürgen Matthäus, eds., *Einsatzgruppen in Polen: Darstellung und Dokumentation* (Darmstadt: Wissenschaftliche Buchgesellschaft, 2008); also see Edward B. Westermann, *Hitler's Police Battalions: Enforcing Racial War in the East* (Lawrence: University Press of Kansas, 2005), 124–62.

36. *X* refers to "Germans." This appears in multiple sources and may have reflected a pattern adopted by those gathering testimonies for the Oyneg Shabes archive. See above, note 22.

last room. My husband opens the door with the key slowly, stalling, trying to gain time. [The German] enters and looks around—no one there, "*und was ist da?*" (and what's there?) Then I come up with, like lightning, a heroic lie, and I say in German: "*Jenes Zimmer gehört zu der Wohnung von jener Seite*" (that room belongs to the apartment on the other side). Struck by the speed of my response and the certainty of my voice . . . he bought it, and goes, saying to the first man that there's no one there. When they knocked on the door of the other apartment, no one answered because there truly wasn't anyone there! But how we felt after they had left is easy to understand since I had risked my life after all. What if he had not believed me and wanted to see for himself. Ha! I know that someone great and powerful was watching over me then, and may he continue to protect me. But those are moments one cannot forget, those are the moments that turn your hair white!

The persecution of the Jews of Lipno on the holiest day of the Jewish year—with the rabbi singled out to move manure on Yom Kippur—can serve as an example of how the Germans treated the Jews. Irrespective of its underlying motives, it worked to undermine both the spiritual and physical foundations of Jewish faith. The uncertainty that the Jews of Lipno experienced—whether to believe the news they had received, whether it would be safe to pray in the synagogue, whether they would be rounded up again for forced labor during prayer—highlighted the extreme shock that the invasion and subsequent attacks on Jews inflicted upon all communities and their members.

Indeed, it is unclear whether, during the first weeks of the war, Jews felt that they had been singled out for special persecution and perceived their suffering to be somehow more severe than that of non-Jewish Poles. It was clear within these weeks, however, that the German campaign targeted not only Jews' lives but also the foundations of Jewish life itself. Synagogue burnings, like those of "*Kristallnacht*" in Germany and Austria in November 1938, took place throughout Poland in September 1939. Multiple sources recount the physical and emotional trauma of the destruction of synagogues for Polish Jewry. Did such measures signal a new type of war, one that targeted Jewish people as a collective whole, or were they merely expressions of an anti-Jewish impulse that would die down once the fighting stopped? Few had a clear sense at the time.

Later, in 1941, Rabbi **Shimon Huberband**, active in Ringelblum's Oyneg Shabes underground archive in the Warsaw ghetto, wrote a study of Jewish religious life in Poland during the war. He titled his study *Kiddush Hashem*, meaning "the sanctification of God's name." Huberband included testimonies from multiple Jewish communities in Poland—Otwock, Serock, Piotrków Trybunalski, Sosnowiec, Będzin, Łódź, Suwałki, and others—and documented the German policy of destroying synagogues, houses of study, and cemeteries.[37] By 1941 the events suggested a pattern not only regarding German persecution but also in terms of Jewish responses. In many instances, Jews—religious and secular alike—risked their lives to rescue and shelter precious Torah scrolls before they could be destroyed by the oppressors. Huberband's account presents a complex picture of the early anti-Jewish violence in Poland, highlighting, among other details, how women were spared the worst violence and pointing to the readiness of certain Poles to help the Jews in these radical new circumstances.

DOCUMENT 4–10: **Shimon Huberband, Warsaw, "The Destruction of Synagogues, Study Halls, and Cemeteries," ca. 1941, USHMMA RG 15.079M (ŻIH Ring. I/108), reel 7 (translated from Yiddish).**[38]

Będzin They [the Germans] marched into Będzin on Tuesday, September 5, 1939. The priest and both rabbis welcomed them [with the traditional] bread and salt. This was an effective gesture. No slaughter took place in Będzin, as had occurred in the neighboring Sosnowiec.[39]

---

37. See (Rabbi) Shimon Huberband, *Kiddush Hashem: Jewish Religious and Cultural Life in Poland during the Holocaust*, ed. Jeffrey S. Gurock and Robert S. Hirt (Hoboken, NJ: KTAV Publishing House, 1987), 274–333.

38. This is also printed in a differently worded translation in Huberband, *Kiddush Hashem*, 274ff.

39. On Monday night, September 4, 1939, German forces invaded Sosnowiec, a town on the road from Katowice to Będzin, about six kilometers (four miles) from the former. In 1939, its Jewish population was around twenty-eight thousand (21.5 percent of the total population). According to Huberband (see his *Kiddush Hashem*, 287), as soon as they entered the town, they arrested three hundred Jews, herded them into the Medical Insurance Building, and shot all three hundred of them that night. The next day all male Jews were interned in a camp within "Schein's factory" where beards were shaved and the prisoners subjected to brutal torture. An additional seven Jews were shot on the pretext that they had been trying to sabotage a German vehicle.

Będzin is about 12 kilometers (7.5 miles) northeast of Katowice in Poland. According to the 1931 census, the Jewish population of the city stood at 21,625, or 45.4 percent of the town's total population. *USHMM Encyclopedia of Camps and Ghettos, 1933–1945*, 2:140–43 and 162–66, entries for Będzin and Sosnowiec.

On the evening of Saturday, September 9, 1939, at the same time as in Sosnowiec, a frightening dynamite explosion was heard across town. It was soon learned that the synagogue was on fire. A number of Jews, including Rabbi Yekhil Shlezinger, his two sons, and his son-in-law, Rabbi Yekhezkel Kon, raced into the burning synagogue to rescue the Torah scrolls. The arsonists shot at them and killed all of them. The martyrs were burned together with the synagogue and its Torah scrolls.

The Jews began to pour out of the surrounding houses to save themselves from the flames. The whole area, however, had been cordoned off by soldiers, and as soon as a Jew was spotted, he was shot. In a short time the streets near the *shul*[40] were filled with the bodies of dead Jews.

At that point Jews no longer even tried to quell the fire. The blaze spread from one house to the next, and everyone inside knew that leaving the house meant certain death. People were driven mad by looking death straight into the eye, and knowing that there was no way they could save themselves from death. The only choice left to them was how to die—burnt by the fire or shot by a bullet.

Women who ran out onto the street were not shot. But many women remained in their homes, although they could have saved themselves from the flames. They perished together with their families.

Fifty-six Jewish houses were burned down that day in addition to the synagogue. Nearly five hundred Jews died, either by being shot or being burned. The synagogue burned, the Torah scrolls burned, the bodies of Jewish martyrs, men and women, burned. But the heavens did not spurt out any fire to burn those who had caused the conflagration.

Only a few Jews managed to save themselves. One man clothed himself in a long dress and put a kerchief on his head. There were six men in all who rescued themselves in such a manner.

There was a church on a hill not far from the synagogue. A steeply curved street led from the Jewish quarter to the church. At a certain moment during the fire, the German guards left this street, and since it was curved and very steep, they couldn't detect from farther away whether anyone was moving there. Six Jews seized this moment, rushing out of a burning house and escaping into the church by way of this street. The priest and the worshippers welcomed the Jews very hospitably and kept them in hiding. As a result, the six were saved from certain death.

---

40. This means "synagogue."

When he wrote this account, Shimon Huberband had managed to hide himself in a different manner: in plain sight of the German authorities, provided with—for the time being—a crucial identity card that attested to his economic usefulness and reduced the risk of falling victim to random abuse and attacks.

DOCUMENT 4–11: **Registration card for Shimon Huberband issued by the Warsaw Labor Office, ca. 1941, USHMMA RG 15.079M (ŻIH Ring. II/385), reel 58 (translated from German).**[41]

Work office: <u>Warsaw Labor Office</u>
Branch: <u>Branch for the Jewish</u>
    <u>Living Quarter.</u>
Registration Card for Jews
Number:<u> 21321</u>
The Jew<u> Huberband Szymon</u>
Born on <u>19.IV.1909</u>
In <u>Chęciny, Kielce District</u>
    <u>Married</u>
Residence: <u>Warsaw</u>
<u>Zamenhof Street</u> number <u>19/19</u>
Job category & type: <u>25-1</u>
has been registered in accordance with the 2nd Implementing Regulations for the decree dated Oct. 26, 1939, pertaining to the introduction of forced labor for Jews in the Generalgouvernement dated Dec. 12, 1939, and is available to the Labor Office for work. Interception [of this person] on the street [*Auffangen auf der Strasse*] is not permitted.
(Seal of the Labor Office)
[signed:] Ziegler

Apart from the antisemitic motives that underpinned attacks on the Jews, another dimension to anti-Jewish violence inevitably arose. Similar to measures

---

41. Underlined text was typed or stamped into the form.

implemented in the German Reich and **Protectorate** earlier, these attacks on the Jews were part of the larger Nazi aim to exploit their resources—labor and property—for the benefit of the German state. Extracting Jewish wealth and using the Jews as a supply of cheap labor were important goals of the early anti-Jewish measures in the German-occupied territories.[42] In many locales in Poland at the beginning of the war (and later), Jewish communities were also compelled to pay large ransoms to secure the release of Jews who had been arrested on various pretexts.

Events in Włocławek (German: Leslau) exemplify this. Here the traumatic destruction of the two largest synagogues on Yom Kippur was accompanied by subsequent seizures of Jewish men for forced labor.[43] The Germans then incarcerated Jewish men for arson—for allegedly setting fire to their own synagogue. In a testimony recorded in Palestine several months later, a Jewish refugee from Włocławek described the chaos on Yom Kippur and the days that followed.

DOCUMENT 4–12: **Testimony on persecution in Włocławek/Leslau, recorded in Jerusalem, Palestine, June 7, 1940, translated from Benjamin Mintz and Joseph Klausner, eds., in** *Sefer ha-Zeva'ot. Eduyot ve-dinim ve-heshbonot al sho'ot ha-yehudim be-milhemet ha-olam ha-sheniya* **(Jerusalem: R. Mass, 1945), 86.**[44]

The Extermination of the Community of Włocławek: Protocol
Organized by the United Community to Aide Polish Jewry in Jerusalem. On July 7, 1940, a man appeared before us, M.P. from Włocławek. The man is now in Jerusalem, and testified to these things:

---

42. On this topic, see Martin Dean, *Robbing the Jews: The Confiscation of Jewish Property in the Holocaust, 1933–1945* (New York: Cambridge University Press in association with the USHMM, 2008); also see Götz Aly, *Hitler's Beneficiaries: Plunder, Race War, and the Nazi Welfare State* (New York: Metropolitan, 2007).

43. Włocławek is a town located about 107 kilometers (sixty-six miles) north-northwest of Łódź. On the eve of World War II, the Jewish population numbered between ten and fourteen thousand people, comprising about 20 percent of the total population. *USHMM Encyclopedia of Camps and Ghettos*, 2:118–20, entry for Włocławek.

44. This document is written in extremely formal, literary Hebrew. In fact, some idioms appear only in biblical rather than modern Hebrew usage. Thus, while neither the document nor the collection explicitly notes this, it is highly probable that the survivor (noted only as "M.P.") dictated his thoughts in either Polish or Yiddish to a transcriber, who then rendered this information into Hebrew. This hypothesis may be confirmed through the consistent use of the author's or speaker's third-person voice that never breaks through and the use of certain terms or notes (the general Hebrew term for money, *zahov*, is used instead of the Polish currency, parenthetical remarks are added, and so forth).

A few days after they entered Włocławek, the Germans burst into a private house where Jews were standing in prayer on the eve of the Day of Atonement, and ordered those present to get out and run. Then they gave the order "Stop," but some of the Jews did not hear this order being given and went on running; then they [the Germans] opened fire and killed 5 or 6 of them. On the Day of Atonement itself the Germans burned down the two large synagogues. The fire also spread to several private homes. The Jews threw their possessions out [to save them] and there they were robbed by the Polish mob. These fires were set mostly by the men of the SS. The Jews tried to save the burning houses. Then the Germans took all the Jewish men from one of the buildings, 26 persons whom they found there, and forced them to sign a declaration that they themselves had set fire to the building. After they had obtained this declaration the Germans informed the men who had been arrested that they would receive the death penalty for committing arson and could save themselves only if they paid a ransom of 250,000 [złoty]. The Jewish population of Włocławek collected the necessary sum amongst themselves and the incarcerated men were released. Then they [the Germans] began to launch hunting expeditions into the houses. They caught about 350 Jews and put some of them in barracks and some of them in the Muehsam factory. From there they were taken out to work every day, but given no food—only their families were permitted to bring them food. After many pleas those who had been arrested were permitted, after much checking, to visit their homes from time to time in accordance with a special leave-of-absence permit, in order to wash, change their clothes, eat, and so on. The work routine of the 350 who had been arrested did not by any means stop Jews from being abducted for work in the streets of the city. And apart from that there was the Jewish Council (*Judenrat*), which had been appointed in place of the former community authorities—it would supply a certain number of Jewish workers every day, in accordance with German demands. Those who had been taken away and those who were abducted for work were beaten and abused unmercifully. How they behaved toward the Jews during working hours is shown by the fact that one of these Jews, Jacob Heiman, 52 years old and too weak for physical labor, was beaten and stabbed with a dagger while he was working, and a few days after he returned home, he died of his injuries. In October the Germans decreed that the Jews must attach a yellow badge to the back of their clothes, and that they cannot be on the sidewalks of the street but rather in the middle of the road. After this they collected the ransom of 250,000 [złoty] from the Jews for the imaginary arson, they imposed a new fine on the Jewish population after a short while, of 500,000 [złoty], for the imaginary offense of not obeying the ban on using the sidewalk. The schools were closed.

A few days after they moved into the city, the Germans closed and confiscated the factories and stores belonging to Jews. The Jews were required to register all their property, and a Jew was not permitted to keep more than 200 [złoty] in his home (in Warsaw—2,000 [złoty]). There were many cases of Jews being beaten and tortured. They used to beat them not only during forced labor and not only when they had some excuse but also for no reason at all: they would simply approach passing Jews in the street, cry "Zhid," and stop to beat them.

WITNESSING THE COLLAPSE OF POLAND

In the midst of the chaos and destruction wrought by war and Nazi brutality, Polish Jewish leaders struggled to find a way to respond to the demands of the new German occupiers and a ravaged Jewish society. The impetus to establish new communal leadership came from within Jewish communities and was imposed from without. SS-Obergruppenführer **Reinhard Heydrich** issued an order on September 21, 1939, calling for the establishment of Jewish Councils to serve as administrative links between the German authorities and the Jewish population. Yet, as historian Isaiah Trunk has noted in his study of Jewish Councils, in some cases Jews formed councils before Heydrich issued his letter ordering their formation.[45] In other places, German troops gathered the entire Jewish community of a particular town before selecting its new "leaders." Indeed, a comparison of diverse locales reveals that the creation of Jewish Councils usually took place in a random and haphazard manner, often before September 21, and was generally accompanied by intimidation, humiliation,

---

45. Isaiah Trunk, *Judenrat: The Jewish Councils in Eastern Europe under Nazi Occupation* (New York: Macmillan, 1972), 15–16. Trunk's book is the classic work on the topic. Early scholarship on the Holocaust tended to point accusatory fingers at surviving members of the *Judenräte*, arguing that they were cogs in the Nazi machinery of destruction, hence Nazi collaborators; see Raul Hilberg, *The Destruction of the European Jews*, 3rd ed. (1961; New Haven, CT: Yale University Press, 2003), 3:1111–12, and Hannah Arendt, *Eichmann in Jerusalem: A Report on the Banality of Evil* (1963; New York: Penguin, 1976), esp. 117–18. Trunk's work presents a more complex picture of Jewish choices under Nazi occupation and inserts the institution of the *Judenrat* firmly into Jewish history. See also Dan Michman, "Judenrat," in *The Holocaust Encyclopedia*, ed. Walter Laqueur (New Haven, CT: Yale University Press, 2001), 370–77.

and even massacres in many communities.[46] Often those who had in fact been prewar leaders managed to escape in the first week of the war, went underground, or simply refused to obey the Nazi edict, which meant that those who ended up becoming representatives of the Jewish community in fact had little prewar political or administrative experience.[47]

In the erstwhile capital of Poland, Warsaw, home to Europe's largest Jewish community, **Adam Czerniaków** wrote in his diary about the efforts of Warsaw Jewish communal leaders to respond to the humanitarian crisis precipitated by the siege of Warsaw and Poland's military defeat. Czerniaków had served as deputy chair of the Jewish community before the war. After the prewar community chairman fled Warsaw, Czerniaków was appointed head of the Warsaw Jewish Community by the Warsaw mayor and head of civil defense, Stefan Starzyński, on September 23, in advance of the German occupation of the city. He was subsequently named head of the Warsaw Jewish Council under the Nazis. Czerniaków served in that capacity until his suicide on July 23, 1942. The *Judenrat* became the sole official body with which the German authorities were willing to deal, facilitating the stranglehold the occupying powers had over the Jews. The complete *Judenrat* staff in Warsaw at its height numbered six thousand persons who worked on a wide range of communal functions.[48]

Throughout the almost three years that he served as chairman of the Warsaw Jewish Council under the Nazis, Czerniaków faithfully recorded entries in his diary. His entries for September and October 1939 regularly return to the themes of hunger and anarchy in the streets of Warsaw. He sketched how he and his colleagues tried to create an organized administrative apparatus to respond to the exigencies of the moment.

---

46. See Trunk, *Judenrat*, 22.

47. For a more extensive discussion of the flight of Polish Jewish elites during the first months of the war and its impact, see chapter 5.

48. Shmuel Zygielbojm described the formation of the Jewish Council in Warsaw (quoted in Trunk, *Judenrat*, 22–23). See also Yosef Kermisz, "The Judenrat in Warsaw," in *Patterns of Jewish Leadership in Nazi Europe, 1933–1945: Proceedings of the Third Yad Vashem International Historical Conference, Jerusalem, April 4–7, 1977*, ed. Yisrael Gutman and Cynthia J. Haft (Jerusalem: Yad Vashem, 1979), 75.

DOCUMENT 4–13: Adam Czerniaków, Warsaw, diary entries for September and October 1939, in *Adama Czerniakowa dziennik getta warszawskiego: 6 IX 1939–23 VII 1942*, ed. Marian Fuks (Warsaw: Państwowe Wydawn. Naukowe, 1983), 48–51 (translated from Polish).[49]

September 23, 1939—For quite a while a shortage of bread. There is no meat. They've started selling horsemeat, praising its taste in the news-papers, even as stock for soup. Mayor Starzyński named me chairman of the Jewish community in Warsaw. A historic role in a besieged city. I will try to live up to it.—The city was bombed all night long, perhaps more heavily than before. Extensive damage to buildings and great loss of life. Sparks from the gutted railroad station fell on our school. At the office (4 Sienkiewicz Street) shrapnel hit the fifth floor for the second time, demolishing two rooms. We are moving to the fourth floor. [. . .]

September 28, 1939[50]—In the morning, planes marked with a cross of as yet unknown origin. At the office salaries are paid out. In the streets people are carving out chunks of flesh from dead horses. There's a guard at the gate from 2 to 5 at night. Wages paid at the office.

September 29, 1939—In the morning a warehouse on Barbara Street was looted. A nightmarish sight. Looting of the warehouse and robbing of the looters. I have offered myself as a hostage to the Germans.[51]

I inspected the community offices. I met Bryl. I met Mrs. Mayzel[52]— her house in ruins, all she was left with was the shirt on her back. The

---

49. This is also printed in a slightly differently worded translation in Raul Hilberg, Stanislaw Staron, and Josef Kermisz, eds., *The Warsaw Diary of Adam Czerniakow: Prelude to Doom* (Chicago: Ivan R. Dee in association with the USHMM, 1999), 76–78.

50. This was the day when Warsaw fell to the Germans.

51. As part of the surrender agreement, the German occupiers of Warsaw demanded twelve prominent hostages; two of them were Jewish, but Czerniaków was not among them.

52. Further information on Mr. Bryl is unavailable; the Polish edition of the diary, *Adama Czerniakowa dziennik getta warszawskiego: 6 IX 1939–23 VII 1942*, ed. Marian Fuks (Warsaw: Państwowe Wydawn. Naukowe, 1983), identifies him as Dr. Bryll, a member of the Capital Committee of Social Self-Help, which dealt with evacuation matters. Mrs. Mayzel was married to Maurycy Mayzel, head of a merchants' association and chairman of the Warsaw Jewish community when the war broke out. Her fate is unknown; her husband fled and was later murdered in Bachowo near Kowel [Kovel] at the beginning of June 1942. See Robert Moses Shapiro and Tadeusz Epsztein, eds., *The Warsaw Ghetto Oyneg Shabes– Ringelblum Archive: Catalog and Guide* (Bloomington: Indiana University Press in association with the USHMM and the Jewish Historical Institute in Warsaw, 2009), 179 (Ring I./997); Moshe Landau, "Mayzel, Maurycy," in *Encyclopaedia Judaica*, ed. Fred Skolnik and Michael Berenbaum, 2nd ed. (Detroit, MI: Macmillan Reference USA, 2007), 13:704.

head of the burial section crushed to death. I buried corpses in the little square near Węgierkiewicz [café]. On my way home there was a woman refugee pulling possessions on a little wooden horse. [. . .]

September 30, 1939—Morning at the offices of the community. I called a meeting for Sunday. I was not accepted as a hostage. At 1 p.m. a meeting of the Jewish Citizens Committee. Poland is to be ethnographic [*etnograficzna*] (15 million people), including 2 million Jews.[53]

October 1, 1939—Division of responsibilities in the community. *Sind Sie ein Jid?* ["Are you a Jew?"—a reference to German soldiers questioning Jewish pedestrians on the street]. Starzyński requested that I issue a proclamation in the name of the community with the goal of inducing the Jewish population to maintain order while food is distributed.

October 2, 1939—Meeting with Mayor Starzyński.

1. Proclamation to the Jewish population
2. Armbands for functionaries of the community
3. Food allocation

Dead horses were buried in the courtyard of the community at 26/28 Grzybowska Street. A meeting of the Jewish Citizens Committee. Proclamation sent to the printers. Meeting of the Community Council. Search for food. Onions purchased at 1.80 złoty per kilogram.

Jews suffered in the siege of Warsaw and endured the German onslaught in the blitzkrieg during September 1939 together with their Polish neighbors. At times, the shared suffering produced feelings of camaraderie and mutual sympathy, as some of the descriptions of Polish neighbors and clergy helping to protect Jews from Nazi persecution demonstrate. Despite many instances of communal cooperation and mutual support, observers also noted the fraying of prewar social bonds. Social, religious, and class differences continued to influence the manner in which Poles treated Jews once the occupation began; in general, the collapse of Poland seemed to expose the fragile nature of Polish-Jewish relations at that time.[54]

---

53. This is an allusion to the creation of the Generalgouvernement and the annexation of parts of Poland into the Reich. Poland's prewar population totaled 33 million, including 3.3 million Jews, of which 2 million fell under German rule in 1939 and 1940.

54. For works on the history of Polish-Jewish relations, see note 5 in the introduction to Part II.

The rapid defeat of the Polish military also quickly vanquished any sense of camaraderie in the military units. Among the roughly four hundred thousand Polish soldiers captured by the Wehrmacht, approximately sixty thousand were Jewish. In the first period of the war, Jewish POWs were detained along with their non-Jewish comrades by the Germans in transit camps located in the Polish cities of Radom, Żyrardów, Siedlce, Krośniewice, Kutno, and others. The treatment of all POWs was inhumane. They experienced harsh conditions, including hard labor, starvation, and incarceration in cells without heat during the difficult winter weather of 1939–1940. Their captors exposed them to daily abuse and torture as well. Many POWs died or were shot. It is estimated that close to twenty-five thousand prisoners of war of Jewish origin had been murdered or died in German POW camps by the end of the spring of 1940.[55] However, no systematic extermination policy had been put in place yet.

In December 1939 the Wehrmacht began releasing POWs and sending them home. Ringelblum's team in the Warsaw ghetto later sought out Jewish soldiers who had fought with the Polish armed forces and preserved their accounts in a section of the Oyneg Shabes archive titled "The September 1939 campaign." It included the testimony of Samuel Zeldman, a Jewish POW from the 14th Infantry Regiment of the Polish army who had survived capture near Kutno by German troops on September 23, 1939. Zeldman, who had been conscripted into the Polish army in March 1938 for eighteen months, found himself battling German forces just weeks before his scheduled discharge date.[56] In document 4–14, he recounts his capture, captivity in German POW camps (at Żyrardów, Ostrzeszów, Brandenburg, Frankfurt an der Oder, and Szubin, near Bydgoszcz), and his subsequent return with eight hundred Jewish POWs to Biała Podlaska and eventually to "his" ruined Warsaw.

DOCUMENT 4–14: Samuel Zeldman, "To Berlin, for a Military Parade," no date (ca. mid-1940), USHMMA RG 15.079M (ŻIH Ring. I/458), reel 17 (translated from Yiddish).

[. . .] The next day when I woke up, I saw that we were surrounded by German soldiers. They were looking at us curiously and offering chocolate and cigarettes. I later found out that we were in the Kampinowski forest,

---

55. See Shmuel Krakowski, "The Fate of Jewish Prisoners of War in the September 1939 Campaign," *YVS* 12 (1977): 297–333.

56. His fate is unknown. Possibly the same man, Szmul Zeldman, was a prisoner in a Lublin labor camp in October 1942. See Ring. II/273/5, summarized in Shapiro and Epsztein, *The Warsaw Ghetto*, 393–94.

where Germans were concentrating Polish POWs. The entire day all kinds of POWs were streaming to our place in groups, some large, others small, until we were about ten thousand. Then they gathered us up, and the next morning we were sent to Żyrardów, where they put us in a big sports field in the open.

We spent two weeks in this "camp." The Germans did not care about us, and therefore a lot of Jewish soldiers had to suffer heavy abuse from their Polish colleagues, who organized themselves in gangs, like criminals in prison cells, and took away by force from Jews their blankets, coats, and better shoes. The anarchy that the Germans permitted within the camp caused demoralization among the POWs. And hunger was getting worse. City people brought plenty of food but demanded high prices.

On a beautiful, bright day, a riot broke out. People tore down the fences and the crowd started running into town. The Germans managed to shoot after us. Some people fell, a few turned back, but very many succeeded to run into town, change clothes and disappear. I managed to reach the town too. I found a Jewish home and asked for civilian clothes. But apparently they were afraid to get into trouble, so they didn't give me any.

I went back out to the street and met many other escapees. We knew we were in great danger here but did not know what to do—try to run farther or to return to camp. Meanwhile a rumor spread that all POWs from Warsaw and its regions would be freed on the spot. So we decided to return. Here we found an entirely different situation. German soldiers were running around with bayonets, machine guns, and pistols and chasing the Polish POWs from one place to another. We didn't get any special treatment, they just intermingled us with the forty thousand strong crowd. For eight days, "iron discipline" ruled. Hundreds of people, who were considered responsible for the riot, were shot, and then the camp was liquidated. They took the entire group to Ostrzeszów near Poznań, into barracks. We stayed for two weeks, with terrible relations prevailing between Poles and Jews. Again the Germans did not intervene in our affairs, they remained indifferent.

After two weeks we went to Brandenburg, into a large POW camp. We were put to work right away, building barracks, burning straw from the previous camp, and the like. I was employed as a waiter, serving coffee in the guardroom. The attitude of the Germans, most of whom were older, was very correct, and there was enough food. After four weeks of this "paradise," they moved us again—this time to Frankfurt an der Oder. There, they sorted us out according to occupation. I got into a sawmill together with four Jews. Every day a car would come for us at eight in the morning, drive us, well-guarded, to Guben, and at four in the afternoon, the same car brought us back. The wage was 1.50 Marks a day, and it remained on paper only. But we were getting enough to eat. The woman who owned the sawmill was very correct in her relations with us, and life in general was not bad at all. This lasted until New Year's.

On New Year's Day, the owner of the mill, her husband, came back on leave. Robert Jokel was a captain in the [German] air force who "worked" the west section. He arranged for us to stay at the sawmill, not to have to commute daily from Frankfurt. There we felt quite well, the people of Guben were quite decent and friendly, they invited us often for a meal. In the homes we met mostly older women, old men, and children. Young men and women were not seen at all.

One day a messenger came from Frankfurt with the news that we were "going home." So we left everything and returned to the camp in Frankfurt, where our belongings were already packed. They gave us provisions for the journey and sent us by train to Szubin, near Bydgoszcz. There we stayed for four weeks in a reformatory building. We were "supervised" by *Volksdeutsche*,[57] with whom we spoke Polish, of course. Their attitude toward us was extremely hostile, they robbed us systematically of mail and packages that we got, they found "work" for us, and the like. At long last, the happy day arrived, March 11, 1940. In the evening they loaded us, about 800 Jewish POWs, into a freight train and transported us to Warsaw. Those who were from Warsaw disembarked here. The others continued, and we heard later that Jews were persecuted at Biała Podlaska.[58]

---

57. The term *Volksdeutsche* denotes members of the ethnic German diaspora outside Germany's borders in central and eastern Europe. Since the Nazi seizure of power in 1933, these German minorities were instrumentalized by Hitler and organized into Nazi-controlled organizations—de facto fifth columns helping to facilitate German aggression after 1939 and later participating in the mass murder of the Jews. On this topic, see Valdis O. Lumans, *Himmler's Auxiliaries: The Volksdeutsche Mittelstelle and the German National Minorities of Europe, 1933–1945* (Chapel Hill: University of North Carolina Press, 1993).

58. Biała Podlaska is a town about one hundred kilometers (sixty-two miles) north-north-east of Lublin. On the eve of World War II, approximately seventy-five hundred Jews lived there. In early 1940, about five hundred Jewish prisoners of war from the Polish army were marched on foot to Biała Podlaska, where they were placed in a POW camp located in a barracks on the road toward Brześć Litewski (today Brest in Belarus). Subsequently, some of these Jewish POWs managed to sneak out of the camp and join the Jews in the ghetto. Inside the ghetto, the Jews were confronted with the terror of the German Gestapo, which carried out frequent shootings. *USHMM Encyclopedia of Camps and Ghettos 1933–1945*, 2:615–619, entry for Biała Podlaska.

But we arrived safely in Warsaw. When I saw "my" Warsaw after an interval of scarcely 15 months, I started to cry. I did not expect such destruction [*khurbn*].

In August 1939, just before the outbreak of the war, estimates put the Jewish population of Warsaw at about 380,000, or about 30 percent of the city's total population. In the first weeks of the war, due to population fluctuations resulting from mobilization, flight, and the arrival of refugees, the number of the city's Jews actually dropped by about twenty thousand. By early 1940, however, it had swelled to some four hundred thousand because Jews from areas annexed to the Reich were being deported to the **Generalgouvernement**, and expellees and refugees were pouring into Warsaw.[59] This further compounded the scarcity of housing, food, and medical supplies in the city. It also appears that many Polish Jews from smaller cities and towns may have believed that they had a better chance of becoming invisible in their Polish surroundings in a large urban area.[60]

Polish Jewish historian Emanuel Ringelblum was keenly interested in the subject of Polish-Jewish relations during the war. The excerpt from his study of Polish-Jewish relations presented in document 4–15 highlights the changing dynamics of relations between Poles, Jews, and Germans at the start of the war. He perceived differences between the religious/racial persecution of Jews and the national persecution of Poles. Perhaps most interesting, however, is how in flux things appear to have been during this period. Poles were trying to figure out where they fit in the new political order. Were they on the same level as Jews in German eyes, or did they hold a more privileged position? And Ringelblum indicates that Jews sought to establish whom they could turn to for support. Which segments of Polish society would come to their defense?

---

59. Barbara Engelking and Jacek Leociak, *The Warsaw Ghetto: A Guide to the Perished City* (New Haven, CT: Yale University Press, 2009), 47–48.

60. This perception had also been widely shared among German Jews, many of whom were already flocking to Berlin in the mid-1930s in search of anonymity in the face of mounting antisemitic persecution by their neighbors. See Beate Meyer, Herman Simon, and Chana Schütz, eds., *Jews in Nazi Berlin: From Kristallnacht to Liberation* (Chicago: University of Chicago Press, 2009).

DOCUMENT 4–15: **Emanuel Ringelblum, "Polish-Jewish Relations in Occupied Warsaw," October 1939, USHMMA RG 15.079M (ŻIH Ring. I/91), reel 7 (translated from Yiddish).**[61]

Relations between Polish and Jewish intellectuals have not changed; previously established cordial relations were maintained. We know of instances when mutual material aid was given. But Jews, whose houses had been destroyed or burned down, were not welcomed in Polish apartments. Those who tried to move in were either politely turned down or received with great reservation by the Poles, who were afraid that they would get into trouble with the Germans for letting Jews into their apartments.

But the mood of the masses has changed radically. Even before the persecution of Jews began, as had been anticipated, the masses made efforts to please the newcomers, pointing out Jews, who were hard to recognize by their appearance.

If, standing in line for water on Oczki Str. [in Warsaw], or in the Central-Railway Station Tunnel, a quarrel arose over a place, Poles eagerly called a passing-by German soldier or a German railroad worker and, indicating that "this is a Jew," demanded the undesirable neighbor's removal from the line. As a result, Jews were, indeed, led away. The same thing happened in lines for bread, meat, etc. Wishing to please the masses, the Germans made a rule that Jews were not allowed to stand in line. At the bakeries, soldiers appeared to take care of "order," which meant to kick out those who had been pointed out or recognized as Jews.

The first street atrocities against Jews, usually Orthodox Jews in *kapote* [traditional garb], who were easily recognizable, found eager spectators among the Polish masses. Some Germans were disgusted by the Poles' reactions. Eyewitnesses relate that sometimes spectators who laughed at a Jew whose beard was being cut or who was caught and taken for forced labor unexpectedly got their own share. From that time originates the following story, told by an eyewitness: A soldier was cutting the beard of an old Jew, clad in his traditional garb, in the street. A Pole was standing nearby, laughing. The Jew asked indignantly: "What are you laughing at? The beard will grow anew, but your Poland will never rise again." The Pole started threatening, ready to beat him. The soldier, who was about to leave after finishing the job, turned back and asked the Jew: "What did he want

---

61. This is also printed in a differently worded translation in Joseph Kermisz, ed., *To Live With Honor and Die With Honor! Selected Documents from the Warsaw Ghetto Underground Archives "O.S." (Oneg Shabbath)* (Jerusalem: Yad Vashem, 1986), 611–14.

from you?" The Jew told him what had happened. "Right, right, your beard will grow anew, but Poland will never exist again." He clapped the Jew's hand and went away, leaving the disappointed Pole behind.

For all Polish Jews—those who stayed in their homes and those who became refugees—the end of the military campaign in Poland failed to relieve their desperate positions. As a result, the European Jewish humanitarian crisis that dated from before the outbreak of World War II and centered on the proportionally smaller populations of central European Jewish communities now reached a theretofore unparalleled scale. To drive home to its readers the magnitude of the crisis of Polish Jewry in the beginning of the war, the *American Jewish Year Book* framed the condition of Polish Jewry as having taken on biblical proportions:

"A work is done in your days,
which ye will not believe though it be told." (Habakkuk I:5)

The story of the Jews in Poland during the past year is the story of what is probably the greatest tragedy in the entire history of Israel. It is a story which no man can write, still less read, with objective composure. Facts and figures, names and dates, become but inadequate symbols and shrunken garments. Three million broken lives cannot be set down on paper.[62]

Well before the onset of genocide, Jewish commentators expressed the inadequacy of language to capture early Polish Jewish wartime experiences.

---

62. "Review of the Year 5700—Poland," *AJYB 5701* 42 (1940): 365.

CHAPTER 5

JEWISH FLIGHT

T HE NOVELTY of the Nazi campaign in Poland consisted of its erasure of the line between the front and rear. In the first weeks of September 1939, everyone was suddenly affected by the war. It is difficult to evoke the panic, chaos, and confusion that the brutal invasion and prospect of Nazi occupation caused among both Jews and non-Jews across Poland. Within days of the Nazi invasion, hundreds of thousands of people in Poland were on the move, in flight from advancing **Wehrmacht** troops. When rumors spread through Warsaw that the government had abandoned the capital on the night of September 6, the panic deepened. Some, especially able-bodied men, hoped to regroup and rebuild lines of defense in the eastern part of the country,[1] although the radio broadcast of September 6, ordering all men fit to fight to leave the city and head eastward, was taken as government sanction for mass flight.[2] Others fled as far as they could, simply hoping to escape the Nazi reach.

---

1. The Polish government hoped to reestablish the line of defense beyond the Vistula River. See Samuel D. Kassow, *Who Will Write Our History? Emanuel Ringelblum, the Warsaw Ghetto, and the Oyneg Shabes Archive* (Bloomington: Indiana University Press, 2007), 104; cf. Debórah Dwork and Robert Jan van Pelt, *Flight from the Reich: Refugee Jews, 1933–1946* (New York: W. W. Norton, 2009).

2. Kassow, *Who Will Write Our History*, 104. The September diary entries of **Chaim Kaplan** testify to the chaos in Warsaw; he makes repeated reference to the refugees pouring both in and out of the city. See his entries for September 6, 11, and 16 in Chaim A. Kaplan, *Scroll of Agony: The Warsaw Diary of Chaim A. Kaplan*, ed. Abraham I. Katsh (Bloomington: Indiana University Press in association with the USHMM, 1999).

Many of the thousands of frightened people who fled Warsaw were Jews, and many of the Jews fleeing Warsaw were quite prominent. Overnight, Jewish Warsaw—the cultural and political nexus of all Polish Jewry but also a large Jewish community in its own right—saw many of its most important leaders leave.[3] In the words of historian Samuel Kassow, "Europe's largest Jewish community lost most of the Jewish Community Council, most directors of relief organizations, and many of the leading political cadres."[4] Jewish politicians who fled spanned the entire spectrum of modern Jewish politics, from Orthodox leaders of Agudes Yisroel, to Zionism and its splinter parties, to **Bundism** and Communism, and to the leaders of many of the Zionist youth movements.[5] They were joined by many rabbis and members of the "intelligentsia," that is to say, those regarded as belonging to the cultural, political, and intellectual elite.

From early October on, many of these Jewish leaders found refuge—temporary refuge, as it eventually turned out—in Vilna (Polish: Wilno; Lithuanian: Vilnius).[6] Long a historic center of Jewish culture, known to eastern European Jews as the "Jerusalem of Lithuania," Vilna had been seized by Poland during the Second Polish Republic (1918–1939). On September 19, 1939, the Red Army occupied the city briefly, but ceded it to Lithuania in October. Most historical accounts of Jewish Holocaust experiences in Vilna take as their starting point the Nazi massacre of five to ten thousand Jews in Vilna in the summer

---

3. Israel Gutman, *The Jews of Warsaw, 1939–1943: Ghetto, Underground, Revolt* (Bloomington: Indiana University Press, 1982), 4–5.

4. Kassow, *Who Will Write Our History*, 104–5.

5. Aharon Weiss, "Youth Movements in Poland during the German Occupation," in *Zionist Youth Movements during the Shoah*, ed. Asher Cohen and Yehoyakim Cochavi (New York: Peter Lang, 1995), 227–44.

6. In the aftermath of World War I and the creation of independent Lithuania and Poland, Vilna was claimed by both states. In October 1920 Poland seized the city and the surrounding area and in early 1922 formally annexed them. Although Kaunas (Polish: Kowno; Yiddish: Kovno) became the temporary capital of Lithuania, subsequent Lithuanian governments maintained their claim to Vilna and the region. On the eve of World War II, more than fifty-five thousand of Vilna's approximately two hundred thousand inhabitants were Jews; the majority of the city's population was Polish. See Yitzhak Arad, *Ghetto in Flames: The Struggle and Destruction of the Jews in Vilna in the Holocaust* (New York: Holocaust Library, 1982), 9–28.

of 1941, followed by the creation of the Vilna ghetto in early September.[7] Yet, from early October 1939, when it became clear that it was possible to cross the border freely into Lithuania from Soviet-occupied Polish territory, Vilna became a hub for exiled Polish Jewish leaders, including large numbers of prominent Jewish political figures, intellectuals, journalists, rabbis, and wealthy tradesmen and industrialists. As soon as they reached the relative safety of Vilna, they set out to organize relief for both Vilna's new refugees and the embattled Polish Jews who had stayed behind.

While the well-to-do and the politically connected had the option of resettling in Vilna, hundreds of thousands of Jews—about 350,000, according to the information collected by the Polish government-in-exile—fled to eastern Poland, away from the advancing German tanks.[8] Along with the general breakdown of order engendered by the collapse of the Polish state, the large influx of these refugees from elsewhere in Poland further complicated the already fragile pattern of ethnic relations in the *kresy*, or eastern Polish borderlands.[9] In eastern Poland—in the provinces of western Ukraine and western Belorussia—Poles and Jews together comprised the majority of the urban population. Nevertheless, their combined numbers barely matched those of the non-Polish-speaking peasant populations of Ukrainians, Belorussians, and other groups whose identification eluded ethnic or national categories and who referred to themselves as "locals."[10] This ethnic mosaic, interlaced with class resentments, anti-Polish sentiments due to the repressive policies of the Second Polish Republic, and general economic underdevelopment and poverty, constituted a dangerous mix.

---

7. Notable exceptions include Yitzhak Arad, "Concentration of Refugees in Vilna on the Eve of the Holocaust," *YVS* 9 (1973): 201–14; Yehuda Bauer, *American Jewry and the Holocaust: The American Jewish Joint Distribution Committee, 1939–1945* (Detroit, MI: Wayne State University Press, 1981), 107–28.

8. Maciej Siekierski, "Jews in Soviet-Occupied East Poland at the End of 1939: Numbers and Distribution," in *Jews in Eastern Poland and the USSR, 1939–46*, ed. Norman Davies and Anthony Polonsky (New York: St. Martin's Press, 1991), 112–13.

9. A Polish term meaning "borderlands," *kresy* is used to refer to the lands in Poland's eastern frontier. From the time of the Russian Empire through the eve of World War II, these lands often changed hands—between Poland, the Russian and Habsburg empires, and Soviet Ukraine and Belarus—and were characterized by a complex ethnic and economic structure.

10. Jan T. Gross, *Revolution from Abroad: The Soviet Conquest of Poland's Western Ukraine and Western Belorussia*, exp. ed. (Princeton, NJ: Princeton University Press, 2002), 4–5. For an authoritative history encompassing this region, see Timothy Snyder, *Bloodlands: Europe between Hitler and Stalin* (New York: Basic Books, 2010).

The situation in the *kresy* was complicated further when on September 17, in accordance with the secret protocol of the **Molotov-Ribbentrop Pact**, Soviet troops crossed the eastern Polish border and, in effect, invaded the country as well. The pretext for the Soviet occupation sounded flimsy at best: after the Nazi invasion, the Polish government was allegedly no longer able to protect the rights of minorities living in eastern Poland, and the Soviet Union claimed it was stepping in to secure those rights and guarantee peace. Most people probably saw through the Soviet rhetoric of claiming to "protect" Ukrainians and Belorussians within Polish borders and regarded the intervention for what it really was: unabashed territorial expansion. Regardless of whether one was a cynic, the fact remained that Red Army troops had now moved into Poland as well, and the Soviets would soon move to incorporate eastern Polish territories into the Soviet Union.[11]

This, then, was the situation in the immediate wake of the Nazi invasion. In tracing Jewish flight in the first months of the war, this chapter investigates some important questions that individual Jews faced in this short yet crucial period. Where could a Polish Jew flee in the early fall months of 1939? It was clear that the Nazis were no friends to Jews, but should one flee from the invading Red Army? Were the Soviets "better" than the Nazis? And what range of concerns did Jewish women and men each have to weigh when deciding whether to flee or not? Finally, what were the consequences of the flight of Jewish leaders for Jewish communal life in territories under both Nazi and Soviet occupation? Was it realistic or even possible for these leaders—their understandable moral and political claims notwithstanding—to command continued authority or influence over the communities they had left behind?

As discussed in chapter 4, the chaos that prevailed during the few weeks of the Polish campaign and the early months of Nazi and Soviet occupation left very little time for people to write down the dramatic developments, let alone ponder their long-term meaning or organize a coherent Jewish "response." Nevertheless, the documents below provide some fragmentary insights into the complex decisions that Polish Jews had to make in the relatively short period between the swift collapse of the Polish state and the introduction of anti-Jewish measures by the Nazis that would change their lives forever.

---

11. On the coordination of Nazi and Soviet moves to partition Poland in August and September 1939, see Gross, *Revolution from Abroad*, 8–13.

FLIGHT ROUTES

Among those who joined in the flight from Warsaw was Herman Kruk, a Bund activist, director of the Yiddish Library at the Cultural League in Warsaw (of which he was also director), and editor of its monthly library journal.[12] Like others who had little time or opportunity to reflect on the fast-moving events triggered by the Nazi invasion, he wrote the story of his flight retrospectively from Vilna in January 1940, possibly based on notes he had taken along the journey. According to that account, Kruk left Warsaw on the afternoon of September 6 and traveled in a wagon with five other men. Like many others, they left their wives behind in Warsaw. Kruk's description of the journey resembles other accounts of the chaos of flight from the capital: "The highway presents an extraordinary picture. Traveling is almost impossible. The road is completely blocked. You drive barely a few feet and have to stand still 15 or 20 minutes."[13] Over the next two weeks, Kruk and his group traveled first to the southeast, finally reaching Łuck on September 19; the town had just been occupied by the Soviets. There they found a number of other prominent political leaders, who had also fled to what, in the meantime, had become Soviet-occupied territory in eastern Poland. While Kruk's account illustrates well the generally chaotic nature of Jewish flight, it also hints at some important aspects of the refugee experience that separated prominent from "ordinary" Jews and men from women. Often, prominent Jews' prewar contacts and friendships facilitated the process of flight, despite the fact that their positions deteriorated rapidly following the foreign invasion.

12. See Herman Kruk, *The Last Days of the Jerusalem of Lithuania: Chronicles from the Vilna Ghetto and the Camps, 1939–1944*, ed. Benjamin Harshav (New Haven, CT: Yale University Press, 2002). Kruk (1897–1944) was born in Płock. Although without formal education, he was active in Bundist circles in interwar Warsaw. The Yiddishist Cultural League, which he had headed since 1936, supervised around four hundred libraries in towns across Poland. During the German invasion in September 1939, Kruk fled Warsaw and arrived in Vilna. For the next two years, he was involved with helping refugees and organizing cultural activities. In anticipation of the German invasion of Lithuania, he booked a trip to the Soviet Far East, hoping to be able to flee to the United States via Japan—a route that his brother had traveled successfully. However, the Soviet authorities would not let him pass through the Soviet Union unless Kruk agreed to join the Polish army in Britain and serve as a Soviet spy—which he refused to do. In the ghetto that the Nazis subsequently established in Vilna, he ran the library and kept a diary, which is one of the most important testimonies of life in the Vilna ghetto. In 1943, he was deported to a forced labor camp in Estonia; he wrote his final diary entry on September 17, 1944, just hours before he was murdered at the Lagedi camp in Estonia.

13. Kruk, *The Last Days of the Jerusalem of Lithuania*, 2.

DOCUMENT 5–1: Herman Kruk, Vilna, diary entries for September 19 to October 6, 1939 (written in January 1940), translated from Yiddish and published in Herman Kruk, *The Last Days of the Jerusalem of Lithuania: Chronicles from the Vilna Ghetto and the Camps, 1939–1944*, ed. Benjamin Harshav (New Haven, CT: YIVO Institute for Jewish Research and Yale University Press, 2002), 21–22.[14]

In Łuck, we came on a new wave of people.

"All Warsaw is in Łuck," claims one of our group.

Among others, we meet the Zionist activist Dr. Kleinbaum;[15] a contributor to *Nasz Przegląd*,[16] Attorney Nowogródzki; one of the directors of the organization of cooperatives in Poland, Shmoysh. We also meet Bella Shapiro and her husband, editor of the *Lubliner Togblat*, who have fled from Lublin. [. . .] The Lublin Bundist councilman Dr. Hershenhorn is here, a captain in the military. There are a great many workers and worker activists from Warsaw: Comrade Hershl Ramet, the veteran president of the Leather Workers' Union in Warsaw, the youth activist Bornstein, etc. Once again, we meet Berke Shnaydmil, whom we met before in Włodawa.

Everyone tells of horrible events. They share their first impressions of the Bolsheviks. But all of them are penniless, they are hungry, and they are naked and barefoot. Shnaydmil calls me aside and shows me: he doesn't have a shirt. On his naked body he simply wears a woolen sweater. I give him one of my shirts and a pair of warm underwear. We, too, especially Rosen and I, are penniless, and we have also been hungry for long days. There is no bread there to be gotten. You can't even dream of other food. Rosen is afraid for my health; he sees that my strength has declined, and he left to ask for food for me.

In fact, a carpenter whom Rosen confided in was strongly taken with our situation, and for a few days he takes care of us like one of his own. He is really extraordinary. But the carpenter doesn't stop there. He brings us into his home. He gets bread for us, fruit, he brings butter, eggs. It does indeed turn out that there is everything. But speculators are hiding it.

Dr. Kleinbaum accidentally learned of our plight. He came to us and said that until today he had been penniless. He got something to

---

14. For the Yiddish original, see Herman Kruk, *Togbukh fun Vilner geto*, ed. Mordechai Bernstein (New York: YIVO, 1961).

15. For more on Moshe Kleinbaum, see the Glossary.

16. This Warsaw-based Zionist daily, founded in 1923 by Jakob Appenszlak and Nathan Schwalb, had a prewar circulation of more than twenty thousand copies.

eat because he was taken in by rich Zionist activists. Only today did he get a little money and he wants to share it with us. We take some and are moved by his extraordinary concern.

A few days later, on my own responsibility, I call a meeting of a few local and refugee Bundists. I propose to do something to get urgent aid at least for a group of close comrades. The meeting decided: the Łuck members collect a little underwear, clothing, bread. We ourselves start getting some financial support for the neediest. Comrade Shmoysh is the first to contribute a big sum. He and Dr. Hershenhorn promise to make an agreement with TOZ[17] about the establishment of a kitchen.

Within a few days, a kitchen is organized at TOZ. We were able to distribute some clothing, bread, and financial support. When I left Łuck on October 6, the TOZ kitchen was distributing 250 lunches a day.

Despite the chaotic and ad hoc nature of the flight, it is not by chance that Kruk and others first headed in the direction of Łuck. Located in the southeast of the country, the town was relatively close to the Polish border with Hungary and Romania, two countries that, despite falling squarely within the Nazi orbit, were not involved in the war and could potentially offer the Jews refuge in their escape from war-torn Poland. For a few brief weeks, this area seemed the only way out of the deadly Nazi-Soviet embrace rapidly choking the rest of the country.

To many Jews, especially the Zionists, the prospect of reaching Romania looked particularly promising. As document 2–19 attests, Romania's Black Sea ports offered an opportunity for clandestine passage to Palestine.[18] Jewish refugees hoping to cross into Romania thus poured into Volhynia and eastern Galicia, the southeasternmost provinces of Poland. Active members of different Zionist organizations in particular harbored these hopes and proceeded to the Polish southeast in an organized manner. In the end, however, it only proved possible to cross into Romania until the Soviet invasion or shortly thereafter. Thus, only limited numbers of Jews—mostly employees of the fleeing Polish government institutions—were able to reach the relative safety of Romania in

---

17. For more on the **TOZ**, see the Glossary.

18. In 1938 and 1939 the Romanian government did not object to Jewish emigration from its shores, and Romania thus became an important center of Jewish emigration to Palestine. See Dalia Ofer, *Escaping the Holocaust: Illegal Immigration to the Land of Israel, 1939–1944* (New York: Oxford University Press, 1990), 77–88; also see Ephraim Ofir, "Aliyah bet mi-Romaniya," *Yalkut moreshet* 30 (1981): 38–74 (in Hebrew).

1939. Once the Soviets established firm control of the areas they occupied, they sealed the Romanian border and arrested Jewish refugees trying to leave.[19]

An early report about the establishment of a refugee self-help committee in Bacău, a town in Romania close to the Polish border, gives us insight into the plight of Polish Jewish refugees who made it across the border. Consistent with other such accounts, it suggests, at least in the beginning, that the refugees were members of Polish Jewish elites. When one reads the whole text, however, the document becomes contradictory; the author makes clear that the refugees came "from every part of Poland, from every town and social class, and a wide range of educational levels." The author may have hoped to present the refugee community as properly bourgeois, just like the imagined reader of his report, in order to improve chances of the **World Jewish Congress** (WJC) office in Geneva sending aid.

DOCUMENT 5–2: Alfred Tisch,[20] Bacău, Romania, to WJC, Geneva office, "Report on the Establishment and Work of the Local Refugee Self-Help Committee in Bacău, Romania," December 1939, USHMMA RG 68.045M (WJC Geneva), reel 2, folder 9 (translated from German).

REPORT
On the Establishment and Work of the Local
Refugee–Self-Help Committee in Bacău (Romania)
by Its President, Alfred Tisch
(end of December 1939)

I. The stream of refugees from Poland that poured across the border points at Kuty and Zaleszczyki on September 17 and 18 consisted primarily of Polish government officials, civil servants from state-owned enterprises, military personnel, and people who had an opportunity to possess vehicles, mainly cars, that enabled them to flee from Poland, currently at war.

Therefore it is clear that the refugees included only a tiny percentage of Jews, as only in a few exceptional cases were Jews employed as officials in the government offices and state-owned enterprises. Among the military personnel too, however, most who came to Romania were

---

19. Arad, "Concentration of Refugees in Vilna," 203–4.

20. Further information about Tisch or how his report was conveyed to Geneva is unavailable.

high-ranking officers, and there also were very few of them in Poland who were Jews. Because most privately owned vehicles had been requisitioned by the military and the state authorities during the war in Poland, and there was a considerable gasoline shortage besides, the civilians who crossed the border into Romania also included very few Jews, as the vehicles of the majority had been confiscated back at home or during the flight, or had had to be abandoned owing to lack of gasoline. So it is understandable that in total, no more than about 1,500 Jewish persons fled to Romania.

In large part, these are people who were quite well-to-do in their native country, because they otherwise would have lacked the opportunity to reach the border. Nevertheless, most of them have left all their belongings on the other side of the border, because so many people were crammed into the vehicles in which they came that absolutely no room was left to carry baggage. In the vast majority of cases, the Jewish refugees brought to Romania only what they were wearing on their backs; in some instances, if time permitted, they brought their personal jewelry and lastly the sum of złoty and other money that was left by the time they reached the border. That amount had shrunk considerably, however, as incredibly high sums were demanded and paid for gasoline and travel expenses. Opportunities to exchange the złoty amounts were limited from the outset, as only 350 złoty per capita could officially be exchanged for 7,000 lei at the banks, and exchange elsewhere was possible only at very poor rates. Thus the result was that large amounts of złoty could be converted only into lei sums that were worth little. These conditions have inevitably forced the work for the refugees into very specific channels.

II. The first city inundated by the refugees was Cernăuți [Czernowitz], and it was here that the refugees principally wished to rest from the physical and mental tortures of their flight and exchange the amounts of lei required for the most necessary clothes, so that they could set forth on their journey farther into Romania. The Jewish community of Cernăuți made an extraordinary effort here and proved that the greatest goods of Jewish life are inherent in the community's members. The refugees were not only accommodated in private homes but also surrounded by so much care, kindness, and concern that they could truly rest from the hardships of the flight and restore their mental equilibrium to the extent possible. But in material terms as well, the Cernăuți Jews made an enormous contribution, because in most cases they gave as much food as possible to the Jewish refugees, who could not get even the essentials for themselves.

On the other hand, the evacuation of the refugees from Cernăuți, which took place in very unpleasant conditions, unfortunately negated a large part of the recuperation in Cernăuți and ruined the items of clothing received or bought there, because traveling for days in overcrowded and unheated railroad cars in wet, damp weather without the necessary food created new physical stress.

III. Around 250 to 300 Jewish refugees reached Bacău between September 25 and 30. Some of them immediately continued on their journey, and about 200 remained there temporarily. And here began the first organized relief effort. The majority of the refugees were housed in private residences through the efforts of the refugee committee that was formed by the Jewish community in Bacău. It must be said, however, that it was hard to persuade some hosts to take in refugees, and the reluctance with which this occurred resulted, only a few days later, in many refugees having to face the need to go out looking for furnished rooms in a strange city with no help at all from the public organizations. At the same time, it also turned out that the high demand and relatively small supply led to exploitation, with the refugees being taken advantage of by the landlords. While, for example, the rent for a room with two beds was still in the range of 600 to 1,000 lei in Bacău in early September, by October it already had climbed to between 1,200 and 2,000 lei. As for the feeding of the refugees, a small number of them were fed by their local hosts in the first few days, and others were subsidized by funds from the committee of the Jewish community, while the rest of the refugees had to eat in restaurants at their own expense. As the financial subsidies from the community ceased after 10 to 14 days and the number of hosts who fed the refugees also became smaller and smaller, the refugees also faced the need to feed themselves.

IV. This necessity forced the refugees to help themselves. As these were people from every part of Poland, from every town and social class and a wide range of educational levels, it took one to two weeks until they became acquainted with each other and the material situation of each individual was ascertained. In the process, the mutual understanding that was created allowed an organization to be formed.

A committee of refugees was created, which was asked to make contact with the local relief committee in order to steer the committee's work in the directions where the refugees were most in distress and, on the other hand, to bring the local committee's attention to those refugees most in need of assistance and keep the emergency from degenerating into a situation where individual refugees were begging from the local committee and private individuals. [. . .]

With regard to food, the committee obtained a lower price by making arrangements with restaurants, so that the owners of several good establishments were ensured a larger number of customers. However, the committee focused on the fact that the refugees have banded together in families and groups, and the refugees' wives themselves are running the household economy or kitchen. This not only lowers the cost of living but also gives the refugees the feeling of "being at home," and they are less aware of their alien surroundings when a provident female hand is taking care of the cooking, laundry, and household. Finally, to prevent the refugees from hanging around in the streets and public restaurants because they have nothing to do and no proper home, the committee rented a relatively large space that has appropriate adjoining rooms in addition. This space, which was appropriately decorated and fixed up by the committee itself, now allows the refugees to take care of their correspondence and to read, and newspapers and magazines are available for this purpose. For various games, chess sets, dominoes, table tennis, and cards are available for use. A cultural department was created, and it plans to offer lectures and musical performances for stimulation and education. A buffet operated by the committee itself provides many refugees with an inexpensive breakfast and supper, and it covers most of the local expenses. Courses in English and Hebrew were set up and made available to all refugees at no cost. They are taught by teachers who are refugees, but the lack of suitable school premises, especially now in winter, is placing more and more new obstacles in the way of continuing these courses. [. . .]

VIII. It goes without saying that our own means for meeting the existing daily needs of the refugees without outside help are diminishing; we also are not in a position to get the refugees to other countries without outside help, countries where they will find opportunities to work and live, but we want to do everything within our power to create, through self-discipline, mutual aid, and maintenance of the mental and emotional level, a state of affairs that makes it possible for the refugees to survive this difficult time and for us to provide help from outside to people who are worthy of this help.

In the spring of 1940, significant numbers of Polish Jewish refugees were still in Romania. As noted earlier, many already intended to immigrate to Palestine in September 1939. Even if their flight had not been sparked by

Zionist motives, however, the Palestine option certainly became appealing once they were in limbo in Romania; Zionist agents in the country were trying to secure passage to Palestine for as many of them as possible. Document 5–3, a letter soliciting funds for such efforts, speaks to the magnitude of this undertaking.

DOCUMENT 5–3: **Letter from Rudolf Katz, director of the Aliyah Committee[21] in Bucharest, Romania, to Simon Mirelmann, Buenos Aires, Argentina, April 20, 1940, USHMMA RG 68.045M (WJC Geneva), reel 140, file 1290 (translated from German).**

You are certainly aware that in the fall of last year as a result of the Polish tragedy approximately 1,500 Jewish refugees came to Romania. Owing to the cooperation of local authorities, these unfortunate persons received temporary permission for residency.

Responsibility for caring for these individuals was taken over by a Polish Central Committee, which is made up of Polish Jews who have been settled here for quite some time already and which is under the leadership of Dr. B. Rosenthal, Jacques Liebermann, M. Berlin, and Engineer A. Eiger. For more than half a year, this committee has provided enormous support for these now homeless persons but naturally faces great difficulties since all sources of money are being successively exhausted.

According to a survey carried out by the central Zionist organizations here, more than half of the approximately 1,500 refugees here expressed the desire to emigrate to Palestine and indicated they would be happier the more swiftly this hope is fulfilled.

You are aware that only very few can reach Palestine by means of immigration certificates, so that other ways and means—naturally significantly more costly ones—must be sought and found to facilitate the Polish refugees' departure for Palestine.

The sums that have been made available by private donors as well as the office of the World Jewish Congress[22] in Geneva, etc., etc., are hardly

---

21. It is unclear whether the Aliyah Committee in Bucharest headed by Rudolf Katz had ties to the illegal immigration wing of the Revisionists or the Haganah, but it was clearly part of this wider effort to smuggle Jewish refugees to Palestine. Ofer, *Escaping the Holocaust*, 11–20. For more on illegal emigration to Palestine (*Aliyah Bet*), see chapter 2, and the glossary entry for *aliyah*. Information on the fate of individuals mentioned in the document is unavailable.

22. For more on the World Jewish Congress, see the Glossary.

sufficient to cover the tremendous transportation costs for hundreds of people.

We have been made aware that you and/or the committee to which you belong would be able to support the unfortunate persons mentioned above with a considerable sum. In regard to how [this money] will be spent, the individuals who are leading this action (Dr. B. Rosenthal, Director Rudolf Katz, Filip Rosenstein, Saul Companet, Ella Gold et al.) offer full moral assurance, and we leave it up to you to obtain information on this matter from either the office of the World Jewish Congress in Geneva or Dr. Mibashan, the K[eren] H[ayesod][23] delegate there.

We request that you kindly make all potential payments to the World Jewish Congress, Executive Committee, Geneva, 52 Rue des Pâcquis (Palais Wilson) while simultaneously informing us, for which we convey in advance the endless thanks of everyone involved.

We eagerly await your news and request that you direct the same to Rudolf Katz, Bucharest, Bdl. Dacia, No. 42.

In exemplary respect,

"ALIYAH"

P.S. The local Polish Central Committee will also contact you about this matter.

Only so many Jews could make it to Romania in the fall of 1939, however. Once the Soviets had sealed the border, the route of escape to Romania was no longer viable. By the time the news broke in early October that it was possible to cross into Vilna, many Jews had already abandoned the idea of leaving Poland for Romania and opted for Lithuania. Japanese diplomat Chiune Sugihara was a vice consul of the Empire of Japan in Kovno (Lithuanian: Kaunas; Polish: Kowno), Lithuania, when the war broke out. Risking his professional career, he granted Japanese transit visas to Jewish refugees stranded in Lithuania against the rules set by the Japanese government, thereby saving thousands of people. Other diplomats in Kovno in this period took similar risks.[24] Refugees were

---

23. Keren Hayesod was the central fund-raising organization of the Zionist movement, established in 1920.

24. On Chiune Sugihara (1900–1986), see Hillel Levine, *In Search of Sugihara: The Elusive Japanese Diplomat Who Risked His Life to Rescue 10,000 Jews from the Holocaust* (New York: Free Press, 1996); also see Jonathan Goldstein, "Motivation in Holocaust Rescue: The Case of Jan Zwartendijk in Lithuania, 1940," in *Lessons and Legacies: New Currents in Holocaust Research*, ed. Jeffry M. Diefendorf (Evanston, IL: Northwestern University Press, 2004), 6:69–87.

thus able to leave Lithuania and travel east in an effort to escape Nazi reach. Stamps in Samuel Soltz's nationality certificate (in effect, his passport), illustrate the path of one such individual—from Białystok, via Kovno, to Japan, China, India, and, finally, Palestine.

DOCUMENT 5–4: Two pages from the certificate of Polish nationality issued to Samuel Soltz by the Polish consul in Kovno, Lithuania, 1939, USHMMPA WS# 86548A, 86548E.

Lithuania thenceforth became the main immediate destination for Jewish refugees from Poland. Herman Kruk and the travelers accompanying him thus did not diverge from this general trend: they made what would have been a complete about face on their journey from Warsaw and left via Równe for Vilna, arriving there on October 10.[25]

REFUGEES IN VILNA

The Red Army had entered Vilna two days after the Soviet Union invaded eastern Poland on September 17, 1939. After several weeks of occupation, however, the Soviets decided to cede the city and the surrounding areas to Lithuania

---

25. For border changes after the beginning of the war, see Map 3, p. xiv.

(although they also decided to keep troops in the countryside surrounding the city). Vilna now became the capital of the Lithuanian state, although it was still possible to move freely between Vilna and the eastern part of Poland for about two months. Many Polish Jews took advantage of this opportunity and fled for the city, despite knowing about the pogrom that had followed Soviet withdrawal from Vilna, in which one Jew was killed and as many as two hundred wounded. Indeed, despite this, Polish Jews found Vilna appealing, not only as possibly the only remaining way out of Poland but also as a long-standing center of vibrant Jewish culture with a well-established Jewish community and infrastructure.[26] According to one refugee, "At first instinctively and spontaneously and then in an organized way, masses of Jews moved to Vilna [. . .] trains going to the city were overcrowded."[27] The number of Polish Jewish refugees in Vilna eventually reached about fourteen thousand, according to **American Jewish Joint Distribution Committee** (AJJDC) data.[28]

Thousands of Jewish refugees from Poland depended on Jewish humanitarian aid for survival in their new place of residence. Jewish organizations such as the AJJDC—in whose Vilna office the photograph in document 5–5 was most probably taken—continued to operate in Vilna with some difficulty after the Soviet Union occupied Lithuania (June 15, 1940) and until the Soviets outlawed foreign aid organizations (December 31, 1940).[29]

---

26. The pogrom was instigated by right-wing Polish circles and in effect supported by the Lithuanian police, who dragged their feet in restoring order and even on occasion beat the Jews themselves. Arad, *Ghetto in Flames*, 10–12. In the complicated political mosaic of eastern Europe, waves of anti-Jewish violence usually accompanied periods of turmoil and change in the late nineteenth and twentieth centuries. For this reason, Jewish communities had reason to fear attacks in uncertain times, such as the periods surrounding the outbreak of war. For the history and analysis of anti-Jewish violence in eastern Europe in the modern period, see Jonathan Dekel-Chen et al., eds., *Anti-Jewish Violence: Rethinking the Pogrom in East European History* (Bloomington: Indiana University Press, 2010), esp. David Engel's introduction, "What's in a Pogrom? European Jews in the Age of Violence."

27. Quoted in Arad, *Ghetto in Flames*, 15.

28. Bauer, *American Jewry and the Holocaust*, 111.

29. Bauer, *American Jewry and the Holocaust*, 116, 127–28.

DOCUMENT 5–5: **Jewish refugees waiting for aid distribution, Vilna, Lithuania, no date (ca. 1940), USHMMPA WS# 20707.**

Writing a year after the fact, Kruk documented the early days of refugee life in Vilna: "The hundreds and thousands who arrived in Vilna were huddled together, terrified, hungry, and exhausted"; "a week ago a landlord, the director of a bank, an industrialist; today hungry, naked, and hunched up. Ten days ago a merchant, a factory supervisor, a cobbler, a baker; today naked and barefoot, crushed." He went on almost nostalgically: "Tortured and worn out, they look fearfully at tomorrow. Fear brings people together, strangers become intimate, people cling to one another. The Jewish engineer befriends a Polish factory worker; a Jewish tailor is with a group of Polish students. Everything was so simple then, so human, so equal. All were brothers and all were close, facing the thousand lurking dangers. If someone is bleeding you tear off your shirt and bandage his wounds. If someone falls down, you carry him along, so as not to abandon him in the wasteland."[30]

Kruk may have idealized the relations among refugees, which to him appeared fraternal. He was, after all, a Bundist, dedicated to Jewish class solidarity and socialism. Yet, he was certainly right about the "thousand lurking dangers." Despite the fact that the group of Polish Jewish refugees in Vilna consisted mostly of the prewar Jewish elites, most refugees could not support

---

30. Quoted in Kruk, *The Last Days of the Jerusalem of Lithuania*, 28.

themselves. They had fled Poland overnight, usually with only the clothes on their backs, and the Lithuanian government did not allow them to work. One of the main Jewish relief organizations that provided aid was the AJJDC, which worked with local Jewish refugee aid committees to find housing, establish soup kitchens, and distribute clothing. Despite such efforts, **Moshe Kleinbaum**, who had returned home from the **Twenty-First Zionist Congress** in Geneva in the end of August 1939 to witness firsthand the outbreak of war, worried that the physical needs of the refugees were not being met. This would prove detrimental, he thought, "when the time comes for them to return home." Kleinbaum, too, had been living as a refugee in Vilna in the late fall and early winter of 1939–1940. Prior to reaching Vilna, he had served in the Polish army during "the entire tragic campaign," as he put it, retreated with the Polish army, and ended up under Soviet occupation in the town of Łuck. He then escaped Soviet arrest and, like many other Polish Jewish leaders, opted to flee Poland, making his way to Vilna, where he was reunited with other members of his family who had fled from Warsaw and managed to smuggle themselves across the German-Soviet demarcation line.[31] In the last report he penned before leaving the European continent (document 5–6), Kleinbaum pleaded for financial support for Polish Jewish refugees in Lithuania, including aid for their emigration efforts. He clearly regarded the refugees' situation in Vilna as temporary, though the duration of their stay in Vilna remained unclear.

DOCUMENT 5–6: **Letter from Moshe Kleinbaum, Geneva, Switzerland, to Nahum Goldmann,[32] chairman of the Administrative Committee of the WJC, March 12, 1940, facsimile reprinted in** *Archives of the Holocaust*, **ed. Henry Friedlander and Sybil Milton (New York: Garland Publishing, 1990), 8:119, 122–27.**

[. . .] Polish Jews under Lithuanian Rule: The number of Jewish refugees who escaped to Vilna is less than 10,000. They comprise, however, the intellectual elite of Polish Jewry. Among these, there are the active Jewish intellectuals of the Zionist and socialist movements, political leaders, writers, journalists, teachers, scholars, rabbis, Chassidic rabbis, and entire Yeshivas, as well as a considerable section of the wealthy Jews who have a good deal of capital abroad. What is the attitude of the Lithuanian government to the refugees? Apart from the Vilna pogrom, which will be

31. Kleinbaum eventually made his way across the European continent to board a ship in Trieste, Italy, bound for Palestine.

32. For more on **Nahum Goldmann**, see the Glossary.

described below, the attitude is favorable.[33] The central administration, to a certain degree, ignores the mass influx of refugees across the frontier, and it is always possible to come to an understanding with the border officials and the local administration, which in the end legalizes the sojourn of refugees who have entered illegally. The authorities of Kowno gave official permission to some thousands of Jewish refugees from Suwalki in the German area to enter. The registered refugees must stay in places to which they are assigned by the police. They may not work or earn anything, and may not participate in politics. As a matter of fact, the Lithuanian economy is not suffering because of the refugees, in view of the relief funds and the foreign currency, which the country needs badly and which are being sent in. [. . .]

It becomes clear then that the situation of the Jewish refugees in Lithuania can by no means be considered secure, although their lot is better than that of the other three million unfortunate Polish Jews. There is scarcely any possibility for emigration. Apart from the lack of immigration countries, there is hardly any means of transportation out of Lithuania. Russia and Germany do not permit the transit of Polish citizens. There remains then only the route through Latvia, Sweden, Denmark, Holland, Belgium, and France. But even on this route the **Gestapo**[34] and G.P.U.[35] prohibit the Riga-Stockholm line from carrying Polish citizens of military age. Furthermore, transit through France is very difficult and it is uncertain whether this route will remain open. Consequently, we must reckon with the fact that the majority of the Jewish refugees must remain in Lithuania for a long time.

---

33. Kleinbaum described the event in his letter as a "real pogrom, Jews were beaten and many were seriously injured." But he warned against viewing it "as a significant episode, for pogroms are not part of the Lithuanian policy toward Jews." See Vladas Sirutaviius and Darius Stalinas, "Was Lithuania a Pogrom-Free Zone? (1881–1940)," in Dekel-Chen et al. *Anti-Jewish Violence.*

34. For more on the Gestapo, see the Glossary.

35. The GPU (Gosudarstvennoye Politicheskoye Upravlenie, or State Political Directorate) was the state security service of the Russian Federal Soviet Socialist Republic from 1922 to 1934. Emerging from the Bolshevik revolutionary secret police, it was reorganized and renamed several times but is often used interchangeably with the NKVD and KGB, two of the most famous names for the Soviet secret service. See Paul R. Gregory, *Terror by Quota: State Security from Lenin to Stalin* (New Haven, CT: Yale University Press, 2009); Paul Hagenloh, *Stalin's Police: Public Order and Mass Repression in the USSR, 1926–1941* (Washington, DC: Woodrow Wilson Center Press, 2009).

The refugee situation is then very difficult. The J.D.C. [AJJDC] and the smaller relief organizations have done a great deal. In Vilna the refugees obtain at the J.D.C.'s kitchens a daily ration which keeps them from starving but is not adequate to satisfy a man's hunger. Each refugee likewise receives 15 lit[36] monthly for shelter. Neither does the clothing aid cover minimum needs, and no one has a groschen [the equivalent of a penny] in cash. When one takes into consideration the relatively high standard of this group of refugees, it is obvious that the J.D.C.'s aid is far from sufficient. This is not said by way of complaint. On the contrary, it must be admitted that almost everything which has been done is the work of the J.D.C. Nevertheless, it is not sufficient, and if the refugees continue in their present plight, when the time comes for them to return home they will be only shadows of their former selves.

It is then urgent to provide additional aid of two kinds: 1. financial help for those who are in a position to emigrate; 2. supplement the J.D.C.'s aid for such organized groups as the Haluzim, Yeshivas, Zionist groups, teachers, and writers association [sic]. The first steps taken by the World Jewish Congress in its relief work were directed for these purposes and must be continued. If the World Jewish Congress should succeed in raising larger sums for this purpose, the relief work should be directed by a committee of our friends in Kowno and Vilna.

While refugees in Lithuania depended on aid to survive, it quickly became clear that the various relief organizations were ill equipped to work together. Disagreements persisted; war and the refugee crisis in Vilna did not resolve long-standing differences in political outlook. For example, Bundist refugees in Vilna fought to have their own relief committee as they refused to sit on a committee with Zionists and religious leaders. Moses Beckelman of the AJJDC complained to his superiors about "the Bund question which is coming out of my ears now."[37] The organizational framework thus presented its own troubles, which only exacerbated the difficulties of organizing relief work. In a report from Kovno sent in late November 1939 to officials of the WJC on relief efforts in Vilna, Dr. Garfunkelis, a member of the WJC's administrative committee,

---

36. The *litas* was the currency introduced in 1922 in independent Lithuania; fifteen *litai* were valued at approximately US$2.80 during this period. See *Financial Times* (London), March 21, 1940.

37. Cited in Bauer, *American Jewry and the Holocaust*, 113.

reported on the conflicts and repetition of efforts among the organizations active in Vilna.[38]

DOCUMENT 5–7: Dr. Garfunkelis, "Report of the Lithuanian Committee on Behalf of Polish Jewish Refugees," November 22, 1939, American Jewish Archives, WJC records, series A, box A2, file 2, *Day Book of the WJC II*, 37–38.[39]

REPORT ON THE WORK OF THE LITHUANIAN COMMITTEE
IN BEHALF OF POLISH JEWISH REFUGEES
Kaunas
November 22, 1939
   The following organizations are concerned with relief for the Jewish refugees from Poland:
   Joint Distribution Committee
   HICEM office in Kaunas
   Lithuanian Jewish Committee of the Red Cross
   There is no possibility of uniting these organizations. The representative of the Joint Distribution Committee works in accordance with instructions issued by the European office. HICEM is guided by instructions from Paris and its own committee in Kaunas, including, among others, Rubinstein, Kelson and myself.[40] As for the Lithuanian Jewish Committee, it is subject to the Lithuanian Red Cross.

---

   38. This was most likely Leib Garfunkel (1896–1977), lawyer, journalist, and activist in Zionist and Jewish cooperative society circles. In the 1920s he edited a series of Jewish newspapers and served in the Lithuanian parliament and on the Kovno city council. He helped to organize aid for refugees from Poland and was detained by Soviet authorities in mid-1940 until Kovno fell into the hands of the Germans. Garfunkel served as an official with the Kovno Jewish Council until July 1944, when he was sent to a satellite camp of Dachau. He survived the war, undertook refugee aid work in Italy, and immigrated to Israel, where he wrote a famous study of the destruction of Jewish Kovno. See Boris Kotlerman, "Gorfinkel, Leyb," *The YIVO Encyclopedia of Jews in Eastern Europe* (New Haven, CT: Yale University Press, 2008), 1:622; *USHMM ITS Collection Data Base Central Name Index*; Leib Garfunkel, *Kovna ha-Yehudit be-Khurbana* (Jerusalem: Yad Vashem, 1959).
   39. See World Jewish Congress records at the American Jewish Archives: www.americanjewisharchives.org/aja/WJC (accessed March 3, 2011).
   40. Kelson may have been Shlomo (Shlioma) Kelson (1897–1945), an agronomist by training, Zionist, and organizer of Jewish cooperative projects before the war; after the Kovno ghetto formed, the Jewish Council appointed him to supervise the communal ghetto vegetable garden. He perished toward the end of the war in Landshut, a subcamp of Dachau. See Avraham Tory, *Surviving the Holocaust: The Kovno Ghetto Diary*, ed. Martin Gilbert and Dina Porat (Cambridge, MA: Harvard University Press, 1990), 87, 116, 119, 205, 229; *USHMM ITS Collection Data Base Central Name Index*.

From telephone conversations with Dr. Nurock and Dr. Kleinbaum, we learn that the present situation in Vilna is chaotic.[41] Every organization is engaged in registering refugees, but not one does so satisfactorily. A committee has been set up under the chairmanship of Chief Rabbi Dr. Rubinstein,[42] and includes the following, who are our friends: Dr. Kleinbaum, Rafael Szerechowski, and Prilucki, Secretary.[43] This committee has undertaken to procure statements from Polish Jewish refugees in Vilna and expects to obtain 2,000. A telegram just received from Dr. Kleinbaum indicates that the Joint Distribution Committee wishes to participate in this committee. The World Jewish Congress is attempting to contribute toward the costs involved in collecting these statements, and has therefore turned to our American friends with the request, so that we may obtain use of this valuable material.

A complete list of refugees in Vilna is promised to us through the good offices of Dr. Jacob Robinson [of the United Refugee Committee], who is to receive a copy of this list thanks to his influential connections, apparently from official sources.[44]

DR. GARFUNKELIS

---

41. Dr. Nurock may have been the Latvian rabbi and Zionist activist Mordechai Nurock (1884–1962), who was a founder of the WJC, delegate to many prewar Zionist congresses, and a member of the World Council of **HICEM**. He survived the war in the Soviet Union, emigrated to Palestine, and became a long-serving member of Israel's Knesset. See Mendel Bobe and Susan Hattis Rolef, "Nurock, Mordechai," in *Encyclopaedia Judaica*, ed. Fred Skolnik and Michael Berenbaum, 2nd ed. (Detroit, MI: Macmillan Reference USA, 2007), 15:350–51.

42. Isaac Rubinstein (1880–1945), born in Dotnuva, Lithuania, became a leading representative of Vilna Jews during World War I and then under first Lithuanian and then Polish rule. Rubinstein managed to move to the United States in 1941, where he taught at Yeshiva University; it is not clear whether he is identical with the Rubinstein mentioned earlier in the document. See Getzel Kressel, "Rubinstein, Isaac," in Skolnik and Berenbaum, *Encyclopaedia Judaica*, 17:517. For more on Dr. Kleinbaum, see the Glossary.

43. The authors have been unable to identify Rafael Szerechowski. Prilucki was most likely Noah Pryłucki, (1881–1941), a refugee in Vilna, renowned professor of Yiddish literature, and long-time editor of a Jewish paper in Warsaw. See Gudrun Schroeter, *Worte aus einer zerstörten Welt: Das Ghetto in Wilna* (St. Ingbert: Röhrig Universitätsverlag, 2008), 291n14; Kruk, *The Last Days of the Jerusalem of Lithuania*, 32, 42, 52n18, 76, 532n25.

44. Jacob Robinson (1889–1977), a legal expert who served with the Lithuanian parliament and foreign office before the war, was active in promoting Jewish rights. He left Lithuania in May 1940 for New York, where he established the Institute of Jewish Affairs. After the war he became a prominent consultant for the Nuremberg trials, the UN Secretariat, the Jewish **Agency for Palestine**, the Israeli Mission to the United Nations, and the Conference on Jewish Material Claims Against Germany. See Maurice L. Perlzweig, "Robinson, Jacob," in Skolnik and Berenbaum, *Encyclopaedia Judaica*, 17:355–56; obituary, *New York Times*, October 28, 1977.

OCCUPIED POLAND: LEADERS, COMMUNITIES, CHOICES

Organizing relief work thus proved a challenge, as old rivalries, political disagreements, and not a few difficult egos were transplanted from Poland. One
may subscribe to Kruk's retrospective idealization of the "leveling" push of the
tragedy and his view of a Jewish refugee community based on solidarity, or one
may endorse Garfunkelis's more sober approach. Regardless, these texts, perhaps
unwittingly, raise the question of how Jewish communities realigned themselves
in this period. Disparate people were brought together by dint of their common refugee experience. But how changed were the communities they had left
behind, since they had fared differently in the maelstrom of the invasion of
Poland and its subsequent occupation? And who were their new local leaders, if
many of the earlier ones had left to find refuge in Vilna and elsewhere?

The case of Zamość highlights the question of Jewish leadership in the face
of the disintegration of traditional communal structures. Due to the chaos of
the invasion, many Jewish communities ceased their work in the first weeks of
September or scaled down their regular operations to a minimum. The situation was exacerbated by the flight, as we have seen, of many Jewish leaders.
Thus, after the Nazi Polish military campaign was over and the Nazi occupation authorities began to establish *Judenräte*, or Jewish Councils, many of the
people who would have been "natural" candidates for council leadership were
no longer there. In his study of 128 *Judenrat* chairmen in the period immediately following the Nazi occupation, Aharon Weiss shows that only 17.2 percent of the leaders of these new entities had formerly been chairmen of Jewish
Community Councils. A further 4.7 percent of *Judenrat* chairmen had come
from the ranks of the former community council members. In contrast, 43
percent of the new leaders had been prominent community members but had
no prior formal experience in Jewish leadership positions.[45] These data by no
means challenge the well-established thesis that, in general, there was substantial continuity in Jewish leadership from the old Jewish communal structures
to the newly established *Judenräte*; after all, "prominent community members"

---

45. Aharon Weiss, "Jewish Leadership in Occupied Poland—Postures and Attitudes," *YVS*
12 (1977): 356. Isaiah Trunk, who studied 740 members of different *Judenräte* over a much
longer period, concluded that 43 percent "had been active in *Kehilas* [Jewish communities]
and municipal organs before the war." The inclusiveness of this category probably conceals a
breakdown between prewar chairmen, council members, and prominent Jewish citizens similar
to Weiss's study; Trunk invoked this percentage to claim that *Judenrat* membership was, "in
fact, an extension of the prewar *Kehila* bodies." See Isaiah Trunk, *Judenrat: The Jewish Councils
in Eastern Europe under Nazi Occupation* (New York: Macmillan, 1972), 574.

were just that, prominent and well-known, and had in most cases been close to communal leadership in the prewar period. It is nevertheless important to understand that the majority among the new cohort of Jewish leaders came from a different background and in many cases had little formal experience in Jewish leadership.

The testimony of Mieczysław Garfinkiel, a prominent lawyer, landowner, and industrialist from Zamość, provides a glimpse into this critical issue.[46] Garfinkiel was summoned as one of the few remaining prominent Jews in town, and he eventually became the head of the Zamość *Judenrat.*

His testimony was written after the war, but its temporal proximity to the events it describes preserves its eyewitness quality. How had several successive German and Soviet occupations over a very short period unsettled and reshaped the complex web of relations between Germans, Poles, Jews, and Soviets? And what does the memoir tell us about the vacuum created in Jewish leadership after the mass flight of the elites?

DOCUMENT 5–8: **Excerpt from a memoir by Mieczysław Garfinkiel, written in 1946, USHMMA RG 02.208M (ŻIH 302/122) (translated from Polish).**

The Germans captured Zamość on Wednesday, September 13, 1939. The occupation was preceded by two aerial bombardments, during which a small number of firebombs were dropped. The bombs fell on the neighborhood inhabited by the poor Jewish population and claimed approximately 500 victims from among the Jews.

The Germans' first stay lasted until September 26, 1939, on which day as a result of the agreement with the USSR the Germans pulled back to around Lublin, giving up the city to the Russians. The Germans' stay in Zamość during that period was not marked by any special anti-Jewish actions. The Germans restricted themselves to taking a fairly large number of hostages, both Poles and Jews, who together numbered around 1,500 persons. The hostages were mistreated and beaten, but none of them was killed. With the arrival of the Russians, the Jews breathed more freely, but already toward the end of September it unfortunately became apparent that the Russians would pull back beyond the Bug [River] and that

46. During the occupation, Garfinkiel was the chief of the JSS in Zamość and, beginning in 1940, chairman of the *Judenrat.* After the liquidation of the ghetto in Zamość, he hid in Warsaw. Garfinkiel's wife perished in Auschwitz in January 1944. See Adam Kopciowski, "Der Judenrat in Zamość," *Theresienstädter Studien und Dokumente* 9 (2002): 221–45.

Zamość would again be handed over to the Germans. This news created a mood of panic among the Jewish population. As if sensing the misfortunes to come, masses of Jews prepared to leave the city along with the Russians, even more so because the Soviet forces gladly provided aid by furnishing means of transportation. Approximately 7,000 to 8,000 Jews left the city together with the Russians. [. . .]

The Germans entered Zamość for the second time on October 7, 1939. Approximately one-third of the Jewish population had remained in the city and they very much feared excesses from the dregs of society that allegedly could and would take place in the so-called transitional period; voices from certain segments had arisen threatening Jews with reprisals for fleeing with "the Soviets." The situation was that much worse because the city council categorically rejected a proposal from certain Jewish circles to raise a mixed Polish-Jewish civil militia for the transitional period. The argument they gave was that the Germans, who were going to take the city, would be displeased. Fortunately, those fears were not realized, and the transfer of the city from the hands of the Soviets to the Germans took place peacefully. At the same time, however, the Jews began to understand from the very outset what the German occupation would mean.

Immediately after the Germans occupied the city, the roundup of Jews for labor began. This bore a mass yet unorganized character, so much so that Jews could not show themselves on the streets and sat hidden away at home. Simultaneously, people began destroying Jewish shops. This was done by German soldiers. Polish youth pointed out the shops to them, and the youth likewise took advantage of the opportunity to plunder. Since they did not see Jews on the streets, the German soldiers entered their homes and dragged them out for work and personal services. The situation prompted several former members of the board of the Jewish community to consider approaching the military commandant of the city with a proposal to normalize relations. It consisted of the Jewish community providing laborers—several dozen Jewish workers—under the condition that the lawlessness and the soldiers' marauding stop. They also appealed for a prohibition on the destruction and plundering of Jewish shops to be issued.

After a certain amount of time had passed, more or less at the start of November 1939, German civil authorities and the Gestapo came to Zamość. Shortly thereafter, the mayor of the city summoned eight Jews, including myself as one of the few members of the intelligentsia who had remained in the city. He informed us that, in accord with an order of the

German civil authorities and the Gestapo, we were to form a so-called Council of Jewish Elders of the city of Zamość.

The Council of Elders was to represent the interests of the Jews before the German authorities and above all to ensure fulfillment of all the edicts and orders made by the Germans. None of my requests or attempts to get myself out of it had any effect.

Another testimony from Zamość, written in 1941 by a far less prominent person, provides more detail about the confusion and fear that gripped the Jewish community during the first uncertain months following the Nazi invasion. In Kraków at the outbreak of the war, this anonymous twenty-two-year-old Jewish woman joined the flood of Jewish refugees fleeing east. Her flight seems to have been the result of a collective decision made by her Zionist political circle, her colleagues from an agricultural training camp at Krzeszowice near Kraków, which ran a program for young Zionists preparing for emigration to Palestine. The German army overtook the group close to Zamość, on the road from Kraków to Łuck, where, as we have seen from Kruk's account, throngs of Jewish refugees were heading. Having occupied the town, the German army nevertheless soon withdrew, in accordance with the secret Nazi-Soviet agreement. Even though the initial days under Nazi rule certainly promised hard times for the Jews, the decision of the German army to withdraw put the Jews in a difficult situation: in the absence of a political or military authority—even one hostile to the Jews—they were left subject to the whim of the surrounding population. In turbulent times, this was almost a guarantee of anti-Jewish violence, and this pattern, which predated the war, sheds light on the woman's reaction in document 5–9. Her text also raises the question of how the local Jewish population fared under the Soviet occupation.

DOCUMENT 5–9: **Testimony provided by unidentified female author regarding the German/Russian occupation of Zamość, no date (ca. 1941), USHMMA RG 15.079M (ŻIH Ring. I/935), reel 42 (translation from Yiddish).**[47]

[. . .] Between Yom Kippur and Sukkot of the year 5700 [between September 23 and September 28, 1939], the Germans left the city, and we learned that the Russians would soon come in.

---

47. This is also printed in a differently worded translation in Shimon Huberband, *Kiddush Hashem: Jewish Religious and Cultural Life in Poland during the Holocaust*, ed. Jeffrey S. Gurock and Robert S. Hirt (Hoboken, NJ: KTAV Publishing House, 1987), 341–42.

Jews were extremely afraid of pogroms and attacks by the Poles in the intervening time, before the arrival of the Russians. Jews closed down their shops and locked the gates. All the men took up positions by the gates, armed with sticks, rods, axes, and iron tools, to defend themselves in case of an attack by the Poles, but no attacks took place.

After three days, Russian tanks and a large military force entered the city. Jews rejoiced and went out to the marketplace. The military forces continued beyond the city. A city council was created and was composed of formerly arrested Communists, for the most part Jews. The local Jewish Communist, Hackman, was appointed to be the head of the council. A militia was soon formed, which was composed of some of the darker elements of the Polish and Jewish population. [Food] products, which had been stored in warehouse of the municipal authorities, were distributed by the city council among the poorer segments of the Polish and Jewish population. Every night there was a meeting in the marketplace, Hackman and others gave Communist speeches in Polish, Russian, and Yiddish.

After a few days, we learned that the Soviets would leave the city and that the Germans would return. Great panic and confusion gripped the Jewish population. Hackman called a special meeting in the marketplace and categorically denied the rumors, but in the morning we found out that Hackman himself had sent off his mother, wife, and child in a horse and carriage.

The next day the retreat of the Soviet forces began in the town. Many Jews, out of fear of the Germans, also fled the city with the Russians. The soldiers gladly picked them up and allowed the Jews to travel on their vehicles. Among the Russian soldiers there were many Jews, among them a great number who still remembered their Jewishness. With great longing, they asked about the Jewish holidays, the Sabbath, and praying.

My husband and I also boarded a military vehicle. On Shemini Atzeret of that year [October 5, 1939], we arrived in Rawa Ruska.

When thinking about Jewish reactions to the arrival of Soviet occupation forces, we need to keep in mind the terribly stark choice Jews in eastern Poland faced: they became subject to either the Nazi or the Soviet order. "The principal clue to the joyous atmosphere [among the Jews] surrounding the entry of the Soviet troops," Jan Gross points out in his excellent account of the chaotic days of the collapse of Poland, is that "where they came, the Germans did not."[48] Where neither army was present, the Jews lived in fear of the rage of the local population,

---

48. Gross, *Revolution from Abroad*, 32.

as attested to by the unidentified woman's testimony from Zamość excerpted in document 5–9. To cite one other example, in the village of Aleksandria, near Równe, the Jews were left to the mercy of the local Ukrainian population in the period between the departure of the Polish army and the arrival of the Soviets. The crowd was ready to start a pogrom and undoubtedly would have attacked the Jews had not a sympathetic police commander, just before leaving, let the Jews arm themselves. After a short period of tension and virtual frontline division of the town between the Ukrainians and the Jews, the Soviet army marched in. It is not very difficult to imagine the relief the Jews felt and thus to understand the nature of initial Jewish reactions to the Soviet occupation.[49]

The question of whether Polish Jews in the main responded positively to the Red Army and the first days of Soviet occupation was a hot-button issue. It reinflamed stereotypes and tensions from the interwar period. On the heels of the 1917 Bolshevik revolution that shook Europe, particularly its eastern parts bordering the Soviet Union, a myth had taken root about a Jewish conspiracy to seize power through communism and spread it to eastern Europe. As in several historical periods in previous centuries, many people tended to make sense of seemingly sudden, inexplicable, and threatening political changes and social transformations by imagining a vast conspiracy plotted behind closed doors by "the Jews."[50] Needless to say, such a conspiracy never existed; its pervasiveness as a myth stemmed from ignorance, fear, and a general lack of understanding of social processes and movements. Nevertheless, proponents of *Żydokomuna*— roughly, "Jew communism" in Polish—saw the Jews everywhere as agents of Soviet-style communism, which they perceived as the major and most immediate threat to ethnic cohesion and national sovereignty. Because the latter concerns topped the political agenda throughout eastern Europe in the 1930s, relations between Jews and non-Jews, already strained by anti-Jewish prejudice and occasional incidents of anti-Jewish violence, deteriorated further.

The situation was especially difficult in the Polish regions bordering the Soviet Union, the *kresy*, an area marked by ethnic and class resentments.[51] To

---

49. Gross, *Revolution from Abroad*, 32–33.

50. For an authoritative history of antisemitism in the modern period, see Walter Laqueur, *The Changing Face of Antisemitism: From Ancient Times to the Present Day* (New York: Oxford University Press, 2006), 71–124.

51. On *Żydokomuna*, see Joanna B. Michlic, "Żydokomuna—Anti-Jewish Images and Political Tropes in Modern Poland," in *Jahrbuch des Simon-Dubnow-Instituts* (2005): 4:303– 29; Joanna Michlic, *Poland's Threatening Other: The Image of the Jew from 1880 to the Present* (Lincoln: University of Nebraska Press, 2006); and Jan T. Gross, *Fear: Anti-Semitism in Poland after Auschwitz: An Essay in Historical Interpretation* (New York: Random House, 2006).

many Polish and Ukrainian nationalists subscribing to the *Żydokomuna* myth, the collapse of Poland in the first weeks of the war—especially the occupation of the eastern part of the country—was the ultimate proof that the Jews aimed to Bolshevize the *kresy*. The rejoicing of many Jews at the arrival of the Red Army further entrenched the myth in the minds of the local population. The excerpt in document 5–10 from Moshe Kleinbaum's lengthy report of March 12, 1940, conveys his awareness of and sensitivity to the question of whether the majority of Polish Jews supported Communist Russia. Kleinbaum was an exceptionally authoritative commentator on events during these first months of the war, with an eye to their broader political and social implications, thanks to his experience as an editor of the Yiddish daily *Haynt*.

DOCUMENT 5–10: **Letter from Moshe Kleinbaum, Geneva, Switzerland, to Nahum Goldmann, chairman of the Administrative Committee of the WJC, March 12, 1940, facsimile reprinted in** Archives of the Holocaust, **ed. Henry Friedlander and Sybil Milton (New York: Garland Publishing, 1990), 8:112–13.**

[. . .] 3. <u>Under Soviet Occupation</u>. I had the opportunity to observe at first hand the Soviet occupation for a period of six weeks in three important places, in Łuck, Lemberg, and Vilna, from September 18 to October 28. I therefore have a right to claim that everything I say represents my own view and reflects the truth.

I saw the Red Army march into Łuck. Thick rows of people lined the main street through which the Soviet tanks, artillery and mechanized infantry marched. Most of them watched the scene out of curiosity. Ukrainian peasants, who streamed in from the surrounding villages, and young Jewish Communists, particularly the girls, applauded and hailed the Army with friendly greetings. The number of Jewish enthusiasts was not very large, but they made more noise than all the others that day. This created the false impression that the Jews were the chief hosts at this festival. In Łuck, the Polish population consisted almost entirely of officials and the military. They and their families kept off the streets on that memorable day. I spoke with Jewish shopkeepers, with a tailor, a shoemaker, a teacher, a salaried man, an unemployed Jewish engineer, with Jews representing all sections, who expressed the reaction of the Jewish population, not to be confused with the tumult raised by a few dozen youthful Jewish Communists, in a clever comment such as issues from Jews in critical times. Already on September 18, the following remarks prevailed among the Jews of Łuck: "We were condemned to death, but our sentence has been commuted to life-long imprisonment." The Nazi danger meant the death penalty for the Jews. The Red Army came and rescued a million and a half Jews from a sure physical and civil death, but the Red Army rescued no more than the bare lives of Jews. The Jewish population views life under Soviet rule as a sentence of life imprisonment. Life continues, but with nothing more than black bread and water, and people are no longer free. You probably know that I am somewhat familiar with the spirit of the masses, and that the gauging of public opinion is, so to speak, my profession. I wish to declare, with the fullest conviction, that at least 80 percent of the Jews think that way, and that they accepted Soviet rule first with a sigh of relief, because of the weeks of anxiety regarding the threat of Nazi invasion, and then with a sigh of deep concern: What will the morrow bring us? Whoever describes the reaction of the Jewish people in eastern Poland to the arrival of the Red Army otherwise, is falsifying the truth.

A memoir Calel Perechodnik from Otwock recorded in 1943, while he was in hiding in Warsaw, casts additional light on the complex emotions that many Jews harbored about the Soviet occupation of Poland.[52] Perhaps most tellingly, Perechodnik felt the need to address the issue of the Jewish reaction to the Soviet invasion four years after the fact. The myth of *Żydokomuna* must have remained very strong even then, if the urgency of addressing it had not faded.

---

52. In September 1939, Calel Perechodnik was living in Otwock, where his family owned a movie theater. He subsequently became a member of the Jewish police in the Otwock ghetto; his wife and daughter perished at Treblinka, and Perechodnik blamed himself for their deaths for the rest of his life. He wrote his memoir while hiding in Warsaw and gave it to Władysław Błażewski in the fall of 1943. The remaining part of the memoir was lost during the 1944 Warsaw Uprising, in which Perechodnik took part. After its failure he hid in the ruins of Warsaw but was discovered and killed by the Nazis. Błażewski gave the memoir to the author's brother, Pejsach Perechodnik, after the war, who in turn allowed the Central Committee of the Jews in Poland to make a copy and then took the original text to Israel. The abridged version of the memoir was published as Calel Perechodnik, *Czy ja jestem mordercą?* ed. Paweł Szapiro (Warsaw: ŻIH and KARTA, 1993); an extended version was published as Calek Perechodnik, *Spowiedź: Dzieje rodziny żydowskiej podczas okupacji hitlerowskiej w Polsce*, ed. David Engel (Warsaw: KARTA, 2004), and, in English, as Calel Perechodnik, *Am I a Murderer? Testament of a Jewish Ghetto Policeman*, ed. Frank Fox (Boulder, CO: Westview Press, 1996).

DOCUMENT 5–11: **Excerpt from a memoir by Calel Perechodnik, written in 1943, USHMMA RG 02.208M (ŻIH 302/55) (translated from Polish).**

I'm not going to go through the history of the war; I'll just say that on September 7, 1939, I heard the order [to go east] broadcast on the radio, left my wife behind, and headed out on foot together with my brother, father, and uncle to the east. On the way, my brother wanted to join with the army, but they didn't let him; they ordered us to go farther east and said that we would be mobilized there. [. . .]

We reached the point where the Bolsheviks had entered the eastern territories, it didn't make any sense to go farther. The Russians caught us off guard in Słonim [in present-day Belarus], the birthplace of my mother and where my uncle had his own apartment. We also had a lot of family there, who welcomed us very kindly, and we stayed there, following the course of further events.

How did the Jews feel when the Bolsheviks entered Polish territory?

This is a very touchy question, but I'll try to be completely honest and objective, writing the truth and only the truth. The first response was boundless joy, which really shouldn't be a surprise. From the one side, the German invaded, proclaiming the merciless destruction and murder of all the Jews. And from the other side, the Bolshevik invaded, proclaiming that for him all people are equal before the law. There was no comparison to be made. The Jews rejoiced, myself included. Although I had opposed the communists for my entire life, I asked God for the Bolsheviks to occupy the area up to the Vistula [River]. I was prepared to lose the movie theater, my business interests, my father's villa, just to live as a free man, without any racial restrictions.

Nevertheless I didn't jump for joy when I saw the Soviet tanks. I won't deny that there were Jews, longtime communists, who disarmed Polish divisions, but can you blame all Jews for that?

It is important to keep in mind that, at the time of the German invasion, it was impossible to predict the Nazi policy of systematic murder of the Jews; while it was clear that Jews could expect nothing good from the German occupation, the ones who decided to flee did not do so out of fear of genocide. Rather, people largely perceived this war as like any other war in recent history. They assumed that able-bodied men would be at risk for labor and even military conscription at the hands of the invading army; as a result, men fled in droves. In some cases, men took their entire families with them, for they harbored no illusions about the Nazis' disposition toward the Jews. But many people also thought that civilians would be safe once the actual military campaign was over and that women, children, and the elderly were not risking their lives by staying at home, even if they would suffer humiliation and harassment by the Nazis. Such assumptions are borne out by Perechodnik's memoir and many other accounts of Jewish flight in the face of the Nazi invasion—including those published in this chapter—which indicate that it was predominantly men who fled.

The women who did end up fleeing their homes experienced the flight very differently from the men. To posit a "typical" Polish Jewish woman's experience would do injustice to the tremendous complexity of Jewish women's experiences in eastern Europe on the eve of World War II. As ChaeRan Freeze and Paula Hyman remind us, the feminist critique of "'universal womanhood' [. . .] raises a fundamental question about the very category of 'east European Jewish women' who resided across a vast geographic expanse in different cultural, political, and social settings."[53] Nonetheless, the memoir of Zofia Dulman[54] gives us clues about how a Jewish woman's experience of flight might have differed from that of a man. Evidently at home in Polish culture, Dulman managed to pass as a Pole where neither a Jewish man of military age nor a more traditional Jewish woman could. Indeed, her ability to pass probably made the difference between life and death. It is also interesting to note the gender dynamic between Zofia and her husband. His order propelled her and their daughter to leave their home in Warsaw; yet, it was Zofia who decided to risk a dangerous trip back to Warsaw—once the family was already safe in Kowel—to retrieve their clothing.

DOCUMENT 5–12: **Excerpt from a memoir by Zofia Dulman, written in 1945, USHMMA RG 02.208M (ŻIH 302/261) (translated from Polish).**

On September 7, 1939, one week after the start of the German-Polish war, nearly all the young men left Warsaw's walls behind and headed east. My husband set out along with the others and, after a week of wandering,

---

53. ChaeRan Freeze and Paula Hyman, "Introduction: A Historiographical Survey," in *Jewish Women in Eastern Europe: Polin*, ed. ChaeRan Freeze, Paula Hyman, and Anthony Polonsky (Oxford: Littman Library of Jewish Civilization, 2005), 18:5.

54. Zofia Dufman (or Dulman; née Chłodnik or Chłodnicka), born in Warsaw in 1906 into an Orthodox Jewish family, became active in Zionist circles as a young woman. After her husband Stanisław was arrested in Kowel in 1941 and presumed killed, Zofia left Kowel with her daughter Dana (Danuta) and survived the war with false "**Aryan**" identity papers. They both emigrated to Israel in the late 1950s, and Zofia settled in Tel Aviv. See "Virtual Shtetl," Museum of the History of Polish Jews, www.sztetl.org.pl (accessed September 8, 2010).

reached Kowel. In October I received word from him. He ordered me to come immediately together with our child [Dana].

The journey to Kowel lasted a week. We left Warsaw on a large wagon, which brought us to Małkinia. I didn't yet know that that was the most dangerous section of the border. The Germans were scrupulously carrying out searches and horribly beating Jews. Worse than anywhere else. I reached an agreement with my Polish guide that I would pretend to be his wife. My heart was beating terribly as I approached the place where the searches were being carried out. A German, fat and red like a pig, was blocking the crossing to the other, safe side. He was angrily waving an upside-down cane about. He let Poles through but ordered Jews to stand to the side so that he could deal with them later. A whole group already stood behind a barbed wire enclosure. I took a look and was overcome with terror. They were completely docile, they only had animal-like fear in their eyes. The same look stayed in their eyes throughout the entire occupation, it even betrayed a few surviving Jews to the Aryans.

When it was my turn, I walked up, trembling, with the guide to get searched. The fat, angry German raised the upside-down cane and, instead of, as I expected, striking me, directed it at my companion and said with a wild shriek: "Jude" [*sic*]. I quickly regained my composure and, laughing, cried out: "Sir, but we're Polish." The angry German looked at us, and then lowered the cane and let us forward with the words: "Voraus" [*sic*].

We had reached the neutral strip. Now we had to solve a new, weightier problem: how to make it to Kowel. We could have stayed for an eternity in the neutral strip and no one would have bothered with us, but our goal was to cross the border. How could we accomplish this? On the one side of the strip stood the Germans, from whom we had fled, and on the other side Soviet soldiers were standing guard and weren't letting anyone through. We begged them, we implored them to take pity on the children. Nothing helped, they remained adamant. In the meantime, night was growing nearer. I was overcome by despair. What were we to do with little children here in the woods? Not having any other choice, we set up the little ones on carts (Dana was three years old at the time), where they soon fell asleep. All night long, I circled around the child, I didn't sit down for even a moment. To make matters worse, rain was continually pouring down. I was soaked to the bone and my knees swelled up like balloons from all the standing, but I was glad that at least the child was warm and, covered by a small waterproof coat, completely dry. The next day, the situation did not improve. The Soviet soldiers were unbending. Suddenly, someone in our group recalled that, at a different section of the border, refugees in a similar situation gathered up their courage and, singing battle songs, went forward. The confused guards let them through. We decided to do the same. We didn't have anything to lose, there was no return for us. We put the children at the front, behind them were the women, and in the rear were the men. When the sign was given, we began the song "Esli zavtra voina" [famous patriotic Soviet song "If Tomorrow There's War"] and started forward. The soldiers, blocking the road, pointed their bayonets at us, but we, determined and not interrupting the song, continued forward with the children in front of us. The soldiers slowly moved back, cursing and not lowering their bayonets, while we pressed on. At a certain point, the soldiers, resigned, dropped their bayonets with the words "Go to hell" [in Russian] and allowed us to go forward. Half unconscious from joy and shouting like madmen "Long live Stalin" [in Polish], we ran to the station. After three days I was in Kowel.

My husband was working as the head of an officers' canteen. We received an apartment and things were going great.

In that same year, 1939, I decided to risk it and cross the border for a second time to bring our clothing from Warsaw to Kowel, where the clothing situation was very difficult. The child stayed with my husband. When I reached the border zone with some others, who were smugglers, night had already fallen. Our group was made up principally of railway men and peasants. They were making their living off the Jewish tragedy. The Germans were searching for Jews—they approached each person individually and shined a torch in our eyes. They removed whomever they identified [as Jewish] from the ranks of the others, then they sent the entire group to the nearby hills. Kicking them and hitting them with their bayonets, they ordered the Jews to march and sing "hatikvah" [popular Zionist anthem "The Hope"]. Later, with a shout they drove them back to the Russian side. We watched dumbstruck. Even the Poles were silent this time, they didn't mock the Jews and didn't help the Germans as they usually did. I trembled from the fear that they might find me out. They shined the light in my eyes but continued on. I breathed easier. All of a sudden I overheard the conversation of two railway men in front of me: "That's definitely a Jew; tell the German to order her to present her documents." I quailed with fear, but, composing myself, I said: "You think I'm a Jew? Go ahead and report it to the Germans. What wonderful times these are when Poles snitch on Poles." My self-confidence threw them off, and they left me alone. After a moment, I noticed movement behind me in the rows of people. A flaxen-haired boy, maybe 12 years old, abruptly began to tremble with fear and dropped a small loaf of bread to the ground which he had been holding to his chest under his coat. The peasants took pity on the Jewish child and, when the Germans approached them with the torch, they moved him between themselves so that he remained in the shadows, unnoticed. Poor child, perhaps he had lost his parents and had set off on the dangerous road to Warsaw in order to find them . . . My journey to the capital lasted six weeks, but I returned to Kowel with all of our clothing, which at the time was our only property. I took my friend Eda and her young daughter Asia with me from Warsaw.

The German invasion of Poland and the partition of the country between the Nazis and the Soviets inaugurated a radically new phase of Polish Jewish history. Many Jews attempted to escape the dangers of this deadly embrace; we have seen some of the issues they faced in trying to get away. Others decided to stay in German-occupied Poland and help their coreligionists. We now turn to their efforts.

CHAPTER 6

THE ORGANIZATION OF RELIEF FOR POLISH JEWS

IN THE FIRST month after the outbreak of war in Poland, Jewish leaders around the world scrambled to organize assistance for Polish Jews. Throughout the 1930s and particularly beginning in 1935, international Jewish organizations had already worked to provide relief for Polish Jews hit hard by the Depression and government-supported economic antisemitism. They now confronted massive new challenges in delivering aid to a country facing occupation and territorial dismemberment. What the future held in store nobody knew, but the Polish situation showed every sign of deteriorating further. Jewish relief organizations and political leaders in the United States, Palestine, and elsewhere in Europe (particularly in Geneva, Switzerland) endeavored to understand what was happening to Polish Jews under the German occupation. Observers described the events of September 1939 in relation to prior massacres in Jewish history. The Crusades and the Khmelnitsky pogroms of 1648 became frequent reference points, as did the more recent pogroms in the aftermath of World War I. With Hitler's unconcealed threat to annihilate European Jewry in the event of another world war, it was obvious to Jewish leaders outside of Poland that action to aid Polish Jewry had become a matter of life and death.

Scholarly treatments of American and Palestinian Jewish leaders' responses to the crisis unfolding in Poland have centered on whether they ought to have done more to rescue Polish Jews. This chapter examines the nature of the crisis as those leaders understood it in the early months of the war, the constraints they faced, and the possibilities they saw for action in organizing relief for

Polish Jews. What steps could they take without legitimizing the pursuit and waging of war? And who would take the lead, American Jews or the **Yishuv** in Palestine? Could Jewish groups put aside their prewar differences and political feuds to organize a united relief action? Did they even have sufficient resources or the political power to do so? Like their Polish counterparts, Jewish organizations and communities in the United States and the *Yishuv* suffered from internal divisions and divergent goals in the prewar period. Henry Feingold has suggested in his work that American Jews were largely unprepared to assume the mantle of leadership of world Jewry in this period. There was no unified American Jewish community to speak of in the 1930s; thus, a communal base for unified action did not exist.[1] At the same time, the leaders of the *Yishuv* did not appear to be in a position to provide central coordination in the relief effort due to their distance from war-torn Europe, their own preoccupation with the future Jewish settlement in Palestine, and internal divisions over the best course of action. Should they continue to pursue **Aliyah Bet**, immigration efforts deemed illegal by the British, and thereby bring as many Jews as possible out of parts of Europe dominated by Germany to Palestine? Or was it more important for them not to antagonize Britain at this juncture, despite their disappointment with Britain's wavering position on a future Jewish state in Palestine?[2] Furthermore, Zionist leaders in the *Yishuv* continued to debate whether they should loosen their strict criteria for whom to welcome as immigrants, a debate that arose, as we have seen in chapter 2, in 1938 in response to the desperation of Austrian and German Jews to flee the Reich.[3]

A combination of factors dominated the course of action taken by Jewish aid organizations well into 1940 to help Jews under siege in Poland. Diverse

---

1. Henry Feingold, "Who Shall Bear Guilt for the Holocaust? The Human Dilemma," in *The American Jewish Experience*, ed. Jonathan D. Sarna (New York: Holmes and Meier, 1997), 285.

2. For a discussion of this dilemma, see Dalia Ofer, *Escaping the Holocaust: Illegal Immigration to the Land of Israel, 1939–1944* (New York: Oxford University Press, 1990), 23–41. The "wavering position" of Britain refers to the White Paper, issued in 1939, which in effect annulled the 1917 British commitment (the Balfour Declaration) to the establishment of a Jewish "national home" in Palestine. See discussion of this issue in chapter 2 of this volume (note 9). The Jewish Agency—in effect, the nascent Jewish government of Palestine—said of the White Paper, "It is in the darkest hour of Jewish history that the British Government proposes to deprive Jews of their last hope. . . . The Jews will never accept the closing to them of the gates of Palestine nor let their national home be converted into a ghetto." Quoted in Dina Porat, *The Blue and the Yellow Stars of David: The Zionist Leadership in Palestine and the Holocaust, 1939–1945* (Cambridge, MA: Harvard University Press, 1990), 14.

3. Ofer, *Escaping the Holocaust*, 24.

prewar experiences with relief work in eastern Europe came into play, as did reactions to the uneven situation on the ground and conflicted visions of what was best for a long-term Jewish future within and beyond Europe. Jewish organizations whose resources were already stretched by the economic depression and the refugee crisis of the 1930s now grappled with a humanitarian crisis rendered all the more complex by the politics of war.

ORGANIZING HELP, CONFRONTING OBSTACLES

For American Jews, the **American Jewish Joint Distribution Committee** (AJJDC) had played the primary role in organizing relief and assistance for Polish Jews within the limits of what was possible after the Great Depression.[4] Complicating matters in the 1930s was the balance the AJJDC had to strike between sending assistance to German Jews while complying with the American Jewish boycott of Hitler's Germany. Nonetheless, the AJJDC supported the **Reichsvereinigung** in Germany and the Jewish community in Vienna at the end of 1939; as a result, over 70,000 people, including 9,555 school-age children, received "winter help."[5] In 1939, of the organization's total expenditure of $8.5 million, $3.25 million supported displaced Jews in European countries of refuge, $2.18 million went to Jews in central Europe, and $1.25 million went to Jews in eastern Europe.[6]

New political developments in the summer of 1939 portending the imminence of war forced AJJDC leaders to realign their budget priorities. At an emigration conference in Paris convened jointly by the AJJDC and **HICEM** toward the end of August 1939, the two organizations' leading representatives (among them, **Morris Troper**, the AJJDC's European director; **Joseph C. Hyman**, vice chairman of the AJJDC based in New York; **Saly Mayer** from

---

4. For the authoritative work on the AJJDC, see Yehuda Bauer, *American Jewry and the Holocaust: The American Jewish Joint Distribution Committee, 1939–1945* (Detroit, MI: Wayne State University Press, 1981). For an overview of wartime relief efforts of HIAS, the New York–based Jewish humanitarian organization, see Valery Bazarov, "HIAS and HICEM in the System of Jewish Relief Organisations in Europe, 1933–41," *East European Jewish Affairs* 39, no. 1 (April 2009): 69–78. For an early postwar account of the activities of the WJC, see Institute of Jewish Affairs of the World Jewish Congress, *Unity in Dispersion: A History of the World Jewish Congress*, 2nd rev. ed. (New York: Institute of Jewish Affairs of the World Jewish Congress, 1948). See also the memoir of its wartime Geneva office director, Gerhart M. Riegner, *Never Despair: Sixty Years in the Service of the Jewish People and the Cause of Human Rights* (Chicago: Ivan R. Dee in association with USHMM, 2006).

5. Bauer, *American Jewry and the Holocaust*, 29–30.

6. Bauer, *American Jewry and the Holocaust*, 25.

Switzerland; Gertrude van Tijn from the Netherlands; Max Gottschalk from Belgium; **Yitzhak Giterman** from Poland; Marie Schmolka from Prague; and **Otto Hirsch** from Berlin) decided to transfer large amounts of money to Poland for the second half of 1939. They hoped that if war broke out, it would be over by the end of that year.[7] Looking back half a year later, Troper summed up the collective sense of anxiety that hung over the joint meeting in Paris:

> The imminence of war had been in the air for several weeks. An atmosphere of gravity and depression prevailed. Everyone sensed that at any moment the conference on emigration might have to be converted into a war emergency meeting. On the very morning of August 22, when the first session took place, the world was startled to learn of the signing of the Russo-German pact. The drama of the occasion was heightened when one of the French delegates was summoned from the opening session, and reappeared a few hours later in the uniform of a French officer to bid his colleagues adieu. [. . .] The meeting proceeded to the end of the scheduled program, but even before the final adjournment, delegates were being flooded with anxious telegrams and telephone calls urging them to return home. Departures were hastened, and many left without knowing whether or not they would arrive at their destinations. Some of the delegates found their homeward paths already blocked and remained in France.[8]

The beginning of the war created a whole new set of political and financial challenges. In the war zone, Jewish organizations struggled to coordinate their response to the overwhelming demands for help. The AJJDC's dedicated staff in Poland proved central to any success they had in coping with the exigencies of these early months of war. Yehuda Bauer has argued that since the 1920s, there had been "a very active and influential JDC office in Warsaw [. . .] which in time became almost autonomous."[9] The response of the AJJDC Warsaw staff to the refugee crisis at Zbąszyń in late October 1938 (see chapter 1) evidenced their

---

7. Bauer, *American Jewry and the Holocaust*, 34–35. See also Bazarov, "HIAS and HICEM."

8. Morris Troper, "On the European Relief Front," *Contemporary Jewish Record* 3, no. 3 (May–June 1940): 227–28.

9. Bauer, *American Jewry and the Holocaust*, 32. Bauer argues further, "The story of Warsaw's JDC office in the twenty-eight months between the conquest of Poland by the Germans in September, 1939, and the Japanese attack on Pearl Harbor in December, 1941 is the story of Polish Jews trying to help themselves, sometimes with the aid of their American brethren, sometimes against the wishes of the U.S. parent organization, in the face of literally impossible odds." Bauer, *American Jewry and the Holocaust*, 67.

dedication and competence. And in the first weeks of the war, when Poland was effectively cut off from the rest of the world, the Warsaw office, rather than waiting for directions from New York, exhibited an independence and resourcefulness that proved crucial in organizing relief on the ground. Men such as **Emanuel Ringelblum**, Yitzhak Giterman, Leib Neustadt, and Daniel Guzik were well-connected figures in Warsaw Jewish society. And unlike many prominent Jewish leaders from Warsaw who fled in front of the German onslaught (see chapter 5), Ringelblum and his circle decided to stay in Poland.[10]

Leaders of the Jewish relief organizations in Warsaw came together at the invitation of the AJJDC, which funded most of them, to form the **Coordinating Commission of Jewish Aid and Civic Societies**. **Michał Weichert** emerged as one of the best-known participants in these developments. According to his memoir, he had proposed this wartime merging of efforts and was immediately voted vice chairman of the commission. The unified vote in favor of this suggestion surprised him, given each organization's well-known desire to protect its turf.[11] However, the enterprise seemed to work. The body was soon known simply as the Coordinating Commission (Yiddish: Koordinir komisiye, or KK). Emanuel Ringelblum—who according to Weichert came to his office one morning and "stayed"—became its secretary-general.[12] The KK commission operated soup kitchens and created temporary shelters for refugees and residents forced to leave bomb-damaged homes.[13] One year after the outbreak of the war, the AJJDC office in Warsaw summarized its efforts to provide immediate aid and assistance to the embattled Jews of Warsaw and the rest of Poland.

DOCUMENT 6–1: Report by AJJDC Warsaw about its work during the thirteen war months from September 1939 to October 1940, USHMMA Acc. 1999.A.0154 (ŻIH 210/6), 10–12 (translated from Yiddish).

The first steps in providing aid/The first aid efforts

During the first month of the war, September 1939, it was, of course, impossible to organize any formal relief assistance for the Jews in Poland. The military campaign had such a blitz-character right from the beginning, that any sort of normal activity was impossible. The bombs and

10. Samuel D. Kassow, *Who Will Write Our History? Emanuel Ringelblum, the Warsaw Ghetto, and the Oyneg Shabes Archive* (Bloomington: Indiana University Press, 2007), 91; on the flight of Warsaw Jewish elite, 114–15.

11. Michał Weichert, *Zikhroynes*, vol. 3: *Milkhome* (Tel Aviv: Urly, 1970), 18.

12. Weichert, *Zikhroynes*, 3:22–23.

13. Bauer, *American Jewry and the Holocaust*, 68.

shrapnel brought death and destruction to Jewish life and property. Just going out into the street put your life at danger. Each day brought new dead, new homeless, masses of people whose homes had burned down; some managed to survive, but they lost everything but the clothes on their body.

Under such circumstances it was difficult to organize an appropriate relief action for the tens of thousands of homeless. Those unfortunate from the first and second categories, who had no relatives in Warsaw, crowded in the dirty, stifling cellars, courtyards and staircases, often holding their tiny, sick children in their arms. First it was necessary to find a roof over their heads and some cooked food for them, but there was no one to whom they could turn; there was not a single representative of a Jewish social organization willing to risk his life in order to organize the necessary help.

The Joint [AJJDC]-Central in Poland was the first to do this. On September 14, the very day when terrible bombings took place in Warsaw, when dozens of homes on Nalewki, Gęsia, Franciszkańska, and other Jewish streets were destroyed and approximately 200 Jews were killed, on this very day the Coordinating Commission was formed. It was established on the initiative of the Joint Central Office, in the local office of the Joint on Jasna 11 (in Warsaw), with the money of the Joint and with the assistance of the Joint directors. The Coordinating Commission was created from a range of Jewish help organizations which the Joint had until then subsidized, e.g., CENTOS, TOZ, Tze-ka-be, the Help Committee for German Refugees, and others.[14] This commission immediately opened soup kitchens for the refugees, relief stations and overnight shelters in synagogues, prayer houses, school buildings and in other public buildings in various locations. [. . .]

The Joint was able to launch a much more generous aid campaign only in October, when the military operations ceased and, as a result of forced expatriations, the second wave of Jewish homeless started to flow.

The Ten Commandments of the Relief Action

From then on, the relief action began to embrace the following areas:

---

14. For **CENTOS** and **TOZ**, see the relevant glossary entries. Tze-ka-be (or CEKABE, the Central Organization of Societies for the Support of Noninterest Credit and Promotion of Productive Work) was a network of Jewish free-loan societies in Poland established in 1926, with a goal of supporting Jewish small businesses (despite its banner calling for "productivization"). The AJJDC initially provided most funds, but local Jewish contributions proved significant as well. The Joint nevertheless continued to control the organization; Isaac Giterman served as its managing director. See Joseph Marcus, *Social and Political History of the Jews in Poland, 1919–1939* (Berlin: Mouton, 1983).

Food for the hungry

Providing shelter for the homeless

Clothing

Fight against epidemics and other illnesses

Children's protection

Aid for the Jewish intelligentsia, clergy, artisans, and the working class

Constructive aid, individual aid, legal aid

Emigration

Contacts with relatives abroad

Organizing self-help action among Polish Jews.

Actions in all these fields were carried out in Warsaw and in the provinces simultaneously.

In addition to its relief efforts, the AJJDC commissioned, in early 1940, a professional photographer by the name of Baum to document the organization's work. The photograph in document 6–2 is from that collection.

DOCUMENT 6–2: **At the Warsaw office of the AJJDC, April 1940, USHMMPA WS# 48208.**

Efforts to coordinate relief work in Poland were hindered by the rapid changes brought about by the war and by the absence of a preexisting organizational infrastructure and effective leadership, beyond the AJJDC, capable of meeting all the challenges that had cropped up. Writing in the Warsaw ghetto later in the war, Emanuel Ringelblum summarized the efforts he and others had undertaken to organize social welfare in these early weeks and months. The study, titled "The History of Social Aid in Warsaw during the War" and included in the **Oyneg Shabes** archive, suggested that "to judge the wartime social aid fairly, one must bear in mind the nature of social aid before the war. Apart from providing for the suffering and health care, which were based on modern European foundations, there was no social aid in any other area." Any philanthropic societies that did exist "were only loosely rooted in Jewish life, [and] their economic basis was weak. [. . .] When the world war broke out, all these societies disintegrated, though some had behind them decades of philanthropic work." Ringelblum argued that the Warsaw Jewish Community had almost no efficient social aid department to speak of at the outbreak of the war, only one that worked according to "obsolete and outlived methods" and communal organizations that the Jewish public felt largely neglected the needs of the four hundred thousand people remaining in the city. Furthermore, Ringelblum lamented "the departure of, or—as some would say—the desertion by, those who had been active in social work at the time the war broke out." Entire offices of social institutions "suddenly became empty." The AJJDC Warsaw office—partly by default and partly as a result of its activists' determination—came to fill this void during the first weeks of the war.[15]

In mid-1940 Morris Troper, chairman of the European Executive Council of the AJJDC, lauded the Joint's prewar work in establishing an efficient relief apparatus, one that proved vital to the successful functioning of the Polish office and its ability to deliver aid at the beginning of the war.

DOCUMENT 6–3: **Morris Troper, "On the European Relief Front,"** *Contemporary Jewish Record* **3 (May–June 1940), 233–35.**

One of the immediate effects of the German invasion of Poland was the complete isolation of that country from the rest of the world. For many

---

15. Emanuel Ringelblum, "The History of Social Aid in Warsaw during the War," in *To Live with Honor and Die with Honor! Selected Documents from the Warsaw Ghetto Underground Archives "O.S." (Oneg Shabbath)*, ed. Joseph Kermish (Jerusalem: Yad Vashem, 1986), 338–40 (original in Yiddish).

weeks and months no word could be gotten into or out of Poland. Our office made repeated efforts, through diplomatic channels and otherwise, to reach its representatives in Warsaw. Nothing helped, and for a long time we were in the position of not knowing whether our office still existed, whether our representatives were alive or dead, or whether any relief activity was being carried on.

The first news concerning Poland which reached us dealt with the refugees from the war zones who had fled to the contiguous countries—Lithuania, Hungary, [Romania . . .]

As the status of Wilno[16] cleared up, we were able for the first time to gain authentic information of just what our Warsaw office was doing. We learned to our amazement and deep satisfaction that it had operated uninterruptedly from the beginning of the war. During the month-long bombardment of Poland's capital, our workers had heroically carried on. They had been able to use the funds which we had sent in at the last minute and had, on their own initiative, utilized the free funds of all of our affiliated institutions. The skeleton structures of the TOZ (central Jewish medical aid society) and CENTOS (central Jewish child-care agency) had been retained. Working under our supervision, these agencies had carried on relief programs. While no other Jewish organization in Warsaw was functioning, it was discovered that our office had, nevertheless, succeeded in maintaining unbroken activity.

Numerous eyewitnesses to the fall of Warsaw came to our offices in Wilno, in Paris and in Amsterdam, overflowing with praise and gratitude for the work of the J.D.C. [AJJDC] in Poland. Differing reports were received as to just how extensive this activity was. At one time we heard that the J.D.C. was supplying 20,000 meals a day in Warsaw. Later, there came to us the figure of 50,000, and still later 100,000. It was not until late in February, however, that we were able to learn the full story.

One thing, however, had by now become clear. This was the tremendous importance of the work that had been done by the J.D.C. over a period of more than two decades in Poland. Particularly valuable were the agencies which had been set up to deal with local problems. During the long years after the first World War when the J.D.C. founded and nurtured these self-help organizations and gradually built them up almost to independent status, there was no inkling that these very agencies would be the only ones in a position to render first aid to Polish Jews when

---

16. Here Troper uses the Polish spelling for Vilna.

the second holocaust[17] struck. The CENTOS, the TOZ, the Gemiloth Hasodim Kassas (free loan societies), the Nurses' Training School of Warsaw—these were the institutions which were able to adjust their activities to a war-time tempo on September 1, 1939, when the Warsaw office sounded a call to action. Were it not for the J.D.C. policy, which had always insisted that its affiliated agencies in whatever country be local organizations, locally staffed and supervised, we might well have been in the position of other foreign relief agencies when Poland was overrun by German troops. Only the fact that our functional units were firmly rooted in Polish soil made it possible for the J.D.C. to continue its operations without interruption at a time when every other foreign body was helpless.

Troper pointed to the importance of the grassroots nature of prewar AJJDC relief work. According to him, only such a decentralized network, firmly rooted in local customs and social relations, could withstand the rupture caused by the Nazi occupation. In a seemingly contradictory vein, Emanuel Ringelblum decried the prewar absence of Jewish social organizations rooted in Jewish life; he did, however, stress the success of AJJDC's prewar organization. It is important to note that both Troper and Ringelblum committed their observations to paper at least several months after the turbulent days of September 1939. By that time, the new relief effort taking shape through the activities of the KK seemed to make the most sense, even though each author accounted for its evolution with reference to a different historical narrative. Troper identified its roots in the prewar AJJDC structure, while Ringelblum lamented the absence of any comparable organization before the war and emphasized its radically new nature in the new circumstances.

This new shape of relief became known by its Yiddish name: **Aleynhilf** (self-help). The dissolution of the prewar, traditional Jewish social aid infrastructure—exemplified by the flight of most of its leaders—mandated a new approach. Jewish leaders who decided to stay in Warsaw were dedicated to doing as much as they could under the new circumstances. But they would no

---

17. It is unclear which historical event, according to Troper, would have constituted the "first" Holocaust. Long before the term became the standard word in English to refer to the Nazi genocide against the Jews of Europe, various authors had employed it to describe historical calamities of various kinds, including acts of mass violence against the Jews. Since the end of World War II, the meaning of the word has been transformed so that today, in its capitalized form, it exclusively refers to the Nazi genocide. For the etymology and history of use of the word "Holocaust," see Israel Charny, "'Holocaust': The Word and Its Usage," in *Encyclopedia of Genocide*, ed. Israel Charny (Santa Barbara: ABC-CLIO, 1999), 1:40–43.

longer provide aid through the top-down, centralized networks that relied on formal and well-defined hierarchies of traditional employees, networks that had unraveled under the German onslaught. Rather, changed circumstances now forced them to embed their work in the surrounding Jewish society and rely on informal Jewish social institutions. One such new institution was a series of "house committees," ad hoc panels of building residents in Warsaw's Jewish neighborhoods. Because all public order had collapsed under the invasion, these spontaneous, informal bodies sought to restore normalcy to at least one dimension of daily life by creating and relying on informal networks for provisioning and aid. Ringelblum quickly seized the potential of this new development and organized this motley network into what, by 1940, had become the nerve center of Aleynhilf. From opening soup kitchens and organizing cultural activities to providing cover for illegal Jewish schools, the Aleynhilf network, coordinated by the "public sector" that Ringelblum led, created an alternative Jewish society characterized by demographic, economic, cultural, and political diversity.[18] In addition to providing aid, however, this new form of social organization also sought to endow Warsaw Jews with a sense of Jewish pride. Ringelblum and other Aleynhilf leaders insisted on Yiddish as the language of self-help, in contrast to Polish, the language of the Warsaw *Judenrat*. With all the obvious and all-too-painful limitations, Aleynhilf provided people with a sense of empowerment. They were finding creative ways to fend for themselves, even under the toughest of circumstances. Because of the density of the Jewish population and the concentration of able leaders, Aleynhilf remained a mainly Warsaw phenomenon. The AJJDC funded the network at least initially; other means of funding included loans provided by wealthy Jews against promises of repayment after the war and local fund-raising, especially through the network of house committees, albeit with predictably poor returns.[19]

Not everyone in Warsaw applauded AJJDC efforts, however. Dissenting voices pointed to the Joint's heavy-handedness and insisted that Aleynhilf efforts had different aims from those of the AJJDC. In his diary entry for March 14, 1941, **Chaim Kaplan**, leader of one of the house committees, noted,

> As long as the Joint had the means, we continued to lay our burden on our rich uncle that he should support us . . . It was our luck that the Joint was reduced to ruins and ended its assistance. When we saw that your problems grew, we had to say, 'If I am not for myself, who will be for

---

18. Bauer, *American Jewry and the Holocaust*, 80; see also Kassow, *Who Will Write Our History*, 112–28.

19. Kassow, *Who Will Write Our History*, 113–14.

me?' and the Jewish Self-Help Society (Aleynhilf) was created. In a short period of time, it became an organization with many branches and affiliates. It had a budget of a quarter million—besides sums which flowed in through other channels, especially through the house committees. The Aleynhilf offered equitable support for those in need. It can be said at this time that in you, the Jews in Poland, has been fulfilled their mission to the greatest heights . . . half a million złotys in assistance to the needy within one month—who had dared even imagine that the Jews of Warsaw were capable of such giving? The Aleynhilf will certainly find a historian of documents and statistics who will tell generations to come of its scope, greatness and educational worth.[20]

Tensions arose in many quarters around relief work within and outside Poland. Indeed, furnishing aid to beleaguered Jews in Warsaw and other occupied Polish cities was a field with many players. Warsaw's new *Judenrat* ran its own relief efforts, and there were often tensions between this official body and the unofficial network of Aleynhilf. The head of the *Judenrat*, **Adam Czerniaków**, harbored deep suspicions about Aleynhilf leaders.[21] In addition, another member of the original KK, Michał Weichert, established a new organization, **Jewish Social Self-Help** (Jüdische Soziale Selbsthilfe, or JSS), which had a mandate to operate in the **Generalgouvernement** under **Hans Frank**; consequently, Weichert soon moved the seat of his organization to Frank's "capital," Kraków. The JSS was funded and given legal cover by the AJJDC, which was technically an American organization that the Nazis tolerated and recognized because the United States remained neutral at that time. However, by early 1940, Frank's civilian authorities had effectively subsumed the JSS.[22]

Aleynhilf and JSS were two distinct organizations based on different rationales. The former sought to build an independent infrastructure rooted in Jewish society, while the latter tried to organize a more conventional network, cooperating with the Nazi authorities. Regardless of the different paths they took, both organizations chose to incorporate "self-help" into their name, insisting that they were Jewish organizations dedicated to helping Jews under the ever-deteriorating circumstances of the occupation. It is also worth noting that both Aleynhilf and the JSS emerged from the original coordinating

---

20. Quoted in Kassow, *Who Will Write Our History*, 425n88. Originally quoted in Israel Gutman, "Kiddush Hashem and Kiddush Hachayim," in *Simon Wiesenthal Center Annual* 1 (1984): 85.

21. Kassow, *Who Will Write Our History*, 111.

22. Bauer, *American Jewry and the Holocaust*, 85.

body of Jewish relief organizations (KK) and that both were supported by the AJJDC, even though, as JSS came under strict Nazi control and the United States entered the war, relations between the JSS and AJJDC cooled.

Outside Poland, the AJJDC found itself at odds with the **World Jewish Congress** (WJC). Whereas the AJJDC held an established position within the network of American Jewish relief organizations and was perceived as the face of American Jewish relief by many Jews in Poland, the WJC was a relative newcomer on the scene. Established in Geneva in 1936, the WJC owed its existence to the idea of creating a worldwide Jewish body to safeguard Jewish minority rights, which had been embraced by ad hoc Jewish committees during World War I, at the Versailles Peace Conference in 1919, and within the framework of the **League of Nations**.[23] Over the course of the 1930s, the incursion of antisemitism into official state policy—in Germany, Romania, Poland, and Hungary—rendered more resonant the call for a permanent, transnational political representation. Yet, at the same time, Jews in many countries worried that such a body would undermine their standing within their respective societies and further boost the antisemitic obsession with the myth of a "world Jewish conspiracy."[24] In fact, the WJC had much in common with the similarly oriented **Jewish Agency** (JA), and many WJC activists, on both the local and international levels, were also Zionist activists. Dr. **Nahum Goldmann**, who since 1934 had represented the JA before the League of Nations, was active in setting the policy of the WJC. He headed the political office of the WJC in Paris, was responsible for its office of judicial affairs, and represented the WJC before the League of Nations in Geneva. Both the JA and the WJC offices were housed at Wilson Palace in Geneva, not far from League headquarters. Goldmann and his secretary, **Gerhart Riegner**, thus found themselves at close quarters with **Richard Lichtheim**, representative of the Jewish Agency, and **Abraham Silberschein**, a Zionist leader from Poland who had decided to remain in Geneva at the end of the **Twenty-First Zionist Congress** and who founded and headed **RELICO**, another Jewish relief organization.[25]

23. See Carole Fink, *Defending the Rights of Others: The Great Powers, the Jews, and International Minority Protection, 1878–1938* (New York: Cambridge University Press, 2004). For an early postwar assessment of the WJC's work and its limitations, see Institute of Jewish Affairs, *Unity in Dispersion*.

24. Raya Cohen, *"Ben sham le-khan": sipurim shel edim la-hurban, Shvaits 1939–1942* (Tel Aviv: Universiṭat Tel Aviv and Am oved, 1999), 127. For a general overview of interwar Jewish history in eastern Europe, see Ezra Mendelsohn, *The Jews of East Central Europe between the World Wars* (Bloomington: Indiana University Press, 1987).

25. Cohen, *"Ben sham le-khan,"* 128.

At the outset of the war, the WJC saw itself solely as a political organization gearing up to fight for Jewish interests at a future peace conference. However, with the realities of occupation, it quickly became involved in the business of relief, much to the chagrin of AJJDC leaders. After all, President Franklin Delano Roosevelt's declaration of neutrality on September 5 complicated the efforts of the AJJDC, for the organization now had to strive even harder to avoid engaging in any relief work that might be construed as providing aid to belligerent countries. When the WJC sought to unite political and relief efforts among the United States, Palestine, and Jewish communities worldwide, the AJJDC feared that the WJC, as a political organization, would thwart the AJJDC's efforts to maintain neutrality and remain apolitical. Such divisions in New York hampered relief efforts.[26] Even in the first month of the war, it became apparent that all of the agencies involved in Jewish relief—the WJC, AJJDC, JA, HICEM, HIAS, and others—not only struggled to remain viable as individual organizations but were in fact ill-equipped to work together. Efforts to marshal some sort of unified relief initiative fell apart in the face of territoriality, squabbling, and competition for limited relief funds. Furthermore, the aggressive, yet highly fluid Nazi policies in the newly occupied areas made unified action a highly attractive goal, if one difficult to achieve.

In October 1939, Silberschein worked together with Goldmann and Riegner from the Jewish Agency to provide an account of what was happening in Poland and to organize relief for Polish Jews. Silberschein summarized relief efforts in the first month of the war in a letter to Rabbi **Stephen S. Wise**, president of the American Jewish Congress. Silberschein stressed the importance of cooperation and the sharing of information among the Jewish relief organizations. Yet, he also sharply criticized the AJJDC's work, which he described in rather different terms from Troper's summary in document 6–3.

DOCUMENT 6–4: **Excerpts from a letter by Dr. Abraham Silberschein, WJC Committee for Polish Relief, Geneva, Switzerland, to Stephen S. Wise, October 11, 1939, American Jewish Archives, WJC records, series A, box A2, file 2,** *Day Book of the WJC I,* **26–28.**

Dear Dr. Wise:

Despite the necessity for relief action as early as the second week of the war, the appropriate organizations such as the Joint, HICEM, and the others, not only undertook nothing but apparently did not even begin to deal with the question [of] how to provide relief. We were the first and for a time the

---

26. Bauer, *American Jewry and the Holocaust,* 37.

only ones who not only were concerned with the question but attempted to do something concrete, and prepared a plan of work, so far as it went, for the establishment of a bureau, for this task for the setting up of committees in the countries concerned, and we began the work without delay.

Only after the lapse of some time did certain organizations, such as OSE, HICEM and then the Joint report regarding their work on behalf of refugees. We were able to determine that at the time of those reports the statements issued were at least very much exaggerated, since they had little to do with work actually conducted. These circumstances have been the chief motive in all our negotiations. We undertook these at a time that was appropriate and favorable and, moreover, at a time when we were in the midst of the work, whereas the others had scarcely begun. This applies to the Joint as well.

The great catastrophe which has overwhelmed the Jewish population of Poland and has destroyed a community of 3 1/2 millions in the course of two weeks has confronted all the relief organizations with tasks to which they are not equal and for which they are in no way prepared. The problem is not only to provide thousands and thousands of refugees with help, clothing, food, and housing, but also to give them legal aid, as, for example, to arrange for their sojourn in foreign countries. Even more important was the work of searching for members of families who disappeared, to enable refugees to communicate with those who stayed behind, to establish contact with relatives abroad, to transfer money held by refugees abroad, and also to arrange for emigration. Not the least of the necessary tasks was to gather documentation which would orientate us in formulating our attitude to the new political problems, and to serve as a basis for relevant demands regarding the safeguarding of Jewish rights during peace negotiations.

It is clear that no Jewish organization alone was and is in a position to fulfill these varied tasks. Yet, on the other hand, it is clear that all aspects of relief overlap, and that it is hardly possible to provide for individual fields of relief by special organizations working independently of one another.

A great concentration of all energies within Jewry for this activity is likewise absolutely necessary for the representation of the interests of Jews affected by the war. We can obviously gain much more if we appear before the international Red Cross, for example, as a unity than if the Red Cross receives requests from various Jewish organizations at the same time.

To meet these tasks also requires large sums of money, even if many of those tasks cannot be handled by expenditures of money.

With these considerations in mind we strove for the unification of relief work involving all organizations. The idea was not to relieve the organizations from any activities but to have an appropriate division of labor so that the organizations will be responsible for those tasks with which they have been dealing hitherto, while all the activities shall be carried out as an organized whole. This seemed important to us not only because of the momentary situation, but as a possible beginning for the establishment of a permanent Jewish relief agency, provided we could win the individual organizations over to the idea.

In order to make the establishment of such an organization possible, we decided to carry on our work as a committee set up by the World Jewish Congress. In this way we expect to build the framework for the federation of all organizations and to give them an opportunity to send their representatives to the committee in order to exercise control over the work.

COORDINATING MORE EFFICIENT RELIEF

Each organization was convinced of its superior qualities, yet needed to look realistically at the circumstances in which it was operating to be effective in helping the Jewish population in Poland. The force of the German assault thus provided the greatest motor to overcoming old animosities. At the same time it constituted the greatest obstacles, throwing up immense practical roadblocks for an interorganizational rapprochement. One month after his letter to Wise, Silberschein summarized the efforts of the WJC in a letter to the AJJDC director in Europe, Morris Troper. He recognized how crucial it was, under the circumstances of boundless problems and limited resources, to cooperate with the AJJDC or any other relief institution operating in good faith.

DOCUMENT 6–5: **Letter from Dr. Abraham Silberschein, WJC Geneva, to Morris Troper, director of AJJDC work in Europe, November 9, 1939, American Jewish Archives, WJC records, series A, box A2, file 2, *Day Book of the WJC II*, 23–26.**

Dear Mr. Troper:
    In our conversations on the 5th and 6th of the present month I explained to you in detail the extensive and varied field of work included, in my opinion, in the relief activity for Polish Jews, and came to the conclusion that no single Jewish organization, including the J.D.C. [AJJDC], existed which would be in a position to undertake alone the fulfillment

of all tasks. At the same time I pointed out that even if the individual branches of the work are so different, despite their diversity they overlap so that they all belong to one field and constitute an organic whole.

If the work is to be achieved with a minimum expenditure for administrative costs, and, what is more important, with the proper results, it must be carried out by the joint efforts of all interested bodies in accordance with uniform methods. It is likewise of no small importance to prevent the individual smaller or larger organizations from duplicating one another and consequently injuring fund raising efforts and lowering the prestige of all Jewish organizations in the eyes of the Jewish and non-Jewish public, for this would present a deplorable picture of our disunity. It is clear that there are difficulties blocking the collaboration of the organizations concerned, some of a psychological character, others of a more material nature, none of which, however, are insuperable.

As was to be expected, Mr. Director, you pointed out the difficulties in the way of cooperation between the J.D.C. and the W.J.C. as a political organization. I thereupon explained to you that the W.J.C., which is above all concerned to have the work done properly and completely, had foreseen this obstacle and had therefore done its work through a committee which works under the W.J.C. This committee consists only of three persons and has been so limited in order not to hinder cooperation with other organizations through too large a group. This committee calls itself "Committee of the World Jewish Congress" only for the present, since the W.J.C. has placed at the disposal of this activity not only its office and staff, but also its financial resources insofar as has been possible, and above all its connections. From the very outset, however, the Committee declared that it wished to establish only the framework for the cooperation of all Jewish organizations, and I am convinced that the W.J.C. will agree to the adoption of a new name when cooperation is established.

I propose the following name: "Joint Committee for the Relief of the War-Stricken Jewish Population of Poland."[27] I can assure you that if you wish to call it by another name that will be no obstacle to cooperation.

---

27. The organization that grew out of the provisional "Committee of the World Jewish Congress"—taking shape at the very time of Silberschein's writing—eventually became known, similar to Silberschein's suggestion in the letter, as the Relief Committee for the War-Stricken Jewish Population (RELICO; see Glossary). It is not clear who the other two members of the initial Committee of the World Jewish Congress were, but it is likely that Gerhart Riegner was one of them. See Bronia Klibanski, "Relief Committee for the War-Stricken Jewish Population," in *Encyclopedia of the Holocaust*, ed. Israel Gutman (New York: Macmillan, 1990), 3:1254–55.

As the result of our conferences, I am to submit to you proposals of an alternative nature which you may transmit to New York in the hope of procuring a decision as soon as possible. I am, therefore, submitting the following proposals:

1. The organizations concerned, particularly the J.D.C. and the Committee of the World Jewish Congress, establish a joint committee for the purpose of comprehensive aid for the war-stricken Jewish population, in which committee all other interested Jewish organizations, such as I.C.A., HICEM, etc., shall be admitted. The committee's seat shall be in Geneva, for reasons which require no explanation, since it is the most suitable place in the neutral countries.

2. This committee shall concern itself exclusively with relief problems for the war-stricken Jewish population. Beyond this, the activities of the individual organizations remain untouched.

3. Within the committee the separate tasks shall be so distributed that the cooperating organizations shall continue to handle independently those fields with which they have concerned themselves hitherto. The arrangement above is to apply to new activities. Thus, for example, emigration is to be handled by HICEM, aid in the form of clothing, food and other social service by the Joint Distribution Committee, legal advice and representations by the World Jewish Congress, etc. [. . .]

In accordance with your wish, I have avoided going into details and have presented my proposals in broad outline. I believe that the general idea is clear to you, and that the two alternatives have taken into consideration the things you have told me. I wish, finally, to repeat what I have stated to you orally. The Joint Distribution Committee will earn a historical reward in Jewry if the collaboration of all the great political organizations should take place under its leadership, even if only within a limited degree.

Very truly yours,
A. SILBERSCHEIN
(Signed)

This initiative came to very little. Throughout the war, the AJJDC and WJC remained, according to Bauer, "enemies"; "the word is not too strong,"

Bauer insists.[28] The overlap in the work of these two organizations proved an insurmountable obstacle, and for the entire duration of the war, they never cooperated in a serious way.[29]

Polish Jews nonetheless did get some help. One of the organizations that managed to overcome seemingly insurmountable problems, bypass internal quarrels, and reach people on the ground across and beyond Poland was Abraham Silberschein's RELICO. Based in Geneva, it set up branches in the Baltic states, Czechoslovakia, Hungary, and Romania to provide assistance for the thousands of Jewish refugees from Poland.[30] In Poland, RELICO first focused on locating scattered Jewish families by working with the International Committee of the Red Cross (ICRC). Silberschein's committee also organized shipments of food and medical supplies despite criticism from those in the United States and England who insisted on upholding the blockade of goods to Germany.[31]

Silberschein had established RELICO as an independent agency, although it was run de facto as part of the Geneva WJC office. As we have seen in his letter to Troper, this arrangement enabled Silberschein to claim that RELICO was not involved in the WJC's political efforts and to operate in the German-occupied lands more easily. Thousands of inquiries directed to RELICO in the first year of the war attest to the expectation held by many Jews inside and outside of Europe that this organization could help them find missing or incarcerated family members and war refugees and secure their release where necessary.[32]

---

28. Bauer, *American Jewry and the Holocaust*, 184.

29. By contrast, relations between the Joint and the Jewish Agency for Palestine would prove decidedly more positive. Throughout the war, the AJJDC was able to maintain its predominant position in the field of overseas work, although the JA would also become increasingly involved in rescue and relief efforts as the war progressed.

30. Institute of Jewish Affairs, *Unity in Dispersion*, 197–201.

31. Cohen, *"Ben sham le-khan,"* 156.

32. Cohen, *"Ben sham le-khan,"* 156–57. RELICO was successful in connecting over ten thousand family members who had lost contact with one another. See Cohen, *"Ben sham le-khan,"* 158.

DOCUMENT 6–6: Letter from Käthe Knöpfmacher,[33] WJC, Geneva office, to Lillie
Schultz, American Jewish Congress, New York City, December 8, 1939, USHMMA RG
68.059M (WJC London), reel 146, folder 1515.

Dear Miss Schultz,

I am very glad to inform you that we have find out [*sic*] the whereabouts of Mr. Chaim Liberman, Bialystok. We have cabled you yesterday: "Congress New York—Inform Biagyer Washington received cable
Bialystok quote everybody safe Chaim Liberman unquote—'Worldcon.'"

This was an enquiry from Mr. Biagyer, Maurice: 1003 K Street N.W.
Washington D.C., to whom I am writing as for the enclosed copy.

We have tried for the first time, with return answer paid, to cable to
Mr. Lieberman in Bialystok (territory occupied by the Russians) as well
as to the other addresses given by Mr. Biagyer in Warsaw and Bedzin.
So far we have had no cable reply of the cities in the German occupied
territories.

You will understand that we cannot cable to every person of the thousands enquiries which are arriving in this office. But I would like to make
a suggestion: the cost of a cablegram to Russian occupied territory (with
answer paid) is amounting to 4,50 $. A night letter to the USA is about
3 $. You could ask the people who wish to have located their relatives
in the most quickest way to pay together with their enquiry these cable
charges = 7 1/2 – 10 $. Payments could be made to your office, and when
you are telling that we shall cable, we will do it, waiting for your gathered
remittans at the end of every month.

Please let me have [an] answer as soon as possible.

Will you be good enough to try to find out a relative of a polish refugee Mr. David May of Chrzanow (Poland) now in Bacou, c/o Smilovici,
str. General Averecu 5. Mr. David May does not know the address of his
relative whose first name is probably Lazar. But he assures that this Mr.

---

33. This document's grammatical inconsistencies reflect the original letter. A cofounder
of the WJC, Käthe Knöpfmacher (Kate Knopfmacher; 1890–1965) worked for the WJC in
Paris and Geneva, emigrating to Mexico after the outbreak of war. She continued working
for the WJC for the remainder of the war in Central America and New York and was married to another WJC official, the economist Ernst Knöpfmacher. See Henry Friedlander and
Sybil Milton eds., *Archives of the Holocaust: An International Collection of Selected Documents*
(New York, Garland Publishing, 1990), 8:xvi. Lillie Schultz (or Schulz; ?–1981) had ties to
the American Jewish Congress in New York and the journal *The Nation*. See obituary, *New
York Times*, April 16, 1981.

Lazar May is a very rich industrialist who will certainly be anxious to help him. We would be very much obliged to you if you would try to find out this man in the USA. I am sorry that I cannot give you more exact data.

With kindest regards

Sincerely Yours

K. Knöpfmacher

Jewish relief organizations also concerned themselves with the wider ramifications of the war in Poland, particularly with the new populations of Jewish refugees who had fled the war zone and were in need of permanent asylum. Outside of Poland, RELICO provided relief through its Lithuanian committee for thousands of Jews in Vilna, locals as well as refugees, thus complementing the work of the AJJDC and JA. The organization also supported penniless Jewish refugees in southeastern Europe as much as limited resources allowed.

DOCUMENT 6–7: RELICO report about the Vilna committee's organizational efforts to assist Polish Jewish refugees in Lithuania, Romania, and Hungary, February 25, 1940, USHMMA RG 68.059M (WJC London), reel 142, folder 1477.

POLISH JEWISH REFUGEE FUND

The position of the Refugees and War Victims in Lithuania, Roumania [sic], Hungary and their present needs.

LITHUANIA

The total number of Jewish refugees [. . .] Lithuania is 14,000, out of which 11,000 are registered with the Refugees Committee in Wilna and 3,000 are registered with the "Ezra" Committee in Kaunas.[34]

The work of the Wilna Committee comprises of:

a. Feeding section in charge of 50 feeding centres where the refugees are receiving their daily meals;

b. Clothing section for distribution of clothing as well as their repairs;

c. Lodging section whose object is to find the necessary accommodation in hostels and private houses;

d. Legal Section dealing with 50–60 cases daily;

e. Child's care section.

---

34. The Ezra aid committee was a local organization in Kovno that worked specifically to provide aid to refugees from Suwalki. See Bauer, *American Jewry and the Holocaust*, 112.

The cost of feeding a refugee per day is about 80 cents.

Whereas there is sufficient food to be obtained in the country there is a great shortage of clothing and underwear. The Wilna Relief Committee so far managed to satisfy the clothing needs of the refugees to the extent of 10 to 15 percent.

The Committee was even obliged to make a loan of the Jewish Burial society of [. . .] pieces of linen destined to be used for shrouds for the dead to make up some shorts for the refugees.

As to the bedding shortage statistics have shown that 20 pillows were used by 270 refugees. Similar shortages also applied to beds. Refugees therefore have to sleep in shifts utilizing the day for their "nights rest." In order to save accommodation the Refugees, particularly the younger ones, are sleeping in double bunks. These bunks as well as other pieces of furniture are being made up by the Refugees themselves. Workshops are attached to some of the hostels carrying out all kinds of carpentry, tailoring, shoe repairing, etc.

The Joint Distribution Committee, who hitherto practically covered the whole of the budget of the Wilna Refugee Committee (50,000 dollars per month) has owing to lack of funds now considerably curtailed its allocations.

In addition to the Refugee Committee in Wilna there is also the Jewish District Committee [LEOPO?] dealing with the Refugees in the Wilna district covering an area of 22 points.

The "Ezra" Committee in Kaunas is dealing with 3,000 Refugees in 14 border points. The American Joint Distribution Committee is contributing only 20% of its budget. This Committee is making a splendid effort to raise funds locally and to collect bedding and old cast-off clothing. They have their own tailoring workshops employing 16 tailors for the repair of Garments.

The Committees through which we are operating are calling upon us to share their monthly budget. But in addition we are also called to help:

1. The Palestine Committee for Jewish Refugees in Lithuania.

Whose object is to arrange the emigration of refugees to Palestine. These refugees can only leave if their passages are obtained by the way of foreign currency brought in from abroad, otherwise they cannot leave the country.

2. The Youth Aliyah (immigration of Jewish Boys and Girls to Palestine).

There are about 300 of them (age 12–17), who are living in the most abnormal conditions. It is essential to remove them to better accommodations to continue their preparatory course for Palestine. 35 of them will shortly be leaving for Palestine and must be provided with passages.

3. <u>Hebrew and English Courses.</u> These courses are organized by the Tarbut organization[35] and must be supported as they are of paramount importance to all these prospective emigrants to Palestine or to English speaking countries.

4. <u>Yeshiboth.</u>[36] The 2,500 Yeshiboth pupils. These Yeshiboth have now reestablished themselves. They must receive adequate support for their maintenance.

<u>30,000 WAR VICTIMS</u>

In addition to the Refugees there are 30,000 Jews in Wilna i.e. 50% of the Jewish population, as well as 20,000 in the province, who have lost every livelihood on account of the denationalization of the Wilna district. They are obliged to be economically assisted by the Relief Organisation. [. . .]

<u>Roumania</u>

In Roumania there are now 1500 Jewish Refugees from Poland. Our Hon. Treasurer Dr. Zeitlyn[37] who has visited the Refugees there was instrumental in organizing a representative body known as the Central Refugee Committee. The budget of this Committee compiled in November last for six months ahead was 35,941,000 Lei. This Committee, which is also dealing with the problem of the emigration of the Refugees to Palestine has received from us 1,500,000 Lei. The Committee will secure funds for the maintenance of the Refugees from other sources, but we must have 4,000,000 Lei immediately for emigration purposes.

<u>Hungary.</u>

The number of refugees in Budapest is 2,500. A Committee was formed there as a result of Dr. Zeitlyn's visit. The main requirements are adequate funds for emigration purposes.

---

35. For more on **Tarbut**, see the Glossary.
36. A yeshiva (pl. yeshivot) is a Jewish religious secondary-level school.
37. The authors have been unable to find information about this man.

The refugees who had managed to reach Lithuania, Romania, or Hungary sought to continue their journey out of Europe. Many were determined to reach the *Yishuv* despite the British disinclination to admit more Jewish settlers in the wake of the May 1939 **White Paper**, with its restrictive rules on immigration and the purchase of land. A total of forty-five hundred legal and thirty-eight hundred illegal immigrants reached Palestine in 1940. At the end of that year, the British clamped down on such illegal immigration and reduced it to a trickle, albeit without managing to stop it completely.[38]

The *Yishuv* leadership felt pressed between the needs of refugees and the demands of British authorities. The *Yishuv* leadership was thus confronted with a difficult choice. They could further pursue Jewish immigration to Palestine (and possibly even loosen the requirements for the new immigrants' Zionist commitment in order to rescue as many people as possible); this option would inevitably alienate the British. Alternatively, the leaders could opt to limit immigration and support Britain loyally in the war in the hope of being rewarded with Jewish political sovereignty in Palestine afterward. The recent White Paper, which seemed to renege on the "national home" promised in the Balfour Declaration, gave a pessimistic cast to this latter choice. In the early days of the war, David Ben-Gurion, chairman of the JA Executive, gave what became the guiding formulation of the Zionist position toward Britain and the issue of Jewish immigration, or *aliyah*: "We must aid the [British] army as if there were no White Paper, and fight the White Paper as if there were no war."[39] Translating Ben-Gurion's dictum into policy, the Mossad l'Aliyah Bet, the JA's illegal immigration arm, intensified its operations in the first months of the war. By February 1940, however, as historian Dalia Ofer has suggested, it appears that those among the *Yishuv* leadership who favored a more constructive policy toward Britain prevailed. Thereafter, the JA suspended its support for illegal immigration.[40]

Still, the attention of the *Yishuv* was focused more on its own situation than on what was happening to the Jews in German-dominated Europe. The *Yishuv*, as Dina Porat has put it, "was engaged in its own urgent problems."[41]

---

38. Porat, *The Blue and Yellow Stars of David*, 9–16.

39. Ben-Gurion on September 12, 1939, quoted in Ofer, *Escaping the Holocaust*, 23. David Ben-Gurion (1886–1973) was a Polish-born Zionist who emigrated to Palestine in 1906. He became a labor leader and served as head of the Jewish Agency (see glossary) from 1935 until 1948. In 1948, he became Israel's first prime minister and minister of defense. See Tuvia Friling, *Arrows in the Dark: David Ben-Gurion, the Yishuv Leadership, and Rescue Attempts during the Holocaust* (Madison: University of Wisconsin Press, 2005).

40. Ofer, *Escaping the Holocaust*, 28.

41. Porat, *The Blue and Yellow Stars of David*, 16.

This situation was exacerbated by the break in lines of communication between the JA executive in Palestine and the occupied Polish territories, with their persecuted Jewish populations. Losing touch with Polish Jews meant that a key source of information about the unfolding emergency was lost. Nevertheless, at the end of 1939, the JA Executive established the Committee for Polish Jewry.[42] **Chaim Barlas**, head of the JA's immigration department in Geneva, detailed his office's efforts to organize the escape of Jews from Europe.

DOCUMENT 6–8: Activity report of Chaim Barlas and the regional office of the Jewish Agency for Palestine in Geneva, Switzerland, between September 1, 1939, and January 25, 1940, USHMMA RG 68.045M (WJC Geneva), reel 20, file 147 (translated from German).

THE JEWISH AGENCY FOR PALESTINE   Geneva, January 25, 1940
IMMIGRATION DEPARTMENT   P.O. Box, 312 Rue du Stand
(Temporary Office)   TEL 5 12 10
CH. BARLAS
Geneva

To the Executive of the Jewish Agency for Palestine
Jerusalem

I find it appropriate at the end of the activity of the "Temporary Office of the Immigration Department, Jewish Agency for Palestine," of which I have been in charge since the outbreak of the war, to provide you with a comprehensive report on the work that I have led in Geneva.

1. After the closure of the 21st Congress in the last days of the month of August 1939, I decided to remain in Geneva and to take charge of the immigration agendas for Palestine, assuming that it was necessary and that it would be possible to develop such work even in war. The immediate tasks that I envisaged at the time were:
a) a rescue action for approx. 2,900 Olim,[43] who had been approved for certificates for the immigration schedule of April–September 1939 and who were stranded in the countries involved in hostilities with no possibility of leaving and no possibility

---

42. Porat, *The Blue and Yellow Stars of David*, 6–7.
43. *Oleh* (pl. *olim*) is a Zionist Hebrew term for a Jewish immigrant to Palestine (and, later, Israel).

of receiving Palestine visas (as the British consulates had been evacuated).

b) transport for a group of approx. 150 congress participants (delegates, workers, and attendees) who had remained in Switzerland.

c) arranging for the further travel of approx. 550 Olim who, while on the way to Palestine, were sent back after the outbreak of war on the SS "Galilea" from Rhodes to Trieste and Sussak.[44]

[. . .]

5. After the conclusion of the immigration work for the 2,900 Olim, I suggested to the Immigration Department of the Jewish Agency that during the war the work of all existing Palestine Offices in Europe be coordinated by a "Central Office of the Immigration Department of the Jewish Agency" in Geneva. Unfortunately there still has been no decision on this question. I am distributing this report about my activities, however, in the belief that the "Temporary Office" in Geneva has done important work, not only saving 3,000 Jewish Olim for Palestine but serving as a ray of light and encouragement for the Zionist movement in what for the Jewish people is the most difficult period of suffering and destruction.

Sgd. CH. BARLAS

VIII. POLAND—CAMPAIGN

As a result of the catastrophe that has befallen Polish Jewry, the Zionist Organization, the Palestine Office, and all Zionist offices were closed. The reports that have arrived by circuitous means from Warsaw portrayed a gruesome picture of the situation in the occupied territories. Communication with Warsaw has stopped and it was only with difficulty that I was able to make contact with some of the remaining Polish Zionist leaders still in Poland. I took all possible steps to rescue some of the well-known leaders of the organization, the Palestine Office, etc. The news of their arrival in Trieste was a sign of the beginning of the Aliyah Movement from the ruins of Jewish Poland to Palestine. I regard it as premature to provide a detailed report on this chapter. With the help of a friendly authority, I was able to establish communication with Warsaw

---

44. Sušak is a port city in Yugoslavia. After World War I, the Austro-Hungarian port city of Fiume (with a majority Italian population) in the northern Adriatic was reestablished as an independent city-state. Under the Treaty of Rome (1924), the city of Fiume was annexed by Italy, while its Slav majority suburb of Sušak was incorporated into the Kingdom of Serbs, Croats, and Slovenes (renamed Yugoslavia in 1929), where it became a moderately important port. Today, Sušak is an integral part of the city of Rijeka (the Croatian name for Fiume) in Croatia.

and set up an aid center for emigration to Palestine. To date ca. 250 Olim and returnees have been saved in Poland. I hope that ways can be found to win the support of the government in Palestine for this campaign for refugee migration from Poland.

"THE SITUATION OF POLISH JEWRY"

Organizations such as the WJC, RELICO, the JA, and the AJJDC based their work on detailed information of what was happening to the Jews under Nazi rule. Access to this information was the precondition for successfully organizing assistance, planning for the future, lobbying governments, and intervening on behalf of the Jews in the affected territories. The picture that emerged following the first months of the war was alarming and confusing. Assessments of Nazi plans for the future differed. Would the conditions for Jews continue to deteriorate, or had the worst already passed? This uncertainty derived from the ongoing radicalization of German war aims and policies. It even affected Nazi officials' own ability to predict the future with any degree of certainty. And beyond a lack of coherent information about developments across Nazi-dominated Europe, Jews and their leaders lacked a reliable frame of reference based on prior experiences for determining how to proceed, how to cope. In reading contemporary assessments of the "Jewish question" from those early months of the war, we have to remind ourselves that only hindsight transforms the opaque, fragmented signs of the time into a clear image. Richard Lichtheim of the JA office in Geneva was among the very few who would astutely combine earlier insights—gained during World War I as a German Zionist emissary in Istanbul during the Armenian genocide—with the news arriving in Switzerland. Lichtheim's early assessment of the situation in Poland would turn out to be all too correct: "I am afraid," he reported to his colleagues in London on October 12, 1939, "we shall have to face the fact that under German rule 2,000,000 Jews will be annihilated in not less a cruel way, perhaps even more cruel, than 1,000,000 Armenians have been destroyed by the Turks during the last war."[45]

Lichtheim's prediction stood out even among Jewish functionaries in Geneva who had access to privileged information. Nahum Goldmann of the WJC political office, together with his secretary Gerhart Riegner and Abraham Silberschein, tried to keep Rabbi Stephen Wise in New York abreast of developments in Poland. Here as elsewhere, we find that the chaos of the first months of the Nazi

---

45. Richard Lichtheim to Joseph Linton, London, October 12, 1939, quoted in Friedlander and Milton, *Archives of the Holocaust*, 4:2.

onslaught on Europe and the lack of reliable information elicited widely diverging conclusions about the situation at hand. Goldmann's letter to Wise on November 4, 1939 (document 6–9), is thus striking for a number of reasons, beginning with its assumptions about the duration and scope of the war.

DOCUMENT 6–9: **Excerpt from letter of Dr. Nahum Goldmann, chairman of the Administrative Committee of the WJC, Geneva, Switzerland, to Dr. Stephen S. Wise, New York, November 4, 1939, American Jewish Archives, WJC records, series A, box A2, file 2,** *Day Book of the WJC I,* **48–52.**

Dear Wise,

[. . .] Most of those who still a month ago in France and Britain believed in a very long war, do not believe in it anymore and very important people hold the view that by next spring or summer the war may be over. The internal situation of Germany seems to be very bad. It is the Germany of the end of 1917, both economically and psychologically.[46] It is naturally possible and even probable that, before his end Hitler will try some mad act of despair, but nobody believes that he can succeed. There is naturally a fear of Bolshevism in Germany and even of Hitler himself turning Communist, but most people believe that the Army will intervene, get rid of Hitler and prevent Communism. These are naturally all guesses, but I am rather inclined to take this optimistic view and think that it is quite probable that by the next year war will be over and Hitlerism crushed. I wanted to transmit to you these impressions in order that with all the terrible news about the Jewish situation in Poland you should also have this encouraging information.

As for the Jewish situation, it becomes worse and worse. In Poland it seems to be worse than hell. Jews starving, driven from their homes, massacred by the Germans and at the time being no real help. You know that the Germans think of creating a kind of Jewish reservate [*sic*] near Lublin. Officials of the Palestine offices in Prague and Vienna have been sent there already to elaborate schemes for the

---

46. The situation within Germany toward the end of World War I (1914–1918) was marked by hunger, discontent, and social unrest; after the war, the German Right blamed Jews, Socialists, and Communists for having allegedly "stabbed" the fighting army in the back by stirring up the flames of the revolution. For the general situation in Germany after World War I and the rise of the Nazi movement, see Peter Fritzsche, *Germans into Nazis* (Cambridge, MA: Harvard University Press, 1998).

transfer of the Jewish population. (The news about the Palestine Office officials should be kept confidential.) First transports of Jews from Czechoslovakia and Austria have been sent already there. I am of the opinion that the time has come to think about some help for the Jews in the Polish territories occupied by the Germans. I know all the difficulties about getting the consent of the Allies to send food to Poland, but something must be done unless hundreds of thousands of Jews will be starved to death. I have reasons to think that the Germans would allow a neutral Jewish commission to go to Poland to organize such help and the question should be discussed and dealt with immediately. The problem of the Polish refugees outside of Poland is not of great importance, as their number is rather small.

As for the Russian part of Poland, the Jews are treated decently, but their bolshevisation and dejudaisation are being forced upon them by all means. I will try and get in touch with the Soviet Government about the possibility of some emigration of the Russian-Polish territory to Palestine, but I doubt very much if I will succeed.

I am awaiting anxiously for your news about the outcome of your negotiations with the Joint. All Jewish organizations in Europe are definitely in favour of creating a united Jewish front for the time of the war and the coming peace conference. I informed you already that the ICA and HICEM favour it and you have probably read that even the [British] Board of Deputies has announced that they are in favour of cooperation with the World Jewish Congress.

Less than two weeks later, a report from Trieste by a Jewish leader who had managed to flee Warsaw in November 1939 painted an even grimmer picture of the Jewish situation in Poland during the first two months of the war. In doing so, the author made two important points. First, while there had been arrests, German violence against Polish Jews seemed less severe in scope than what the world had witnessed in terms of Nazi activism in the prewar period. Second, the author found it hard to differentiate clearly between violence used by the occupiers specifically to address the "Jewish question" and German atrocities of a more general kind, the destructive fallout of any war for a civilian population under siege: hunger, homelessness, and disease. These problems—the absence of a clearly discernible, linear progression in German anti-Jewish radicalism and the difficulty of perceiving a distinctly anti-Jewish bent in German war policy—were to present major obstacles to assessing the plight of the Jews in Nazi-dominated Europe.

DOCUMENT 6–10: Author unknown, Trieste, Italy, "The Situation of Polish Jewry: A Letter to the World Jewish Congress," November 16, 1939, American Jewish Archives, WJC records, series A, box A2, file 2, *Day Book of the WJC II*, 31–33.

Dear Mr. Director:

I shall attempt to give you a most brief report regarding the present situation of Polish Jewry. I must point out that all my information goes down to November 9, the day on which I had to leave Warsaw.

In general, it must be said that the arrests among the Polish Jews did not have as much of a mass character as those at the time of the annexation of Austria and Czechoslovakia. On the other hand, there can be no doubt that many individual actions, to a certain extent involved in the military action, caused more serious losses among Polish Jews than in the aforementioned countries.

Polish Jewry insofar as it is under German rule is on the verge of complete destruction. The sacrifices which the Polish Jews, as a result of military movements, individual actions, epidemics and famine, have suffered in the course of the last ten weeks must be estimated without exaggeration at 250,000 persons. In Warsaw alone some 30,000 Jews fell directly or indirectly victims of the war. Many other cities inhabited by Jews have been burned, the men dragged off to labor camps, while the wives and children camped among the ruins or in the open air. The Jewish merchant and petty trader who has not managed to shift into street hawking, has no means of livelihood. As a result of various actions, the Jewish merchant has no goods in stock and even if some money remains, he can obtain nothing from the warehouses. In Łódź and vicinity trade with leather and manufactured articles has been explicitly forbidden Jews.

The plight of the destitute population, easily 90% of Polish Jewry in the large cities, where the essential foodstuffs have risen fourfold, is very bad. A kilo of bread which formerly cost 25 groschen has risen to seven times that amount, as has the cost of potatoes. Jewish intellectuals are completely without employment. When it is considered that 25% of all houses in Warsaw were completely demolished during the war and another 25% badly damaged and that the reconstruction of these houses is to begin in the Spring, one will have a picture of the immeasurable privation of the Jews in the former Polish capital. Under such circumstances it is no wonder that the epidemic of typhus is reaching disturbing proportions in Warsaw and Łódź.

The catastrophe in Warsaw has been made even more serious by a Ghetto decree. By November 13, about 50,000 Jews will be compelled to leave the Christian streets and move into the Jewish neighborhood.

The Jewish press is no longer in existence in Poland. Jewish societies are inactive. The Jewish schools have not yet opened and many teachers have been arrested. But the existence of Polish Jewry is not fundamentally menaced by persecution. The chief danger is death from starvation. Such is the opinion of all the leaders left in Poland, who view the immediate future with the gravest concern.

It is not questionable whether in such a situation one can talk of any general rescue. It would be a great deal if the horrible poverty and the threatening danger could be checked even to a slight extent.

All possible avenues of emigration must be used. The German occupation authorities should not cause any difficulties. One will have to reckon with emigrants who have nothing to take with them and who will be unable to pay for their passage in currency. There is under consideration a Jewish body for emigration, apparently with the participation of Hartglas.[47]

At least fifty certificates for Palestine are urgently needed in order to rescue those Zionist and other Jewish leaders who are threatened with immediate danger. When you come to Trieste, I shall give you their names.

A few hundred certificates for the Jewish youth in Poland will be no solution, but will have a tremendous moral effect. They will be a ray of hope showing that everything is not yet lost and that help may yet be expected. [. . .]

In the spring of 1940, **Moshe Kleinbaum,** the prominent Polish Zionist leader, summarized his assessment of the situation of Polish Jewry after nearly six months of war. Despite the devastation wrought by the conflict, cultural and social life "still throbs amid the ruins of former Polish Jewry." But, he insisted, Polish Jews could simply not be financially abandoned despite concerns over the boycott of Germany. He advocated the creation of alliances with Poles

---

47. Maximilian Meir Apolinary Hartglas (1883–1953), prominent lawyer, parliamentary deputy, and Zionist leader in Poland, was a member of the Warsaw City Council at the time of the invasion. He briefly served on the Warsaw *Judenrat* before fleeing in late 1939 and settling in Palestine. See Shlomo Netzer, "Hartglas, Maximilian Meir Apolinary," *Encyclopaedia Judaica*, ed. Fred Skolnik and Michael Berenbaum, 2nd ed. (Detroit, MI: Macmillan Reference USA, 2007), 8:374.

and formation of the broadest possible representation of Polish Jewry before the world community under the auspices of the WJC. "Above all," he argued, "Polish Jews under Nazi rule must not be abandoned to their horrible fate."[48] When Kleinbaum issued this call for action, Jews in western Europe were themselves on the brink of experiencing a dramatic deterioration in their situation and status, which in the following months would transform them from givers into recipients of relief.

---

48. Letter from M. Kleinbaum to Nahum Goldman, March 12, 1940, facsimile reprinted in Friedlander and Milton, *Archives of the Holocaust*, 8:111–12.

PART III

WAR AND ITS REPERCUSSIONS IN THE REST OF EUROPE

SEPTEMBER 1939 TO DECEMBER 1940

A S GERMAN tanks, airplanes, and soldiers overran Poland, Europeans outside Poland readied themselves for war. Even in those first days, government officials, journalists, and ordinary civilians recognized that the "hostilities begun" on September 1, 1939, would not remain confined to Poland.[1] The Polish campaign was not Czechoslovakia redux. In the final days of August, Great Britain signed an alliance with Poland, thereby formally abnegating its policy of **appeasement** toward Nazi Germany. France, too, was bound to defend Poland by a long-standing treaty, reaffirmed and extended in May 1939. As a result of such guarantees and the general sense that accommodating Hitler was no longer defensible, the British and French declared war against Germany on September 3, 1939. Those declarations, as well as the Soviet occupation of the eastern part of Poland from September 17, 1939, ensured that, this time,

---

1. "Hostilities Begun" was the headline of an article on the front page of the *New York Times* on September 1, 1939.

the Third Reich's aggression had triggered a conflict that would encompass all of Europe.[2]

Jews formed part of the stream of those joining the armed forces of France and Britain and, later, of the other western European countries threatened by German aggression, be it as draftees or volunteers. Many refugees from the Reich or other parts of Nazi-dominated Europe also enlisted.[3] Despite their seeming readiness to fight, however, the Western Powers' declarations of war did not translate into offensive operations. On the contrary, assurances that they would support Poland in the event of attack notwithstanding, Britain and France maintained a defensive position. From September 1939 through April 1940, during what was soon referred to as the "phony war," the only major military clashes in western Europe took place at sea, and even they were largely of a defensive character, aimed at protecting Allied shipping and enforcing a naval blockade against Germany. Indeed, during the five weeks in which Poland suffered the effects of blitzkrieg and over the subsequent months when Poles were introduced to life under Nazi and Soviet occupation regimes, Britain and France mobilized their armed forces and intensified their rearmament programs but avoided full-scale military conflict. And Hitler, who had originally hoped to initiate war in the west in early November 1939, was forced to postpone that campaign for six months because of unfavorable weather conditions.[4]

The "phony war" dragged on, yet peace was not on the horizon. Since it was in the German interest to take a brief respite from the hostilities before moving against western European nations and the Soviet Union, various agents of the Nazi regime sought to reestablish diplomatic connections with Britain and France. In the winter of 1939–1940, Hitler, Hermann Göring, and a few other German officials, some acting independently of the Führer, explored the possibilities for establishing a peace without concessions. These were half-hearted attempts to legitimize the status quo in Europe and get Britain and France to recognize de facto the results of the German aggression toward Austria, Czechoslovakia, and Poland. Several other countries, among

---

2. In his eagerness for war, Hitler was determined that Britain's policy of appeasement would fail. He guaranteed that the crisis he had precipitated with Poland could not be resolved by diplomacy, unlike his dismantlement of Czechoslovakia the preceding fall and spring. See Gerhard L. Weinberg, *A World at Arms: A Global History of World War II* (Cambridge: Cambridge University Press, 1994), 46, 51, 64–65.

3. For a review of secondary literature regarding this topic, see chapter 12, note 75.

4. Weinberg, *A World at Arms*, 67–73, 106, 110–11. Not that all of Europe beyond Poland was spared fighting in this period. The Soviet-Finnish war, lasting from November 30, 1939, until a peace treaty was signed in mid-March 1940, resulted in the deaths of two hundred thousand Soviet and twenty-five thousand Finnish soldiers.

them German allies and countries that had chosen to remain "neutral," also briefly attempted to advance peace negotiations. With Germany's refusal to restore Polish and Czechoslovak independence, such efforts were nonstarters in a France and Great Britain that no longer believed Hitler's regime could be trusted to uphold an agreement.[5] There could be no peace with a Third Reich determined to dominate Europe.

Germany extended the arena of war in April 1940 with a surprise attack on Denmark and Norway.[6] Despite the fact that it took Germany two months to secure Norway's complete surrender, the attack's initial successes meant that Hitler could now launch the battle that he and the rest of the world had long anticipated against Great Britain and France. War in the west proceeded apace. On May 10, the German army invaded the neutral Low Countries and France. That month, the Netherlands, Belgium, and Luxembourg surrendered. But the true shock came on June 22, when the newly appointed French prime minister and octogenarian hero of World War I, Marshal **Henri-Philippe Pétain**, signed an armistice agreement with Germany, acceding to all German and Italian conditions of surrender.[7] Within weeks, Germany had overpowered an enemy it had found impossible to defeat during four years of fighting in World War I. Barely avoiding annihilation at Dunkirk, British troops withdrew from the continent; the French Third Republic ceased to exist. France was divided into an Occupied Zone in the north, placed under direct German occupation, and an Unoccupied Zone in the south, to be ruled by a new French regime, the collaborationist **Vichy regime**, named for the spa town that became home to Pétain's government.[8]

Nazi Germany's military victories in April through June 1940, in combination with the strengthening of alliances with satellite states, established Germany as the hegemonic power over much of the continent of Europe. Europe's future seemed to lie in German hands; new antisemitic measures soon followed. Indeed, by the end of 1940, every European country within

---

5. Weinberg, *A World at Arms*, 89–95.

6. Germany invaded Denmark and Norway in order to control strategic naval ports. In the wake of this latest round of German military triumphs, the government of France fell and Paul Reynaud replaced Edouard Daladier as prime minister. The British government was next: Neville Chamberlain resigned, and Winston Churchill became the head of a coalition government in the early days of May. Weinberg, *A World at Arms*, 113–21.

7. Saul Friedländer, *Nazi Germany and the Jews:* (vol. 2) *The Years of Extermination, 1939–1945* (New York: HarperCollins, 2007), 66–67.

8. See Michael R. Marrus and Robert O. Paxton, *Vichy France and the Jews* (New York: Schocken, 1981); Renée Poznanski, *Jews in France during World War II* (Hanover, NH: University Press of New England in association with the USHMM, 2001).

the orbit of Nazi Germany (the only exception being Denmark) had introduced anti-Jewish laws and decrees. In western Europe, Jews in the Occupied and Unoccupied Zones of France, as well as in Belgium, Luxembourg, and the Netherlands, were subjected to anti-Jewish decrees for the first time. The Jewish populations of Romania, Hungary, Slovakia, and Italy were subjected to the amplification of antisemitic measures first introduced in the late 1930s. Though hardly identical from one satellite state or even one occupied territory to the next, the racial laws, it could be said, focused in aggregate on defining who could be counted as a Jew and on excluding those so defined from participating in broader economic, social, and cultural life. As varied as the measures adopted across German-dominated Europe outside of Poland were the Jewish reaction to these policies were equally varied, a topic explored in the next three chapters.

CHAPTER 7

OUTSIDE POLAND
WAR AND ITS REPERCUSSIONS

E VEN IN THE absence of fighting in the west, Jews and non-Jews alike faced a changed landscape in September 1939. Outside of Poland, to what extent were Jewish perceptions of the war similar to those of non-Jewish Europeans? German Jewish writer Gertrud Kolmar, living in Berlin, described in a letter to her sister of October 1, 1939, how time had seemingly accelerated in those early weeks of the war. Kolmar's response to the atmosphere of that period could also be read as a reflection of the specific situation of Jews in Germany at that time: she described herself as removed from, rather than participating in, world events as they were unfolding.[1]

> The days were all bursting with events . . . with world affairs . . . It's not as though I'm particularly moved by or entranced by these world affairs, which was once the case. It seems to me that nowadays the face and shape [*Gesicht und Gestalt*] of things are changing at a frantic pace; everything is changing, yes, whirling by, nothing stands [still], and everything that once took years, even decades to alter is now completely transformed in just a few days. And in the meantime I have withdrawn ever more into

---

1. This contrasts with substantial evidence from oral histories in which non-Jewish Germans remember fondly their sense that they had been active participants in the history of this period. See, e.g., Margarethe Dörr, *"Wer die Zeit nicht miterlebt hat . . .":* *Frauenerfahrungen im Zweiten Weltkrieg und in den Jahren danach* (Frankfurt am Main: Campus Verlag, 1998).

that which endures, into Being [*das Seiende*], the eternal occurrences [*das Ewigkeitsgeschehen*] (these things that occur eternally don't have to be "religion"—they can also be "nature" or even "love"); from this perspective I can view current events almost as though they were apparitions in a kaleidoscope: an image has barely formed when a shake and a turn brings the brightly colored glass fragments together in a different way—and it is almost impossible, pointless, to recall individual beams and stars among all the different shapes and colors. Sometimes I do in fact participate in something the way I used to, talk about it, warm up a bit; but afterwards I always wonder a little about myself and ask myself why I spoke so fervently about things that at heart barely touch me.[2]

In concrete ways, too, the war affected Jewish populations seemingly untouched by the hostilities in Poland. An **American Jewish Joint Distribution Committee** (AJJDC) report from February 1940 offered an overview of Jews in various locales. Although the situation of Jews, depending on the national and even regional context, was far from uniform, the general picture conveyed by the AJJDC Bulletin was one of deterioration. German, Austrian, and Czech Jews in the Reich were suffering disproportionately from food and clothing shortages under the ration system the Nazi regime had introduced with the start of the war. Emigration remained their only escape, but visas, a means of leaving, and currency exchange had receded even further from reach in wartime. As a result, the Jewish population of the Reich became all the more impoverished and dependent on foreign assistance. Meanwhile, outside the Reich, in countries with substantial numbers of German, Austrian, and Czechoslovakian refugees—France, Italy, and the neutral countries Belgium, the Netherlands, and Switzerland—the newcomers found themselves in increasingly precarious positions, as did the native Jewish populations that had taken on responsibility for supporting them. The AJJDC Bulletin warned that "the share of the burden assumed by local committees has now dwindled almost to the vanishing point because of the drain on their resources created by the

---

2. Letter from Gertrud Kolmar, Berlin, Germany, to her sister Hilde, October 1, 1939, in Gertrud Kolmar, *Briefe*, ed. Johanna Woltmann (Göttingen: Wallstein, 1997), 37–38 (translated from German).

exigencies of war and national requirements."[3] Perhaps the most stringent new restriction introduced in the early months of the war in western Europe was the internment of "enemy nationals." France interned all central European (German, Austrian, and Czech) male refugees, Jewish and non-Jewish, between the ages of seventeen and sixty-five, sometimes in the same internment camps, leaving the women and children who depended on them without any means of subsistence.[4] Under the circumstances, European Jews came to rely more and more heavily on American Jewish aid.

Inside the Reich, throughout the rest of Europe, and on other continents, people were forced to grapple with the war, with what it meant and might mean for their lives. Jews, like others outside Poland, absorbed the news of world events. When the war expanded, first into Denmark and Norway in April 1940, then into the Low Countries—Belgium, Luxembourg, and the Netherlands— and France the following month, Jews in western Europe moved from the sidelines to firsthand experience of Nazi German rule. Throughout the fall and winter of 1939 and 1940, Jews outside Poland began assessing the ways in which their situation as Jews in their respective countries might be altered by the war and how they would deal with the new exigencies.

WAR IN POLAND VIEWED FROM AFAR

The invasion of Poland directly affected German, Austrian, and Czech Jews trapped inside Nazi Germany in two distinct ways. First, flight from the Reich became less achievable, despite the Nazi regime's continued commitment to emigration as the means of solving the Reich's "Jewish question." The war rendered many routes over land and sea impassable. It also divided countries into "belligerents" and "neutrals," resulting in new visa restrictions for people from enemy countries. For example, on the day the British declared war, they shuttered their consulates in Germany, in part to stave off the threat of enemy agents entering the United Kingdom. Jews inside the Reich consequently had

---

3. "Bulletin #6—Present Activities of the J.D.C. (Germany and Its Possessions and the Refugees)," New York, February 21, 1940, facsimile reprinted in *Archives of the Holocaust: An International Collection of Selected Documents*, ed. Henry Friedlander and Sybil Milton (New York: Garland Publishing, 1990), 2/2:11 and cf. 4–8. Another AJJDC report by **Morris Troper**, "On the European Relief Front," published in the spring of 1940, offered a similar assessment; see document 6–3.

4. Vicki Caron, *Uneasy Asylum: France and the Jewish Refugee Crisis, 1933–1942* (Stanford, CA: Stanford University Press, 1999), 242–43.

no way to obtain new visas for Britain. Nor could German nationals issued visas prior to September 3, 1939, make use of them; Britain announced that it would no longer recognize them as valid.[5] A second direct consequence of war was that it restricted the movement of letters and goods. With family and friends strewn across continents—by the end of 1939, according to one AJJDC report, 70 percent of Austrian Jews alone had fled Austria—central European Jews were especially dependent on letter writing.[6] The war attenuated their long-distance connections with loved ones.

In a diary entry from the day after the German invasion of Poland, **Willy Cohn** evocatively rendered the interpolation of world events into daily life away from the war front. To a certain extent, that admixture was no different for German Jews than for non-Jews, for all learned about the war from the same news sources and were subjected to the same blackout measures to guard against nighttime raids. Yet, even on the second day of the Polish campaign, Cohn articulated some concerns brought on by the war that were unique to Jews. Indeed, the three main concerns he expressed in this entry, presented in document 7–1, were widely shared by German Jews in this period. How the war would impede German Jewish emigration efforts and how it would affect communication with relatives abroad were of central importance. A third and no less important issue evident in the entry was heightened antisemitism, the "pogrom-like" atmosphere that predominated. Cohn feared that the war would bring about the intensification of anti-Jewish measures.

---

5. Debórah Dwork and Robert Jan van Pelt, *Flight from the Reich: Refugee Jews, 1933–1946* (New York: W. W. Norton, 2009), 191; Henry L. Feingold, *The Politics of Rescue: The Roosevelt Administration and the Holocaust, 1938–1945* (New Brunswick, NJ: Rutgers University Press, 1970), 81; Saul Friedländer, *Nazi Germany and the Jews:* (vol. 2) *The Years of Extermination* (New York: HarperCollins, 2007), 82–84.

6. "Bulletin #6—Present Activities of the J.D.C.," in Friedlander and Milton, *Archives of the Holocaust*, 2/2:7. Between 1933 and 1939, more than 285,000 Jews—or more than 57 percent of the Jewish population—had left Germany. Avraham Barkai and Paul Mendes-Flohr, *Deutsch-jüdische Geschichte in der Neuzeit*, vol. 4: *Aufbruch und Zerstörung 1918–1945* (Munich: C. H. Beck, 1997), 226. In addition, it is estimated that twenty-seven thousand Czech Jews emigrated between 1939 and 1941 by legal channels and one thousand by illegal channels. See Livia Rothkirchen, *The Jews of Bohemia and Moravia: Facing the Holocaust* (Lincoln and Jerusalem: University of Nebraska Press and Yad Vashem, 2005), 302. On Allied economic measures against the Nazis, see W. N. Medlicott, *The Economic Blockade*, vol. 1 (London: HMSO, 1952).

DOCUMENT 7–1: **Willy Cohn, diary entry for September 2, 1939, translated from** *Kein Recht, Nirgends: Tagebuch vom Untergang des Breslauer Judentums, 1933–1941*, **ed. Norbert Conrads (Cologne: Böhlau Verlag, 2007), 2:683–84.**

Breslau, Saturday. The first blackout night, thank G-d, has passed uneventfully. Sat on the balcony. The air was quite good, and one could look out over the darkened city. Toward evening, Trudi [his wife] returned from shopping with the news that the airport in Warsaw has been bombed and Pless in Polish Upper Silesia apparently has been leveled. Now this morning, we'll learn how much truth there is to all those things.

I wasn't in the synagogue in the evening, and we didn't light the *Kiddush* candles either. Lay in bed awake for a long time and thought about Wölfl [his son Wolfgang from his first marriage, who had emigrated to France in 1934]; we're completely cut off, and only our thoughts are still a bond between us. Sometimes it's very hard to dismiss these thoughts. Inwardly, I've practically lost all hope that immigrating to Palestine could still work for us. One surely must also expect the loss of the money that would have made the transfer possible for us. But there's no point in agonizing over it now; one can only live from one hour to the next. At the moment, I still don't know what position the other powers are taking on the German-Polish war.

Afternoon. I want to stay true to my longtime habit and write down everything that goes through my mind, even on such a critical day. Reading the *Schlesische Zeitung* provided a certain picture. The war with Poland has really gotten going, and the Germans have invaded Poland at various points; on the other hand, the Poles have shelled [the German city of] Beuthen.[7] Listening to foreign radio stations is outlawed; a remarkable decree. It will be a dreadfully bloody war, as the Poles appear to be putting up fierce resistance; but people here have the feeling that it will be over in two weeks. There will be a rude awakening when the numbers of dead and wounded are made public. The first death notices have already appeared in the *Schlesische Tageszeitung*. Even now, close to 4 p.m., I still know nothing definitive about the stance of France and England and whether it will be possible to localize the conflict. France has ordered general mobilization, starting today.

From the Jewish point of view, the following must be said about the situation. The mood of the Aryan population certainly is not favorable to

---

7. Today Beuthen is the Polish city Bytom.

us, and if Germany fails in Poland, pogrom-like outrages can surely be expected; possibly even if England gets around to intervening on Poland's side. But you can't look at everything from this standpoint, of course, even if, as a faithful family man, you're concerned about the family; but which way do you turn first with your worries? Today, for the first time, I heard an antisemitic comment from two older men on the street: "The Jews have to go." It wasn't aimed at me; but it was all the more significant. [. . .]

Romanian Jewish writer Mihail Sebastian[8] also used his diary in September 1939 to reflect on news of the war in Poland. Viewed from Bucharest, the conflict in Poland seemed all too near. Romania's oil fields and strategic ports made it likely that the country would soon be drawn into the conflict. And as a thirty-three-year-old man, Sebastian reckoned that he would be forced to serve in the military "in the event of a general mobilization."[9]

Greater than his dread of military service, however, was the panic he experienced over the attempted coup d'état by the Romanian fascists, the **Iron Guard** (also known as the Legion).[10] Since 1930 Romania had been ruled by a succession of parliamentary governments under the reinstated monarch King Carol II. With the worsening of the Romanian economy and the influence of Nazi Germany on Romanian politics over the course of the 1930s, the extreme Right posed an increasing threat to Carol II's regime. The king initiated a new campaign of repression against the Iron Guard in 1938 (in the early 1930s, three different governments had outlawed it for brief periods), which included the murder of its founder, Corneliu Codreanu, and the establishment of a one-party corporate state ruled by the king. In 1939 the Legionnaires retaliated, assassinating the

---

8. Mihail Sebastian (1907–1945), born Iosif Hechter in Braila, Romania, became a playwright and author of fiction and literary criticism. In the interwar period, he was a member of a circle of prominent intellectuals (such as Emil Cioran, Mircea Eliade, and Nae Ionescu), who in the 1930s drifted into far-right exclusionary Romanian nationalism. As a Jew, Sebastian became increasingly marginalized from the intellectual scene and bitter about his position and his former friends' fascist allegiances. His diary, covering the years 1935 to 1944, chronicles the ultimate demise of democracy in Romania and the worsening plight of the Romanian Jewish population under successively more extremist antisemitic regimes. For biographical details, see Radu Ioanid's introduction to Sebastian's diary, in Mihail Sebastian, *Journal, 1935–1944* (Chicago: Ivan R. Dee in association with the USHMM, 2000), vii–xx.

9. Sebastian, diary entry for September 8, 1939, in *Journal*, 236. Sebastian was called up to serve in the army in December 1939.

10. For an analysis of Romanian fascism and the ideology of the Iron Guard, see Constantin Iordachi, "Charisma, Religion, and Ideology: Romania's Interwar Legion of the Archangel Michael," in *Ideologies and National Identities: The Case of Twentieth-Century Southeastern Europe*, ed. John R. Lampe and Mark Mazower (Budapest: Central European University Press, 2004), 19–53.

country's prime minister, Armand Călinescu.[11] Sebastian's diary entry, presented in document 7–2, reveals how vulnerable he felt in the immediate aftermath of Călinescu's assassination and in the face of a war that threatened to overtake Romania, despite the superficial normalcy of street life in Bucharest. As much as Romanian Jews were already suffering from a series of discriminatory laws implemented by successive recent governments under Carol II, Sebastian seemed to fear the antisemitism of the Legionnaires even more.[12]

DOCUMENT 7–2: **Mihail Sebastian, Bucharest, Romania, diary entry for September 21, 1939, in** *Journal, 1935–1944* **(Chicago: Ivan R. Dee in association with the USHMM, 2000), 239–40.**

I was in court, waiting my turn for an adjournment, when a woman pale with fright leaned across the counsels' bench and whispered to someone: "They've shot Armand Călinescu; it was on the radio."

I took a taxi and raced home, where I found everyone downstairs at the Pascals, panic-stricken around the radio, though it was broadcasting a normal musical program. [. . .]

Back at my place in Calea Victoriei, however, I received a call from Alice Theodorian with news from Armand's sister-in-law (whom I met myself at Alice's the day before yesterday). Yes, Armand was murdered today in his car between one and one-thirty; a group of Legionaries had waited beneath a timber cart and opened fire several times when his car approached. At the same time, another group burst into the radio station and broadcast the news. Both groups captured—but Armand is dead.

---

11. Armand Călinescu (1893–1939) was a Romanian politician and served as prime minister between March and September 1939, when he was murdered. He was a pronounced opponent of the Iron Guard and its influence in Romanian society and a fervent critic of pro-Nazi sentiments in the country.

12. The Romanian Jewish population was the third largest in Europe, numbering approximately 757,000 people, according to the 1930 census. Under the short-lived government of Octavian Goga (1881–1938) and Alexandru C. Cuza (1857–1947)—lasting only from December 1937 to February 1938—Romanian Jews were subjected to a series of discriminatory laws that culminated with the Decree-Law on the Revision of Citizenship of January 21, 1938, which stripped 270,000 Romanian Jews of their citizenship and, in many cases, their sources of income. After the Goga-Cuza government was toppled by a royal coup, King Carol II kept the antisemitic decrees in force. Radu Ioanid, *The Holocaust in Romania: The Destruction of Jews and Gypsies under the Antonescu Regime, 1940–1944* (Chicago: Ivan R. Dee, 2000), xx–xxi; Ezra Mendelsohn, *The Jews of East Central Europe between the World Wars* (Bloomington: Indiana University Press, 1987), 203–7; *The Final Report of the International Commission on the Holocaust in Romania*, USHMM, November 11, 2004, taken from www.ushmm.org/research/center/presentations/features/details/2005-03-10/pdf/english/chapter_01.pdf (accessed July 19, 2010).

If it is true, the situation is disastrous. It is a question not only of the internal situation (which could be dealt with one way or another), but also of the Germans and the Russians, who might enter the country "to establish order" and "to protect their kith and kin."

From one hour to the next, one day to the next, we could lose everything: a roof over our heads, bread to eat, our modicum of security, even our lives.

And there is nothing, absolutely nothing, to be done about it.

It is a wonderfully sunny autumn day. I lie on the chaise longue on my terrace and look at this city, which can be seen so well from above. The streets are full of life, cars drive along in every direction, traffic policemen direct the traffic from their boxes, the shops are open for customers—the whole machinery of this great city seems to be working normally, and yet somewhere at its heart a terrible blow has been delivered, without yet being felt. It is as if we were a city strewn with dynamite due to explode in five minutes' time—a city which, for the moment, carries on unawares, as if nothing has happened.

A short while ago I saw a group of Polish refugees coming toward my block. They were raggedly dressed, each carrying a battered backpack, but they were alive—do you know what I mean?—alive and saved. Maybe we (Benu, Mama, Tata, myself) won't even be that by this evening, tomorrow, or the day after—not even refugees who have escaped the fire with nothing but our lives.

I am probably one of those who are made to await death with resignation, to accept it. I don't see any defensive gesture I could make; no thought of escape or refuge crosses my mind.

Listening to the radio and reading the newspapers in the small Dutch coastal town of Scheveningen, just three miles from The Hague, German Jewish refugee Grete Steiner also devoted the lion's share of her diary entries in early September 1939 to war news and analysis.[13] Her projections about the war's outcome are strikingly more optimistic than Willy Cohn's or Mihail Sebastian's. Whether this difference in outlook can be attributed to each diarist's temperament or particular circumstances, such as political outlook, geographic vantage point, age, or

13. Grete Steiner (1874?–1944?) started keeping a diary in Scheveningen in May 1937. From a wealthy German Jewish family, she was already a widow at the time of arrival, with her children, as a refugee in the Netherlands. Her two sons integrated well into Dutch society and got married; her daughter emigrated to Palestine, eventually settling in **Kibbutz** Hefzibah in Jezreel Valley. When Germany occupied the Netherlands in 1940, Grete went into hiding, nevertheless maintaining connections with the Dutch underground. The last entry in her diary was written on March 3, 1944; Grete was arrested by the Dutch collaborationist police soon thereafter and subsequently deported via Westerbork to Auschwitz, where she perished.

personal situation, is not easy to ascertain. Despite her own uncertain status—Steiner was one of some twenty thousand Jewish refugees from the Reich who remained in the Netherlands in this period although the Dutch government policy did not allow refugees to take up permanent residency—she betrays no particular concern about what the war might mean for herself or for Jews elsewhere.[14] Beyond political prognostication, she imparts a sense of the surrounding population's mood in the first days of the war and of how her own existence, like Willy Cohn's, was inflected by her distance from her loved ones.[15]

DOCUMENT 7–3: **Grete Steiner, Scheveningen, Netherlands, diary entries for September 1, 3, and 6, 1939, Ghetto Fighters' House Archives (Beit Iohamei hagetaot), Israel, 1064 (translated from German).**

Sept. 1. As I now have two grandchildren, whom I perhaps will never see, I want to write down for them the history of this second world war as I experience it and understand it. One year ago, I thought it would begin. [. . .] An entire year of tension, danger, and constant fear of war is behind us. In this year, Germany destroyed and occupied Czechoslovakia, Italy seized Albania,[16] and Franco, with the help of Italy and Germany, was victorious in Spain.[17]

---

14. On Dutch government policy toward refugees and relations between Dutch Jews and Jewish refugees in the 1930s, see Bob Moore, *Victims and Survivors: The Nazi Persecution of the Jews in the Netherlands, 1940–1945* (London: Arnold, 1997), 29–36.

15. Grete dedicated her diary to Tamar, her granddaughter, who was born in Palestine to her daughter Sabine.

16. In early April 1939, Fascist Italy invaded Albania, sending King Zog into exile and proclaiming the country an Italian protectorate. Italian Albania was enlarged by the incorporation of parts of Kosovo, Montenegro, and Yugoslavian Macedonia in the aftermath of the German dismemberment of Yugoslavia in April 1941. After the Italian collapse in 1943, German troops occupied the country. For a history of World War II in Albania, see Bernd J. Fischer, *Albania at War, 1939–1945* (West Lafayette, IN: Purdue University Press, 1999).

17. In July 1936, a group of right-wing Spanish army generals led by Francisco Franco (1892–1975) carried out a coup against the democratic Spanish republic of president Manuel Azaña (1880–1940). For the following three years, until Franco defeated the Republicans and established his rule over the entire country, a fierce civil war raged in Spain. It was fought between the democratic forces, aided by anarchists and Communists and supported by the Soviet Union and large numbers of international volunteers, on the one hand, and Franco's clerical fascist phalanxes, aided by Fascist Italy and Nazi Germany, on the other. The Spanish Civil War served, in a sense, as a prelude to World War II: a struggle between democracy and totalitarianism, a proxy war in which the main actors in the upcoming global conflict tried out different military and propaganda strategies. For a detailed history of the war, see Anthony Beevor, *The Battle for Spain: The Spanish Civil War, 1936–1939* (New York: Penguin, 2001).

All countries armed themselves to the limit of their ability—endless messages were sent back and forth—lies were spread and denied [. . .]

Sept. 3, Sunday. Today, on the third day, England issued a short ultimatum to Germany—and after its expiration—when no reply followed—declared war on Germany, at 11:20 Dutch time. Thus World War II now has broken out, irreversibly. I hope it will end in a decisive abolition of the Nazi regime—and thereby Europe's liberation from a blemish on mankind will be accomplished. That I would like to live to see to the finish.

Sept. 6. Nothing is actually happening; there is a piercing, expectant hush. [. . .] There is no "eagerness to fight" anywhere. But I don't doubt for a minute England's strong will to overthrow Hitler. It's high time, too, for Germany and the whole world to breathe freely again. [. . .] Here you see nothing but soldiers. Yesterday I was at the fish market, where there were scarcely any fish and only two vendors. Nevertheless, the fishing fleet was just going out again this morning when I was on the beach at 6:30. We also have food ration cards, but they're not in use.

Alfred Berl,[18] editor of the prominent French Jewish weekly *Paix et Droit*, also allowed himself to conjecture about the future defeat of Nazi Germany just days after Poland's capitulation. In contrast to Grete Steiner, Berl did not feel reassured by the postwar order he envisioned. The disruption of Jewish life in central Europe and Poland was already so profound, in Berl's estimation, that there could be no return to the pre-Nazi days. He forecast that the refugee crisis from before the war would continue to plague the world with the resumption of peace.

Of particular interest in the piece presented in document 7–4 are the language and concepts Berl employed. Well before the establishment of Jewish ghettos in Poland, Berl wrote about "ghettos" enclosing Jews and the "extermination" of Jews. How are we to interpret Berl's portrayal of Jewish suffering as a "cataclysm" and a "martyrology without precedent"? Given our knowledge of what was to come, it is difficult not to read this piece from October 1, 1939, as sensationalistic journalism or a left-wing interpretation of nazism. Yet, Berl indirectly countered such a reading of his news analysis. As a journalist, he touted the necessity of "accurate and restrained documentation," which he

---

18. On Berl, a prolific writer, see Michel Abitbol, *Les deux terres promises: Les juifs de France et le sionisme, 1897–1945* (Paris: Olivier Orban, 1989), and accounts in passing by his nephew, Emmanuel Berl, and Jean d'Ormesson, *Tant que vous penserez à moi* (Paris: Grasset, 1992), 25; Emmanuel Berl and Patrick Modiano, *Interrogatoire par Patrick Modiano suivi de Il fait beau, allons au cimetière* (Paris: Gallimard, 1976), 15. The authors have been unable to trace Berl's fate after *Paix et Droit* ceased publication in 1940.

insisted would be more effective than "the most literary passages" in helping the governments and publics of France and England "to comprehend the danger that threatens all peoples and the urgency with which solidarity imposes itself on all who want to live freely, independently, with respect for the law [*contrats*], for human life, and for peace." It would appear that he saw his own editorial as a contribution to such an effort.

DOCUMENT 7–4: **Alfred Berl, Paris, France, "The Frenzy of Barbarism and the Jews of Central Europe,"** *Paix et Droit*, **October 1, 1939, 1ff. (translated from French).**

The incredible catastrophe unleashed by the insane ambition and arrogance of one man is turning Europe upside down, not only in its political and economic status but also in its moral foundations. Today it is no longer a question of replacing a hegemony, territorial expansions or decreases, social transformations: what is at stake is much more serious; it is our civilization itself, civilization inherited from the Greco-Roman ideal, improved and perfected by the Decalogue and the Gospel. [. . .]

What a miracle, if, in such a universal disaster, the people of Israel had been spared! Alas, this people has followed its traditional and painful destiny, which is to suffer always, before and after all and more than all. [. . .]

The damages to Jews do not stop at the Reich's boundaries; wherever the German Attila[19] puts his destructive foot, even in the countries least inclined to anti-Judaism, the Jewish plant withers without any hope of coming alive again.

After being excluded from their civic homeland, the Jews are also declined the right to belong to their own country; they are uprooted from the soil where they were born, where they have lived for centuries, where their homes and cemeteries are. They are deported to distant countries— just like herds pushed to other pastures and they are penned in huge ghettos, with no funds, no clothing, left to perish of misery or despair.

To satisfy the racist fury, it is not enough to exterminate Jewry; it must be made to suffer, must be tortured in the flesh. [. . .] Whatever the height of suffering attained today by the Jews of Central Europe, that is, by more than 2 million human beings, they are locked in a vicious circle.

Rescuing them at the moment is both necessary and practically impossible. Even assuming that—and it is not the case—organizations

---

19. This is a reference to the leader of the Huns, Attila (406–453), known in European memory for his extreme cruelty, mercilessness, and capacity for destruction.

and philanthropic societies were rich enough to provide effectively, not for the distress of two hundred or three hundred thousand persons, but considering the scale of the cataclysm, we are talking about millions of people, how could they physically help these masses, thrown to the cruelty of their executioners because of their birth or military conquest? One should know that, locked up in their ghettos, these masses are absolutely unable to communicate with the outside world; and the reverse is no less true. [. . .]

It is therefore less the present hour than the future that it is important to envisage; we mean the day after victory. Perhaps its date is not very close, but, for the entire world, it cannot be in doubt. [. . .]

Yes, indeed, the ghettos will be destroyed, and the emergency laws will be repealed. The principle of equality will be in force again, and tens of thousands of Jews born in Germany will certainly want to go back there. But will they regain their jobs, their fortunes? All that is, or will be, nothing but a memory.

The fate of Polish Jews is even worse. Most of the Polish Jews will not be able to live where they were born. Even before the collapse caused by the German invasion, the Polish economy couldn't meet the needs of the Jewish population. How could it support its burden now, being so weak, exhausted, and ruined?

Polish Jews will need to migrate, en masse. But to what land can they head? [. . .]

After a crisis that is shaking the entire world to its depths and from which it will be necessary to rebuild, the United States, which has such a keen sense of duty and morality, will know how to match its actions to its resources, to its potentialities. [. . .]

Robert Weltsch, the leading German Zionist journalist who had emigrated to Palestine in 1938, also interpreted the outbreak of the war as ushering in a new world order. Already in March 1939 in the *Jüdische Welt-Rundschau,* the newspaper he founded and edited, Weltsch had declared the definitive end of German Jewry. He saw in "*Kristallnacht*" the symbol of the total destruction of German Jewish culture, which would survive for the time being among the refugees who had fled Nazi Germany.[20] In the first volume of the *Jüdische Welt-Rundschau* published in Jerusalem after the beginning of the war, Weltsch's edi-

---

20. Christian Wiese, "Resisting the Demonic Forces of Nationalism: Robert Weltsch's Response to Nazism and Kristallnacht," *Jewish Quarterly Review* 121 (winter 2008): 50–53.

torial discussed what he perceived to be major shifts in the Jewish world of the future, particularly in the position of the *Yishuv*, thanks to the war.

DOCUMENT 7–5: **Robert Weltsch, Jerusalem, Palestine, "Changed World,"** *Jüdische Welt-Rundschau* **(special issue), October 27, 1939, 2 (translated from German).**

The hectic, dramatic events of the last days of August, when the great international political conflicts that have manifested themselves with increasing intensity in the past few years heated up once again, and at the same time, frantic attempts to avoid a global catastrophe were made— these days of feverish excitement, dying hope, and manly resolve have been superseded by a new era; we are in a radically changed world. The die is cast. [. . .]

In this time of war, when everything is astir again, everyone filled with uncertainty, the Jewish colony in <u>Palestine</u> is a fixed point in all Jewish hopes for the future. At present, Palestine is not directly caught up in the war, and anyone coming here from belligerent countries in Europe is surprised at the peaceful and normal course of daily life. It would be wrong, of course, to allow oneself to be deceived by a superficial observation. In actual fact, Palestine is deeply strained by the convulsions of war, and the effects undoubtedly will come to light in short order. [. . .]

One thing is certain: The Jews of Palestine are <u>firmly resolved to continue their work</u>, despite all the restrictions and hardships that may be necessary. Next to <u>American Jewry</u>, whose position of Jewish leadership is uncontested today, and which is aware of its enormous responsibility, Palestinian Jewry can be termed one of the most important Jewish communities at this moment in history. In the previous world war, to be sure, Palestine was an object of political desires and considerations, but the Jewish colony was in its infancy and was not a social reality. Things are different today. Today, the Jewish community of Palestine is a powerful factor in the larger Jewish macrocosm. It has a wealth of moral, intellectual, and material strengths, which are now being put to the test. The Jews of Palestine have always seen themselves as an outpost of the Jewish people <u>as a whole</u>, and in this hour too, it cannot be otherwise. They must remain in <u>close contact</u> with every fragment of the Jewish people that is within reach, in a constant give-and-take. In their struggle to maintain the positions that are threatened by the war (with its disruption of commerce and transportation), Palestinian Jews are relying on the <u>help</u> of those Jews in the world who still can offer help. This does not mean offering support of a personal kind but preserving a large social and cultural organism, whose moral and constructive value for Jews in the present day, and probably still more so in the future, cannot be overestimated.

Understandably, contact between Palestine and other countries was disrupted in the first weeks of the war. Doubtless this will change as general circumstances worldwide increasingly adjust themselves to the war. Despite all the technical difficulties, we believe that <u>the link between Palestine and world Jewry must be maintained</u>. It is perhaps one of the most important tasks of Jews in this hour. Where all peoples are prepared to make the ultimate sacrifices, the Jewish people too, in its entirety, will prove itself. Each of us, in his place, must do his duty. <u>We are convinced</u> that after a chaos that may yet severely test all of us—and here we mean <u>all human beings</u>—there will come a time of cleansing and of economic and political reconstruction. The Jewish people must prepare to take its place in this reborn world of new building and development.

Despite the continued absence of fighting in western and central Europe into the late fall and winter of 1939 and 1940, the war disrupted people's lives in diverse ways. The situation of Jewish refugees in western European countries in particular and of all Jews in the Reich deteriorated. Describing circumstances inside Germany, an AJJDC report called special attention to "the plight of some 35,000 male Jews between the ages of 15 and 65 of Polish nationality living in Germany and Austria who were interned at the beginning of the war and who are being held in Nazi concentration camps under indescribable conditions of hunger and cold. Kept on a starvation diet, they are not permitted to receive food from the outside and have been forbidden visitors."[21]

Now with the start of the war, the mass detainment of Jews became a reality in western countries as part of internment measures adopted there. In

---

21. "Bulletin #6—Present Activities of the J.D.C.," in Friedlander and Milton, *Archives of the Holocaust*, 2/2:6. According to Saul Friedländer, however, only approximately 11,500 Polish Jews still lived in the Reich in the late summer and early fall of 1939; they were all arrested in the first week of September as enemy aliens and deported to the Buchenwald and Sachsenhausen concentration camps. The AJJDC report thus probably unknowingly inflated the numbers of Polish Jewish men in detention. Friedländer, *Nazi Germany*, 2:60. For a discussion of the fate of foreign Jews in Nazi Germany through September 1939, see Trude Maurer, "Ausländische Juden in Deutschland, 1933–1939," in *Die Juden im nationalsozialistischen Deutschland/The Jews in Nazi Germany, 1933–1943*, ed. Arnold Paucker with Sylvia Gilchrist and Barbara Suchy (Tübingen: J. C. B. Mohr, 1986), 189–210.

September 1939, France decreed that all male "enemy aliens" aged seventeen to sixty-five were to be rounded up and held in one of over eighty camps designated for this purpose and spread around the country. The rationale offered by the French government was fear of fifth-column activity.[22] Surely the widespread antirefugee sentiment in France played a role, as did the surge of antisemitism that had emerged in an especially pernicious form among detractors of **Léon Blum**'s Popular Front government in 1936. In contrast to the Nazi camps, the French permitted relief organizations to furnish the internees with food and other necessities. The pressure on such organizations was enormous: the expenditures incurred by French refugee organization Comité d'assistance aux réfugiés for the month of December 1939 alone were the equivalent of its entire 1938 budget. Despite such allowances, the French policy was considerably harsher than policies toward refugees in Belgium, the Netherlands, and Great Britain in this same period. As a result, French refugee policy came under attack from various groups and individuals, who attempted to intervene with the French government to improve conditions in the internment camps and release people who might be able to contribute to the war effort or emigrate abroad.[23] The letter in document 7–6 from **Nahum Goldmann**,[24] head of the Paris and Geneva offices of the **World Jewish Congress** (WJC), to WJC president **Stephen S. Wise** reveals the congress's strategy on behalf of interned Jewish refugees. It also raises the question of when it is reasonable and just for a government to abrogate an individual's rights for the sake of national security during wartime.

---

22. The term *fifth column* originated during the Spanish Civil War: in 1936, in the early period of the siege of Madrid (which the Republican government defended until 1939), a nationalist army general, Emilio Mola, used the term in a radio address to signal that the nationalist forces had clandestine supporters in the city, ready to undermine its Republican defenses. In addition to Mola's four army columns attacking the city, there was allegedly a "fifth column" in the city itself. Subsequently, the term *fifth column* has referred to traitorous clandestine activities of groups of people plotting to undermine larger, usually unsuspecting groups, such as nations. The French government's pretext for detaining "enemy aliens" in September 1939, in other words, was the alleged suspicion that refugee foreigners would secretly act as agents of the German government to undermine France. In the case of Jewish refugees fleeing from Nazi persecution, this of course sounded flimsy and ill-conceived at best.

23. Caron, *Uneasy Asylum*, 242–45, 248–49, 268–69, 316.

24. For a collection of essays discussing the various aspects of Goldmann's life, thought, and political involvement, see Mark A. Raider, ed., *Nahum Goldmann: Statesman Without a State* (Albany: State University of New York Press, 2009).

DOCUMENT 7–6: **Letter by Dr. Nahum Goldmann, Geneva, Switzerland, to Dr. Stephen S. Wise, New York City, November 17, 1939, facsimile reprinted in** *Archives of the Holocaust*, **ed. Henry Friedlander and Sybil Milton (New York: Garland Publishing, 1990), 8: 88–89.**

Dear Wise,

I am writing you today concerning a matter which requires your urgent action. It concerns the 15,000 German and Austrian Jewish refugees in France who have been interned by the military authorities. I have dealt with the matter during all the last weeks. In my opinion the measure is stupid and cruel. It would have been understandable, if the French authorities had interned, like the English have done, all suspect people, but to intern all the men till the age of 65, among them 90% Jews who have fled from Germany, is idiotic and can only be explained by the spy complex which dominates the French authorities since the outbreak of the war. The accommodation of the refugees is very bad and many of them suffer from cold and disease. There have been famous writers, Jews and non-Jews, among the interned people. [. . .] The French Jews behaved cowardly and did not really intervene for fear to be accused of "solidarity with enemies." The Joint Distribution Committee tried to intervene in a few individual cases.[25] The only organisation which really dealt with the whole question is the World Jewish Congress. From my negotiations with the French military authorities about the Jewish Legion I know the General who is in charge of all questions relating to foreigners in France.[26] So I took up the question with him. He personally is a charming and very human man. I got him to give instructions that all the interned refugees who have visas to leave France (certificates for Palestine or visas for the States, etc.) should be released. Finally, a governmental commission was

---

25. The AJJDC provided close to 90 percent of the funds to feed and shelter the eighteen thousand refugees in French camps and their families who lacked other means of support. Caron, *Uneasy Asylum*, 316. See also Yehuda Bauer, *American Jewry and the Holocaust: The American Jewish Joint Distribution Committee, 1939–1945* (Detroit, MI: Wayne State University Press, 1981), 152–77.

26. Jewish men serving in the French Foreign Legion were frequently subjected to anti-semitic discrimination and harassment. Beginning in September 1939, WJC officials met with French military authorities to discuss the possibility of creating exclusively Jewish units within the French Foreign Legion. Nothing came of these negotiations (see USHMMA RG 11.001M.36, Records of the Executive Committee of the World Jewish Congress, Paris, fond 1190, reel 107, folder 303). On Jews in the French Foreign Legion, see Renée Poznanski, *Jews in France during World War II* (Hanover, NH: University Press of New England in association with the USHMM, 2001), 19–20, and Zosa Szajkowski, *Jews and the French Foreign Legion* (New York: KTAV Publishing House, 1975).

set up to investigate the individual cases in order to release those who are unsuspected. The World Jewish Congress and the French office of the Jewish Agency for Palestine have submitted lists of people for whom they can guarantee, but owing to the very slow and disorganized working of the French bureaucratic machinery none of them has been released till now. To illustrate [to] you the absurdity of the whole procedure I want to tell you that the French authorities in the Mediterranean took off Italian boats Jewish refugees who never were in France and were on their way to the States.[27] [. . .]

In order that the situation should change I have come to the conclusion, after discussion of the matter with many friends in France, that America must intervene. Naturally you cannot protest publicly against France in these days. But a delegation should go and see the French Ambassador. I am sure (quite confidentially: people in the French Foreign Office encouraged me to do so) that when Saint-Quentin [the French Ambassador] will send a report about this intervention saying that American Jewry begins to become worried and nervous about this treatment of the refugees in France, something will be done by the authorities. It is not so much lack of good will and human understanding as the slowness of the bureaucracy and the spy complex which has made impossible till now the release of the unsuspected refugees. [. . .] Naturally you should not say a word about me or the [World Jewish] Congress, but tell them that you have got the news from the press, and as many reports have been published, you can easily base your intervention upon them. Speak friendly, but firmly to the Ambassador and tell him how cruel and stupid this measure is. Thousands of Jewish refugees in France, which were enthusiastic for the Allied cause, have been turned into bitter and disappointed people who feel they have a reason to complain about the attitude of the French authorities towards them. He will probably tell you that there have been some spies among the Jewish refugees. This may be the case, but nobody would resent the internment of all suspect people. But 15,000 refugees cannot be punished, because there may have been a few spies among them. Refer to the English example. Don't forget to mention the scandal of taking Jewish refugees off the Italian boats sailing to America. Please intervene quickly, as winter is approaching and the accommodation of the refugees in the camps is very bad and many of them will fall sick in the winter months. [. . .]

Please deal with the matter immediately: it is really important.

Yours as ever

---

27. The British also seized refugees from the ships operated by neutral countries. See Caron, *Uneasy Asylum*, 248.

The plight of Jewish refugees in neutral countries in western Europe also worsened after the outbreak of war. Resources became scarcer as the refugee crisis dragged on without end. Moreover, the need for aid grew dire and the competition for American Jewish funding fierce with the situation confronting Polish Jewry.

Document 7–7 attests to the crisis of German Jewish refugees in the Netherlands during the months of the phony war.[28] The report's author, Gertrude van Tijn,[29] worked for the Committee for Jewish Refugees in the Netherlands as one of two senior aides under its director, David Cohen.[30] Since its establishment in 1933, the committee had organized, coordinated, and taken full responsibility for financing aid to refugees in Amsterdam and at the national level. However, in the months after the start of the war, the committee found its financial burden to be increasingly untenable. Before turning to the

---

28. The "phony war" was a period of World War II between the Nazi invasion of Poland in September 1939 and the Nazi campaign against the Benelux countries and France in the late spring of 1940. Germany was technically at war with Britain and France, which went to war because of their obligations to guarantee Polish sovereignty, violated in September 1939. However, the phony war period was characterized by the complete lack of engagement between the warring sides in continental Europe, with the exception of the Nazi invasion of Norway, which spurred Britain and France to intervene briefly in April 1940; they eventually withdrew from this conflict because of the Nazi invasion of France.

29. Gertrude van Tijn-Cohn (1891–1974) was born in Braunschweig, Germany, a daughter of assimilated German Jews. After a period of living in England, she moved to the Netherlands at around age twenty and became active in the Council of Jewish Women in Amsterdam. She later joined the Committee for Jewish Refugees and became, with David Cohen, one of its most prominent members. During the war, she was a member of Amsterdam's Jewish Council; in 1943, she was deported to Westerbork and, subsequently, Bergen-Belsen. In 1944, she was exchanged with a number of other Bergen-Belsen inmates for German civilians interned in Palestine and thus saved. In the immediate aftermath of the war, she worked for AJJDC in Europe and Shanghai, eventually settling in the United States.

30. The Committee for Jewish Refugees carried over in several substantive ways to the Jewish Council (*Joodsche Raad*) of Amsterdam, which was established in February 1941 at the behest of German occupation authorities in the Netherlands. Cohen (1882–1967), a well-known academic and Zionist, became the Jewish Council's cochair, Gertrude van Tijn one of its senior staff members, and the committee's offices became the seat of the Jewish Council. Most significantly, the continuity of leadership and staff meant that the Jewish Council of Amsterdam took a similar approach toward German occupation authorities as the committee had taken toward the Dutch government. Indeed, the Jewish Council's compliance has been the object of considerable criticism among historians of Dutch Jewry during the Holocaust. See Joseph Michman, "The Controversy Surrounding the Jewish Council of Amsterdam: From Its Inception to the Present Day," *The Nazi Holocaust: Historical Articles on the Destruction of European Jews*, ed. Michael R. Marrus (Westport, CT: Greenwood, 1989), 6/2:821–43, and Moore, *Victims and Survivors*, 106–15.

Dutch government for assistance—something the committee had never done since its creation—van Tijn pleaded for additional funds from the AJJDC. Here again, as in Goldmann's letter to Wise above and as in German-dominated Poland, we see European Jewish officials looking to the United States for help.[31]

DOCUMENT 7–7: **Gertrude van Tijn, Amsterdam, Netherlands, "The Refugee Problem in Connection with the General Situation in Holland. Confidential Report for the Joint Distribution Committee," February 29, 1940, USHMMA Acc. 1997.A.0117 (NIOD 217a), reel 448, 1, 3–4, 7–9.**

> The war has made an enormous change in Holland also as far as the refugee problem is concerned. First of all the frontiers have now been definitely closed and for the last months [*sic*] or two practically no new refugees have been allowed to remain in Holland. With the exception of a group of Aliyah children and perhaps a few single cases no new permits to come to Holland will be given. It is therefore that for the first time we can gauge the size of our task. [. . .]
>
> Apart from the fact that, as we have seen, the legal position of the refugees in Holland is unsatisfactory, there is no doubt that the moral condition of the whole group, no matter how much our Committee may do to mitigate their fate, is tragic to a degree. From self-supporting valuable citizens they have suddenly become paupers. They are unwelcome strangers in a strange land. They know what is happening to Jews from all the countries now under the sway of Germany; the fear that in addition to all they have endured and are enduring the same fate may befall them any day is constantly with them. They are not allowed to work, they know that the Committee which gives them only just enough to not actually starve may not even be able to continue to do this in the near future. A few years of such an existence must sap the vitality of anybody and it is therefore also in the interest of those countries to which eventually the refugees will emigrate that they should get these before some years in exile have turned them into physical and mental wrecks. [. . .]
>
> During the 3 1/2 months until we handed over the work at the end of December, we handled 3,894 cases, for which your organization gave us

---

31. In late April 1940, the committee did turn to the Dutch government for help. The government agreed to help fund the committee's activities but then never had to deliver on its pledge because of the German invasion and subsequent occupation of the Netherlands. On the history of the committee, see Dan Michman, "The Committee for Jewish Refugees in Holland (1933–1940)," *YVS* 14 (1981): 205–32.

the funds amounting to over 860,000 [Dutch guilders].[32]—We are proud to say that, notwithstanding our inexperience and notwithstanding the fact that the temporary aspect of the arrangement made it undesirable to increase our office-staff, we managed to do the work in such a way that all the organizations concerned were satisfied.[33]

Moreover, since the war the number of transmigrants has increased greatly. During the few days preceding the departure of a boat to the United States our offices, both in Amsterdam and Rotterdam are crowded with transmigrants in need of advice and/or help.

How considerable this work is may be gathered from the fact that during the year 1939 the Rotterdam office looked after 4385 transmigrants and the Amsterdam office after 1939 transmigrants. [. . .]

This report is specially made for the Joint Distribution Committee. We know (and every personal contact makes us terribly conscious of the fact) that your organization is the point where the fate of all Jewry is reflected. One hour in the office of the Joint where uninterruptedly telegrams and telephone messages come in, each reporting of new disasters and urgent appeals for help, is enough to make one realize that by comparison Dutch Jewry and the refugees in Holland are still fortunate indeed. Yet, even with the best will in the world, and knowing how much the money is needed in places where the world is in flames and Jewry in ruins, we still plead for financial assistance from America, be it on a more moderate scale than heretofore; for we know that the burden is too heavy to bear alone. [. . .]

It is our deep felt conviction that it would be detrimental to the interests of all Jewry if the Dutch link in the chain of relief-organizations would break, and if here too chaos were to reign.

---

32. According to Yehuda Bauer, the total AJJDC expenditure in Holland (the Netherlands) in 1939 was $439,000; this number apparently partly covered **HICEM**'s expenses in Holland as well. Yehuda Bauer, *My Brother's Keeper: A History of the American Jewish Joint Distribution Committee, 1929–1939* (Philadelphia: Jewish Publication Society of America, 1974), 171, 320n81.

33. With the outbreak of the war, HICEM, which was responsible for the bulk of Jewish emigration from the Nazi-controlled territory, had to stop its operation briefly because it was formally registered in France, a country at war with the Reich. In the several months between the outbreak of the war and the move of HICEM's headquarters to neutral Belgium, Cohen and van Tijn's Committee for Jewish Refugees in Amsterdam took over this task, with the AJJDC funding that van Tijn references in this document. Bauer, *American Jewry and the Holocaust*, 38. For more on HICEM, see the Glossary.

EXPANSION OF THE WAR

As in the early weeks of the war in Poland, Jewish experiences during the military campaigns fought in western Europe during April through June 1940 did not diverge substantially from non-Jewish experiences. Like other Norwegians, Danes, Dutch, Belgians, and French, Jewish citizens of those countries fought as soldiers, prayed for an Allied victory, tried to protect themselves from bombardments, and took to the roads to flee the advancing German army. Willem Friedman (b. 1919), who grew up in Antwerp, joined the Belgian army after finishing high school. He fought against the invading German army in May 1940, was taken prisoner, and was eventually released. Friedman and his entire family managed to flee Belgium via France, Spain, and Portugal, eventually emigrating to the United States in 1940.

DOCUMENT 7–8: **Willem Friedman, a soldier in the Belgian army, poses next to a piece of artillery, winter 1939–1940, USHMMPA WS# 20481.**

Leo Krell (b. 1913), born in Poland but raised in The Hague, served in the Dutch military. He managed to survive the war in hiding, while his wife, Emmy, lived in Rijswijk with false papers. Their baby son Robert was sheltered by a non-Jewish Dutch family. After the war, the Krells emigrated to Canada.

DOCUMENT 7–9: **Leo Krell, a soldier in the Dutch army, poses on a motorcycle, ca. 1940, USHMMPA WS# 73215.**

In May and June 1940, the exodus of Belgians and Dutch fleeing to France and of Parisians fleeing south and west was nothing short of massive. In all, an estimated 7 million people took to the roads. If the word "refugee" had been associated largely with Jews fleeing Hitler, now its meaning expanded to encompass these millions eager to leave their homes to avoid the fighting.[34] Because so many men had been mobilized to serve as soldiers, the majority of people fleeing were women, and one-quarter to one-third were children.[35] One AJJDC relief worker from Brussels writing several months later on another subject could not "help mentioning the dramatic scenes which I witnessed at La Panne [De Panne], the French border point open to automobiles. More than 200,000 persons came through this small health resort in three days. The streets were so crowded that it was almost impossible to pass through. The food was insufficient, the water poor, and there was an epidemic of dysentery among the children."[36]

Acts of altruism and self-interest, of courteousness and incivility, abound in people's accounts of flight from the German offensive. In an eyewitness account published in *Aufbau* in New York on May 31, 1940, one German Jewish refugee, who numbered among the three hundred refugees from the Reich living in Norway at the time of the German invasion, described the evacuation of people from Oslo and his own escape to Sweden.[37] He dwelled on the acts of kindness shown him and the eleven other refugees with whom he traveled by different Norwegians they encountered along the way: "A Norwegian soldier flagged down an empty truck and induced the driver to give us a lift for part of the journey. In this way we managed to get out of the danger zone. A farmer put us up for the night. Far from being a socialist, he read the semifascist *Nationen*. But what he did for us, he did out of human decency."[38]

The decision to flee one's home was anything but easy. In his account of the first days of war in Belgium, Salomon Van den Berg, a prominent member of

---

34. Most refugees were repatriated in the summer and fall of 1940. Nevertheless, close to 1 million people had still not returned home as of March 1941; see Hanna Diamond, *Fleeing Hitler: France 1940* (New York: Oxford University Press, 2007), 5–6, 163. For an updated bibliography of published and unpublished works on the exodus of May and June 1940, see Diamond's "Further Reading" section, 241–45.

35. Diamond, *Fleeing Hitler*, 5–6.

36. "Report on the Events of May 10th to July 30th, 1940," September 26, 1940, facsimile reprinted in Friedlander and Milton, *Archives of the Holocaust*, 10/2:706.

37. There were seventeen hundred Jews total in Norway at the time, according to Hugo Valentin, "Rescue and Relief Activities in Behalf of Jewish Victims of Nazism in Scandinavia," *YIVO Annual of Jewish Social Science* (1953): 228–29, 231.

38. C. P., "Flucht aus Oslo. Bericht eines Flüchtlings," *Aufbau*, May 31, 1940, 4 (translated from German).

the Brussels Jewish Community, conveyed his reluctance to leave Belgium and the factors he weighed in choosing whether to stay or go.[39]

DOCUMENT 7–10: Salomon Van den Berg, May 1940 diary entry, WL PIIIi (Belgium) no. 275 (translated from French).

The question remains: will you stay or will you go. Given that André [his son] is in the army in Belgium, we are not thinking of leaving Belgium. However, the news [of the war] is bad. [. . .] Friday, at the stroke of noon, David Van den Berg telephones that he will leave by taxi for La Panne with Van Cleef, who has not found the time while living in the same house to come say goodbye to us. These are the first departures. Called Arnold, who is not thinking of leaving, for he has some information from a very good source that there is no danger. [. . .]

Saturday morning, at the office, nothing, no mail. Just in case, I make some arrangements for possible departure. The bombings make all of us jumpy, and we would like to get away from them while still remaining in Belgium. Saturday was spent by the radio, which gives us news every half hour. Naturally everything is fine, we are holding up, but the Germans are advancing. Our friend B. told us that it would be better to leave, but that it was not urgent. [. . .]

On Sunday, given that everyone I know is getting ready to leave, that I see hundreds of cars that are getting ready by loading up all that they can carry, mattresses, crockery, food, etc! I also decide to leave at 3 o'clock, especially since B. has told us again to leave if we don't want to be caught at the last minute. He advises us to head for the French border, which is open to us. Having loaded many trunks onto the car, we're on our way at about 3 o'clock, headed for Tournai. I was thinking above all of two

---

39. Salomon [M. S.] Van den Berg (1890–?), a furniture wholesale dealer by profession, returned to Brussels with his wife and daughter later in 1940. Upon being repatriated, he was nominated to the board of the Association des Juifs en Belgique (AJB), a Jewish body created under the German Military Administration. Van den Berg was subsequently named president of the Brussels Committee of the AJB. He was held briefly in the Breendonk camp in the autumn of 1942 but went into hiding after his release and survived the war. Maxime Steinberg, "The Trap of Legality: The Association of the Jews of Belgium," in *Patterns of Jewish Leadership in Nazi Europe, 1933–1945: Proceedings of the Third Yad Vashem International Historical Conference, Jerusalem, April 4–7, 1977*, ed. Yisrael Gutman and Cynthia J. Haft (Jerusalem: Yad Vashem, 1979), 356, 369; Insa Meinen, *Die Shoah in Belgien* (Büttelborn: Peter Lohse, 2009), 248.

things: to bring Mama and Nicole [his daughter] to safety and to remain in contact in Belgian territory with the office and with André.

If in the fall of 1939, Belgium and Britain could be favorably compared to France for their more selective internment policies, in May 1940 both countries' policies concerning "enemy nationals" became more sweeping and repressive. The Belgian Ministry of Justice ordered "all refugees of military age," that is, between the ages of sixteen and sixty, to report to the police. Britain introduced policies of a similar nature at the same time. By late June and early July, nearly eighty thousand people were being held in various internment camps in continental western Europe, with an additional twenty-eight thousand in Britain.[40]

On May 10, Albert Magsamen, a German Jewish refugee and businessman who had been living with his wife and child in Belgium, was taken into custody as an "enemy national." Beginning that same day, in a Belgian prison, he recorded entries in his diary, which he continued to keep in subsequent months. His internment under the German occupation would continue as he was moved from one camp to another in France, from Le Vigeant, Beauvoir, and St. Cyprien, to the southwest of France, and finally to the Gurs camp.[41]

DOCUMENT 7–11: **Albert Magsamen, from Brussels, Belgium, to the Belgian-French border, diary entries for May 10 through 13, 1940, YVA RG 09, no. 267 (translated from German).**

10 May   We were rather rudely awakened around 5:00 a.m. by a heavy bombardment of Brussels. It was only a few hours later that we learned from the radio that the Germans had attacked Belgium, Holland,

40. "Report on the Events of May 10th to July 30th, 1940," in Friedlander and Milton, *Archives of the Holocaust*, 10/2:703, 706; Maxine Schwartz Seller, *We Built Up Our Lives: Education and Community among Jewish Refugees Interned by Britain in World War II* (Westport, CT: Greenwood, 2001), 69.

41. Albert Magsamen (1904–1983?), born in Habitzheim, Germany, ended up in Switzerland as a refugee in late April 1943 until the end of the war, along with his wife, Agnes (née Hahn), and daughters Ruth (born in Brussels) and Jeanne (born in France in mid-1942). The family emigrated to the United States in 1947, where Albert had once lived for a year from 1933 to 1934 to escape the anti-Jewish climate in Germany. See New York Passenger Lists, NARA I; records of Jewish refugees in Switzerland, USHMMA RG 58.001M, reel 203 (from the Swiss National Archives, series N, RG E 4264–1985/196, E 4264–1985/197). For a first-person account by a German Jewish refugee in Great Britain who, like Magsamen, was interned in May 1940 and transported from one camp to another, see Janis Wilton, ed., *Internment: The Diaries of Harry Seidler, May 1940–October 1941* (Sydney: Allen and Unwin, 1986).

and Luxembourg. Around midday I reported as required to the nearest police station (in Ganshoren), where both our reception and our treatment were very friendly and kind. Jakubowski, Silberschmidt, Popper, and I (we were the only Jews among about 15 Germans) immediately teamed up. My wife visited me during the course of the afternoon. We spent the night on chairs and benches in the corridor of the community center—naturally there was no question of sleep. However, we hear the arrival of French troops.

11 May   Visits by my wife and child in both the morning and the afternoon. My wife brought a few belongings as well, as I have begun to have doubts about the length of my detainment, which supposedly is for 48 hours.—Around evening we were suddenly taken away in a half-covered truck to the Etterbeek Barracks. We drove within 50 meters of my apartment, which I saw for the last time. After just 30 hours, the city is completely changed. A stream of refugees has flooded the streets, everything appears transformed. We were taken to the gymnasium at the barracks, which was already terribly overcrowded. The air was so thick you could cut it and laden with indescribable tension. We spent the night on the bare floor—naturally again without sleep. The food is tolerable, but we are already completely cut off from the outside world.

12 May   There's no place where we can wash. The day passed uneventfully. One rumor follows another, like the air raid sirens. All this leaves me completely indifferent, however, I can think only of home. Toward evening we were suddenly given marching orders. We each received 1 loaf of bread and had to line up in rows of 4. What then happened in the barracks square can be described as Prussian militarism, from a superficial point of view, but it was not worthy of civilized Belgium. Perhaps it was only an abuse perpetrated by lower-ranking officials, but nevertheless it will eternally remain as our last memory of our beautiful Brussels. We were forced to hand over our tobacco, matches, knives, razor blades, razors, etc. Many other small objects were likewise taken. A purely arbitrary measure, or better, theft. Finally we had to do a forced march to the Etterbeek Railway Station, opposite the barracks. On this very short route we were verbally abused by women.—We had to wait for ages and finally, when it was completely dark, we were loaded into cattle cars like livestock, 40 men to a car. It was terribly confining and we had bad air or none at all. On the journey—naturally we did not know our

destination—we constantly heard air raid sirens and bombing. It was only with a lot of luck that we escaped this danger, whereas a car in another transport with our comrades was hit, with 21 dead.

13 May   It was only around midday when we arrived finally in Tournai on the French-Belgian border. It took us 16 hours for this journey—normally you only need 2! Unloaded, we had to get in formation and parade through this small provincial town in wonderful, but very hot weather, and we were spat upon and insulted by the population. A terrible torture! We were taken to barracks and told that we would definitely be interned here.—There is nothing to eat.—We write immediately to our families, letters that probably never arrived.[42]—We sleep (?) on a bare stone floor and are constantly disturbed by air raid sirens.

Defeat brought millions of additional Europeans, among them Jews from Scandinavia and western Europe, into direct contact with Nazi German rule for the first time. It also forced back under Nazi dominion the tens of thousands of German, Austrian, and Czech Jews, as well as the stateless Jews of eastern European origin, who had been living as refugees in western Europe. One such individual was Jacob Müller, a German Jewish businessman and bachelor who had resettled in Amsterdam in the 1930s with his mother and father. Thanks in part to his fluent Dutch, he had established extensive business and personal connections in the Netherlands prior to the start of the war.[43] He described the first days of the German occupation of Amsterdam in his wartime memoir, which he began in 1942 after going into hiding. Looking back on this earlier period, he recalled how Jews' panic contrasted sharply with the reticence of the Dutch non-Jewish population.[44]

---

42. His mother and sister were living in Chicago. His wife was not from a Jewish background, and they had married in contravention of the **Nuremberg Laws** in 1938 after a long acquaintance. USHMMA RG 58.001M, reel 203, Swiss refugee file.

43. On September 9, 1940, Jacob Müller (1894–1967) was arrested and imprisoned, first in Amsterdam and then in Kleve. Upon his release from prison in March 1941, he returned to Amsterdam, where his mother and father were living as well. After the death of his father in June 1942, Müller made the decision to go into hiding, acting on the mistaken belief that the Nazis would leave his mother, an elderly woman, alone. He had a false identity card in his possession. With that card and fishing gear in tow, he was emboldened to get on his bike and ride thirty-five miles to Driebergen, where he knew a family from prior fishing trips that was willing to hide him. He moved from one hiding place to another and survived the war.

44. On this point, see Moore, *Victims and Survivors*, 50–51.

DOCUMENT 7–12: Jacob (Köbes) Müller, memoir entry written ca. late spring or early summer 1942, LBINY ME 1028 (translated from German).[45]

[. . .] Thus Holland had capitulated, and the war was apparently over. Everyone breathed a sigh of relief, but wondered: what now? And the Jews in particular waited for what might come. Many had lost their wits, and suicides were the order of the day. In Amsterdam alone, 800 suicides are said to have occurred. For the time being, however, nothing happened at all. Everything took its usual course; people did their work, to the extent that there was still something to do, and they waited. The German troops had occupied the city, but they were not much in evidence, for most of them were quartered outside of the city. The military behaved very properly. The soldiers were well-dressed and very well-equipped. On various occasions I tried to sound out the soldiers on the Jewish question, but I always got the answer that they had nothing to do with these things, they were soldiers and had to fight, and everything else was of no interest to them. The behavior of the population was calm and dignified, no public gatherings were seen while the Germans were entering the city, and the Dutch, who otherwise are very inquisitive, stayed at home or went their own way. Infrequently one saw people standing on the wayside who gave the Hitler salute, and these were members of the German colony. It was very quiet in the stores, there were almost no customers to be seen, only in the grocery stores was there intense activity, and the shop windows were so choked with goods that one might have assumed that Holland would never run out, but everything took a different turn.

It didn't take long before Amsterdam was full of soldiers and women in uniform, who were used as auxiliary troops. These people bought whatever they could get hold of; the most outrageous things, which had gone unsold for years on end, found a buyer, and in such quantities besides that the Dutch finally realized what was going on. Everybody bought until there was literally nothing left, and then—but too late—rationing was introduced! [. . .]

---

45. Müller started writing down his memoir of the occupation on June 1, 1942, when he went into hiding at the house of Jan van den Assem in Driebergen, a town just outside Utrecht. A year later, in June 1943, he had to stop writing because the **Gestapo** broke into his hiding place and he was forced to flee. He completed the memoir after the liberation, but certainly before 1946. Some dates in it refer to the approximate time of events rather than the actual day on which Müller wrote them. The above entry was written under "May 9, 1940"; the entry after this one is dated "June 26, 1940."

Less than three weeks after the Dutch capitulation, the newly instated German occupation authorities were already targeting Jews in Amsterdam. The Daily Information Bulletin issued by the **Jewish Telegraphic Agency**'s Paris bureau on June 4, 1940, reported on the violent measures to which Jews in Amsterdam were being subjected, as well as on the continuing plight of Jewish refugees. These stories reveal what information was reaching Paris and London from the occupied Netherlands.

DOCUMENT 7–13: **Daily Information Bulletin issued by the Jewish Telegraphic Agency, Paris, France, June 4, 1940, USHMMA RG 11.001M.25, reel 106 (SAM 674-1-130) (translated from French).**

The situation in Holland: epidemics, arrests, murders
London, June 3 (J.T.A.)

According to the "Jewish Chronicle," a telegram has been received from Amsterdam announcing that the influx of refugees from the provinces has provoked an explosion of epidemics in the ancient ghetto of Amsterdam. The food shortage aggravates the situation.

Mass arrests of Jewish journalists, industrialists, and shopkeepers have occurred in Amsterdam. Many Jews have been shot. The Gestapo has closed the offices of the Jewish community in Amsterdam, Rotterdam, and The Hague.

For the immediate admission of refugees to the United States
London, June 3 (J.T.A.)

The Manchester Guardian is publishing an appeal to the United States government for the immediate admission of all refugees from Germany who find themselves at present in Allied countries. Such a gesture would conform to American humanitarian traditions and would free the Allied countries from a responsibility made particularly delicate by the circumstances.

If the mass evacuation of the refugees is impractical for the moment, at least the refugees already in possession of the first papers that should assure them of obtaining an American visa could be admitted to the United States without delay, the author of the appeal thinks.

Jewish refugees in the south of France who had either escaped internment camps or never been interned devoted all of their energy to finding a way out. Despite the fact that the Unoccupied Zone was under French authorities, remaining there did not seem to promise security. One Belgian refugee reported on "the complete change of the 'climate' of France within those few weeks [before and following the French surrender]. The democratic ideal which seemed to be the essence of France itself, has yielded to xenophobia, to poorly understood totalitarianism, and to low standards. These profound changes in France have prompted me, like so many others, to seek a possibility of emigrating from Europe."[46] Thus, from this time forward, many western European Jews commenced the process of trying to obtain visas, as their coreligionists from central Europe had been doing for years. Still, exit, transit, and entrance visas were no easier to attain; the expansion of the war only made transport more inaccessible, and most Jews had exhausted the resources at their disposal. Of the several million Jews across Europe who desperately wanted to escape Nazi rule or its orbit in 1940, thirty-seven thousand emigrated to the United States, ten thousand to Palestine (half of whom arrived illegally and were held by British authorities), and another ten thousand to other countries around the world.[47]

Some refugees managed to reach Portugal by boat from French ports like Marseilles; other escape routes were by land and entailed first reaching one of the two neutral countries bordering France: Switzerland or Spain. Historians estimate that perhaps as many as several tens of thousands of Jews passed through Spain between June 1940 and July 1942.[48] The firsthand report published in *Aufbau* by Jewish journalist Eugen Tillinger (document 7–14) offers a remarkable description of the complex emotions and unceasing insecurity generated by leaving France.[49] After reaching Spain—in this case by walking across the bridge from Hendaye, France, to Irún, Spain—Jewish refugees continued

---

46. "Report on the Events of May 10th to July 30th, 1940," in Friedlander and Milton, *Archives of the Holocaust*, 10/2:706.

47. Caron, *Uneasy Asylum*, 262; Dwork and van Pelt, *Flight from the Reich*, 196.

48. Haim Avni, "Spain," in *The Holocaust Encyclopedia*, ed. Walter Laqueur (New Haven, CT: Yale University Press, 2001), 601.

49. Born in Lemberg (Polish: Lwów; Ukrainian: Lviv), Poland, Eugen (Eugene) Tillinger (1908–1966) worked for a German tabloid from 1928 to 1933 in Berlin, where he secured support from Manfred George, later a long-serving editor of *Aufbau*. In 1933 Tillinger evidently left Germany with his brother and mother, moving first to Vienna and then to France. He arrived in New York from Lisbon in late 1940. (His brother and a cousin had preceded him, and his mother managed to follow them in 1942 on a ship from Casablanca.) Tillinger published extensively in *Aufbau* through the late 1940s (sometimes under the byline "E.T." or "e.t.") and continued working as a correspondent for the French and U.S. press until his death. He also achieved brief notoriety through his attacks on Thomas Mann's political leanings in the late 1940s. See New York Passengers Lists, NARA I; Wolfgang Elfe, James N. Hardin, and Günther Holst, eds., *The Fortunes of German Writers in America: Studies in Literary Reception* (Columbia: University of South Carolina Press, 1992), 140; obituary, *New York Times*, October 15, 1966.

on to Portugal, where they could wait in relative peace for visas to the United States or Latin America.

DOCUMENT 7–14: Eugen Tillinger, "The Bridge of Hendaye: Eyewitness Account of the Mass Flight to Spain," *Aufbau* (New York), August 30, 1940, 2 (translated from German).

Closed border

And now people are standing in line before the bridge. Before the bridge that has often been mentioned in the world press, before the famous bridge at Hendaye. Just a few meters ahead of us, the *tricolore* still flies. The French officials are unusually friendly. And barely a hundred meters away lies Spain. We hear the radio: the German troops are advancing, the cease-fire was signed yesterday. Many people are growing impatient. Believe that the border could be closed any minute. One man, who is sent back because his papers are not in order, has a crying fit.

It is 1:00 in the afternoon now. Our turn has come. All the formalities are done with, we walk the few steps toward the French border barriers, show the official a white slip of paper; he takes it, says "Merci" one last time, and gives a signal with his hand. The toll bar rises slowly . . . One step and we're no longer in France. Just a few more steps . . . We look behind us. Stand still here in no-man's-land for a moment, quietly. We think back with melancholy: Adieu, France . . . Glorious, beautiful France! Why did it have to come to this? Why? Slowly we walk toward the opposite end of the bridge. And only a lively dispute abruptly rouses us from our dreamlike state. What has happened? . . . A few seconds later we catch sight of a man talking insistently to the Spanish officials and gesticulating energetically all the while. The discussion grows louder and louder. It is clear: the Spaniards are unwilling to let the man pass through. In vain, he shows his visas, his diplomatic passport . . . Nothing helps: Mr. Titulescu, Romania's former foreign minister, is not allowed to pass . . . He has to go back. Back to France. . .

And 24 hours later, as we arrive at the Portuguese border, the swastika flag is already flying at the Hendaye bridge . . .

In a December 1940 edition of *Aufbau*, Tillinger published a piece about how refugees in Portugal were faring. This subsequent article, presented in document 7–15, served to remind *Aufbau* readers in New York how difficult life continued to be for Jewish refugees on the margins of Nazi-occupied Europe.

Tillinger also offered some advice about how best to guarantee the delivery of parcels and money to relatives stuck in France.

DOCUMENT 7–15: Eugen Tillinger, "You've come from Lisbon? . . . Do tell! . . . ," *Aufbau* (New York), December 20, 1940, 2 (translated from German).

> When you run into friends and old acquaintances just after you've arrived in New York, people you haven't seen for years, the same question is repeated every time: "You've come from Lisbon? . . . Tell us about it!"
>
> What should one say in reply? . . . That the mood among the refugees is not precisely rosy . . . that only a relatively tiny fraction of them have a chance of getting a visa . . . that the news arriving from France is getting worse by the day? [. . .]
>
> Here, at this juncture, it is important to give some advice to those who still have loved ones in Portugal and France. [. . .]
>
> As regards the <u>food parcels</u> that can be sent from Lisbon to France, I would suggest sending only small, 500-gram "sample without commercial value" parcels, because the others rarely reach their destination. Any grocery store in Lisbon will arrange for the shipping.
>
> Anyone wishing to send <u>sums of money</u> to loved ones living in the <u>unoccupied</u> zone should do this directly through a bank, ideally by wire, even if it costs a few dollars for the charges. Avoid a more complicated payment transaction, because the French authorities require the German and Austrian emigrants, even the women, to provide detailed proof that they have money available or that they really are getting money from America. But this proof, which in many cases can save the refugees from being interned anew in a camp, is valid only if they can produce a receipt from a French bank. . . . [. . .]

France's invasion and defeat also had an impact on the sizable Jewish populations of Algeria, Tunisia, and Morocco.[50] Refugees fleeing Europe began to arrive in North Africa in June 1940, using these three French colonial possessions as way stations.[51] The local Jewish communities suddenly found them-

---

50. The Jewish population of Algeria numbered 150,000 in 1950; of Morocco, 200,000 in 1940; and of Tunisia, 100,000 in 1945. Haim Saadoun, "North Africa" in Laqueur, *The Holocaust Encyclopedia*, 444.

51. In the two years between the 1940 German-French armistice and 1942, some twenty thousand Jewish refugees passed through French Morocco, Tangiers, and Algeria: as transients in Casablanca (some ten thousand), as civilian refugees, as camp internees deported from **Vichy** France, and as "foreign workers." Michel Abitbol, *The Jews of North Africa during the Second World War* (Detroit, MI: Wayne State University Press, 1989), 92–93.

selves responsible for aiding newly arrived Jews from Europe. In the letter in document 7–16, part travelogue, part report, by an unknown Jewish individual who appears to have had connections to Swiss Zionist circles, we glimpse how the expansion of the war in 1940 thrust the refugee crisis on North Africa's Jewish populations. In Casablanca, the Moroccan Jewish community adapted the existing organizational infrastructure to respond to the needs of refugees.

DOCUMENT 7–16: **Letter from an unnamed Jewish correspondent in Casablanca, Morocco, August 28, 1940, USHMMA RG 68.045M (WJC Geneva), reel 1, 203–20 (translated from German).**

[. . .] Incidentally, Casablanca is the most curious city I have ever seen— an American-style cocktail with a shot of megalomania and a Moorish flavor that fits the area well. Directly after seeing skyscrapers, you again catch sight of the most splendid gardens, like something out of *1001 Nights*. One can find the grandest and most powerful American cars such as Packards here, and the small donkeys ridden by a Moroccan must tread cautiously so as not to be run over. Nowadays horse-drawn carriages straight out of grandma's day make their way through traffic, since the fuel shortage has also arrived in these parts. And the elegant residential area here lies directly next to the old medina, the native quarter of the Arabs—but also of the Jews—who live in unimaginable misery. Apart from that, Casablanca during the last two decades must truly have been the city where people became millionaires overnight. [. . .]

The Jews of Casablanca have by and large attained a highly respected position. Not only in an economic respect; they also have had a knack for gaining the favor of the Moroccan dignitaries and of members of other faiths through their extraordinary charitable endeavors. The Alliance Israélite in particular has made a name for itself here by founding a series of charitable institutions that are viewed as exemplary. The Alliance also maintains a number of its own schools for the benefit of the poor Jewish population. Casablanca, like Algeria, remained completely untouched by the stream of Jewish refugees over the last seven years. This changed with the tragic days of June, when the Germans swiftly advanced through France. A hundred ships lay anchored off Bayonne, Biarritz, and Saint-Jean-de-Luz on the southernmost Atlantic coast [of France] ready to take on board refugees. It was precisely on those three critical days before the armistice that it rained horribly. The refugees stood in the downpour on the beach for hours, all night, because they were willing to board the ships only if they were truly going to depart. Some sailed to England, but these steamships mainly took only English passengers as well as whole units of Polish and Czech troops, while smaller and medium-sized French ships initially set course for Portugal. However, the Portuguese port authorities refused to let the ships offload their cargo of hundreds of refugees, including very many non-French Jewish refugees. The term "cargo" [*Last*] is fitting here because the people were penned up, there was in most cases nothing to eat, and some ships even ran out of drinking water. The Joint and HICEM in Lisbon were not informed in time. Hundreds of passengers had to be transferred from the smallest ships to a larger cargo ship while out at sea but within the three-mile zone. Some of the steamers set course for Casablanca. Here, too, port authorities initially refused to let them disembark. Their position changed quickly after they learned that these were refugees from France, many of whom had served France loyally. The refugees were first placed in a quarantine camp. In a humanitarian gesture, the Moroccan Jewish community in Casablanca very quickly attended to the refugees, who stemmed from 12 different nations and included four Christian families. Alongside some French notables, the Alliance Israélite as well as members of the foreign colony provided financial guarantees, and a great humanitarian service was thus performed. Those [newcomers] who were not deemed suspicious and who did not have a criminal record were by and by released [from the camp]. The Alliance set up sleeping quarters at its various institutions, families were housed with private individuals, and a communal kitchen was created to provide kosher meals three times a day for individuals without means. All this work showed the same initiative and generosity as the aid provided for the Austrians in Switzerland during the fall of 1938. Provisions were also made to ensure that the refugees obeyed all police regulations. No new steamers arrived after the armistice because the French government followed its provisions to the letter. A few stragglers still arrived, but only by land and having traveled in part through Spain. The Aid Committee is well organized and seeks to help above all emigrants who already hold visas (indeed, only genuine visas). And yet various difficulties have arisen, since France remains bound to certain conditions; for instance, men fit for military service may not leave, and, moreover, the English blockade has brought travel by sea to an almost complete standstill. Very occasionally merchant vessels set sail for Portugal. These belong to a Portuguese company and charge "only" 3500 French francs for a passage to Lisbon but are of course already sold out.

That is how things stand here. Incidentally, a few good acquaintances from Switzerland are here as well. The head of the Aid Committee, incidentally, is a Zionist who represented Morocco at the last [Zionist world] congress, Herr Tuers or something like that. I intend to remain here for a period of time. Please send me the little green newspaper [*Blättli*]—one cannot get a Jewish paper here.

Romania became an important transit station for those Jews who tried to navigate a particularly challenging passage as part of Zionist efforts to enter Palestine via **Aliyah Bet** or another illegal channel. They traveled by boat on the river Danube through the Black Sea into the Mediterranean. As we saw in chapter 2, in addition to the hurdles all would-be emigrants had to overcome, already in peace time the risks involved in taking this escape route included crammed and unhealthy conditions aboard barely seaworthy ships, exposure to the elements and bad provisions, and extended stays at inhospitable border crossings and encounters with often ill-willed officials. After the beginning of the war, those passengers traversing the Danube and the Mediterranean aboard derelict ships like the *Milos, Atlantic,* and *Pentcho* faced an even riskier odyssey. The diary extract presented in document 7–17, partly written en route to Palestine, partly from memory in 1946, describes key points in the journey of young Egon Weiss from the German-annexed part of Czechoslovakia.[52]

---

52. Egon Weiss was born to Emil and Olga Weiss in 1920 in Karlovy Vary (German: Karlsbad) in what was then Czechoslovakia. His sister, Edith, was born in 1923. After the German annexation of the **Sudetenland** in late 1938, the entire family applied for American visas under the sponsorship of an aunt in the United States. The family worried that the Germans could conscript Egon as forced labor, so they decided he should go to Palestine while the rest of the family waited for their American papers to come through. On January 20, 1942, Emil, Olga, and Edith Weiss were deported to Theresienstadt, where Olga Weiss gave birth later that year to another child, Tommy. None of Egon's immediate family survived: Edith was deported to Auschwitz in 1943, and the rest of the family was deported in 1944. Egon left Palestine for the United States in 1947.

DOCUMENT 7–17: **Egon Weiss, en route to Palestine, diary entries written in 1940 and 1946,**[53] **USHMMPA, private collection (translated from German).**

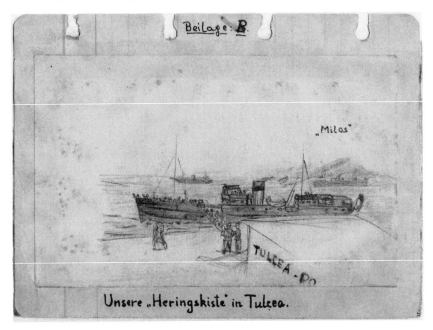

[. . .]

II. My Emigration

Like all the other Jews in the Protectorate, I too had to look around for an opportunity to emigrate, and so I signed up [here Weiss inserted: Dec. 39] for an illegal Revisionist Zionist transport to Palestine. Mail often came, saying that the transport was leaving, but the departure time was repeatedly postponed. Again on Saturday, September 1, 1940,[54] I received a message that the date had been set for September 3 and that I should inquire once more by telephone on the 2nd. On Sunday afternoon

---

53. According to information kindly supplied by Egon Weiss in October 2010, he wrote the diary copy that constitutes the basis for this document in ca. 1946; it represents a verbatim transcription of his original (no longer available) diary notes for the events after October 30, 1940. For events before that date, a mixture of early postwar memory and original notes survived the sinking of the *Patria*. The drawing of the *Milos* was done in the Athlit camp by a friend of Mr. Weiss.

54. This and the following September date are misdated in the diary copy for November 1940.

I learned that this time it was really in earnest. [. . .] Monday afternoon I phoned the transport office and received the surprising news that I needed to be at the train station that very evening, ready to go. [. . .] After I had said goodbye to my d.[ear] parents and my sister, I took my knapsack and rode the tram, crammed full, to the train station. The whole thing was happening so suddenly that I couldn't take it all in. I couldn't grasp that it would be a long parting. Not until I reached the ship did I realize what it means to know that people you've loved are far away. Another state of mind also set in: I saw my entire past life as something that was finished, over, something that I thought about sometimes with a certain melancholy but that already lay far, far in the past.

[. . . Trip by train to Vienna, and then by ship "Melk," reaching Ruse, Bulgaria, on September 7, 1940]

On the 20th [of September], our "herring box" (the expression came from the shortage of space) was renamed, and besides the Panamanian flag it also was given the lovely name "Milos." Five days later, the passengers quartered in the warehouse by order of the Romanian authorities were supposed to reboard the ship. We protested vigorously and did not let anyone board our "little rowboat." By so doing, we wanted to force the Romanian government to extend permission for our stay. That's not how it turned out, however. The police seized two of our stewards and refused to release them until everyone from the warehouse was accommodated on board.

Our transport was organized along the following lines: Each room was under the control of a room commander. The highest authority was the warehouse management. To maintain order, there was a security police force [*Schutzpolizei*], armed with wooden clubs. In addition to the security police, there were stewards, who managed communication and other technical matters. A lavatory service, arranged by each block of quarters, was responsible for keeping the toilets and washrooms clean.

On October 10, supplies, in particular hardtack, were taken on board the "Milos," and from that we concluded that we soon would sail. It was also possible for us to trade fountain pens, cigarette lighters, and other items with the Romanian military in exchange for food. A bath in the Danube could be obtained by bribing the guard with cigarettes. [. . .]

The food we were given was inadequate in terms of both quality and quantity. The bread and hardtack were moldy, and we had to cut out the mold before we could manage to eat the food at all. The hardtack was especially awful: it looked like dog biscuits and tasted like flour paste. Sometimes there were also sausages or jam, both full of worms.

[. . . Onward journey via Piraeus and Cyprus; on November 7, they reached the shores of Palestine and were transferred by British authorities to a ship known as the *Patria*.]

13. [November 1940] Everyone was given a life belt. We don't know what that is supposed to mean. Rumor has it that we are to be deported to Australia. I hope it's not true.

16. [November 1940] There were demonstrations in the evening. Jewish songs were sung, people chanted in unison, demanding our release, and above all, we protested against deportation to Australia.

17. [November 1940] Everything points to a speedy departure. Coal was loaded, crew came on board, emergency staircases were built, etc. The following was read in the Chosen (newsletter): The T.L. [transport management] sent the Palestinian authorities a petition in which our release is demanded and a vigorous protest is made against deporting us to some colony.—That is the first official report, which proves to us again that the rumors are true and not made up out of thin air. At the same time, in today's Chosen, the spreading of information was strictly prohibited.

18. [November 1940] Coal was loaded again. We are pondering what we can do to oppose the planned "Australia trip."

One week later, on November 25, 1940, Weiss witnessed—and survived—the sinking of the *Patria* in Haifa harbor, organized by Zionist resisters against the British detention policy.[55] He spent the following eleven months in the Athlit camp, cut off from his friends and relatives back in his home country.

Germany's spring campaign in northern and western Europe emboldened the Soviet Union to press forward with its territorial expansion in the Baltic and Balkans. In mid-June, the Red Army moved into Lithuania, Latvia, and Estonia as a first step toward those countries' incorporation into the Soviet Union as Soviet Socialist republics. In the same month, the Soviet Union insisted that

---

55. See Meir Chazan, "The Patria Affair: Moderates vs. Activists in Mapai in the 1940s," *Journal of Israeli History* 22, no. 2 (2003): 61–95; Tuvia Friling, *Arrows in the Dark: David Ben-Gurion, the Yishuv Leadership, and Rescue Attempts during the Holocaust* (Madison: University of Wisconsin Press, 2005), 41; Yehuda Lapidot, "The Irgun's Role in Illegal Immigration," Jewish Virtual Library, www.jewishvirtuallibrary.org/jsource/History/irgunill. html (accessed March 4, 2011).

Romania surrender the provinces of Bessarabia and northern Bukovina. The Red Army was poised to invade if Romania did not willingly comply.[56]

When Romanian troops evacuated those two provinces a mere two days later, according to historian Radu Ioanid, it "was a heavy blow to Romanian prestige and triggered severe reactions in the country's internal political life." Just one week earlier, on the same day that France signed its armistice with Nazi Germany (June 22, 1940), Romania's King Carol II had taken drastic action to preserve his regime amid ever-mounting pressure from the fascist Iron Guard movement. Carol II had declared Romania a "totalitarian" state and established the Party of the Nation with active participation by the Iron Guard. Now he faced additional external pressure with the situation in Bessarabia and Bukovina.

Heightened antisemitism was one response to the Soviet incursion. Romanian propaganda and intelligence reports portrayed Jews as Communists and traitors who had welcomed Soviet troops and insulted Romanian soldiers as they were in the process of withdrawing from Bessarabia and Bukovina. In the last days of June and first days of July 1940, Romanian soldiers and mobs of Romanians and Ukrainians massacred Jews, including Romanian Jewish soldiers, in a series of seemingly uncoordinated attacks. The deadliest pogrom occurred on July 1 in Dorohoi, in Bukovina, where an estimated 160 to 200 Jews were killed.[57]

The telegram in document 7–18 illustrates the efforts of Bucharest's **Sephardi** Jewish community to abate the wave of attacks against Jews. In response to reports alleging the lack of patriotic feeling among Bessarabian and Bukovinan Jews, the Sephardi community of "Old Romania" asserted its unwavering patriotism.[58] Such a strategy of emphasizing shared national history and patriotic fervor was common to Jews throughout Europe in times of crisis and in response to antisemitism.

---

56. Gerhard L. Weinberg, *A World at Arms: A Global History of World War II* (Cambridge: Cambridge University Press, 1994), 135–36.

57. Ioanid, *The Holocaust in Romania*, 38–43. The quote in the previous paragraph appears on 38.

58. "Old Romania," also known as the "Old Kingdom" or Regat, refers to the provinces of Wallachia and Moldavia, which comprised Romania prior to World War I. Most of the Sephardi community of Romania lived in the Regat in the capital, Bucharest.

DOCUMENT 7–18: **Telegram sent by the Israelite Community of Spanish Rite, Bucharest, Romania, to King Carol II, July 2, 1940, USHMMA RG 25.021 (CSHJR file III:2), reel 1, 51 (translated from Romanian).**

THE ISRAELITE COMMUNITY
OF SPANISH RITE OF BUCHAREST
49 Banu Maracine St
Tel.: 3.22.04
<u>Copy</u>
<u>of the Telegram Sent to His Majesty the King on July 2, 1940</u>

SIRE,

During its general assembly, the Israelite Community of Spanish Rite[59] of Bucharest, gathered around the Throne, through his Eminence Head Rabbi Sabetay Djaen,[60] raised fervent prayers to our God, the God of all, for Your Majesty and for the Country.

In our mourning and heartfelt grief for the precocious loss of Bessarabia and Northern Bukovina—[two] Romanian territories—we can only find consolation in the hope and conviction that, soon enough, our precious Fatherland and August Sovereign will come to see better and more just times once again.

We are Your Majesty's most humble and loyal servants.

President,

Attorney Iosif G. Cohen   General Secretary,

                                                                        I. Campus

If such a telegram sought to communicate that Romanian Jews remained steadfast, other documents reveal ambivalence, a sense of betrayal, and even anger on their part. Another Bucharest native, Emil Dorian, a Romanian Jewish doctor, writer/poet, teacher, and diarist, pondered the meaning of his Romanian patriotism upon learning about the atrocities committed in Bessarabia and

---

59. This appellation, "the Israelite Community of Spanish Rite," appears in all of the Sephardi community's official communications with the Romanian government in this archival collection.

60. Sabetay I. Djaen (1883–1947) was a well-known rabbi and Jewish teacher. Born in Plevna (today Pleven, Bulgaria), he went to Buenos Aires in 1928 from Monastir (now Bitola, Macedonia). He later returned to Romania, where he assumed the chief rabbinate of the Union of Communities of Spanish Rite in 1931. Djaen remained in Romania through World War II but returned to Argentina after the war, where he died in 1947.

Bukovina against Jews.[61] The violence perpetrated by Romanian soldiers against their Jewish comrades in arms particularly outraged him.

DOCUMENT 7–19: **Emil Dorian, Bucharest, Romania, diary entry for July 16, 1940, in *The Quality of Witness: A Romanian Diary, 1937–1944*, ed. Marguerite Dorian (Philadelphia: Jewish Publication Society of America, 1982), 107–8.**

[. . .] During this half century, my existence unfolded between the cry of "Down with the kikes" in 1800-and-something and that of "Down with the kikes" in 1940. During all this time, I gave the best of myself, over and over, loving and waiting, understanding and loving. What I saw and heard around me all this time—Jewish beards torn out, synagogues desecrated, insults and beatings, injustice done to my daughters, the whole gamut of infamies, of injuries and insanities, of refined or cruel brutalities—I suffered, in the belief that someday everything would be accounted for, paid for. Yet today the balance of this half century closes with new humiliations and new crimes. After all this time, when I loved and sang, understood and forgave, what kind of change for the better can I expect for my family, for my country, for this whole continent?

Unbelievable, the stories told about the endless number of crimes committed on trains in the last two weeks. [. . .] Today we know more about what happened in Bessarabia and Bukovina when the Romanian army withdrew: acts of revenge by the Communists, who had been persecuted before, retaliation and destruction by the withdrawing soldiers, violence on the part of the population that stayed behind. All this, common occurrences under such exceptional circumstances. I can understand that the embittered soldiers behaved cruelly. What I cannot comprehend is that later, as the army passed through a peaceful little Romanian town, it shot down like dogs a group of Jews in the cemetery where they were praying at the grave of a Jewish officer. Such senseless savagery! Let us admit that, in some frontier village, the recent frustration and anger could have led to

---

61. Emil Dorian (1893–1956) was a pseudonym of the son of Herman and Ernestina Lustig. Born in Bucharest, Dorian began to publish poetry and other writings early in life but went on to study medicine. In the interwar period he published essays, satire, books of popular medicine, and children's literature. In 1937 he began keeping a diary, which documented the most difficult period in the history of Romanian Jewry. After the war, he briefly served as secretary-general of the Jewish community of Bucharest and director of the documentary libraries and archives of the Federation of Jewish Communities of Romania. He soon resigned, however, and practiced medicine until his death.

attacks against a population of odd and dirty-looking Jews with side curls. But how can one explain the cold-blooded, organized crimes committed on trains against Jewish officers and soldiers on their way to perform their duty or returning from its performance? How can a soldier push another soldier out a train window? We are no longer dealing with the misguided zeal of some youths on their way to a rally who have fun molesting a few Jews and pulling out their beards. We are dealing with the senseless murder of innocent people at the very moment when they were showing devotion to their country, although insulted by legislation and threatened with starvation. How far can the authorities go and shamelessly continue to call Jews to military service? Is it cynicism or an invitation to massacre?

Germany's hegemony over much of Europe by the middle of 1940 made the situation of Jews in Romania, France, the Netherlands, Belgium, and several other European countries more vulnerable. As battle fronts quieted, Hitler's regime and other like-minded governments turned their attention to waging legislative assaults against Jews under their control.

CHAPTER 8
JEWISH DAILY LIFE IN WARTIME

JEWS IN THE Reich and the **Protectorate of Bohemia and Moravia** contended with worsening persecution during the first two years of the war.
In the months leading up to the war, German and Austrian Jews had suffered
the loss of jobs, the liquidation of businesses, the seizure of property, and acts
of violence and degradation. Now they also faced hunger, forced labor, and
removal from their homes into "Jew houses." In the Protectorate, the timing
and content of decrees affecting Czech Jews were slightly modified, but their
thrust remained the same. Making life more unbearable still, fewer antidotes
were available to Jewish individuals seeking a way out of their social isolation,
with radios confiscated (on Yom Kippur), curfews imposed, and leisure activities and venues declared off-limits. And emigration was less feasible than ever.
The Nazi regime's official stance until September 1941 was to allow Jews to
leave the Reich; yet, as we have seen in previous chapters, the hurdles to emigration became increasingly insurmountable.[1]

In the same period, German occupation authorities and regimes allied with
Nazi Germany in western, central, and southeastern Europe, including **Vichy**
France, Belgium, Luxembourg, the Netherlands, Hungary, Italy, Slovakia,
and Romania, all introduced or extended discriminatory measures against
their respective Jewish populations. Native and foreign-born Jews residing in

---

1. Marion A. Kaplan, *Between Dignity and Despair: Jewish Life in Nazi Germany* (New
York: Oxford University Press, 1998), 146, 150–54, 173; Livia Rothkirchen, *The Jews of
Bohemia and Moravia: Facing the Holocaust* (Lincoln and Jerusalem: University of Nebraska
Press and Yad Vashem, 2005), 110, 114–18.

Nazi-dominated continental Europe found themselves subject to a barrage of legislation and decrees restricting their economic livelihoods, social relations, and cultural pursuits. The dynamics of the relationship between the Nazi regime and local authorities differed in each national context, as did the history of Jewish-Gentile relations. Nevertheless, Jews in all of these European countries were forced to cope with the circumscription of their spheres of activity and with hardships that set them apart from their non-Jewish compatriots.

This chapter aims to tease out the similarities and differences among the situations and response strategies of Jews in many different European countries in the first year and a half of the war, prior to the German invasion of the Soviet Union. It excludes Poland, where the brutality of German occupation policies during this period and the complexity of Jewish responses necessitate a separate examination (see Parts II and IV of this volume). When we study in parallel the responses of Jews who were either under direct Nazi control or within the Nazi orbit, how homogeneous does "European Jewry" appear to have been in the early years of the war? What were the main elements of shared identity in this period? And what influence did individuals' definitions of self and community have on their responses to antisemitic persecution? In seeking answers to these questions, we must keep in view the variations in the European Jewish landscape. Individuals continued to understand themselves in reference to national, regional, local, communal, and personal frameworks of belonging. Hence, to whatever extent antisemitic decrees and Jews' responses may give the impression of uniformity when viewed in retrospect, specific contexts and identities remained distinct and meaningful from the perspective of people at the time.

DIRECT APPEALS TO AUTHORITIES

Antisemitic laws and decrees elicited a host of written protests by Jewish leaders and average Jewish citizens. Read separately, Jewish letters to authorities reflect the history and political traditions of a given nation, including most significantly the history of Jewish-Gentile relations and Jewish emancipation. When looked at together, such letters reveal an overarching faith in the rule of law and the force of public opinion. To varying degrees, European Jews from many countries maintained faith in the national ties forged from allegiance to liberal political traditions. They also conveyed a hope in the power of petition to effect change.

In the letter to the Italian Fascist leader Benito Mussolini, presented in document 8–1, Italian Jewish writer Luciano Morpurgo protested the antisemitic measures introduced in Italy beginning in August 1938.[2] Morpurgo's letter numbers among more than a thousand such letters written by Italian Jews between 1938 and 1942 to Mussolini and King Victor Emmanuel III. In those letters, Italian Jews registered their shock at being set apart from the general population, for they had perceived no tension between their identities as both Italians and Jews. Rather than remaining passive, these letter writers defended their rights as citizens. In many instances, they also made rational arguments appealing for exemptions, referred to as "discriminations" [*discriminazione*] in Italian, from different sections of the antisemitic legislation.[3]

Italy's racial laws of 1938 and 1939 affected the Italian Jewish population (approximately forty-seven thousand) and the foreign Jewish population residing in Italy (some ten thousand) in different ways.[4] Foreign Jews were given six months to leave Italy and all Italian overseas territories. If they remained as of March 12, 1939, they faced imprisonment. Jews who had been naturalized citizens since 1919 lost their citizenship and were treated thenceforth as foreigners. Italian-born Jews had as a whole thrived since being granted full political rights with Italian unification in 1870 and were well-integrated into the Italian nation, rising to prominent positions in national politics and even in the Fascist Party itself.[5] They now found themselves

2. Luciano Morpurgo (1886–1971) was a writer, photographer, and publisher. His books of photography based on his travels in Italy, Palestine, Egypt, and elsewhere were well-known in his day. Morpurgo lived in Rome throughout the years of the war, going into hiding in October 1943 when Germans began rounding up Jews in Italian cities. He survived the war living underground with false papers. Susan Zuccotti, *The Italians and the Holocaust: Persecution, Rescue, and Survival* (Lincoln: University of Nebraska Press, 1996), 108, 144, 194.

3. For the estimate of the number of such letters in the Italian State Archives, see Iael Orvieto, "Letters to Mussolini: Italian Jews and the Racial Laws," in *Remembering for the Future: The Holocaust in an Age of Genocide*, ed. John K. Roth and Elisabeth Maxwell (New York: Palgrave Macmillan, 2001), 468, 477. See also Iael Nidam-Orvieto, "The Impact of Anti-Jewish Legislation on Everyday Life and the Response of Italian Jews, 1938–1943," in *Jews in Italy under Fascist and Nazi Rule, 1922–1945*, ed. Joshua Zimmerman (New York: Cambridge University Press, 2005), 175–76.

4. These population figures are based on the census of Jews taken in August 1938 and cited in Zuccotti, *The Italians and the Holocaust*, 5.

5. See Zuccotti, *The Italians and the Holocaust*, 23–27. According to Susan Zuccotti, 4,920 Italian Jews had become members of the Fascist Party by October 1933. Cf. the membership numbers presented by Renzo De Felice, *The Jews in Fascist Italy: A History*, 1st Eng. ed. (New York: Enigma, 2001), 65–67, and the related discussion in Michele Sarfatti, *The Jews in Mussolini's Italy: From Equality to Persecution* (Madison: University of Wisconsin Press, 2006), 15–17, 66–67, 116–17. At the same time, the Jewish presence in the ranks of antifascists remained very strong.

subject to a slew of regulations similar to Nazi Germany's **Nuremberg Laws** and discriminatory decrees. These prohibited intermarriage, introduced restrictions on Jewish ownership of businesses and property, barred Jewish participation in many professions and in public schools and universities, and banned Jews from Fascist Party membership and from serving in the military.[6]

These and other anti-Jewish measures took Italian Jews by surprise. Unlike in Nazi Germany, antisemitism was not central to Fascist ideology, nor had Jewish assimilation come to an abrupt halt with the coming to power of Mussolini's Fascist regime in 1922. Indeed, the Italian racial laws appear to have been motivated more by international political considerations than by the steady escalation of antisemitic sentiment in the Fascist Party or in Italian society as a whole. Racism against Jews and blacks did intensify in Italian right-wing and Catholic circles during the mid-1930s as part of the propaganda supporting Italy's involvement in the Spanish Civil War and the invasion of Ethiopia; most of all, however, Mussolini had decided to tie Italy's fortunes to the Axis alliance with Nazi Germany in this period, and it appears he used racial policy to prove his camaraderie with Hitler.[7]

There are different ways to interpret why Italian Jews addressed their petitions to Mussolini directly. Morpurgo was moved to write in September 1939 when he learned about the most recent anti-Jewish decree eliminating the organizations that Italian Jews had formed in the 1930s for the purpose of helping German Jewish refugees. He attempted to engage Mussolini's attention in a number of ways, among others by reminding him of Italian Jews' love of the "Italian people and our blessed land."

---

6. Meir Michaelis, *Mussolini and the Jews: German-Italian Relations and the Jewish Question in Italy, 1922–1945* (London and Oxford: Institute for Jewish Affairs and Clarendon Press, 1978), 206; Zuccotti, *The Italians and the Holocaust*, 13–21, 25–27, 36–41. For findings of the commission led by Tina Anselmi on the expropriation of Italy's Jews, visit www.governo.it/Presidenza/DICA/beni_ebraici/index.html (accessed September 2, 2010), which includes English-language summaries.

7. Michaelis, *Mussolini and the Jews*, 206; Zuccotti, *The Italians and the Holocaust*, 23–27, 33–34, 40–41. For different interpretations of the motivations behind Mussolini's antisemitic policies, see Orvieto, "Letters to Mussolini," 467–70, 474.

DOCUMENT 8–1: Letter by Luciano Morpurgo, Rome, Italy, to Benito Mussolini, September 9, 1939, in Luciano Morpurgo, *Caccia all'uomo! Vita sofferenze e beffe: Pagine di diario, 1938–1944* (Rome: Casa Editrice Dalmatia S.A., 1946), 42–45 (translated from Italian).

Duce! One year has now passed since the racial laws came into effect. I do not want to and cannot discuss what you, in your wisdom, have decided; I am not in a position to pass judgment; I seek only—as an Italian, as a man, and as a Jew—to set forth some considerations, which you, in your graciousness, humanity, and wisdom, may wish to examine.

My letter will be audacious: but nothing ventured, nothing gained, as the Latin proverb tells us.

In the greatest book on earth, the Bible, it is written: ". . . and Abraham replied, 'Now behold, I have ventured to speak to the Lord, although I am but dust and ashes.'" (Genesis, 18:19)[8]

I can hardly compare myself with Abraham but would wish to defend—if possible—this small core of Italian Jews, who so love Italy, who have always done so in both past and present, and who I believe are not guilty. If there is one or more who are guilty among the many, they should be known to everyone, declared guilty, and punished.

Not all the Italians were fascists in the beginning: many opposed you and still do, they opted for a life in exile, and they were and are still your enemies in the world outside of Italy; but you did not punish all the Italians who remained in the motherland [*patria*] because of it. The same holds true among the Jews: there have definitely been enemies of Italy and of fascism at home and abroad [among them]. But you should not punish all the Jews for this.

Did all the Christians, Catholics or Protestants—in and outside of Italy—always view you favorably? Are not some of them your enemies? And can you punish all the Catholics in Italy for that?

I am brave enough to speak to you and tell you, Your Excellency:

Those Jews who are struck by your iron laws do not raise their voices; those who can, leave Italy.[9] But they do not become your enemies; rather, they promote Italian products, be it through commercial ventures or by teaching in schools and in universities (if they are teachers), offering the same disciplines they taught in Italy.

---

8. This passage is actually from Genesis 18:27.

9. Approximately six thousand Jews emigrated from Italy in this period. See Nidam-Orvieto, "The Impact of Anti-Jewish Legislation," 169.

They leave in silence and without protest, and inside them they carry the flame of being Italian and carry with them a pride of the Italian motherland and of their language.

Jews they may be, but many—perhaps all—allow me to say this—feel a double pride in being Italians and being Jews. And so they submit to their destiny surprised, still have a hard time believing what is happening to them, consider the laws that separate them from their Italian brothers with whom they shed blood on the battlefield for a common cause impossible and inapplicable.

When I had an audience with you years ago and you received my collection "Italy," you asked me if I had any special request.[10] I never asked for anything for myself; but now, with the distance of some years, I beg you to forget any faults of which I was not aware. I beg you not to allow this small group of Jews, Italians to the core, to perish. I beg you not to exasperate those who have always carried the Italian motherland with them. [. . .][11]

While the Vichy regime—officially called the *État français*—started to introduce antisemitic legislation aimed at recently immigrated and naturalized Jews barely a week after its founding in July 1940, the Jewish Statute (Statut des Juifs), enacted without much fanfare in early October 1940, came as a shocking betrayal to French Jews, much like that experienced by Italian Jews during the preceding two years in response to comparable laws. Despite the intensification of antisemitism in France in the 1930s, French Jews had continued to trust in the French republican tradition and the French state. After all, France had been the first European nation to emancipate its Jewish minority, in 1790 and 1791, and the French state had protected the rights of Jews throughout the intervening century and a half, even in the face of heightened antisemitic agitation during the Dreyfus affair in the 1890s. Now French-born Jews found

---

10. Here he may have been referring to the lavishly illustrated book he published on public buildings and public works projects under Fascist rule, *Roma mussolinea: Anno decimo dell'era Fascista*, ed. Giuseppe Lugli and R. Ricci (Rome: L. Morpurgo, 1932).

11. According to a note added by Morpurgo in the 1946 published edition, he also sent copies of this letter to Felice Guarneri, then minister of foreign exchange and Morpurgo's "dear friend from school," and to Father Pietro Tachi Venturi, secretary-general of the Jesuits. See Luciano Morpurgo, *Caccia all'uomo! Vita sofferenze e beffe: Pagine di diario, 1938–1944* (Rome: Casa Editrice Dalmatia S.A., 1946), 42n1.

themselves the target of anti-Jewish legal measures for the first time in modern French history.[12]

In the months immediately following the armistice, many Jews still held out the hope—and were reassured by different parties—that French republican values would prevail in some form in the *État français* despite its subservient role vis-à-vis Nazi Germany. The director of the French office of Keren Kayemet (the Jewish National Fund), Nahum Hermann,[13] articulated this sense in a letter he wrote on July 22, 1940, the same day that Vichy announced it would begin to review the citizenship status of all individuals who had been naturalized since 1927: "I have the clear impression that <u>for the moment</u> neither pride nor good French sense will accept the radical political practice of the neighboring countries. Some of these officials insisted earnestly that it would be an insult to France to believe it capable of such an attitude. We understand that there will not be at present, under French authority, legislation that would undermine the equal rights of Israelite citizens of the country." Hermann recognized that the measures just introduced by Vichy against naturalized French citizens, as well as possible future measures against them and foreigners, would have a disproportionate impact on "our coreligionists." But he called attention to the fact that, "strictly speaking," such measures were not anti-Jewish and would also affect the large number of non-Jewish Italians and Belgians in France. Hermann could not imagine that the French would so soon adopt the "sympathies and antipathies" of its still-loathed enemy. He concluded on an uncertain note, tinged with optimism: "In conclusion, I do not believe that the situation of the Jews in France will be altogether compromised by the current rulers in France. Everything will depend on the German influence, more or less great over the

---

12. For a general history of Jews in France, see Paula E. Hyman, *The Jews of Modern France* (Berkeley: University of California Press, 1998); Pierre Birnbaum, *The Jews of the Republic: A Political History of State Jews in France from Gambetta to Vichy* (Stanford, CA: Stanford University Press, 1996); and Susan Zuccotti, *The Holocaust, the French, and the Jews* (New York: Basic Books, 1993). Renée Poznanski, *Jews in France during World War II* (Hanover, NH: University Press of New England in association with the USHMM, 2001), 1–18, calls into question the "uniformity of the category 'French Jews'" and differentiates, based on the perceptions prevailing at the time, between "foreign Jews" and "French Israelites."

13. Nahum Hermann (?–1944), a Ukrainian Jew, studied in Odessa and later at the Sorbonne. He worked as a journalist and insurance agent in Paris in addition to pursuing his Jewish National Fund activities. After the German invasion, he fled to Vichy with his wife and one daughter; another daughter became active in OSE child-rescue work. In January 1944 Hermann was arrested in a **Gestapo** raid on OSE offices in Limoges and deported to Drancy, then to Poland, where he perished. USHMMPA WS# 38347.

country. Or, with the European war not yet finished, it is impossible to make a clear prognosis."[14] Subscribing to similar reasoning, two-thirds of the Jews who had fled the advancing German army in May 1940 preferred to take their chances living in the Unoccupied Zone under Vichy rule.[15]

Vichy's October 1940 Jewish Statute, applicable to Jews in both zones of France, put an end to speculation about whether the new French regime would oppose racial politics aimed at French-born Jews.[16] At the end of September, the German military administration in the Occupied Zone had promulgated an ordinance that defined Jewish identity in religious terms and required all Jews to register their names and places of residence with the police.[17] German influence fast merged with homegrown French antisemitism, and Vichy ministers proved all too eager to take the initiative. They signed into law a series of statutes revoking Algerian Jews' French citizenship (granted in 1870 by the Crémieux Decree), defining Jewish identity on the basis of race, and banning altogether or limiting Jewish participation in a host of professions, most prominently the civil service, the military, journalism, film and theater, and many commercial professions. According to a report penned in July 1941, close to 50 percent of Jews in France lost their livelihoods as a result of the legislation enacted by the *État français*.[18]

French Jewish leaders missed no time in protesting against the Jewish Statute. One of the first to convey his outrage was the chief rabbi of France

---

14. Letter from Nahum Hermann, Vichy, to Arthur Hantke, Jerusalem, Palestine, July 22, 1940, USHMMA RG 68.045M (WJC Geneva), reel 1 (translated from French; emphasis in the original).

15. Poznanski, *Jews in France during World War II*, 24.

16. The Jewish Statutes were announced to the public on October 3, 1940, but their full content only became known on October 18, 1940, when they were printed in the government publication, the *Journal officiel*, and in French newspapers. Vicki Caron, *Uneasy Asylum: France and the Jewish Refugee Crisis, 1933–1942* (Stanford, CA: Stanford University Press, 1999), 348; Poznanski, *Jews in France during World War II*, 34.

17. This ordinance defined a "Jew" as a person of the Jewish religion or with two grandparents who subscribed to the Jewish religion. In the Occupied Zone, according to Poznanski, "By October 21, 1940, some 149,734 Jews had thus registered with the census. Of these, 86,664 were French Jews, and 65,070 foreigners." See Poznanski, *Jews in France during World War II*, 31–33.

18. Report cited in Poznanski, *Jews in France during World War II*, 42; Robert O. Paxton, *Vichy France: Old Guard and New Order, 1940–1944* (New York: Columbia University Press, 1972), 174; Caron, *Uneasy Asylum*, 324–27. In the same period, Vichy banned "secret societies" (i.e., Freemasons) and began to arrest Communists, foreign Jewish refugees, and others deemed threatening to the security of the nation. Julian Jackson, *France: The Dark Years, 1940–1944* (Oxford: Oxford University Press, 2001), 151.

(*grand rabbin de France*), Isaïe Schwartz, who wrote the letter presented in document 8–2 to Vichy head of state Marshal **Henri-Philippe Pétain** even before the clauses of the new law were made public.[19] Schwartz challenged the legitimacy of the Statut des Juifs and saw fit to remind Pétain of French history, international legal principles, and French Jewish patriotism.[20]

DOCUMENT 8–2: Letter from the chief rabbi of France, Isaïe Schwartz, Vichy, France, to Marshal Pétain, French head of state, October 10, 1940, USHMMA RG 43.069M (Consistoire Central collection BCC-19a), reel 4 (translated from French).

Monsieur le Maréchal,

According to an official communiqué, "the adjustment of the status of the Israelites was pursued" at the Council of Ministers meeting on October 1 [1940].

This information has caused a great stir: for the first time in France, an official text mentions a "status" that would be peculiar to Israelites.

Monsieur le Maréchal, the Head of State is the defender of the rights of all French people.

Therefore, any discrimination against a category of French people due to their religion or their ancestry would be contrary to the rules of public law in this country, contrary to the principles of public international law. Contrary, as well, to the ideal of civilization that our country represents in France and all its territories and in the entire world.

1. All the constitutional and organic laws promulgated under the different and successive regimes in France since 1789 declare the equality of citizens before the law. This means in particular freedom

19. Isaïe Schwartz (1876–1952) was born in Alsace (now in the Bas-Rhin department of France), served during World War I, and was elected chief rabbi of France in March 1939, after holding a series of similar appointments in Bayonne and Strasbourg. During World War II, Schwartz worked to aid refugees and counteract the Vichy regime's racial laws, narrowly avoiding arrest in 1944. See obituary, *New York Times*, July 22, 1952.

20. In a telegram to Pétain one month earlier, Schwartz had echoed the catchwords of Vichy—patriotism for the fatherland, family, and labor—in underscoring French Jewish loyalty to the French state. Yet, over the course of the next two years, his position toward the state underwent a transformation. Schwartz was among the earliest of the **Central Consistory**'s leadership to support noncompliance as a stance of resistance toward Vichy antisemitic legislation. Adam Rayski, *The Choice of the Jews under Vichy: Between Submission and Resistance* (Notre Dame, IN: University of Notre Dame Press in association with the USHMM, 2005), 26.

of access to professions and admission to public functions based only on merit. As far as Israelites in France are concerned, their civil rights were explicitly recognized by decrees of the National Constituent Assembly on January 28, 1790, decrees adopted as state law by King Louis XVI.

2. The principles that inspired the members of the Constituent Assembly and the legislators have been defended by all French governments in the international realm. In particular, France was triumphant with these principles twice: in 1919 after the victory, but also in 1878 after the defeat.

3. France leads an empire of millions of people of all origins. What would be the effect in the colonies, protectorates, and countries under mandates if the news spread that France has entered upon a path of distinctions based on minority or race?

4. France's greatness also includes the high ideal of human civilization that she represents in the concert of nations. There remain great countries in the world that love France because she is faithful to this ideal.

These, Monsieur le Maréchal, are some of the arguments based on law and history that I would like to emphasize to the Head of State, for every State is founded on justice and on tradition.

Should I also appeal to your generosity?

Yesterday, you uttered words that went directly to the heart of all French people.

You assured the "populations of Alsace and Lorraine that have been forced to abruptly quit their towns and villages" of your deep sympathy. As you surely know, the Israelites were the first victims of this duress, not only as Israelites but also because they were among the supporters of French Alsace.[21]

You also reminded the French of the necessity of "the equality of all in the face of the sacrifice imposed on them by defeat and the con-

---

21. On July 16, 1940, German authorities rounded up all Jews remaining in Alsace along with other Alsatians who displayed what they considered to be a pronounced affinity for France. This expulsion resembled earlier expulsions from the Reich carried out by Nazi authorities in being sudden and brutal. In all, around three thousand people were pushed over the border, joining the fifteen thousand Jews who had been forced out of Alsace in the fall of 1939. They resettled in Paris and in several different cities in the Unoccupied Zone of France. See Poznanski, *Jews in France during World War II*, 27.

queror's will." Monsieur le Maréchal, the French Israelites are among the conquered: they ask the Head of State for equality in the face of sacrifice.

Please accept, Monsieur le Maréchal, my deepest respect.

Later in October, after the full text of the Jewish Statute had become official, Schwartz followed up with another letter that merged expressions of protest with the assurance of "unswerving devotion to our country." Neither this nor Schwartz's earlier letter to Pétain was acknowledged by Vichy authorities. Only after the chief rabbi of Paris, Julien Weill, had written to the head of the *État français* that French Jews would remain faithful to France "whatever the rigors of the new law may be" did the marshal reply with a general expression of faith that all French citizens would display the "spirit of sacrifice" needed under the circumstances.[22]

Unlike Jews in France, and to a lesser extent in Italy, the president of the Union of Romanian Jews (Uniunea Evreilor Români, or UER), Bucharest lawyer Wilhelm Filderman, could not rely on a long-standing tradition of liberalism and political emancipation in defending the rights of Romanian Jews. Romania had only extended political equality to its Jewish population after World War I, and it did so then under pressure from the victorious Allied powers. Thus, in protesting the discriminatory legislation introduced by successive Romanian governments in the late 1930s and 1940, Filderman advanced rational arguments about Romanian self-interest, not grandiose political principles. The memorandum reproduced in document 8–3 exemplifies his approach.

The diversity of Romania's sizable Jewish population transcended the divide between native and foreign-born Jews typical of most western European communities: historian Ezra Mendelsohn counted "at least five, and perhaps as many as seven, distinct Jewries" in interwar Romania.[23] Filderman, the country's most prominent Jewish leader in this period, belonged to the affluent, Romanian-educated segment of the Jewish population from Wallachia

---

22. For Schwartz's and Weill's letters to Pétain of October 22 and 23, 1940, and Pétain's reply dated November 12, see Poznanski, *Jews in France during World War II*, 88–89.

23. Romania's Jewish minority comprised 4.2 percent of the overall Romanian population, but percentages varied considerably by region. Ezra Mendelsohn, *The Jews of East Central Europe between the World Wars* (Bloomington: Indiana University Press, 1987), 173, 178, 189–98. For more on the Romanian Jewish population, see chapter 7, note 12.

and Moldavia in the Old Kingdom, or Regat, the core Romanian territory.[24] Throughout the 1920s and 1930s, Filderman's UER pursued a version of Jewish politics that defended Jewish civil rights on the Romanian national stage and strove to integrate Jews into the Romanian body politic. At the same time, the organization's leaders sought to reinforce a Jewish cultural sensibility based primarily on an ethnic and religious understanding of Jewish identity. In so doing, the UER's position contrasted with the Jewish political parties and youth movements of Bukovina, Bessarabia, and Transylvania, territories that Romania had acquired only after World War I and would lose again in June 1940 following France's defeat. Whereas the UER tried to advance Jewish interests by working with Romanian political parties, these other Jewish organizations were critical of such tactics in their support of a range of Zionist, nationalist, Socialist, and Orthodox positions. Yet, differences in ideology and strategy did not impede Filderman from maintaining a productive working relationship with Romanian Zionist leaders. In 1936, they banded together to form the Central Committee of Romanian Jews (Consiliul Centrala Evreilor din România) to fight mounting antisemitism.[25]

Given his past experience, Filderman—now as leader of the Federation of Jewish Communities in Romania, which after 1938 became the main institution representing Romanian Jews—was well-positioned to continue his and the UER's past work, advocating for Jewish interests in the face of an onslaught of antisemitic measures introduced in the summer and fall of 1940. Following the loss of Bessarabia and Bukovina, King Carol II's government issued racial

---

24. Wilhelm Filderman (1882–1963), born in Bucharest and a World War I veteran, first joined the Union of Romanian Jews' central committee in 1913. After the war he became both president of the union and the Joint representative in Romania, working for Jewish civil rights through a number of initiatives. He went on to become a Liberal Party member of parliament and leader of the Federation of Jewish Communities, which was dissolved in December 1941, to be replaced by a Jewish Council–like organization. He continued to fight discriminatory measures and deportations of Romanian Jews and suffered expulsion to Transnistria for a time. Upon his return he intervened on behalf of other deportees to Transnistria, with some success. After the war he resumed a number of his posts and continued his work for Jewish rights but eventually fled to Paris in 1948 after repeated conflicts with the new Communist regime. Theodor Lavi, "Filderman, Wilhelm," *Encyclopaedia Judaica*, 2nd ed., ed. Fred Skolnik and Michael Berenbaum (Detroit, MI: Macmillan Reference USA, 2007), 7:19; Jean Ancel, "Filderman, Wilhelm," in *Encyclopedia of the Holocaust*, ed. Israel Gutman (New York: Macmillan, 1990), 2:482–83.

25. Yehuda Bauer, *American Jewry and the Holocaust: The American Jewish Joint Distribution Committee, 1939–1945* (Detroit, MI: Wayne State University Press, 1981), 336–37.

laws that prohibited Jews from serving in the army, owning land, and participating in public life, including attending universities and schools. When in September Carol II was forced to abdicate and **Ion Antonescu**, together with the **Iron Guard**, formed the new National Legionnaire government, the vise on Romanian Jews tightened.[26] The Romanian state instituted a policy of "Romanization" modeled on the Nazi policy of "Aryanization."[27] Iron Guard members expropriated Jewish property and businesses in a manner often tantamount to robbery and plunder. A former schoolmate of Antonescu, Filderman met in person with him and other high officials, including generals and ministers, to try to alleviate the plight of Romanian Jews. In those face-to-face meetings and in correspondence like the memorandum presented in document 8–3, Filderman and other officials of the Federation of Jewish Communities protested the legality of particular anti-Jewish measures and called out violations and inconsistencies in their implementation around the country.

---

26. King Carol II's dictatorship was toppled after public opinion turned against him. Carol's attempts to ally with Hitler's Germany only resulted in further Romanian territorial concessions. Romania was forced to turn over a portion of Transylvania to Hungary and part of Dobruja to Bulgaria only two months after ceding Bukovina and Bessarabia to the Soviet Union (see chapter 7). All of these lands had been annexed by Romania after World War I, and although they had substantial Romanian populations, they also had large populations of other nationalities, including Russians, Ukrainians, Hungarians, Germans, and Jews, depending on the region. The ever-closer ties of the Romanian regime to Nazi Germany brought the joint government of Ion Antonescu (1882–1946) and the Iron Guard to power. Under the leadership of Horia Sima (1907–1993), who now became deputy prime minister, the Iron Guard instigated waves of further antisemitic legislation and perpetrated pogroms and political assassinations of Jews and political opponents. Mendelsohn, *The Jews of East Central Europe*, 171–73.

27. "Aryanization" and "Aryanize" (German: *Arisierung, arisieren*) are words derived from the vocabulary of *völkisch* antisemitism. It denotes the process of expropriating Jewish property and excluding the Jews from the economy for the purpose of establishing a racially "purified" state. Between 1933 and late 1938, Nazi functionaries, government officials, professional associations, and private businessmen deployed a range of different, increasingly violent means to achieve "Aryanization" in Germany. Other European countries occupied or dominated by the Reich adopted their own measures. The result was the systematic and organized theft of Jewish property. See Martin Dean, *Robbing the Jews: The Confiscation of Jewish Property in the Holocaust, 1933–1945* (New York: Cambridge University Press in association with the USHMM, 2008). For more on "Aryan," see the Glossary.

DOCUMENT 8–3: **Letter from Wilhelm Filderman and Dr. I. Brucăr, Federation of Jewish Communities of Romania, Bucharest, to Ion Antonescu, Romanian prime minister, September 30, 1940, in** *Documents Concerning the Fate of Romanian Jewry during the Holocaust,* **ed. Jean Ancel (New York: Beate Klarsfeld Foundation, 1986), 1:528–30 (translated from Romanian).**

[. . .] Through the regular application of the Jewish Statute Law, over 25% of the current Jewish population—at least 80,000 souls—will be starving by February 9, 1941, when the legal interval of six months allowed for the termination of professions forbidden to the Jews will expire. [. . .]

In reality, against the formal orders of Your Excellency and in violation of the current legal norms and of the Jewish Statute laws, some authorities extend, based on their [own] decisions, the list of professions forbidden to the Jews; others deny [the Jews] the right to carry out business throughout the legally established interval of 6 months; others cancel contracts, although the Statute explicitly stipulates their fulfillment; others have required the immediate closure of all Jewish stores in certain locations; others have demanded the closure of firms; others deny access to the customs offices at ports to Jewish merchants who wish to see or export merchandise; professional associations demand that the Jews be completely or indirectly excluded from professions, which the Statute allows them to practice; or require regulations that cancel lease contracts [signed by Jewish individuals], etc., others allow individuals to stand by the entrances to Jewish shops in order to prevent customers from entering; or by the entrances to residences and stores of Romanian manufacturers, in order to prevent them from selling their products to Jews, etc. [. . .]

Generally, every authority and every citizen seems to wish to appear more legionary than the Legionnaires, more puritanical than his neighbor, instead of following Your Excellency's decisions regulating the phased Romanization, beginning with those who entered the country—legally or illegally—after 1913. [. . .]

We cannot help but point out the legal and humane attitude of the Prefect of Dorohoi, who convened all leaders of the Jewish Community and declared that he would guarantee the maintenance of order among all; and invited Jewish merchants to provision themselves with goods so that normal commercial activity may be reestablished. [. . .]

We hope, Mr. Prime Minister, that you will appreciate the sentiments that have compelled us to bring these facts to your attention and that you will be so kind as to ensure that Justice be dispensed to us. Please remain assured of our utmost consideration.

GENERAL SECRETARY,   PRESIDENT,
Dr I. Brucăr[28]   Dr. W. Filderman

During the same period that the National Legionnaire government transformed ideology into practice with a spate of antisemitic laws, Iron Guard members initiated a new wave of anti-Jewish terror, often with the support of local groups. Representatives of the UER and other Romanian Jewish organizations protested the random acts of violence inflicted on Jews, just as they spoke out against corruption and violations of the law. They doggedly sent memoranda and met with government officials when granted an audience. In response to perhaps the most flagrant incident of anti-Jewish violence perpetrated by Iron Guard members and their sympathizers during these months, Filderman tried to secure the release of the sixty Jews falsely charged and detained by police acting on behalf of the Iron Guard in the town of Ploieşti.[29]

---

28. Born in Bukovina, Isac Brucăr (1888–1960) was a lawyer, journalist, and leading philosopher who specialized in Baruch Spinoza's thought. Active in Jewish affairs, he headed the Cultural Institute of the Choral Temple, a scholarly Jewish organization, and served as a high official of the Federation of Jewish Communities until the Antonescu regime disbanded the organization in 1941. After the war he taught at the Institute of Philosophy of the Romania Academy but, owing to the long-lived antisemitic climate in Romania, some of Brucăr's major works were only published after his death and the fall of communism. See Hary Kuller, ed., *Evreii din România: Breviar biobibliografic* (Bucharest: Hasefer, 2008); Camelia Crăciun, "Brucăr, Isac," in *The YIVO Encyclopedia of Jews in Eastern Europe*, ed. Gershon David Hundert (New Haven, CT: Yale University Press, 2008), 1:249.

29. Ioanid, *The Holocaust in Romania*, 46.

DOCUMENT 8–4: **Memorandum from Wilhelm Filderman and Matatias Carp to the minister of the interior, November 25, 1940, in Matatias Carp, *Cartea neagră: Suferint, ele evreilor din Romania in timpul dictaturei fasciste, 1940–1944* (Bucharest: Atelierele grafice Socec, 1946), 1b:340 (translated from Romanian).**

UNION OF THE JEWISH COMMUNITIES

November 25, 1940

OF THE OLD KINGDOM

No. 2034

MR. MINISTER:

On November 15, on the occasion of an audience that the General Director of State Security[30] was kind enough to grant our President, Dr. W. Filderman, we brought to [his] attention the arrest on November 10 in the city of Ploești[31] of a group of approximately 50 Jews, peaceful people, against whom there is not a single charge. The detainees, among whom one may find veterans and heroes of the war of unification, were apprehended, some off the street, others—including Rabbi David Friedman—from the synagogue, during the religious service.[32]

These facts were exposed in our memorandum No. 1988, a copy of which is enclosed here but which we did not submit, since the General Director of State Security communicated to us that: 1) He had been informed of this fact; 2) He had been to Ploești, accompanying Mr. Horia Sima, interim President of the Council of Ministers; 3) He ordered that 10–11 of the detainees, suspected of having communist ties, be sent to trial in a military court and that all others be released immediately.

On November 18, we were informed that none of the detainees had been released, and we informed the General Secretary of State Security of

---

30. The authors have not been able to ascertain who occupied this post at this particular time. The office itself (Serviciul Siguranței Statului) was under the Ministry of the Interior, in contrast to the Special Intelligence Service (Serviciului Special de Informații), which was under the general staff of the Romanian army and thus under Antonescu's control. The Special Intelligence Service was headed by Eugen Cristescu (1895–1950), who assumed his post in mid-November 1940 after serving as general director of state security; it is possible that the meeting of November 15, referred to by Filderman and Carp, was with him. For a broader context for the anti-Jewish policies of the Romanian regime under Antonescu and the role of security agencies, see Ioanid, *The Holocaust in Romania*.

31. This is the old spelling; today, the city is known as Ploiești.

32. The phrase "war for unification" refers to World War I.

this fact through our memorandum No. 1943, a copy of which we have also enclosed here.

Since this order has not been executed up until today, we have the honor of requesting that you be kind enough to take urgent and efficient measures to release those arrested and prevent such deeds from recurring in the future.

Please remain assured, Mr. Minister, of our utmost consideration,

President, Secretary General,

Dr. W. Filderman   Matatias Carp[33]

Filderman's efforts may have played a role in the new release order issued to the Ploieşti police by Horia Sima, the Iron Guard leader and vice president of the Council of Ministers. But in this instance we see how local authorities could flout the commands of their superiors: The Ploieşti police ignored the release order and massacred eleven of the men they had detained. Their bodies were dumped on the edge of town. Thus, as much as Filderman tried to apply pressure on officials in Bucharest, he had no influence over their actions, much less over what local officials and police were doing outside the capital city.[34]

In Germany and in areas directly under the Reich's control as well, local officials sometimes acted independently in devising and carrying out

---

33. Matatias Carp (1904–1953) was born into an assimilated Jewish family in Bucharest. His father, Horia Carp, was a major intellectual and political figure involved in fighting discrimination against Jews. Matatias worked as a lawyer in the 1930s until he was excluded from the bar in 1940. He subsequently took on the post of secretary-general of the Union of Romanian Jews, working closely with Wilhelm Filderman, and in June 1940 began collecting documentation on the persecution of Romanian Jews. In 1941 he and his father were arrested, tortured, and subjected to a simulated execution by firing squad. Later that year, he resigned from the union but continued to work with Filderman and collect material for his documentary project with his wife, Ella Carp. The *Cartea Neagra* (black book) collection was first published in three volumes in Bucharest from 1946 to 1948 but was kept out of circulation during the Cold War. The Carp family emigrated to Israel in 1952, shortly before the author's death. See Alexandra Laignel-Lavastine, "Introduction. Cartea Neagra, de Matatias Carp: Un monument pour l'histoire," in Matatias Carp, *Cartea Neagra*, Fr. ed. (Paris: Denoël, 2009), 13–14, 21ff.

34. Corruption and random acts of violence brought about the demise of the Iron Guard. Ion Antonescu did not object to the Legionnaires' goals but found their methods problematic. With Hitler's approval, Antonescu succeeded in definitively removing the Iron Guard from power in January 1941. During their final attempt to retain power in an unsuccessful coup, the Iron Guard went on a murderous anti-Jewish rampage in Bucharest, killing more than a hundred Jews. Subsequently, Antonescu successfully eliminated the organization from the government and exiled its leaders. Ioanid, *The Holocaust in Romania*, 19–24, 46, 50–61.

antisemitic measures.[35] Unlike Antonescu, however, "Hitler would hardly have received representatives of German Jewry or overturned anti-Jewish measures."[36] Nevertheless, German Jewish communal leaders and private individuals wrote letters to officials at all levels in an effort to improve their situation. Here as elsewhere no one letter can represent this diverse body of source material. Even looking at a single such letter, however, can reveal something of German Jewish strategies of contestation, in particular the types of appeals that individuals thought might meet with the sympathy of Nazi officials and that utilized inconsistencies in the law for the purpose of subverting anti-Jewish goals.[37] The letter presented in document 8–5 by Albert Koppenheim from Leipzig contains a request for an exemption not only for himself but also for others in his position, as well as a call for "clarification" regarding his wife, an "**Aryan**." The outcome of the request is unknown.[38]

DOCUMENT 8–5: **Letter from Albert Koppenheim, Leipzig, Germany, to the Leipzig mayor/City Office for the Facilitation of Residential Construction, June 24, 1940, USHMMA RG 14.035M (Leipzig Jewish Community), reel 9 (translated from German).**

With reference to the public notice prohibiting the Jews here from entering public parks and using benches in them, I politely request that I be granted an exemption for the following reasons.

I am a 100-percent disabled war veteran with a corresponding pension, including a basic care allowance and a pension supplement. I took part in the world war, serving in the German army at the front from 1914 until the end. I was discharged with the rank of *Vizefeldwebel* [a senior NCO], and because of serious injuries, I was not released from the military hospital until September 1921. I was awarded the Iron Cross 1st Class and the Iron Cross 2nd Class.

---

35. See Jürgen Matthäus and Mark Roseman, *Jewish Responses to Persecution*, vol. 1: *1933–1938* (Lanham, MD: AltaMira Press in association with the USHMM, 2010), 290–304.

36. Ioanid, *The Holocaust in Romania*, 44.

37. For an analysis of Nazi linguistic strategies of assault and the linguistic strategies of contestation employed by "Germans of Jewish ancestry," see Thomas Pegelow Kaplan, *The Language of Nazi Genocide: Linguistic Violence and the Struggle of Germans of Jewish Ancestry* (New York: Cambridge University Press, 2009).

38. Albert Koppenheim (1889–?) survived the war, possibly because of his wife Dora's status as a non-Jew. See "German 'Minority Census' of 1938–1939"; *Aufbau*, June 1, 1945, 19.

I have a brain injury and am paralyzed on my right side as a result of the war injuries I received, so that my entire right side is paralyzed. My papers are located at the Leipzig Pension Office and are marked with reference number K.28315. The service-related injury is described as follows:

> spastic weakness on the right side, organic speech disorder, and nervous complaints after being shot in the head and suffering a brain injury.

The doctors certify that being outdoors in fresh air is important for me, though on the other hand my disabilities cause me to tire quickly when walking. Therefore I request that I, along with a companion—I am married to Dora Koppenheim née Leischker—be allowed to use the benches in the city parks, including those outside the area specially designated for Jews.

A few severely disabled Jewish war veterans in Leipzig whom I know personally are in the same situation as me. Therefore I would be especially obliged to you if you would be so kind as to give me an affirmative answer for these men as well.

According to the wording of the regulation, it applies to everyone who receives food ration cards with the letter "J" [marking used for Jews]. In principle, this includes my wife as well, although she is an Aryan, because my marriage is childless and my household thus counts as a Jewish one. For this reason, I am requesting, at the same time, clarification as to whether my wife—despite her Aryan status, which is also recognized by the Election Office [*Wahlamt*]—is subject to the prohibition herself, or whether women in mixed marriages are allowed to enter public parks and so forth.

COMMUNAL SURVIVAL, COMMUNAL SOLIDARITY

In countries across Europe, Jewish men, women, and youth struggled by different means to adapt to and counter the particular forms of persecution to which they were subject. As we have seen, Jewish communal leaders and some private individuals appealed to political authorities in their countries, protesting anti-Jewish measures and seeking improvements. But since the opportunity for writing such appeals was limited, as were the chances of success, most people's efforts focused internally, within Jewish communities and organizations, as well as their own families. In their capacity as Jewish leaders, social workers, parents, writers, and youth group members, as well as in other roles, they endeavored to mitigate their plight. They looked for ways of supporting, emotionally and practically, their communities, their loved ones, and themselves.

For Jews who had subscribed to assimilation as a means of countering antisemitism, the revocation of Emancipation, with its promise of liberty and justice for all citizens, posed a challenge to their cherished ideals. Italian Jews writing to Mussolini or French Jews writing to Pétain constructed arguments in opposition to official discrimination and in support of the viability of that long-standing belief in acculturation. Were Jews who remained assimilation-ists naive? Before arriving at any judgment, we must consider not only the complex connotations and different manifestations of assimilation but also the particular circumstances of Jews in each country and across time. The case of Hungarian Jewish community leader Géza Ribáry points to the need for care-ful consideration of the situation at the time.[39] Ribáry was vice president of the Neolog (similar to Reform) community of Pest, the largest Jewish congregation in Hungary. In contrast to Orthodox Hungarian Jews, those who belonged to Neolog congregations shared the mainstream western and central European Jewish commitment to acculturation.[40] This political and ideological current did not attain the position of dominance among Hungarian Jews that it had among Jews in pre-Nazi Germany and Austria. Nevertheless, it did achieve suf-ficient influence that the majority of Hungarian Jews identified as "Magyars of the Jewish faith." Even Hungarian Zionist and other national Jewish move-ments embraced the values of Emancipation. Their trust in the Hungarian conservative-aristocratic ruling classes dated back to before World War I, when the liberal political elite had protected Jews from antisemitic outbreaks, and

---

39. A lawyer, law journal editor, and prolific writer for the Jewish press, Géza Ribáry (1889–1942) organized cultural opportunities for Jewish artists after the first anti-Jewish law was issued in 1938. He also headed the National Hungarian Jewish Assistance Campaign (OMZSA), which launched its activities in late 1939, and was active in the Pest Jewish Community's Social Work Committee until his death in May 1942. See eulogies in *OMZSA-Évkönyv 5703* (1942–1943) (OMZSA Yearbook); Randolph L. Braham, *The Politics of Genocide: The Holocaust in Hungary*, rev. ed. (New York: Columbia University Press, 1994), 1:89–90, 154.

40. According to a 1941 census, there were 725,007 Jews in Hungary, comprising 4.94 percent of the Hungarian population, 400,981 Jews lived in the borders of pre-1938 Hungary, known as Trianon Hungary, and 324,026 Jews lived in the territories annexed by Hungary from 1938 to 1941 that had formerly belonged to Czechoslovakia, Romania, and Yugoslavia. In Trianon Hungary, according to the 1930 census, 65.5 percent of Jews were members of Neolog congregations, and 29.2 percent were members of Orthodox congrega-tions. Braham, *The Politics of Genocide*, 1:86–92.

in return Hungarian Jews demonstrated fierce patriotism and became active agents of "Magyarization" within what was then a multinational empire. In interwar Hungary, Jewish leaders such as Ribáry remained true to the values of the traditional Hungarian political-social order. The introduction of the First Anti-Jewish Law on May 29, 1938, and then of the Second Anti-Jewish Law on May 4, 1939, did not shatter their identification with the Magyar people.[41]

Ribáry and other Hungarian Jewish leaders regarded this antisemitic legislation as a necessary evil. They hoped that the economic restrictions and racial definitions it introduced might stanch more radical concessions to Arrow Cross supporters.[42] In response, they devised new tactics to cope with the overwhelming burden of organizing and administering relief to the thousands of Hungarian Jews who now lacked a means of support. Ribáry played a pivotal role in bringing the different Hungarian Jewish congregations together, despite their religious-doctrinal and political differences, to build a new network of social welfare and cultural organizations. And he helped open Hungarian Jewry to international Jewish relief organizations, which constituted a shift in Hungarian Jewish attitudes toward outside philanthropy and political advocacy on their behalf.[43]

Nonetheless, the guidance Ribáry offered fellow Hungarian Jews in his contributions to Jewish periodicals reflected the constancy of his faith in assimilation. And why not? After all, Hungary remained an independent country, and antisemitic policies were neither predetermined in their trajectory nor

---

41. The First Jewish Law, officially called the Law Providing for a More Effective Safeguard of Equilibrium in Social and Economic Life, introduced a 20 percent ceiling on Jewish employment in the professions and in all enterprises with more than ten employees. The Second Jewish Law dropped the ceiling to 6 percent and defined who was to be counted as a Jew on the basis of complex religious and racial criteria. The combined impact was severe, especially due to the fact that one hundred thousand converts to Christianity were now counted as Jews and subject to the economic restrictions. See Braham, *The Politics of Genocide*, 1:125–30, and 151–60, and László Csősz and Gábor Kádár, *The Holocaust in Hungary* (Lanham, MD: AltaMira Press in association with the USHMM, forthcoming 2012).

42. The Arrow Cross Party, a Hungarian fascist party led by Ferenc Szálasi (1897–1946), combined several interwar far-right nationalist and antisemitic movements into a loose ideology it termed *Hungarism*. It contended with various Hungarian prewar and wartime governments for primacy until October 1944 when, with Hitler's help, it seized power in a coup and intensified the deportations of Jews to their deaths in Auschwitz, as well as implemented murderous fascist policies in general. After the war, Szálasi was tried and executed. For a short history of the party, see Stanley Payne, *A History of Fascism, 1914–1945* (Madison: University of Wisconsin Press, 1995), 271–76, 415–20.

43. Braham, *The Politics of Genocide,* 1:88–90; "Review of the Year 5700—Hungary," *AJYB 5701* 42 (1940): 363–65.

uncontested among Hungarians. Despite the fact that the radical Right had gained in prestige with each expansion of Hungary's borders and despite its clamoring for a Third Jewish Law beginning in the fall of 1940, the Hungarian regime continued to offer asylum to thousands of Jewish refugees and to allow its substantial Jewish community to remain more or less intact.[44] Indeed, according to the report on Hungary in the *American Jewish Year Book's* "Review of the Year 5701 [1940–1941]," there had been "manifold manifestations of sympathy toward Jews emanating from high-standing political leaders, aristocrats, important organizations, such as that of the war veterans, and notably, of a new group of patriots called the 'Hungarian Family,' devoted solely to the task of holding together in spiritual unity 'the Hungarian family of all those who, without difference of race or creed, are, in their souls, true children of the nation.'" Seemingly bolstered by the "sympathetic attitude of millions of Hungarians," Ribáry continued to espouse his Magyar outlook. At the same time, by calling for the "intensification of our virtues," he echoed appeals that Jewish leaders in many countries, including Germany, had voiced since the nineteenth century despite their proven futility as a weapon against antisemitism by 1940.[45]

DOCUMENT 8–6: **Géza Ribáry, Pest, Hungary, "The Most Important Present Tasks and Duties of Hungarian Jewry," 1941, translated from Hungarian and published in** *The Holocaust in Hungary: An Anthology of Jewish Response*, **ed. Andrew Handler (University: University of Alabama Press, 1982), 43–44.**

[. . .] Our lives and future are inextricably fused with the destiny of the Magyar people. It is for that reason that we must participate in the constructive work of the Magyar people with unabating enthusiasm and unbroken faith in the reaffirmation of our emancipation, notwithstanding the likelihood that in certain respects we may not reap the fruits of our labor in the near future.

In addition to our commitments, we must be on guard to defend our right to live and protect our future against antisemitism, that dangerously menacing disease. [. . .]

---

44. Livia Rothkirchen, "Hungary—an Asylum for the Refugees of Europe," *YVS* 7 (1968): 127.

45. Quotations from Eugene Hevesi, "Review of the Year 5701—Hungary," *AJYB 5702* 43 (1941): 225.

The atmosphere created around us by the ideologies that are saturated with antisemitism renders the weapon of persuasion useless. It is for that reason that we must resort to the other weapon in the struggle against antisemitism. We must increase our virtues a hundredfold and eliminate our mistakes. With iron will gained by heavy physical work, with spirit made exalted by knowledge and culture, and with a soul made noble by unselfish, helpful service to others we must create an atmosphere around us in which the weapons of antisemitism will be rendered ineffective.

I cannot repeat often enough that there are two virtues in particular which we must inculcate in our coreligionists: modesty and steadfastness. Unfortunately we have often witnessed the manifestation of immodesty on the part of our wealthy coreligionists. Spinelessness, however, is an attribute of the shipwrecked in Jewish life. Due to the enduring tradition of generalization, all of us are victimized by the disadvantages that these seemingly conflicting qualities, which evoke both hatred and contempt, have created. Speaking for myself, I believe that our most important tasks are the elimination of mistakes due to immodesty and spinelessness, and the institutionalization of the virtues of modesty and steadfastness. We must strengthen them in all walks of life, in the area of mental and physical work as well as in recreation and social contacts.

The elimination of our seemingly conflicting shortcomings and the intensification of our virtues will undoubtedly provide a middle course on which we shall advance, leaving behind the harmful atmosphere of antisemitism, until we regain the position in this land that we had earned by the common destiny we share with the Magyar people, and by our passionate devotion to the Magyar ideal.

In Romania as in Hungary, Jewish communities struggled to meet the demands placed on them as a result of the more repressive anti-Jewish laws of 1940. Document 8–7 details the efforts of the small but wealthy **Sephardi** community of Bucharest to expand its social welfare work in response.[46] As evidenced by Géza Ribáry's appeal in document 8–6, the representatives of the Sephardi community portrayed themselves as continuing to espouse Romanian patriotism despite their persecution by their compatriots. Such sentiments had

---

46. The community had around six thousand members in 1940. Alexander Avraham, "Sephardim," in Hundert, *The YIVO Encyclopedia of Jews in Eastern Europe*, 2: esp. 1691–92.

deep roots in history as well, for the Sephardim were the most acculturated of all the Jewish communities in Romania.[47]

DOCUMENT 8–7: The Council of Representatives of the Israelite Community of Spanish Rite, Bucharest, Romania, "Bulletin of the Council of Representatives," no. 33, report on January 1 to December 31, 1940, USHMMA RG 25.021 (CSHJR, file III:2), reel 1 (translated from Romanian).

Beloved members of the community,

[. . .] We did not hesitate for a second. Not for a moment did we allow the adversity of events to bow us, and we did not lose hope in the viability of our cherished Community, [which is] the nucleus into which our millenary faith, culture and tradition flow. [. . .]

Spiritually prepared, we are determined to do everything humanly possible for the good of the society. But we also ask from our beloved coreligionists the same sympathy and indisputable capacity for sacrifice that they have demonstrated until today. We live in times when we need to dedicate all our verve, all our work to the Community. Support this institution in all its efforts. Do not forget that it represents you, that you can make your voice heard through it. Do not forget that it is destined to find the cure for our pain, and it is also its fate to prepare the future. [. . .] With dignity, honesty, and trust in the leaders of our beloved Homeland Romania, to which we are bound by old sentiments and blood sacrifices, [you should] await the solution to the Jewish question [*chestiunii evreiești*], which can only be achieved in the spirit of the true and traditional Romanian justice.

Economic survival and emigration were the paramount considerations for Czech Jews in 1939 and 1940. German occupation in Bohemia and Moravia rapidly transformed daily life for all Czechs, but Jews were subject to particularly harsh treatment akin to that of German and Austrian Jews in the Greater Reich. Among other prohibitions, they suffered from a host of antisemitic decrees restricting their economic activities and freedom of movement (including expulsions from some towns and cities and the first deportations

---

47. Even convinced antisemites in Romania set the Sephardim apart from the majority of the Jewish population of Romania, as Octavian Goga did in an interview with the French periodical *Paris-Soir* in January 1938. Quoted in Ioanid, *The Holocaust in Romania*, 18.

to Poland).[48] In response, Czech Jewish leaders attempted to find constructive means of improving the lives of their constituents. They reorganized and expanded the work of the central Jewish organization, the Jewish Religious Congregations (JRC). Like Jewish communal leaders in Hungary, Czech Jewish leaders had to overcome ideological differences, particularly pronounced between Zionists and assimilationists in the Czech context, in order to work most effectively. JRC leaders met with German authorities, facilitated emigration opportunities (including illegal ones), and tried to furnish material aid in various forms to the destitute members of their congregations.[49]

The articles in documents 8–8 and 8–9 from the *Jüdisches Nachrichten-blatt Prag/Židovské listy* exemplify the focus of the JRC in the first two years of the war. This bilingual newspaper emerged in November 1939 under the editorship of lawyer and writer Dr. Oskar Singer as the German-mandated organ of Czech Jewry in the Protectorate, the Prague-based equivalent to periodicals issued in Berlin and Vienna.[50] The lack of free speech evident in its carefully worded texts notwithstanding, contributors to the *Jüdisches Nachrichtenblatt* advised readers about strategies they ought to adopt to prepare for the future. In the first article included here, the author insisted that economic survival entailed more than occupational restructuring.[51] To be successful, Czech Jews would have to rethink the ideas and values underpinning their professional lives. To counter middle-class prejudices against manual labor and crafts, the author recast them within Jewish history and ethics.

---

48. For more on the deportation campaigns of 1939 and 1940, see chapter 9. On the antisemitic decrees introduced in the Protectorate in these years, see Rothkirchen, *The Jews of Bohemia and Moravia*, 110–14.

49. Rothkirchen, *The Jews of Bohemia and Moravia*, 116–20, 134.

50. Dr. Oskar Singer (1893–1945) was deported with his wife, Margarethe (née Kornfeld) from Prague to Łódź on October 26, 1941, where he worked as head of the archives and editor of the official chronicle of the Łódź ghetto. Deported to Auschwitz during the final liquidation of the Łódź ghetto in August 1944, he appears to have been killed on a death march from Auschwitz in January 1945. Sascha Feuchert, Erwin Leibfried, and Jörg Riecke, eds., *Die Chronik des Gettos Lodz/Litzmannstadt: Supplemente und Anhang* (Göttingen: Wallstein Verlag, 2007), 393. On the *Jüdisches Nachrichtenblatt Prag*, see Rothkirchen, *The Jews of Bohemia and Moravia*, 118–20.

51. "W. Sch." wrote other occasional articles for the newspaper with advice on career or occupational training from late 1939 through late 1940. The authors have been unable to uncover his or her identity.

DOCUMENT 8–8: **W. Sch., "Schooling, Retraining,"** *Jüdisches Nachrichtenblatt Prag/ Židovské listy*, **December 15, 1939, 4 (translated from German).**

Retraining [*Umschichtung*] is today the watchword of Jewish occupational counseling, just as it was when such counseling began. In those days few people understood the term, and in many hundreds of speeches and essays the occupational counselor had to battle complacency, prejudice, and ignorance. Today, everyone has most likely grasped the concept behind the watchword "retraining." Nonetheless, it is necessary to say a few things about retraining.

Many believe that the <u>decision</u> to choose a new occupation or to let one's child become a carpenter instead of a lawyer is sufficient. That is merely <u>external retraining</u>. This external process, however, must be preceded by an <u>internal</u> retraining. A lawyer who does carpentry is not yet a carpenter. The decision to retrain must go hand in hand with the decision to transform one's entire lifestyle. Above all, retraining means a complete change in one's previous set of social concepts and professional ethics. If the person to be retrained feels proletarianized, or believes that the retraining is only a temporary thing and that he can return to his old occupation at the first good opportunity, these are dangerous self-delusions. Retraining is not proletarianization, and for the Jews retraining now amounts to the prerequisite for a <u>permanent condition</u>. The retrained person must recognize that retraining cannot be approached with a resigned shrug and the words, "there's no choice but to retrain." Manual labor has moral values and potentialities that can satisfy the <u>entire</u> person. But retraining can succeed only when all the forces of the personality contribute to the process. In the person being taught a trade, there must be an active will to build a new life, in a different social milieu, under new, realistic occupational and social conditions. The ability to effect this <u>restructuring of the entire person</u> is the criterion for the success or failure of the retraining. Learning a new occupation, therefore, is only half the battle.

Many people who face retraining fear that they will deteriorate psychologically and intellectually and no longer have access to the fruits of a general education. This very mind-set, however, is not only wrong but also un-Jewish. In the old Jewish writings, we repeatedly find the admonition to perform manual labor. Thus Rabbi Yehuda says: "Every father is obligated to teach his son a trade; if he fails to teach him a trade, he is teaching him to steal." The types of the worker who studies and the teacher who works (the famous Rabbi Itzhak was a blacksmith, Rabbi Yochanan was a shoemaker, and the great philosopher Spinoza was a lens grinder) are typical of the Jewish mentality. In ancient times, the Jews were tillers of the soil and stockbreeders. Only through the scattering of Jews all over the world, the uprooting of Jews from their native soil, did Jewish farmers become business people. Yet the longing to return from working with their heads to working with their hands was always present in the Jews. Although the guilds in the Middle Ages waged an intense fight against the Jews' endeavor to pursue trades, many young Jews nonetheless persisted in their attempt to take up a manual trade. According to the census of Jews in Prague in 1729, which included more than 10,000 people, there were about 660 Jewish master craftsmen living in Prague at that time: one-third of the gainfully employed Jews in Prague. There were Jewish goldsmiths, hosiery knitters, rope makers, glaziers, cutlers, furriers, milliners, saddlers, wainwrights, button makers, makers of braids and tassels, metal workers, sword makers, potters, bag makers, lorimers, glove makers, shot casters, silk workers, bead stitchers, tailors, shoemakers, tawers, butchers, bakers, confectioners, bookbinders, printers, canvas printers, coppersmiths, etc. There were also female artisans, such as women who sewed linens and undergarments, did gold embroidery, made and repaired fur garments, made buttons, and even made shoes. [. . .]

There are no figures more miserable than people who repeatedly parade what they once were, forgetting in the process to look the truth and the future in the face with their eyes wide open. What one was is past; only what one will become and can become is valid!

Job retraining was but one of the responsibilities that fell to Jewish communal organizations in the many different countries in which Jews were being forced out of their previous economic roles. Indeed, support for the masses of Jews who had become dependent on welfare exceeded the resources of European Jewish communities. The editorial in document 8–9, also from the Prague edition of the *Jüdisches Nachrichtenblatt*, conveys how acute the situation had become in the Protectorate.[52] Communal survival depended on each individual's commitment to self-sacrifice. Above all, this Czech Jewish author called for Jewish solidarity.

---

52. Specific information on JRC welfare activities in this period can be found in Rothkirchen, *The Jews of Bohemia and Moravia*, 120.

DOCUMENT 8–9: **"The Meaning of Jewish Sacrifices,"** *Jüdisches Nachrichtenblatt Prag/Židovské listy,* December 28, 1939, 1 (translated from German).

Moral duties are not obvious at all times and to all people. Frequently we take note of them only reluctantly, and even then are more inclined to construe them one-sidedly. Therefore it is not pointless to say a few more words about the meaning of Jewish sacrifices. The Jewish community's primary options for building a sustainable bridge across the stormy course of time into a better future amount to sacrificing, donating, and holding out a helpful hand. Plainly, sacrifices no longer have their old, religious meaning; they are not made to appease gods or to invoke misfortune; they stem not from fear but from compassion, from a strong internal emotion, in the grip of which people cease to ask why and wherefore. Jewish sacrifice, in addition, is the means of Jewish self-help, without which winning our way out of the present situation is simply inconceivable. [. . .]

One consequence of the special nature of the Jewish situation is the special meaning of Jewish sacrifices. Just as people in a lifeboat pass around their last water bottle and, when the boat rocks, toss all their belongings overboard to escape with nothing but the clothes on their back, the Jews of our day must make exceptional sacrifices. In so doing, they not only fulfill a commandment of philanthropy but also abide, first and foremost, by a very mundane law of self-preservation.

These days, Jewish sacrifice is more than mere charity [*Spenden*]. It must acquire a valid meaning, and therefore Jews, in whatever they do and omit to do, must be guided exclusively by consideration of the needs of the community. The sacrifices that are made alleviate Jewish suffering and supply the passage money for Jews who are entering upon the path to a new life. However, a more general self-sacrificing Jewish bearing has helped—through tact, restraint, and understanding—make possible the difficult and responsible redirection of Jewish lives to other countries and continents without causing disruption or undue excitement. Because misery produces panic and despair in the people involved, elemental distress that becomes widespread only leads to fresh consternation and complications. [. . .]

The more poor Jews there are who are starving in the world, the less peace will be found by affluent Jews, however great the distances separating them from the hardships of their brethren. As long as starving, freezing wanderers tug at the bell of Jewish houses at night, seeking to be let in, the more fortunate Jews who already have gained access will also find no sleep.

That is the meaning of the Jewish sacrifices, both active and passive. Any Jew who has not grasped that meaning does not comprehend his own fate.

Whereas this editorial was directed at Jews who still had some means of support and thus reflected their point of view, the letter in document 8–10 offers the perspective of a Jewish man in Luxembourg who was reduced to penury after five months of German occupation. Joseph Pradelski and his wife, along with the three thousand or so Jews of Luxembourg, suffered from a rash of antisemitic decrees introduced subsequent to the Nazi invasion of that country in May 1940. Luxembourg was to be incorporated into the Greater Reich, and toward that end, the German chief of the civil administration, Gustav Simon, issued a decree on September 7, 1940, modeled on the Nuremberg Laws that forbade sexual relations between those defined as "Jews" and "Aryans," as well as another decree restricting Jewish economic activity in various realms.[53] Driven to desperation by such measures, Pradelski turned to the Luxembourg Jewish Community (Consistoire) for help. His original letter contained many grammatical lapses, suggesting that he had had little schooling or, as a native of Poland, knew only rudimentary German.[54]

DOCUMENT 8–10: **Letter from Joseph Pradelski, Luxembourg, to the Jewish community of Luxembourg, October 7, 1940, USHMMA Acc. 1999.A.0013 Consistoire Israelite Luxembourg, reel 5, folder 37 (translated from German).**

Luxembourg, Oct. 7, 1940
Dear Sirs,

I have struggled greatly not to become a burden on the community— my wish was always, don't sink to that. now I am powerless. I haven't

_____

53. Martha Jelenko, "Review of the Year 5701—Luxembourg," *AJYB 5702* 43 (1941): 175–76.

54. Joseph Pradelski (b. 1901 in Szczekociny, Poland, later stateless) and his wife, Jetta or Jeta (b. 1905 in Przeworsk), both ended up in France in mid-December 1940. After spending time in the Rivesaltes camp, Joseph (and probably Jetta) was sent to Drancy and then to Auschwitz on September 9, 1942, where they perished. See *USHMM ITS Collection Data Base Central Name Index*; Yad Vashem, "Central Database of Shoah Victims' Names," www .yadvashem.org.

earned anything for five months now, I'm asking for at least some aid to
pay the rent. haven't paid rent for 4 months. pay 250 francs a month,
work as a vendor at the market, barely made ends meet with my wife,
[have] been in Luxemburg [*sic*] for 11 years and have never asked the
community for anything. unfortunately at the breaking point now, must
turn to you gentleman of the community and ask you for help. with my
thanks in advance

> Joseph Pradelski
> Talstrasse 81
> Luxembourg

Pradelski's request for assistance generated "1 month of [soup] kitchen
access/250 fr[ancs]," according to a note scribbled on his letter by someone
in the Consistoire office. That the Luxembourg Jewish Community furnished
him with aid for such a limited duration suggests that dependence on welfare
was, at best, a stopgap measure. Indeed, for Jews under German authority, emigration continued to offer the sole chance for a brighter future. Yet, with the
start of World War II, emigration ceased to seem like a real possibility, despite
the Nazi regime's ongoing commitment to emigration as the primary "solution" to Germany's "Jewish question." "Castles in the air" is how one woman in
Prague characterized her emigration hopes in October 1939.[55] Individuals continued to turn to communal organizations like the Czech JRC and the German
Reichsvereinigung der Juden in Deutschland for help navigating the governmental bureaucracies and arranging transportation in wartime. People also tried
to optimize their situation by other means. Personal ads from a 1940 edition of
the *Jüdisches Nachrichtenblatt Prag* indicate that emigration status became one
of the main criteria for men and women seeking marriage partners.

---

55. Letter from Hansi Pick, Prague, Protectorate of Bohemia and Moravia, to Rudi
Kohner, Bradford, England, October 17, 1939, in Nancy Kohner, *My Father's Roses:
A Family's Journey from World War I to Treblinka* (New York: Pegasus Books, 2009),
249. Hansi Pick was then in her early twenties. Kohner and the authors lack conclu-
sive information about Pick's fate. Articles in the 1939–1940 Berlin edition of *Jüdisches
Nachrichtenblatt* also reflected the limited opportunities for Jewish emigration. See
Clemens Maier, "The *Jüdisches Nachrichtenblatt*, 1938–43," in *Jews in Nazi Berlin: From
Kristallnacht to Liberation*, ed. Beate Meyer, Hermann Simon, and Chana Schütz (Chicago:
University of Chicago Press, 2009), 114.

DOCUMENT 8–II: **Marriage ads, *Jüdisches Nachrichtenblatt Prag/Židovské listy*, January 12, 1940, 10 (translated from German).**

Marriages
SŇATKY[56]

Widow living alone
age 55, youthful looks,
pleasant appearance
and nature, well-spoken,
industrious and enterprising,
seeks intelligent partner
for the purpose of remarriage.—Reply to Box
"Serious 810," at this newspaper office.
Sň. [Sňatky] 656

Seeking
for my brother, 37-year-old academic
now in retraining,
pleasant appearance,
for purpose of emigration:
truly beautiful, personable
marriage partner. Send offers with photo
to "Eretz" at this newspaper office,
Sň. [Sňatky] 631

[. . .]

Attention
Immigration to USA
as soon as possible
Seeking suitable young woman
who will provide an affidavit
for my 22-year-old son
and can go to the USA
as soon as possible
as a result of this marriage.

---

56. This is Czech for "marriages."

Constitutes a prerequisite.
—Reply to Box USA 1940
at this newspaper office.

Viennese businessman,
skilled craftsman with
possibility of emigrating,
wants to meet only a pretty lady
with ideal disposition
and good character, up to age 33.
Reply to Box "Not Anonymous," at this
newspaper office
Sň. [Sňatky] 556

Intell., 30-year-old,
superior craftsman
with commercial training
seeks, for the purpose of marriage,
young, pretty girl
up to age 26, also
employed in trade, immigration
to USA facilitated,
affidavits on hand.
Reply to Box "Offers with Photo,"
at this newspaper office.
Sň. [Sňatky] 644

In addition to social welfare and emigration, culture and education became newly important for many Jewish communal organizations and individuals in response to antisemitic persecution during the first two years of the war. Indeed, occupational retraining programs often encompassed courses in Hebrew, the Bible, and Jewish history. Depending on the particular context, a person's increased interest in culture and education signified different things: political engagement, emotional retreat, social interaction, or employment opportunity. We must also bear in mind that for many European Jews, a Jewish cultural and educational agenda was consistent with religious or nationalist ideas that predated their experiences of antisemitism under Nazi occupation and collaborationist regimes.

The Jewish scout movement in France, the Éclaireurs Israélites de France (EIF), was one such Jewish organization that seamlessly adapted its prewar mission to the situation Jews faced in both zones of France after the armistice with Germany.[57] In the 1920s and 1930s, the EIF had brought together French- and foreign-born Jewish youth in a movement that valorized manual labor and agricultural work in conjunction with the study of Hebrew, Jewish history and literature, and religious practice.[58] Vichy's anti-Jewish measures in the fall of 1940 endowed the EIF's work with greater urgency and meaning. Beginning in September in the Unoccupied Zone, the movement established group camps to train new youth leaders. Within those groups, Jewish youth could pursue jointly the goals of occupational "reorientation" and the revitalization of Judaism. The report in document 8–12 offers a description of life in one of the first EIF group camps. According to historian Renée Poznanski, "Within a year, more than two thousand young Jews were grouped together under the auspices of twenty-six Scout units in the Unoccupied Zone, thus providing support for young French Israelites who were bewildered and distressed as well as for young foreign Jews who had lost their ties with society."[59]

---

57. Founded in 1924, EIF was a national Jewish scout organization; the first Jewish scout group was founded in Paris in 1923. The purpose of the organization was to provide a scouting experience in a Jewish environment. In terms of Jewish politics, the organization endorsed a pluralistic understanding of Judaism and Jewishness and worked with various groups, although Zionism permeated its leadership in the late 1920s and 1930s. The organization continued its activities after the defeat of France in 1940; the Vichy government even allowed it to function until 1943. It did so under the framework of the Union générale des israélites de France (UGIF), the new central Jewish organization established in late November 1941 in both the Occupied and Unoccupied Zones in France, which was subordinated to the commissioner general for Jewish affairs. The UGIF encompassed all Jewish relief organizations operating in France, as well as other French Jewish social bodies. See Paula Hyman, *From Dreyfus to Vichy: The Remaking of French Jewry, 1906–1939* (New York: Columbia University Press, 1979), 191–98.

58. Hyman, *The Jews of Modern France*, 142–44.

59. On the EIF during the first year of Vichy rule, see Poznanski, *Jews in France during World War II*, 137–40.

DOCUMENT 8–12: Report by Nina Gourfinkel, Unoccupied Zone, France, "First Attempts at the Organization of Professional Restructuring," to Arieh Tartakower of the WJC, Relief Department, New York City, October 15, 1940, USHMMA RG 68.045M (WJC Geneva), reel 1 (translated from French).[60]

[. . .] The Land-Clearers Camp—a nice name, which makes one think of the pioneers and the Halutzim—was set up a month ago in Viarose, in the Moissac hills (Tarn-et-Garonne [district]); it was founded by the Jewish Scouts Movement to train people in agricultural work in order to encourage Jewish youth to return to the land.

Before the establishment of the Land-Clearers Camp, an 8-day camp for leaders was held, to give the young people the necessary spiritual instructions and enthusiasm for a living Judaism and a physically and morally healthy communal life.

22 land clearers (16 males and 6 females), supervised by a Jewish Scout leader, make up a community of pioneers that will spend six months learning to work the land. Then they'll become instructors able to train other young people. They are all between 20 and 25 years old. Their number, limited for the moment, should increase. Among them, there is an expert agricultural trainer.

These young people are diverse in origin: some are French, but most are Polish, and there also are many Hungarians and Russians. Most of them have military service behind them. One of them, a soldier of the Polish Legion, came back from Norway, where he took part in the Battle of Narvik. The head of the Jewish Scouts is a pilot, also returned from Norway.

---

60. Born in Odessa, Nina Gourfinkel (1898?–1984) studied in Russia and moved to Paris in 1925, where she lived and worked until the occupation. In the summer of 1940 she became involved in relief work for people displaced by the war. In 1941 she helped to found an organization with Joseph Weill (of OSE) and Abbé Glasberg that set up hostels in the Unoccupied Zone for men and women released from French internment camps, mainly Jews. She continued working for the Lyon-based organization after the war, when it began serving other groups of displaced persons, and became a woman of letters. See Poznanski, *Jews in France during World War II*, 193, 524n108; Zuccotti, *The Holocaust, the French, and the Jews*, 37–38, 74–75, 77, 309n17. Born in eastern Galicia, Arieh Tartakower (1897–1982) became a sociologist in Warsaw and a founder of a Zionist labor organization. He ran relief and rehabilitation operations for the WJC after emigrating to the United States in 1939 and remained active in the WJC after his move in 1946 to Palestine, where he also continued his work in sociology at Hebrew University. See Natan Lerner, "Tartakower, Arieh," in Skolnik and Berenbaum, *Encyclopaedia Judaica*, 19:523.

The abandoned farm with a smallholding and a plot of land where the land clearers are was lent to them by a local French landowner. The house is ramshackle and bare, but habitable, because they [the scouts] themselves have made repairs and continue to make them on a daily basis.

The young girls, supervised by an older qualified housekeeper, take care of the cooking, the housework, and the laundry and clothes-mending. They knit warm clothes for winter. Some of them also help local peasants.

Many of the young people were not prepared for the tough work and the rough living conditions, but nevertheless they devote their evenings to cultural activities, reading, and courses in literature, Hebrew, history, Jewish folklore. Every newspaper brought to them is devoured. They are hoping to set up a small library (for which **RELICO**[61] is granting them a small monthly sum, and at the moment books are being sought in Toulouse and Lyon) and thus to pursue at the same time agricultural jobs and intellectual development. One needs a great desire for culture to return to books in the evening after a physically exhausting working day. [. . .]

Friday evening, we went to the Land-Clearers Camp. [. . .] There was a real table surrounded by real benches, all that built by the two carpenters of the house. Not an amateur job, really good work! Pewter tableware, pitchers, bread baskets decorated with flowers by the girls. [. . .] The instructors who come regularly to give courses and chatty lectures at the camp have arrived. They are Jewish Scout leaders. The young land clearers, freshly dressed for the festive evening, gather. The songs of Shabbat rise up.

After the meal, Hebrew and Yiddish songs, stories from Jewish folklore, and discussions go on for an hour longer than usual. Saturday is the only day when the land clearers sleep late. The day is devoted to rest. Oneg Shabbat closes the day in the afternoon, outside on the grass, weather permitting. [. . .]

The endurance, good will, and vitality of these young people, who deserve the interest and support of four great institutions, are one of our reasons to hope for the future.

The song in document 8–13 also conveyed the continued faith in a brighter future. It was one of several copied down in a notebook by Henri Pohyrles, a teacher at the **Œuvre de secours aux enfants** (OSE) children's homes in France. Prior to World War II, OSE created several homes for refugee children from central and eastern Europe whose parents could not take care of them.

---

61. For more on RELICO, see the Glossary.

After the armistice between France and Germany, OSE evacuated children to the Unoccupied Zone administered from Vichy and took in hundreds more children who had no other place to go while their parents were being held in internment camps. Pohyrles was a teacher at the home in La Bourboule, in the Unoccupied Zone about three hundred miles south of Paris. In the following song, titled after the Hebrew name for the youngest age group in the Hashomer Hatzair youth movement, hope coexisted uneasily with an implicit acknowledgement of the uncertainty that lay ahead and the difficult lives these youths were leading.[62]

DOCUMENT 8–13: **Song titled "Benei-Midbar," La Guette, France, USHMMA Acc. 2004.435 Naomi Elath papers (translated from French).**

---

62. Poznanski, *Jews in France during World War II*, 140–43.

We are young, the world is large
For us, happy Benei-Midbar,[63]
Working together now
Is our greatest happiness
We want to sing together!
"Let's be cheerful and brave"
Refrain:
We are young, the world is large
For us, happy Benei-Midbar.

Go to work! Our slogan is
Do it cheerfully
We never lack the will
Even for big duties
Obey always without a word and with a good heart
Refrain

Head held high in tough times
Even when all goes wrong
We don't want fights
Everyone is a brother to us
We are proud of our people
Let's follow its path without fear
Refrain

(melody: Wir sind jung . . . [German for "we are young"])

INDIVIDUAL COPING STRATEGIES

Letters and diary entries reveal different dimensions of Jewish responses during the first two years of the war. They offer glimpses of individuals' emotions and psychological coping strategies as they contemplated the meaning of antisemitic measures and the radical disruptions to their families, social worlds, and physical existences. The documentation presented in this section provides a smattering at best. It is arguably impossible to generalize about the emotional and psychological responses of Jews across Europe when one considers the diversity of men and women's national contexts, political orientations, and sociocultural backgrounds, not to mention their ages, family circumstances, and individual dispositions. Still, it is important for our understanding of the range of Jewish responses to lay out and scrutinize some portion of the period's complex emotional range as reflected in the documentation of the time.

---

63. "Benei-Midbar" was one of the appellations given to the youngest age group of youth in the Hashomer Hatzair youth movement.

The diaries and letters of Czech, German, and Austrian Jews from this period suggest that resignation and depression predominated. Prior to the start of World War II, in the months after "***Kristallnacht***," Jews in the Reich and the Protectorate seemed almost frantic as they tried to flee Nazi rule. After the war began, as emigration became less imaginable, many individuals wrote about their exhaustion and sense that everyday activities lacked meaning. In a November 1939 letter, a Czech Jewish woman described to her friend who had emigrated to England, "I am still working at the Kindergarten and have at present fifty children to look after, so there is plenty of work. The Jewish Community is taking over the Kindergarten and I am now getting a proper teacher's contract and better pay. It's something I'd have felt proud of in the past but gradually these things seem to matter less and less and one gets to the point where one doesn't really care."[64]

As we have seen in previous chapters, a principal feature of central European Jews' lives during this period was the scattering of family members across Europe and the world. Lotte Meissner and her husband, Norbert, were among the thousands of Jewish parents who bid farewell to their children and remained in Nazi-occupied Europe. Parenting at a distance, via written communications through the mail, replaced the direct and often intense interactions that take place within an intact family. After their sixteen-year-old son, Frank, arrived in Denmark in October 1939 as part of a **Youth Aliyah** group, Lotte and Norbert wrote to him every couple of days, enclosing vouchers to cover the cost of postage for his return letters to them in the Protectorate, in their hometown of Triesch (Czech: Třešť). Their letters betray the extent to which their separation from their son marked their emotional lives, both as a burden that added to their daily tribulations and as a source of hope emanating from the knowledge that he had gotten out of Nazi central Europe.[65]

---

64. Letter from Hansi Pick, Prague, Protectorate of Bohemia and Moravia, to Rudi Kohner, Bradford, England, November 26, 1939, in Kohner, *My Father's Roses*, 250. See also on Hansi Pick, note 55 above.

65. Frank Meissner (1923–1990) escaped from Denmark to Sweden in October 1943 as part of the grassroots rescue operation that saved seven thousand Jewish lives. After a year in Sweden, he enlisted in the Czechoslovak army in Great Britain, where he finished out the war years. He eventually emigrated to the United States. Lotte Meissner (Charlota Meissnerová; née Grunenberger, b. 1894) and Norbert Meissner (b. 1884) were deported from Triesch (Třešť) to Theresienstadt (Terezín) in May 1942. They and their son Leo (b. 1920) were subsequently deported from Theresienstadt to Auschwitz in October 1944, where they were presumably killed. See *USHMM ITS Collection Data Base Central Name Index.* For additional biographical information, see Frank Meissner, "A Young Czechoslovak Jew in Denmark," *Kosmas* (a publication of the Czechoslovak Society for Arts and Sciences) (1983): 115–31. On Jewish parents attempting to maintain relationships with their children from a distance after the start of the war, see Alexandra Garbarini, "Family Correspondents," in *Numbered Days: Diaries and the Holocaust* (New Haven, CT: Yale University Press, 2006), 95–128.

DOCUMENT 8–14: Letters by Lotte Meissner, Triesch, Protectorate of Bohemia and Moravia, to her son, Frank ("Mokele"), Denmark, March 21, 1940, and June 8, 1940, USHMMA Acc. 2007.228 Frank Meissner collection (translated from German).[66]

50th letter, Triesch, March 21, 1940
My dear Mokele!
[. . .] And in fact your letter of March 7 arrived today, in which you tell about moving into your room. Did you move the furniture in by yourself, or did somebody help you? I hope it's not such a cold attic room again as at the Petersens.[67] Now that summer is coming, it is not so important, but when it gets too cold there, surely Mrs. Nielsen will understand and will let you sleep in the room with her son again. I already asked you previously to describe the rest of the apartment, but it's not always easy to get information from you. Now I would like to request that you not take too much advantage of your freedom and not come home too late, to avoid creating any unpleasantness. First of all, for your landlords, and secondly, one can also experience unpleasantness on the country road [*Landstrasse*] at night. Now that, thank God, you are doing well and are satisfied, you should not abuse your freedom. I was happy to read that you had lots of guests and feasted so well at the dinner. Have you ascertained yet why the lady of the house sat with you instead of with the guests? I thought that you eat with the family, but now I see that the personnel eat separately. Or is that only when there are guests? Please report, I'd like to be informed about that. I hope Mr. Nielsen wasn't too angry with you for talking with the son in the stables instead of working. Does Werner have such a sweet tooth that he had to snatch extra sweets after he already had enough to eat at the table[?] Please do not imitate him, even if you would enjoy that. In your case it could be considered stealing and could have grave consequences for you. You always have to remember that you are the foreigner and that you can't act like him. Surely, as the youngest in the family, he is being spoiled and allowed to get away with a lot. As you do not mention it again, I assume that the crate arrived in good shape and that you are again able to put all your things in good order. Please make sure that the winter things are well laundered, so that you can keep them for the next winter.

---

66. Lotte's letter to her son was written on the verso of Frank's father's letter to him.

67. Frank was originally placed with a Danish family, the Petersens, on a farm about one hundred kilometers (sixty-two miles) south of Copenhagen. In the early months of 1940, he moved to live with a second farm family, the Nielsens, about forty kilometers (twenty-five miles) south of Copenhagen. As a member of the Hehalutz, or agricultural pioneers in a Zionist youth group, Frank was being trained in agriculture with the intention of settling in Palestine. For more on Hehalutz, see the Glossary.

The sweaters and woolens also have to be laundered well, so that they don't attract moths during the summer. I'm sure that Mrs. Nielsen, who is such a good housewife, will take care of that, and you should ask her very politely to make sure that the things will be laundered with good soap flakes. You always have to consider that these things are all you possess and are good, and that you have to protect them like the eyes in your head. How would you have the opportunity to acquire anything new? Also shoe lasts should always be put into the shoes that you are not wearing so that they don't lose their shape. If you don't have enough, maybe you could buy some, that is very important so that the shoes remain in good shape. Do you have enough clothes hangers? Please consult Mrs. Nielsen, she will understand all this and will not find it laughable, as you may. I have repeatedly asked about your finance minister in my letters but have never received an answer. You wrote the Winternitzes only a postcard, you must at all costs write another letter to them, it can't be so difficult.[68] Or did you have some falling out with them that makes it so difficult for you to write them a proper letter? Your letters are no longer forwarded on to Prague since Leo [Frank's brother] is no longer there. Why did you let Aunt Rosa wait so long for an answer? Aside from Vienna, you don't write anything there. I have now run out of paper.

A thousand kisses from

your Mom

Easter greetings to the Nielsens.

[June 8, 1940]

My dear Mokele!

[. . .] Tomorrow we are going to the cemetery, because it is the anniversary of the death of my blessed mother, she is at peace and was spared a great deal. It is also a good thing that Bobisek [her father] is a good sport and finds it easy to overcome adversity. He misses both of you [Frank and his brother, Leo] and would very much like to see you again. We hope that this will happen one day, and we will be happily together again. You have already gotten used to being abroad and surely have so many distractions that you don't feel homesick. But this feeling may come over you once in a while, and you would like to see us and speak with us. Certainly I am sufficiently occupied that I, too, have distractions, but when I can't sleep at night, I feel very lonesome, and what I wouldn't give to have you both close to me. I don't want to make you anxious, and I won't write about this anymore. [. . .]

---

68. The Winternitz family may have been the "finance minister" in question, providing financial help for Frank.

How long will we still be able to enjoy your dear letters, you can't imagine how much joy they give us. I don't want to spoil your mood with my lamentations, and so I'll close with the fondest regards and loving kisses,
    Your mother

Like Lotte Meissner, **Jenny Marx**, living in Mannheim, Germany, with her partner Siegmund Mayer, did not seem to envision an improvement in her situation after the start of the war. Writing to her brother, Max, and his new family in Palestine, she now regarded emigration as a remote possibility. And in a manner characteristic of this correspondent but atypical of letter writers overall, Marx did not affect a cheerful tone for the sake of her family abroad. Indeed, she regularly called attention to the difference in perspective of people abroad and how impossible it was for them to understand the dire nature of Jewish life in Nazi Germany. Living in poverty and burdened with responsibility for her ailing parents, Jenny Marx did not appear to derive any sense of comfort from her correspondence with her brother.

DOCUMENT 8–15: **Letter by Jenny Marx, Mannheim, Germany, to Max Marx and family, Jerusalem, Palestine, January 14, 1940, private collection (translated from German).**

My dear Three:
    I thank you for your two letters and am happy that you all are well. Unfortunately, I cannot say the same of us. Papa is very gravely ill and is slowly declining. There is no chance for improvement, as cancer of the lung is incurable. He has had this illness for 4 years now, and he is bedridden, can no longer get up. He was in the hospital for 10 weeks without any improvement, and the doctor tells us that the end could come fast.[69] We have to face the facts, because there is no sense in deceiving each other. Mother is also an old, sick woman; 70 years is no longer youth. The daily sorrows take their toll. I'm certain, dear Max, that you cannot imagine how poor we have become. I hope that you will always be spared such a sad condition. We are entirely dependent upon the Jewish Community; otherwise, we have nothing left at all. Completely without means. You will also understand that this is hard on the nerves. Siegm. [Siegmund] and I carry the entire responsibility. It is very sad that we have to start building our new life in such poverty. To set up a comfortable home, from what? It is out of the question. Our bedroom is my white bed and your old bed, painted white, that is my home. I've gotten past it. Siegm. is unemployed at the moment,

69. Jenny Marx's father, Herz, died of his illness in January 1940.

as work was stopped because of the cold weather. But daily life goes on. One has to live, the rent has to be paid, and we have to have some heat. We sit here often without heat. Can you imagine that? I don't think so. [. . .] I think you couldn't stand this misery. This is my lot. Who wants impoverished people? Nobody. Nobody is left here, they all have emigrated. The only one with some human compassion is Uncle Schlösser. Uncle Josef also promised the parents that he will help, but nothing so far. Please remind him of his duty. Now you have a picture how poor we have become. Sometimes I would want to end my life, if I did not love Siegm. so much. Therefore I am making a sincere request of you, please send Uncle what is meant for us, because we are in dire need. Please write once more to Martin Dreyfuss, and ask that he get the matter of the house sale in Malsch in order. It is already a year since they left, and we're already dead as far as they are concerned. Uncle Salomon has owed us 1,000 Marks for 10 years. He has yet to pay back a penny, and now we would need it desperately. Please see to it that they help us in whatever manner. Siegm. and I can <u>no longer</u> carry this burden alone. Otherwise there is little news. My in-laws visit us from time to time, they are also in bad shape financially. I have a question, has your affidavit for America expired? Are you still interested in it? If not, see whether it can be transferred to us, Siegm. has none, in the event that you cannot let us come to you. I thank you all for your congratulations on our wedding. It had to be postponed, since I have been very sick, we hope that we can do it this month. [. . .]

Women writing diaries, as opposed to letters, sometimes gave more complete expression to their hopelessness. This was certainly the case for Mignon Langnas, a Jewish woman living with her elderly parents in Vienna who gave voice to the unrelenting misery of her existence in the diary she kept during these years.[70]

---

70. Mignon Langnas (1903–1949) was born in Borysław, then part of the Austro-Hungarian Empire, and moved to Vienna with her family just before World War I. She married Leon Langnas (1895–1978) from Lemberg (Polish: Lwów; Ukrainian: L'viv) in 1928. Leon was a passenger on the ill-fated MS *St. Louis* voyage in May 1939, and when the ship was forced back to Europe, he was sent to England and an internment camp for over a year. He managed to get to New York in 1940, where their children Manuela (b. 1933) and Georg (George; b. 1935) had already arrived under the care of a family friend. The children were temporarily placed in a Jewish orphanage until their father and other relatives could provide for their care. During the war years, Mignon remained in Vienna, working as a nurse at a children's hospital, and both of her parents died of natural causes. She followed her husband and children to New York in 1946. Only a portion of Mignon's diary and some of her correspondence with relatives scattered abroad survived the war. See *Aufbau*, October 12, 1945, 31; *USHMM ITS Collection Data Base Central Name Index*; Elisabeth Fraller and George Langnas, eds., *Mignon, Tagebücher und Briefe einer jüdischen Krankenschwester in Wien, 1938–1949* (Innsbruck: Studienverlag, 2010).

Mignon's husband, Leon, and her two children had managed to get out of the Reich by December 1939, but she remained, apparently because responsibility for her parents fell to her. She started the diary in 1939, before the start of the war, addressing the first entry to "Leochen, my dearest" and explaining, "I write these lines only for you, so that in case fate does not bring us together, you will be able to read this and will know everything." Beyond depression and loneliness, her diary entries also point to a source of comfort for some Jews: religious observance.

DOCUMENT 8–16: Mignon Langnas, Vienna, diary entries for February 11 and March 24, 1940, private collection (copy at USHMM Collections Division; translated from German).

Sunday, February 11, 1940, 4:30 a.m.

What is there since [word missing/erased] and today?! A long stream of hot tears, and now, while writing, I also don't know why and for what purpose I am alive. The little children left on December 6, then came the death notice of your dear father. And I have only sorrow and grief— only tears. The state of my beloved mother has worsened, and how much we suffer for her, only God knows! On Saturday, the 29th of December, Mother had a terrible night followed by a terrible day; she just lay there, indifferent to everything. We're having a Siberian winter—the windows are frozen all the way to the top—there is no heating here because it is Saturday, and father and I are sitting, crying and freezing, and full of anguish about our most precious possession. Shall I ever forget this Saturday? This "shir ['song' in Hebrew] hamalvis min-ha-amakim" [from a Psalm] to which my most beloved mommy suddenly wakes up. Will Gusti or Nelly [two of Mignon's sisters] ever know the spiritual greatness of our wonderful mother? How I love Mother's ways, her voice! And each day I renew my thanks to God when I hear this voice! [. . .]

It is 5 in the morning, and God sees our room with three broken human beings: sick, miserable, and poor. What will become of us? All are given notice to leave the apartments. They don't give us coal, and on top of it, the longing I feel in recent days for the children is so painful that soon I cannot live any longer.

Purim, Easter Sunday, March 24, 1940

I've gone to bed, it is 9 in the evening. I am in such a mood that I don't want to live anymore. Don't be angry, Leochen, but understand: for us it is so unspeakably sad—Mother suffers so much and the longing for the children—it has become unbearable. Yesterday we sat by Mother's bed and Father carried the Megillah scroll, and today we sat lonely at the table. Where are you all? Our little children and you, you sit at strangers' tables—and to whom have we done bad things—by which we would deserve such a lot? [. . .]

In their correspondence and diaries from these years, Jewish men typically showed greater emotional reserve than Jewish women. Nevertheless, in framing the details of daily life within broader analyses of current events and history, they still managed to convey a great deal about their emotional states and coping strategies. The richly detailed daily entries recorded by Gabriel Italie, a Dutch Jewish teacher of classical languages in The Hague, are exemplary for what they reveal about the impact of antisemitic measures on one man and his social and professional world in the months following Dutch capitulation. Italie was himself an observant Orthodox man who came from a long line of esteemed rabbis, teachers, and cantors in the Netherlands. The day after Nazi Germany defeated his country, Italie gloomily contemplated what German occupation would mean for his family and for all of Dutch Jewry: "If present conditions persist, the outlook for my children's future appears very dark. I will probably be dismissed and can only <u>hope</u> that I will be left alone, but then, I am already old: my temples are gray and the rest of my hair will quickly turn gray as well; above all I <u>feel</u> myself getting very old these last years. Only God can save us. [. . .] I ask myself anxiously what lies in store for Jews. If we will only be excluded from communal life (which I certainly expect) or if more serious measures will be taken." At that time, he described how two of his friends were taking comfort in Jewish learning and how he felt some consolation from the visits of sympathetic Dutch colleagues who "paid [him] a 'condolence call' (that is how I'll refer to it)."[71]

In a series of entries from the fall of 1940, presented in document 8–17, Italie contended with the unrelenting legislative assault against Dutch Jews by the German occupiers. He captured something of the complexity of daily life and the mounting tension between the Germans and the Dutch on account of German policies toward the Jews.[72] He also alluded to the different interpretive

---

71. Gabriel Italie, diary entry for May 15, 1940, in *Het oorlogsdagboek van dr. G. Italie: Den Haag, Barneveld, Westerbork, Theresienstadt, Den Haag, 1940–1945* (Amsterdam: Contact, 2009) (translated from Dutch; emphases in the original).

72. On February 25, 1941, Dutch Communist sympathizers in Amsterdam staged a general strike to protest the arrest of hundreds of Jewish men three days before. The strike spread, and soon Social Democrats and other Dutch patriots joined in. The Germans violently suppressed the rebellion. They also reevaluated their way of proceeding against Dutch Jewry in response. Bob Moore, *Victims and Survivors: The Nazi Persecution of the Jews in the Netherlands, 1940–1945* (London: Arnold, 1997), 72–73.

frameworks he drew upon to help him make sense of Dutch Jews' current predicament, from contemporary comparisons to historical ones and from religious concepts to secular nationalist ideas.[73]

DOCUMENT 8–17: **Gabriel Italie, The Hague, the Netherlands, diary entries from October 27, November 28 and 29, and December 5, 1940, in** *Het oorlogsdagboek van dr. G. Italie. Den Haag, Barneveld, Westerbork, Theresienstadt, Den Haag, 1940–1945* **(Amsterdam: Contact, 2009), 88–89, 101–3, 104–5 (translated from Dutch).**

Oct. 27

Again a new edict [*gezera*]: all Jewish establishments are required to register before the end of November with disclosure of assets and liabilities, etc. It appears that they want to be done with the "liquidation [of the assets]" of Netherland's Jews in 1940. And there has to be a great miracle—too great to hope for—to avoid this calamity. The thoroughly decent Dutch people will feel shame because of this officially organized exclusion [*broodroof*], but to what end? [. . .]

For my mood it is best that I am at school or busy preparing lessons and correcting exams. Because there is already too many reasons to be anxious about all the things that hang over the heads of the Jews and me personally. The children are fortunate that because of their youth, they have no sense of worrying ahead of time; and that accounts for the fact that the mood at home is still not that depressing.[74] But I see everything as very dark, very hopeless; though I do admit that they have left us alone for several months, more than I had expected earlier. But I think, for example, about Norway where the Quisling administration immediately discharged all "unreliable" public servants or about France, where the Jews again are deprived of their rights.[75] A consolation? Oh, yes, in the Middle Ages they robbed and murdered us; nowadays they refrain from the latter. [. . .]

73. Gabriel Italie (1895–1956) taught until late 1940, when he lost his job for being Jewish. He began keeping his diary in 1936. After the war he resumed teaching at a lyceum in The Hague and published a number of books on classical Greek figures. He continued writing in his diary until 1951; it was published in 2009 in an abridged Dutch-language edition.

74. He had three children. Ralf and Ida survived Theresienstadt, but his son Paul died in 1942.

75. The Norwegian political leader Vidkun Quisling was sympathetic to the Nazi takeover of his country, and he ran its Nazi-controlled puppet government between 1942 and 1945. His name thus became synonymous with traitors or collaborators. Quisling was sentenced to death and executed after the war ended. See Jacqueline Rokhsar, "Quisling, Vidkun," in Gutman, *Encyclopedia of the Holocaust*, 3:1203–4.

November 28

Now the newspaper finally carries the news that Jews in public service positions must be dismissed because of the activities of the Jewish community against Germany. "To assure the order, safety, and peace in the occupied territory." The announcement begins approximately with those words! And there is the added information that "because of a misunderstanding of the intent of the regulations, students in Delft and Leiden allied themselves with the Jews, so that it became necessary to close the T. H. [Technische Hoogschool] and the Academy until further notice. The dismissal of the Jews will be granted with a retention of their monetary rights.["] [. . .]

November 29

This morning the dismissal notice arrived neatly by registered mail. At the end of this curious document it (in)humanely states that the Reichskommissar[76] has determined that the dismissed will "temporarily" retain their salaries. The piece is dated 22 November, so that I taught a week too long since the dismissal was effective "as of today" (that should be tried some time with domestic help!).

The first use I made of my involuntary vacation was that I paid a Shiva visit with Rose and Paul to the Becker family.[77] Very fortuitously Rose learned from Martin's accountant that Mr. Becker passed away. It happened Sunday. [. . .]

Just before coffee I received a visit from my (ex-)colleague Schippers who on behalf of the father of a student offered an opportunity for private lessons and who—very carefully and delicately—offered to help should that become necessary at some point. I could tell him from the bottom of my heart that it felt good to encounter Christian conviction where there is so much happening that is un-Christian. He is namely a faithful Protestant and, as such, very indignant about the dismissal.

Ralf did not have a class for the last hour this afternoon because of the dismissal of Zeldenrust. Van Ijzeren came to make the announcement

76. Hitler appointed Arthur Seyss-Inquart (1892–1946), an Austrian lawyer, to a series of posts in Austria and Poland, then in May of 1940 assigned him to the highest-ranking post in the Dutch occupation administration, Reich commissioner of the occupied Netherlands. Seyss-Inquart carried out a range of harsh anti-Jewish measures in this capacity. He received a death sentence at the postwar Nuremberg war crimes trials. Jozeph Michman, "Seyss-Inquart, Arthur," in Gutman, *Encyclopedia of the Holocaust*, 4:1344–46.

77. Rose (née Hausdorff) was his wife, and Paul (b. 1922) was his older son.

to the class with tears in his eyes. The decency of the Dutch is one of those things that a German can never understand. [. . .]

December 5

The last few days I have again been diligently busy with my Euripides papers. That is something I can indulge in during this "vacation." [. . .]

Sarcasm was another means of resisting the assault on individuals' sense of identity and personal dignity. In their private writing, people could derive some sense of superiority over their persecutors by means of what one French Jewish diarist called "secret intellectual and moral victories."[78] Such an attitude is evident in document 8–18 by Czech Jewish writer and poet Jiří Orten.[79]

DOCUMENT 8–18: **Jiří Orten, Prague, Protectorate of Bohemia and Moravia, diary entry for October 26, 1940, translated from Czech and published in** *The Jews of Bohemia and Moravia: A Historical Reader*, **ed. Wilma Abeles Iggers (Detroit, MI: Wayne State University Press, 1986), 361–62.**

Prohibitions

I could not fall asleep for a long time last night and I contemplated and tried to make sense of all the prohibitions that affect me, even if only slightly. Because it is Sunday morning, snowing for the second day, and I have a few hours before I have to go to Košíře,[80] I will set down on paper all the prohibitions that I can recall when I am done, I will leave a large blank space for the ones that will be issued after today. Unfortunately, I have no reference on hand to use, and so both the order and the number will be arbitrary. These, then, are the prohibitions:

---

78. Lucien Dreyfus, Nice, France, diary entry for December 22, 1940, USHMMA RG 10.144.04 Lucien Dreyfus collection, 1903–1943.

79. Jiří Orten (Ohrenstein; 1919–1941), eminent Czech lyrical poet, was born in Kutná Hora. A number of his works appeared under a pseudonym during the occupation, and his poetic references to the prophet Jeremiah hinted at the world tragedy to come. He was killed in a traffic accident in Prague, run down by a German military vehicle. His collected works were published posthumously under his own name in Prague in 1946. See Wilma Abeles Iggers, ed., *The Jews of Bohemia and Moravia: A Historical Reader* (Detroit, MI: Wayne State University Press, 1986), 394; Egon Hostovsky, "Participation in Modern Czech Literature," in *The Jews of Czechoslovakia: Historical Studies and Surveys*, ed. Society for the History of Czechoslovak Jews (Philadelphia: Jewish Publication Society of America, 1968), 1:445, 452.

80. Košíře is a district of Prague.

I am prohibited from leaving the house after 8 o'clock in the evening.

I am prohibited from renting an apartment for myself.

I am prohibited from moving anywhere but to Prague I or V [municipal districts], and then only as a subtenant.

I am prohibited from visiting wine restaurants, coffee houses, taverns, movies, theaters, or concerts, except for the one or two coffee houses allocated to me.

I am prohibited from going to parks and gardens.

I am prohibited from going to the municipal woods.

I am prohibited from traveling outside the Prague city limits.

I am thus prohibited from going home, to Kutná Hora,[81] or anywhere else, without the special permission of the Gestapo.

I am prohibited from traveling in the engine cars of the trams; I can only go in the last car, and if that has a center door, then only in the rear section.

I am prohibited from shopping in any stores except between 11 a.m. and 1 p.m. and between 3 p.m. and 5 p.m.

I am prohibited from acting in a play or taking part in any other public activity.

I am prohibited from belonging to any associations.

I am prohibited from going to any school.

I am prohibited from having any social contact with members of the National Union[82] and they are prohibited from associating with me. They may not greet me nor stop to talk to me except about essential matters (e.g. while shopping, etc.).

---

81. Kutná Hora (German: Kuttenberg) is a city in Bohemia.
82. The right-wing National Union was the only legal political party in the Protectorate.

CHAPTER 9

DEPORTATIONS FROM THE REICH

IN HIS DIARY entry for August 11, 1940, **Victor Klemperer**, living in a crowded "Jew house"[1] in Dresden, reflected on his own situation as well as on the general situation of Jews in Germany and in Romania, Slovakia, and Poland. He concluded, "Everything points to a constant worsening of the situation for Jews."[2] Devoid of optimism, Klemperer's summation cannot help but strike readers as astute. As we have seen, the relentless piling on of antisemitic laws and decrees throughout 1939 and 1940 left Jews in many countries in Europe increasingly impoverished, isolated, and vulnerable. Furthermore, as we know, the following summer would witness the Nazi invasion of the Soviet Union and, with it, the onset of the "Final Solution." But what did Klemperer mean in August 1940 when he projected into the future and envisioned the "constant worsening" of Jews' plight in Europe? And what did his Jewish contemporaries know and invest with significance as they analyzed their own predicaments and those of Jews elsewhere on a European continent now dominated by Nazi Germany?

The year 1940 struck many European Jews as a watershed in modern Jewish history. Yet, in general, Jewish men and women's view of this period focused not on the unforeseeable events of the future but on what had already

---

1. See discussion of "Jew houses" in chapter 3, p. 99.
2. Victor Klemperer, diary entry for August 11, 1940, in *I Will Bear Witness, A Diary of the Nazi Years, 1933–1941* (New York: Random House, 1998), 1:351–52.

come to pass. France, the beacon of republicanism and foe of German fascism, stood defeated. They regarded France's military defeat in catastrophic terms. Without France, would Great Britain stand firm? With Italy squarely in the German corner, large parts of western Europe occupied by the Reich, and southeastern Europe moving ever more into the sphere of Axis influence, did a safe haven remain for Jews on the Continent? Would the Allies be willing and able to mount a forceful response, one that held out true protection for Europe's besieged Jews?

The era of European Jewish Emancipation appeared to be over.[3] That macro perspective, however, emerged alongside a continuing concern with the local. Indeed, Jews in different national-political contexts, and even in different locales within the same territory, did not generally perceive the situation of Jews in other places as having direct relevance for them. Given the disparity of anti-Jewish policies within and beyond the Reich, this was hardly a surprising phenomenon. Local contexts continued to appear as meaningful in mediating and moderating—or escalating—the implementation of antisemitic policies. How did Jews perceive the threat to their existence in this period? Of particular concern to Jews in the Greater Reich beginning in the fall of 1939 was their vulnerability to deportation, which appeared to them to be a critical new stage in Nazi Jewish policy. The following therefore examines what individuals and groups of Jews knew about expulsions, deportations, and related policies—and how they responded to the knowledge they acquired. About half a million people, overwhelmingly non-Jews, were uprooted between 1939 and 1941.[4] Jewish responses to these policies

---

3. In the historiography of modern European Jewry, the term *Emancipation* refers to the granting of full civil rights to Jews in European nation-states in the aftermath of the French Revolution (1789). In some cases, as in France, the acceptance of Jews as equals in all areas of life happened overnight and by a stroke of the pen (1790 and 1791); in others, as in the various German states, a protracted, nearly century-long debate about whether the Jews should be, or were even capable of being citizens followed. Emancipation decrees were passed (e.g., in Austria-Hungary in 1867, the newly unified German Empire in 1871, and Serbia in 1878). See Pierre Birnbaum and Ira Katznelson, eds., *Paths of Emancipation: Jews, States, and Citizenship* (Princeton, NJ: Princeton University Press, 1995).

4. For a detailed account of the Nazi expulsion policy between 1939 and 1941, see Christopher R. Browning with contributions by Jürgen Matthäus, *The Origins of the Final Solution: The Evolution of Nazi Jewish Policy, September 1939–March 1942* (Lincoln and Jerusalem: University of Nebraska Press and Yad Vashem, 2004), 36–110; see also Götz Aly, *"Final Solution": Nazi Population Policy and the Murder of the European Jews* (London: Arnold, 1999), 1–148.

constitute an important dimension of Jewish "knowledge" and illuminate what Jews regarded as meaningful in their attempts to make sense of their situation in the early years of the war.

EARLY "RESETTLEMENTS" TO THE EAST

Between September 1939 and March 1941, the Nazis forced more than five hundred thousand people to abandon their homes and property in the Polish and French territories incorporated into the Reich (as distinct from those territories German authorities were occupying but not annexing). These expulsions were part of much grander schemes involving millions of people and meant to put the vision of creating *Lebensraum* into practice. Nazi planners sought to remove from German "living space" all inhabitants defined as "harmful" or "undesirable"—which included all Jews, most Poles, Roma ("Gypsies"), and those residents of Alsace and Lorraine who were found to be politically suspect—and to resettle ethnic Germans from the Baltics and other eastern European areas in an expanded Reich. During this period, Jews comprised approximately 12.5 percent of the expellees.[5]

Historians emphasize that, in the main, these expulsion plans did not make Jewish populations their central focus. While expulsion in conjunction with ghettoization certainly constituted the "crux of Nazi Jewish policy in Poland before the Final Solution," **Heinrich Himmler**'s priority at this time was to facilitate the resettlement of ethnic Germans, not to devise and implement the "Final Solution to the Jewish Question."[6] When resources permitted, Nazi officials pursued both population policies simultaneously in 1939 and 1940. However, Nazi officials impatient to press forward with anti-Jewish policies also had to suffer delays in their efforts to rid the Reich of Jews from time to time. Ghettos in Poland were devised as but a stopgap measure until Jewish expulsion could be completed.[7]

The **Nisko**-Lublin Plan provides a prime example of the friction that emerged among Nazi officials around these sometimes competing expul-

---

5. For a detailed chronology of expulsions from September 1939 through March 1941, see Browning, *The Origins of the Final Solution*, table on 109.

6. Browning, *The Origins of the Final Solution*, 36.

7. Browning, *The Origins of the Final Solution*, 42–43, 108; Saul Friedländer, *Nazi Germany and the Jews:* (vol. 2) *The Years of Extermination, 1939–1945* (New York: HarperCollins, 2007), 31.

sion plans. **Adolf Eichmann** and several eager *Gauleiter* seized upon the opportunity presented by Germany's defeat of Poland to reinvigorate a "territorial solution" to the "Jewish question." The mounting obstacles to emigration during wartime compelled Eichmann, as the official within **Reinhard Heydrich**'s Security Police and SD apparatus tasked with organizing Jewish emigration, to seek other options for removing Jews from the Reich. In early October 1939, he began to explore the idea of establishing a "reservation" for German, Austrian, and Czech Jews near the Polish city of Lublin. He settled on a location called Nisko on the San, on the western border of the Lublin district within the **Generalgouvernement**. Indeed, the Lublin reservation proved the first of several relocation schemes that various subordinates of Hitler dreamed up between 1939 and 1941 as a means of transferring, and in the process decimating, the Jewish populations of German-occupied Europe. After Hitler approved Eichmann's plan, transports of several thousand Jews began to leave in the third week of October for Nisko from Ostrava (German: Mährisch Ostrau) in the **Protectorate**, Vienna, and Katowice. No arrangements were made for accommodating these people upon arrival, and within weeks the **Reichssicherheitshauptamt** (RSHA; Reich Security Main Office) in Berlin had put a halt to any new transports. It seems that Himmler had decided to allocate all resources at his disposal to assisting incoming Baltic Germans; deporting Jews from the Reich and the Protectorate could wait. The Lublin reservation proved to be a failure, and the camp was dissolved in April 1940.[8]

What information reached Jews in different places about these policies? The Lublin scheme was by no means kept secret. As early as October 9, an Associated Press story reported that Jews from the Reich and Protectorate would be deported, along with 3 million Polish Jews, to a newly created "reservation."[9] The *Jewish Chronicle* (London), in an October 27, 1939, article titled "Vienna Jews Leave for Lublin," speculated about whether the Nazis were "Preparing the 'Jewish Pale'?"[10] If friction and poor planning characterized the conduct of Nazi officials around these plans, the deportations of Jews from the Reich

---

8. Browning, *The Origins of the Final Solution*, 36–43, 45–47, 54, 64–65, 106–7; Friedländer, *Nazi Germany*, 2:35–36.

9. Quoted in the front-page article "Ghetto-Staat von Hitlers Gnaden?" in the German-language, New York–based newspaper *Aufbau*, October 15, 1939, 1. For more on *Aufbau*, see the Glossary.

10. "Vienna Jews Leave for Lublin," *Jewish Chronicle* (London), October 27, 1939, 10–11.

to Poland constituted a confusing and alarming new policy development for Jewish observers. In a letter to **Stephen S. Wise**, dated November 10, 1939, the Central Bureau of the **World Jewish Congress** (WJC) in Geneva reported what it thus far knew about the Lublin plan and the impact it was having on the Jewish populations it had targeted.

DOCUMENT 9–1: **Letter from the Central Bureau of the World Jewish Congress, Geneva, to Dr. Stephen S. Wise, New York, November 10, 1939, American Jewish Archives, WJC records, series A, box A2, file 2, American Jewish Conference, *Day Book of the WJC II*, 27–30.**

[. . .] The Lublin Plan: The reports regarding the compulsory settlement of the Jews from Austria and Czechoslovakia in Lublin are becoming steadily more alarming. In Vienna anxiety and terror prevails among the Jewish population. I received directly from Vienna the "Instructions for the Transfer of Jews Residing in Vienna to the Polish Territory."[11] [. . .] The wives and children of the Jews transported have remained temporarily in Vienna. The house furnishings have been sold through the Jewish community. The proceeds must, however, be turned over to the Winter Relief of the Nazis.[12] On what the families are living is not known.

From Czechoslovakia we have learned through an absolutely reliable source that the Jews of the city of Bruenn [Brno in the Protectorate] have been shipped off in the same way to the Lublin region. Their house furnishings have been disposed of by the Jewish community in the same fashion as in Vienna, the proceeds going to the Winter Relief.

THE GERMAN OCCUPIED AREA: From a letter written at Bielitz [Polish: Bielsko] on the German frontier, dated October 26, we quote the

---

11. See "Deportation of Jews from Austria to Nisko (Lublin), October 1939," in *Documents on the Holocaust: Selected Sources on the Destruction of the Jews of Germany and Austria, Poland, and the Soviet Union*, ed. Yitzhak Arad, Israel Gutman, and Abraham Margaliot (Lincoln and Jerusalem: University of Nebraska Press and Yad Vashem, 1999), 143–44.

12. Winter Relief (Winterhilfswerk des deutschen Volkes, or Winter Aid Work of the German *Volk*," known more popularly as Winterhilfe) was a Nazi welfare program established in 1933. It consisted of an annual drive to help the poor and victims of the economic depression and, later, the war. See Cornelia Schmitz-Berning, *Vokabular des Nationalsozialismus* (Berlin: Walter de Gruyter, 2007), 695–97.

following: Bielitz has over night become a German city. All Poles and Jews up to the age of 60 must leave.[13] No one knows whither they are being sent. All Jewish and Polish business, houses and factories are under the administration of the commissar.

In the widespread reportage about the Lublin reservation, we repeatedly encounter the same question: what did these policies mean? In his diary entry of October 25, 1939, **Chaim A. Kaplan** recorded from Warsaw, "Yesterday we heard over the London radio that the Jews of Vienna have received an order to be ready to leave their native city and migrate to the Lublin district of Poland. This means: Prepare yourselves for total destruction [*kliyah gemorah*]."[14] A London *Times* article from two months later titled "Lublin for the Jews. The Nazi Plan. A Stony Road to Extermination" called attention to the horrific reality concealed by Nazi language, asserting "it is clear that the scheme envisages a place for gradual extermination, and not what the Germans would describe as *Lebensraum*. [. . .] The number of the dead rises into tens of thousands, and of refugees into hundreds of thousands. But again the size of the programme is very nearly irrelevant: it amounts to a mass massacre such as Nazi imagination can conceive but even Nazi practice can hardly carry through in full. Meanwhile it serves as a means of torture for many thousands and of terror for all the rest."[15]

As farsighted as these pessimistic assessments appear from our perspective, at the time they carried an air of undue alarmism in view of the fact that German anti-Jewish policy had not yet reached genocidal proportions; furthermore, the Lublin plan soon disappeared from newspapers, making it look more like a figment of Allied propaganda reminiscent of World War I than an important step in the Reich's path toward the mass murder of Jews.[16] The testimony excerpted in document 9–2, written by a Jewish man deported to Lublin from the Reich on October 21, 1939, presents a different perspective.

---

13. On Germanization policy in Poland, see Richard C. Lukas, *The Forgotten Holocaust: The Poles under German Occupation, 1939–1944*, 2nd rev. ed. (New York: Hippocrene, 1997), and Jan T. Gross, *Polish Society under German Occupation: The Generalgouvernement, 1939–1944* (Princeton, NJ: Princeton University Press, 1979).

14. Chaim A. Kaplan, diary entry for October 25, 1939, in *Scroll of Agony: The Warsaw Diary of Chaim A. Kaplan*, ed., Abraham I. Katsh (Bloomington: Indiana University Press in association with the USHMM, 1999), 57.

15. "Lublin for the Jews. The Nazi Plan. A Stony Road to Extermination," *Times* (London), December 16, 1939, 9.

16. John Horne and Alan Kramer, *German Atrocities, 1914: A History of Denial* (New Haven, CT: Yale University Press, 2001), 366–418.

It registers how little these early deportees knew about what was happening to them. It also suggests that a few Jews even tried to generate hopeful readings of their fate, supported by the fluidity of reality on the ground as well as by the Nazi use of euphemistic language. Most of all, this account offers an early narrative of what would become an archetypal feature of postwar Jewish Holocaust survivors' testimonies: the degrading and often deadly experience of being crammed into a cattle car and transported to Poland.[17] The author of the testimony, S. Moldawer, a Polish-born Jew from Leipzig, had been scheduled to sail from Hamburg to the United States when the war broke out.[18] The description of his experiences in transit to Lublin was published in January 1940 in New York's largest circulating Yiddish-language newspaper, **Forverts**, and again three months later in English translation in the *Contemporary Jewish Record*. Moldawer's story reached these American Jewish publications in an interesting manner. Because he had retained possession of an American visa, the American consul in Warsaw intervened with German authorities on his behalf. Moldawer was released from the Nisko camp with his wife and child on November 15, 1939, and subsequently made his way to New York.[19]

DOCUMENT 9–2: S. Moldawer, "The Road to Lublin," *Contemporary Jewish Record* 3 (March–April 1940): 119.

> [. . .] Twelve hours in the foul and filthy car. Not even a drop of water to drink. The few scraps of food we were able to buy at Hamburg with our last couple of marks have long since been exhausted. What we had has

---

17. Indeed, a reference to such transit experiences in an **AJJDC** report written at the same time is striking for its description of "the cattle cars" as "by now the traditional Nazi vehicles for Jewish transportation." They had become so familiar, suggested this report, as to render extensive description of them unnecessary: "The inhumane conditions under which these transports are sent out are by now too well-known to merit description here." See "Bulletin #6—Present Activities of the J.D.C. (Germany and its Possessions and the Refugees)," New York, February 21, 1940, facsimile reprinted in *Archives of the Holocaust: An International Collection of Selected Documents*, ed. Henry Friedlander and Sybil Milton (New York: Garland Publishing, 1990), 2/2:8. For an analysis of representations of deportation experiences, see Simone Gigliotti, *The Train Journey: Transit, Captivity, and Witnessing in the Holocaust* (New York: Berghahn Books, 2009).

18. Once the proprietor of a prosperous fur shop, he had lived in Leipzig for over two decades; he was held in Buchenwald for many months—presumably after "*Kristallnacht*"—until his wife secured his release.

19. The authors have been unable to track the later story of Moldawer and his family.

been divided among the women and children or given to old people. We men have had nothing. For us it has been a real *Yom Kippur*.[20]

Suddenly the door of the freight car is opened. The captain of the guard pokes his head in and orders us all to get out. We form fours on the platform. The chief of the Berlin Gestapo calls the roll.[21] One hundred and twenty-two "pieces of baggage." "No one dead?" he remarks ironically. "Wait till they get to Lublin, and we'll put them to bed with a shovel."

It's the first time anyone has mentioned a destination. Now we hear it, we can scarcely believe our ears. What has Lublin to do with us? Naturally, we had heard of it. City in Poland. Once played a role in Jewish history.[22] That's all. No one, of course, has the faintest idea that this is to be the capital of Hitler's "Ghetto-State," the republic that is somehow to rise from the ruins and smoke. For five weeks we have been cut off from the outside world and seen no papers.

The formalities are over. We are herded back into the car, into our living grave.

In heaven's name, we cry, what is to become of us? What does it all mean? Here we are, hungry and frozen, without a penny or a morsel of bread, without even a drop of water, and once again we are ordered out. This time they prod us in the back with the butts of their rifles. At four o'clock, they stuff us in again and padlock the door. The train moves off. So there is no reprieve.

In a corner of the truck, stifled sobbing. Every now and then a piercing shriek. Everywhere tears, everywhere terror. Presently pandemonium. People start knocking their heads against the walls. It goes on like this for a couple of hours. Then, a platform, crowds, human faces. People begin to hear us. They stop in their tracks. They look around.

---

20. This is an ironic reference to the Day of Atonement, during which pious Jews observe a fast.

21. The author may have meant Kurt Lischka (1909–1989), who joined the SS in 1933 and Gestapo in 1935 and became head of the Reich Center for Jewish Emigration in Berlin in late 1938 or early 1939. In 1940 he headed the Cologne Gestapo headquarters and later in the war played a critical role in organizing the deportation of thousands of Jews from France. Robert S. Wistrich, *Who's Who in Nazi Germany* (London: Routledge, 1982), 157–58.

22. Between 1580 and 1764, Lublin was the seat of the Council of Four Lands, a Jewish body uniting representatives from four provincial Jewish Councils (Greater Poland, Little Poland, Red Ruthenia, and Volhynia); this constituted an unprecedented instance of Jewish self-government in eastern Europe in the early modern period. See Joseph Marcus, *Social and Political History of the Jews in Poland, 1919–1939* (Berlin: Mouton, 1983), 8–10.

The bolt slides back. The Gestapo officer comes in. He is livid with rage. He wants to know the reason for the din.

"We are hungry," cry some.

"We want to know where we're going."

"Where?" bellows the officer, foaming with rage. "To Lublin, of course, to the Jew state."

Is the world gone crazy? It's the second time we've heard that name. Lublin. We are going to Lublin. A Jewish state. What does it all mean? Are we dreaming? Are we mad? A Jewish state in Lublin? Hitler the Savior of the Jews? Hitler the Messiah?

An order is rapped out. Whoever has money can buy food. Whoever hasn't can rot.

We run through our pockets for our last few pennies and frenziedly hand them over. The Gestapo agent runs to the buffet. The place is cleaned out. Only sweets and chocolates. Better than nothing.

The train moves on. Over and over again the word Lublin is muttered. But now it is not merely Lublin. It is the Jewish state. The words ring like magic. Now, at least, our journey has [a] point. Instead of New York, Philadelphia, or Chicago, they are taking us to Lublin. One hundred and twenty-two Jewish souls packed in a filthy freight car. [. . .]

In their reporting on the Lublin reservation, Jewish commentators abroad tried to determine the connections between its formation and other antisemitic policies introduced by the Third Reich in this period. An article that appeared in the *Canadian Jewish Chronicle*[23] on January 12, 1940, speculated about the possible causal relationship between the difficulty of absorbing Jews from the Reich into the reservation and the Nazi move to establish Jewish ghettos in the Generalgouvernement.

---

23. The *Canadian Jewish Chronicle* was a Montreal-based, English-language Jewish weekly. In 1966, it merged with the moderately Zionist *Canadian Jewish Review* to become the *Chronicle Review*, which was in circulation until 1976. Louis Rosenberg, *Canada's Jews: A Social and Economic Study of Jews in Canada in the 1930s*, ed. Morton Weinfeld (Montreal: McGill-Queen's University Press, 1993), 198.

DOCUMENT 9–3: **"Nazis Establish More Ghettos in Poland,"** *Canadian Jewish Chronicle*, January 12, 1940, 5.

NAZIS ESTABLISH MORE GHETTOS IN POLAND

NEW YORK (WNS) Establishment of ghettos in various towns in Nazi-occupied Poland not incorporated in the Reich, to segregate Jews in separate districts, besides the Jewish "reservation" in Lublin, is reported to Jewish organizations in Paris, according to a Paris dispatch to the *New York Times.*

Warsaw Jews, who paid several million złotys in November for postponement of the ghetto orders, now again are menaced with formal separation. Already certain streets in the centre of the city are closed to Jews. The dispatch further disclosed that in Radom, Minsk and Mazowiech,[24] Jews already have been ordered to settle in separate districts. To these ghettos have been transferred many inhabitants from surrounding villages and townships.

Before ghettos are created detailed registration of Jewish property is undertaken. Jews are compelled to deposit sums of more than 2,000 złotys and any valuables they possess.

Informed sources were of the opinion that this policy of separating Jews in various towns confirms recent information that the Nazis decided to slow down deportations to Lublin. According to the dispatch, Dr. Hans Frank, Governor General of Nazi-occupied Poland, visited the "reservation" recently and expressed dissatisfaction with the state of affairs there, asserting that the idea of the "reservation" is difficult to work out and too costly, as foreign Jews are unwilling to pour relief money into a reservation.

The widely publicized experiences of German, Austrian, and Czech Jews deported to the Lublin district generated a formal protest by French and Algerian Jewish leaders in early 1940 (document 9–4). The French **Central Consistory**'s formal statement represents their dire understanding of these resettlement policies. Particularly noteworthy is how they couched their advocacy on behalf of German Jews, now technically enemy nationals in the French context, in terms of a broader concern they felt for all Nazi victims. Like former French prime minister **Léon Blum** in his speech in document 1–8, French Jewish leaders here, too, profess a continued faith in French republican ideals.

---

24. This is most likely a reference to Mińsk Mazowiecki, near Warsaw.

DOCUMENT 9–4: "The Central Consistory of Israelites of France and Algeria Protests against the Creation of the Lublin 'Reserve,'" JTA bulletin, January 6, 1940, USHMMA RG 11.001M.63, reel 218 (SAM 186-1-8), 68 (translated from French).

Hitler's persecutions seemed to have exhausted all the forms of barbarism. Nothing of the kind. Having been unable to chase out or exterminate all the German Jews, the Nazis have found in their perverse imagination a diabolical way to destroy them under the pretext of applying to them the principle of population transfers.

To that end, a reserved zone has been created in Poland, southeast of Lublin. After chasing out all the Poles, they plan to pen up there, like cattle, not only the Jews of Germany but also all those whom they have subjugated. Left to themselves, in a swampy region where fever, dysentery, and all kinds of contagious diseases are raging, these unfortunates, who have been stripped of everything and have neither clothing nor food, are destined for certain death. The Nazis' fierce and refined hatred will never be assuaged. Already, thousands of these people have been driven into this gigantic concentration camp, torn from their families, from all that is dear to them. Many even, in desperation, have voluntarily hastened the certain death that awaited them.

Bruised by so many unspeakable miseries, the Central Consistory of Israelites of France and Algeria sends to its brothers in distress, as to all the unhappy victims of the Nazis in Austria, Czechoslovakia, and Poland, the fervent expression of its grief.

These barbarous methods dishonor the civilized world and, convinced that the principles of Justice and Humanity will stand up, avenging, against those who have trampled them underfoot, [the Consistory] expresses its certainty that France and its Allies, by the strength of their moral and combined material forces, will gain—over the spirit of evil— the victory necessary for the Peace of the world and the reign of God on Earth.

ANOTHER WAVE OF DEPORTATIONS FROM THE REICH TO THE EAST

Between February 10 and March 15, 1940, eighteen hundred more Jews were deported to the Lublin district from the Pomeranian towns of Stettin and Schneidemühl. These new transports were part of a larger operation in which more than forty thousand Poles were expelled from the **Warthegau** in order to provide apartments and houses for additional Baltic Germans. In this instance, **Hans Frank** prevailed upon Hermann Göring to put a halt to these expulsions. As was the case with those from the Reich and Protectorate in the fall of 1939, Jewish and general newspapers reported on this set of deportations in the days and weeks that followed. The *New York Times*, for example, ran its first article about the roundup of the Jewish population of Stettin just four days after it was carried out, although the article was hardly front-page news, appearing on page ten.[25]

In addition to foreign press reports, letters written by Jewish deportees from the Reich comprised a crucial source of information about conditions in the Lublin district. Jews deported from the Reich in February and March 1940 wrote to their friends and family members back in the Reich or in other permitted locations (German allies or neutral countries). They described the misery of daily existence in surprisingly frank terms, thus providing accounts of recent events and their devastating consequences, accounts that press reports did not feature or only addressed in abstract terms.

After being deported in February 1940 with her husband, Max, from Stettin to Piaski in the Lublin district, Martha Bauchwitz regularly wrote letters to their daughter, Luise-Lotte Hoyer-Bauchwitz.[26] Their daughter remained in Stettin, protected from deportation by her "privileged mixed marriage" to a non-Jewish man and by the fact that they had raised their children as Christians. The three letters presented in document 9–5, which are representative of the many that Martha Bauchwitz wrote to her daughter, convey little speculation about what the future held, although Martha's reference to the futility of "petitioning" in the final letter excerpted here suggests that she held out little hope of their situation improving. Most of all, with their hurried syntax

---

25. "Transport of Jews in Stettin Reported; Nazis Said to Have Sent 800 to Lublin Area of Poland," *New York Times*, February 14, 1940, 10.

26. Martha Bauchwitz (née Cohn; 1873?–1942) and Max Bauchwitz (1871–1942) were both born and raised in Stettin. They married in 1897. Martha was active in volunteer work for the Red Cross and a variety of women's organizations, including Stettin's association for promoting home economics. Max was a dentist who, despite his age, volunteered to serve in World War I as a dental medic. Sustaining a serious injury in 1916, he was released from active duty. One of their three sons, who also volunteered to serve in World War I, died in France in 1918. Another son emigrated to Argentina, helped his surviving brother to emigrate, and made unsuccessful efforts to get his parents out of Poland. The couple was arrested in Stettin in January 1940 and sent to the Piaski ghetto near Lublin. Their letters stopped after they were sent out of Piaski to an unknown destination in April 1942, and the Bauchwitzes did not survive. See Else Behrend-Rosenfeld and Gertrud Luckner, eds., *Lebenszeichen aus Piaski: Briefe Deportierter aus dem Distrikt Lublin, 1940–1943*, unabr. ed. (Munich: Biederstein Verlag, 1968), 30; *USHMM ITS Collection Data Base Central Name Index.*

and mix of details, these letters communicate the living conditions that the recent German Jewish deportees from Stettin confronted, as well as Martha's restrained condemnation of the Reich.

DOCUMENT 9–5: **Letters by Martha Bauchwitz, Piaski, Lublin district, Generalgouvernement, to Luise-Lotte Hoyer-Bauchwitz, Stettin, Germany, February 27 and March 1940, translated from Else Behrend-Rosenfeld and Gertrud Luckner, eds.,** *Lebenszeichen aus Piaski: Briefe Deportierter aus dem Distrikt Lublin 1940–1943,* **unabr. ed. (Munich: Deutscher Taschenbuch Verlag, 1970), 32–33 (emphases and ellipses in the original).**

February 27, 1940

Your first message just came! We are happy that you're well.

<u>We</u> are healthy. Father is in the office [or "a practice"], where there's no doctor today. But not much opportunity, since we're here in the wild, wild east [*Wild-Ost*]

Tomorrow is market day—we want to have cheese <u>bought for us</u>.

Perhaps <u>one</u> egg. Very expensive.

We are doing well compared to many others, relatively speaking.[27] Straw is in short supply. We can sometimes heat. But there are always ten or more people sharing a confined space.

We have been wearing the [same] stockings and undergarments since the eleventh! Day and night. Very little water.

My boys should love us—despite everything—Mother.

. . . we are enjoying sunny brisk winter days and hoping for a better future soon . . . Father.

March 1940

Haven't brushed my teeth for two weeks.

I recite Goethe, lots of Schiller to myself. *Captive au rivage du mort;*[28] *Les hirondelles*; etc. etc. For myself, of course.

We're close to Russia. German military personnel pass through a lot.

Commandant visiting yesterday, with a <u>delicious</u> meal. Fidelio.

---

27. Despite the unimaginable poverty of their landlords, Martha and Max Bauchwitz were given space with a Jewish couple who had four small children and slept in a hallway on a sofa. Most people had to sleep on straw beds on the ground.

28. This is a reference to "Captif au rivage du Maure," the first line of "Les Hirondelles," a poem by Pierre-Jean de Béranger (1780–1857).

But what's ahead, nobody knows. Inform P. P. Pommerland![29] I wish I could find some soap! Insulin! Father's face is fine. Just the color still![30] Pray! Please send twelve-cm-wide white armbands and cornflower-blue embroidery thread! . . . Thanks to the parcels, we're doing fine. We have skin irritations, but no vermin. Hosts are clean. Our hosts fed us for three days! Purim.[31] The children run around in masks, like Carnival. People bake for nights on end. It's a great day of rejoicing.

We're envied for our "home." And Father suffers from it so much, you know.

What about the charcoal tablets? They would do us good! Today German soldiers passed through. We know nothing of the war!—

We're healthy, but have no handkerchief or soap. Suitcases lost!!!

Theo dead. Many. Eating only carbohydrates. Noontime soup in the house of prayer. In the evening, bread sine.[32] Would like to be young and Zola, Leibl, Thoma. Experience Breughel, Steen, Murillo with all the pots and figures. But without alcohol.

Weather's good, cold. Think of you all in gratitude and prayer. Lots of dirt, more misery here. Father—no instruments. If only tweezers and cotton!

Please send money and food and medicines, dressing material. One becomes a realist for others and oneself. We don't have any frostbitten limbs. We will accompany the dead to the cemetery as soon as the north wind stops. It's very cold. Send immediately!

We lie in the passageway, covered by our fur coats, in woolens and wearing stockings.

Father suffers from lack of dressing materials etc., and can't help. Is the Reich asleep? . . .

We're glad that you're well. Thanks very much for everything! But will anything help us ever again? Nobody believes it. Deported Cayenne. Dead bodies every day. Father substitutes for the doctor, runs around all day in north wind and freezing temperatures or deep mud.

---

29. This is a reference to Pastor Pompe, who was serving as a soldier not far from Lublin and rendered services to the Bauchwitzes. Behrend-Rosenfeld and Luckner, *Lebenszeichen aus Piaski*, 32n2.

30. According to the editors of *Lebenszeichen aus Piaski*, Max Bauchwitz had been beaten.

31. This is a Jewish holiday commemorating the saving of the Persian Jews, recounted in the Book of Esther.

32. Latin for "without" (i.e., bread without anything on or with it).

The children are delighted with the checkers game. Do you still have candles from Christmas? None here! Darkness!

. . .

Insulin syringe broken—clock has stopped.

You should only say prayers of thanks for yourselves. Here, petitioning is powerless against hell. We give thanks whenever another person is dead. We've been away for three weeks now and each day gets harder.

Hunger and thirst. Everything sticks to our skin. It's the same for all of us here . . .

Personal correspondence from Jews who had been deported to the Lublin district also reached family members in neutral countries in western Europe. Walter Steinbach, a German Jewish refugee living in the Netherlands, learned of his father's deportation from Stettin to Bełżyce from a letter his father wrote to him, which arrived just a few short weeks later. Upon receiving this alarming news about his father, Walter immediately wrote to his brother, Hans, who had also emigrated from Nazi Germany and was living in Cairo, Egypt. He copied his father's letter verbatim within the letter to his brother, as well as a note from a woman named Erna (his father's second wife), who was in Bełżyce with their father. Walter's letter thus conveys the dual perspective, in first-person voice, of German Jewish deportees and of Jews outside the Reich who were trying to respond to their loved ones' pleas for help.[33] How did each interpret the meaning of the deportations? What end was in sight, and what possibilities for rescue seemed to exist? What connections did Walter draw between the Nazi policies affecting his father and his own situation as a Jewish refugee in Holland?

---

33. Walter Steinbach was born in 1921 in Nörenberg, Pomerania (then part of Germany). He left Germany in March 1939 and settled in Tonden, where he worked as an agricultural laborer until he was sent to the Vught camp in April 1943. He was killed in Sobibór in the summer of 1943. His mother was Anna Steinbach (née Lewin; 1890–1934) and his father, Gustav Steinbach (b. 1884), probably perished in Bełżec. Erna Steinbach (née Kaatz; 1889–1940?), Gustav's second wife, also most likely perished in Bełżec. Walter's brothers Hans (1916–2007) and Rudolf (Rudi) Steinbach (b. 1922) survived the war and later immigrated to the United States. The authors have been unable to find more information about other persons mentioned in the letter. See donor's information, USHMMA RG 10.074M; *USHMM ITS Collection Data Base Central Name Index*; *Gedenkbuch*, www.bundesarchiv.de/gedenkbuch.

DOCUMENT 9–6: **Letter by Walter Steinbach, Tonden, Netherlands, to Hans Steinbach, Cairo, Egypt, February–March 1940, USHMMA RG 10.074 Steinbach family letters (translated from German).**

[. . .] Now Hans—what can one do to save Father, I am interested in Father alone, let Kurt D. look after Erna, Frau Davidsohn, and Frl. Unger. Get in contact with him! I know the following. Willi Lewin, the father of my comrade [*chavera*] Kläre stayed in St[ettin] to run the Palestine Office. I asked him to inquire about Father and he told me yesterday that Meineke Street[34] alone can deal with people from Germany proper [*Altreich*]. They are still waiting for regulations for the Lublin region. Point 2. It is also impossible to get Father to Holland, as Holland only allows foreigners in for a transit of 2 days and 1 night. So, as I thought, it is impossible to have him stay in a Dutch refugee camp. Everyone now tells me: "Your older brother is now the only one who can do something." Hans, I am already half *meshugge* [mad] from writing so many letters, running around, and brooding. Now it's your turn to get worked up at last. Please speak with Uncle Carl, but politely(!), try Schocken or wherever you think you can achieve something! Each day the newspapers report on the persecution of the Jews in Poland. Many are dying, but we <u>must</u> save our father's life. Put all your energy into getting Father out of this adversity. Get the S. H. involved on his behalf. Try and get some money together that I can give to Father for now to keep him alive. Remember, he has nothing and is freezing and starving in addition to the emotional distress! So, Hans, [illegible] you, maybe also Rudi through his peasant,[35] must achieve something really positive quickly! This is the only way out. At the moment, I am sacrificing all my earnings for Father—just forgetting a lot of personal matters.

Hans, act, but above all give me information immediately—it is really deadly serious!

Heartfelt kisses to you and Rudi
Your brother Walter

Father writes the following from ca. 8.III from Belzyce near Lublin:
"My dear, good Walter! It is three weeks since we left Stett[in]. I sleep together with a J. in one bed. [. . .] I have one suit, no underwear.

34. Meineke Street was the location of the **Jewish Agency**'s Palestine Office (Palästina-Amt) in Berlin.
35. Steinbach uses the Hebrew word אכר (*ikar*, "peasant") here, perhaps a reference to a Zionist friend of Rudi's.

We were given 20 złoty each. As everything here is terribly expensive, you can't buy anything. We have not been given our luggage. The only solution for us is for our emigration to be expedited, otherwise we will perish here. Frau Koh and old Glasfeld have died here, also Mati Kaatz and wife. People are dying each day. We are customers for everything, but it is too difficult to send from there. The Hilfsverein[36] is working in Bel[Bełżyce], but whether it will take care of us, we'll have to wait and see. I have written to Hertha that she should send us something. I have also written to Uncle Max that he should send me socks. Small packets get here [illegible], if it is at all possible send us something to eat! All of our things are still in St[ettin]. You can be happy that you are not here. Perhaps you can do something about the emigration. For now, greetings and kisses from your father.—Dear Walter! (so writes Father's wife). We long for a sign of life from you. Can't you help us? There is no end to our unhappiness and despair. We only have the clothes on our backs. So what is going to happen? Write <u>immediately</u> to my nephew Kurt and your brother Hans and ask whether they can, from there, do something for us 4. For Father and me, my sister, and Käthe Unger. If we are not rescued here, we all are going to die. The conditions here are indescribable. We are freezing appallingly, there is no little spot that's warm. You can't even be sick here because then you are lost right away. Write soon, dear Walter, it is the only ray of light in our sad existence. I can't write any more now. Regards, Erna.["]

So, what do you think about this? Once again, try <u>everything</u> to save them. Get in contact with Kurt D.! We have to succeed. How are you getting along, is the café a success!? I am okay otherwise—not counting on *Aliyah* at the moment! Last week was my first anniversary in Holland! Ask Rudi to write again. Kisses. Your brother Walter.

The deportations of Jews from the Reich presented the leaders of the **Reichsvereinigung der Juden in Deutschland** with a host of issues to resolve. Which agency had initiated them, what could be done to help the deported, and, even more importantly, how could further deportations be prevented? In the case of deportations from Stettin, it turned out they had been planned by local Nazi Party officials without prior consent from the major players in Berlin, most notably the RSHA. Because the Reichsvereinigung had been created by the Security Police and SD for the purpose of organizing the systematic emigration of as many Jews from German soil as possible, its leaders could argue with

---

36. For more on the **Hilfsverein**, see the Glossary.

some level of success that interference in their efforts would prove counterproductive. Indeed, German Jewish functionaries managed to intervene to stop at least two deportations, one in January from Stettin and another involving some one thousand Jews from East Frisia and Oldenburg, by adopting a dual strategy that made use of muddled lines of communication and unclear competences within the German bureaucracy.[37] This approach worked as long as the German agencies involved in anti-Jewish measures had not sorted out a further course of action.

The minutes from the Reichsvereinigung's board meeting of February 29, 1940, give muted expression to the problems the board had to tackle in the wake of the deportations from Stettin and its vicinity earlier that month. Aware of the **Gestapo**'s watchful presence, German Jews in general and their leaders in particular were long accustomed to censoring their written communications. The minutes from the Reichsvereinigung's weekly meetings offer but a bare-bones account of the items discussed. The set of minutes excerpted in document 9–7 is no different. Action-oriented, it itemizes the board members' decisions pertaining to responsibility for the Jews of Stettin but offers no elaboration on how these German Jewish leaders perceived the deportations. Nor do these minutes reveal anything about the official protests the Reichsvereinigung had lodged against the deportations from Stettin and would continue to deploy later in the year at great risk to the officials involved.[38]

---

37. See Beate Meyer, "Between Self-Assertion and Forced Collaboration: The Reich Association of Jews in Germany, 1939–1945," in *Jewish Life in Nazi Germany: Dilemmas and Responses*, ed. Francis R. Nicosia and David Scrase (New York: Berghahn Books, 2010), 149–69; also see Otto D. Kulka, "The 'Reichsvereinigung of the Jews in Germany' (1938/9–1943)," in *Patterns of Jewish Leadership in Nazi Europe, 1933–1945: Proceedings of the Third Yad Vashem International Historical Conference, Jerusalem, April 4–7, 1977*, ed. Israel Gutman and Cynthia J. Haft (Jerusalem: Yad Vashem, 1979), 45–58. A forthcoming monograph by Beate Meyer explores the Reichsvereinigung's history in greater depth.

38. See Meyer, "Between Self-Assertion," 153–54.

DOCUMENT 9–7: Protocol of board meeting of the Reichsvereinigung held February 29, 1940, Berlin, March 4, 1940, USHMMA RG 14.003M, folder 4 (BAB R 8150), 187 (translated from German).

Present: **Dr. Baeck**[39] as chairman
Dr. Eppstein[40]
Henschel[41]
Dr. Hirsch[42]
Kozower[43]
Dr. Seligsohn[44]
excused (owing to illness):
Dr. Lilienthal[45]
as persons responsible from the Reichsvereinigung:
Dr. Berliner[46]
Fürst[47]
Karminski[48]

---

39. For more on Rabbi Leo Baeck, see the Glossary.

40. For more on Paul Eppstein, see the Glossary.

41. Moritz Henschel (1879–1947), a lawyer, served as the last head of the Berlin Jewish Community during the war and was deported to Theresienstadt in June 1943, where he served on the Council of Elders (*Ältestenrat*). He survived the war and emigrated to Palestine.

42. For more on Otto Hirsch, see the Glossary.

43. Philipp Kozower (1894–1944) practiced law in Berlin until 1933 and became an official in the Berlin Jewish Community, the Reichsvertretung, and its successor organization, the Reichsvereinigung. He was deported to Theresienstadt in January 1943 and murdered in Auschwitz in October 1944.

44. Julius L. Seligsohn (1890–1942), a Berlin lawyer and World War I veteran, became a leading figure in several German Jewish organizations and served on the board of the Reichsvereinigung. Arrested in December 1940 as a result of a planned protest day of fasting against the deportations of Jews from southwestern Germany, he died in the Sachsenhausen camp in the spring of 1942.

45. For more on Arthur Lilienthal, see the Glossary.

46. Cora Berliner (1890–1942), a professor of economics in Berlin until 1933, played a lead role in several national Jewish organizations, including the Reichsvertretung and its successor organization, the Reichsvereinigung. Deported in the summer of 1942, she probably died in the Minsk ghetto.

47. For more on Paula Fürst, see the Glossary.

48. Hannah Karminski (1897–1943), child-education specialist, long served on the executive board of Germany's national League of Jewish Women. She worked in the education division of the Reichsvertretung and then Reichsvereinigung from 1933 until her December 1942 deportation to Auschwitz, where she was most likely killed.

Meyerheim[49]

as person responsible from the Berlin Community:
Brasch[50]

[. . .]

3. The board resolves:

a. to transfer the duties of the Bezirksstelle für die Juden des Reg. Bez. Stettin [District Office for the Jews of the Stettin Administrative District] to the Bezirksstelle Nordwestdeutschland [District Office for Northwest Germany] in Hamburg

b. to transfer the duties of the Bezirksstelle für die Juden des Reg. Bez. Köslin [District Office for the Jews of the Köslin Administrative District] to the Bezirksstelle Brandenburg [Brandenburg District Office]

c. to cede the reorganization of the responsibility for determining and collecting the emigration tax in the Köslin and Stettin Administrative Districts to the head of the Community Department

d. to keep Paul Israel Hirschfeld,[51] the member of the Board of the Kultusvereinigung, in this position until further notice.

[. . .]

6. There is a report on efforts to provide for the Jews transported out of Stettin and on the arrangement for control of the assets they left behind.

With regard to the former, the Reichsvereinigung is not permitted to become active; with regard to the latter, applications can be made to the appropriate authority.

---

49. Paul Meyerheim (1896–1945), a civil servant and official in various Jewish organizations, served in the finance department of the Reichsvertretung and later Reichsvereinigung. Sent first to the Theresienstadt ghetto in May 1943, he was later deported to Auschwitz in October 1944 and died in the Flossenbürg concentration camp in February 1945.

50. This may have been Martin Brasch (1906–1941), a Breslau-born assessor who served as an official for the Berlin Jewish Community and last head of the Jewish Cultural League (**Judischer Kulturbund**) in Germany; he died in the Sachsenhausen concentration camp.

51. Paul Hirschfeld, a member of the Jewish community of Stettin, had been informed of the earlier deportation attempt planned by local Nazi Party board but had not passed this information on to the Reichsvereinigung; he was later removed from his post. Meyer, "Between Self-Assertion," 153–54. The authors have been unable to establish his later fate.

7. A report is given on the temporary accommodation of the Jews from the former Grenzmark in Schneidemühl and on suggestions for their permanent accommodation in various localities in the Old Reich.

[. . .]

[signed:] Dr. Hirsch

THE PERSISTENT THREAT OF DEPORTATIONS

Despite the fact that, as of April 1940, Nazi officials deemed the Lublin reservation a failure, the threat of deportation in various guises did not disappear. In the summer and fall of 1940, some Jewish families received notification that their "mentally ill [*geisteskranke*]" relatives had been "evacuated [*abtransportiert*]" to an institution in the Lublin district. Indeed, over the course of 1940, the program to murder the Reich's mentally ill and disabled population—a program approved by Hitler under the cover of war—expanded considerably, and in June 1940 Jewish asylum patients who had been segregated in Jewish-only institutions began to be killed.[52] As was the case with the population resettlement policies pursued most energetically by Himmler in 1939 and 1940, what Nazi officials referred to as "mercy killings" did not center on Jews. Nevertheless, Jewish men, women, and children deemed mentally ill or physically handicapped were among those targeted by Nazi "euthanasia" by dint of both their diagnosis as hereditarily diseased and their racial status as Jews.[53] In all, the adult

---

52. The first mass killings of patients in asylums were carried out in occupied Poland and northeastern Germany immediately after the conclusion of the Polish campaign. The SS murdered three thousand or more patients by shooting. They buried them in mass graves in the woods. These massacres were distinct from the "euthanasia" program, although they constituted the first mass killing of disabled people. Michael Burleigh, *Death and Deliverance: "Euthanasia" in Germany, 1900–1945* (Cambridge: Cambridge University Press, 1994), 130–33. See also Henry Friedlander, *The Origins of Nazi Genocide: From Euthanasia to the Final Solution* (Chapel Hill: University of North Carolina Press, 1995), 271–83.

53. The terms and definitions of hereditary disease used by psychiatrists and other medical "experts" during the Third Reich hardly resemble current scientific conceptions; nor were they consonant with mainstream science of the early twentieth century. Nazi psychiatrists brought together ideas from negative eugenics and Nazi racial science to construct new categories of incurable disease, including such diagnoses as "feebleminded," "work-shy," and "asocial." Individuals found to be hereditarily diseased, it was argued, were "lives unworthy of life" or "ballast" weighing down the German Reich in a time of war and in the midst of its campaign of racial purification. Burleigh, *Death and Deliverance*, 47, 59–60, 89; Friedlander, *Origins of Nazi Genocide*, 14–22.

and children's "euthanasia" programs would take the lives of more than seventy thousand adults and at least six thousand children. Adult patients were typically gassed en masse in one of six mental institutions that the Nazi regime converted into its first killing centers. Doctors and security personnel worked together to carry out these murders covertly. They sent written notification to the victims' families, first about their relatives' transfer to another institution and then about their sudden death from unknown causes.

Notification of these transports elicited strong suspicions. Individual family members wrote concerned letters to the directors of institutions or to other Nazi officials requesting information about the whereabouts and condition of their relatives. People's misgivings about the actual meaning of such moves are evident in many such letters. One father, Adolf Hähnlein, inquired anxiously,

> In your last card, you wrote me that my son had been transferred to the Generalgouvernement and that I would receive notification of this from the Bielefeld District Office. So far I have received no information and thus I paid a visit to the city welfare office, which advised me to turn to you once again, because the patients must be somewhere, after all, or else there is some reason for secrecy, such as serious illness or death.[54]

In other cases, German Jews appealed for their sons or daughters, brothers or sisters, nieces or nephews to be released into their custody. Reichsvereinigung officials also tried in certain instances to save Jewish patients of mental institutions.

DOCUMENT 9–8: Letter by Else Demang[55] of the Reichsvereinigung, Hannover, to the Wunstorf mental institution, September 21, 1940, translated from Asmus Finzen, *Massenmord ohne Schuldgefühl: Die Tötung psychisch Kranker und geistig Behinderter auf dem Dienstweg* (Bonn: Psychiatrie-Verlag, 1996), 81–82.

> We respectfully request that you provide us with the names of all Jewish inmates of your mental hospital or mentally ill patients assigned from other institutions to whose release there are no further medical objections.
>
> If the persons concerned have relatives, we would arrange for them to take in, wherever possible and without delay, those who are released.

---

54. Letter from Adolf Hähnlein, Gelsenkirchen, Germany, November 5, 1940, translated from Asmus Finzen, *Massenmord ohne Schuldgefühl: Die Tötung psychisch Kranker und geistig Behinderter auf dem Dienstweg* (Bonn: Psychiatrie-Verlag, 1996), 102. The authors have been unable to learn the later fate of Hähnlein.

55. The authors could not locate further information on Else Demang.

Because of the urgency of the matter, we take the liberty of asking that you inform us immediately, possibly by telephone (3 – calls at
our expense). We note that we can also be reached tomorrow, Sunday,
September 22, in the morning.

On behalf of the Reichsvereinigung der Juden in Deutschland,

Else Sara Demang[56]

Identity card: Hannover A= 2390

In this instance, the Reichsvereinigung's persistence paid off, and it managed to secure permission for the release of three Jewish patients from the
Wunstorf institution. No further documentation exists about one of those
patients, Martha Cohn, but the other two, Johanna Lohn and Heinz Fränkel,
were saved at this time from "evacuation," that is, from transport and murder.[57]

In the fall of 1940, Hitler authorized a further set of deportations of
sixty-five hundred Jews from Baden and the Saar-Palatinate region of southwestern Germany to the **Vichy** zone of France. These areas of the Old Reich
were going to be combined with Alsace and Lorraine to form new administrative districts. Hitler's viceroys saw an opportunity to render these areas
"free of Jews" by piggybacking illegitimately on the terms of the armistice
agreement with France, according to which Germany would annex Alsace
and Lorraine while France was required to absorb the Jewish population
of its former provinces. This time the Reichsvereinigung intervened at the
RSHA and tried to call on rabbis for a Germany-wide day of fasting—an
attempt at resistance, immediately squashed by Reinhard Heydrich's officers,
that led to the arrest of Reichsvereinigung board member Julius Seligsohn.[58]
The Vichy regime protested, too, against being saddled with these additional
Jews from Germany and proceeded to confine them with other foreigners

---

56. Effective January 1, 1939, Jews in Germany were required to use "Sara" for women
and "Israel" for men as compulsory middle names and had to include their official identity
card (*Kennkarte*) number in their correspondence. See Jürgen Matthäus and Mark Roseman,
Jewish Responses to Persecution, vol. 1: *1933–1938* (Lanham, MD: AltaMira Press in association with the USHMM, 2010), 449–50.

57. However, Lohn (b. 1878) was eventually deported to Theresienstadt in late July 1942
and from there to Auschwitz in May 1944. Fränkel (b. 1908) was deported from Berlin in
early April 1942, probably to the Trawniki camp near Lublin. See *USHMM ITS Collection
Data Base Central Name Index*; *Gedenkbuch*, www.bundesarchiv.de/gedenkbuch; Finzen,
Massenmord, 82–85.

58. He later died in the Sachsenhausen concentration camp. See above, note 44;
Friedländer, *Nazi Germany*, 2:65, 93, 104.

already in custody in internment camps. Most were sent to the Gurs camp in the foothills of the Pyrenees.[59]

The deportations of October 1940 caught the Jews from Baden, Mannheim, and elsewhere in the Palatinate entirely unaware. In an account written ten months later, Clara Suess from Mannheim remembered how policemen had given them one hour to pack—they were permitted to bring no more than fifty kilograms (110 pounds) of luggage, including provisions—before she and her husband were taken from their home: "They brought us to the Pestalozzi School. We waited there until 8:00 p.m. I was surrounded by desperate, half-crazed people, old people, children, sitting on their few meager belongings. Everyone speculated about what would happen to us. Poland, some said. Others seriously doubted if we would even live to see the next day. I myself was totally in shock." Apparently possessing knowledge of the few previous transports of Jews from the Reich to Poland, some people assumed they were to share that fate. Once on the train, people realized they were being sent westward to France, and, as Suess recalled, "We thought and felt deeply that we were at last free of the terrible oppression of Germany."[60] That sense of relief soon disappeared upon arrival in Gurs.

Conditions in Gurs were abysmal. Practically overnight, the population of the camp increased from 440 women and 1,000 men to more than 12,000 prisoners without a corresponding expansion of the camp's infrastructure.[61] Overcrowding, infestation, hunger, and disease made life miserable for the diverse population of Jews trapped behind barbed wire in the impassably muddy tract of land that was Gurs. Further compounding the wretched conditions was the separation of women and men into separate barracks. According to a WJC report of November 22, 1940, mortality rates had reached fifteen people per day by the middle of November. The Jews deported to Gurs from

---

59. Renée Poznanski, *Jews in France during World War II* (Hanover, NH: Brandeis University Press in association with the USHMM, 2001), 172–73.

60. Clara Suess (née Mars; 1882–1968), "Meine Erlebnisse ab 22. Oktober 1940," LBINY ME 1498. Suess wrote her diary-memoir on a ship, the *Navemar*, en route to New York from Spain, in August 1941. She and her husband, David Suess (b. 1878), were interned in Gurs from October 1940 until their release in February 1941, thanks to their U.S. visa applications proceeding to the next stage. On May 16, 1941, their American visas were issued, and they traveled from France, via Spain, to the United States, where they were reunited with their two daughters.

61. Jewish refugees in France who had been interned in other camps were transferred to Gurs at this same time, accounting for the population figure.

southwestern Germany were the most vulnerable to the cold and hunger due to the number of people over the age of sixty.[62]

From the outside, the situation of the recent deportees to Gurs appeared no different from that of other Jews interned in the camp. After all, most of the people already being held in French internment camps had escaped from Nazi Germany at most seven years before. From the perspective of those inside the camp, however, the physical and mental condition of those recently deported from Germany to Gurs was quite distinct. Hans J. Steinitz, who had left Germany for Switzerland and then France in 1934, described the state of these other German Jews in the clandestine diary he kept in 1942 after he was transferred from Gurs to another internment camp, Les Milles.[63]

DOCUMENT 9–9: Hans J. Steinitz, undated diary entries about his internment in Gurs, France, USHMMA RG 04.072 Hans J. Steinitz collection (translated from German).

The arrival of these 4,000 Jews from Baden and the Pfalz was a shocking and heartrending sight. These people had not the faintest idea what had happened to them; many of them explained in broken French to the other internees across the barbed wire fence, while they were waiting for their block allocation, that they were Jews and had been expelled from Germany as a result: they assumed that they were among French people and wanted to explain to them their fate. Hundreds of tiny details revealed that these people had completely forgotten that there were such things as charity and sympathy and that there could be solidarity with them: an old man showered an internee with effusive thanks, shaking both of his hands, when the internee gave him through the barbed wire a match to light his cold pipe; a little farther along a white-haired woman kissed a hand that

---

62. Poznanski, *Jews in France during World War II*, 178–79, 181; "Report on the Situation of Interned Refugees in Gurs," Lyon, France, November 22, 1940, USHMMA RG 68.045M, reel 1, WJC (Geneva).

63. Hans J. Steinitz (1912–1993), born in Berlin, was a former lawyer and journalist who retrained as a sports teacher. He moved via Switzerland to France in February 1934 and served briefly in the French army when the war broke out. After France's surrender to Germany, the French police arrested him and sent him to Gurs, where he remained through the summer of 1942, at which time he was moved to Les Milles camp. On Yom Kippur 1942, he escaped to Switzerland to avoid deportation, smuggling his diary with him. However, his fiancée, Martina Gruber, was deported from France to Germany and may not have survived. Steinitz remained in Switzerland for the remainder of the war as a refugee and emigrated to the United States in 1947. See USHMMA RG 58.001M Jewish Refugee Records, reel 104.

held out a glass of water to her through the barbed wire. At other locations the "old Gurser" gave their new comrades some of their coffee, their thin soup, or even a slice of bread—gifts that were accepted with unbelievable astonishment and respectful whispers—"See, here is someone who has helped us." After eight years of living in the Third Reich, the transport in cattle cars to France, and the reception in Gurs, these unhappy people had forgotten what it is like to be regarded as human beings. [. . .]

And while new trucks continued to roll in, hour after hour, day after day, the newly arrived established themselves in their barracks. There were no beds, no blankets, no straw, and so these deflated people lay on the bare floor, while the autumn wind whistled through the unsealed bar-rack walls, and the rats crawled around the floor, inquisitively sniffing the new arrivals. In the first few nights there were mass outbreaks of hysteria, screaming, anxiety attacks, heart attacks; doctors and nurses were busy all the time; and this hellish spectacle went on for days until the new arrivals, for better or worse, had settled into their new living conditions.

The letter in document 9–10 imparts the perspective of the "newly arrived" in Gurs. It was written by Hilda Stras, who was deported from Brücken in the Rhineland-Palatinate, along with her husband, Simon.[64] Apparently sent to a neighbor back in her hometown, the letter contains convivial, chatty greetings and details of everyday needs interspersed with descriptions of extreme depri-vation, shocking death rates, chronic hunger, and cold. Most of all, it conveys how confusing it was for German Jews who had been forced to pack a few belongings and leave their homes in a matter of hours to sort through their experiences of the last few weeks and their homesickness. Missing home meant, first and foremost, missing creature comforts. But it also seemed to include nostalgia for the Germany that had once been their home and to which, despite Nazi antisemitism, they continued to feel connected.

---

64. Hilda Straass (also Hilde or Hildegunde Stras, née Mann; 1901–1942?) was born in Heinach. In the late summer of 1942, she was deported to Drancy and then Auschwitz, where she was presumably killed. Simon Lazarus Straass (or Stras; 1893–1942?) was born in Bergzabern/Pfalz and may have worked as a miner originally. He spent time in the Dachau concentration camp after "*Kristallnacht*." After being held in Gurs, he was deported in the autumn of 1942 to Drancy and Auschwitz, where he was murdered. See *USHMM ITS Collection Data Base Central Name Index*.

DOCUMENT 9–10: **Letter by Hilda Stras, Gurs, France, to Staab family, Brücken, Germany, December 6, 1940, USHMMA RG 10.150 Walter Stras collection (translated from German).**

Dear Staab family,

Today is the first opportunity that I have to write to you. I hope you all are fine and healthy. Unfortunately I could not write to you earlier, after we parted. I fell about four weeks ago and injured my right arm. It still has not healed. Nevertheless, I think of you each day and have dreamed about you so often. After four days and nights of wandering, we have landed here and were supposed to go to the Mediterranean, but since [there was] such severe flooding, we were sent back here. I still can't get my thoughts straight. If you were to see me now—I am not half the person I was—I've lost a lot of weight, and my hair has become somewhat gray. There are 5 women and children in our barracks. The men are housed in other barracks. We have been interned here and are living behind barbed wire. Simon is a Red Cross medical orderly for the men, and I did night duty at the very beginning. Dear Frau Staab, how I would thank God if I had my duvets and my pillows here. We lie on straw sacks on the ground, and the blankets don't give any warmth. We don't have a table or a chair, and we don't have any windows either, just hatches, and when we open these, we have some light. We have a stove but very little wood for heating. Ruth and my sisters are also here. We are constantly hungry and freezing. We are not far from the Spanish border, and our gaze is often directed toward the Pyrenees, which are constantly covered with snow. We had freezing temperatures for days, and for the last 4 days it has rained. The weather and the climate are completely different from Germany. We have heard nothing from our Walter, unfortunately, even though a lot of letters and packages have arrived from Germany.[65] What has happened to my belongings? You can keep what was standing in the hallway and in the cellar. Did you get my bicycle from Otto Bauer? Dear Lisbeth, did you collect the jacket, the georgette dress, the blue pleated skirt, and the coat fabric from Anna Staab? You can also keep the laundry that you washed.

---

65. Walter Straass (later Stras; 1924–1995), Hilde and Simon's son, had lived in a variety of places since 1939, including the Zionist youth agricultural training farms at Gut-Winkel and Ahrensdorf near Berlin. In April 1943 he was deported to Auschwitz from Berlin, then in January 1945 to Buchenwald and Altenburg, before he escaped. He survived the war, married a fellow survivor, Malvina, and emigrated to the United States in 1948. See *USHMM ITS Collection Data Base Central Name Index*.

The mail comes straight here, and you can send up to 2 kilos. Dear Frau Staab, can you send from my clothes the following things: my aprons, 2 brassieres, Simon's and my handkerchiefs, and stockings, which we badly need, the one summer dress, because I have almost nothing, and if there are shirts then those as well, please. You can send 2 kilos per month. I have written to Walter 3 times, once from Dijon and from here via the Geneva Red Cross, and direct. Mildred has written three times and is missing us terribly, but the roundtrip costs 600 francs, which we don't have.[66] She also asked after you and sends greetings. I sent her two photos of us with Lisbeth, and she was very glad to have them. Have you heard anything from Otto and Bernhard? Give them our greetings. I have written to both families in Berlin but have not yet received a reply. Dear Frau Staab, I really need the brown jacket. Our Aunt Johanna died a month ago, and there were 70 burials this week.[67] I began to write on St. Nicholas Day [December 6] and am continuing today, Sunday. How much has changed since then! [. . .] Dear Lisbeth, have you heard anything from Ernst and Kurt? Give them our greetings. We hope and wish that we will soon hear from you, as I am longing for my beautiful German homeland, which we had to leave so disgracefully. Stay well, and from far, far away, heartfelt greetings to you. Thinking of you often, Hilda and Simon.

A host of Jewish and non-Jewish relief organizations that were still active after the armistice in the Unoccupied Zone of France devoted themselves, among other things, to helping improve people's living conditions inside the internment camps. Working sometimes independently, sometimes jointly, they made it a priority in these first months after the armistice to provide internees with supplementary food rations and medical supplies. They also tried to influence Vichy authorities to institute changes in the camp system as a whole.[68] Document 9–11 presents part of a series of **World Jewish Congress** (WJC) reports written between August and December 1940 on Jewish refugees in France. The report detailed the living conditions in Gurs: the filth, cold, and overcrowding, as well as the below-subsistence food rations and the physical effects already evident among prisoners in the camp, who were suffering from severe malnutrition. In conclusion, this report argued for the necessity of reor-

---

66. The authors have not been able to identify this woman.
67. Johanna Mann (1868–1940), a resident of Mannheim, was deported to Gurs with her relatives in late October 1940 and died there on November 10. See *USHMM ITS Collection Data Base Central Name Index.*
68. Poznanski, *Jews in France during World War II*, 185–87.

ganizing Vichy's internment camps. The arguments proffered suggest that relief agencies were torn between wanting to shoulder responsibility for maintaining the people interned in camps and fearing that the state would then divest itself of any and all responsibility for helping to support refugees.

DOCUMENT 9–11: WJC report on the situation of refugees in Gurs, sent from Lyon, France, November 22, 1940, USHMMA RG 68.045M (WJC Geneva), reel 1 (translated from French).

[. . .] It does not appear that a reorganization of the camp will be possible. When it is a question of a clustering of 20,000 people, the resources to be used come from State planning and exceed those of private charities. It is not for the representatives of the latter to offer suggestions but, concerned about the human drama that is playing out at Gurs, they take the liberty of very respectfully expressing some wishes that they believe likely to improve the present state of affairs.

Insofar as it cannot be reorganized, it would be desirable to dissolve the Gurs Camp, which has become like an antechamber of a morgue.

It would be desirable for the screening commissions to speed up their work, so as to quickly release the greatest possible number of internees, particularly those who are engaged in emigration proceedings, those who possess personal means for subsistence, and those for whom parents, friends, or charitable societies are ready to take responsibility. Each day, each hour of delay is fatal to hundreds of people worn down by cold and hunger.

Conditions of liberation such as those expressed [earlier in the report] at present rarely attain their goal. Thus, anyone eligible for release is required to present a residence permit endorsed by the Prefecture of the department[69] to which he could go. But the Prefectures usually refuse to grant this visa, and the internee, although recognized to be worthy of release, is turned down in the camp.

It would be desirable to transfer the internees who are not eligible for emigration or release, in particular those who lack means, to camps of a new kind, family camps, "home centers," which, while remaining under the surveillance of the authorities, effectively could be supported and organized with the aid of private charities.

---

69. France is divided into regions, which are subdivided into administrative units known as departments. Each department has a prefecture, an administrative body that represents the Ministry of the Interior at the local level and is responsible for managing such documents as identity papers and work or residency permits for foreigners.

Confining tens of thousands of people in internment camps, this WJC report suggested, was unsustainable in the long term. But what was to be the future of European Jewry? Jews throughout Europe and the rest of the world anxiously assembled the fragments of news that reached them from Poland, for it was in Poland that the venomous potential of Nazi anti-Jewish policy revealed itself most plainly. By the end of 1940, Jews throughout the European continent were more vulnerable than they had ever been to economic discrimination and social isolation. Jews in the Reich and the Protectorate, in particular, lived in the shadow of threats of deportations and other acts of terror. But over the course of that same year, Polish Jews, the largest Jewish community in Europe, had their world turned upside down. The humanitarian crisis unfolding in Jewish communities throughout Poland in the early months of the war continued to deepen.

PART IV
PRECARIOUS SHELTER
LIFE IN THE EMERGING POLISH GHETTOS

I N LATE 1939 and throughout 1940, no centralized occupation policy existed
across the annexed Polish territories and the **Generalgouvernement** beyond
the push to marginalize the Jews and steal their property. In the **Warthegau**,
German authorities created a ghetto structure in Łódź under the aegis of **Chaim
Rumkowski** but displayed what Christopher Browning has described as "great
reluctance" in replicating the Łódź "model ghetto" elsewhere in that district.
In the Generalgouvernement, from the spring of 1940 into the first months
of 1941, local German leaders followed a different "model of shrinking the
Jewish urban populations through expulsion to the rural towns and villages
and then ghettoizing the remnant."[1] The ghettos that came into existence varied considerably. In Warsaw and Łódź, walls clearly marked the border beyond
which Jews could not pass without running the risk of severe punishment.
Other ghettos often lacked such a rigid delineation of space between the Jewish
residential district and the Polish and German areas. Beyond geography, Jewish
leadership and governance took many different forms. Where *Judenräte*, or
Jewish Councils, were constituted to carry out the new rulers' demands, they
exercised control to varying degrees within their respective communities. The
power Chaim Rumkowski wielded within the Łódź ghetto, for example, contrasted substantially with that of **Adam Czerniaków** in Warsaw, whose *Judenrat*
constantly struggled to maintain some level of control over the multitude of

---

1. Christopher R. Browning with contributions by Jürgen Matthäus, *The Origins of the
Final Solution: The Evolution of Nazi Jewish Policy, September 1939–March 1942* (Lincoln and
Jerusalem: University of Nebraska Press and Yad Vashem, 2004), 114, 135.

projects initiated by house committees, youth groups, and community activists. And some communities did not even have a Jewish Council in place.

Due in part to the inconsistency of German policies and in part to the diversity of Jewish communities, a wide spectrum of responses to the occupation took form. More impromptu than coherent, they manifested Jewish efforts to cope with the ever-changing situation, with mounting German demands and communal burdens. The physical features of ghetto environments, such as space limitations, infrastructure, and the quality of housing, contributed to survival or death. Indeed, where boundaries and borders proved more permeable, ghetto inhabitants could sometimes seize an opportunity to escape to the "**Aryan**" side temporarily or permanently. Furthermore, the intensity of German terror through direct interference or economic exploitation had fundamental ramifications for ghetto populations, for their vitality and endurance. In addition to the living conditions within the newly created ghettos, the range of Jewish responses to the first year and a half of German occupation also reflected a multitude of interconnected factors stemming from prewar Polish Jewish history. Prewar patterns of Jewish leadership were part of the mix, as were the presence of alternative leadership structures and the backgrounds and personalities of each *Judenrat*'s members. The size and composition of ghetto communities, including their social, political, and religious stratifications, the number of refugees present, and the existence of prewar and newly formed groups, likewise played a role in shaping Polish Jewish responses. These final chapters explore these factors, as well as the synergistic effect created by their interaction.

As we shall see, the picture that emerges from contemporary documentation offers a different perspective on the history of the ghettos in the early years of the war than that typically rendered by commentators and scholars writing after the conflict ended. Postwar discussions about the ghettos centered less on broader parameters such as the interactions among German oppressors, local non-Jews, Jewish leaders, and the ghetto population.[2] Instead, they

---

2. The most notable exception is Isaiah Trunk's groundbreaking study *Judenrat: The Jewish Councils in Eastern Europe under Nazi Occupation* (New York: Macmillan, 1972); more recently and for individual ghettos, see Dan Michman, "Reevaluating the Emergence, Function, and Form of the Jewish Councils Phenomenon," in *Ghettos, 1939–1945: New Research and Perspectives on Definition, Daily Life, and Survival: Symposium Presentations*, ed. Center for Advanced Holocaust Studies, USHMM (Washington, DC: USHMM, 2005), 67–84; Barbara Engelking and Jacek Leociak, *The Warsaw Ghetto: A Guide to the Perished City* (New Haven, CT: Yale University Press, 2009); Barbara L. Epstein, *The Minsk Ghetto: Jewish Resistance and Soviet Internationalism* (Berkeley: University of California Press, 2008); Andrea Löw, *Juden im Getto Litzmannstadt: Lebensbedingungen, Selbstwahrnehmung, Verhalten* (Göttingen: Wallstein, 2006); Sara Bender, *The Jews of Bialystok during World War II and the Holocaust* (Waltham, MA: Brandeis University Press, 2009).

focused on two narrower, closely related, and highly charged issues: the role of *Judenrat* leaders and Jewish policemen in the different ghettos. Members of both institutions, according to the standard argument, abused their authority by abandoning their responsibilities toward their communities and becoming instruments of the Germans. Interestingly, harsh verdicts about the Jewish Councils, especially about Chaim Rumkowski and the Jewish police, began to emerge in 1940, well before the advent of mass deportations to murder sites and the transformation of the councils into cogs in the machinery of destruction. In contrast to many postwar verdicts, however, this early criticism did take into consideration the highly restrictive conditions under which Jews in positions of authority had to operate. There could and can be no doubt that the men on the Jewish Councils (few women served on them) had been put in place by German taskmasters interested only in the swift and effective execution of their orders, not in creating harmonious relations or quelling discontent within the ghettos. Thus, irrespective of whether they were located in the parts of Poland annexed to the Reich or in the Generalgouvernement, Jewish Councils were subject to the demands of German authorities, who could have disposed of Jewish Council leaders at any time.[3] Nevertheless, the Jewish public expected the *Judenrat* to provide for community welfare, given that large segments of the ghetto population had become destitute, malnourished, and vulnerable to illness and disease after a few months of German rule. The persistence of inequality among social groups and the appearance of new elites only exacerbated social tensions in the ghettos. Thus, Polish Jews writing in 1940 noted the pressure that the Germans exerted on local councils and the councils' small successes in mitigating Nazi terror, though most apparent to them were the *Judenräte*'s austerity measures and the worsening inequality and destitution.

In addition to overlooking the severe constraints under which German-appointed Jewish leaders operated during the war, by looking at this story from our vantage point of the twenty-first century, we can easily fall into the trap of seeing ghettos as a fixed, almost self-evident element of Nazi policy in occupied eastern Europe, an institution that led straight to the death camps where millions of Jews were later murdered. In the words of eminent Holocaust scholar Raul Hilberg, "The Jewish ghettos mark an interim phase between prewar freedom and wartime annihilation," and they became "a form of organized

---

3. See Yisrael Gutman, *The Jews of Warsaw, 1939–1943: Ghetto, Underground, Revolt* (Bloomington: Indiana University Press, 1982), 38–39.

self-destruction."[4] Important case studies notwithstanding,[5] the prevailing retrospective image of life in the ghettos is one of relentless terror from German overseers, abject destitution, and a lack of hope on the part of residents. This perception indeed describes what the vast majority of Jews ultimately experienced. Yet, it downplays the important differences that also existed within and between ghettos and, perhaps more importantly, over time. It causes us to lose sight of how Jews lived as individuals, with their families, and as members of broader communities in situations not predetermined to end in mass death, but containing an element of hope.

If only for a brief period after the Germans had conquered Poland and claimed "their share" of the country, the appointment of a Jewish Council—sometimes but not always followed by the establishment of a ghetto—seemed to offer a faint chance for stabler, more tolerable conditions, at least for the duration of a war whose end was not yet in sight. As Hilberg reminds us, "Czerniaków, as well as most of the other Jewish leaders, acted on the premise that *there would be a future.* From the outset, the councilmen at their desks and the crowds in the streets bore their crushing burdens as temporary inflictions to be suffered until liberation."[6] Exposure to hunger, overcrowding, disease, and forced labor seemed bearable as a temporary phenomenon, not as part of a continuing crisis that would escalate over time. Every day and in almost any situation, an individual had a choice between complying with a *Judenrat*'s orders on behalf of "the authorities" or overstepping the narrow boundaries of the permissible. Many leaders and members of Jewish Councils labored on out of a sense of responsibility and assumed it would be better for the community if the Jews themselves administered German orders and decrees, not the conquerors.[7] Improving Jews' living conditions depended on factors mostly out of their control, yet Jewish leaders tried to foster a sense of hope among their

---

4. See Raul Hilberg, "The Ghetto as a Form of Government," *Annals of the American Academy of Political and Social Science* 450, no. 1 (1980): 98–112, reprinted in *The Nazi Holocaust*, ed. Michael R. Marrus (Westport, CT: Meckler, 1989), 6/1:184, 190; Raul Hilberg, *The Destruction of the European Jews*, 3rd. ed. (New Haven, CT: Yale University Press, 2003), 3:1320, Table B-1: "Deaths by Cause."

5. See especially Gutman, *The Jews of Warsaw*, and the essays on ghettos in Philip Friedman, *Roads to Extinction: Essays on the Holocaust*, ed. Ada June Friedman (New York: Conference on Jewish Social Studies and the Jewish Publication Society, 1980).

6. Hilberg, "The Ghetto as a Form of Government," 186 (our emphasis).

7. See Trunk, *Judenrat*, 14–35.

community members, a sense that things would change for the better. And to a certain extent, a council's legitimacy depended on the degree to which key groups—members of the elite or important organizations, communal leaders such as rabbis, and others with informal authority—as well as the more general Jewish public perceived it as indeed providing for their needs and preventing a steeper deterioration of living conditions. The chapters in this section look at the ways in which Polish Jews, despite worsening discrimination and growing internal fragmentation, organized their lives in the emerging ghettos with hope for a better future.

CHAPTER 10
SETTLING INTO CONFINED SPACES

WHETHER IN the areas annexed to the Reich or those incorporated into the **Generalgouvernement**,[1] the threat of dislocation or its reality defined the lives of Polish Jews, be they urban or rural dwellers, lifelong residents or refugees. To many, this fate was not completely unexpected. "Resettlements" of groups had accompanied armed conflict since the late nineteenth century, at times resulting in mass murder. Those who were ethnically different from the majority population in a nation-state were especially vulnerable to such resettlements.[2] For the Jews, who had no territory of their own, as Hannah Arendt observed in early 1940, there could be no "re-importation" into a state

---

1. The areas annexed to the Reich comprised the western provinces (*Województwa*) of Poland, renamed and reorganized as Reichsgau Wartheland, Reichsgau Danzig-Westpreussen (Reichsgau Danzig-West Prussia), Distrikt Zichenau (Ciechanów), and Ostoberschlesien (East Upper Silesia). The remaining central and southeastern parts of Poland were incorporated into the Generalgouvernement administered by Hans Frank, with regional subdivisions (Distrikte) around Warsaw, Lublin, Kraków, Radom, and the Galicia region. See Isaiah Trunk, *Judenrat: The Jewish Councils in Eastern Europe under Nazi Occupation* (New York: Macmillan, 1972), ix–xii; Map 3, p. xiv.

2. Donald Bloxham, *Genocide, the World Wars and the Unweaving of Europe* (London: Vallentine Mitchell, 2008), 7–8; Mark Levene, *Genocide in the Age of the Nation State* (London: I. B. Tauris, 2005).

where they were in the majority, but "only deportation" to some other place.[3] And, at least initially, the German rulers' wide-reaching expulsion policies, in conjunction with the disparate and seemingly random anti-Jewish measures, suggested that the fate of Polish Jews was part of a broader wartime sweep to "Germanize" the conquered territory. As discussed in chapter 9, more than half a million people, the vast majority of them Poles, along with at least sixty-three thousand Jews, were forcibly uprooted between the fall of 1939 and the spring of 1941. The Jewish expellees were pushed into Soviet territory, deported into the Generalgouvernement, driven from their homes in Stettin in northeastern Germany after the Polish campaign, or forced from Alsace-Lorraine or Baden-Saarpfalz into French territory beginning in the summer of 1940.[4]

While expulsion formed a pervasive feature of Nazi wartime policy, the ghetto emerged by early 1940 as a distinct phenomenon largely restricted to Jews in eastern Europe.[5] Ghettoization entailed the removal of all Jews from spaces claimed for German use and their concentration in designated places elsewhere. At the time it was not at all clear to those about to be ghettoized or to their overlords what conditions Jews would face living in a ghetto. As

---

3. Hannah Arendt, "The Minority Question (Copied from a letter to Eric Cohn-Bendit, Summer 1940)," in *The Jewish Writings: Hannah Arendt*, ed. Jerome Kohn and Ron H. Feldman (New York: Schocken Books, 2007), 129.

4. See Christopher R. Browning with contributions by Jürgen Matthäus, *The Origins of the Final Solution: The Evolution of Nazi Jewish Policy, September 1939–March 1942* (Lincoln and Jerusalem: University of Nebraska Press and Yad Vashem, 2004), 109, which provides a breakdown of individual "resettlement actions." On German policies toward the non-Jewish Polish population, see Phillip T. Rutherford, *Prelude to the Final Solution: The Nazi Program for Deporting Ethnic Poles, 1939–1941* (Lawrence: University Press of Kansas, 2007). On the impact of the broader resettlement policy for anti-Jewish measures in Poland and beyond, see also Götz Aly, *"Final Solution": Nazi Population Policy and the Murder of the European Jews* (London: Arnold, 1999).

5. For a general overview, see Dan Michman, "The Jewish Ghettos under the Nazis and Their Allies: The Reasons Behind Their Emergence," in *The Yad Vashem Encyclopedia of the Ghettos during the Holocaust*, ed. Guy Miron and Shlomit Shulhani (Jerusalem: Yad Vashem, 2009), 1:xiii–xxxix. See also Michman's *The Emergence of Jewish Ghettos During the Holocaust* (New York: Cambridge University Press, 2011), and Christopher Browning's introduction to vol. 2 of *USHMM Encyclopedia of Camps and Ghettos*. For a discussion of Jewish "resettlement" policy outside eastern Europe, in Amsterdam and Salonika respectively, see Raul Hilberg, *The Destruction of the European Jews*, 3rd. ed. (New Haven, CT: Yale University Press, 2003), 2:600–32, 738–55. For the history of the Łódź ghetto, to which some five thousand Roma were deported, see Isaiah Trunk, *Łódź Ghetto: A History*, ed., Robert Moses Shapiro (Bloomington: Indiana University Press in association with the USHMM, 2006).

reminiscent as the German methods seemed of medieval anti-Jewish persecution and as pessimistic as most forecasts were about the Nazis' future course of action, the architects of German "*Judenpolitik*" had not yet settled on the means to achieve their utopian aim of "solving the Jewish question." **Reinhard Heydrich**'s September 21, 1939, order to the *Einsatzgruppen* was vague about the creation of *Judenräte*, or Jewish Councils, and how the desired "concentration of the Jews in the cities" would be achieved. His stated goal was "to facilitate subsequent measures," which seemed to refer to expulsions from the Reich, particularly "resettlements" like the **Nisko** deportations (see chapter 9) or the planned large-scale deportation of European Jews to Madagascar.[6] A similar decree issued by **Hans Frank** for the Generalgouvernement also failed to provide clear guidelines for the creation of ghettos or specifics on the workings of the Jewish Councils beyond the expectation that their compliance with German commands would be absolute.

The absence of central direction caused ghettoization policy to unfold differently in different places on the basis of German regional interests and local needs. Despite sharing common features, the ghettos were ultimately "far from homogeneous in their internal, demographic, and economic structures."[7] In some areas, the German military had already created Jewish Councils during the first days of its Polish campaign, as in Piotrków-Trybunalski, where the first ghetto was established on October 8, 1939.[8] In the annexed **Warthegau**, the new German authorities appointed **Chaim Rumkowski** to be "eldest of the Jews" in Łódź in mid-October 1939 and established a ghetto there in March–April 1940. In still other cases, the Reich authorities set up a whole regional network of Jewish Councils, such as in East Upper

---

6. "Schnellbrief" to the chiefs of the *Einsatzgruppen* in Poland, September 21, 1939, quoted in *Documents on the Holocaust: Selected Sources on the Destruction of the Jews of Germany and Austria, Poland, and the Soviet Union*, ed. Yitzhak Arad, Israel Gutman, and Abraham Margaliot (Jerusalem: Yad Vashem, 1981), 173–78. See also Saul Friedländer, *Nazi Germany and the Jews:* (vol. 2) *The Years of Extermination, 1939–1945* (New York: HarperCollins, 2007), 30–31, and Dan Michman, "Why Did Heydrich Write the Schnellbrief? A Remark on the Reason and on Its Significance," *YVS* 32 (2004): 433–47.

7. See Trunk, *Judenrat*, xvii–xviii, who stresses that "the entire [Jewish] Council phenomenon cannot be analyzed in general terms."

8. *USHMM Encyclopedia of Camps and Ghettos*, Piotrków-Trybunalski entry, 2:279–83.

Silesia under the leadership of **Moshe Merin**.[9] In Hans Frank's fiefdom, the Warsaw ghetto was only sealed in November 1940, greatly restricting residents' movement inside and out. Meanwhile, in the three other regional centers in the Generalgouvernement—Kraków (Frank's seat of government), with some 200,000 Jews in July 1940; Lublin, with 250,000; and Radom, with 310,000—a still different pattern emerged. Jews were expelled from these cities to alleviate the housing crisis, and ghettos were only formally established in the spring of 1941.[10] The ostensible reasons for the creation of ghettos also varied: in Warsaw the ghetto was supposedly set up to prevent the spread of epidemics, while in Łódź it was linked to resettlement of ethnic Germans.[11] When over the course of 1940 the need for more permanent administrative policies in German-controlled Poland grew, German attitudes toward ghettos changed. According to Christopher Browning, the ghettos, "intended as temporary way stations on the road to complete deportation, now became a factor with which local German authorities unexpectedly had to cope on a long-term basis."[12]

How were Jews to know what ghettoization would ultimately entail if German officials in Poland and the Reich were themselves grappling with the question of how overall goals regarding Jewish policy should be translated into concrete measures and what role the ghetto would play? Yet, even with such uncertainty and lack of uniformity, even if Heydrich's order did not lead to the immediate creation of ghettos across German-dominated Poland, the anti-Jewish measures introduced had a massive impact on the perceptions and actions of Jews. A new form of Jewish self-government, Jewish Councils (*Judenräte*), supplanted long-standing Jewish community structures and often elevated new individuals to positions of leadership. All councils had to oversee the distribution of scarce resources and abide by German rules while facing the constant threat and reality of terror. Each Jewish Council controlled an administrative

---

9. Moshe Merin's position was different from that of most other heads of a *Judenrat*. Beginning in early 1940, he was made head of what Isaiah Trunk has called a "central Jewish Council" for an entire region (annexed East Upper Silesia), encompassing more than thirty communities in ten counties and comprising close to one hundred thousand Jews. To a more limited degree than Merin in East Upper Silesia, the Łódź *Judenrat* also had influence outside the city perimeter. Trunk, *Judenrat*, 39–40. For a character sketch of Merin, see Philip Friedman, "The Messianic Complex of a Nazi Collaborator in a Ghetto: Moses Merin of Sosnowiec," in his *Roads to Extinction: Essays on the Holocaust*, ed. Ada June Friedman (New York: Conference on Jewish Social Studies and the Jewish Publication Society, 1980), 353–64.

10. Browning, *The Origins of the Final Solution*, 131–37. These population figures stem from German statistics.

11. Friedländer, *Nazi Germany*, 2:38–39. For a more extensive discussion of early ghettoization policy in Poland, see Christopher R. Browning, *The Path to Genocide: Essays on Launching the Final Solution* (New York: Cambridge University Press, 1992), 28–56.

12. Browning, *The Origins of the Final Solution*, 113.

apparatus—some large and long-lived, as in Warsaw and Łódź, others smaller and more ephemeral—that tried to reconcile the implementation of German orders with the Jewish interest in restoring a semblance of normality and stability in the daily life of the community. As irreconcilable as these goals might have already appeared at the time, many Jews hoped that a central Jewish authority would be better able to represent Jewish interests before local German authorities than fragmented groups or individuals. Furthermore, despite the fact that the composition of a *Judenrat*, the personalities of its members, and the specific conditions in a town, city, or region played an important role in determining the degree to which ordinary Jews suffered, the belief was widespread among Polish Jews in this period that the concentration of Jews in an urban setting offered them the chance to improve the efficiency of social and relief work. Pooling resources, finding comfort among others who shared a similar fate, and establishing networks—official as well as clandestine—were concrete ways to mitigate the effects of German terror. Under the circumstances, the Polish Jews appointed to Jewish Councils had little alternative but to act under the assumption that there was a logic to the Germans' demands and expectations and that German interest in exploiting Jewish labor and other resources for the war effort was strong enough to justify the continued existence of the ghetto.

UPROOTING AND RELOCATION

Less than half a year into the German occupation, twenty-five-year-old Jan Karski, a non-Jewish Pole sent by the Polish government-in-exile on a fact-finding mission to his country, reported the following about "the Jews in the Homeland":

> The forbearance, the submissiveness, the exhaustion, the atmosphere, the conditions in which the extensive pauperized classes of the Jews live in the territories annexed to the Reich and even in the Generalgouvernement often exceed what one can imagine of human misery. Their only reaction consists of attempts to escape to Bolshevik occupation, or more often literally not to appear in the light of day.[13]

Karski, a keen observer, also noted that the German attempt to find a "solution" to the "Jewish question" provided "something akin to a narrow bridge upon which the Germans and a large portion of Polish society are finding agreement"

---

13. For an annotated reprint of the report, see David Engel, "An Early Account of Polish Jewry under Nazi and Soviet Occupation Presented to the Polish Government-in-Exile, February 1940," *Jewish Social Studies* 45, no. 1 (1983): 1–16. For a broader context, see David Engel, *In the Shadow of Auschwitz: The Polish Government-in-Exile and the Jews, 1939–1942* (Chapel Hill: University of North Carolina Press, 1987), 60–64, 163–69.

based on the strong antisemitic current within Polish society.[14] He was certainly right in stressing the Jews' desperation to cross the Bug River in an attempt to escape German rule and find a way into or beyond the Soviet Union (see chapter 5). He did not, however, have sufficient insight into the situation in which Jews were living to foresee their resilience, resourcefulness, and courage in the face of a plethora of discriminatory measures.

The Jews of Poland were uprooted geographically, economically, and socially as a consequence of German policy. As Karski suggested in his report, the fates of those living in the territories annexed to the Reich appeared particularly bleak when they were pushed into the Generalgouvernement to "make room" for Germans. By the end of 1939, the Jewish population in the annexed territory had decreased from 692,000 to 460,000, mostly due to organized expulsion to the Generalgouvernement; according to historian Yehuda Bauer, the combined Jewish population of the annexed territory and the Generalgouvernement numbered between 1.8 and 1.9 million at the time.[15] Despite Frank's initial enthusiasm for the "reception" of the expelled Jews in the Generalgouvernement, the project was so haphazard and caused such humanitarian problems in the Generalgouvernement—and here we should keep in mind that not just Jews but also hundreds of thousands of Poles were being forcibly "resettled"—that Frank succeeded in halting the deportations temporarily in April 1940. By then the number of Jews expelled from the annexed territory and resettled in the Generalgouvernement had reached two hundred thousand.[16] By September 1940, over 600,000 Polish Jews had become refugees; in Warsaw alone by early 1941, the Jewish refugee population still numbered 130,000 people (of a total of 445,000 Jews in the city, up from roughly 360,000 in late 1939).[17] Across Poland

---

14. On the Karski report of February 1940, see Engel, "An Early Account," 12–13.

15. Yehuda Bauer, *American Jewry and the Holocaust: The American Jewish Joint Distribution Committee, 1939–1945* (Detroit, MI: Wayne State University Press, 1981), 69.

16. Friedländer, *Nazi Germany*, 2:36–37.

17. It is impossible to provide accurate numbers of Jewish refugees and ghetto inhabitants in Warsaw for this chaotic period. Israel Gutman cites 130,000 Jewish refugees in Warsaw by April 1941, while Yehuda Bauer estimates the number of Jewish refugees in the city at 150,000 after September 1940. Regardless of whether the actual number was closer to Gutman's estimate or Bauer's, it was further affected by a massive influx of Jews from the Warsaw district into the city itself, the bulk of which took place between September 1940 and March 1941, bringing into Warsaw as many as fifty thousand Jews. Yisrael Gutman, *The Jews of Warsaw, 1939–1943: Ghetto, Underground, Revolt* (Bloomington: Indiana University Press, 1982), 63; Bauer, *American Jewry and the Holocaust*, 69. Barbara Engelking and Jacek Leociak estimate the peak number of inhabitants of the Warsaw ghetto at 460,000 in March 1941 (15,000 more than Gutman's number for the same month) and quote Nazi documents that put the number as high as 490,000. Engelking and Leociak, *The Warsaw Ghetto: A Guide to the Perished City* (New Haven, CT: Yale University Press, 2009), 49.

and despite relief efforts, refugees were the first to be hit by widespread starvation, disease, and mass death.[18] But even where Jews managed to stay in their communities, they faced the ramifications of German measures designed to force them out of their jobs and rob them of their possessions.[19]

The plight of the Jews in Poland was to some degree the result of a shift in the power structure and a refocusing of efforts within the Nazi system. With **Heinrich Himmler**'s appointment in October 1939 as Reich commissioner for the strengthening of Germandom (**Reichskommissar für die Festigung deutschen Volkstums**, RKFDV) in charge of both resettling ethnic Germans (*Volksdeutsche*) and eliminating the "harmful influence" of non-German populations in the areas to be Germanized, the SS apparatus began to wield a growing influence on population policy. Other agencies, most notably Frank's Generalgouvernement administration, demanded their own say in the matter, thus adding to the radicalization of German measures. As a result, Poles and Jews in the German-occupied territories of Poland became the objects of more sweeping "resettlement" plans designed to make room for ethnic Germans "repatriated" from the Soviet Union and other areas.[20]

The meanings and consequences of these expulsions went far beyond physical displacement. The uprooting severed existing ties that linked Jews to their non-Jewish surroundings. Compounding matters, Polish Jews were stigmatized for everyone to see. As of December 1, 1939, all Jews aged ten and over in the Generalgouvernement were required to wear a white armband with a Star of David. This decree standardized a practice of marking Jews that had already begun after September 1939 and nevertheless continued to produce different variations throughout German-occupied Poland. Except in the concentration camps in the Reich, Jews were not required to wear Jewish badges or armbands elsewhere in German-controlled Europe at this time. The wave of exclusionary prohibitions spread to all arenas of Polish Jewish daily life, affecting where Jews

18. For a literary illustration of the increasingly desperate circumstances of the Jewish refugees in Warsaw, see Yisrael Vinik, *Tsvishn lebn un toyt: proze-shafungen*, ed. Bernard Mark (Warsaw: Farlag "Yidish Bukh," 1955), 39–45.

19. Bauer, *American Jewry and the Holocaust*, 70. One survey cited by Bauer from May 1940 found that only 40 percent of ninety-five thousand Jewish workers had some form of work under the Nazis. For Nazi policies on Jewish property, see Martin Dean, *Robbing the Jews: The Confiscation of Jewish Property in the Holocaust, 1933–1945* (New York: Cambridge University Press in association with the USHMM, 2008).

20. Browning, *The Origins of the Final Solution*, 43. For an in-depth analysis of German resettlement policies and Himmler's role, see Aly, *"Final Solution"*; Robert Koehl, *RKFDV: German Resettlement and Population Policy, 1939–1945: A History of the Reich Commission for the Strengthening of Germandom* (Cambridge, MA: Harvard University Press, 1957).

could live and the jobs they could hold and banning them from use of public transportation and other public places.[21]

The Jews of Kalisz in the annexed part of occupied Poland were among the early victims of Germanization plans. In 1939 over twenty thousand Jews were living in Kalisz (almost 50 percent of the total population). On November 20, 1939, ten thousand of them were evicted from their homes to make room for Baltic *Volksdeutsche* being resettled in Kalisz, which by then had been renamed Kalisch and incorporated into the Reich as part of the Warthegau. The city's Jews were then deported to the Lublin district of the Generalgouvernement during the first two weeks of December. For many, the odyssey continued. Over the course of 1940, nearly seven thousand Kalisz Jews found refuge in the Warsaw ghetto.[22] A Jewish resident of Kalisz later provided the testimony presented in Document 10–1 on their expulsion via Łódź to Warsaw. Despite describing by now familiar features of German abuse, the testimony reveals a different pattern from initial wartime flight experiences, for it became evident to this narrator that Jews were being targeted as Jews and could expect little if any comfort from their non-Jewish Polish compatriots.

DOCUMENT 10–1: Testimony by unidentified author, "From Kalisz to Warsaw," August 23, 1941, USHMMA RG 15.079M (ŻIH Ring I/830), reel 39 (translated from Polish).[23]

[. . .] The Jews were in a dispirited mood when their train reached Koluszki, where they again had to get off and spend many hours waiting for the right train. And here the train station was brimming with people. Thousands of Jews walked up and down the platform, looking out impatiently for a train to approach. Koluszki was a station on the border between the territories incorporated into the Reich and the Generalgouvernement. On the road from Łódź to Koluszki, the Jews took the liberty of taking off their armbands, assuming that they would no longer be compulsory in Koluszki. They were terribly mistaken. The Germans recognized that many Jews were at the station—so how could

---

21. Friedländer, *Nazi Germany*, 2:38; Arad, Gutman, and Margaliot, *Documents on the Holocaust*: 178–82.

22. See Kalisz entry in *USHMM Encyclopedia of Camps and Ghettos*, 2:60–61; "Kalisz," in Miron and Shulhani, *Yad Vashem Encyclopedia of the Ghettos*, 1:274–75.

23. Robert Moses Shapiro and Tadeusz Epsztein, eds., *The Warsaw Ghetto Oyneg Shabes–Ringelblum Archive: Catalog and Guide* (Bloomington: Indiana University Press in association with the USHMM and the Jewish Historical Institute, Warsaw, 2009), speculate that the author was Natan Koniński.

they not take advantage of such an opportunity and entertain themselves at their expense? And our experience from the Łódź train station was again repeated, albeit with some variations. The German railway workers rounded up the Jews in one area and beat them, cursing and swearing at them for not wearing armbands. The Jews hurriedly put them on, but it didn't help much for the railway men decided to toy with the Jews and torment them a bit. One young railway worker in particular sought to unload all his anger and fury on the Jews gathered there. He paced back and forth in front of the fearful women and men and pushed them, all the while repeating the words: "*die ferfluchten Juden*" ["the damned Jews"]. But for him, apparently this still didn't suffice. Suddenly, he stood in front of the Jews and ordered them to shout loudly all together several times: *Wir wollten den Krieg* ["we wanted the war"]. The Jews had to follow his order, and a rather considerable group of traveling Poles gathered around him who laughed at the Jews and tried to signal to the railway man their approval of his wonderful ideas. Among them was even a man who graciously offered to translate the railway man's orders into Polish for the Jews. Seeing [this as an encouragement, the railway man] came up with even more things. With the help of his eager translator, he ordered all the Jews who had served in the Polish army to step forward. A group of a dozen or so men came forward. The railway man arranged them in two rows and heaped abuse upon them for shooting at German soldiers. Next, he drilled them and gave the commands "down" and "up," which the Jews had to carry out eagerly since he was pressing them and prodding them with his leg. In the end he ordered them to take whichever bundles, suitcases, and rucksacks each of them had and to run 100 meters ahead across the rails, embankments, and tracks. He drove them along the way, and many among those who were running stumbled and fell. Before the train departed, the Germans carried out the same baggage search as in Łódź and again took whatever they liked.

Everyone sighed with relief when we finally somehow managed to board the train to Warsaw. This was not at all easy. People literally pushed themselves into the cars through the windows, stood on the steps, and climbed onto the roofs. Yet in the end, tired and worn out, these Jews made it to the Central Station in Warsaw, where they expected to find some peace and quiet. The train pulled into Warsaw at night, so we had to wait at the station until dawn to go out into the city. At the train station, aside from numerous Jews, there were also many peasants from near and far waiting at the station who had brought all kinds of items to Warsaw, like salt, kielbasas, fats, and other goods since, as a result of military operations, the supply of basic goods to the city was still very deficient.

After several long hours of waiting at the station, everyone finally set out into the city, where they began the search for a new home and a new livelihood.

Many Jewish Councils tried their best to accommodate the newcomers. In Włoszczowa, in the Radom district of the Generalgouvernement, the Jewish Council established in October 1939 under the leadership of Aleksander Fargel had to take care of a besieged but not yet ghettoized Jewish community. Numbering roughly twenty-seven hundred, the Jewish population comprised almost half of the town's total population.[24] The council's troubles were aggravated by the influx of refugees, whose number would ultimately double the size of the prewar Jewish community. In December 1939, the arrival of 217 displaced Jews from the area around Posen (Poznań) prompted the council to organize its welfare work in a more rational manner and to seek greater financial support for its activities. In early 1941, Fargel reflected on these earlier events in Włoszczowa from the perspective of the Jewish Council.

DOCUMENT 10–2: Aleksander Fargel, "Account of the Social Welfare Measures Taken by the Aid Committee for Refugees and the Poor of the Jewish Council of Włoszczowa in 1940," no date (ca. January 1941), USHMMA RG 15.073M (ŻIH 223/1), reel 1 (translated from Polish).

The population of Włoszczowa heartily welcomed the unfortunate ones [from the Poznań area]. A special reception committee for the displaced persons was organized which awaited their arrival at the train station. There, a first hot meal for the displaced persons was also prepared, and in the meantime living quarters were readied in town, a very weighty problem in light of the already cramped living conditions. The premises of the Beth Hamidrash [local Jewish house of study] were set up as a gathering point, to which the population of Włoszczowa at its own initiative brought food for the newcomers throughout the day. From there, only individual families were taken to living quarters, a process that lasted several days. The displaced persons arrived with almost no money, so the organization of meals became the most important matter after housing.

---

24. See Włoszczowa entry in *USHMM Encyclopedia of Camps and Ghettos*, 2:342–44; "Włoszczowa," in Miron and Shulhani, *Yad Vashem Encyclopedia of the Ghettos*, 2:938–39.

We immediately set about establishing a communal kitchen for the refugees. Unfortunately, a lack of funds and the mounting financial difficulties of the Jewish community delayed this initiative. It was at this time that the plan surfaced to turn to the American Joint Distribution Committee for help. A delegation comprised of Dr. Chaim Fargel and Josef Kochen was immediately dispatched to Warsaw with the aim of obtaining subventions for social welfare. On January 7, 1940, the delegation returned, having obtained a first subvention in the amount of 2,500 złoty and bringing back a rather ample amount of clothing and even medicine from the TOZ.[25] Social welfare activities, which to this point had been carried out in a chaotic and unsystematic fashion by several groups of individuals willing to perform this work, now had to be organized in a manner consistent with existing financial capacities to achieve maximum efficiency.

To this end, on January 10, 1940, a consolidated Aid Committee for Refugees and the Poor [Komitet Pomocy Uchodźcom i Biednym] was created under the authority of the Jewish Council of Włoszczowa. From that moment it took upon itself the burdens of and responsibility for the welfare of displaced persons and the poor.

The committee immediately set about expanding the communal kitchen and distributing clothing that it had received. Beds were also provided for many of the refugees. At this time a large wave of refugees from Łódź reached Włoszczowa. Hundreds of persons arrived who required aid in the form of food and medicine. A second communal kitchen became necessary and construction began immediately. Lack of food and fuel, the harsh winter, and the resulting lack of supplies hindered the work to such an extent that at times it proved completely impossible to carry on. To make matters worse, a typhus epidemic broke out and the German authorities ordered the Jewish Council to organize and equip an epidemic hospital within two days and to maintain it at its own cost, and this under the discipline of a compulsory financial contribution imposed upon the town. With superhuman efforts, the hospital successfully opened on the designated date, January 27, but without medicine and medical instruments. Over the course of 48 hours, a thorough overhaul of the entire building designated to be the hospital was carried out; in the course of a single day, 25 beds were constructed, 25 quilts were sewn, and several hundred pieces of bed linens and underwear were collected. The scope of

---

25. For more on the American Jewish Joint Distribution Committee and **TOZ**, see the Glossary.

the work and the effort was so monumental and the time for completion so short that it is possible to assess it properly only from the perspective of the present day.

Fargel went on to detail how the increasing impoverishment of the Jewish community of Włoszczowa coincided with the arrival of another group of Jewish refugees (from Włocławek). The harsh winter also seriously hindered the scope and efficacy of the social welfare activities of the Aid Committee, which in turn was compelled to turn repeatedly to the American Jewish Joint Distribution Committee (AJJDC) and TOZ for financial support. As the funds available from those two organizations progressively dwindled, the Aid Committee had to rely more and more upon donations, both monetary and in kind, from the local Jewish population. Yet, as dire as the financial straits of the Jewish Council and the Aid Committee became, there were isolated instances of success. During Passover in 1940, for instance, a subsidy from the Joint and local donations enabled the Aid Committee to distribute an array of different products (matzoth, potatoes, beets, eggs, soap, and so forth) to 2,225 individuals from 595 families at a total cost of 8,500 złoty.[26] Still, the conditions for social welfare activities in Włoszczowa generally worsened over time. The establishment of a ghetto for Jews in the summer of 1940 marked a new low point in this downward trend.

In their search for shelter and relative security, thousands of Jews headed for the largest Polish Jewish community, Warsaw. As numerous sources detail, however, refugees in Warsaw soon realized that their expectations of being greeted with great hospitality or generosity would go unmet. If nothing worse, a sense of confusion and loss engulfed those who found that their Jewish badge marked them as outsiders even among fellow Jews. In his diary, **Chaim Kaplan** recorded his impressions of the Łódź Jews he came into contact with on the streets of Warsaw, remarking on the brutal treatment they had endured during the expulsions and the hardships they bore as refugees in Warsaw.

---

26. For the AJJDC Passover shipment of 1940, see Bauer, *American Jewry and the Holocaust*, 98.

DOCUMENT 10–3: Chaim Kaplan, Warsaw, diary entries for December 19 and 30, 1939: for December 19, USHMMA Acc. 2004.405 Chaim Kaplan diary copies; for December 30, Abraham Isaac Katsh, Nachman Blumental, and Bernard Mark, eds., *Megilat yisurin: yoman geto Varshah 1 be-september 1939–4 be-ogust 1942* (Tel Aviv and Jerusalem: Am Oved and Yad Vashem, 1966), 126–28 (translated from Hebrew).[27]

December 19, 1939

The savage and rapacious Nazi has mercilessly stabbed his claws into the Jews of Łódź, and without pity, like an animal, he is sucking their blood and breaking their bones. Since I live in Warsaw, I am far from the place where this is happening and I am unable to collect precise information to record in an organized manner. But the exiles of Łódź are fleeing to Warsaw, and there is no house that does not provide shelter for a Łódź refugee and his family. You can recognize them in every street and on every corner. The more you encounter them, the more their horrifying stories shake your entire existence and fill your eyes with shame and disgrace, and make you feel more like a worm than a man. Never, since the day that robbery and violence were created, were humans robbed or oppressed in such a cruel and cynical fashion. [. . .]

December 30, 1939

The conqueror admits in his press reports that up to 50,000 refugees have entered the capital. However, as always, he lies. Over 100,000 Jews have actually come to Warsaw.[28] Their carts, piled with personal belongings and living babies, line the city streets. No organized help is provided. Each person helps himself in his own way and with his own capabilities. Some stay with a relative, a friend or a distant acquaintance. The poor fill the synagogues, which have become shelters. One cannot describe the crowdedness, the stress and the filth in these shelters. The catastrophe has overwhelmed the Joint; they do not have the ability to restrict or control it.

---

27. This was published, using slightly different wording, in Chaim A. Kaplan, *Scroll of Agony: The Warsaw Diary of Chaim A. Kaplan*, ed. and trans. Abraham I. Katsh (Bloomington: Indiana University Press in association with the USHMM, 1999), 88–89, 93–94.

28. From November 1939 until October 1940, around ninety thousand Jews expelled from the Polish areas annexed to the Reich were deported to Warsaw. Engelking and Leociak, *The Warsaw Ghetto*, 48.

One can recognize the deportees and fugitives by their faces, the way they walk through the busy city. They stop passers-by and ask directions. Occasionally, one will see a provincial Jew who is truly an exotic sight in a European city. Even his brethren from Warsaw are not accustomed to him. In the eyes of the Gentiles, he is an object of mockery and ridicule. Some of them go out to the streets wearing "their yellow badges" that are shaped as the "Star of David."[29] It is simply the yellow badge of the Middle Ages. On those occasions, they are rebuked and forced to change the star for the blue and white armbands, the symbol of the Jewishness of the Jews of Warsaw.

DOCUMENT 10–4: **Warsaw Jews, wearing armbands, sell their possessions out of suitcases in a makeshift market on a bombed-out street in the ghetto district, December 1939, USHMMPA WS# 31515.**

Less than one year later, when the ghettoization order came down in Warsaw, long-time residents faced being uprooted within their own city. A Jewish woman named Helena Gutman-Staszewska, who until the closing of the

---

29. Because all Warsaw Jews over ten years of age were required to wear white armbands with a blue Star of David on their right sleeves, the yellow patch distinguished the refugees as "provincial Jews." See Gutman, *The Jews of Warsaw*, 29.

Jewish public schools in Warsaw in December 1939 had worked as a teacher, described the confusion surrounding the edict and the frantic scramble for new accommodations in the ghetto.[30]

DOCUMENT 10–5: **Helena Gutman-Staszewska, Warsaw, "Recollections from the German Occupation, August 1939–November 1940," USHMMA RG 02.208M (ŻIH 302/168) (translated from Polish).**[31]

[. . .] The declared boundaries of the Jewish district were continually altered, even over the course of a day there were several changes. In our apartment building [at 20 Chłodna Street] there were 50 Jewish tenants and 10 Christian families. We did not know for sure whether we would be added to the Jewish district because the situation was subject to constant revision. It was on Sądny Dzień (Yom Kippur) when the news spread that we would have to move and that we had the right to exchange [our current apartment] for Aryan apartments. Since our building was modern—even the smallest apartments had modern appliances—from the very break of dawn it was as if a siege had begun, like a swarm of locusts. As soon as day broke, there was constant knocking at the door and questions about the exchange. The mood in the courtyard was terrible, some were yelling, some were crying, people were cheating each other, numerous shady characters were lurking about who wanted to take advantage of the situation. Someone approached my neighbor, an old woman, and tried to force her to give up her apartment without an exchange. Evidently the law still carried some weight because she was able to get out of the situation. The district state police officer[32] took our administrator's apartment and gave

---

30. For biographical information on Helena Gutman-Staszewska (1894–?), see *USHMM ITS Collection Data Base Central Name Index*; Michał Grynberg, ed., *Words to Outlive Us: Voices from the Warsaw Ghetto* (New York: Metropolitan Books, 2002), 462–63. She survived the war hiding in Warsaw.

31. Parts of her testimony have been published in Grynberg, *Words to Outlive Us*, 25–26, 28.

32. This person was a Polish police officer responsible for a district within the city. In 1939, the German occupiers put the existing regular Polish police force under the control of the Schutzpolizei; its commanders were Germans. This collaborationist police force was known as the "Blue Police," after the color of its uniform. It was used for general policing tasks but also for various roundups of both Jewish and non-Jewish Poles, guard duties in the ghettos, aid with the deportations, and other tasks ordered by the Germans. On the Blue Police, see Gunnar S. Paulsson, *Secret City: The Hidden Jews of Warsaw, 1940–1945* (New Haven, CT: Yale University Press, 2002), esp. 144–48 and passim.

him an apartment in ruins in a neighborhood that would be incorporated into the Aryan district. The administrator did not consent to this but he was forced and his belongings were thrown into the courtyard. Witnessing all these scenes, I was literally afraid that I would go insane; I left to try to shake it off. After I returned, the apartment caretaker informed me that my apartment was reserved by the state police commissioner, 7th precinct, and I was not allowed to move until his arrival nor to exchange with anyone because the new buyer and I would be thrown onto the pavement. Since I already had an exchange in mind, I began the move to 6 Ogrodowa Street at the very crack of dawn and, making use of the crowd, I stole away like a thief. I do not know whether the caretaker simply did not notice me or whether he let me be for other reasons. In fact, the next day the police commissioner called on my apartment with a large escort and, faced with a fait accompli,[33] merely scolded the caretaker. In this case, I was lucky that I only had to make one move. But in our building, there were many instances where people moved from 20 Chłodna Street to 80 Żelazna, then to Łucka Street, and from Łucka to Krochmalna. There was another case: one of my relatives lived at 22 Poznań Street, she exchanged apartments with some magisterial official at 52 Ogrodowa Street but, because the building on Ogrodowa was being added to the Aryan district, she did not agree to the exchange and was beaten by Gestapo men sent by that official and thrown out of the apartment without being allowed to take anything with. From Ogrodowa she moved from Sienna to 30 Chłodna Street, from Chłodna to Twarda 7, from Twarda 7 to Dzielna 61, from Dzielna 61 to Leszno 12. During the apartment exchanges, the view on the street was extraordinary: handcarts, wagons with possessions going in every direction, constant fear of whether the gendarmes would take your things since this was indeed often the case. [. . .]

On November 25, 1940, the final deadline for the closing of the district is announced. We are surrounded by fences, walls; we are left with a few outlets to cross to the Aryan side.

GHETTO ECONOMIES AND FORCED LABOR

In this early phase of the war, the economic conditions in the ghettos differed as widely as the circumstances of their creation. Well into 1941, German economic policy regarding the Jews was dominated by what Christopher Browning

---

33. The author added in the margin that "the apartment was transferred to an Aryan family, and theirs to me."

has called "a split between 'attritionists' and 'productionists.'" "Attritionists" focused on the radical and swift extraction of Jewish wealth, whereas "productionists" were oriented toward a longer-term utilization of the Jews' economic potential for the German war effort.[34] The Germans were supposed to deliver provisions to Jewish communities, but they often did so irregularly, sometimes not at all, and always at a high price. Left to the initiative and inventiveness of their leaders, organizations, and rank-and-file members, the Jewish communities of Poland had to harness support wherever they could find it. No Jewish Council could amass sufficient material resources to ensure tolerable living standards for the majority of its population for any length of time. Yet, some were successful in rallying or drawing on solidarity within the ghetto and organizing help from the outside, despite constant, often large-scale disruptions by the Germans.

Jewish Councils struggled to create stable, long-term sources of income for the majority of the Jewish population. Irrespective of the circumstances under which a particular Jewish Council came into being, all Jewish Council leaders needed to establish an infrastructure that would sustain basic communal services and other crucial aspects of Jewish life. For that purpose they had to interact with German and Polish authorities. Particularly in dealing with Germans, Jewish community representatives often tried to stretch the narrow limits of their official roles. They resorted to techniques that borrowed from long-standing negotiation strategies, yet also went beyond what Jewish leaders had ventured prior to the war on behalf of their communities. In this early stage of ghetto history, as Isaiah Trunk observes, Jewish interventions "were at times daring in that they openly stated objections to and requested relief from the persecutions imposed by the Germans."[35] Given the degree of corruption and spoliation inherent in German anti-Jewish policy, bribery could provide a crucial supplement to Jewish protests and appeals. Nevertheless, it involved considerable risks and was not always successful.

In Zamość in the Lublin district of the Generalgouvernement, as Mieczysław Garfinkiel recalled shortly after the war, the *Judenrat*—with him at the helm—adopted a strategy that exploited weaknesses in the German system of subjugation, especially the element of personal greed. Garfinkiel's account conveys a sense of the pressure Jewish leaders felt as they tried to use whatever leverage they could to protect their communities from disaster. This required constant awareness of impending danger, creativity in handling acute problems,

---

34. Browning, *The Origins of the Final Solution*, 113–31.

35. Trunk, *Judenrat*, 389–90, also provides examples of this behavior in the 1939–1940 period.

adaptability to new circumstances, courage when approaching German authorities and their Polish collaborators, and a willingness to put pressure on the relatively well-off segments of the community to aid the poor and the general public. After describing early German measures in Zamość (see document 5–8), Garfinkiel addressed the basic problems he and his fellow *Judenrat* members faced once the German version of normalcy in the Generalgouvernement had set in.

DOCUMENT 10–6: Memoirs by Mieczysław Garfinkiel about Zamość, written in 1946, USHMMA RG 02.208M (ŻIH 302/122) (translated from Polish).[36]

[. . .] Thus we began our work in the building of the Jewish community. In addition to our daily obligation to provide Jewish laborers, who were demanded in continually greater numbers, reaching a figure of 500–600 laborers per day, [the Germans] began to demand other services from us. [. . .] After several days, we were summoned to the German in charge, a certain Wei[?]henmayer, from Stuttgart. This character, after telling us off in the bitterest terms and berating us indiscriminately, demanded that we pay a sum of 75,000 złoty to the Zamość city administration. Mayor Michał Wazowski, as I later learned, had given him the idea. The money was intended to help the masses of Polish repatriates passing through Zamość who were returning from Soviet territory to the territory of the German occupation. We had to collect *this* sum from among broader segments of the Jewish population. I personally deposited with receipt nearly the entire sum, in the amount of 73,000 złoty, to the account of the Zamość city administration. Moreover, [the Germans] continually demanded we set up all different sorts of sites designated for German offices, quarters for German officers where beds, bedding, and linens had to be provided, furniture, etc.

Two or three days after paying the aforementioned sum to the city administration, we were summoned for the first time to the Gestapo. The head of the Gestapo at the time was Schturmannführer [*sic*] Blak,[37]

---

36. A short extract from the account is published in Trunk, *Judenrat*, 395.

37. This is most likely SS-Sturmbannführer (Major) Hans Block (1898–1944), who had been transferred to the Lublin district after serving in the Vienna **Gestapo** office and in 1942 was involved in the murder of the Jews in Drohobycz, East Galicia. See Thomas Sandkühler, *"Endlösung" in Galizien: Der Judenmord in Ostpolen und die Rettungsinitiativen von Berthold Beitz, 1941–1944* (Bonn: Dietz, 1996), 440.

from Vienna. After he was transferred from Zamość, he became head of the Gestapo in Borysław. Blak, in the presence of an interpreter named Bernardt (a Silesian) read through an entire litany of Jewish faults and crimes. The most serious accusation was provocation of the war, after which he gave us a prepared protocol to sign "confirming" German authorities' good treatment of Zamość's Jews and also that the Jews of Zamość had not yet made any tribute payment. Having concluded the official part, as it were, of the audience and after coercing us to sign, he made the following declaration: "Listen carefully to what I'm going to tell you, it's more important than the written protocol you signed. You Jews have to do everything we demand and provide us with everything—you'll live as long as we're happy."

At this point, the Jewish population of the city increased because Jews from surrounding towns and villages, where the situation was much more horrible, began to arrive in great numbers. Even before centralized ghettos had been established, every larger Jewish center attracted the surrounding Jewish population, dispersed across smaller settlements, like a magnet. The problem of employing them and caring for a significant number of the poor population consequently arose. These people found employment working for the Germans because, from the very beginning, the Jewish Community introduced the principle of remuneration for such work. We obtained the funds for this goal in the following manner. We introduced forced labor two days per week for the entire Jewish population from the age of 14 to 60 without regard to sex. Better-off Jews, merchants, or those involved in some other way in factory work could pay the community a sum amounting to the daily wage of a laborer, and with these monies the Jewish workers were paid who, due to the lack of other work, eagerly reported every day for the German jobs. The Germans did not pay for those jobs, but in the course of time certain sites crystallized where Jews were eager to work, particularly for the Wehrmacht, on account of the relatively humane treatment and the support through occasional small handouts of food.

The successor of the aforementioned military commandant Harms was Captain Paul Wagner, an older man, a factory owner from Chemnitz, a calm and comparatively decent man. We came to an arrangement with him according to which all German enterprises interested in Jewish laborers had to submit a corresponding request to Wagner a day ahead of time and then he, after collecting all the applications, would send them on to us. The assignment and dispatch of the laborers were handled by two of his subordinate officers together with Azriel Szeps,[38] a member of the Council of Elders, a tailor by trade, and an old, prewar social actor. This took place every day at 6 a.m. on the square in front of the local head-quarters [*Ortskomenda*]. From this time on, Jews could calmly come to this location and engage in gainful employment since the roundups had ceased. [. . .]

At the start of December 1939, I was called before the German city administrator, who informed me that a transport of Jews deported from the so-called Wartegau [*sic*] was to arrive in Zamość. In connection with this, he demanded that I create an Aid Committee that would see to hous-ing and caring for these people. He directed me to the head of the local NSV—NationalSocjalischtischeVolksvohlfahrt [*sic*][39]—a certain Schultz wearing a party uniform. He informed me that the Aid Committee which was to be created would be directly subordinate to him and that I would have to submit monthly reports on its activities to him. In response to my requests and appeals, he promised to support me in this matter. And he in fact provided us with a field kitchen, since I considered our first task to be getting a canteen up and running for the settlers who were to arrive.

On December 18, 1939, at night, I received notification from the German city administrator that a transport of Jews from Włocławek [German: Leslau] would arrive early the next day. At dawn, I—together with the Aid Committee, which had already been organized—was at the railway station, where the transport of Jews in closed freight cars soon arrived. They were indeed the Jews from Włocławek, numbering around 550 persons who had been in transit for nearly a week without sustenance. We wanted to start immediately unloading the people from the cars and

---

38. Azriel Szeps (1886–1942) was a well-known tailor and Zionist from Zamość. During the war, he was vice chairman of the Zamość *Judenrat*. In October 1942 he was deported to Izbica and a month later to Bełżec, where he was tortured and shot on arrival. His wife, son, and daughter perished in Bełżec as well. See Adam Kopciowski, "Der Judenrat in Zamość," *Theresienstädter Studien und Dokumente* 9 (2002), 221–45, and Rudolf Reder, *Bełżec* (Kraków and Oświęcim: Fundacja Judaica and Państwowe Muzeum Oświęcim-Brzezinka, 1999).

39. The "Nationalsozialistische Volkswohlfahrt" (literally, the National Socialist *Volk* Welfare Association), better known by its German acronym, NSV, was a Nazi Party charity organization founded in Berlin in 1931. It became the exclusive Nazi social welfare organiza-tion under the leadership of Erich Hilgenfeldt and, after the Nazis' seizure of power, pushed aside or forcibly co-opted others, such as church organizations or the Red Cross. For a brief overview of the history of NSV, see Michael Burleigh, *The Third Reich: A New History* (New York: Hill and Wang, 2000), 219–28.

providing them with food, above all drinking water, of which they had been deprived for so long. But the German authorities who had also come to the station forbade us from helping and initially did not even want to let us through to the cars. As it turned out, the city administrator did not want to allow these Jews onto the territory of the city at all but intended to send the transport on to the Russian border in order to pass them off forcibly to the other side.

Following strenuous efforts, we succeeded in "freeing" the women, children, and elderly, while the men in their prime, numbering about 150, were placed in what was the first Jewish camp organized on the territory of Zamość. They were housed in the synagogue, where they stayed under guard of the SS.

After placing the children and women in unoccupied apartments left behind by Jews [*pożydowskich*; literally, "post-Jewish"], we turned our attention to organizing aid for this first camp. The men stayed in the closed-off synagogue for approximately four weeks. And again after long-lasting efforts, we succeeded in getting these people released, yet on the condition that they would not remain in Zamość but be settled in the closest village, Szczebrzeszyn, located 20 kilometers from Zamość. On January 15, 1940, I personally took them there and asked them not to show themselves in Zamość for at least a few days because, as the Germans had threatened, they would be shot if they did so. I added that they at least have freedom of movement and could go to Warsaw or other cities. However, all of my pleadings to the German authorities and all my pronouncements on the absurdity of an edict dividing families, separating wives and children from husbands and fathers, had no effect—the prohibition on these men residing in Zamość was categorical.

As could have been foreseen, on the next day, immediately after being sent to Szczebrzeszyn (where I had even organized an Aid Committee), these Jews, not paying heed to [my warnings], began sneaking [back] to Zamość. In doing so, they provoked the first serious Jewish tragedy on the territory of Zamość. The road from Szczebrzeszyn to Zamość led past barracks where SS detachments under the leadership of Fritz[40] were stationed. I should add here that he was later commandant of Oświęcim for a period of time. Upon noticing the Jews filing along the road, the SS men caught

---

40. This is most likely SS-Hauptsturmführer (Captain) Karl Fritzsch (1908–1945), who from 1940 until the end of 1941 served as "protective custody commander" in Auschwitz and from 1942 was commandant of the Flossenbürg concentration camp; see Danuta Czech, *Auschwitz Chronicle, 1939–1945* (New York: Henry Holt, 1990), 811.

17 of them and, after bestially torturing them for several days, murdered them. As I was later able to learn, these people were stripped naked in minus-30-degree cold [–22°F], and cold water was poured on them, turning them into pillars of ice. They were literally frozen to death. I recall that among these martyrs were the following Jews from Włocławek: Ber Czarny, the owner of a mill, Blas, Praszkier, a merchant, Stupaj, a young man, a student, the son of a gymnasium teacher.

Despite prior harassment and instances of individual Jews disappearing without a trace, this was the first tragic shock that the Jewish population of Zamość experienced.

The Jewish Quarter and Its Administration

As I have already mentioned, shortly after the occupation of the city the Germans established the so-called Council of Elders composed of eight members. Aside from myself, the following individuals were appointed to the council: Bencjan Lubliner,[41] formerly chairman of the administration of the Jewish Community and a merchant, Azriel Szeps, a tailor by trade, an old social activist, and a member of the administration of the former community, Eliasz Epsztein,[42] a merchant, Wiktor Inlender, a merchant, Stanisław Hernhut, the owner of a printing press, Szulim Tyszberg, an old social activist and a merchant, and Samuel Kahan, an industrialist. At that time, I dealt principally with organizing the Aid Committee and directing its work, particularly in connection with the influx of ever-greater numbers of Jews deported from Koło, Konin, and Włocławek as well as new arrivals from Warsaw and Łódź seeking greater calm, since a lack of accommodations had not yet made itself felt in Zamość, and since the situation with respect to provisions did not differ from the prewar situation.

It was roughly in January 1940 that the Germans issued an edict creating the so-called Jewish Council—*Judenratt* [*sic*]—envisaged in the

41. Bencjan Lubliner (1873–1942?) was president of the Zamość Jewish Community at the outbreak of the war and subsequently the first chairman of the *Judenrat*. In January 1940 Mieczysław Garfinkiel replaced him. Lubliner perished in Bełżec. See Mordechai Bernstein, *The Zamosc Memorial Book* (Mahwah, NJ: Jacob Solomon Berger, 2004), and Kopciowski, "Der Judenrat in Zamość."

42. Eliasz (or Eljasz) Epsztein (1875–?) owned a pharmacy in Zamość before the war and was a member of the city council. During the war he became a member of the *Judenrat*. He managed to escape deportation to Bełżec in November 1942. He hid with his two sons in the vicinity of Zamość, then in the village of Poronin near Zakopane, and eventually in Kraków, where he lived with forged papers until the liberation. After the war, he returned to Zamość, where he stayed until the end of his life. See Kopciowski, "Der Judenrat in Zamość."

directive of Governor Franck [*sic*], who at the time had just arrived in Zamość.

Making use of the vagueness of the decree's provisions stipulating that in cities with more than 10,000 inhabitants (but without explicitly referencing the Jewish population) the councils were to be comprised of 24 persons, the *Judenrat* in Zamość was also established with 24 members.

I was in Warsaw at the time, trying to gain a subsidy from the Joint for the Aid Committee, and when I returned to Zamość, I was informed that I had been unanimously selected by the *Judenrat* as its head. None of my efforts to decline this duty produced a positive outcome, and all the members of the council categorically demanded that I take over leadership. I was also summoned by the mayor, who at the order of the city administrator demanded that I accept leadership of the Jewish Council.

Without interrupting our ongoing work, we first dealt with the inner organization of the newly established institution. We initially organized the following departments:

I. Registry of addresses

II. Civil registry [births, deaths, marriages]

III. Finances

IV. Labor

V. Provisions

The following departments were subsequently created:

VI. Supervision of camps

VII. Post

VIII. Taxes

In response to the considerable growth of the Jewish population as a result of the aforementioned influx from outside, a census was taken and a directory established. The census showed some 8,000 Jews in June 1940.

Since a prohibition on Jews communicating with Aryans was soon issued and Jews were not allowed to visit any German or Polish government offices, we began keeping our own records on marital status, registering births and deaths, and issuing marriage certificates and temporary proof of identity. Juljan Goldsztejn, the nephew of Leon Perec, was the head of the civil registry department.

Our officials also had to settle all the affairs of Jews in all government offices, in particular those pertaining to taxes, patents, and other matters.

The ideal situation on our territory with regard to provisions did not last long. The Germans soon established a system of ration cards for the entire population, whereby the Jewish population was allotted minimal rations. Provisions for the Jews were organized as follows: the *Judenrat* received a lump sum of food, which it in turn distributed among the Jews by means of its own system of ration cards.

The provisions department, headed by Szulim Tyszberg and Adam Galis, both members of the council, had more and more work in the course of time and, due to certain circumstances which I will discuss below, played an important role until the end of the existence of Zamość's Jewish settlement.

Until May 1, 1941, Jews occupied their old apartments throughout the city, aside from sporadic cases where individual Jews were kicked out of their apartments by Germans or Poles, in the latter case as compensation for their own apartments being taken over by Germans.

Despite the rigid hierarchy imposed by the Germans, groups other than the Jewish Councils endeavored to create sustainable living conditions for Jewish communities. Since early 1940, workers' cooperatives and organizations such as the (largely AJJDC-financed) **Jewish Social Self-Help** (Jüdische Soziale Selbsthilfe, or JSS) had cooperated with Jewish Councils to set up workshops for the production of trade goods and thereby a means of subsistence. This took place in a number of towns and cities, from Łódź in the Warthegau and Radom in central Poland to Drohobycz in Galicia. In many instances, workshops used materials that originated from illegal sources, while the resulting products in turn supplied the black market.[43] Still, destitution was rampant: in mid-1940, more than half of the roughly 160,000 residents of the Łódź ghetto had registered as unemployed. In Warsaw alone, the JSS had to assist 160,000 Jews in need.[44]

Warsaw became the setting for a special grassroots initiative that sprang up in response to this new crisis: house committees. These committees were centered in the seemingly more secure inner courtyards (*hoyf*) of the large apartment buildings in the Jewish quarter. As Samuel Kassow suggests, "The house committees quickly became the basis of public life in the Warsaw ghetto," providing communal kitchens, child care, shelter for the sick, and a safe place for social interaction.[45] By April 1940, 778 such committees had been set up in the Jewish quarter of the city; eventually this number would reach 1,518, covering

---

43. Trunk, *Judenrat*, 78–80.

44. Trunk, *Judenrat*, 88; Bauer, *American Jewry and the Holocaust*, 67–73.

45. Samuel D. Kassow, *Who Will Write Our History? Emanuel Ringelblum, the Warsaw Ghetto, and the Oyneg Shabes Archive* (Bloomington: Indiana University Press, 2007), 121.

more than two thousand houses. The committees received contributions from their members as well as from the JSS and other organizations.[46]

An **Aleynhilf** report from 1941 summarized the work of the committees in the first year of the war. It noted their crucial role in providing aid and assistance to the entire Jewish population of Warsaw and conveyed the hope that a united Jewish public could save many people from hunger, pain, and death. The author struck a note reminiscent of prewar social reform movements, stressing that "the residents of each house must remember at all times that they are a cell, a member of a great Jewish family, one part of a whole."[47]

A later, less elevated description of life in an apartment building in Warsaw sought to capture some of the early initiatives of the house committee at Gęsia Street 19, where residents apparently engaged in more modest pursuits as compared to those of other house committees elsewhere in the city.

DOCUMENT 10–7: **[Stefa Szereszewska], "Account of Activities of the House Committee at Gęsia Street 19," Warsaw, April 1942, USHMMA RG 15.079 (ŻIH Ring. I/297), reel 12 (translated from Polish).[48]**

[. . .] Inside, there is a 4-story house that resembles military barracks; 45 tenants, 25 subtenants, housing 138 people. The house is very poor. Street peddlers and vendors, each of them currently lacks not only a workplace but also any opportunity to earn a living. Twenty of the families are refugees who either still live off what is left of their vanishing savings or keep afloat without means to support themselves . . . and there is one financial tycoon, Blajman the baker, or rather Blajman's bakery, which is located in the house.

Generally speaking, the House Committee's year of prosperity was 1940. In 1941 signs of decline were visible, yet it was only in the fall of that year that we entered the period of ruin. [. . .]

The House Committee began its work on a larger scale in the spring of 1940, without betraying significant [. . .][49] in obtaining money and

---

46. Gutman, *The Jews of Warsaw*, 45–47; Friedländer, *Nazi Germany*, 2:148.

47. Jewish Welfare Society (Aleynhilf), The House Committee, report of August 1941, in *To Live with Honor and Die with Honor! Selected Documents from the Warsaw Ghetto Underground Archives "O.S." (Oneg Shabbath)*, ed. Joseph Kermish (Jerusalem: Yad Vashem, 1986), 346.

48. For a slightly differently worded translation, see Kermish, *To Live with Honor*, 148–52.

49. This spot in the text is illegible. Kermish reads "inventiveness."

without organizing social events or card-playing parties (conditions for this were not favorable, even though the winter of 1940–41 was to be, if anything, rather too heavily exploited in this respect). The House Committee fulfilled its mission of providing social care in the best and most upstanding sense of the word. Monthly contributions of approximately 300–400 złoty were collected and benefits were distributed. In terms of local conditions, this was quite a bit, but it was not much in comparison to the "profits" of other house committees. In the summer of 1940, a kitchen operated that provided supplemental meals for twenty children. Housewives took turns cooking at home. The scope of the work was not great, its character was rather "provincial," but at the same time it was marked by great caution and care for one's fellow man [. . .].

Informal networks of trade sprang up alongside more organized efforts to address the dire economic conditions in the ghettos. Individuals participated in shadow economies based on barter, smuggling, embezzlement, and bribery in order to meet their short-term needs. Over time, these activities made some people newly rich and deepened the gulf between the haves and the have-nots. In his diary entries for January 1940, **Emanuel Ringelblum** called attention to "the question of the new-made rich from different cities."[50] He expressed concern about total economic collapse and the resulting dissolution of any sense of Jewish communal feeling. He also noted some details about the types of informal economic activities in which the Jews of Warsaw were engaged.

---

50. Emanuel Ringelblum, *Notes from the Warsaw Ghetto: The Journal of Emmanuel Ringelblum*, ed. Jacob Sloan (New York: Schocken Books, 1974), 12. The first English edition, published in 1958, was based on the selection of Ringelblum's diary entries published in *Bleter far geshikhte* (1948) and the volume published in 1952 by the Jewish Historical Commission in Warsaw. The first full Yiddish edition is Emanuel Ringelblum, *Ksovim fun geto: Togbukh fun Varshever geto* (Warsaw: Farlag yidishe bukh, 1961).

DOCUMENT 10–8: **Emanuel Ringelblum, Warsaw, diary entries for January 1940,** translated from Emanuel Ringelblum, *Ksovim fun geto: Togbukh, 1939–1942* (Tel Aviv: I. L. Peretz, 1985), 65–69.[51]

The economic situation is extremely difficult; there is no basis for a normal economic life. We are cut off from the supplies of raw material which are being shipped elsewhere on a large scale. Jewish merchants from Łódź are bringing certain items from Łódź and then selling them here for three times their value, because in Łódź they still have prewar prices. They have to pay 40 to 50 percent of the merchandise's value to have it transported. The goods are sold by street peddlers and in private homes, behind the doors. All this will probably stop in a month or two, because the merchants are "robbing" their own warehouses in Łódź. The goods are brought out with the help of smugglers, who are carrying them on their backs. [. . .]

Yesterday, on January 5 [1940], an ordinance concerning trading in the street was published. Jewish trading is restricted to streets within the ghetto, beginning with [the following streets:] Krakover Przedmieszcie [Krakowskie Przedmieście], Karowa, Krolewska [Królewska], Sienna, etc. You have to have a special commercial card. The decree limiting the right of Jews to resettle is being interpreted as aimed against Jewish trade, smuggling, and against the migration to Warsaw. Those who apply [for a permit] to resettle to the other side, to the areas closer to Russia, are not subject to these restrictions.

Jewish subsistence was further threatened by forced labor. As with the marking of Jews and the appointment of Jewish Councils, a flurry of decrees beginning in the fall of 1939 transformed forced labor from an early feature of random persecution into a staple item of German anti-Jewish policy. A precedent existed. Many adult male Jews in the Reich had already been used as forced labor during their detention in the concentration camps and, on a larger scale, throughout Germany and Austria since 1938.[52] Jewish groups outside of Poland watched with grave concern when not only men but also women and

---

51. Because the original diary (ŻIH 789; copy in USHMMA RG 15.079M, Ring. I/507/1) has faded and is not readable, we have based the translation of this document on the version published in *Ksovim fun geto.*

52. Wolf Gruner, *Jewish Forced Labor under the Nazis: Economic Needs and Racial Aims, 1938–1944* (New York: Cambridge University Press in association with the USHMM, 2006).

youth became subject to compulsory labor. In early 1940, Hanns Winter, the representative for **Youth Aliyah** in Geneva, was especially alarmed by reports of forced labor in the Generalgouvernement for Jewish children over the age of thirteen. He wrote to **Henrietta Szold** in Jerusalem to discuss possible responses and avenues by which Jewish youth might ultimately be "deployed in Galilee rather than along the San River."

DOCUMENT 10–9: **Letter from Hanns Winter, Jewish Agency for Palestine, Youth Aliyah Section, Geneva, Switzerland, to Henrietta Szold, Jewish Agency, Youth Aliyah Division, Jerusalem, Palestine, February 6, 1940, USHMMA RG 68.045M (WJC Geneva), reel 20, file 147.**

[. . .] Forced labor for children 13 and older!

(With regard to the decree on the introduction of compulsory labor for the Jewish population of the General-Gouvernement for the occupied territories, an implementing provision (the second) has been enacted. It stipulates that all Jewish residents in the area of the General-Gouvernement who are between the ages of 13 and 60 are categorically subject to forced labor. Normally this legal compulsion will remain in effect for a period of two years; the term will be extended in the event that "its educational objective" has not been accomplished within the specified time.)[53]

It is not the purpose of these lines to deal with general issues that arise in this context and to describe what this means for the Jewish population in Poland. Rather, their purpose is to point out the relatively low age limit that has been set, and to ask the relevant bodies to consider and take the

---

53. On December 23, 1939, Himmler's representative in the Generalgouvernement, SS-Obergruppenführer Krüger, issued a decree on "compulsory labor," along Frank's guidelines of October 26. According to this decree, all Jews between the ages of fourteen and sixty in the Generalgouvernement were "on principle, subject to compulsory labor," which "as a rule" would last for two years. The length of a forced labor sentence could be increased "should its educational purpose not be achieved within this period." The regulations also threatened penal servitude of up to ten years for any Jew who evaded forced labor or for *Judenrat* members who helped them in evasion. For the English translation of the decree, see "Compulsory Labor," *Contemporary Jewish Record* 3 (May–June 1940): 316–17. The source of Winter's interpretation (thirteen to sixty years of age, as opposed to fourteen to sixty years appearing in the published decree) is unclear; it is worth mentioning that paragraph 3 of the order, while noting that "for the time being" only male Jews were subject to forced labor (presumably in contrast to the letter of the law, which, in paragraph 1, stipulated that *all* Jews aged between fourteen and sixty were subject to this measure), listed the age of these Jewish males as between twelve and sixty years of age. The editors of the *Contemporary Jewish Record* regarded this as a typographical error and added a "[sic]" in the text.

possible actions, in order to keep youngsters between 13 and 17 from having to spend these years of their youth in Polish swamps, under the supervision of SS men.

I need not describe to you what this commonly means, especially for children and teens in this age group, and what it signifies from an educational standpoint for these young people, precisely in these critical years of their development, to be in this atmosphere and to be forced to spend at least this two-year period—which easily can be extended to who knows how long—together with men up to the age of 60.

I think it is necessary to make every possible effort to rescue and help these youngsters, to the best of our ability, and to the extent now possible. What a blessing it could be for this portion of the Jewish youth and for Eretz Yisrael if these work gangs could be deployed in Galilee rather than along the San River.[54]

Certainly, money and certificates are needed to accomplish that.

But I have no doubt that American Jews, who are linked to the Jews in Poland by so many ties of kinship, will respond to a special appeal concerning this issue, in spite of the great demands now being made of them. I even believe that a large part of the sums required in this situation could be raised through a so-called <u>family members' campaign</u> by relatives of the children in question.

In addition, the situation in Poland, which in this form affects only the Jews there, is so grave that I believe many national and international committees and relief committees, Polish aid programs, etc. will do their part to come to the rescue of those members of the Jewish population whom Palestine can accept, even in these times of war: the children.

The issue of the certificates certainly is an especially difficult matter. Only two days ago, however, I had an opportunity to discuss this with Mr. Moshe Shertok,[55] and I think I can infer from this conversation that at the

---

54. In interwar Poland, the San was located in the south-central part of the country, a tributary of the Vistula River some 270 miles in length. During the Nazi occupation, the San was in the Generalgouvernement. Today, it is in southeastern Poland and western Ukraine.

55. Moshe Shertok (1894–1965), better known as Moshe Sharett, was born in Ukraine and emigrated to Ottoman Palestine at the age of twelve. An Ottoman citizen fluent in Arabic and Turkish, he fought in the Ottoman army in World War I. After studies in Istanbul and London, he joined the **Jewish Agency** in 1933. Until Israel's declaration of independence in 1948, Sharett headed the political department of the Jewish Agency, the post second only to Ben Gurion, who was the chairman of the agency. After 1948 he became a prominent Israeli politician, holding the posts of minister for foreign affairs and prime minister. See Gabriel Sheffer, *Moshe Sharett: Biography of a Political Moderate* (Oxford: Clarendon Press, 1996). For more on the Jewish Agency, see the Glossary.

very least, a final decision on the further emigration of children up to a certain age from the regions in question, in the future as well, has not been made thus far, and that there are still grounds for hope.

If, in the presentation outlined here, I have stayed within the limits of what is possible as far as these two requirements (financing and certificates) are concerned—as I believe I have—then an energetically conducted campaign might really succeed in creating the prerequisites for putting this plan into practice.

Now I will wait for your reaction to this explanation and also for an opinion statement from London, where I am sending a copy of this letter. Where appropriate, I would be willing to offer you additional suggestions about the problems related to this subject, particularly about the conduct of the preliminary work in the relevant region itself. How much happiness and joy we could bring to the youngsters we would rescue from their distress in this way!

With best regards,

Shalom

Hanns Winter

Possibly in response to this plea, the **World Jewish Congress** put together travel subsidies for thirty-five Polish refugee children who were holders of so-called Palestine Certificates.[56]

Szmul Zygielbojm,[57] a **Bundist** leader and one of the original representatives on the Warsaw Jewish Council (before his escape from Poland in

---

56. Letter from Hanns Winter to Dr. Knöpfmacher (WJC Geneva), March 1, 1940; letter, Ch. Barlas, Immigration Department, Jewish Agency for Palestine, Geneva, to Knöpfmacher, March 1, 1940, both in USHMMA RG 68.045M (WJC Geneva), reel 20.

57. Szmul Zygielbojm (1895–1943) was a prominent Polish interwar Bundist. In Warsaw at the outbreak of the war, Zygielbojm was appointed member of the first Warsaw *Judenrat* but soon left, for he disagreed with *Judenrat* policies of compliance with Nazi orders. He left for the United States, where he resumed his work in Bundist circles there. In 1942, he became the Bund's representative in the Polish National Council in London, an advisory body to the Polish government-in-exile. He soon became disillusioned with the apathy of the Polish government-in-exile circles, the British political leadership, and the world at large to the Nazi genocidal policy against the Jews in Europe. Upon hearing news of the destruction of the Warsaw ghetto in the aftermath of the uprising in the spring of 1943, Zygielbojm committed suicide in protest of the world's lack of action to prevent the mass murder of the Jews. Daniel Blatman, "On a Mission against All Odds: Szmuel Zygielbojm in London (April 1942–May 1943)," *YVS* 20 (1990): 237–71; Isabelle Tombs, "'Morituri vos salutant': Szmul Zygielbojm's Suicide in May 1943 and the International Socialist Community in London," *H&GS* 14, no. 2 (2000): 242–65.

December 1939), detailed the efforts of the Warsaw council to intervene and to prevent random kidnappings of Jews for forced labor in the fall of 1939.

DOCUMENT 10–10: Szmul Zygielbojm, "Kidnapping for Labor," no date (ca. December 1939), translated from *Zygielbojm-bukh* (New York: Farlag "Unzer tsayt," 1947), 142–50.[58]

One of the most awful torments overwhelming Jewish life in Poland under the Nazis is kidnapping for labor service. The Germans are seizing young and old in the streets and taking them away to perform the hardest labor. [. . .] Jews are also brutally beaten with regularity and often murdered . . .
     [. . .]
[The morning after Warsaw fell to the Germans, on October 2, 1939,] trucks parked near the places where Jews were standing in long lines waiting to obtain a piece of bread. Nazis in blue uniforms, holding rifles, revolvers, and whips, undertook to cleanse the lines of Jews. Jewish women, young and old, were beaten out of the lines with fists, pulled out by the hair, knocked out with kicks to the stomach. Jewish men were grabbed by the collar, dragged out of the lines and thrown into dark, closed trucks . . .
     That was the beginning. Where the people were being taken, what would happen to them—no one knew. [. . .]
     [Since then] groups of Germans stand on street corners, looking at the faces of passersby. Whoever is a Jew is ordered, "Jew, come here!" When that happens he is already lost, a captive. Often young Polish anti-semites would stand with the Germans and help the Nazis recognize who is a Jew. The decent Poles are angry about this. [. . .]
     I will never forget the faces of some Jews who came to the offices of the Jewish community [*yidishe kehile*] to tell about the horrors. [. . .] One young and strong worker banged his fist against his own face and wailed . . . "Look! I'm being forced to soak myself in blood. I won't survive this! Help, do something, help save me from this, because I'm liable to commit some horrible deed." [. . .] Another man who came was one of the best-known and finest Yiddish actors. His clothes were torn and smeared with mud and blood. His hands were cut and torn from the hard labor he was forced to perform. [. . .]

---

58. This was also published in a slightly different translation in David Engel, *The Holocaust: The Third Reich and the Jews* (New York: Longman, 2000), 105–6.

We [at the Jewish community] could not bear to see the humiliation that Jews were kidnapped from the streets the way dogcatchers catch
dogs. We tried to figure out how to put an end to this. The Warsaw Jewish
Community approached the Gestapo with a proposal: if the German
occupation authorities need people for labor, they should obtain them
in an organized fashion, but the kidnapping of people in the street must
stop. Let the daily quota of Jews required by the Germans be determined,
and the community will provide people.

The Gestapo accepted the proposal on the surface. From that time
(November 1939) the Warsaw Jewish Community did, indeed, provide
two thousand Jews a day for labor service. But the kidnappings of Jews
from the streets did not stop.

When the community protested, the Gestapo replied [. . .] that the
military authorities were the ones doing the kidnapping, and the Gestapo
had no control over them. Nonetheless, the obligation that the Jewish
community took upon itself remained in force: it had to continue providing two thousand workers every day, even though kidnappings from the
street went on anyway.

To eliminate kidnappings, the Warsaw *Judenrat* created a work battalion,
the Batalion Pracy, which supplied a daily quota of one thousand laborers in
November 1939. It would grow to almost nine thousand by August 1940.[59]
Similar regulations were put in place in other ghettos. As historian Saul
Friedländer notes, this sort of arrangement between Jewish Councils and the
German authorities meant that those with means and money could often buy
their way out of forced labor while the poorest segments of the population
got stuck.[60] The less access a person had to material means and positions of
power, the bleaker his or her prospects were in every respect. At the same time,
the bribe money richer Jews paid to avoid work camps made it possible for
the Jewish Councils to provide forced laborers with clothing, blankets, and
other essential items beyond the means of those who needed them most. In the
process, Jewish administrations invariably became intermediaries between the
German occupiers and the Jewish communities. And, indeed, Jews at the bottom of the social spectrum saw these administrations as the prime agents of the
misfortune of the masses.[61]

---

59. Bauer, *American Jewry and the Holocaust*, 72.
60. Friedländer, *Nazi Germany*, 2:42.
61. See Engel, *The Holocaust*, 68.

In addition to providing forced labor in the immediate vicinity of Warsaw, the Warsaw *Judenrat* was forced to send fourteen hundred workers to labor camps in the Lublin district.[62] Reports of terrible conditions filtered through to Warsaw, and the city's *Judenrat* began sending food and blankets. The partially illegible report in document 10–11, from the **Oyneg Shabes** archive, summarized what the *Judenrat* in Warsaw was able to learn about the Józefów forced labor camp, established at the end of 1939 approximately seventeen kilometers from Opole Lubelskie. According to *Pinkas ha-kehilot*, the camp initially dragged Jews from Opole to dig drainage ditches close to the Vistula River but expanded in 1940 with Jews brought in from distant Warsaw and other towns.[63]

DOCUMENT 10–11: Report on the labor camp at Józefów, Generalgouvernement, November 1940, USHMMA RG 15.079M (ŻIH Ring I/3), reel 1 (translated from Polish).

Information on the Józefów Work Camp

[1.] Location: 17 km by road from Opole (arrival in Opole by train [illegible]) or directly to Józefów by boat from Warsaw.

[2.] Population: 667 persons, including 306 Varsovians (as of August 16, 1940).

[3.] Living Conditions:

[illegible] live in 3 buildings:

1. The former synagogue—270 persons

2. The former *beth ha-midrash*[64]—260 persons. The manor house— the rest [. . .] on mats covered with straw (that is not changed) and spread across three stories.

4. Working Conditions: Reveille at 5 o'clock in the morning. The distance from the worksite to the camp is 2 km. Piecework until 3–4 o'clock in the afternoon. One extremely difficult type of work: regulation of the river and the construction of a protective embankment. Some of the teams work in ankle-deep water.

---

62. Bauer, *American Jewry and the Holocaust*, 72.

63. Entry on Józefów in *Pinkas ha-kehilot, Polin: Encyclopedia of Jewish Communities, Poland* (Jerusalem: Yad Vashem, 1999), 7:256–58.

64. A *beit midrash* (pl. *batei midrash*, "house of study" or "house of interpretation" in Hebrew) is a hall for the study of traditional texts in Judaism. It is distinct from a synagogue, although many synagogues have *batei midrash*, and sometimes the terms are used interchangeably.

5. <u>Hygienic Conditions</u>: There is no water for washing on-site; it is delivered by water cart. There is no dining room. People sleep in their boots and in dirty, louse-infected, stinking rags. A sick ward is lacking.

6. <u>Sustenance</u>: For breakfast unsweetened black coffee, 400–500 grams of bread (on November 1, bread rations were reduced to 200 grams daily); for lunch about one liter of soup (porridge, potatoes); for dinner unsweetened coffee.

7. <u>Wages</u>: Wages were supposed to be regulated in the following manner: no wages were to be paid for the first two weeks; after two weeks 100 persons were each to receive 1.50 złoty daily (the best workers and the officials), half of those remaining were each to receive 50 groszy daily, and the rest nothing. But as workers' accounts indicate, they received almost no payment whatsoever for their work.

8. <u>General Conditions</u>: Clothing in very bad condition; more than 100 persons lack boots. Dirty, ragged, emaciated, malnourished. It is teeming with lice and insects; many have a fever. Instances of flight are growing.[65]

9. <u>Aid from Local Authorities</u>[66]: A permanent delegate and a doctor from the local authorities are on site. Aid in sustenance (500 grams of bread every other day, 75 kilograms of meat twice a week for the preparation of soup), the distribution of various items (blankets, pants, shirts, undergarments, etc.)

10. <u>Return</u>: Aside from individuals returning on medical grounds, the return of 120 persons on November 23 was noted and the return of the rest at the start of December. Several deaths were noted, both at the camp and after returning from the camp (in the hospital).

Reports from the forced labor camps confirmed that the actual intent of the German authorities was not "education," as stated by Frank and reported abroad, but ruthless, if not murderous exploitation. The continued abuse increased despair in the Jewish population, already angered by the seemingly conciliatory position of the Jewish Council. For its part, the council waged an ongoing struggle to reconcile the conflicting demands of supplying labor for the Nazis with working to ameliorate conditions for its own constituents. Was there a way to appeal to "the authorities" with rational economic arguments? In the early fall of 1940, an unknown AJJDC official drafted a memo along those

---

65. It remains unclear to where the escapees fled.

66. The use of the Polish term *gmina* suggests that local Polish authorities provided aid, although additional details are unavailable.

lines. This Jewish relief official made a case for the value of moving from the precarious "state of temporariness" (*Zustand der Vorläufigkeit*), with its disastrous effects for the Jews in the Generalgouvernement, to more viable, even humane conditions.

DOCUMENT 10–12: Draft memo by JDC (Warsaw or Kraków office) on the state of Jewish affairs in the Generalgouvernement, no date (probably early fall 1940), USHMMA Acc. 1999.0154 (ŻIH 210/5) (translated from German).[67]

Introduction

The previous directives of the authorities regarding Jewish affairs are conspicuously negative in nature. There is no realm of life and of social, economic, or cultural activity in which the Jews have not been subjected to severe restrictions, and quite frequently they are faced with the complete paralysis of their functioning in one area or another. Even where the regulations of the authorities represent a positive decision, the foundations for real activity over the long term are lacking. As an example, we will cite the instituting of representation of the Jewish population in the form of the Jewish Councils. A large sphere of influence passed to these institutions in terms of organizing forced labor, welfare work, and public health; however, there is no basis at all for this activity in the form of subsidies or donations for these purposes, which are of a general social nature. Jewish society, which is impoverished and continues to deteriorate, cannot raise sufficient means for these purposes, of course. That applies also to the Jewish philanthropic institutions, which, though they are tolerated, cannot keep up with the profusion of their responsibilities on their own.

In short: in the realm of Jewish life, there is an absence of real, positive directives. But no population segment can base its life merely on restrictions, merely on prohibitions and on commands that burden people with taxes and personal services. The life of every social group must have firm foundations, such as the possibility of retaining a residence and pursuing a gainful occupation in a place that is favorable for this work, as well as a certain freedom of movement, etc. Without these basics, the given social group is deprived of the potential for economic reproduction; it has no significance as a producer and as a consumer; it is unable to feed itself

---

67. The German used by the unknown document author is neither good nor graceful; in addition, he uses many terms drawn directly or indirectly from Marxist economics (e.g., "economic reproduction").

and perform social services. The state for the time being, which is based on the consumption of what remains of meager supplies, which is linked with the constant degradation of the already low standard of living, cannot be maintained in the long run without bringing this segment of the population to the point of obliteration.

Therefore it is imperative to take steps that would <u>make possible a renewed integration of the Jewish population into productive economic processes and the restoration of the Jews' capacity for economic reproduction and adaptability</u>. It must be noted that even the discontinuation of the current prohibitions in and of itself will not be enough to bring about the result mentioned above in the form of the Jews' capacity for economic reproduction. For that to happen, positive steps must be taken, steps that aim at the <u>economic restoration of this population.</u> In addition, there is the fact that the Jewish population absolutely does not desire the restoration of its former economic structure. The watchwords of social restructuring[68] have long since found a lively response in Jewish society, particularly in view of the proliferation of small, insubstantial workshops and enterprises in the trades and in commerce, and in view of the moderate encumbrance with an economically passive element.

Thus there is a pressing need to implement an economic redevelopment program linked with achieving productivity and social restructuring. Simultaneously, hand in hand with this program, there must be a <u>rebuilding of social welfare</u>, or more precisely, a guarantee of the foundations of its activity, which it lacks at present. Entry into <u>cultural, instructional, and educational work</u> must also be made possible.

---

68. In German the word is *Umschichtung* (literally, "relayering"). "Restructuring" or "productivization" had been the catchwords of the Zionist movement since its inception. Envisioning a new, Palestine-based Hebrew culture that dispensed with the alleged Jewish pathologies of centuries of Diaspora life, the Zionists insisted that the path to normalcy involved economic restructuring and productivization. In other words, according to the Zionists, to become a normal nation, Jews needed to change their economic structure, which for historical reasons had been skewed toward trade, banking, and the free professions but remained devoid of "productive" professions, such as farming, industry, artisanal production, and the like. At the same time, the Zionists were sensitive to the fact that Jewish overrepresentation in "nonproductive" professions fueled antisemitic prejudice. This document is thus very interesting in its echoing of Zionist rhetoric and its insistence that the Germans should understand that "the Jewish population does not desire the restoration of its former economic structure." For a case study in productivization, see Israel Oppenheim, *The Struggle of Jewish Youth for Productivization: The Zionist Youth Movement in Poland* (Boulder, CO: East European Monographs, 1989).

Now—against the backdrop of the present situation in every area—we want to consider the postulates that result from the <u>constructive solution of the Jewish problem.</u>

<u>Economic and Demographic Matters</u>

It is a notoriously well-known fact that despite the outflow of a certain part of the Jewish population toward the east, factors that favored an <u>increased concentration of the Jewish population in the territory of the Generalgouvernement</u> were predominant. It was in that direction that the resettlement directives of the German authorities exerted their influence, particularly the expulsions of the Jews from the regions annexed by the Reich, especially from the former Łódź *województwo*, part of the Kraków *województwo*, the Dąbrowa coal region, and the western provinces. Also operative here, besides the forced expulsions, were voluntary migrations out of fear that the situation in the regions annexed by the Reich would deteriorate.

This fact, therefore, resulted in an increase in the Jewish population in the territory of the Generalgouvernement, which was further intensified by the return of a certain number of refugees from the east. An additional consequence of this fact was the concentration of the population in isolated urban settlements, reinforced by the last expulsions, now within the scope of the Generalgouvernement (Kraków, among others). The expulsions are causing destruction of the centers of productive work and of previous forms of social welfare, as well as blockage of previous means of livelihood. This only leads to a further increase in pauperization, due to the immediate and indirect consequences of the war, and to a surplus of a passive element that has been deprived of the potential to earn a living.

Thus it is to be expected that the return to economic productivity of the Jewish population, especially of recent newcomers, will frequently require resettlement. This is all the more necessary as some Jewish centers are unable to provide for the upkeep of the expellees. This resettlement operation, however, is possible only subject to the provision of employment opportunities or retraining and maintenance in other localities, subject to the provision of centers of work that would ensure the expellees and their families a livelihood, and subject to housing resources.

Although the present placement of the Jewish population is not in accordance with possibilities for employment and even for sustenance, the previous forms of resettlement further exacerbate this situation. Therefore, fundamental requirements for improvement of the circumstances are: <u>a</u>

complete break with the method of forcible expulsions of the Jewish population; repeal of the artificial restrictions placed on settlement in individual localities; a break with the method of creating closed ghetto quarters
whose artificial separation condemns the local population to compulsory
unproductiveness.

Instead of the previous expulsion practices, it is necessary to consider,
arrange for, and implement the following two items:

Repatriation of part of the population influx to a place where an
opportunity exists in terms of chances to find work or sources of livelihood (payments from ventures and assets that are under temporary
administration).

Settlement in regions that guarantee the possibility of employment
for craftsmen or workers or in regions where new centers of production
for craftsmen and farm laborers come into being.

We do not know whether this proposal was ever considered within the
AJJDC or by any other Jewish organization to pass along to German authorities. Regardless, the memo attests to the author's firmly held belief, shared by
many other Jews one year after the German conquest of Poland, that as bleak
as things might have appeared at the time, there was some reason to hope for a
brighter future. By means of negotiation, bribery, rational argumentation, and
greater efficiency, Polish Jews in councils and relief organizations, as well as at
the grassroots level, worked to improve their living conditions and adapt to the
new wartime regime.

CHAPTER 11

FORMAL AND INFORMAL LEADERSHIP

B Y THE END of 1940, Jewish life in German-controlled Poland had been walled in. All interactions with the outside world were restricted to official contacts, funneled through Jewish Councils. To be sure, the structure that the Nazis imposed on communities positioned the *Judenräte* at their center. These bodies had not been elected by the people they represented. They had no power to change the overall German course of action. They did not possess sufficient resources to improve deteriorating living conditions, much less to level the acute inequality between the upper and lower strata of the community—and some were not even invested in trying. Still, despite their problematic genesis, the councils did at times try to push beyond their designated purpose by seeking redress from the Germans, by circumventing or otherwise diluting the effect of German orders, and by appealing to other Jewish bodies for solidarity and help.

The personalities, interests, and abilities of individual Jewish leaders mattered a great deal, as did other factors. In Łódź, for example, Jewish Council head **Mordechai Chaim Rumkowski** managed to monopolize most ghetto functions by the end of 1940, either personally or through an elaborate system of offices and agencies. In Warsaw, by contrast, the *Judenrat* under **Adam Czerniaków** continued to coexist with a wide range of Jewish communal groups, including house committees, political groups, and youth associations such as **Left Poalei Zion**, the **Bund**, and **Hehalutz**. The composition of the Jewish community in each city, town, or village played an equally important role. Towns in Poland differed tremendously in terms of the social, political, and religious stratification of the Jewish community; the existence of alternative leadership structures, including political groups and youth movements; the number of refugees that had appeared in the aftermath of the German invasion; and relations with Polish society as a whole. Many other material factors shaped the quality of Jewish life under Nazi rule: the quality of housing, available space and resources, the permeability of boundaries, public health issues, and, of course, the intensity of German terror and level of German interference. Throughout German-dominated Poland—in the annexed territory and in the **Generalgouvernement**—a multitude of interconnected factors shaped the nature of Jewish leadership and governance. As we shall see, as early as this first year and a half of the war, when Jews still hoped for stabilization and improvement of their situation under German authority in the future, the impediments to solidarity within individual Jewish communities and across Poland were already substantial.

INTERCEDING WITH GERMAN AUTHORITIES

As their living conditions deteriorated in Polish cities and towns, Jews became more willing to confront their overlords. With its nearly half million Jews facing a massive humanitarian crisis, the *Judenrat* in Warsaw did not waste time in approaching the German authorities. In November 1939, through a series of bribes, as well as by taking advantage of an internal conflict between the **Wehrmacht**, **Gestapo**, and SS, Adam Czerniaków and his council colleagues managed to stave off the creation of the ghetto and thus prevent the further deterioration of conditions for the city's Jewish population. This success led the Warsaw Jewish leadership to believe, as Yisrael Gutman put it, "that discord between the various German authorities could be exploited."[1] Their success proved short-lived. The Germans had not abandoned the idea of creating a ghetto in Warsaw, and on March 27, 1940, they ordered the *Judenrat* to build a wall around the Jewish residential area. German authorities told the Jews that the walls were intended to protect them from possible Polish violence, while the Poles were told that a ghetto would protect them from typhus emanating

---

1. Yisrael Gutman, *The Jews of Warsaw, 1939–1943: Ghetto, Underground, Revolt* (Bloomington: Indiana University Press, 1982), 50; Isaiah Trunk, *Judenrat: The Jewish Councils in Eastern Europe under Nazi Occupation* (New York: Macmillan, 1972), 389–94.

from the Jewish area.[2] Such rational arguments overlay a policy driven by a mix of ideology, self-interest, and improvisation. The Warsaw Jewish Council tried to refute the logic presented by such arguments with similar reasoning. In the appeal presented in document 11–1, written in German apparently for a readership of German officials, the council tried to explain that epidemics resulted not from Jewish customs but from the inhumane conditions Jews had been forced to endure.

DOCUMENT 11–1: **Warsaw Jewish Council, "Memorandum on the Causes of Typhus in Warsaw and Proposals for Combating It," May 1940, USHMMA RG 15.079M (ŻIH Ring I/85), reel 7 (translated from German).**

[. . .] Epidemic Typhus and the Jews in Warsaw

Following the general observations above, the issue of "Epidemic Typhus and the Jews in Warsaw" will be dealt with now in greater detail.

It must be pointed out emphatically that before the present war, the position of the Warsaw Jews with respect to health was in no way inferior to that of the city's non-Jewish population. This is confirmed by a comparison of the mortality rate for Jews in the past decade with that of the non-Jewish population. According to official materials for the years January 1, 1931, to June 25, 1939, the mortality rate for Jews was even lower than for non-Jews. In fact, in that eight-year period in Warsaw, 990 of every 100,000 Jews died, while the comparable figure for non-Jews was 1,167. Thus the mortality rate of Jews was 85 percent of the rate for non-Jews. The causes of death reveal several differences between the Jewish and the non-Jewish populations. Among the Jews, a relatively larger number died of diabetes, kidney disease, respiratory diseases, and heart disease, while a smaller number died of tuberculosis, syphilis, and enterocolitis (the latter affects children), and there was not a single death due to alcohol poisoning. As for typhus (abdominal typhus and epidemic typhus), the Warsaw

---

2. German officials often invoked medical and hygienic pretexts to justify the radicalization of their anti-Jewish policies. In December 1939, for example, Eduard Könekamp, sent by the German Foreign Institute to observe the resettlement operations in occupied Poland, wrote in his report, "[The ghettos] are just about the filthiest places you can imagine. [. . .] The hygienic and moral conditions are simply appalling. [. . .] Exterminating these subhumans would be in the best interests of the whole world." Quoted in Götz Aly and Susanne Heim, *Architects of Annihilation: Auschwitz and the Logic of Destruction* (London: Weidenfeld & Nicolson, 2002), 127.

Jews are less [*sic*] susceptible than the non-Jews: the mortality rate from typhus was 12 per 1,000 deaths for Jews, in comparison with 9 per 1,000 for non-Jews.[3] Of 1,000,000 inhabitants, 12 Jews and only 10 non-Jews die each year of typhus. In the rank order of causes of death, typhus holds [24th place ?] among Jews and 20th place among non-Jews. The figures cited above indicate that before the war, as previously mentioned, the Jews were no worse off than the non-Jewish population with regard to health, but they were indeed more susceptible to certain diseases and, moreover, exhibited a certain susceptibility to typhus.

During the last six months, an enormous increase in the mortality rate appeared among the Jews of Warsaw, due primarily to pandemic diseases (abdominal typhus in the past two months). From November 1, 1938, to March 1, 1939, 1,712 Jews died in Warsaw, while in the same period of 1939–1940, 5,155 Jews died. In the non-Jewish population, too, a rise in the mortality rate is to be noted, but to a less alarming extent. These prewar conditions have undergone a great change in the last months, and the pandemic diseases among the Jewish population have had devastating effects; the causes of this phenomenon, however, are to be sought not in Jewish customs but exclusively in the living conditions of the Jewish population in Warsaw.

The primary emphasis must be placed on the overcrowding in Jewish homes, which is a consequence of the destruction caused by the war, but second to that in importance is the great influx of evacuees and refugees. As is well-known, a large number of Jewish apartments fell victim to acts of war. The homeless, many of whom had lost all their belongings, sought refuge with relatives and friends: that is to say, in already crowded apartments. Then came the flood of evacuees and refugees seeking accommodations in the Jewish areas, which again were already densely populated. Their number should total at least [60,000 ?]. The vast majority of these people were unable to bring with them essential articles of personal use. Moreover, the migrations of the evacuees and refugees took place in circumstances that were in no way apt to enhance the sanitary condition

---

3. The numbers the author cites show that Jews were indeed more, not less, susceptible to typhus than non-Jews (twelve per one thousand deaths for Jews, as opposed to nine per one thousand for non-Jews); since this fact is part of the larger point that the author is making— that "before the war [. . .] the Jews were no worse off than the non-Jewish population with regard to health, but they were indeed more susceptible to certain diseases and, moreover, exhibited a certain susceptibility to typhus"—the "less" in this sentence is apparently an error and should read "more."

of these people. While evacuees and refugees of other nationalities could find accommodations in the countryside and the entire urban population remained at the prewar level, the Jews had to go to the [illegible] towns. This led to overcrowding of the neighborhoods inhabited by Jews and created [illegible] [. . .]

Now, in addition, there is the lowered resistance of the Jewish population, which worsens daily and is a result of malnutrition and the shortage of [illegible]. The impoverished Jewish population eats poorly, and a great many Jews literally are suffering from hunger. The repeated instances of fainting due to malnutrition—recorded by the Immunization Office—offer evidence of this. The Jewish welfare organizations, which have banded together to form a Coordinating Committee, tried to remedy this malady. In the period from October 1, 1939, to February 29, 1940, about 4,750,000 bowls of soup were distributed to adults and about 1,300,000 to children. On March 1, the number of bowls of soup distributed daily to adults reached 67,357, while children received 16,890 bowls. To assess this effort correctly, one need only compare it with welfare activity in the 1914–1918 war years in Warsaw. The Citizens Committee of the City of Warsaw, which looked after the entire population regardless of religious affiliation, distributed 4.2 million bowls of soup in the last five months of 1915: that is, only two-thirds of what the Jewish public soup kitchens achieved in the same length of time.

The activity of the Jewish social welfare groups, which required the expenditure of considerable effort and resources, is certainly saving people from death by starvation but is unable to prevent the impending consequences of long-term malnutrition. The management of the public soup kitchens determined beyond a doubt that although the caloric content of the soups is decreasing continuously, these soups nonetheless are the only hot food the people assisted get during the day. The saddest thing, however, is that the number of bowls of soup distributed lags far behind the actual demand. Right now, about 50,000 adults and about 20,000 children are knocking at the doors of the soup kitchens in vain, and the number of those waiting is constantly growing. The lack of funds, as well as the [illegible] distribution of the currencies subject to a quota, completely rules out the opening of new soup kitchens or expansion of the existing ones for the time being.

The Jews are also at a disadvantage in terms of the distribution of foodstuffs on the basis of food ration cards in Warsaw. As of February, food ration cards were introduced in Warsaw in different colors for the

Jewish and the non-Jewish populations. After that time and until May 14, the Jews received only bread, while the non-Jews also were given a roll every other day and an additional 250 grams of bread each week. As of May 14, Jews receive only 1,000 grams per week, and non-Jews, 1,750 grams. More coupons from the food ration card were distributed among non-Jews than among Jews. No wonder the epidemics claimed their victims precisely among the undernourished Jewish population, for countless numbers of homeless people and evacuees were by no means equipped with underwear and clothing for the extremely harsh winter, and the clothing assistance service of the social welfare groups could help only a tiny percentage of those in need.

From the foregoing it is quite clear that the epidemics among the Jews are a consequence of overcrowded residences, destitution, and lack of a way to earn a living. Mere regulatory actions, therefore, will do nothing to enhance the state of health of the Jewish population and eliminate the danger of epidemics. Similarly, a mechanical closing off of the neighborhoods where Jews live will do little to protect the rest of the population against the threat of epidemics. The typhus bacilli will not be deterred by warning signs and barbed wire. The surest means of combating the epidemics are as follows: provide a halfway adequate diet and at least humble clothing; rebuild the dwellings destroyed by the war; and reintegrate the Jewish population into active working life. [. . .]

Despite the Warsaw Jewish Council's well-reasoned explanations that an impoverished Jewish population imprisoned behind walls and barbed wire would not be able to cope with disease (and that typhus did not discriminate between Jews and non-Jews), its efforts to prevent the creation of the ghetto failed. Making matters worse, on April 13, 1940, Czerniaków noted in his diary that the Jews of Warsaw had been ordered to pay to build their own ghetto walls.[4] Twenty sections of the wall were completed by the beginning of June 1940; two months later, Warsaw had been divided into three sections for Germans, Poles, and Jews, each with starkly different living conditions. Finally, on November 15, 1940, the Warsaw ghetto was sealed.[5]

The creation and sealing of ghettos in the parts of Poland ruled by the Germans was not a foregone conclusion; indeed, in the months following the

---

4. Raul Hilberg, Stanislaw Staron, and Josef Kermisz, eds., *The Warsaw Diary of Adam Czerniakow: Prelude to Doom* (New York: Stein and Day, 1979), 140.

5. Gutman, *The Jews of Warsaw*, 51.

end of the military campaign, some Jewish leaders dared to plan for a different future. In the city of Oświęcim (German: Auschwitz), located in the region of East Upper Silesia that was incorporated into the German Reich, the recently appointed local Jewish Council tried to make use of the seeming advantages of being located within the newly drawn German borders.[6] In November 1939, its chairman, Leo Schönker, a well-known local businessman and former owner of a fertilizer plant,[7] traveled to Berlin with other council members to request relief assistance from the Berlin Jewish Community and the **Reichsvereinigung der Juden in Deutschland**. There they found that the central organization for the remaining Jews in Germany had, as Schönker put it in a letter to the **American Jewish Joint Distribution Committee** (AJJDC) office in Amsterdam, "only words for us and no concrete help."[8] Much as the Jewish leaders in the Reich would have liked to help their fellow Jews from Oświęcim, they had to comply with the demands of **Reinhard Heydrich**'s Security Police, which kept a firm grip on the budget of the remaining Jewish organizations in Germany.

As revealed by documents in the first volume of this series,[9] Heydrich's men radically transformed German Jewish organizational life in the wake of "*Kristallnacht.*" They sought to ensure compliance with their demands and to guarantee that Jews would flee the country (in line with the dominant policy of enforced emigration). Consequently, **Leo Baeck** and the other leaders of the Reichsvereinigung had been forced into a role that resembled that of the Jewish Councils in German-dominated Poland, with the difference that they represented a central body for all Germany and that no local *Judenräte* or ghet-

---

6. It should be noted that the reference to Auschwitz deals with the city, not the camp located near Oświęcim or Auschwitz. During the period covered in this volume, the Auschwitz camp first housed Polish POWs and in the spring of 1940 was taken over by Himmler's SS as a concentration camp. It had barely evolved, to borrow a phrase from Raul Hilberg, as "a site in search of a mission." See Debórah Dwork and Robert Jan van Pelt, *Auschwitz: 1270 to the Present* (New York: W. W. Norton, 1996), and Sybille Steinbacher, *Auschwitz: A History* (New York: Ecco, 2005).

7. See his postwar account in Józef Schönker (aka Schenker), "The Jewish Shtetl: The Beginning of the Shoa," in *The Book of Oshpitsin: Oświęcim-Auschwitz*, ed. Chaim Volnerman, Aviezer Burstein, and Meir Shimon Gashuri (Jerusalem: Oshpitsin Society, 1977), 161–65 (Hebrew), as referred to in Steinbacher, *"Musterstadt" Auschwitz* (Munich: K. G. Suar, 2000), 47f., 165f.

8. Ältestenrat der Juden in Auschwitz to AJDC Amsterdam, January 4, 1940, facsimile reprinted in *Archives of the Holocaust: An International Collection of Selected Documents*, ed. Henry Friedlander and Sybil Milton (New York: Garland Publishing, 1995), 10/2:649–51.

9. Jürgen Matthäus and Mark Roseman, *Jewish Responses to Persecution*, vol. 1: *1933– 1938* (Lanham, MD: AltaMira Press in association with the USHMM, 2010), 273–74.

tos existed in the Reich proper.[10] By the time of Schönker's visit to Berlin, the consultations of Reichsvereinigung officials with the Gestapo had deteriorated to such an extent that distinguished Jewish leaders were receiving orders from increasingly junior SS officials. In a letter that Baeck sent shortly after the start of the war to a colleague who had emigrated to the United States, he confided, "We are immersed in work which again and again shows a different face, sometimes rather Medusa-like. But we try to achieve what we can and to give people the feeling that everything that's possible is being done."[11]

While in Berlin, Schönker took a bold step: he wrote a letter to SS-Untersturmführer (Lieutenant) Kurt Lischka, one of the Gestapo officers in charge of the so-called **Reichszentrale für Jüdische Auswanderung** (Reich Central Office for Jewish Emigration), requesting Gestapo-controlled funds to concentrate Silesian Jews in the city of Oświęcim. This constituted a first step in a highly ambitious emigration scheme involving the AJJDC, the **Jewish Agency**, and American Jews with relatives in Silesia. Financial transactions would be routed through Amsterdam, Auschwitz, and the German national bank (Reichsbank). In writing to Gestapo officer Lischka, Schönker tried to appeal as closely as possible to the prevailing German interest—that Jews should get out of the Reich while paying for it themselves—and to what he must have perceived as the German preference for orderliness and planning over chaos and improvisation. He even inquired about the location of the widely rumored German plans for a "Jewish reservation," intended for all Jews under German domination.

---

10. See Beate Meyer, "Between Self-Assertion and Forced Collaboration: The Reich Association of Jews in Germany, 1939–1945," in *Jewish Life in Nazi Germany: Dilemmas and Responses*, ed. Francis R. Nicosia and David Scrase (New York: Berghahn Books, 2010), 149–69. Ghettos existed in the Polish territories annexed to the Reich but not within Germany's prewar borders. Concentration of Jews in Germany proper did take place during the war in many cities, especially in the form of forcing local Jews out of their dwellings into local "Jew houses" (*Judenhäuser*) and in the final stages of preparation for deportation to "the East." See Wolfgang Benz, *A Concise History of the Third Reich* (Berkeley: University of California Press, 2006), 219–20; "Judenhäuser in Germany," in *The Yad Vashem Encyclopedia of the Ghettos during the Holocaust*, ed. Guy Miron and Shlomit Shulhani (Jerusalem: Yad Vashem, 2009), 2: 999–1001.

11. Leo Baeck, Berlin, to Friedrich Brodnitz, New York City, September 12, 1939, printed in Jürgen Matthäus, "'You have the right to be hopeful if you do your duty': Nine Letters by Leo Baeck to Friedrich Brodnitz, 1937–1941," *LBIYB* 54 (2009): 333–55.

DOCUMENT 11-2: **Letter by Leo Schönker, chairman of the Jewish Council in Auschwitz, to Berlin Gestapo office, November 30, 1939, facsimile reprinted in** *Archives of the Holocaust,* **ed. Henry Friedlander and Sybil Milton (New York: Garland Publishing, 1995), 10/2:652–53.**

Translation[12]

Leo Schönker

Chairman of the Aeltestenrat

der Juden in Auschwitz,

at present Berlin W 15, Meinekestr. 16,

Pension Chilcott

To the Secret Police,

Att. Mr. Lischka (Member of the Government-board)[13]

Berlin.

Dear Sirs,

As leader of the delegation of district-Aeltestenraete, who came to Berlin to enable the direct emigration of the Jews of the occupied territory of Silecia [Silesia], I herewith enclose a confirmation issued by the commander of the troops who occupied our districts (VI/Dinafü/ dated October 23, 1939) stating that I am appointed as such. Our visit to Berlin has been approved by the Secret [State] Police at Bielitz, in order to enable us to contact the competent authorities in Berlin. I herewith request an audience with the competent authority to discuss the problem.

1. To enable the concentration of all Jews who will probably have to leave Silesia we propose an orderly provisional resettlement at Auschwitz (occupied territory) which place counts already 8,000 Jews and which after thorough examination could absorb 18–20,000 Jews. Hospitals, old-age homes and other social institutions have formerly been established at that place. The concentration of all Jews from Silesia in Auschwitz requires a support of about RM [Reichsmark] 200,000. The Reichsvereinigung der Juden in Deutschland together with the Berlin Jewish Community shall be permitted [by the Gestapo] to give us this amount.

2. With regard to the resettlement of the Jews an exact control of decrease and increase is necessary to enable quick emigration.

3. The emigration will be financed by Jews in America whose relatives are still living in the occupied territory. The money will have to be

---

12. The translation, presumably from German, was in all likelihood solicited by the AJJDC in January 1940. Obvious errors have been corrected here, but the stylistic peculiarities of the translation have been retained. The original German letter is no longer available.

13. This is most likely an incorrect translation of the title *Regierungsrat.*

deposited with a bank in Amsterdam on behalf of relatives living in the occupied territory.

4. Besides [in addition], a second emigration cassa [fund] shall be established in Auschwitz to which emigration charges in our own currency are to be paid, and which also will receive the equivalent of blocked Reichsmark and Zloty accounts which have been sold in foreign countries and which so have been released.

In return for release of the blocked accounts the German Reichsbank will participate in the foreign currency which we will receive for a certain percentage still to be determined. The equivalent of foreign currency deposited at Amsterdam will be paid to the relatives living in the occupied territory, at a rate which depends whether [depending on whether] the amount originates from blocked Mark-accounts or Zloty-accounts, for support by the emigration cassa at Auschwitz.

5. The payment of boat tickets, transport charges etc. will be made by the bank at Amsterdam.

With the great number of our Jewish Landsmannschaften [regional community organizations] in America and with the support of the American Joint Distribution Committee whose Amsterdam representative should have to come here to discuss the whole problem, the immediate organization of this plan would be possible, and both the balance of foreign currency of the German Reichsbank as well as the balance of foreign currency at Amsterdam would increase rapidly.

The Polish Jews in the occupied territory represent immense possibilities. The Polish Government used to collect large amounts in foreign currency here. No other organization than we from the occupied Polish territory approach our relatives in America without creating suspicion. It is therefore necessary to establish a central representation of the Jews living in the occupied territory, based on the same norms as those of the Reichsvereinigung der Juden in Deutschland.

6. The emigration can take place by making use of the Palestine certificates which as a result of the war could not be used, and would go via Trieste, for which purpose a personal discussion with Dr. Scheps, leader of the Jewish Agency in Geneva, is necessary.[14] Further there is a possibility

---

14. Samuel Scheps (1904–1999) was a Polish Zionist leader and head of the Jewish Agency office in Basel (1933–1939) and Geneva (1939–1945). After the war, he stayed in Switzerland, where he represented Israeli companies and businesses. Dina Porat, *The Blue and the Yellow Stars of David: The Zionist Leadership in Palestine and the Holocaust, 1939–1945* (Cambridge, MA: Harvard University Press, 1990), 316–17.

via Sulina (Danube).[15] Besides there are other emigration possibilities to overseas countries.

7. If it is already possible to give an explanation of the territory to be reserved only for Jews, concerning extension and its legal status, we request to grant this audience so that we may be able to explain the whole situation on our return.

Berlin, November 30, 1939

Schönker and his colleagues did not achieve anything from their overtures to the Gestapo in the Reich's capital city. Moreover, in their absence, the Oświęcim synagogue that had escaped damage during the military campaign was burned down by the same Gestapo office in Bielitz that had authorized the Oświęcim *Judenrat*'s trip to Berlin. Prior to destroying the synagogue, the Gestapo ordered the Oświęcim Jewish Community to remove the relics. And less than a month later, in December 1939, Schönker was forced from his position as council head.[16]

Although German functionaries ignored Schönker's proposal, they soon developed their own means of exploiting the economic value of Silesian Jews. The idea floated by Schönker of a somewhat more centralized system of Jewish organizations modeled on the Reichsvereinigung found favor with the Germans in the region. While the Germans made no attempt to establish a central organization for all Jews in Poland, in early 1940 they did appoint **Moshe Merin** head of a regional Jewish Council for East Upper Silesia, which comprised more than thirty communities, with roughly one hundred thousand Jews.[17] In late October 1940, **Heinrich Himmler** ordered an SS commander to establish a system of Jewish forced labor camps in the region ("Organisation Schmelt").[18] These decisions resulted from internal delibera-

15. Sulina is a Black Sea port town in the Danube delta in Romania. During this time, it served as an important stop for ships ferrying Jewish refugees along the Danube from central Europe to Romania and on to Palestine, as part of *Aliyah Bet*. See Dalia Ofer, *Escaping the Holocaust: Illegal Immigration to the Land of Israel, 1939–1944* (New York: Oxford University Press, 1990).

16. Sybille Steinbacher, *"Musterstadt" Auschwitz*, 165–66.

17. Trunk, *Judenrat*, 36–37; Philip Friedman, "The Messianic Complex of a Nazi Collaborator in a Ghetto: Moses Merin of Sosnowiec," in his *Roads to Extinction: Essays on the Holocaust*, ed. Ada June Friedman (New York: Conference on Jewish Social Studies and the Jewish Publication Society, 1980), 353–64.

18. Wolf Gruner, *Jewish Forced Labor under the Nazis: Economic Needs and Racial Aims, 1938–1944* (New York: Cambridge University Press in association with the USHMM, 2006), 214–20; Steinbacher, *"Musterstadt" Auschwitz*, 138–53.

tions or improvisations, however poorly synchronized. They certainly did not stem from Jewish initiatives. Schönker's letter nonetheless highlights the proactive resolve and willingness of local Jewish leaders to take risks at a time of rapid change.[19]

Jewish leaders dared to approach local authorities at a number of junctures. In the process, they attempted to exploit weaknesses in the sometimes chaotic German administrative structure without apparent disobedience. The letter presented in document 11–3 from the administrators of the Jewish old-age home in Falenica[20] to the AJJDC office in Warsaw triggered a chain reaction. They sought to annul an evacuation notice received from the local Jewish Council (on order of the German authorities).

DOCUMENT 11–3: **Letter by the administration of the old-age home Ezra in Falenica near Warsaw to the AJJDC office in Warsaw, March 5, 1940, USHMMA Acc. 1999.A.0154 (ŻIH 210/34), 28 (translated from German).**

Administration of the "Ezra"   Warsaw, March 5, 1940
Old People's Home in Falenica
6 Marshal Pilsudski Str.
To
      The JOINT DISTRIBUTION COMMITTEE
      in Warsaw
      On February 16 of this year, we received from the Jewish Council in Falenica the news that our old people's home must be vacated by March 1 of this year. On February 19, we received from the same Jewish Council another letter saying that the eviction deadline had been postponed to April 1 of this year.

---

19. The emigration cum financing plan Schönker proposed was similar to the scheme still being discussed at this time on a much higher level between Intergovernmental Commission head George Rublee and German representatives; see chapter 2, note 8; Debórah Dwork and Robert Jan van Pelt, *Flight from the Reich: Refugee Jews, 1933–1946* (New York: W. W. Norton, 2009), 98–102; and Saul Friedländer, *Nazi Germany and the Jews:* (vol. 1) *The Years of Persecution, 1933–1939* (New York: HarperCollins, 1997), 314–16.

20. Falenica, today part of the Warsaw municipality, was a village southeast of Warsaw, with a population of just over five thousand in January 1940. In October 1940 the Germans established a ghetto in Falenica, which eventually housed some sixty-five hundred Jews. The ghetto was liquidated on August 20, 1942. See the "Falenica" entry in *USHMM Encyclopedia of Camps and Ghettos*, 2:369–71.

In the old people's home at present are elderly people between 65 and 85, from various towns in this country [Poland], including a few who are blind and several who are ill. Now these people are perplexed, desolate, and without care of any kind; they have no relatives of any kind who would be able to assist them. The vacating of the home would be an incalculable catastrophe for these most unfortunate of the unfortunate.

We now are turning to you, dear gentlemen, and as we are aware that the JDC has always tried to help the old people's home and underwritten large sums for it and for the upkeep of the residents, we consider it our duty to inform you of this matter and to request most fervently that you intervene with the appropriate authorities to call off the vacating of the home and allow the old folks to remain in the home.

In the hope that you will spare no effort to achieve what we wish,

Yours respectfully,
Signed /-/
[Signature illegible]

The AJJDC office in Warsaw sidestepped the local authorities and forwarded the request to the Generalgouvernement's Interior Department in the Warsaw district. The office explained to the German authorities that the Joint had been supporting the Falenica home with its 150 elderly residents "with the aim of taking in occupants from evacuated old peoples' homes" in the annexed parts of Poland. The evacuation order "seriously affects our care for old people as we have no other building at our disposal to provide the old people removed from the home board and lodging," which compelled the Joint to "humbly request that you will allow us to maintain the Falenica old peoples' home."[21] In response, the German authorities' Warsaw district office for social welfare requested additional information from the organization about the building's owners. It also asked on what basis the evacuation order had been issued, thereby signaling the lack of communication between occupation agencies.[22] Surviving documentation of the incident suggests that the AJJDC's intercession on behalf of the home met with some measure of success, for the Interior

21. Letter dated March 7, 1940, from the AJDC to the Social Welfare section of the Internal Administration Department of the Office of the Head of the Warsaw District, USHMMA Acc. 1999.A.0154 (AJJDC records from the Jewish Historical Institute Archives in Warsaw) (ŻIH 210/34), 31.

22. Letter dated March 14, 1940, from the Social Welfare section of the Internal Administration Department of the Office of the Head of the Warsaw District to the AJDC, USHMMA Acc. 1999.A.0154 (ŻIH 210/34), 32.

Department administrators indicated their willingness to allow the AJJDC to hunt for another unused building in Falenica. German authorities in Warsaw in this period allowed the Joint to be active, recognizing it as a relief organization "which provides extensive aid and whose work should thus not be impeded."[23] The episode supported hopes among Jewish functionaries that what one German authority ordered might be revoked by a higher one.

Confrontations with Germans were a daily occurrence for members of a *Judenrat*. Many such episodes went unrecorded, especially in those instances that involved Germans inflicting physical violence on Jewish officials. But on several occasions, always under extremely lopsided circumstances, records were preserved documenting meetings between Jewish leaders and German functionaries in Poland. In early 1940, Jewish leaders and German representatives met several times to discuss the large-scale problem of supplying food to large urban communities; Yehuda Bauer argues that both the AJJDC and the Nazis had some interest in "normalizing" the situation, albeit for entirely different reasons.[24] One such meeting, held on February 29, 1940, in Kraków, the seat of the Generalgouvernement administration, brought together SS-Sturmbannführer (Major) Fritz Arlt, resettlement expert for the SS and head of the Generalgouvernement's Office for Population and Health Affairs, and two of his associates[25]; Isaac Borenstein of the AJJDC[26]; Marek Biberstein, chairman of

---

23. Letter dated March 28, 1940, to the Operational Administration Reichsbahn, Falenica, USHMMA Acc. 1999.A.0154 (ŻIH 210/34), 46.

24. Yehuda Bauer, *American Jewry and the Holocaust: The American Jewish Joint Distribution Committee, 1939–1945* (Detroit, MI: Wayne State University Press, 1981), 86.

25. Before the war, Dr. Fritz Arlt had been active as a "race expert" in the German city of Breslau, where he had solicited the help of Jewish scholars for his ancestry research, including **Willy Cohn**; see Willy Cohn, *Kein Recht, Nirgends: Tagebuch vom Untergang des Breslauer Judentums, 1933–1941*, ed. Norbert Conrads (Cologne: Böhlau, 2007), 667–71. Later during the war, Arlt was also involved in early planning for the expansion of the Auschwitz concentration camp; see Aly and Heim, *Architects of Annihilation*, passim, and Götz Aly and Karl Heinz Roth, *The Nazi Census: Identification and Control in the Third Reich* (Philadelphia: Temple University Press, 2004), 75–78.

26. Isaac Borenstein was a Warsaw-based AJJDC activist at the beginning of the war. When the JSS established an office in Kraków in 1940, he moved there to head the AJJDC office and coordinate the channeling of funds to JSS. His fate is unknown, although according to Yehuda Bauer, he probably was included in one of the deportations of the Kraków Jews. See Bauer, *American Jewry and the Holocaust*, 79, 86, 328.

the Kraków *Judenrat*[27]; and **Michał Weichert**, head of the Kraków-based **Jewish Social Self-Help** (JSS). The meeting culminated in a rare exchange of plain language. Biberstein, who was both the chairman of the *Judenrat* and a member of the JSS presidium,[28] spoke first and discussed the Kraków Jewish Community's difficulties in trying to support a hospital, three orphanages, and eight soup kitchens for eighty thousand refugees and the poor. As he suggested, resources for the community had become extremely limited, for Jews of greater means had largely left and *kehilla* taxes were now almost nonexistent. Arlt agreed that it was impossible to squeeze—and here, the writer of the minutes leaves the word in the original German, *herausschlagen*, meaning literally "to beat out"—any more from the Jewish population. In his response, Weichert recapitulated some aspects of the wartime history of organized self-help in Kraków and Warsaw, before pointing "bluntly" to the only realistic alternatives remaining.

DOCUMENT 11–4: **Report of a conference in the Generalgouvernement in Kraków, February 29, 1940, USHMMA RG 15.079M (ŻIH Ring II 1/28), reel 48 (translated from Polish).**

[. . .] Dr. Weichert in turn reported on the work of the Coordinating Commission in Warsaw,[29] briefly describing its origins, the problems with which it has had to deal, and the goals it needs to fulfill in the near future. Above all, he underlined the fundamental difference between Kraków, where one form of social aid—based in the community—has

---

27. Marek Biberstein, a prominent figure in Kraków before the war, was appointed first chairman of the provisional Jewish administration in the occupied city. This institution soon officially became the *Judenrat*, and Biberstein remained its head; he was also a member of the presidium (executive committee) of JSS, which had its headquarters in the city. The Germans arrested him in 1941 on charges of financial violations, but the real reason seems to have been his attempt to forestall the expulsion of Jews from Kraków. He spent the next year and a half in a prison in Tarnów before being deported to the Płaszów labor camp, where he died in 1944. See Aharon Weiss, "Biberstein, Marek," in *Encyclopedia of the Holocaust*, ed. Israel Gutman (New York: Macmillan, 1990), 1:214, and Trunk, *Judenrat*, 339, 438.

28. Close cooperation between JSS and the Jewish Councils can be seen in the fact that many *Judenrat* chairmen were also members of the JSS executive committee. By contrast, the Warsaw *Judenrat*'s relations to the grassroots Aleynhilf effort coordinated by Emanuel Ringelblum were more strained (see chapter 6). Biberstein attended the meeting described above, probably as a leader of JSS. Trunk, *Judenrat*, 339–40.

29. For more on the **Coordinating Commission of Jewish Aid and Civic Societies**, see the Glossary.

taken shape, and Warsaw, embodying a separate form of aid, organized by volunteer organizations, which at the outbreak of the war joined together to form the Coordinating Commission. The tasks facing the Coordinating Commission have grown to exceed its capacities as a result of the extensive damage suffered by Warsaw and the large number of refugees and evacuees. More than 60,000 adults and 20,000 children currently receive hot meals from the kitchens of the Coordinating Commission and more than 20,000 refugees are vying, without success, for this meager soup. The most vital problem for us now is to obtain the allotted provisions, which we unfortunately have not been able to do thus far. We received the first allotment of 20 tons of flour on the day of our departure for Kraków. This will suffice for merely two to three days. At the conference, Mr. engineer Hahn, manager of the Department of Provisions of the City President, announced to us that provisions for Warsaw are secured and that we can count on further allotments. [. . .]

Dr. Weichert apologized for putting the following issue so bluntly: either we take the position that the Jews must be exterminated [*wytępić*] and that it is therefore unnecessary to bother with their fate in the least, or, taking an interest in Jewish social aid, it becomes necessary to think seriously about the sources from which funds for aid will be drawn. The A.J.D.C., which so far has almost single-handedly borne the burden of social aid in Warsaw, probably at great expense to the provinces, will not be able to do so in the future. [. . .]

At the time, "extermination" had not yet become the preferred German way to solve the "Jewish problem." But nor were the authorities willing to provide supplies sufficient to stave off starvation and disease in the ghettos, irrespective of pleas by Jewish Councils or organizations. The following section uses a case study of Łódź to show the practical problems communities faced throughout German-occupied Poland. Notwithstanding the specificity of the setting and the Jewish leadership in that city, Łódź was hardly unique in terms of the social and economic difficulties confronting its Jewish population and the approaches pursued by ghetto leaders and rank and file to stand up against oppression.

CENTRALIZED AUTHORITY AND THE PLIGHT OF THE JEWS IN ŁÓDŹ

The 160,000 Jews of Łódź, living approximately eighty miles southwest of Warsaw in the annexed **Warthegau**, formed the second-largest Jewish community in prewar Poland.[30] With the Germans came the terror. In mid-November 1939, more than a hundred Jewish intellectuals and members of the first Jewish Council in the city were arrested; the Germans shot forty-six men and released the others only after the community paid a ransom. By early 1940, tens of thousands of Łódź Jews had been expelled from the city. They made up more than half of the 140,000 Jews forced out of the territory soon to be renamed Reichsgau Wartheland. Those who remained were subject to a decree issued on December 10, 1939, creating a ghetto in the city, a "temporary measure" (*Übergangsmaßnahme*) that formed part of "Germanization" and "beautification" plans for the city. The implementation of the decree took months.[31] In February 1940 the Germans pushed Łódź Jews into the northeastern section of the city. Where the two main roads divided the ghetto into three segments, bridges acted as connectors. During the forced "resettlement" into the ghetto, brutal German interventions caused hundreds of deaths and spread panic among Jews in the city. An Order Service (Ordnungsdienst, or OD) that was subordinated to Rumkowski's Jewish Council assisted in the relocation; later the OD became the ghetto police.[32] When the ghetto was sealed on April 30, 1940, it was not only "the first major ghetto in the German empire, but it became the model to be studied before the creation of other ghettos." By the summer of 1940, ghettoization had been completed throughout the Warthegau, as well as in some other parts of German-occupied Poland.[33]

Mordechai Chaim Rumkowski had been a member of the prewar *kehilla*. From the time of his appointment as *Älteste der Juden der Stadt Łódź* (eldest of the Jews of the city of Łódź) by the German city authorities on October 13, 1939, he came to play an even more prominent role in the affairs of the Łódź community. With the arrest by the Germans of the original Jewish Council

---

30. For more on the Łódź ghetto, see, e.g., Isaiah Trunk, *Łódź Ghetto: A History*, ed. Robert Moses Shapiro (Bloomington: Indiana University Press in association with the USHMM, 2006); Gordon J. Horwitz, *Ghettostadt: Łódź and the Making of a Nazi City* (Cambridge, MA: Belknap Press, 2008); Andrea Löw, *Juden im Getto Litzmannstadt: Lebensbedingungen, Selbstwahrnehmung, Verhalten* (Göttingen: Wallstein, 2006); Josef Zelkowicz, *In Those Terrible Days: Notes from the Łódź Ghetto*, ed. Michal Unger (Jerusalem: Yad Vashem, 2002); Michal Unger, ed., *The Last Ghetto: Life in the Łódź Ghetto, 1940–1944* (Jerusalem: Yad Vashem, 1995); Alan Adelson and Robert Lapides, eds., *Łódź Ghetto: Inside a Community under Siege* (New York: Penguin Books, 1989).

31. Trunk, *Łódź Ghetto*, 10–17, 19–21; Horwitz, *Ghettostadt*, 26–29, 30–61.

32. Löw, *Juden im Getto Litzmannstadt*, 105–6.

33. Christopher R. Browning with contributions by Jürgen Matthäus, *The Origins of the Final Solution: The Evolution of Nazi Jewish Policy, September 1939–March 1942* (Lincoln and Jerusalem: University of Nebraska Press and Yad Vashem, 2004), 115.

members and their replacement with men lacking both leadership abilities and ambitions, his influence only grew in scope. The German city commissar authorized Rumkowski to "carry out all measures concerning the members of the Jewish race" as ordered. To fulfill his duties, the German authorities allowed him "to move about freely in the streets at any time of day or night," to have access to the agencies of the German administration, to select a Council of Elders to work with him, to publicize his decisions through posters, and to inspect the assembly points for Jewish labor. The city commissar's letter of authorization summarized Rumkowski's powers: "Every member of the Jewish race is required to obey unconditionally all instructions given by Elder Rumkowski. Any opposition to him will be punished by me."[34] Following the creation of the ghetto in March and April 1940, the German mayor of Łódź charged Rumkowski with organizing and maintaining "an orderly community life in the residential district of the Jews." Rumkowski was given license to exert his power over economic life, the food supply, labor, public health, and public welfare through the Jewish police (OD) under his control. He, in turn, was directly subordinated to the German *Ghettoverwaltung* (ghetto administration) led by Hans Biebow, a former coffee merchant.[35]

Rumkowski was ambitious and an able leader. He also believed that by presenting his ghetto population as productive workers essential to the German war machine, he might create an economic basis for the future of the community. "Our only path is work" became his watchword. The main theme of the *Judenrat*'s official proclamations was order. He invoked that theme in dealings with both the Jews struggling to make a living and the Germans who had invested the council with as much power as seemed useful to them. Correspondence preserved in the archive of the Łódź ghetto administration attests to the way in which the *Judenrat* asserted its authority, even in matters as seemingly trivial as the requisition of the horse and buggy owned by a man named Zalomon Mojżesz.

---

34. Authorization letter for Rumkowski issued by Judenrat City Commissar Albert Leister, quoted in Trunk, *Judenrat*, 8.

35. Łódź mayor Franz Schiffer to Rumkowski, April 30, 1940, quoted in Trunk, *Judenrat*, 9–10. On German planning and policy making in conjunction with the creation of the Łódź ghetto, see Browning, *The Origins of the Final Solution*, 114–20.

DOCUMENT ɪɪ–5: **Letter by Łódź ghetto Council of Elders of the Jews to Zalomon Mojżesz regarding his horse and buggy, February 28, 1940, USHMMA RG 15.083M (PSAŁ, file 6), reel 2 (translated from German).**

THE ELDEST OF THE JEWS   Chairman of the
IN THE CITY OF ŁÓDŹ   Council of Elders of the Jews
LODSCH, February 28, 1940
Nr. 734/40
Mr.
Zaloman Mojżesz
    Lodsch
    Wesoła Street, Nr. 9 [8]
    With reference to my personal discussion with the Mayor of the City of Lodsch [Łódź] and until definitive regulation and designation by the authorities, I temporarily confiscate
    1 horse and 1 wagon No. 1946,
    which represent your property, for the needs of the Jewish population and to be placed at the disposal of the Jewish community.
    /-/ Ch. Rumkowski

Eldest of the Jews
In the city of Lodsch

[Seal]
THE ELDEST OF THE JEWS
Chairman of the Council of Elders of the Jews
in Łódź

Rumkowski's office referred constantly to "the authorities," which made the confusing array of German institutions seem to be a unified body to ordinary people living inside the emerging ghetto. Rumkowski's proclamations also avoided any appearance of criticizing German measures, while brimming with a paternalistic determination to get things done and the expectation that the ghetto's residents would comply with orders. In this way, these pronouncements present a doubly unreal picture of Jewish life in the Łódź ghetto. The protocol of a meeting of officials from the Łódź ghetto Council of Elders on April 30, 1940, written in German, provides some clues as to how Rumkowski imposed his authority and perceived his role.

DOCUMENT II–6: **Protocol of meeting of Łódź ghetto Council of Elders of the Jews, April 30, 1940, USHMMA RG 15.083M (PSAŁ, file 1), reel 1 (translated from German).**

Present were

Members of the Jewish Council of Elders

The heads of the various departments of the

Eldest of the Jews and invited guests (according to accompanying list)

Protocol

President Rumkowski opened the meeting and handed over the chair to Dr. Helman.

President Rumkowski delivered a short report about his previous activities and briefly outlined a new plan for the continuation of work in the ghetto for the benefit and maintenance of the Jewish population.

The President has had a lot of work and great difficulties in determining the ghetto borders. As a result of his many interventions, the ghetto area has been considerably increased, but following the increase in area, many streets again have been cut in two by the ghetto. However, the President was successful in getting the ghetto accepted in its current size.

The President has also had many difficulties with the hospital on Hanseaten Street. He intervened many times, and with much difficulty was able to acquire this large hospital. As a result we have: the Northern Hospital at 34/36 Hanseaten Street, the Maternity Clinic (formerly St. Josef Hospital) at 75 Holz Street, and the Hospital for Infectious Diseases at 12 Wesoła/5 Bazarna. There are also several outpatient clinics and pharmacies. The President thus has done everything possible to maintain the health of the Jewish population in the ghetto. The President has taken part in many difficult discussions about the life of the Jews in the ghetto, in the course of which the following items were dealt with: economic life (opportunities to work and thereby earn a living); nutrition (food supply); and the general financial question, to maintain the ability of the poor and less well-off Jewish population to survive.

The President then reported that he has been able to get permission to collect rent for all real property in the ghetto. There are 2,300 houses which will bring in an average monthly rent of RM [Reichmarks] 6–700,000.00. Taxes and other duties on the houses are to be paid to the city treasury.[36] However, the President has reached agreement that these

---

36. Presumably such taxes were collected by the German authorities to pay for "feeding" the Jewish population of the ghetto. For more on the economic situation of the Jews in Poland and the activities of the Jewish Councils, see Trunk, *Judenrat*, 61–114.

sums do not need to be paid in the first few months. He also established that the taxes and other duties for the houses will be based on their rental income, as a large part of the ghetto population is poor and must be relieved of the burden of paying rent.

Other sources of income will be:

Charging shared costs (municipal taxes)
Issuing trade licenses

Everyone who operates a business or is engaged in a trade must have a license, which will be issued by the Eldest of the Jews in return for payment of a fixed fee.

The Finance Department will decide on other sources of revenue, which will be administered by experts.

The community was to receive a subsidy from the authorities by way of reimbursement for the Jewish capital held by the banks. However, this has been refused.

The President then turned his attention to the program of work (employment of the craftsmen and blue-collar workers in the ghetto), which must be considered the most important task and the guarantee of the existence of the Jewish population in the ghetto. In the opinion of the President, 30,000 craftsmen can be employed, so that 90,000 people will have enough to sustain life. The craftsmen have to be registered with the community so that the work can be tackled as quickly as possible. The raw material will be delivered by the authorities. The completed parts will be disinfected and then delivered by the Eldest of the Jews to the authorities. The President will make available large rooms for the assembly of the parts. Not only must craftsmen be given work, but it is essential that unskilled laborers also be given work.

Craftsmen who have assembled parts will not be paid in cash by the authorities. The sums will be transferred to an account set up for the Eldest of the Jews.

The Eldest of the Jews will pay wages to the workers, partly in coupons and partly in foodstuffs.

On this occasion President Rumkowski declared that German currency will not circulate in the ghetto, but rather, special coupons which will be distributed by the Eldest of the Jews. Money will be exchanged in the community for the coupons.

The weekly bank support transfers and all domestic and foreign currency transfers will be deposited in the account of the Eldest of the Jews.

The Eldest of the Jews will then pay the recipient the equivalent value, partly in coupons and partly in food. [. . .]

In conclusion President Rumkowski expressed the hope that those persons entrusted with work in the community would be fully committed so as to maintain the life of the Jews in the ghetto. [. . .]

As noted in the protocol, Rumkowski directed a burgeoning bureaucracy responsible for shelter, food, labor, and public order, with departments overseeing industry, education, hospitals, and social welfare. Its maintenance of schools in the ghetto in particular gave the council the appearance of a forward-looking, well-run, and compassionate apparatus, a strong and positive image that the *Judenrat* under the leadership of Rumkowski cultivated among its constituents. Indeed, schools furnished young Jews with a sense of normalcy and a routine that included shelter and the camaraderie of classmates. During the 1939–1940 school year, over eleven thousand children studied in ghetto elementary, secondary, or vocational schools.[37] Perhaps most importantly, the children also received one meal a day at school, providing vital nourishment often unavailable elsewhere. On June 21, 1940, the ghetto administration announced the opening of a summer camp for children aged four to seven, located in Marysin, a district on the ghetto's northeastern border. By September 1940, more than one thousand children, the majority of them orphans, had enjoyed a stay at the camp, which employed instructors, teachers, doctors, nurses, and hygienists.[38]

DOCUMENT 11–7: Announcement of summer colony for children ages four to seven in the Łódź [Litzmannstadt] ghetto, summer 1940, USHMMA RG 15.083M (PSAŁ, file 1627), reel 380 (translated from German).

PUBLIC ANNOUNCEMENT
No. 69
Re: Children's Summer Camp

So that the children may recover during the summer and also sustain their health, I have decided to establish within the greater ghetto area

---

37. See Trunk, *Łódź Ghetto*, 54–55. The schools were closed in October 1941, when the buildings were converted into shelters for Jewish refugees from western Europe. For more on schools in the Łódź ghetto, see the online exhibition of the USHMM, "Give Me Your Children: Voices from the Łódź Ghetto," at www.ushmm.org/museum/exhibit/online/lodz.
38. See Trunk, *Łódź Ghetto*, 61.

REST HOMES [*Erholungsheime*]

The children will be under the supervision of female Fröbel preschool teachers.[39] Particular attention will be paid to health, and doctors will be retained specifically for this purpose; in addition, there will be an outpatient clinic and a pharmacy.

Registration of children between the ages of 4 and 7 will take place on

Sunday, June 23, 1940

Monday, June 24, 1940

Tuesday, June 25, 1940

between 9:00 and 3:00 p.m.

at the following locations:

7 Bleicherweg

23 Hamburg Street

27 Franz Street

Children's birth certificates must be presented upon registration.

Children who are attending school have already been registered and do not need to register again.

Children who registered at the children's home at 6 Smugowa Street and were not accepted will now be automatically accepted for the rest homes and therefore do not need to register again.

Children of POOR parents are not required to pay any fees, while all others must defray the costs.

Parents who receive support from the Welfare Department must present proof of identity upon registration.

Litzmannstadt Ghetto, June 21, 1940

> (- -) Ch. Rumkowski
> Eldest of the Jews
> in Litzmannstadt

Even more prominent than his concern for the children of the ghetto was Rumkowski's obsession with creating a population of workers efficient enough to prove the economic utility of the ghetto to the German authorities. Rumkowski's approach was not unique; in other communities, *Judenrat* leaders also believed that creating an indispensable workforce and demonstrating its productive potential to the Germans might be the only way to save their Jewish communities. Nevertheless, the Łódź ghetto stood out, for it "possessed a

---

39. Friedrich Fröbel (1782–1852) was a German pedagogue and originator of the kindergarten concept.

substantial percentage of skilled workers and craftsmen in various fields, especially in such important industries as textiles and metal."[40] It also had a leader determined to mobilize labor resources to the maximum and to stamp out displays of dissatisfaction or unrest. Workers' wages were mostly symbolic and bore no relation to the cost of staples, be it on the "official" market, where there was little to buy, or on the black market, which offered items that only the few remaining wealthy or well-connected individuals could afford. Still, people signed up for work in the ghetto (or for forced labor assignments on the outside from the very end of 1940), if not out of a sense of solidarity, then in the expectation of food from the workshop kitchen, or in an effort to avoid sometimes severe punishment.[41]

By mid-1940 the Łódź Jewish Council's administrative apparatus had grown to thirty-five hundred employees working in an ever-growing range of offices.[42] Yet, its expansion stood in marked contrast to the dearth of services it delivered. No matter the personal effort employees might have put into their work and the energy Rumkowski expended as chairman, he and his staff could only administer, not alleviate, scarcity. Situated in the poorest part of the city, the ghetto housed 160,000 Jews in roughly thirty-two thousand apartments, of which almost 90 percent had only one or two rooms, and 95 percent had no toilet or running water. Everyday the ghetto grew more dilapidated, its inhabitants more despondent and physically weak. In the spring of 1940, a dysentery epidemic debilitated an estimated ten thousand ghetto dwellers, killing more than a thousand; typhus and a range of other diseases were rampant. Clothing was unavailable other than what people had managed to bring with them into the ghetto. Many people, lacking fuel for heat, froze to death during the winter of 1940–1941, one of the coldest on record.[43] As living conditions worsened, rich and poor alike sought refuge from the cares of daily life in their private memories and in communal forms of entertainment.

People also fought back. Especially early on in the history of the ghetto—one that we now know survived until the summer of 1944—Rumkowski had to work hard to ensure compliance with his demands. "In no other ghetto," Isaiah Trunk wrote after the war, "did the Nazi *Führerprinzip* or authoritarian principle adapted to the ghetto conditions take on such proportions as in Łódź." And in few other ghettos was there "a single address to which the social protest

---

40. Trunk, *Łódź Ghetto*, 403.
41. Trunk, *Łódź Ghetto*, 157–59, 172.
42. Löw, *Juden im Getto Litzmannstadt*, 100.
43. Löw, *Juden im Getto Litzmannstadt*, 155–57.

was directed: this was Rumkowski."[44] In the spring and summer of 1940, what Trunk referred to as "hunger demonstrations" challenged the Jewish Council's leadership role. Residents began demanding more food and greater participation in running the ghetto. Members of the Bund were particularly outspoken critics. Spontaneous or organized strikes and attacks on *Judenrat* offices extended into the next year, 1941. Rumkowski dealt with such disturbances by both placating the dissatisfied and employing harsh tactics against them when the former approach failed. He would offer extra short-term food rations to the dissenters or devise some new form of entertainment for the ghetto's population at large; at the same time, he would also refuse to listen to demands, denounce protesters as public enemies, and resort to police action, even calling in support from the German police that guarded the outer ghetto perimeters.[45] German authorities generally viewed dissent as an "internal" Jewish matter to be sorted out by the Jewish ghetto leadership and its agents.

From the very beginning, the ghetto walls obscured residents' sense of who was really responsible for their plight. Hans Biebow, his local helpers, and other German officials at a distance from the city were literally outside Jews' field of vision. Compounding ordinary Jews' perspective, Germans would appear on the scene only rarely and then as the final resort in restoring "order." Thus, while everyone knew that without the Germans in Poland there would have been no war and no ghetto, average Jewish men and women perceived their main "enemy" to be the ghetto oligarchy. On occasion, this distorted perception resulted in demands that can only strike us as bizarre in retrospect. In late August 1940, for example, Communists in the ghetto posted protest leaflets containing a "call for the community to be dissolved and to give ourselves

---

44. Trunk, *Łódź Ghetto*, 400, 402.

45. On August 10, 1940, a number of hungry people demonstrated in the streets of the ghetto; the following day the number of demonstrators increased, and the Jewish police, who had dispersed the crowd the previous day, refused to obey Rumkowski's order to intervene. Rumkowski then notified the German authorities, who dispersed the crowd with shots into the air; several people were wounded. This was the first major demonstration in the ghetto. When a hungry crowd looted a potato store in October 1940, Jewish and German police drove them back, leaving two dead and four wounded. In the following months, several further demonstrations and strikes took place, one of the best-organized of these taking place on March 6, 1941, when about seven hundred workers demonstrated in the streets. The ghetto police made numerous arrests. See Trunk, *Łódź Ghetto*, 109, 329, 531, 533–34, 540–41; Löw, *Juden im Getto Litzmannstadt*, 158–60.

momentarily over into the hands of the German government, because we have no[thing] more to lose."[46]

The view at the top was different. Rumkowski knew that if the ghetto was to have a future as a haven for Jews, one capable of outlasting the war, the German demands for internal order and economic productivity had to be met. In a speech he delivered in May 1941 to an audience of Jews from Łódź living in Warsaw, Rumkowski provided a retrospective account of his accomplishments in the Łódź ghetto one year after its creation, at a time when conditions seemed to have taken a turn for the better. Behind his egotistical grandstanding, Rumkowski's listeners could detect a glimmer of hope. His strict tactics with workers and use of rationing were justified in his eyes because they served the greater good of the Jewish people and lessened the strain on relief organizations.

DOCUMENT 11–8: Report of the Chairman of the Council of Elders of the Łódź ghetto, May 15, 1941, USHMMA RG 15.079M (ŻIH Ring I/856), reel 39 (translated from Polish).[47]

Report of the Chairman of the Council of Elders, city of Łódź
Ch. Rumkowski
Delivered on the 15th of May, 1941 to the representatives
of the Łódź community in Warsaw.

When responsibility for leading the community of the Łódź ghetto was imposed upon me, I did not think that my health, intellect, or education qualified me for the position; nevertheless, I was compelled to take on the responsibilities of the chairman of the Council of Elders.

In the beginning, the Jews in Łódź suffered as much as the Warsaw Jews now suffer. When I thought about how best to alleviate their misery, I concluded that only the realization of the motto "work, bread, aid for the sick, aid for children, and order in the ghetto" could bring about a normal situation. I proceeded along these lines. I opened up factories, the Łódź ghetto became a city of labor, so much so that even the authorities

---

46. Protest leaflet against the ghetto regime (in Yiddish) by the "Temporary Committee," August 25, 1940, quoted in Trunk, *Łódź Ghetto*, 372. According to Trunk, the leaders of the protest were Communists.

47. A Yiddish version of the text, which in places differs significantly from the Polish version, can be found in USHMMA RG 15.079M, reel 10, Ring I/193; selections from the Yiddish are published in Joseph Kermish, ed., *To Live with Honor and Die with Honor! Selected Documents from the Warsaw Ghetto Underground Archives "O.S." (Oneg Shabbath)* (Jerusalem: Yad Vashem, 1986), 297–99, and *Biuletyn Żydowskiego Instytutu Historycznego*, no. 54 (1965): 23.

acknowledge our accomplishments. It's true that in the beginning the workers started to play politics, protests broke out, and I had to clamp down with a strong hand. I established prisons, arrested the rebels, and closed the factories, and, as a result, after the protests had been liquidated, work in the factories took place according to plan, and the factories are still in operation today. There are 34 factories, including 12 tailor shops. The workers are devoted to their jobs. They have guaranteed pay rates as well as lunch for 15–20 pfennig (a nutritious lunch). All workers, no matter in what field they are employed, receive lunch in special kitchens. The population receives meat twice a week and 400 grams of good bread daily. Each newborn child is provided with a food ration card, with which the parents receive corresponding portions. Milk is distributed to children up to 3 years old. The price of bread is 2 RM [Reichsmark] for two kilo. The price of potatoes is 22 Pf [pfennig] per kilogram. The ration quotas are established as follows: each person who makes use of services in the kitchens receives in addition to bread a two-week allotment consisting of 4 kg of potatoes, 1 kg of carrots, 1 kg of beets, 1 kg of fish, 100 grams of flour, 400 grams of oil, 20 [text missing] for the price of 2.30 RM. Those not making use of services in the kitchens, in contrast, receive in addition to the aforementioned allotment, 5 kg of potatoes, 2 kg of beets, 1 kg of carrots, [text missing], 250 grams of radishes, 2 kg of fish, 150 grams of cabbage, 300 grams of flour, 600 grams of oil, 100 grams of kasha, 10 [text missing], 200 grams of salt, 1/2 cake of soap, 300 grams of laundry detergent, 100 grams of meat, 100 grams of butter, [text missing] for the price of 6.04 RM. For the holidays we distributed 1/2 kg matzo per person. In this way two slogans [text missing] were realized: all have the right to [food], medical care, and medicine. [. . .]

My goal is to increase the amount of work and to employ as many people as possible [text missing] to lower the expenses associated with public aid. Authorities give us orders and from [text missing] receive income. They also receive income from rents; only those making use of public aid are exempt from paying rent. I established an issuing bank and ordered that all [text missing] gold in the hands of private persons be sold to the bank at a price established by [the authorities]. In this way I got the money. I, of course, encountered objections and accusations from the propertied classes. I ignored them. I believed that by acting for the common good, not just [that of] a few individuals, I would not be condemned by Łódź Jewry. The authorities have so much trust in us that on April 20 of this year, the value of raw materials received on credit for our factories amounted to 4,300,000 RM. I have created a commune, we have reached the point where all are equal, there is no begging on the streets. Seven thousand people work full-time for the community and 20,000 part-time. 3,000 people work at sites outside the ghetto, earning 18.80 RM per week plus full board. They are treated well. The community provides clothing and shoes for all. They reported voluntarily.

<u>Hospitals</u>: At present there are 1,200 beds available; 40 more will soon be added. Five pharmacies are in operation. Pregnant women benefit from free medical care and receive supplemental food as prescribed by physicians. After giving birth, women stay in the clinic for 14 days. After leaving the clinic, they receive additional food for three months.

<u>Children</u>: This is my only joy. The school system has been active since the very beginning. Fourteen thousand children attend primary school; 1,800 are in gymnasiums and lyceums. All the children receive supplemental food rations (lunch either for free or for a payment of 10 Pf). Children from the ages of 4 to 7 are fed in the kindergartens. In Marysin a children's republic was established for 1,400 children.[48] There are three physicians and two dentists active on site. Malnourished children receive a special fourth meal consisting of semolina with butter. The children have clothing and shoes. The language of instruction is Yiddish. More broadly, Hebrew and Polish are also represented. Concerts take place on a daily basis. Two evenings are specially designated for workers with an entrance fee of 10 Pf. We have opened a music school as well as an art school. Synagogues are active. The legal system is Jewish; public prosecutors, judges, [courts?] of inquiry [text missing]. To fight theft and bribery I established a court of summary justice. Sentences are severe, even for petty larceny. There are fewer and fewer crimes. The prisoners who behave well are allowed to go home at night.

No unions are allowed in the ghetto. Only professional meetings are allowed to take place, and these only in the presence of a representative of the community.

I appointed the so-called Supreme Control Chamber, which controls the activities of all departments of the community in their entirety and carries out reviews of all factories and suspends any worker from his duties as soon as an abuse has been confirmed.

In this way I have accomplished all my goals. I am not saying that the situation is ideal. I am saying, however, that no one is dying of hunger. I do not see any children roaming the streets. I have a clear conscience.

---

48. This is a reference to the summer camp. See document 11–7.

Everything I have done has been for the benefit of the Jews. If there are errors in my actions, they do not stem from ill will. Perhaps I am harsh toward people, but I have to be this way toward individuals in order to benefit the common good. I appeal to those present here to help the Warsaw community attain an improvement of conditions. I wish that the situation in Warsaw were no worse than in Łódź.

Despite Rumkowski's claims that everything he did was for the benefit of the Jews, criticism of his actions resounded well beyond the walls of the Łódź ghetto. Warsaw *Judenrat* head Czerniaków had no great regard for his counterpart, nor did **Emanuel Ringelblum**. Echoing many popular comments on Rumkowski's alleged megalomania, they referred to him respectively as "King Chaim" and "God's Anointed."[49] Many of these negative assessments of Rumkowski persist to the present day. At the time, however, hostility like Ringelblum's was perhaps mainly directed against Rumkowski's posturing as a savior and not against his ability to resolve the problems the community faced.[50] In a similar vein, contemporaries looked down on his reliance on a Jewish police force and Jewish court system as a sign of his dictatorial ambition. After the war, Trunk regarded the Jewish police as "a peculiarity of the so-called 'ghetto self-government,'" which tried to reconcile the harsh reality of German demands with the illusion of internal Jewish autonomy.[51]

The concept of a Jewish police force, complete with courts and prisons to secure law and order, drew on precedents in Jewish history in the premodern era. Communal policing and adjudication had once resided outside the realm of state prerogatives.[52] Nevertheless, in the ghetto the *Judenrat*'s judicial and executive branch was the most visible symbol of the glaring imbalances of wealth and power. The fact that the wealthy and influential could bail themselves out, while the poor had little access to justice when they felt wronged, made the ghetto police the most hated institution in the ghetto. The testimony in docu-

---

49. Hilberg, Staron, and Kermisz, *Warsaw Diary*, 191; Emanuel Ringelblum, *Notes from the Warsaw Ghetto: The Journal of Emmanuel Ringelblum*, ed. Jacob Sloan (New York: Schocken Books, 1974), 48.

50. For more on Rumkowski's initiative in shaping ghetto policy and creating a "working ghetto," see Michal Unger, *Reassessment of the Image of Mordechai Chaim Rumkowski* (Jerusalem: Yad Vashem, 2008).

51. Trunk, *Judenrat*, 180.

52. See Aharon Weiss, "The Relations between the Judenrat and the Jewish Police," in *Patterns of Jewish Leadership in Nazi Europe, 1933–1945: Proceedings of the Third Yad Vashem International Historical Conference, Jerusalem, April 4–7, 1977*, ed. Israel Gutman and Cynthia J. Haft (Jerusalem: Yad Vashem, 1979), 201–17.

ment 11–9 details the experiences of one individual who, in the fall of 1940, fell victim to ghetto police corruption and abuse of power while attempting to obtain bread. It is unclear when and by whom the account was recorded; even so, this gripping testimony describes a dimension of reality in the Łódź ghetto that contrasted markedly with the official line, which used statistics to paint a purposefully optimistic portrait.

DOCUMENT 11–9: **Author unknown, diary entry from the Łódź ghetto, December 15, 1940, USHMMA RG 02.208M (ŻIH 302/191) (translated from Polish).**

It happened on Friday, November 1, 1940. For three days already there had been no bread in the house, the child was constantly wailing "give me bread, mommy!" but there is no bread in the house. For supper my wife put some potatoes in to bake, but because the flame was too weak, we couldn't wait for the potatoes [to be cooked]. After supper, the neighbors came by and we agreed that early in the morning one of us would wake the other so that we could go together to wait in the bread line. We also decided to go to the Szmulewicz bakery, which is located at Lutomiersk 8, since we could get there through the back entrance, i.e., from our courtyard at Zgierska 12 to Zgierska 14 and from there to Lutomierska 6. We worked all this out so that we could get up before 7 a.m. (*schperschtunde*[53]) and avoid the barbed wire. All night long my little daughter couldn't sleep because of hunger, and her crying prevented us from sleeping. At 5 a.m. our neighbor Ostrowicz knocked on the shutter, my wife and I got up, we quickly got dressed and went out into the courtyard. We placed the child in the bed of the elderly woman who lived in the first room. Suddenly our other neighbor, Zylbersztejn, also came down into the courtyard and we together woke up the watchman to open the gate for us. Arriving a couple of minutes after 5, a considerable line of people was waiting for us near the bakery, one line in the direction of Zgierska Street and another in the direction of Stodolniana Street. We all joined the Zgierska line. We stood there without a problem until 7 o'clock. At 7 the crowd began to demand that the baker begin distributing bread. The baker did not want to give out any of the bread because, as he explained, there was no (police officer) there yet. A couple of minutes after 6 [*sic*;

---

53. *Schperschtunde* is a Polonized form of the German *Sperrstunde* (curfew). The author reasoned that if he and his companions were to reach the bakery before the nightly curfew had ended, they would have an advantage over those who could not or would not risk moving about during curfew hours.

most likely meaning 7], six men arrived, all of whom were wearing navy blue hats, the same ones the Jewish police wore at the time, and began to violently push their way to the window of the bakery. I didn't know who the six were, but I heard that it was the "Berk" family[54]—well known in the area. They worked their way to the window and the baker started giving them two loaves of bread each. And as soon as they had gotten their bread, the baker stopped handing it out. The crowd raised a cry, demanding that the baker keep handing out bread, and because the baker didn't want to, the crowd began throwing rocks at the bakery's windows, breaking a few panes and wounding the baker's apprentice. The baker then said that without the police there he wouldn't hand out bread, and he didn't. The "Berks" had already managed to bring home the bread that they had received and then to come back. They began pushing again and beat up somebody who was standing in their way. Somebody from the line went to get the police and two policemen came. The "Berks" together with the police began establishing order just as they pleased. And it was at this time that a cart arrived alongside the bakery and the driver, wanting to get bread, got down from the cart. Since he was an acquaintance of the "Berks," he began to help them "establish order." One of the "Berks" then took the driver's whip and began whipping the people in the line to disperse them, and the police pulled people out of the line. I was among those pulled out of the line. They ordered us to form a chain and promised that we would get bread. We stood in the chain for about ten minutes, then four more policemen arrived. Feeling stronger now, they began to disperse the chain with truncheons, and I got hit by one several times. So, I went up to one of the two policemen who had first arrived and asked him to allow me to return to the line I had been waiting in. The policeman's name was Fuchs (I learned the name later). He raised his truncheon and wanted to hit me, but I said to him: "Sir, I left a child at home who has not eaten bread for three days, but instead of bread you want to beat me." In the meantime, policeman no. 357 rushed up to me and hit me in the eye with his leather briefcase so hard that I went blind for a few minutes. And I don't know who it was, but a couple of the policemen beat me pretty badly. When my brother Mojżesz, who was standing in line, saw that they were beating me, he raised a cry. Then the police rushed over to him and began beating him. As I was regaining my sight, I saw that the police were encircling my brother from the other side of the sidewalk and

---

54. For unknown reasons, the author of this document put certain names in quotation marks. Biographical information about persons mentioned in the document is unavailable.

that my brother was gushing blood. I ran over to ask why they were beating him, the answer: they were trying to take us by force to the police station. Being naïve enough to believe that I would find justice at the station, I turned to the policemen who were leading us away and told them that I would go on my own to the station. And this is how we entered the reserve police station at 4 Kościelna Street. A policeman named "Görin" began to take down the report and while doing so and in front of the noncommissioned officer raised his hand and hit my brother in the face. I then asked whether it was permitted to beat people at the station as well. Then I got hit by a policeman too! As I was already at my wits' end by this point, I raised my hand and hit the policeman "Görin" in the nose—the one who had hit my brother while he was taking down the report. Forty policemen, who were in reserve, then began to rain blows down upon me and my brother. After I regained consciousness several minutes later, I had bumps on my head the size of an egg, my watch had been knocked off my wrist, and I didn't even notice until my brother told me that the watch was lying on the ground. I picked it up. They held us at the station for a few more minutes, then an escort led us off in handcuffs to station no. 1. We were taken there by six policemen. The noncommissioned officer left the protocol at station no. 1. It was only while sitting there in the office that I found out that the police get the order to beat people as forcefully as they can. For this was the order the policemen who went to the line at 20 Żydowska Street had gotten from noncommissioned officer Szpic. They weren't averse to beating us at station no. 1 either. The beating was led by Szpic himself. [. . .]

At the [ghetto] courthouse we waited while one case ended. The next case was mine. The court calls forward the defendants and the witnesses. Everyone takes their seats. The judge reads out the indictment and gives me the first word, and I respond by explaining what happened. My brother does the same and my witnesses confirm what happened. Then comes the cross-examination of the police's witnesses. [. . .] Everything that the police's [witnesses] state is a lie, except that I hit the policeman "Görin" in the nose in my own defense and that of my brother. Everyone sees this and the judge sees this as well, so I remain calm about the outcome of the case. [. . .] The court deliberates and returns. For a few minutes I sit as if turned to stone, not knowing what will become of me and whether I had misunderstood [the verdict]. Nine months and a tenth on top of that? [. . .]

In the end, the author spent time in two Łódź ghetto prisons and suffered greatly under the difficult conditions (which included beatings, disease, lice infestation, hunger, and dampness). Following his release from prison, he was no longer as naïve or optimistic and described his view of the Jewish authorities, particularly the Jewish police, as forever changed.

Widespread frustration and anguish directed at the Jewish Council found an outlet not only in protests and attacks on council offices, but also in a highly politicized ghetto culture. People expressed their expectations and frustrations, hopes and anxieties, partly in forms familiar from before the war, partly in new ways. One popular activity seems to have been diary writing. The few diaries that survived the war attest to the growing desperation of their authors.[55] Music also continued to have broad appeal. People listened to and performed traditional music and wrote new compositions. One of the best-known songs composed in the ghettos, written by a tailor and gifted lyricist, Yankel Hershkowitz, and titled "Rumkowski Khayim," took as its subject the Łódź *Judenrat* chairman. In it, Hershkowitz delicately raised questions about the chairman's rule.[56]

The ghetto leadership recognized the power of culture and tried to use it to serve its own ends. Rumkowski attempted to shape public opinion in his favor with an eye toward the future. To that end, he created a new office in November 1940 for the sole purpose of documenting life in the ghetto. Over the next four years, the men and women entrusted with writing this ghetto chronicle produced an extremely rich collection of texts. While avoiding outright criticism of the ghetto leadership, they undoubtedly spoke to a broader range of ghetto realities than Rumkowski had desired.[57] Among the thousands of topics contained in its pages, the Łódź ghetto chronicle described Hershkowitz's song in

---

55. See, e.g., Dawid Sierakowiak, *The Diary of Dawid Sierakowiak: Five Notebooks from the Łódź Ghetto*, ed. Alan Adelson (New York: Oxford University Press, 1996); Shlomo Frank and Nachman Blumental, eds., *Togbukh fun Lodzsher Geto* (Buenos Aires: Tsentral-farband fun Poylishe Yidn in Argentine, 1958); Jakub Poznański, *Dziennik z getta łódzkiego* (Łódź: Żydowski Instytut Historyczny, 2002). A vast collection of unpublished diaries and notes from the Łódź ghetto exists in archival collections; for example, see Harry Fogel, USHMMA Acc. 1995.A.963; Leon Hurwicz, USHMMA RG 02.208M (ŻIH 302/11–13); Szmuel Rosenstajn, USHMMA RG 02.208M (ŻIH 302/115).

56. It is very difficult to locate the original version of the song because many versions were reworked from memory after the war. For one version, see "Rumkowski Khayim," by Yankl Hershkowitz, USHMMA Acc. 2000.134 Joseph Wajsblat collection; for a slightly different version, see Gila Flam, *Singing for Survival: Songs of the Łódź Ghetto, 1940–45* (Urbana: University of Illinois Press, 1992), 40.

57. Lucjan Dobroszycki, ed., *The Chronicle of the Łódź Ghetto, 1941–1944* (New Haven, CT: Yale University Press, 1984). Complete editions of the chronicle are available in German and Polish: Sascha Feuchert, Erwin Leibfried, and Jörg Riecke, eds., *Die Chronik des Gettos Lodz/Litzmannstadt: Supplemente und Anhang* (Göttingen: Wallstein, 2007); Julian Baranowski, Paweł Samuś, and Feliks Tych, eds., *Kronika getta łódzkiego* (Łódź: Archiwum Państwowe w Łodzi and Wydawnictwo Uniwersytetu Łódzkiego, 2009).

an entry for December 5, 1941, noting its widespread popularity and usefulness to Hershkowitz and his accompanist, violinist Karol Rosenzweig from Vienna, as a source of income. It also mentioned that, strangely enough, the chairman himself liked it.[58]

A song from another location, a refugee camp in Sowliny near the town of Limanowa, conveys similar tensions around a leader of a Polish Jewish community under German occupation. Unlike the song about Rumkowski, which is quite well-known among Holocaust survivors and often reworked from memory, the text in document 11–10 was written down in 1940. The scope of the responsibilities of the *Judenrat* chairman in Łódź, of course, differed significantly from that of the Jewish leader of a remote community, and the settings in which these two songs were written diverged markedly. Still, they shared a common tone, revealing some of the misgivings Jews harbored about their leaders.

DOCUMENT 11–10: Pola Mordkowicz, "On Lustig," poem written in the Sowliny refugee camp, April 15, 1940, USHMMA RG 15.079M (ŻIH Ring I/2), reel 1 (translated from Polish).[59]

[The poem is prefaced, "Dedicated to the community chairman of the foothill town of Limanowa, for his minimal efforts in easing our plight."]

Farewell, Mr. Lustig,
Chairman of the *kehilla*,

58. Dobroszycki, *The Chronicle of the Łódź Ghetto,* 92. On Rosenzweig, see Flam, *Singing for Survival,* 24.

59. Pola Mordkowicz, the author of the poem, was interned in the Sowliny refugee camp, close to the town of Limanowa in southern Poland, after being resettled from Łódź. According to the 1931 census, 1,002 Jews lived in Limanowa, but in the fall of 1939 and the spring of 1940, a large number of refugees arrived there from other towns in Poland. By March 1940, five hundred refugees from the city of Łódź, including Pola Mordkowicz, were confined within the newly established refugee camp near Limanowa, at Sowliny. This camp was, however, soon closed down without warning in mid-April. This song is a kind of farewell from Mordkowicz to the town of Limanowa. She and the other refugees were sent to Nowy Sącz, Grybów, and Mszana Dolna. On Limanowa, see "Limanowa" entry in *USHMM Encyclopedia of Camps and Ghettos,* 2:540–42. Following her release from Sowliny and after sojourns in Nowy Sącz, Kraków, and Sochaczew, Mordkowicz wound up in the Warsaw ghetto and was probably killed in Treblinka in one of the deportations of the summer of 1942. Mordkowicz's account of her wanderings can be found in the same file of the Ringelblum Archive (USHMMA RG 15.079M [ŻIH Ring I/2], reel 1).

You did nothing for us,
I'm not sorry to see you go!!!
You showed up here often,
It's hard for me to describe,
You were flooded with requests,
It's boring for me to remember!
But now you've suddenly gone silent,
You don't come by at all!
Is there really that much work for him
In the Limanowa *kehilla*?
You're shunning the rabble,
I understand it perfectly,
You haven't been here since Saturday,
There's no glory in that at all!!!
You sought better guests,
You didn't find them among the hoi polloi
You didn't know about the many proud fellows here
Who don't know how to pay homage!!!
May you be accompanied
By my silent accusation,
No one will sense it here,
No one will hear it here!!!
Farewell, Limanowa,
Our dear [illegible]!
It wasn't healthy here,
In this camp of doom!!!

RELIEF NETWORKS ACROSS POLAND

Prior to the formation of ghettos and intensifying thereafter, a staggering array of responsibilities and demands fell on Jewish communal leaders. The new councils had not only to provide the core services of the *kehilla* (performance of religious tasks, provision of welfare and education) but also to fulfill functions that previously would have been accomplished by Polish municipalities and for which neither appropriate Jewish institutions nor traditions even existed. As discussed in chapter 6, a range of larger relief organizations as well as local initiatives and grassroots committees tried to fill the void immediately after the beginning of the war. Here we examine more closely how the new Jewish Councils interacted with these organizations during the first year of German occupation.[60] While the previous section presents a snapshot of Łódź, with its centralized leadership structure, the remainder of this chapter looks at a broad sweep of Jewish communities across German-controlled Poland and the links Jews attempted to forge across them.

Communities in different parts of Poland had different resources at their disposal. In part, access to resources depended on the administrative status of a region under German control. The AJJDC was able to operate in both the Generalgouvernement and the annexed territories; other organizations such as the JSS were only authorized to work either in **Hans Frank**'s fiefdom or in the incorporated regions.[61] Indeed, because of its wider geographical range, international status, relative means, and experience on the ground and in cooperative projects, the AJJDC served as the most important source of support for all Polish Jews. The organization was able to undertake major relief operations in 1939 and 1940 thanks to mounting awareness of the humanitarian crisis in Poland among its American supporters. In Warsaw alone, between October 1939 and September 1940, the Joint counted 10,101,963 meals distributed.[62] Emanuel Ringelblum in fact feared that it might have been too generous in the early months of the war, creating the impression among Warsaw Jews that their rich American relatives would take care of all of the community's problems. He was concerned that long-term relief work would be more difficult as a result.[63] And, as it turned out, the drying up of outside resources and the channels to distribute them led to a severe reduction in what the AJJDC could do. In the course of 1940, the Joint spent over 14.735 million złoty on relief work before dropping to a mere 8 million złoty in 1941.[64] As the letter in document 11–11 to its Kraków office attests, at the height of its relief activity, the AJJDC was the address to which those in need could turn with some expectation of success.

---

60. For an overview of public welfare in the ghettos, see Trunk, *Judenrat*, 115–71 and 332–51.

61. See Trunk, *Judenrat*, 116–18.

62. See "Thirteen Months of JDC Work in Warsaw," USHMMA Acc. 1999.A.0154 (ŻIH 210/6); Bauer, *American Jewry and the Holocaust*, 72–76; Samuel D. Kassow, *Who Will Write Our History? Emanuel Ringelblum, the Warsaw Ghetto, and the Oyneg Shabes Archive* (Bloomington: Indiana University Press, 2007), 114–15.

63. Kassow, *Who Will Write Our History*, 114.

64. See Bauer, *American Jewry and the Holocaust*, 73, on official JDC expenditures for 1940; on the crucial role of the AJJDC for ghettos in Poland, see Trunk, *Judenrat*, 135–42.

DOCUMENT 11–11: Letter from the Skawina *Judenrat* to the AJJDC office in Kraków, Generalgouvernement, requesting *lulav* and *esrog*, October 16, 1940, USHMMA Acc. 1999.A.0154 (ŻIH 210/79), folder 12 (translated from German).

Judenrat
Skawina

Skawina, October 16, 1940

To the "Joint," <u>Kraków</u>

I request that the bearer of this be presented with a *lulav* and *esrog* for the Jewish community in Skawina.[65] I ask that you make it possible for the bearer, Mr. Barber Isucher, to <u>obtain</u> the *lulav* and *esrog* <u>today</u>. The local Jewish population is very poor and cannot raise the necessary sum for an *esrog*. As it is very pious, however, it asks that a *lulav* and *esrog* be allocated to it.

Respectfully yours,
[Stamp of Judenrat Skawina]
[Signature illegible]

While the Polish Jewish public benefitted from and acknowledged the efforts of relief organizations, the need knew no bounds. The communal fabric had become threadbare. A poster, translated in document 11–12, called upon Jewish women and especially Jewish mothers (or *mames*) to do all they could to support Jewish orphans and the organizations working on their behalf. In this most heart-wrenching offshoot of the crisis, Jewish philanthropy dared to hope that community members still could and would extend a helping hand to those beyond their own overstretched families.

---

65. Together, the *lulav* (a ripe, green, closed frond from a date palm tree), *etrog* (the fruit of a citron tree; *esrog* in Yiddish), *hadas* (myrtle leaves), and *aravah* (willow leaves) are necessary to fulfill the commandment prescribed by the Torah (Leviticus 23:40) in ritual observance of the holiday of Sukkot.

DOCUMENT II–12: **"Save the Jewish Child!" JSS poster, Warsaw, no date (ca. 1940), USHMMA Acc. 1999.A.0154 (ŻIH 210/46), folder 40 (translated from Yiddish).**

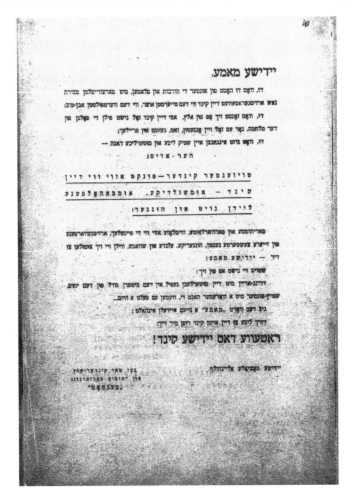

JEWISH MOTHER,

You, who have rescued your child, your dearest treasure, your most precious jewel from under the ruins and flames;

You, who will sacrifice anything just so that your child should not feel the effects of the war, so that he should have clothes and food, be healthy and happy;

You, the embodiment of maternal love and concern—

Listen to this:

Thousands of children—just like your child—innocent and helpless, are suffering in need and hunger!

Orphaned and abandoned, homeless like little birds, thrown out of their destroyed nests, hungry, lonely, and weak, they would like to cuddle up to you—Jewish mother!

Don't push them away!

Use your maternal instinct to feel the bitter fate of the orphan, support, with a warm hand, anyone lacking a home . . .

Give the word "mother" a new, delicate meaning!

Through the love of your own child we appeal to you:

SAVE THE JEWISH CHILD!

Jewish Social Self-Help

Organization for the Protection of Children and the Welfare of Orphans "CENTOS"

Efforts to provide for needy children in the ghettos tried to build on the prewar organizational infrastructure. Document 11–13 highlights such continuities. A Jewish "foundlings' home" created by wealthy assimilationists in Warsaw kept its doors open even after the war began. Until October 1939 it was run by the city of Warsaw; after November 1, it was transferred to the *kehilla*, which could only provide eight thousand złoty a month for its upkeep (compared to fifty thousand before the war), supplemented by some aid from **CENTOS**.[66] Forced to operate with a barebones staff, the home cared for five hundred babies. In view of these challenges, its director surmised that while the ghetto poor gave their last crumbs, the more affluent in Jewish Warsaw had grown coldhearted.

DOCUMENT 11–13: "A Visit to Unfortunate Children,"[67] Warsaw, no date (ca. August 1940), USHMMA RG 15.079M (ŻIH Ring II/107), reel 49 (translated from Yiddish).[68]

A VISIT TO UNFORTUNATE CHILDREN

A few weeks ago a month of the needy child was proclaimed. In our present circumstances there is no need to explain the word "needy"; every Jew knows well what it means. However, a new, special kind of need

---

66. See Kermish, *To Live with Honor*, 396–401.

67. The guide to the Ringelblum Archive indicates that the author of the account was probably Menachem Mendel Kon. Kon was a founding member of the **Oyneg Shabes** project and one of its most dedicated activists, in charge of its financial division. According to his identity card issued in Warsaw in 1938 (USHMMA RG 15.079M [ŻIH Ring I/1124 (1443)], reel 45), he was born in Ostrów on December 9, 1881. He died in the Warsaw Ghetto Uprising in the spring of 1943.

68. Published in Kermish, *To Live with Honor*, 396–401.

appeared recently, a need which transcends any previous understanding of the concept: the need of the poor, lonely, and forsaken child in Warsaw.

For this need, the strongest word is too pale for description; the most shocking term is too weak to render it, its image too barbaric for the human imagination. Here is a fragment of a nightmare that I witnessed with my own eyes in a public institution, which until recently was a warm, kind, loving children's home, and has turned into a punishment corner of the worst, most cruel sort, a guillotine for the unfortunate little babies.

[. . . The writer describes the superior prewar conditions at the "foundlings' home" on Leszno 127–Wolska 18 street.]

The onset of the [1939–1940] winter was the first challenge. The cold was growing sharper day by day until it became unbearable. There was no money for replacing the windowpanes shattered during the bombardment, and the windows remained open holes until January. In an institution for children (and many toddlers and newborn babies among them), they neglected to secure coal for the winter. The temperature could not be kept higher than 4 degrees Celsius! The personnel—doctors, nurses, aides, etc.—worked in winter clothes and gloves, while the children were practically naked and barefooted. The reason for this was quite plain: during the bombardment, and in the confusion of the first days of the war, various crooks and thieves stole everything from the institute, leaving no blanket or pillow, no diaper or children's clothing. The worst part was that there was no food. This terrible situation, the cold and starvation, led to the death of 56 children during November alone!

After long, sustained efforts, the community, together with CENTOS, set up a supervisory council, which was charged with taking care of the needs of the children. But none of the said institutions was in a position to accomplish this task. The community appropriated a monthly sum of 8,000 złoty for the maintenance of the children's home, while CENTOS acted in accordance with its momentary potential; thus, a period of quiet ensued. The 8,000 złoty from the community left the management wondering what to do first, and the subsidy from CENTOS was occasional. It was not until the second half of May 1940 that CENTOS began supplying the home with products on a regular schedule, albeit in very scant quantity. In addition, most products were suitable only for older children. For babies you need milk, eggs, sugar, butter and wheat meal, and all these provisions were either completely missing or given only in a negligible quantity. Thus, for example, for the necessary 50 liters of milk, the home received only 5 liters, or sometimes 10 liters at most, and even this was not whole milk but skimmed. As for eggs or butter—there were none of these. Meat had been obtained only twice, and horse meat at that.

The situation is no better with regard to clothes, underwear, shoes, etc.

[. . . The writer quotes statements by managers Epstein and Fridman] "From November 1939 until July 1940, 226 children died: 56 in November, 42 in July, and the rest during the months in between. And no wonder, since the children are so emaciated, so weakened, that the slightest illness kills them."

[. . .] Everything is being blamed on the conditions of wartime, but this is wrong! There are still quite a few wealthy people in Warsaw. If only there was also strong will and warm, human feelings, it would be possible, even now, to ease the pain and the poverty significantly. But alas, the hearts are frozen stiff, and whatever is brought to us by the poor of Warsaw, by the proletariat, is of no use.

"Here you have it"—says Mrs. Dr. Friedman pointing with her hand—"a mound of bread crumbs, collected from poor, destitute Jews, wrapped in dirty newspaper—there is nothing we can do with these gifts. We must get some constant, permanent, and assured support, which could secure the existence of this institution; or, if not, we will abandon our five hundred helpless little babies."

Let Jewish Warsaw, the largest Jewish community in Europe, decide this question.

In Warsaw, as in other communities, lack of solidarity remained an important issue. It came in many forms, from council-sponsored nepotism to corruption organized by "crooks and thieves," blamed in document 11–13 for the destitution of the "foundlings' home." In some cases, the fraying of communal ties was manifest in the failure of functionaries to do their jobs. In the letter in document 11–14, the Kraków Jewish Council office charged with helping refugees alerted the city's *Judenrat* main office to an official utterly disinterested in the well-being of those he was supposed to help. The document provides a view not only of conflicts and "red tape" within a Jewish Council, but also of the limitations officials confronted in their attempts to remedy problems.

DOCUMENT 11–14: **Letter from the Center for Refugees in Kraków to Wilhelm Goldblatt,[69] vice president of the Jewish Council in Kraków, April 19, 1940, USHMMA RG 15.072M (ŻIH 218/17), reel 1 (translated from Polish).**

The Center for Refugees at 10 Stanisława Street kindly reports that the directive of the president [of the Jewish Council] from April 16 of this year in the matter of issuing 25 beds to the epidemic hospital has been fulfilled.

On the 17th of this month, the leadership [of the Center for Refugees] issued the confirmation for 25 beds to the Council's coachman and made available 75 mattresses. On that day, however, the coachman did not pick up the mattresses, and on the 18th of this month took only 33 mattresses and was to pick up the rest that same day.

The condition of the aforementioned mattresses, it is true, leaves much to be desired. But if we recall that young girls previously slept on those same mattresses for several years at a boarding school and that various people, including many women and children, slept on them starting in September [1939] without bed linens, then we must accept that the outward condition of the mattresses must be as it presently is.

The leadership feels obligated to thank heartily the respectable Council members Dembitzer[70] and Morgenbesser[71] since, thanks to their visit, the residents of the center gave up the beds without a "major row" [*bez 'generalnej awantury'*].

---

69. Wilhelm Goldblatt was a deputy to Marek Biberstein on the Kraków *Judenrat* from the fall of 1939 through the spring of 1940. From the scant information available on Goldblatt, we know that he was arrested along with Biberstein and three other members of the *Judenrat* for trying to stop the Nazi expulsions of Jews from the city, which started in May 1940 and continued into April 1941. He was soon released, however. The authors have not been able to ascertain the details of his later fate. Trunk, *Judenrat*, 438.

70. Teodor Dembitzer (1897–?) was a member of the Kraków *Judenrat* in charge of its secretariat and construction department. He survived the war, most likely as part of the group of Jews saved by Oskar Schindler. Aleksander Bieberstein, *Zagłada Żydów w Krakowie* (Kraków: Wydawnictwo Literackie, 1985), 16–17; Erika Rosenberg, ed., *Ich, Oskar Schindler: Die persönlichen Aufzeichnungen, Briefe und Dokumente* (München: Herbig, 2000), 61.

71. Rafał Morgenbesser (1900–?) was a member of the Kraków *Judenrat* in charge of organizational matters and general affairs. He survived the war, also most likely as part of the group of Jews saved by Oskar Schindler. Bieberstein, *Zagłada Żydów*, 16–17; Rosenberg, *Ich, Oskar Schindler*, 56.

While fulfilling the aforementioned directive, the leadership [of the Center for Refugees] encountered many obstacles on the part of Mr. Scherer, the Council's clerk for social welfare.[72]

For the good of the refugees of the center, the leadership cannot let this matter pass in silence: Mr. Scherer, when sending for the beds, did not want to think that those people from whom he would take away the beds would not have anything to sleep on. He did not instruct the leadership to prepare pallets ahead of time, and he himself did not provide pallets, which significantly hindered fulfillment of the directive.

On the 17th of this month, after issuance of the beds, the leadership, upon the recommendation of the Honorable Vice President, requested that Mr. Scherer issue pallets and straw to the center. Mr. Scherer then set up a "public inquiry," which soon produced the following results: "Well, and? You got a proper scolding from Dr. Goldblatt. Did you pull some strings to get a hold of the beds? I'll settle things here. I, Scherer, will shut down this whole center. Quit acting like you own the place."

Considering that we act for the good of the poor and that I was not permitted to leave without resolving the matter, I requested that Mr. Scherer issue me the desired pallets. Mr. Scherer instructed me to report [to him] anew at 1:15 in the afternoon. I appeared at the designated time together with Mr. Zimmer, and then he instructed us to wait until 2:30, after which he informed us that it was possible to get the pallets only after dinner. I then firmly requested that Mr. Scherer kindly accompany us to the store immediately because the people did not have anything to sleep on.

We then got the material for the pallets, and it was already 4 o'clock when we returned with our "loot," which President [Marek] Biberstein can confirm as he was then returning to the office.

We delivered the material to be made into pallets and then demanded straw. Mr. Scherer provided us with straw, which, however, could not be accepted unconditionally, as the attached protocol [not printed here] demonstrates.

Mr. Glücksman, the commandant of the building, and Mr. Dominitz hand-delivered the protocol to Mr. Scherer together with a letter from Mr. Zimmer with a request for allocation of straw suitable for use in the

---

72. The authors have not been able to find information about Scherer. The person in charge of social welfare at the Kraków *Judenrat* in this period was Leon Salpeter. Bieberstein, *Zagłada Żydów*, 16.

center.[73] Mr. Scherer, however, deemed it appropriate to resolve the matter by rejecting the letter and, with a raised voice, delivered "a speech," which the leadership encloses [not printed here].

Given this state of affairs, the leadership of the center requests that the Honorable Vice President kindly suggest to Mr. Scherer that he:

> a. immediately provide straw suitable for use, i.e., in long stalks and, above all, clean, for the poor people who for two nights have not slept because their beds were taken away;
>
> b. not provide false information in the future because Dr. Biberstein, as he informed us, was led into error by Mr. Scherer because he believed that Mr. Scherer had beds in reserve and, if he had known that the beds that are currently earmarked for the hospital would have to be taken away from poor refugees, he never would have acceded to the establishment of the epidemic hospital;
>
> c. should bear in mind in the future that, before issuing a directive to the center, conditions must first be in place that allow fulfillment of that directive.

Finally, the leadership dares to request that the Honorable Vice President kindly instruct Mr. Scherer that politeness, which is the duty of all social activists, must also be the duty of Mr. Scherer toward all, as long as he remains in the position of social welfare clerk at the Council.

Respectfully,

[Illegible signature]

In the course of 1940, "resettlement" and other German measures aimed at pushing out "unwanted" parts of the population had cut deep into communities. While the need for assistance grew, resources available for relief became even more limited. In the town of Zagórów, renamed Hinterberg after its incorporation into Germany as part of the Warthegau, the Jewish Council had its hands full with trying to care for a community in which refugees suddenly outstripped the number of local Jews by more than two to one.

---

73. The authors have been unable to find biographical information on Glücksman, Dominitz, and Zimmer, mentioned in the document.

DOCUMENT 11–15: **Letter from the Jewish Council in Hinterberg (formerly Zagórów) to the AJJDC office in Warsaw, December 12, 1940, USHMMA Acc. 1999.0154 (ŻIH 210/738), 8–9 (translated from German).**

Jewish Council of Elders
in Hinterberg
Konin Administrative District

Hinterberg, December 17, 1940

To the American Joint Distribution Committee, Warsaw:

In polite reply to your kind letter of December 10 of this year, no. /140–9/40, we inform you of the following:

Around July 15, 1940, all Jewish inhabitants were resettled to Hinterberg (Zagurow [Zagórów]) from the Konin Administrative District, specifically from the following towns: Lehmstädt (Kleszewo [Kleczew]), Golin [Golina], and Wolfsberg (Wilczyn). Immediately after the arrival of the expellees, the local Jewish community set up a relief operation for the purpose of assisting the resettled people with housing, food supplies, and medical attention. This effort is led by the local relief committee, which was acknowledged by the Gendarmerie Kreisführer in Konin as the "Jewish Council of Elders" in Hinterberg.

The Jewish Council of Elders performs the following relief work:

1. Housing registry. In fact, owing to the great shortage of housing, several families had to be accommodated in a large room.

2. The establishment of the communal kitchen, which operates steadily and distributes around 400 midday meals, consisting of a nutritious, well-prepared soup and 200 grams of bread per person.

3. Support of the elderly and ill. For this purpose, a special home was created, which is under medical supervision.

4. Procurement of straw, mess tins, and dishes.

5. Sanitary facilities and medications.

With the onset of winter, we are faced with the insoluble problem of supplying those in need with heating, beds, wooden clogs, and the like, because our funds are completely exhausted. An exception was made for the 120 men who were moved from here to the Jewish labor camp in Konin, as wooden clogs had to be acquired for part of this group.

To the inquiries addressed to us, we reply as follows:

1. Number of Jews, 2,170 persons.
2. Number of refugees or resettled persons, 1,582.
3. Number of people cared for, 68 persons.
4. Returnees: none.
5. Communal kitchen operates daily.
6. The number of midday meals is around 400 per day.
7. ——————————— [left blank]
8. Child care not provided.
9. A home for the sick and elderly is available.
10. Budget of the social welfare office for the month of November 1940 [. . .]

Communal kitchen	RM 848.04
Support for heating	184.80
Support for men moved to Jewish labor camp in Konin	34.75
Wooden clogs, 51 pairs	240.–
Sanitary purposes—medications	28.–
Postage and writing materials	5.25
	1,340.84

11. The subsidy of 500 Reichsmark on October 5 was used for the following purposes:

250 RM for purchasing supplies of potatoes and vegetables for the communal kitchen
200 RM for the acquisition of 50 beds for sick and elderly people
50 RM for heating purposes

From the enclosed letter, you have seen what a great task we must contend with. It is no longer possible to obtain the requisite funds from the previous Jewish inhabitants of Hinterberg, as they all are financially ruined.

In the hope that the worthy Joint will continue to support us in our great relief operation,

Respectfully yours,
[Stamp]
Jüdischer Ältestenrat

zu Hinterberg
Konin Administrative District
[Three signatures, partly illegible]

As help from abroad became increasingly difficult to obtain, appeals to once affluent community members increased. In desperation, Jewish relief organizations also solicited support from other Jewish communities across Poland. To address an acute crisis caused by the expulsion of Jews from the Lublin area in December 1940, for instance, the Kraków JSS sent the appeal in document 11–16 to the Jewish Council in Lublin.

DOCUMENT 11–16: Letter from the Presidium of Jewish Social Self-Help in Kraków, to the Jewish Council of Lublin, December 21, 1940, USHMMA Acc. 1997.A.0124 (ŻIH 211/644) (translated from Polish).

Regarding: aid for displaced persons
For several days we have been receiving telephone calls and telegrams from various localities in the Lublin district appealing for aid of all sorts for thousands of displaced persons who have settled there from various areas, particularly from Mława and Kraków. The state of the displaced persons is simply indescribable, they are threatened by hunger, epidemic, frostbite, and an elevated mortality rate.

Desiring to alleviate this misery even if only minimally and to come to their aid in the first hour, we are currently dispatching, in agreement with the American Joint Distribution Committee, two delegates to the Lublin district with a sum of 15,000 złoty with the goal of familiarizing themselves [illegible word] with the situation, establishing suitable liaisons in individual areas, and allocating available funds for the most pressing needs.

On the basis of the reports of the delegates we are dispatching, we will then put together a program on how one ought to satisfy the most necessary demands and provisionally alleviate the misery prevailing there, even if only in part.

Since this matter requires funds that exceed our financial capacities as well as those of the Joint, we feel obligated to turn to the largest Jewish communities in the G[eneral] G[ouvernement] with the polite request for aid, even if small in size, for the aforementioned purpose. The Jewish Councils in Kraków and Warsaw have already taken upon themselves certain obligations pertaining to certain fixed services; we now appeal to you, respected sirs, kindly to recognize the needs of the moment and to contribute the appropriate sums to the aforementioned goal.

We request that you inform us which monthly sum or larger one-time sum we can expect from you so that we may accordingly formulate an appropriate plan for disbursement of the resources to partially satisfy the needs of the displaced persons.

We greatly appeal for rapid, better immediate, aid.

Respectfully,
[No signature]

The Lublin *Judenrat* informed the JSS Kraków that it could do a much better job with helping the Lublin needy were it not forced "to pay craftsmen working for the German authorities," including Polish workers, in the local workshops.[74] Indeed, already in 1940, Jewish forced labor outside the ghettos had begun to place a heavy burden on communities. It would only grow over time.[75] German authorities not only took Jewish men away more or less randomly, with dire consequences for their families, but also charged the councils for the cost of running the labor camps. Nevertheless, some Jewish community leaders continued to have faith in the power of Jewish self-help. Aleksander Fargel, head of the *Judenrat* in Włoszczowa in the Generalgouvernement, whose report describing the burdens his council confronted with the arrival in Włoszczowa of Jews expelled from Poznań and Łódź featured in document 10–2, discussed in that same report the deterioration of conditions and his ongoing hope and defiance.

DOCUMENT 11–17: Aleksander Fargel, "Account of the Social Welfare Measures Taken by the Aid Committee for Refugees and the Poor of the Jewish Council of Włoszczowa in 1940," no date (ca. January 1941), USHMMA RG 15.073M (ŻIH 223/1), reel 1 (translated from Polish).

[. . .] On July 10, 1940, the Jewish community of Włoszczowa sustained a heavy blow with the introduction of a ghetto. More than 4,000 persons were crammed into about a dozen small streets, with groups of about

---

74. Letter from the Jewish Council in Lublin to the JSS presidium in Kraków, December 11, 1940, USHMMA Acc. 1997.A.0124 (ŻIH 211/644).

75. See Gruner, *Jewish Forced Labor,* 177ff.

a dozen persons sharing small rooms. Merchants and craftsmen were deprived of their workshops and their only sources of support, pushed in an instant into the ranks of those to whom they had up to that point provided considerable aid. The situation became catastrophic as all revenue streams to the committee's treasury dried up. As a result, the shipment of dry foodstuffs for refugees was discontinued and the rest of the funds in our possession were directed toward helping to resettle the poor. Our appeals and calls for help to external institutions had, unfortunately, very little effect, since the financial situation of the Joint was worsening considerably at the time. Desiring despite everything to keep the community kitchens running, we introduced a system of partial payments for meals, which resulted in a massive drop in the number of individuals making use of the kitchens. Existing debts, which had already reached the sum of 7,000 złoty, led to credit being cut off, and we were ultimately forced to close the community kitchen in Włoszczowa on September 1. [. . .]

The conscription and dispatch of Jewish youths to the labor camp in Cieszanów led to such immense dejection, particularly among the families of those sent off, that aid activities were directed only at helping those in the labor camp. The majority of those sent off, among whom were also refugees, found themselves in extremely difficult working conditions and without suitable food, clothing, or footwear. Thus a collection was organized as quickly as possible on the territory of the town, and within two days nine sacks and a box of clothing and food were sent to the camp. Aside from this, an average of 15 to 20 packages of food with bread, sugar, marmalade, etc. were sent each day. The cost of the aid activities for those in the labor camp exceeded 10,000 złoty in the course of six weeks. [. . .]

In the meantime, the long-awaited return of the workers from the labor camp finally came, but unfortunately it was accompanied by the sad news of the death of seven young men. With the return of the workers, a great burden immediately fell from the division for social welfare. [Their] medical care at first proved indeed very costly since the returnees' health was poor, but their return in any case made it possible once again to engage in broader aid activities in the territory of the city. The lack of external aid obliged us this time as well to obtain funds from among the local population. The designated quota of potatoes had to be picked up quickly in light of the rather advanced time of year and the light frosts that had already begun to set in. An action to supply refugees and the poor with potatoes was swiftly put into motion. While we had not envisioned carrying out the action in full in light of disruptions to the potato supply, we distributed 100 kilograms of potatoes per person free of charge to all the refugees in Włoszczowa, Kurzelów, and other nearby villages and to nearly all the local poor. [. . .]

The year of work of the Jewish Council's Aid Committee for Refugees and the Poor, a year of taxing and strenuous work, was characterized above all by great dedication on the part of all its employees and the local community, whose contribution to the financing of all social welfare activities was very significant. If the aid that was provided was not as we desired and was not particularly great when measured against our vision or that of its beneficiaries, this was not our fault. The lack of necessary funds stood as an obstacle upon which more than one plan faltered.

Enriched by the experiences of this year, we go about our work in the new year in even more difficult conditions, yet with the same slogan: HELPING WITH JOINT FORCES!

Polish Jews confronted geographic dislocation, hunger, disease, orphaned children, rampant unemployment, forced labor, and social inequalities in the first year and a half of the war. Subsistence was undoubtedly people's primary concern. Individuals looked after themselves and their families, and workers for relief organizations and employees and leaders of Jewish Councils tried to alleviate suffering on a large scale. Yet, in the midst of this massive humanitarian crisis, some Polish Jews in some communities expended energy on other pursuits—pursuits that seemed to complement and lend meaning to their struggle for survival.

CHAPTER 12

BEYOND BREAD
FAITH, FRIENDSHIP, AND THE FUTURE

BEYOND PHYSICAL nourishment, what sustained Jews in Poland emotionally and spiritually during the first eighteen months of the war? How did they understand what was happening to them? And what prospects did Jews inside and outside Poland see for Jewish life in the future? As varied as the answers to these questions, the experiences of war and occupation as of the end of 1940 overwhelmingly led European Jews to conclude that their lives would never be the same. In Poland in particular, Jews came to believe that even Germany's defeat would not allow for the resumption of life as they had known it. True, Jews in prewar Poland had faced increasing antisemitism, but in many other European countries, Jewish citizens had also been subjected to legal discrimination and outbursts of violence. The Third Reich's assault in Poland, however, had destroyed the feeble basis on which Jews and Poles had coexisted for centuries and introduced in its place an ideology-driven system of subjugation in which the Jews were resolutely expelled from common society. Polish Jews found themselves grappling for even tenuous ways to carry on.

By the end of 1940, the cumulative effect of German anti-Jewish policies had taken a heavy toll on communities, families, and individuals. Under the circumstances described in chapters 10 and 11, it is reasonable to assume that few Polish Jews had the wherewithal to think of anything but subsistence or ways to escape the dragnet of German measures. Indeed, in addition to attempts to flee from German-controlled Poland, some Jews—especially in large urban centers—were evading persecution already in this early phase of the war by posing as "**Aryans**" or by committing suicide.[1] Yet, perhaps astonishingly, Polish Jews in urban and rural communities also undertook a dazzling array of activities. Some were officially permitted, some clandestine; they were in different instances organized by the Jewish Councils, sponsored by political and other groups, or assumed on a purely private basis. In sum, these social, cultural, and religious pursuits distracted those who participated in them from the daily sorrows and enticed them to look forward to better times.

People's prewar beliefs and ideas played an important role in their attempts to transcend bleak reality. For many, particularly Orthodox Jews and those living in smaller communities, religion provided an orientation and protection against despair. Others clung to Zionist hopes or leftist ideologies that promised a more secure and just postwar world. Men, women, and even children tried to carve out private spaces amid the crammed apartments of the ghettos by confiding their experiences and thoughts in diaries, notebooks, and letters. In so doing, they used the space of the page to make sense of the perils they faced and the dilemmas presented by this situation of the Germans' creation. And some even came to the conclusion in this first year and a half of German occupation that the situation called for the amassing of eyewitness accounts, news, and rumors about German actions and Jewish reactions so that future generations might one day comprehend what had unfolded in wartime Poland and assess its historical significance. This chapter provides a glimpse of what Polish Jews thought and did in their efforts to cope mentally with a disastrous reality and its incalculable trajectory.

PRESERVING THE SPIRIT

Historian and social activist **Emanuel Ringelblum** in Warsaw was among the first to grasp the fact that Jews needed more than bread to overcome the challenges of the present. Since the outbreak of the war, he had focused simultaneously on responding to the immediate needs of Jews under the occupation and

---

1. No reliable figures exist on the number of Polish Jews who procured false "Aryan" papers or those who took their own lives. Both evasion strategies were forbidden under religious law. For a classic early study of evasion and hiding during the Holocaust, see Michał Borwicz, *Arishe papirn* (Buenos Aires: Tsentral-farband fun Poylishe Yidn in Argentine, 1955). For a case study focusing on Warsaw, see Gunnar S. Paulsson, *Secret City: The Hidden Jews of Warsaw, 1940–1945* (New Haven, CT: Yale University Press, 2002). The number of suicides among Jews in occupied Poland was not substantial until the summer deportations of 1942. Yisrael Gutman, *The Jews of Warsaw, 1939–1943: Ghetto, Underground, Revolt* (Bloomington: Indiana University Press, 1982), 218.

on documenting the persecution of Polish Jewry. In addition to playing a leader-ship role in relief efforts, Ringelblum helped to found a society for the advance-ment of Yiddish culture (Yidishe kultur organizatsiye, or YIKOR). His most important initiative, however, was the creation of the **Oyneg Shabes** under-ground archive, the secret archive of the Warsaw ghetto from which we have selected several documents for this volume. Ringelblum's project took a similar approach to documentary preservation as prewar efforts at the **YIVO**, the Jewish research institute based in Vilna in whose historical section Ringelblum actively participated since the institute's founding in 1925. Oyneg Shabes *zamlers* (col-lectors) tried to cover all aspects of Jewish life and capture what later came to be called "history from below": the day-to-day struggle of Polish Jewry to survive. Other projects, such as the "official" chronicle of the Łódź ghetto begun in late 1940, also tried to capture a broad cross section of Polish Jewish ghetto life, though Ringelblum's stood out for being a grassroots undertaking.[2]

Through his contacts in the **Aleynhilf** network, Ringelblum brought in key people to work with him on Oyneg Shabes, such as Hersh Wasser[3] from Łódź, and he also recruited heavily from his former colleagues at the prewar YIVO and **American Jewish Joint Distribution Committee** (AJJDC).[4] Among Ringelblum's most vital and active collaborators until his death in 1942 was a young rabbi from Piotrków Trybunalski, **Shimon Huberband**. According to Samuel Kassow, "No one in the Oyneg Shabes worked on as wide a range of topics as Huberband: religious life, labor camps, ghetto folklore, Jewish women, and Jewish life under the Soviet occupation."[5] Huberband recorded the more mundane aspects of life in Warsaw by depicting the religiously inflected humor of Polish Jews, a brand of humor that built upon a legacy of often cynical and

2. For Ringelblum's prewar training and work, see Samuel D. Kassow, *Who Will Write Our History? Emanuel Ringelblum, the Warsaw Ghetto, and the Oyneg Shabes Archive* (Bloomington: Indiana University Press, 2007), 27–48, 78–89. On the Łódź chronicle, see Sascha Feuchert, Erwin Leibfried, and Jörg Riecke, eds., *Die Chronik des Gettos Lodz/Litzmannstadt* (Göttingen: Wallstein Verlag, 2007); in English, Lucjan Dobroszycki, ed., *The Chronicle of the Łódź Ghetto, 1941–1944* (New Haven, CT: Yale University Press, 1984).

3. Hersh Wasser (1912–1980) was a Left Poalei Zion activist who arrived in Warsaw in 1939 as a refugee. He soon joined the Oyneg Shabes effort led by Emanuel Ringelblum. He was one of the handful of Oyneg Shabes activists to survive the war, after which he left Poland and settled in Israel. See Kassow, *Who Will Write Our History,* esp. 149–51.

4. See Kassow, *Who Will Write Our History*, 1, 145–208, on the various contributors who made up the Oyneg Shabes team; on Ringelblum's work, see 116–18. For a full sense of the archive's contents, see Robert Moses Shapiro and Tadeusz Epsztein, eds., *The Warsaw Ghetto Oyneg Shabes–Ringelblum Archive: Catalog and Guide* (Bloomington: Indiana University Press in association with the USHMM and the Jewish Historical Institute in Warsaw, 2009).

5. Kassow, *Who Will Write Our History*, 167.

self-deprecating jokes long practiced as a form of social criticism.[6] In a situation dominated by fear and the yearning for a positive turn, rumors and jokes filled the void created by the absence of reliable information. They provided a release from daily pressures, as well as a vehicle for keeping communication and human interaction alive.[7] Huberband's collection of "wartime folklore" mixed puns and satire with playful allusions to religious themes. Some jokes mocked Jews for their pitiful present condition: "Jews are now very pious. They observe all the ritual laws: they are stabbed and punched with holes like *matzahs*, and have as much bread as on Passover; they are beaten like *hoshanas*, rattled like Haman; they are as green as *esrogim* and as thin as *lulavim*; they fast as if it were Yom Kippur; they are burnt as if it were Hanukkah, and their moods are as if it were the Ninth of Av."[8] Others targeted the oppressors, like the joke in which a teacher asks his pupil, "Tell me, Moyshe, what would you like to be if you were Hitler's son?" The student responded, "An orphan."[9]

Huberband captured a sense of what historians later came to refer to as "spiritual resistance," or alternately as *amidah* (from the Hebrew for standing up against), a term encompassing many forms of Jewish nonconformism.[10]

---

6. See Steve Lipman, *Laughter in Hell: The Use of Humor during the Holocaust* (Northvale, NJ: J. Aronson, 1991); more generally, see Moshe Waldoks, *The Big Book of Jewish Humor* (New York: HarperCollins, 2006), or Joseph Telushkin, *Jewish Humor: What the Best Jewish Jokes Say About the Jews* (New York: HarperCollins, 1992). Telushkin's chapter 5, "Persecution and the Jewish Sense of Homelessness," is particularly useful in this regard.

7. See Barbara Engelking, *Holocaust and Memory: The Experience of the Holocaust and Its Consequences* (London: Leicester University Press, 2001), 185–86.

8. *Matzah*, the unleavened "bread of affliction," is consumed on Passover to commemorate the Israelites' exodus from Egypt; like a cracker, it is dry, thin, and punctured with holes. At the end of Sukkot, on the holiday of Hoshana Rabbah, it is customary to shake the *lulav*, a long, thin frond of a date palm tree; the *etrog* (*esrog* in Yiddish), a citrus fruit, is used in the custom as well. On Purim, which commemorates the deliverance of the Jews in the Persian Empire from the plot to annihilate them—as recounted in the Book of Esther—participants rattle noisemakers when the name of Haman is read from the Purim scroll or *megillah*. On Hanukkah, the Festival of Lights, Jews burn oil or candles in the Hanukkiyah (a special menorah for Hanukkah) for eight nights. The Ninth of Av (Tisha b'Av) is a day of mourning on the Jewish calendar that commemorates the destruction of the First and Second Temples in Jerusalem, as well as other catastrophes throughout Jewish history, including the Crusades, the Spanish Inquisition, and the Khmelnitsky Massacres of 1648.

9. Shimon Huberband, "Wartime folklore," no date, USHMMA RG 15.079M, reel 8, Ring. I/109, and cf. Shimon Huberband, *Kiddush Hashem: Jewish Religious and Cultural Life in Poland during the Holocaust*, ed. Jeffrey S. Gurock and Robert S. Hirt (Hoboken, NJ: KTAV Publishing House, 1987), 113–29.

10. See Huberband, *Kiddush Hashem*, 165–69. For the concept of *amidah*, see Yehuda Bauer, *Rethinking the Holocaust* (New Haven, CT: Yale University Press, 2002), esp. 119–66.

His and others' descriptions of Jews maintaining religious rituals despite Nazi death threats comprise a particularly vivid example of such acts of defiance in which Jews subverted the practice or spirit of Nazi policies indirectly, in ways less confrontational than armed resistance. Indeed, as in Germany after the Nazi takeover, restricting religious freedoms was high on the list of anti-Jewish measures introduced by the occupation regime. Through a somewhat familiar mix of official decrees and actual practice, German authorities generally prohibited ritual slaughter; desecrated, destroyed, or shuttered many synagogues; restricted the observance of religious holidays and ceremonies; and targeted for abuse those Jews with the outward appearance of piety, especially men with beards and side locks. Consequently, many aspects of Jewish religious life were pushed into illegality. With the emergence of ghettos, Jewish Councils could only partially provide or sustain communal activities, a telling indicator of the true weakness of "Jewish self-administration" and its function as a subterfuge for hiding German interests.[11] Nevertheless, religiously observant Jews used all available means at their disposal, often moving well beyond what German orders defined as permissible. In September 1940, Ringelblum estimated that six hundred underground minyanim (or prayer quorums) were meeting in the courtyards of the Warsaw Jewish quarter.[12] Lending further support to people's efforts to maintain religious observance, rabbis interpreted religious law more leniently than under prewar circumstances.[13]

On Yom Kippur in 5741 (October 12, 1940), the Day of Atonement, the holiest day in the Jewish calendar, the day on which Jews confess their sins and ask forgiveness from God and their fellow human beings, Rabbi **Kalonymus Shapira** refused to adapt religious law to suit German proscriptions. According to Rabbi Shapira, despite (and even because of) the conditions of the occupation, one had a sacred duty to immerse oneself in the *mikveh*, the Jewish ritual bath, on Yom Kippur in order to cleanse the soul. Despite all protests to the

---

11. See Isaiah Trunk, *Judenrat: The Jewish Councils in Eastern Europe under Nazi Occupation* (New York: Macmillan, 1972), 187–96.

12. Emanuel Ringelblum, *Notes from the Warsaw Ghetto: The Journal of Emmanuel Ringelblum*, ed. Jacob Sloan (New York: Schocken Books, 1974), 47. A minyan (pl. minyanim; Hebrew) is a Jewish community of prayer. This community must include at least ten Jewish men over thirteen years of age.

13. For a more thorough treatment, see Menashe Unger, *Der geystiker vidershtand fun yidn in getos un lagern* [*The Spiritual Resistance of Jews in Ghettos and Camps*] (Tel Aviv: Menorah Publishing House, 1970). See also Esther Farbstein, *Hidden in Thunder: Perspectives on Faith, Halachah and Leadership during the Holocaust* (Jerusalem: Mossad Harav Kook, 2007), and Steven T. Katz, Shlomo Biderman, and Gershon Greenberg, eds., *Wrestling with God: Jewish Theological Responses during and after the Holocaust* (New York: Oxford University Press, 2007).

contrary, the students of Rabbi Shapira could not convince him that it would be too dangerous to journey to the *mikveh* in defiance of the German order not to use it. Kalman Huberband, brother of Shimon, recorded an account of the journey of the rabbi and other men to the *mikveh*, combining a sense of irony about the "dangerous expedition" with the sensation that they were walking in the footsteps of their forefathers in Spain, who had suffered during the Inquisition, prayed silently in cellars, and rescued Torah scrolls at great personal danger.

DOCUMENT 12–1: Kalman Huberband, Warsaw, "The 'march' into the *mikveh*," October 1940, USHMMA RG 15.079M (ŻIH Ring I/218), reel 11 (translated from Yiddish).[14]

> Among all the other cruel decrees which the evil regime issued was the one forbidding Jews to immerse themselves in the *mikveh*. All the *mikvehs* were sealed, and a notice was hung on their doors saying, "Opening or using the *mikveh* will be considered sabotage and will be punished by ten years in prison to death."
>
> The rebbe [Rabbi Kalonymus Shapira] made a decision, an ironclad decision, that one must immerse oneself in the *mikveh* before Yom Kippur. Members of his inner circle tried to argue that immersion in the *mikveh*, or even just approaching it, would endanger people's lives, and especially the rebbe's, but to no avail. The rebbe did not alter his decision, and we made plans to implement it. But how? As mentioned, all the *mikvehs* were sealed, and their use was subject to such dangerous consequences. Finally, after a number of secret consultations between the rebbe and a *mikveh* owner, the matter was arranged.
>
> At dawn of the day on which the Thirteen Divine Attributes are recited [Yom Kippur], at exactly 5:00 a.m., the hour when Jews are first permitted to walk in the street, a small group of people, lead by the rebbe, assembled and began the "dangerous march" to the *mikveh*.
>
> Luckily it is still pitch-dark outside. We wish that the darkness would thicken even more and last even longer. Maybe we can hide in the darkness, maybe they won't notice us, and we can carry out this "dangerous expedition" successfully.

---

14. This was also printed, using different wording, in Huberband, *Kiddush Hashem*, 199–210.

The distance between the rebbe's home and the *mikveh* is quite long. The wagon that we had ordered has not arrived. The clock is showing ten minutes past five already. The group is getting nervous, because everything had been planned according to the exact minute. We decide to begin "the march" by foot, in the hope that the wagon might meet us en route. It would be rather difficult to find another wagon at this hour of day, and you can't trust just any wagon, since all the arrangements had been made in great secrecy, and the coachman we had hired already knew all the "strategic" information—how to travel, which streets to take, and where to stop. Apparently he had encountered some sort of obstacle, as is so often the case.

Quietly, on our tiptoes, we walk down the stairs, but there is a new, unanticipated problem: the janitor [*struzh*; (non-Jewish) guard] doesn't feel like getting up so early to open the gate, and he wants to know why the Jews need to go out to the street so early. We grease his palm, and this softens his heart instantly; he agrees to let us through the gate.

We are walking with soft footsteps, in pairs, leaving some space between each pair. Our hearts beat like hammers. Our eyes strained, we are staring into the depths of the night, looking at each approaching silhouette, to see whether it isn't one of "them." When we hear heavy footsteps ahead of us or behind us, our limbs are numbed with fear. Suddenly an approaching night trolley is ringing. We run quickly to the station to get on the trolley, since it is going exactly where we need to go. But as we come nearer, we realize that it is an Aryan trolley—off-limits to Jews. It would be a long time until a "Jewish" trolley arrived, since Jewish trolleys do not run so early in the morning.

So we walk from street to street. Suddenly we hear the sound of an approaching automobile. Its blinding headlights shine into our eyes. We stop as if paralyzed, because meeting an automobile on the street can be very unfortunate these days. In most cases, one is "invited" to a place from which there is no return . . . There isn't a gate behind which to hide; they are all still locked, since it's very early. But we were graced with a stroke of luck. The automobile passes by without noticing us. Holding our breath, we manage to walk past the more dangerous points and reach the entrance to the *mikveh*.

The courtyard is pitch-dark. Mysterious shadows creep along the walls and disappear into a cellar on the side. A secret emissary is already waiting for us. Without uttering a single word, just by waving his arm, he begins to lead us. We descend into a deep, dark cellar. The door locks above us. We are groping in the darkness. We have instructions to walk straight and then to turn left. We reach a chiseled hole in the wall. With great difficulty, we push ourselves through it and find ourselves standing on some wooden boards. After a successful jump we land in a corridor that leads to the steps of the *mikveh*.

Despite the great danger in which we found ourselves, we were mesmerized by the whole event. Our forefathers in Spain appeared vividly in our imagination—how they celebrated seders and prayed with a minyan in secret cellars, fearful of the Inquisition. They certainly never imagined that four hundred years later their descendants would find themselves in a much worse situation and that in order to immerse themselves in honor of a festival, they would be forced to follow the same kind of dangerous procedures.

In the *mikveh* we found a large group of people who had received secret word that the *mikveh* would be open for an hour. Silently and in great haste we undressed and immersed ourselves in honor of the festival. A few minutes later, we repeated the same procedure we had used to enter. By the time we reached the courtyard, day was beginning to break, and we could see on the seal on the entrance to the *mikveh* the well-known notice: "Opening or using the *mikveh* will be considered sabotage and will be punished by ten years in prison to death."

Documents attest to the continuation of prayer services, religious study and education, and the observance of the Sabbath and holidays in many Polish towns and cities. Some pious Jews even saw the German assault as an opportunity to deepen their faith in the hope that the messianic age was at hand. Occasional success in defying German proscriptions on religious practices notwithstanding, things were evidently changing for the worse. Though it is more difficult to assess how Nazi persecution challenged Jewish faith at the time, it appears from the sparse documentation on this question that for some people, the severity of Nazi persecution began to call into question the existence of God. In the spring of 1940, **Chaim Kaplan**, the astute observer of Jewish life in the Warsaw ghetto, had written with confidence about the resilience and fortitude of Polish Jewry. "We ought to have been completely annihilated," he described in a diary entry from that period; yet, he insisted, "a certain invisible power is embedded in us, and it is this secret which keeps us alive and preserves us in spite of all the laws of nature."[15] Half a year later, on Yom Kippur, when

---

15. Chaim A. Kaplan, Warsaw, diary entry for March 10, 1940, in *Scroll of Agony: The Warsaw Diary of Chaim A. Kaplan*, ed. Abraham I. Katsh (Bloomington: Indiana University Press in association with the USHMM, 1999), 131.

the creation of the ghetto became known among the Jews of Warsaw, Kaplan's view underwent a radical transformation. He struggled with faith, as, seemingly, did many others.

DOCUMENT 12–2: Chaim Kaplan, Warsaw, diary entry for October 14, 1940, USHMMA RG 02.208M (ŻIH 302/218), 148–52 (translated from Hebrew).[16]

October 14, 1940

A rumor is spreading among the people that in one of the minyanim, the prayer leader, dressed in his white prayer robe [*kitel*],[17] prepared to lead the poor and downtrodden of the congregation in the closing Yom Kippur service [*neilah*],[18] when a young man dashed into the minyan and brought "news" of the [closing of the] ghetto. Immediately, the same Jew refused to pray, removed his robe, and returned to his place.

"One cannot pray when our prayers are forsaken! He who hears our prayers has closed the Gates of Compassion. Why should we lie to ourselves?"

I am not sure that this is exactly what happened; but if the people invented such a rumor, it is a sign that this could be true, since the masses began to think heretical thoughts . . ."[19] One should note: the number of unbelievers and heretics has grown amongst the people of Israel. Faith in "the great leader" whose "ways are all just, a God of faith, without injustice, who is righteous," has run out. Between each other, people murmur:

Is there no God of Israel? Why has He ceased to come to our aid in these times of trouble? We have not had a day as bitter as today! If we use the phrase of the prophet [Isaiah]: "a day of tumult and confusion and din,"[20] we still do not capture the nature of this "day of atrocity," the likes of which have not been seen since I came to Warsaw forty years ago. The wrath of the conquerors and of our God is poured upon us all at once. Our sins have provoked his anger; He has thrown down his rage with his

---

16. For a somewhat different version of this entry, see the English translation in Kaplan, *Scroll of Agony*, 209.

17. A *kitel* (Hebrew) is a white prayer robe used during Yom Kippur, or the Day of Atonement, as a sign of purity and repentance. It is meant to resemble a burial shroud.

18. The *neilah* (Hebrew) is the final service that concludes the Yom Kippur observance and indicates the closing of the gates of heaven for the year.

19. Ellipsis appears in the original manuscript.

20. Isaiah 22:5. Kaplan quotes this passage incorrectly: the correct sequence is "a day of tumult and din and confusion."

hands "to take [his] spoil and seize [his] booty, and to make [us] a thing trampled like the mire of the streets."[21] And still his anger is not quenched and his arm is outstretched. There were days when I thought that these verses of Isaiah were only rhetorical flourishes. On this "day of subordination," I am convinced of their truth, because this hard prophesy has been fully realized.

Finally, the ghetto has been created for the people of Israel in Warsaw, a community that totals half a million Jews. This ghetto is a place of refuge for many people. A narrow quarter has been allotted, which is destined to become a place for all manners of atrocities and evil deeds. Approximately one thousand people still live in the Aryan quarter. In the next twenty days, this entire mass of people must uproot themselves from their apartments, stores, and businesses and come to these narrow, overcrowded streets that have been filled from end to end with refugees from the small towns and provinces. In the ghetto there is not one open corner; there is not an empty crack, not even an unoccupied hole. They have expelled us from the streets that they walk, once renowned for hundreds of years of Jewish life.

Urban religious leaders formed but one group among the variety of Jewish cultural elites. Others included members of the prewar intelligentsia, political activists, and youth leaders and educators, all of whom were eager to participate in the effort to improve the conditions of the Jewish population, be it by working with or against the *Judenrat*.[22] On the political Left, the **Bund** still saw itself as aligned with the Polish working class in its struggle against capitalist exploitation, Nazi oppression, and Stalinist terror. In this sense and in contrast to Zionist groups, Jewish Socialists' striving for solidarity transcended the ghetto to include Polish workers.[23] The article in document 12–3 from the Bundist youth movement paper *Yugnt Shtime* includes a lengthy discussion of the significance of Soviet foreign minister Vyacheslav Molotov's visit to Berlin at a time when Great Britain was left to fight German aggression alone.[24] The author demonstrated Bundist leaders' continuing concern with political alignments and ideology in the midst of the daily struggle for survival. Such "clarity"

---

21. Isaiah 10:6.

22. See Trunk, *Judenrat*, 196–229.

23. For the history of the Bund and its ideology, see Jonathan Frankel, *Prophecy and Politics: Socialism, Nationalism, and the Russian Jews, 1862–1917* (New York: Cambridge University Press, 1981), 171–257.

24. The United States remained neutral at this point.

may have held a special appeal to readers who were grappling for orientation and order in a rapidly and radically changing world.

DOCUMENT 12–3: **"Molotov in Berlin, and What Next?"** *Yugnt shtime* **(Warsaw), October 1940, 3–4, USHMMA RG 15.079M (ŻIH Ring I/685), reel 29 (translated from Yiddish).[25]**

"A WAR AGAINST FASCISM"

The events follow one another at a dizzying pace. All the fig leaves have fallen. We are experiencing a time when all stones have been turned, and they are rolling down the hill.

The fascist dictators now stand as naked as the first man. They started the war with the slogan of liberating their peoples, and Hitler only demanded Danzig. Today the whole world knows that it is about power and control of the world. The individual has no importance. His rights and freedom have been trampled. Entire peoples can be drenched in blood, ridiculed, and shamed. Small countries have two choices: either the shameful fate of a slave (Romania) or the bloody struggle for freedom (Greece).[26] The masses are blinded and deceived by heinous propaganda; the youth is poisoned with the hatred, brutality, and sadism of the rulers.

The god of imperialism, war-crazed capitalism, revels in its disgusting orgies. The war is about who will control the world. But at the same time the bloody wheels of the war machine are destroying the freedom of the working class, of individuals, and of nations. The very existence of culture and human morals is at stake.

It is true, England and America are capitalist countries. Their governments have, in fact, always favored the interests of the wealthy, propertied classes. They have exploited and oppressed not only their own working classes but also hundreds of millions of colonial peoples. But will Hitler and Mussolini be the liberators, the guardians of justice, the builders of a more righteous regime in the world?

25. This was published in Hebrew translation in Yosef Kermish, ed., *Itonut ha-mahteret ha-yehudit be-Varshah* (Jerusalem: Yad Vashem, 1979), 1:151–52.
26. The Romanian "fate of a slave" refers to the rapid deterioration of Romania's international position in the summer and fall of 1940. See the discussion of political events in Romania in chapters 7 and 8. For an excellent study on the Transylvanian question, see Holly Case, *Between States: The Transylvanian Question and the European Idea during World War II* (Stanford, CA: Stanford University Press, 2009). The Greek army successfully repelled the Italian Fascist invasion in the fall and winter of 1940–1941.

It is enough to take a look at Europe under Hitler's occupation and at England in the year 1940. On one side—laws against Jews, ghettos and yellow patches, concentration camps, physical and spiritual displacement of millions, from the Atlantic Ocean to the Bug [River]; prisons in France filled with French Socialists and Communists (!). In France, Belgium, Holland, Norway, etc., the political parties and professional organizations have been disbanded. The press has been subject to *[G]leichschaltung*.[27] Caballero has been arrested in France; the Fascist International has stretched itself across Europe with Hitler's blessing: Laval in France, Degrelle in Belgium, Mussert in Holland, Quisling in Norway.[28] On the other side—in England the influence of the working class is growing both in the country and in the government; in Australia the Labor Party won the elections. The English workers are fighting for higher wages to offset the growing prices and for control of industry because of the war. [. . .] In America, Roosevelt triumphed in the elections, and even though he is really a bourgeois politician, he is also an outspoken opponent of fascism. Even in wartime[,] America and England have remained democratic countries, in which there is opportunity for growth of the workers' movement and antisemitism [*sic*; perhaps meant to read "fight against antisemitism"], where all emigrants from Europe (who are persecuted due to political or national reasons) find refuge, where the fight for national liberation and independence of all oppressed European nations is supported.

Millions who suffer under the fascist yoke tie their destiny and hope in a better future to [words illegible; likely to read "the victory of England"] over Germany.

---

27. *Gleichschaltung* (literally, "synchronization") was a Nazi term for asserting control over all sectors of society in the aftermath of the Nazi seizure of power in 1933.

28. Francisco Largo Caballero (1869–1946), a Spanish trade union leader and Socialist politician, served as prime minister of Spain in 1936 and 1937, the first years of the Civil War (1936–1939). Pierre Laval (1885–1945) was the head of the French collaborationist Vichy government. Léon Degrelle (1906–1994) headed the *Rex*, a Belgian Walloon authoritarian and later collaborationist movement; Degrelle later joined the SS and remained prominent in neo-Nazi circles after the war. Anton Mussert (1894–1946) was one of the founders of the National Socialist movement in the Netherlands and its leader during the war. Vidkun Quisling (1887–1945), a Norwegian politician, served as prime minister of the collaborationist Norwegian government from 1942 to 1945. For a history of fascism and its national variants in Europe, see Stanley Payne, *A History of Fascism, 1914–1945* (Madison: University of Wisconsin Press, 1995).

Hitler took control of Europe, but he has not won the war. Mussolini is stuck in the burning sands of the Egyptian desert,[29] and he has failed even in the tiny country of Greece.

Under these circumstances comes the sensationalistic piece of news: Molotov travels to Berlin with great fanfare in order to conduct negotiations with Hitler. Russia conducts the war in a cold and calm, business-like manner. Until now Soviet Russia has made "excellent" business from the war. She sold merchandise to Hitler, raw materials, and has provided moral support, which in the eyes of the Soviet rulers has cost her nothing. In return, she has received part of Poland, the Baltic lands, Bessarabia, the right to invade Finland, and German machinery. There is a befitting capitalist saying: "Money does not stink." The Soviet politicians are practical merchants. They believe that blood leaves no stains. Their main slogan is to exploit the situation as long as possible. The interests of the international working class and the Communist parties in France and Germany (or whatever has remained of them) have little meaning to them. Long live the imperialistic business of the Russian regime! And while Hitler holds the knife of partition—long live Russo-German friendship! Let's hurry—perhaps it is still possible to get something in the Balkans, maybe even a fat piece like the Dardanelles? Meanwhile, they will make deals: they will buy machines, they will sell produce and oil. Friendship with Germany, friendship with Italy, friendship with Japan—betrayal of the Russian Revolution, Communist ideology, the European working class, the struggle of the Chinese for freedom, and all in the name of the dictatorial, bureaucratic regime that rules over the Russian masses.

We still do not know the contents of the new agreement that has been decided in Berlin. What can still come after all that has occurred until now? What else?

But history is not only made in the cabinets of heads of state, of "führers" and generals. Marx taught us that when the masses awaken from their deep slumber and enter into the historical arena with their steady march, the dictators disappear, together with their slaves and their "heroes"—and then true history is made. For this we wait.

---

29. Refers to the stalled Italian campaign in North Africa; see Gerhard L. Weinberg, *A World at Arms: A Global History of World War II* (Cambridge: Cambridge University Press, 1994), 209; MacGregor Knox, *Mussolini Unleashed, 1939–1941: Politics and Strategy in Fascist Italy's Last War* (Cambridge: Cambridge University Press, 1982), 150–55.

Some community activists and members of the secular intelligentsia saw the war as an opportunity to forge a new sense of Jewish identity, one centered on culture, language, and common experience. The concrete manifestations of these efforts ranged widely, including *Judenrat*-sponsored education efforts, Zionist youth group gatherings, and the activities of the leftist Bund and other organizations. All such efforts vied to satisfy a thirst for intellectual stimulus and moral support—or, as a document circulated in Warsaw put it, "moral supply."[30]

Groups with different orientations were especially concerned about the future of Polish Jewish children and youth. Zionist leaders who before the war had prepared the "elite" among Jewish youth for *aliyah* to Palestine in *hakhsharah* now began to broaden their educational activities by establishing **kibbutz** groups and underground schools.[31] They worked within and across local communities to improve Jewish morale and to nurture an increasingly alienated, isolated, and demoralized youth. In so doing, they provided what Yisrael Gutman has called an "alternative leadership," one that challenged the authority of the Jewish Councils.[32] And in view of the prevailing material plight, it was no coincidence that soup kitchens became centers for educational work and underground meetings. In Warsaw, political and youth groups joined relief organizations like Aleynhilf in opening soup kitchens where their members could discuss party matters and distribute underground newspapers. In a

30. "A call for the establishment of an organization for 'moral support in the Warsaw ghetto,'" by an unknown author, "Warsaw," n.d. (ca. 1940), USHMMA RG 15.079M, reel 7, Ring. I/89, in *To Live with Honor and Die with Honor! Selected Documents from the Warsaw Ghetto Underground Archives "O.S." (Oneg Shabbath)*, ed. Joseph Kermish (Jerusalem: Yad Vashem, 1986), 456–57.

31. See Zivia Lubetkin, *Biyemei kilayon u-mered* (Tel Aviv: Hakibbutz Hameuhad, 1989), 49–52. For other discussions of youth movement activities, see Gutman, *The Jews of Warsaw*; Herman Kruk, *The Last Days of the Jerusalem of Lithuania: Chronicles from the Vilna Ghetto and the Camps, 1939–1944*, ed. Benjamin Harshav (New Haven, CT: Yale University Press, 2002); Tikva Fatal-Knaani, *Zo lo otah Grodno: kehilat Grodno ve-svivatah be-milhamah uveshoah, 1939–1943* (Jerusalem: Yad Vashem, 2001), 227–40.

32. Later in the war, many Zionist, Bundist, and other youth leaders became involved in resistance activities. See Israel Gutman, "The Youth Movement As an Alternative Leadership in Eastern Europe," in *Zionist Youth Movements during the Shoah*, ed. Asher Cohen and Yehoyakim Cochavi (New York: Peter Lang, 1995), 7–18; Daniel Blatman, *Lema'an Herutenu ve-Herutkhem: ha-Bund be-Polin, 1939–1949* (Jerusalem: Yad Vashem, 1996); Aharon Weiss, "Youth Movements in Poland during the German Occupation," in Cohen and Cochavi, *Zionist Youth Movements*, 233; Dina Porat, "Zionist Pioneering Youth Movements in Poland and the Attitude to Eretz Israel during the Holocaust," in *Polin* 9 (Oxford: Basil Blackwell, 1996), 195–211.

similar vein, the Socialist group **Left Poalei Zion** ran four adult kitchens and a children's kitchen, the latter located in the Borochov School at Nowolipki 68 and run by three leading party members: Feige Hertzlich, Natan Smolar, and Israel Lichtenstein.[33] They crafted a plan for educational work in the kitchens that reflected broader Zionist concerns about Polish Jewish youth. Presented in document 12–4, the plan outlined the group's ambitions and goals for educating undernourished children.

DOCUMENT 12–4: **"Plan of Educational Work in the Food Supply Points at Karmelicka 29, Nowolipki 68, Krochmalna 36," Warsaw, no date (ca. 1940), USHMMA RG 15.079M (ŻIH Ring I/204), reel 10 (translated from Yiddish).**[34]

The Aims of Our Work.

We strive to turn food supply points into educational centers where we can supervise and influence the children.

Our primary concern is the children's health, so we first try to develop in them a sense of hygiene and aesthetics.

In view of the present dangers, we also try to include in our work the emotional life [*neshome-lebn*] of the child.

In order to create an atmosphere conducive to any educational influence, we try to convert the food supply group into a children's collective that is cemented by common and mutual interests.

We try to offer the children emotional outlets and we make a special effort to create as many joyous experiences for them as possible.

The social and ethical education of the child is a subject of special consideration, through fostering a sense of comradeship, collectivity, and responsibility, with particular stress on punctuality.

---

33. Kassow, *Who Will Write Our History*, 118–19. See also Barbara Engelking and Jacek Leociak, *The Warsaw Ghetto: A Guide to the Perished City* (New Haven, CT: Yale University Press, 2009), 673. Kassow and Engelking and Leociak note that the kitchen also served as a hiding place for the Oyneg Shabes and the Ringelblum Archive. Apart from being party activists, Hertzlich, Smolar, and Lichtenstein were also teachers. The authors have been unable to trace the fate of Feige Hertzlich (Fejga Herclich). Natan Smolar (1898–1943) probably died in the ghetto uprising with Israel Lichtenstein (1904–1943) and Lichtenstein's family. See Yad Vashem, Central Database of Shoah Victims' Names, www.yadvashem.org; Kassow, *Who Will Write Our History*, 313, 359.

34. Published in *Bleter far geshikhte* 28 (1990): 15–17; in English, Kermish, *To Live with Honor*, 474–75.

As much as circumstances permit, we try to advance the intellectual development of the child.

We try to implant in the child a love of and devotion to the Yiddish language and culture.

The Manner of Our Operation

In order to achieve the aims described above, our work is being conducted in the following manner:

The groups should be as homogeneous as possible, in terms of intellectual level of children and their age.

The children are under constant sanitary and medical supervision by a doctor, a hygienist, and an educator.

We train the children to take care of personal cleanliness and proper neatness of appearance themselves.

We teach the children various cultural norms, especially in connection with eating.

We encourage the children to take care of the aesthetic and orderly appearance of their group rooms and of the house in general, through growing flowers, decorating the walls with drawings and paintings, etc. Taking care of plants is particularly stressed as a means of bringing the child in closer relation with nature and of fostering their appreciation of aesthetics.

We strive to influence the children's life in the home by encouraging them to exercise the useful habits they had acquired at home, too, and by maintaining contact with the children's homes.

We draw the child into participation in all the tasks set for the group by creating situations where they can take leadership positions, such as supervisor at meals, in the wardrobe, in the washroom, at gardening, cleaning, etc.

In connection with the topics mentioned, we conduct talks on the following: (a) hygiene and culture in daily life; (b) comradeship and readiness to help; (c) wildlife and nature (connected with growing plants or as a suitable occasion arises); (d) holidays.

We tell or read aloud suitable tales and literary works. For instance, to younger children—"The Innkeeper," "The Seven Good Years," "A Question," "The Case against the Wind,"—by Peretz. "The Penknife," "Methuselah," "Motl the Cantor's Son," "The Fiddle," "The Ruined Passover"—by Sholem Aleichem. And Pinocchio, Robinson Crusoe, biblical stories (the sale of Joseph), selected Greek myths, etc. For older children—"Tevye the Dairyman," "Stories from Kasrilevke," "A Page from the Songs of Songs"—by Sholem Aleichem, "Folktales" by Peretz, "Kiddush Hashem," "The Neighbors"—by Sholem Ash. And "Uncle Tom's Cabin," "The Microbe Hunters," "The Chained Hero," "From the Epos of the Bible."[35]

We sing with the children, teach them to recite poems on occasion, and perform dramatized versions of stories and songs.

We play with the children (see the book "Games and Entertainment" by Gilinksi, Grundman, and Waffner).

Five minutes may be spent on physical exercise before meals.

On suitable occasions, we organize children's holidays and entertainments.

THE SPACE OF CORRESPONDENCE

The dismemberment of Poland and the physical and geographical marking of Jews made it difficult and dangerous for members of political and youth groups, as well as of families and friendship networks, to maintain contact with each other.[36] Still, some were determined to carry on. Among political and youth groups, women often took on the job of couriers, traveling across the country using false papers to conceal their Jewish identities. Female couriers like Tosia Altman, a Hashomer Hatzair activist who later became prominent in the Warsaw Ghetto Uprising in 1943, risked their lives smuggling an increasing range of materials and information, and helping people get in and

---

35. The provisional list of these "suitable tales and literary works" reveals that the authors had in mind a curriculum that combined classical Jewish literature (Peretz, Sholem Aleichem, Sholem Ash) and general classics (Harriet Beecher Stowe, Carlo Collodi, Daniel Defoe). Isaac Leib Peretz (1852–1915) was one of the greatest Jewish authors from the Pale of Settlement; Sholem Aleichem (1859–1916) was a classic Jewish author from the Russian Empire and one of the towering figures of Yiddish literature; Sholem Asch (1880–1957) was a Polish-born American Jewish author; Harriet Beecher Stowe (1811–1896) was an American writer and abolitionist, whose novel *Uncle Tom's Cabin* (1852) depicts lives of African Americans during slavery; Carlo Collodi (1826–1890) was an Italian children's writer, most famous for his serialized work *The Adventures of Pinocchio* (1881–1883); and Daniel Defoe (1661–1731) was an English writer famous for several novels, among them *Robinson Crusoe* (1719).

36. Gutman, *The Jews of Warsaw*, 136.

out of ghettos.[37] In the process, they performed vital functions for the emerging Jewish underground. They also undermined prevailing gender perceptions and practices—visible in the composition of the Jewish Councils—according to which leadership and communal activism remained predominantly male domains.[38]

In maintaining lines of communication, mail service complemented the work of underground couriers. Polish Jews were permitted to send and receive letters to people in other areas of German-occupied Europe and in neutral countries. In the Łódź ghetto, in the first year of its existence alone, according to the official chroniclers employed by **Chaim Rumkowski**'s *Judenrat*, "the post office delivered 135,062 parcels mailed from the Reich (and territories incorporated into it), and 14,229 from abroad. The telegraph service processed 10,239 wires, and the number of letters and postcards handled reached 1,074,351."[39] People frequently adopted coded language to refer to Germans or other politically sensitive topics that might attract the attention of the censors.

Document 12–5 exemplifies how letter writers commonly used Hebrew in their correspondence to communicate information covertly. It also shows

---

37. Tosia Altman (1918–1943) was raised in Włocławek, where her Zionist father ran a store. When the war broke out, she fled with other Zionist youth activists, eventually reaching Vilna. From there she returned to occupied Poland, traveling extensively and working to gather and rally youth leaders for clandestine work. She carried news of the onslaught against Jews with her and encouraged Jewish youth to organize resistance. Altman also forged contacts with the Polish and Communist underground organizations and, as an emissary of the Jewish Fighting Organization (ŻOB), worked to gather weapons for an armed uprising. Trapped in the ghetto during the April 1943 uprising, she made her way out through the sewers but was later burned in a fire that broke out in a fighters' hiding place in a Warsaw suburb, then captured and killed by the Germans. See Zivia Lubetkin, *In the Days of Destruction and Revolt* (Tel Aviv: Hakibbutz Hameuchad, 1981), 287; Ziva Shalev, "Tosia Altman," Jewish Women's Archive, www.jwa.org/encyclopedia/article/altman-tosia (accessed March 5, 2011).

38. For more on the role of women in resistance activities and as couriers in occupied Poland, see Dalia Ofer and Lenore J. Weitzman, eds., *Women in the Holocaust* (New Haven, CT: Yale University Press, 1998), esp. Lenore J. Weitzman, "Living on the Aryan Side in Poland: Gender, Passing and the Nature of Resistance," 187–222; Nechama Tec, *Resilience and Courage: Women, Men, and the Holocaust* (New Haven, CT: Yale University Press, 2003), 263–65. On the history of Jewish women in eastern Europe and gender, see ChaeRan Freeze, Paula Hyman, and Anthony Polonsky, eds., *Polin* 18 (Oxford: The Littman Library of Jewish Civilization, 2005).

39. Lucjan Dobroszycki, ed., *The Chronicle of the Łódź Ghetto, 1941–1944* (New Haven, CT: Yale University Press, 1984), 35. For more on letter writing among Jews under German occupation, see Alexandra Garbarini, *Numbered Days: Diaries and the Holocaust* (New Haven, CT: Yale University Press, 2006), 64–70, and chapter 4, "Family Correspondents," 95–128.

how Jewish leaders and functionaries tried to reestablish the network of Jewish organizations that the war had damaged, as well as the constraints that prevented letter writing from being a reliable medium of contact. From his post in Geneva, **Jewish Agency** representative Nathan Schwalb worked to stay connected with the members of Zionist youth movements.[40] To Jewish youth affiliated with the **Hehalutz** organization throughout Europe, Schwalb's office in Geneva had become the central nexus in their efforts to flee the Germans and make contact with the **Yishuv**. A letter he received from a Hehalutz member in Bratislava in the German satellite state of Slovakia expressed concern over the lack of contact with Palestine and the ongoing difficulties with which the organization was contending.

DOCUMENT 12–5: **Letter from Szlomo Czigelnik,[41] Bratislava, Slovakia, to Nathan Schwalb, Geneva, Switzerland, December 23, 1940, USHMMA RG 68.045M (WJC Geneva), reel 25, file 169 (translated from German).[42]**

Dear Nathan, shalom!

I'm just now getting around to answering your letter and want to explain to you, first of all, why we've written so little and why many of your letters and your friends' letters went unanswered. The censorship provisions didn't allow even 10 percent of the emeth [truth] to be told. Many of our letters weren't even sent, and therefore much was left undone. We have very poor contact with Eretz. Our only point of contact with Eretz is

---

40. Nathan Schwalb (1908–2004), a native of Stanisławów, had immigrated to Palestine in 1930 as a member of the Zionist youth movement and a Hehalutz representative in Czechoslovakia. Like many among the leadership of the Zionist movement, Schwalb was in Geneva at the end of the **Twenty-First Zionist Congress**. After a failed attempt to visit family in Galicia during the outbreak of the war, he returned to Geneva to work with **Chaim Barlas** in the Jewish Agency's temporary *aliyah* office. He would spend much of the next two years (and indeed much of the war) trying to help Jewish youth in possession of *aliyah* certificates depart from Europe. See document 6–8 on Barlas's work in September 1939.

41. Szlomo Czigelnik was a Hehalutz activist who managed to cross into Slovakia in November 1940 and organize a transit post in Bardejov near the Polish border, the aim of which was to smuggle Hehalutz members out of Poland and transport them to Palestine. Several members did indeed reach Slovakia and continued on to Hungary. In the spring of 1942, Slovak authorities arrested Czigelnik and deported him to Poland, where he was murdered. Ruth Zariz, "Attempts at Rescue and Revolt—Attitude of Members of the Dror Youth Movement in Bedzin to Foreign Passports As Means of Rescue," *YVS* 20 (1990): 213.

42. This document has been translated into English from a copy of the letter. The original letter is missing from the WJC file. All parenthetical insertions appear in the original copy of the letter; all bracketed insertions have been added by the translators.

Wilno [Vila, Vilnius], although there is censorship there, too. That's why we couldn't answer your questions about our Hakhsharah work (retraining activity), and I ask you to clarify for us who the N. Lloyd is who is mentioned several times.

Hakhsharah (retraining). In summer, the news was spread that all the young people had to go to work camps. Therefore we planned to set up a large agricultural Hakhsharah facility, so that our friends didn't have to join up. There were new chaverim [friends, comrades] there, as well as older chaverim and plitim (refugees) in particular, from Łódź and many cities of the Brit-Hamoazot (Russian-occupied part of Poland). It was possible to do regular and normal work in the plugot (groups), and the atmosphere was kibbutz-like and typical of Eretz. The number of chaverim in Hakhsharah (including Bendzin [Będzin]) was 1,500 and could have been many times larger, given sufficient means. Grochów[43]: we rebuilt this retraining site. The Joint enabled us to build this facility by giving us a subsidy of 60,000 złoty. From 80 to 100 people from all movements were housed here. In the winter, Grochów has 50 chaverim. Despite the ghetto established in Warsaw, Grochów remains in existence, and we have oral approval for it. Because of the establishment of the ghetto and the lack of means to keep supporting agricultural groups, all the sites had to be shut down, and the friends got together mainly in Warsaw, where they form a kibbutz (larger group), consisting mainly of people who have done four to five years of retraining work. This kibbutz has 80 members. Besides hairdressing workshops, no others could be set up because of the shortage of funds, although we had been thinking especially of workshops for shoemakers and tailors. In Będzin, on the other hand, we have our own workshops, a shoemaking and tailoring workshop, and we also farm on our own land. All the tnuot [movements] are enlarging their workshops, to the extent, of course, that means are available to them.

Each movement has its own base, and the Central Committee head office [Merkaz Hehalutz] consists of one representative from each. The office is located at the kibbutz, and both general activities and retraining activity are run from there. The establishment of the ghettos lends great urgency to the expansion and creation of new retraining groups, as the making of independent products within the ghettos is of the greatest importance. I can also tell you that the same importance is attached to the groups of craftsmen.

---

43. In 1939, Grochów was a village on the outskirts of Warsaw; today it is part of the city.

<u>Funds</u>: I can't tell you much about the funds. They're not operating right now, all the officials have fled to Wilno and not one of them is in Warsaw today. To the extent that any money was left over from the kranot [funds], it was transferred to the administration of the Joint.

<u>Haavara</u> (money transfer): I'll write you at home about our friend kessef (money). The old zehuvim (złoty) are not in circulation, new ones have been issued. It's very important to provide assistance immediately, as the situation is grave and dismal. Please do your best to help Zivia [Lubetkin][44] and all the others at once (friends of the central office in Warsaw). I advise you not to look for any ways other than through private individuals. With regard to various pratiim (private individuals), I'll write to Zivia, and she'll answer you directly about different possibilities.

<u>Leaving the country</u>: A group of 12[?] people from different movements arrived here with me. The exit of each chaver costs 200 złoty as far as the g'vul (border). It is achieved with many understandable difficulties (bad roads, on foot). You'll hear from the central office here about the local expenses and placement [illegible . . .] to Eretz. We need help at once and expect your earliest reply.

Shalom

Schlomo

Individuals trying to maintain ties with family members and friends across Poland typically resorted to letter writing to communicate their concern and unceasing affection for loved ones. Beyond sharing news and practical matters, writing letters afforded individuals the opportunity to reflect on daily life, to put into writing their thoughts and feelings. The series of letters in documents 12–6 to 12–11 provides an extraordinary example of how letter writing could function to connect friends during this period. Edith Blau, a young Jewish woman living in Minden, Germany, received this correspondence from her sweetheart, Lutek Orenbach, in Tomaszów Mazowiecki, and from her close

---

44. Zivia Lubetkin (1914–1978), born in eastern Poland, was active in the Zionist labor youth movement and represented Hehalutz on the National Jewish Council. After the German invasion she became active in underground work in Warsaw, helped to found ŻOB, the Jewish Fighting Organization, and fought in the Warsaw Ghetto Uprising. Lubetkin survived the war, moved to Palestine, and helped to found the ghetto fighters' **kibbutz**. B. Mordechai Ansbacher and Michael Berenbaum, "Lubetkin, Zivia," in *Encyclopaedia Judaica*, ed. Fred Skolnik and Michael Berenbaum, 2nd ed. (Detroit, MI: Macmillan Reference USA, 2007), 13:240–41; Tikva Fatal-Kna-ani, "Zivia Lubetkin," Jewish Women's Archive, www.jwa.org/encyclopedia/article/lubetkin-zivia (accessed March 5, 2011).

friend Ruth Goldbarth in Warsaw. Lutek's and Ruth's letters allow us to glimpse the acuity of their personal impressions and the creative ways they found to share them with loved ones under adverse circumstances.

Edith, Lutek, and Ruth were all around nineteen years of age at the beginning of the war. Edith met Lutek and Ruth, who seem to have known each other already, in the Polish city of Bydgoszcz in the summer of 1939; the three became close friends. The war soon intervened, dispersing them and their families. Edith, who had grown up in Danzig in a German Jewish family, fled to Minden with her mother. They found shelter in the house of her uncle Hermann Bradtmüller, an "**Aryan**" married to Edith's aunt Frieda. Meanwhile, Ruth went to Warsaw with her mother and father, a dentist, and her younger sister. Despite being newcomers, Ruth's father quickly established a dental practice where Ruth worked during the day, and they associated with the Warsaw ghetto's elite. Lutek's family moved to Tomaszów Mazowiecki in the Łódź district of Poland, which was incorporated into the Radom district of the **Generalgouvernement** under the German rule.[45] Lutek worked for the Tomaszów *Judenrat*, but his heart was in theater, and he took advantage of any opportunity he could find to organize cultural evenings in the ghetto for its elite. What survives of the letters exchanged by these three young adults is unusual in its intensity and style, rich with allusions, insider jokes, and code words. The following sampling represents but a fraction of the entire correspondence. Nevertheless, these extracts convey a sense of the liveliness, passion, and intimacy with which some young Jews tried to overcome barriers, restrictions, and deprivation.

---

45. In 1939, approximately thirteen thousand Jews resided in Tomaszów. In the fall of 1939, a Jewish Council (*Judenrat*) was established under the leadership of Baruch Schoeps and his deputy, Leibush Warsager. In December 1940, the German authorities ordered the establishment of three separate Jewish residential districts (open ghettos), which the Jews were forbidden to leave. See Tomaszów Mazowiecki entry in *USHMM Encyclopedia of Camps and Ghettos*, 2:335–38.

DOCUMENT 12-6: Letters by Lutek Orenbach,[46] Tomaszów Mazowiecki, Generalgouvernement, to Edith Blau, Minden, Germany, September 15 and October 18 and 19, 1940, USHMMA RG 10.250 Edith Brandon collection, folder 7 (translated from Polish).[47]

[September 15, 1940]

My dearest Edith!

I went to a funeral today. Grandpa died on Friday. Those days were terrible. It was the first time that I saw death up close, and I understood life again. Apart from the sadness, there was a sort of wild, inner joy—that I'm alive! It was the first time that I was at a cemetery. The weeping still echoes in my ears . . . I can't cry. Mama no longer has a father.

I won't write you much today. I just want this letter to reach you in time for your birthday and to bring you my sincerest congratulations and wishes and a thousand kisses. Do you remember the rose that didn't really exist? I'm sending you the most beautiful rose, a rose that doesn't exist, just like there are no kisses . . .

I'm very sad that I can't send you even the smallest memento, but you won't be cross, you'll forgive me. What more can I give you than my love, what can be worth more than that? You have everything that I can give.

I'll never forget last summer. I can forget how you look and I can forget who you are, but I won't forget that summer or that experience. You don't understand me very well. There are moments when I don't remember whether you're out there, when I don't know who you were, and then there are others when I remember you as if you were right next to me, when I see your eyes and I feel your kisses.

But this is best expressed in the poem by Tuwim:

"My quiet ponderings, oh the ponderings of a young mind,

Tell her, tell her that I don't remember her,

Tell her, tell her that I deeply long for her,

---

46. Lutek Orenbach was born in 1921 and lived in Tomaszów Mazowiecki. The last letter he wrote to Edith that has been preserved is dated December 2, 1941; that same month, Edith and her mother were transported to Riga as forced laborers. The last letter Lutek wrote to the Blau family in Minden is dated February 5, 1942. Any trace of him disappears after that point. The Nazis liquidated the ghetto in Tomaszów Mazowiecki in late October and early November 1942. Most of the Jews were deported to their deaths in Treblinka, and only about nine hundred able-bodied Jews were left. They were transferred to the local labor camp, which was liquidated in May 1943. Only two to five hundred Jews from Tomaszów Mazowiecki survived the war. See Barbara Engelking, "Miłość i cierpienie w Tomaszowie Mazowieckim," in *Zagłada Żydów: Pamięć narodowa a pisanie historii w Polsce i we Francji*, ed. Barbara Engelking et al. (Lublin: Wydawnictwo Uniwersytetu Marii Curie-Skłodowskiej, 2006), 74.

47. This was partly published in English in Edith Brandon, *Letters from Tomaszow* (London: Self-published, 1994), 27–28, 30–31.

Sighs, oh sighs, float to where she is,
Tell her, tell her that I no longer know who she is,
Tell her, tell her that my heart is dying from grief."

It's already fall here, a golden, Polish fall, the most beautiful in all the world. It's too bad you're not here, and we can't walk down the sad Mazovian road a bit and listen to the sparrows.

I'll stop here because I can't and don't have the need to write more. My parents send you heartfelt birthday wishes. Fred and Bella will write you themselves.

A most powerful kiss on your most precious lips.

Always yours,
Lutek

Cordial greetings and congratulations to your mother.

I apologize for my ghastly writing, but the pen fell to the ground and broke. Aside from that, there's also the irritation.

I'm putting together an album of caricatures. When it's ready, I'll send it to you. You'll just have to be patient.

[October 18, 1940]
My dearest Edith!

Your letter arrived the day before yesterday. I've had it now for three days already—high time that I respond to you.

I should write to you . . . but how? How can I gather my thoughts when I don't know what to think about in the first place. We have so many new worries here that my head's bursting. I'd gladly spare you this news, but, after all, you need to know! So . . . things are starting to go badly in Tomaszów. 1,500 Jews are leaving town in the next few days and are going to smaller places. We are staying for the moment but that's only . . . for the time being. But the scene . . . these people . . . the crying, the crying, the crying! The carts! "Wagons are heading out . . . loaded with people." I am very fearful for us because, even though we're native [to Poland], we haven't lived here [in Tomaszów] long and . . . and what's going to happen? We could move to some half-dead little hole but what would we do there? What will we live on? There's terrible chaos at the moment. The whole [Jewish] community is "on the street" with the carts—the mood is awful. What's the point of living . . . there's nothing left, nothing, nothing. It's only that instinctive will to live that keeps us going; only that last, most basic hope.

We're already getting used to everything; nothing can throw us off balance any more. Friends are already cracking sad jokes: "Lutek, let's meet in Odrzywół, or rather in Żarnów, or Nowe Miasto. We'll perform theater there, we'll create an association for the advancement of culture in Odrzywół, we'll open a kitchen . . . you'll see, it will be alright." "Long live Odrzywół." "Somehow it will be alright."[48]

[October 19, 1940]
I'm not going out of the house today. I don't want to see those carts, those people, that weeping. Sewek's coming over. We're going to play bridge, happen what may. There's already frost outside. You just have to take a look to see that a hard winter is right around the corner. I recently got a letter from Ruth [Goldbarth in Warsaw]. I don't envy her what's going on there, but then one can't envy us either.

I feel like I'm falling ever more deeply into the night, the black, hopeless night. Hopeless?! False! Day must come at some time after all, I will be able to breathe the fresh air of daybreak again and the happiness of love. Everything sleeps in the meantime. My love also slumbers, there with you, far away.

"Drink wine, go dream! But day won't break, wine must be turned into blood; the transformed wine must be drunk!" That's [poet Juliusz] Slovak. For the time being I have to wait. I'm always waiting. In the evening, when I'm lying in bed, I hear the rumbling of a *droshky* [coach] beyond the windows (all are asleep, it's quiet). I listen . . . what do I expect from the *droshky*? I don't know. The *droshky* goes farther and farther until the rumbling goes silent. A quiet sorrow remains in my heart because there's again nothing, because time still passes. Perhaps I'm waiting for you?

A bit later . . .

Sewek was here. He was terribly upset. Oh! What the hell! What will be, will be. You just stay put where you are and, God forbid, don't come here. You're fine where you are. And for now, I will have to wait with my love until . . . "the dawn." I'm twenty years old, I'll get a little older yet! My youth is passing.

I bid you farewell for the time being. Goodbye, my beloved. Accept a most-heartfelt and most-loving farewell kiss.

Always only yours,
Lutek

In place of the old saying "write to me in Berdyczów,"[49] "write to me in Odrzywół."

---

48. The word "alright" is crossed out in this sentence.
49. This is a Polish idiom that roughly means "Leave me alone."

DOCUMENT 12–7: **Letter by Ruth Goldbarth,**[50] **Warsaw, to Edith Blau, Minden, Germany, September 22, 1940, USHMMA RG 10.250 Edith Brandon collection, folder 2 (translated from German).**

My dearest Dita-girl,

I want to quickly start answering your letter of September 16 now after all, because I definitely won't get around to it tomorrow, and I really have to give you a report on the exciting events of the past few days. So just imagine: on Thursday, you know, I got the letter from Bowleg [*O-Bein*],[51] in which he hinted that he had something to take care of here and might be here on Friday, but would let me know in advance. Well, this advance notice never came, but on Friday afternoon, when I was just about to leave for the dentist's office,[52] the doorbell rang. Luckily, I (and not our "maid") went to open the door, and before me stood Herr Berthold, in full regalia. He looked quite impressive indeed, mind you, but I still felt a little funny at the sight of him. In any case, he was in such a dither that he scarcely opened his mouth, and to tell the truth, I was in not much less of a dither. Then we made a date for 6, but on the condition that he would come in civilian clothes, which he faithfully promised to do. I can tell you, honey, I spent two really nice days, packed full of variety. As an old Warsaw resident, I played "bear trainer" and showed all the city sights to *O-Bein* and his friend, a nice boy who allegedly doesn't know what sort of girl I am.[53] I left Mogen at home, of course, after all I really couldn't take the child along everywhere.[54] For that reason, I also got to go everywhere I usually can't go with Mogen, to parks, movies, cafés,

---

50. Ruth Goldbarth was born in 1921 in Bydgoszcz. Her father, Rudolf, was arrested immediately after the German invasion. After his release in December 1939, he decided to move his family from their hometown, which was annexed to the Reich. One month later, in January 1940, they moved to Warsaw in the Generalgouvernement. Ruth belonged to the "privileged" stratum in the Warsaw ghetto: she worked as a receptionist in her father's dental practice and learned English in her free time. Ruth and her family were most likely deported to their deaths in Treblinka in the summer of 1942. See Klaus-Peter Friedrich, "Die Brombergerin Ruth Goldbarth im Warschauer Getto, 1940/41," *Jewish History Quarterly* 1, no. 225 (March 2008): 35–46.

51. This was later identified as "Herr Berthold," an "Aryan" acquaintance.

52. Her father maintained his practice as a dentist in the Warsaw ghetto until after the ghetto was sealed.

53. This is a reference to Ruth hiding her Jewish identity. Her mention of being an "old resident" of Warsaw is a joke since she had only spent about a year in that city.

54. This is a reference to her not wearing her armband bearing a Star of David (Yiddish: *mogen Dovid*). See chapter 10 documents 10-3 and 10-4. According to Gutman, *The Jews of Warsaw*, 29, being caught without the armband was punishable with a prison sentence.

and I even rode on the suburban railway, so in a nutshell—I let off a bit of steam. You can't imagine how much freer one feels immediately, and I wasn't worried about Mogen at all, you know. [. . .]

10:30 p.m.

Now, a little tipsy, I'm going to finish your letter. My father bought a bottle of cognac again, and we've just sampled it. (It went straight to my head, of course.) Day after tomorrow, when it's my friend Edith's[55] birthday, we'll drink a toast to her—

Dear, I got a letter from Juli and Lolo[56] dated August 6, which contains absolutely nothing, and apparently they don't even know what they should write. Otherwise, no news of Musia and Onkel Arthur. Oh, but yes there is, Ninka Klotz wrote that Musia has a job, but nobody knows where or how, etc. [Broneczka's ?] grandmother has died in the Łódź ghetto. The old woman had a very, very bad time.—I absolutely have to write to Lutek [Orenbach], but the news of his grandfather has shocked me so badly that it's damned hard for me to write. Oh, Edith, everything is so terribly lousy [*bescheiden*]![57]

Dear one, promise me something: you have to fight against the nagging fear that you write me about. Don't think about how you have it "too good," instead think about how all of us who love you are so happy that you have nicer and more enjoyable surroundings than all of us here. Surely, we have to live with awareness, especially in these times, and consciously embrace every joy and every happy hour and be grateful for them, and try to use the time for as much goodness and beauty as possible. And it's definitely hard to rid oneself of the thought "Who knows how much longer," but we have to try to do so, for our own sakes.—

Dita, we actually expected to see Onkel Bubi[58] today, but he didn't come. Imagine, my sister,[59] who has a distinct inclination toward sloppi-

---

55. This refers to Edith Blau, recipient of the letter.

56. These and the following names might pertain to common acquaintances from Bydgoszcz.

57. The German word *bescheiden* (literally, "modest") used here may have been a tongue-in-cheek substitute for the crasser *beschissen* ("shitty").

58. This refers to Hermann (Bubi) Bradtmüller, Edith's non-Jewish uncle who sheltered her and her mother, Meta, in the German town of Minden, Westphalia, beginning in the autumn of 1939. Edith and Meta Blau stayed there until December 1941, when they were deported to Riga as forced laborers. Bradtmüller carried letters and goods between Warsaw and Minden before and after the Warsaw ghetto had been sealed. For Edith's story as told by her in the 1990s, see Brandon, *Letters from Tomaszow*; also see Friedrich, "Die Brombergerin Ruth Goldbarth," 36.

59. This refers to Ruth's sister Dorothea (Dorka), who was five years younger.

ness and carelessness, even combed her hair and dressed properly and was very unhappy that it was all for naught (saying something like "now I'm healthy and don't have to go to the doctor anymore and am sitting here with my neck freshly washed"), well, but there'll be another time, and this way we still have the visit to look forward to.

So, my dear, my little sister is already in bed and mutters ungraciously from time to time, to show me that even though she's not asleep yet, she still really wants me to turn off the light, so I'll stop now!

Goodbye, my dear, write to me very soon, especially about how you spent and celebrated your birthday,

and I send you a big fat kiss,

Ruth

DOCUMENT 12–8: Letter and caricatures by Lutek Orenbach, Tomaszów Mazowiecki, Generalgouvernement, November 26, 1940, USHMMA RG 10.250 Edith Brandon collection, folders 7, 12 (translated from Polish).[60]

My dear!

It's a scandal! I know it's a scandal. You should beat me, beat me to death for so mercilessly making you wait for this letter. But I've had so many problems this week. Something was supposed to happen and I wanted to write to you about it all in a single letter. But so far nothing has happened. Things continue as before. Lately I've been very irritated and worried again. All this is driving me mad. But why should I upset you. I'll give you a list of the people in the caricatures (the numbers are on the back of each sheet):

Norek H., member of the Jewish Community Council. Cynic, wit and Master of Law (*loi*) [French for "law"]

Uncle Jacob

Ignaś K., a good bridge partner

Lawyer H., member of the Council of Elders. I hate him. No one can stand him.

Fredek. Don't be frightened—he's much better looking in the flesh.

Mr. B. from Kraków

---

60. This was partly published in English in Brandon, *Letters from Tomaszow*, 34–35.

Bolesław Szeps,[61] chairman of the Community Council

Fredek H. ("Fric")—the son of Lawyer H.—official of the Jewish Community Council

Kasik W., son of the Estonian consul, the biggest braggart in Tomaszów

Sewek R., you have a photo of him

My father

Mr. K, member of the Council of Elders

Uncle Knopp

Mr. P., official of the Jewish Community Council

Abram M., the Don Juan of Tomaszów and a poser

A self-caricature

Mr. W., member of the Council of Elders

Heniek Leiberman (in place of his photo)

That's everybody. And what will you do with the caricatures?

I once again ask that you forgive me for the delay. But you're not here, after all, and you don't know what sometimes goes on here and the kinds of troubles I have. My only pleasure is organizing artistic evenings. I recall the old times, I recall the theater. I act a little, I do recitations . . . Wherever I will be, I will not want or be able to forget about the theater. It's the only thing I dream of, it's my calling.

I bid you farewell for now and kiss you again, and kiss me for my apology. Okay then.

Always always yours,
Lutek

---

61. This refers to Baruch Schoeps. According to the entry for "Tomaszów Mazowiecki," in *The Yad Vashem Encyclopedia of the Ghettos during the Holocaust*, ed. Guy Miron and Shlomit Shulhani (Jerusalem: Yad Vashem, 2009), 2:840, the **Gestapo** arrested Schoeps and beat him to death in late 1940.

Left to right: Lawyer H. Ignaś K., Uncle Jacob; Norek H., Fredek, Mr. B; Boleslaw Szeps, Fredek H. ("Fric"), Kasik W.

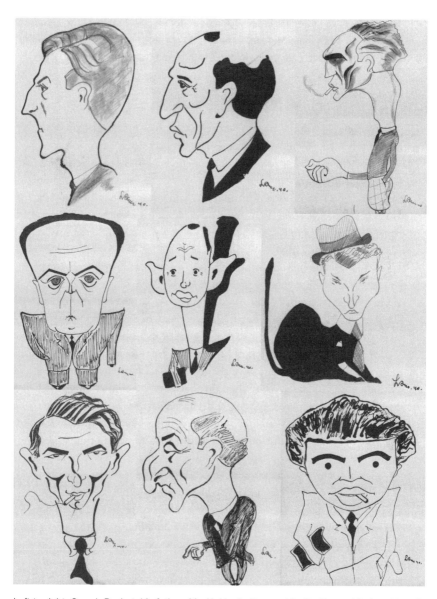

Left to right: Sewek R., Lutek's father, Mr. K; Uncle Knopp, Mr. P., Abram M., Lutek's self-carciature, Mr. W., Heniek Leiberman.

DOCUMENT 12–9: **Letter by Lutek Orenbach, Tomaszów Mazowiecki, General-gouvernement, to Edith Blau, Minden, Germany, December 9 and 10, 1940, USHMMA RG 10.250 Edith Brandon collection, folder 7 (translated from Polish).[62]**

My dearest Edith!

I've finally found the right evening and the right mood to write you. I know, I know—I'm the cruelest person in the world for making you wait and wait; but you should know that I too get upset when I can't talk a bit with my beloved, that I too feel such loneliness and, not being able to write, as if something were missing. I got your letter—so sad—and your postcard, from which I finally learned that you got my caricatures and in which you write that you didn't receive my letter. It's a shame. I'll have to explain all the caricatures for you again. I'll just wait for your letter, maybe everything is already okay.

Actually, you ought to be pleased that I've been so busy lately. I very, very much regret that you weren't here yesterday. We had a lovely evening of poetry for the council chairman's birthday. I arranged everything just like I used to . . . I picked out the performers and we had some pianists. And . . . all of a sudden, I became famous in Tomaszów. "Famous" . . . what an odd word. I don't like to boast, but that's how it is. The chairman's guests (and these were the real intellectuals) haven't stopped talking about the party. They thought that they were in an enchanted theater. Bela did a spectacular job with her recitation. I played the part of "Dancing Socrates,"[63] all made-up, with all my emotion and the talent which reawakened after such a long slumber. Music and improvised lighting created an appropriate atmosphere. I recited two pieces of erotic verse—just for you. I was surrounded by the rapt faces of the guests but I was speaking only to you and . . . why weren't you there. I'll send you a photo of "Socrates." The ear, unaccustomed to poetry and music in the present time of work and grime, greedily took it all in.

That's all on "art" for now. Otherwise, everything is the same as usual—gray reality, gray sky, gray mud and rain, and gray everyday sorrows. If one really wants to, one can forget about the grayness, whether at such a birthday party or in the hustle and bustle of the council. I'm working on the population register now. I feel at home at the council (but what

---

62. This was published in English in Brandon, *Letters from Tomaszow*, 35–36.

63. "Sokrates tańczący," or "Dancing Socrates," is a famous poem by the Polish Jewish poet Julian Tuwim (1894–1953).

of it when I'm still not paid a penny). The chairman is harsh, nervous, loony, but I like him.

Well, that's everything. That's to be my "career": scribbling on bits of paper at the council, drawing caricatures, and reciting poems at somebody's birthday party. And the money keeps on disappearing . . . and disappearing . . .

Let's not talk about it.

How are things with you, my dear? I yearn so much to have a little chat with you (on paper, naturally, because we probably won't see each other again). I'll tell you that I am very concerned about your lungs. Your work is not particularly healthy.

What'll happen to you? What'll happen to me? What'll happen to us? Does God know? Will I see you—so close—beside me? Will I smell the scent of your velvet cheeks and will I again whisper something, something wonderful, in your ear? Will I taste your lips again? Will I? Will I? Will I? . . . Who can answer?

Good night, my dear. I'll finish this letter tomorrow and send it off since you've already been waiting and waiting . . . I kiss you again with a good night kiss.

December 10, 1940

I got a card from Ruth today. Everything is in order with your letters now. Boria has become a policeman. We also have a police force. Dad employs my friends there too.

For now I don't have anything to write to you. I'll wait for your letter, but I may not be able to wait it out. Farewell, then, dear. Greet your mother for me. Bella sends her warmest greetings.

And from me the warmest kiss. Goodbye!

Always yours,
Lutek

DOCUMENT 12–10: Letters by Ruth Goldbarth, Warsaw, to Edith Blau and Hermann Bradtmüller, Minden, Germany, December 17, 1940, USHMMA RG 10.250 Edith Brandon collection, folder 2 (translated from German).

W[arsaw], December 17, 1940

My little best friend,

Yesterday at noontime, your nice long letter arrived, with the cigarettes, and your card with the notification of the sample "*bez wartoszczi* [*wartości*]" [without commercial value]. Sweetie, have you become one of the big earners, just throwing presents around? Mom was quite touched (she's going to write on her own), and I'm waiting expectantly, as eager as a kid waiting for a birthday, for the things that are supposed to come. You're really too kind; I'm afraid that when you got your wages you thought about all the people you care for, and in the end nothing at all was left over for you, right? Anyway, many thousand thanks, honey, and for now settle for a "wireless" kiss sent through the air! (I wish I could give you a real one! Won't you come visit us sometime? There's plenty of room here!) [. . .]

Sweetie, you're young, and you're getting so little out of your youth! Just think how often you would have danced and had fun in normal times. You have so little opportunity to enjoy yourself, and whenever you do have such an opportunity, you simply must take advantage of it and store up as much joy and gaiety in yourself as you possibly can. You write that you should have thought about Lutek [Orenbach], about Heinz, about us. Well, Dita, are you taking anything away from us? On the contrary, we share in your happiness, and you can pass on to us some of what you yourself have enjoyed. And don't you think Heinz would be thoroughly pleased if he knew that, for once, you were truly gay and exuberant for a few hours? No, my dear, you certainly don't need to get any gray hairs on that account!—And now Christmas is just around the corner, you're sure to have a few days of rest again then! Or are you off the whole week until New Year's? At the factory where an uncle of mine works, they've been doing overtime for weeks now, in order to have Christmas week off. Is it the same where you are?—The doorbell just rang! I hope it's not a patient, I'd really like to keep on writing!—No, not a patient, sweetie, but—can you guess? Your parcel! Oh my gosh, Dita girl, my dear! I'm so thrilled! You really are a frivolous soul, you know! Such beautiful stationery! I'll use it to write my very next letter to you, that is, if I can decide to use it at all. For now, I'm still enjoying the sight of it. Once again, then: an extra big thank-you kiss![64]

In the evening: This is the first chance I've had to write any more. I couldn't get around to it all afternoon. Things are a little busy in the office again at the moment, it's really nice, especially for Dad, but nothing comes of it, you know. But the general situation is to blame for that. You can't imagine how many doctors and dentists there are here. And all in

---

64. According to her postwar memoir, Edith Blau tried to send at least one parcel per week to both Ruth in Warsaw and Lutek in Tomaszów. Brandon, *Letters from Tomaszow*, 94.

this little piece of the city, which is dead, after all. In every building there are at least two doctors and three dentists, most of them on the brink of starvation; each one—bowing to necessity—has to be even cheaper than the next; and at the same time, food prices are merrily climbing. A fairly hopeless situation. But what can be done? Wait and see! Things will work out! [*Jakoś to będzie!*]

Shortly before supper, Boria[65] and Hanka were at my place. Boria had just come off duty and was terribly cold, chilled to the bone. The fellow really doesn't have an easy time of it—and the strangest thing of all: he doesn't gripe and doesn't play the hero or the martyr. After all, it's no small thing these days to be at roll call at 6 in the morning and later to do road patrol for 8 to 10 hours without a break. Either he's on sentry duty with the German guard at the exit roads, or he's making patrol rounds in the streets, or he has to control the traffic. Just picture Boria! Hanka and I laughed ourselves sick recently, but give him his due: it worked out, and at a very active corner besides. Naturally, traffic management here, where the walls and exit roads squeeze all the traffic together into a few streets, mostly quite narrow ones besides, is of the utmost importance.—Oh yes, I have a new line of trade: Hanka and I are knitting sweaters, scarves, and gloves for a shop! What do you have to say about that? The pay is fairly poor, of course, and I don't have much time to concentrate on the work either, but it's a little additional income. In addition, I'm making a sweater for Dorlein [her sister Dorothea] now, as a birthday present. It's turning out quite nicely, but the wool alone costs around 55–60 złoty. *Metsiehs* ["bargains"], right? I'm enclosing a sample for you.

In the meantime I also was at a concert again, but it wasn't as good as the first time. The *Pathétique*[66] on the saxophone is sometimes more than one can bear. You see, there are no j. [Jewish?] wind players here, and as practical people, they do the best they can! But it's not pretty. Next week is *Peer Gynt*.[67] Have to see whether we'll go again. I really don't have such a lot of time! I always think the day is too short. [. . . News follows on several common acquaintances and the fact that "there is no more telephoning."]

---

65. "Boria" was Ruth's code for a member of the Jewish police in Warsaw. Friedrich, "Die Brombergerin Ruth Goldbarth," 37–38.

66. This refers to Beethoven's Piano Sonata No. 8 in C minor, op. 13, written in 1798.

67. This work by Norwegian playwright Henrik Ibsen in 1867 inspired composer Edvard Grieg to write two musical suites in 1888 and 1891.

You ask whether Boria got involved with Adi[68] back then. Not a bit, however. You have to understand that the boy just gets cold when he has to stand for so long, and then he whiles the time away a bit, and often does gymnastics, but not alone. You can't hold that against him, after all. Sunday morning he was at our place again. Selected amiably and not longer than 10 minutes. [. . .]

We're taking English lessons now from a young dentist, a university friend of Mr. Walter's. It's usually quite an enjoyable time.

[Separate letter from Ruth to her (non-Jewish) uncle Hermann Bradtmüller]

Dear Uncle Bubi! Actually I wanted to write to you too in my previous letter, but I was in a great hurry at the time, and when I write to the good uncle I have to have time and peace and quiet, after all. I don't need to tell you how glad we all were about your kind letter back then, and surely you also know how very, very sorry we were not to have seen you again. But now that you're back at home, I have a request for you: please look out for my little friend [Edith Blau]! Don't let her overwork or smoke too much, and tell her to try combing her hair for Sunday sometime, and not to bite her fingernails! You can go right ahead and smack her fingers!—Edith surely has told you how we're doing. Gradually one gets used to everything, and if things don't get any worse, we'll be quite content. Only it could get a little warmer again! Today the temperature was minus 12 degrees [Celsius], which was a vivid reminder of the past winter, and we're not at all interested in going through two months that cold again! Maybe you could get in touch with St. Peter sometime? We no longer have a phone, and besides, he's probably cross with us!

Kind regards to you and your loved ones,
Yours,
Ruth

---

68. This was code for the SS used by Ruth and Edith. The passage seems to indicate "Boria" was harassed by the German police or SS while on guard duty for the Jewish police. Friedrich, "Die Brombergerin Ruth Goldbarth," 37–38.

DOCUMENT 12–11: **Letter by Ruth Goldbarth, Warsaw, to Edith Blau, Minden, Germany, December 25–26, 1940, USHMMA RG 10.250 Edith Brandon collection, folder 2 (translated from German).**

W[arsaw], December 25, 1940,

My dear little Dita-girl,

I'm afraid you'll be concerned about my silence, because, as I learned yesterday, either you won't get my last card and the good wishes for the whole family at all, or you'll only get them in eight to ten days. We haven't gotten any mail in more than a week either, and it probably will take a few more days until "our" post office finally gets around to it. Supposedly there's a lot piled up at the post office, but nothing is being delivered yet, and at the moment the mailboxes aren't being emptied either. So let's be patient; but so that you don't have to wait so very long, I want to hurry and write you today, because Mr. Weynerowski is coming tomorrow, and then I'll give him the letter for Jurek too.[69] But you can go ahead and write to me directly; by then, I hope, everything will be worked out.

Last night I was so vividly reminded of you, and I imagined you sitting under the Christmas tree and, in your mind, probably somewhere else entirely. But believe me, Dita, I've missed the Christmas atmosphere and all the trappings much more than I ever would have believed. We were so closely bound with the setting in which we lived, after all, and we could relate to all of it, even though we didn't belong to it. Here, of course, there was naturally no trace of all that, and even Hanukkah isn't being celebrated any longer. But Mr. Weyn[erowski] had given us a liter of liqueur (really nice of him, don't you agree? He's a charming fellow in general), and so we had a celebration just for ourselves. And little Ruth immediately got a bit tipsy, because she hadn't eaten any supper.

Here in the building, a "ball" is being held on Saturday. I'm curious to see how it turns out. In particular, you need to know that in every building here there is a committee, of which all the residents are members. The buildings here are much bigger than the ones we're familiar with from home. Usually there are two big courtyards, each with a right and a left wing and a rear building accessible through the courtyard. And because, owing to the present circumstances, there's usually one family per room (we always feel like con men, though strictly speaking we live in just one

---

69. A Mr. Weynerowski was the person—possibly an "Aryan"—who carried Ruth's letters to the "Aryan side." "Jurek" was Ruth's code for a non-Jewish Pole. Friedrich, "Die Brombergerin Ruth Goldbarth," 37–38.

heated room, too), there are more than 300 of us here in this building. We also have two youth groups, one for younger kids and one for older ones, a bridge squad for card players, a music group, and so on and so forth. Since we all have to be home by 9 p.m. anyway [due to the curfew], it's very nice, of course, that we aren't thrown on our own resources night after night, sitting in our own four walls and going to bed at 9:30 (although that also has its good aspects). And there are really a few very nice folks among them; in my group, a few young married couples, a few quite agreeable young girls (mostly older than me), two medical students, a scholar of language and literature, etc. At the moment we're involved in setting up a library, and I've already been appointed as librarian. For the time being, however, my job consists of running from one tenant to another and collecting books, but you can imagine how happy I am about being chosen for this position. I hope the thing will work out. Some residents actually are putting all their books at our disposal, and that means we're counting on 600–700 volumes. Great, isn't it? At any rate, I'll always have something to read. Then from the dues, which also have to be paid, of course, we can also make new acquisitions. We certainly don't have any other libraries now! [. . .]

By the way, package distribution has been in "our" hands for quite some time now and is working better than we expected. We get our parcels from Aunt Hertha regularly[70]; admittedly, now it costs about twice as much in terms of customs duty and postage charges, but we're quite happy that we get them at all. Dad often orders dental supplies, and mom, odds and ends that aren't available here: polishing stones for knife blades, coffee additives. In addition, Aunt Hertha sends us soups in cans, cubes, and packets, which are considerably better there than here, and all other practical and impractical things. Did she actually send you the newspaper? I assume you will have found it interesting, although, of course, it absolutely does not give a complete picture either. You just can't imagine how Adi often behaves. Anyone who hasn't personally experienced it simply can't believe it. I thought it was an exaggeration too, until one day I observed it myself and almost participated.[71]

In the dental office, things continue to be fairly quiet. The general situation is probably the main reason, and besides, it may be that our location is somewhat unfavorable. I don't quite know how to explain it to

---

70. It is not clear whether "Aunt Hertha" refers to a relative of Edith's or is used as code.

71. This passage seems to imply that Ruth almost fell victim to SS persecution. Friedrich, "Die Brombergerin Ruth Goldbarth," 37–38.

you. The area where we live looks roughly like this [drawing (see facsimile page 476)], and where the *X* is, that's where we live, and where the dots are, sentries are posted.

What have you gotten in the mail? What does your "cutie" write? Do you have news of Lutek? I have no idea what's going on with him. Since the short card in which he informed us of his new address, I've heard nothing more from him, and I must say that it concerns me a bit, especially because he promised me in the card that he would write a detailed letter, and very soon. Now, of course, this business with the post office has gotten in the way, so it's possible that I haven't received his letters.

December 26, 1940

I couldn't keep writing last night, the folks from upstairs came down and asked me up, and we sat there until 12:30 a.m. and carried on until the noise got too much for the neighbors on the right and left. In any case, I have to keep it short now, because Mr. W[eynerowski] really ought to be here already.—I have something else to tell you that is sure to interest you: the day before yesterday, Dr. Kerz[72] got a telegram from Lisbon, saying that ship tickets to New York for him and his family are paid for and waiting at the shipping line office; all the formalities are taken care of, and they want him to send a telegram saying when he plans to embark. What do you say to that? The question is only how he is to get out of here. If he has enough money, he may manage it.—Incidentally, that reminds me of a "Chicago story" that Dr. Kerz and I got involved in last week. He was living here quite near us, not in a very nice place, and that's why he moved. His wife was ill, and he asked me to help him, which I was glad to do, of course. So we packed all his suitcases, bags, etc., full, took them to the new apartment, emptied everything out, and went back again to pack them up once more. On the way, a crush of people suddenly arose, and somebody jostled us back and forth and yanked the suitcases and briefcase out of Dr. Kerz's hands. I saw the thief, cried out, and everybody turned around—the thief was gone, vanished off the face of the earth. And all of it happened in only a second! We came back home, very gloomy; although the suitcases were empty, it still was a big loss. When Dr. K. told the story to an acquaintance, the man said, "A very similar thing happened to me

---

72. Adolf (or Abram) Kerz was born in Gorlice in 1898. He lived with his family (wife Helena and one daughter) in Bydgoszcz but, like Ruth's father, fled to Warsaw when the city was annexed to the Reich. He perished in the Warsaw ghetto. Friedrich, "Die Brombergerin Ruth Goldbarth," 45n93.

not long ago; these aren't common thieves, they belong to a special organization; just wait and see, you'll get your things back." The next morning the two of them set out and went to a very shady area, to a little restaurant in a cellar, where they were admitted only with a special password, and talked to one of these people. This person sent them to someone else, and after much ado and all kinds of go-betweens and passwords, they came to a third middleman and philanthropist who is "helpful" to the poor people who have been robbed in "locating" their things. He had them tell their story, held forth about the carelessness of people on the streets, but promised his "help," provided it would be well paid for, and told Dr. K. to come back later around midday. So at 2 p.m. he set out again, to learn that the things in all likelihood had been found and that he should pick them up in the evening. Then in the evening, after a hundred and one formalities, the things were given back, in return for 110 złoty. What do you say about that?

So, dear, that's all for today! Mr. W. wants to go. With warmest regards from our house to yours,

and a big kiss for you,

Ruth

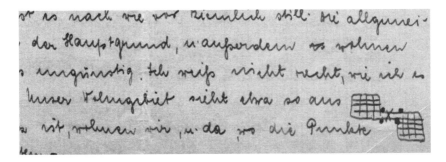

INTO THE SECOND YEAR OF THE WAR

At the end of 1940, while Polish Jews anxiously tracked news and rumors for clues about the future and looked abroad for help, those outside German-occupied Poland tried to get a better sense of the condition of Polish Jews and what the future held for European Jewry as a whole. Looking closely at contemporaneous source materials, we discover a range of perspectives articulated by Jews in 1940 in different parts of Europe concerning what lay ahead and what avenues for action were open to them. Whether the events of 1940, particularly

France's defeat, would prove to be the climax of the war or an intermediate stage in an ongoing escalation of events was far from evident. Different predictions about the war's outcome necessarily led people to different conclusions about the fate of European Jews. Would they be able to restore the lives they had led prior to the war, or even prior to the advent of national socialism? Put differently, would the future resemble the past, or did recent events constitute a fundamental rupture in Jewish history? And if the return of what had been was no longer possible, what would emerge in its place?

To start, the question arose what the status of Polish Jews in a liberated Poland would be. They might have hoped for the support of the Polish government-in-exile under Prime Minister Władysław Sikorski in London.[73] Yet, despite their shared experience of national disaster and a common enemy, the relationship remained strained. Polish leaders failed to dissociate themselves from the country's strong antisemitic tradition and instead seemed inclined to perpetuate prewar policies, which included plans for the resettlement of Jews (to Madagascar or elsewhere) once the exiled government had reestablished its sovereignty in Warsaw. Indeed, not until early November 1940 did the Polish exile authorities issue a declaration promising, "The Jews, as Polish citizens, shall in liberated Poland be equal with the Polish community, in duties and in rights."[74] Even so, these leaders were aware of public sentiment in their home country. As Jan Karski reported in February 1940 (quoted in chapter 10), the Polish public had some sympathy with the Germans' anti-Jewish policy. Even in the ranks of Polish army units supported by the British army, Jewish soldiers complained about widespread discrimination in the summer of 1940. The Jewish and general press lent widespread support to their demand to serve in British uniform instead. And the Polish government-in-exile's reluctance to protect and guarantee the rights of the Jewish minority in postwar Poland made it the object

---

73. Władysław Eugeniusz Sikorski (1881–1943) was a Polish politician and military leader. In the interwar period, he held the post of prime minister of Poland. After the German invasion, he became prime minister of the Polish government-in-exile, eventually based in London. On the history of this government, see Bernadeta Tendyra, *The Polish Government in Exile, 1939–45* (London: Routledge, 2011).

74. Declaration by Jan Stańczyk, labor minister in the Polish government-in-exile, November 3, 1940, quoted from David Engel, *In the Shadow of Auschwitz: The Polish Government-in-Exile and the Jews, 1939–1942* (Chapel Hill: University of North Carolina Press, 1987), 80.

of both public and behind-the-scenes criticism from Jewish functionaries in the ranks of the **World Jewish Congress** (WJC) and other organizations.[75]

Ignacy Schwarzbart[76]—a long-time Zionist from Kraków and one of the two Jewish representatives on the Polish National Council (Rada Narodowa), an advisory body to the government-in-exile also based in London—was not in fact among those Jewish activists demanding greater concessions from Polish exile authorities.[77] In the wake of the November 3, 1940, declaration by the Sikorski government, Schwarzbart presented a report titled "A general outline concerning the Polish-Jewish question." It summed up what he regarded as the critical issues that would extend into the future, beyond the immediate plight of his fellow Jews under German occupation.

DOCUMENT 12–12: **Report No. 4 by Ignacy Schwarzbart, member of the Polish National Council, London, United Kingdom, November 20, 1940, facsimile reprinted in** Archives of the Holocaust, **ed. Henry Friedlander and Sybil Milton (New York: Garland Publishing, 1990), 8:141–44.**

[. . .] I. The Polish-Jewish question: the aim and the ways leading to it.
[. . .]
    3) The principle aim.
    What are we striving for? What is the principal aim of our activity? The aim is: A harmonious living together, in the new Poland, of the Polish and Jewish communities. The concept "harmonious living together" has to cover the sphere of law, facts, physical unity for the State. In short, a complete

---

75. Engel, *In the Shadow of Auschwitz*, 70–71. On the idea explored in 1938 by the Polish government to resettle their Jews to Madagascar, see Engel, *In the Shadow of Auschwitz*, 40; more generally, Magnus Brechtken, *"Madagaskar für die Juden": Antisemitische Idee und politische Praxis, 1885–1945* (Munich: Oldenbourg, 1997). On Jewish fighters and soldiers in Allied armies, see Mordechai Altshuler, "Jewish Warfare and the Participation of Jews in Combat in the Soviet Union as Reflected in Soviet and Western Historiography," in *Bitter Legacy: Confronting the Holocaust in the USSR*, ed. Zvi Gitelman (Bloomington: Indiana University Press, 1997), 151–66; Deborah Dash Moore, *GI Jews: How World War II Changed a Generation* (Cambridge, MA: Harvard University Press, 2004); Peter Leighton-Langer, *The King's Own Loyal Enemy Aliens: German and Austrian Refugees in Britain's Armed Forces, 1939–45* (London: Vallentine Mitchell, 2006); Howard Blum, *The Brigade: An Epic Story of Vengeance, Salvation, and World War II* (New York: HarperCollins, 2001).

76. Ignacy Schwarzbart (1888–1961) was a well-known Polish Zionist and member of the National Council of the Polish government-in-exile. Along with Szmul Zygielbojm, he played an important role in exposing Nazi atrocities against the Jews in Poland.

77. The other Jewish representative on the Polish National Council was Szmul Zygielbojm, a Bund leader from Poland. On Zygielbojm, see chapter 10, note 57, and document 10-10.

change of the situation as it was in the past. In view of this ultimate aim, we have come to the conclusion that secondary problems have to be subordinated to the general and chief aim. Let me give you one drastic example: a young Jew, beaten and expelled from a Polish university, is now on emigration [sic]. Insulted as a human being, despised as a Jew, full of bitterness—he does not want to join the Polish Army. This reaction, completely comprehensible from the psychological point of view, is all wrong politically, and can seriously hamper our work towards the ultimate goal. That is why I have always demanded in cases like this that the individual forget his personal wrongs and be guided by the political aim of the future. [. . .]

II. General Outlook on Jewish Affairs in this War

[. . .]

3) Documentation of sufferings, sacrifices, and the situation of Jewry during the war.

I have the impression that with respect to that there is a waste of energy, as many organizations are collecting material. On the other hand, there is the lack of a central office, which would collect these materials and work on them. The propaganda of the sufferings and plight of European Jewry is at the moment far from being satisfactory. This is a great task for the World Jewish Congress.

4) The so-called Jewish War Aims.

Although not organized in a separate state, the Jews have to prepare their war aims. First of all steps have to be taken to create a centrum, based on the most inclusive possible understanding, which will prepare and elaborate the aims in order to submit them at the right place when the time comes. If we will not do it we shall have a repetition of the Evian Conference.[78] It is my opinion that we should arm ourselves in time against the projects of exotic territorialism which degrade the Jewish nation to the level of export goods. Our war aims should be concentrated on Zionism and the full equality—both as community and individuals—of Jewry in all countries. The problem of the social reshuffling of the Jews in the countries in which they are now living in order to avoid their present concentration in some branches only should become our concrete slogan. There is still one danger, which comes from Jewry itself, it is the theory of liquidating the "Goluth" [Diaspora]. This theory should be opposed by our claim of guaranteeing the development of Jewish culture within our connection with the culture of the nations among whom we live. The most ideal solution of Zionism—and we do not know today what shape it will take—cannot solve the numerical problem of Jewry. Zionism does not claim it.

---

78. For more on the **Évian Conference**, see the Glossary.

5) American Jewry

American Jewry is of decisive importance today in shaping the future of European Jewry. If there is to be any help by non-Polish Jews for Polish Jewry and European Jewry in general, this help can be organized only by the American Jews. Propaganda on a serious scale is required to make American Jewry more active. American Jewry has to play the same part with regard to European Jewry, as the United States with regard to Great Britain, which is fighting for a new Europe, against barbarism, brutal force, and fascism. I emphasize: the awakening of the political consciousness of this historical importance amongst American Jewry and the organization of an adequate help is the most realistic entry into the discussion about our war aims. [. . .]

Like Schwarzbart, other Jews refused to abandon their commitment to life in the Diaspora in states governed democratically. In looking to the future, they clung stubbornly to the conviction that humanist values would prevail. Many French-born Jews in particular, despite feeling shaken by France's defeat and betrayed by **Vichy**'s anti-Jewish laws, would not abandon France and what it stood for. In his diary entries from late 1940, Raymond-Raoul Lambert gave voice to this anguish. Lambert represented the dominant current of thought within French Jewry. As a fervent French patriot who insisted on the complementary relationship between his French and Jewish identities, he shared the outlook of most of his Jewish compatriots represented by the **Central Consistory**. His affinal ties to his country ran too deep to abandon his trust in France's ultimate victory at this time. Moreover, he recognized that his position was relatively privileged compared to the plight of refugees residing or held in France. Lambert's sensitivity to their plight reflected his ongoing activism in defense of the rights of Jewish refugees in France.[79]

---

79. Raymond-Raoul Lambert (1894–1943), an assimilated French Jewish leader and intellectual, was secretary-general of the Comité d'assistance aux réfugiés (CAR) from its creation in 1936. In that role and as editor of the Central Consistory's publication *L'Univers Israélite*, he became a vocal critic of France's increasingly restrictive immigration policies in the late 1930s, calling for France to reverse such policies and keep its borders open to asylum seekers. His views on immigration put him in conflict with some of the most prominent leaders of French Jewry. With the outbreak of the war and then in the wake of France's defeat, Lambert's commitment to helping refugees did not flag. He relocated to the Unoccupied Zone with his family and resumed his work for CAR. When in late November 1941 the new central Jewish organization, Union générale des israélites de France (UGIF), was established, Lambert became one of its most prominent leaders in the Unoccupied Zone. Lambert was deported and murdered in Auschwitz in 1943. For more on his life, see Richard I. Cohen's introduction to Raymond-Raoul Lambert, *Diary of a Witness, 1940–1943* (Chicago: Ivan R. Dee in association with the USHMM, 2007).

DOCUMENT 12–13: Raymond-Raoul Lambert, Unoccupied Zone, France, diary entry for December 20, 1940, translated from French and published in *Diary of a Witness, 1940–1943*, ed. Richard I. Cohen (Chicago: Ivan R. Dee in association with the USHMM, 2007), 25–26.

[. . .] I have been putting more emotion and energy than ever into reflecting on the Jewish question since this *Statut* was decreed; it has really shaken up my inner life. . . . It is so true that I am still completely French in my heart, in my mind, as a family man, in the love I had for my mother and that ties me now to my sons! But this is precisely what makes this such a tragic situation and makes me doubt the future, even though I am still convinced that this represents only an eclipse, an interruption, of the freedoms that are necessary for modern man. . . . I am French in my culture, in my blood, and by inclination. I am being made less than that. It hurts me terribly, but it makes me suffer even more when I realize that there are truly stateless Jews, both at the top and the bottom of the social ladder. The unfortunate pariahs who escaped from eastern ghettos and wandered about central Europe, who are now wandering or are interned in France, have never succeeded in becoming integrated into the nation where they have been temporary guests. They are still living on the margins of our society. On the other hand the leading capitalists, who are kings of their banks and industries, felt like internationalists and made a cult of wealth, of the Golden Calf, of "titles," rather than becoming attached to any soil. . . . If I was an internationalist, it was in the dream of humanitarianism, it was my Judeo-Christian culture, catholic in the etymological sense of the word. But through the bones of my ancestors, which have been mingled for more than a century with this ground, I feel closer to the French serfs, to French artists and French writers, than to any others. So I shall have to suffer and to wait. [. . .]

It is easy to dismiss the perceptions of people like Schwarzbart in London or Lambert in southern France as too detached from the Polish ghettos to be of any immediate help for those in the greatest need. But most Jews in Poland had little time for reflection on the meaning of the events then transpiring. Ringelblum in Warsaw did take a step back at the time of the sealing of the ghetto to reflect on its meaning. He saw it as a regression to an earlier period in Jewish history, when Jews could live without interference from the outside world. He added, however, that "The Ghetto is much more painful now than it was in the Middle Ages, because we that were so high and mighty are now fallen so low."[80] Despite the strong sense of loss, and notwithstanding the uncertainty as to what Germany, its allies, or its enemies would do, many Jews inside and outside ghetto walls remained hopeful as they witnessed how resilience, resourcefulness, and determination could be mustered against despair and destitution. On the occasion of the beginning of the Jewish New Year 5701 (October 3–4, 1940), the WJC issued an appeal written in English, French, and German to Jews in the United States to do what they could on behalf of their oppressed people in Europe.

DOCUMENT 12–14: **WJC Geneva, appeal to Jews, fall 1940, USHMMA RG 68.045M (WJC Geneva), reel 1.**

Jews!

Europe enters into the second year of the war. For us as Jews the past year was one of the hardest of our history. European Jewry is menaced with extermination. From Poland and Rumania, from Belgium and France, from all of the *Jeshuvim* [sic] of Europe one great wail arises across the world. The Jewish people have never lived through such a catastrophe.

On the threshold of the Jewish New Year and the coming Holy days we address to you, American Jews in this dark hour: Will you remain impassive while your brothers and sisters are exposed to hunger and misery?

The winter approaches; it is war's second winter. What will it bring? What can it bring? Still cold, hunger, epidemics and indescribable suffering! Where will one find the wood and coal for heating, where a drop of milk for the children, medicine for the sick, warm clothing protecting against cold and rain?

Jews! All of you who have in Europe a father or mother, brother or sister, relatives or friends, all you who do not remain indifferent to the destiny of European Jewry, all you who were spared the terrible fate of your brethren, from you and you alone aid can come!

Expelled from Cracow, the ancient Jewish community, behind the ghetto walls of Warsaw and Lodz, on the roads of France, behind the barbed-wire of concentration or internment camps,—European Jewry awaits anxiously a brotherly word of encouragement and a helpful hand.

---

80. Ringelblum, diary entry for November 8, 1940, in Ringelblum, *Notes from the Warsaw Ghetto*, 85.

Jews! To you our appeal is addressed. As long as a Jewish heart beats in your breast, as long as you breathe free air, do not forget your brothers on the other side of the sea! As long as hundreds of thousands of Jews do not know where to lay their tired heads at night, you do not have the right to sleep tranquilly.

Jews, arise from your apathy; save European Jewry! Help, Jews, help!

Working out of Geneva, Jewish Agency representative **Richard Lichtheim** was remarkably well informed about the situation of Jews across Nazi-occupied Europe. In one of a series of reports he sent to Jewish Agency officials in Jerusalem, Lichtheim reflected in December 1940 on the larger implications of the circumstances unfolding. He expressed his conviction that, whether or not a new calamity struck European Jews, the events of the last few years meant that the European Jewish future would look entirely different from the past. The triumph of Anglo-American democracy and, with it, the restoration of Jews' political rights would not remedy the economic straits produced by recent antisemitic policies. Return to the past was no longer possible.

DOCUMENT 12–15: **Letter by Richard Lichtheim, Geneva, Switzerland, to Dr. Leo Lauterbach,**[81] **Jerusalem, Palestine, December 11, 1940, facsimile reprinted in** *Archives of the Holocaust*, **ed. Henry Friedlander and Sybil Milton (New York: Garland Publishing, 1990), 4:24–25.**

[. . .]

6.   What will become of the Jews of Europe? I feel that a word of warning to the happier Jews of England and America is necessary. It is impossible to believe that any power on earth will be able (and willing?) to restore to the Jews of Continental Europe what they have lost or are loosing to-day. It is one of the superficial beliefs of a certain type of American and British Jews that after Great Britain's victory—for which of course the Jews all over the world are praying—everything will be allright again with the Jews of Europe. But even if their civil rights can be restored—what about the property confiscated, the shops looted, the practice of doctors and lawyers gone, the schools destroyed, the commercial undertakings of

---

81. Leo Lauterbach (1886–1968) practiced law in Vienna before serving in the Austrian army during World War I. In 1919 he began working for the executive of the Zionist Organization in London under **Chaim Weizmann** and became an official in the organization, in 1936 moving with the office to Jerusalem, where he spent the war. See Leo Lauterbach, *Chronicle of the Lauterbach Family*, new ed. (Jerusalem: Lauterbach Family Fund, 1961), 19, 47.

every description closed or sold or stolen? Who will restore all that and how? Who will drive away the "Gentiles"—or shall I say the natives?—who have taken possession of all that, or have simply destroyed it? And what will be left of the Jews of Europe? I am not speaking of the hundreds of thousands who have lost their lives or will die from hunger and exposure before this war ends, but of those who will be found alive after the war is over! There are several hundred thousands who during these years of persecution have managed to escape and are now trying to build up a new life in Palestine, in U.S.A., in South America, Australia, San Domingo or elsewhere. Then there are the refugees in Europe who tried to escape but did not go fast and far enough. The tens of thousands in Holland and Belgium, Portugal, Switzerland and France, who are now living on the rest of their possessions or on public charity or have been herded into camps. What will become of them after the war? These refugees together with the remnants of the dispossessed and destitute Jews of Greater Germany and Rumania, of Hungary and the Balkan States (where economic persecution is steadily going on in this or that form) will present a problem which cannot be solved by the simple formula: Restore their rights.

Jewry and the governments of the civilized nations will have to find new methods, a new approach to the whole problem. Some new forms of organized help must be found. In Palestine this should take the form of developing the Community as a whole on a much larger scale than before, thus enabling the economic absorption of thousands of immigrants who will go there. In other countries assistance will be needed in a more individual form. And then there will be a mass of several hundred thousands who are in a permanent no-man's land, who are now drifting from one frontier to the other, from concentration camps to labour camps, from there to some unknown country and destiny. For most of these people it will be impossible for economic reasons to return to their old homes and many of them will refuse to do so also for moral reasons. They must be helped to build up a new life somewhere else. It is certainly too early to formulate any definite policy or to make detailed plans now, but the Jews of England and America must know that the problems cannot be solved by using only the old watchwords and slogans which under the radically changed conditions of present and future life in Europe have lost much of their meaning.

One week later, in the closing days of the year 1940, Franz Werfel published the reflection on the fate of European Jewry presented in document

12–16. The Prague-born Jewish writer had escaped from Vienna to France in the days following the *Anschluss* in 1938.[82] In October 1940 he made the treacherous journey on foot across the Pyrenees into Spain and from there traveled by ship to New York. Werfel was one of the two thousand refugees, including many prominent intellectuals and artists, whom Varian Fry rescued in 1940 and 1941 while working clandestinely for the American Emergency Rescue Committee.[83]

Werfel had spent much of the preceding decade writing fiction about the persecution of minorities in recent history, particularly about victims' responses to persecution. His best-selling novel *The Forty Days of Musa Dagh*, published the year Hitler came to power, offered a dramatic rendition of Armenian suffering and resistance in the face of Ottoman Turkish efforts to exterminate the Armenian population during World War I. During Werfel's first year in exile in France, he worked on another historical novel, *Cella oder die Überwinder* (literally, "Cella, or the Overcomers"), which took up a topic from his own immediate past: the experiences of Austrian Jews during the first months of Nazi rule. He continued to write about Jewish themes in subsequent years, reflecting on his own identity and that of the Jewish people.[84] The essay he published shortly after arriving in the United States in the German Jewish emigré newspaper *Aufbau* explored the meaning of recent Jewish suffering in relation to world history, religion, and human nature.

DOCUMENT 12–16: Franz Werfel, "Our Path Continues," *Aufbau* (New York), December 27, 1940, 1–2 (translated from German).

It is not easy for me to speak about the thing that is blazing like a bonfire. I am only one of the hundreds of thousands who have experienced in their own lives the stupefying fate of our tribe, one of the vast number whose previous life—homeland, security, house, possessions, family, achievements, and names—has dissolved into a painful haze. Again and again,

---

82. Franz Werfel (1890–1945) gained renown as an expressionist playwright, poet, and novelist. Having fled from Austria to Paris in 1938, he and his wife left France after the German invasion and arrived in New York in October 1940. See Hans Wagener, *Understanding Franz Werfel* (Columbia: University of South Carolina Press, 1993).

83. Varian Fry, *Assignment Rescue: An Autobiography* (New York: Scholastic, 1992); Anne Klein, *Flüchtlingspolitik und Flüchtlingshilfe, 1940–1942: Varian Fry und die Komitees zur Rettung politisch Verfolgter in New York und Marseilles* (Berlin: Metropol, 2007).

84. *Cella oder die Überwinder* remained unfinished and was published posthumously in 1982. Wagener, *Understanding Franz Werfel*, 139–49.

it is necessary to give an answer to the dreadful question, "What shall we do?" I can make only a faint attempt to face head-on the other question: "How do we make sense of this?"

How are we to understand what has been going on here, for almost a decade now? How are we to comprehend this hatred from the abyss, which is massing more horrifyingly than ever around an ethnic group that has preserved its existence among the nations for several millennia now? Antisemitism? What a foolish, feeble, and imprecise word for this diabolical phenomenon! [. . .] Viewed superficially, difference in type, competition, envy, the so-called biological causes play a role in antisemitism, but they certainly do not explain it. They are the modern costume of a thousand-year-old phenomenon that has always managed to wear different disguises, according to the historical circumstances.

In earlier times, hatred of Jews was always parochial, limited in scope. Today, in our technical age, it is global. Let no one think that an inch of social territory on this earth exists that is not insidiously weakened from beneath by this volcano![85] Let no one surmise that here or there, wherever Jews live, the same thing that is now happening in Europe cannot occur. It can happen, in an even worse way and in proportions yet unknown. How, therefore, should we understand this immutable hatred? I will be so immodest as to quote a few lines that I put down on paper more than twenty years ago. They go like this: "Israel has given the world a God. Every gift signifies a kind of humbling of the person receiving it. The psychological resistance of the recipient increases in proportion to the magnitude of the benefit." [. . .]

What is taking place in the world today seems to us to be a social revolution of enormous import. In its external form, it is a social revolution, too; at its core it is far more. It is the most monumental religious war of all time, a war that the human race is waging against the 2,000-year-old paradox, against the spirit of Israel, the biblical spirit in all its manifestations. History knows no wars more terrible than wars of religion. And now we also understand why modern antisemitism, the current hostility against the Jews, is taking on such inconceivably horrendous forms.

This time, unlike the previous times, it is not a matter of the disenfranchisement and robbing of parts of the Jewish people in certain countries. Far more is at stake. Everything is at stake. The enemy's goal is the

---

85. On the volcano as a trope for Jewish persecution in this period, see chapter 1, note 17, and document 1–4.

utter eradication of the Jewish spirit from this planet, indeed, in all its forms and repercussions. But if Israel's God and spirit are to vanish from this planet, the physical vehicle of this spirit—the Jewish people—must first be annihilated, down to the very last man. For as long as a single Jew lives, the flame of the demanding spirit can continue to ignite. In this respect, antisemitism has diabolically clear vision. Just as Israel's spirit has its physical vehicle, so too does antisemitism have a carrier of its own. This carrier is not only national socialism, fascism in its various hues; it is a new biological type of modern-day youth, a type that extends right across all continents and peoples and social classes. You can encounter this new type by the dozen in the street. It is waiting here and everywhere for its hour to come. In my last book, I called this type the "motorized golem." He dreams with strange fanaticism of a value-free, spiritless, and soulless world that resembles a technically elaborate frozen hell.—It is against this dreadful foe that the war is being fought. It is indeed a holy war. Only how terrible it is that the fronts are so very blurred and that the enemy is found in our own ranks everywhere. England is fighting on the forwardmost line of this holy war. (Is it only a symbolic coincidence that the Puritans trace the origin of the British nation back to the ten lost tribes of Israel?) If England falls, the American democracy falls. If England and the American democracy fall, the last hour of the Jewish people has struck, and its long path has reached an end. If the Jews succumb, the Christian churches will fade away to mere shadows and quickly vanish. The endeavor of every intellectual culture will be dropped, and man can once again be what he was on his lowest rung of development: a technically gifted animal.

It must not happen! This despairing cry escapes our breast. England must not fall! The American democracy must not topple in its wake. The path of the Jewish people, of the biblical spirit, must not end! We Jews are fighting today for more than the continued existence of our communities in the Diaspora, for more than the development work in Palestine, yes, for more than our lives. We are engaged in God's struggle for the salvation of the entire world.

My faith lies in these words! It is one of the great mysteries of human history that Israel from time to time must again fight God's fight for the well-being of the world, whether this people wants to do so or not. Therein, if anywhere, lies the proof of its being "chosen," or more correctly and unassumingly put, of its being "singled out" among the nations. But it would be entirely mistaken if this faith were to make us haughty and proud. No, it summons us to self-awareness, to atonement, and to sacrifice. [. . .]

Therefore, everything that is going on is insufficient. Therefore, the sacrifices of wealth and possessions, of support and aid, which so quickly put our conscience at rest, are insufficient. All too many people still believe that the enemy's intent to destroy does not apply to them personally. Until we have saturated our consciousness with the significance of these events, with the terrible need into which we have been hurled, we will continue to be poor fighters. But we must be good fighters at this most significant and most perilous moment of our history!

At the end of 1940, after more than a year of German triumph in Europe, the feeling of unprecedented catastrophe and fear of still greater future challenges had grown among Jews in Europe and around the world. Uneven patterns of German persecution, different approaches by Jewish groups in response to a wide range of problems, and uncertainty about what lay ahead contributed to a general sense of bewilderment. The collective fate of the European Jews had never before seemed so precarious, so impervious to reason, and so far removed from self-determination. Millions of Jews had never been as isolated as they were within their segregated communities, whether behind closed ghetto gates or left for a time to continue life among non-Jews. It was clear that the options open to Jews in the face of new crises had been massively reduced, while the paths of action still open had narrowed and become far more difficult and treacherous.

LIST OF DOCUMENTS

PART I: FROM "*KRISTALLNACHT*" TO WAR

1: Responses to "*Kristallnacht*" outside of Germany

Assessing the Damage

Document 1–1: Letter by Emanuel Ringelblum, Środborów, Poland, to Raphael Mahler, New York City, December 6, 1938, Moreshet, Mordechai Anielevich Memorial Archive D.1.4927 (translated from Yiddish).

Document 1–2: Jewish expellees from Germany in the refugee camp in Zbąszyń, Poland, fall/winter 1938–1939, USHMMPA WS# 13547.

Document 1–3: "The Destruction of the Jews in Germany," *Olami* (Warsaw) 7, no. 55 (November 21, 1938): 99, USHMMA Acc. 2003.300 Sztejnsznajd family collection (translated from Hebrew).

Document 1–4: "Before the Final Verdict," *Beys Ya'akov: A Literary Publication for School and Home* (Łódź, Warsaw, Kraków) (Kislev/November–December) TRZ"T (5699/1938): 152:1 (translated from Yiddish).

Document 1–5: E. G. O., editorial, *Aufbau* (New York), December 1, 1938, 5 (translated from German).

Forward Action

Document 1–6: "The German Pogrom," *Jewish Chronicle* (London), November 18, 1938, 7.

Document 1–7: Ovadia Camhy, "Under the Sign of Satan," *Le Judaïsme Séphardi* (Paris) 7, no. 66 (December 1938): 135, 140 (translated from French).

Document 1–8: Speech by Léon Blum delivered at the banquet dinner at the ninth annual meeting of the International League against Antisemitism, November 26, 1938, Centre de documentation juive contemporaine, fonds LICA, CMXCVI/Série I/3.2.2, dossier no. 42, 2–12 (translated from French).

Document 1–9: Prayer inserted into a Dutch prayer book following the "*Kristallnacht*" pogrom of November 1938, USHMMA Acc. 2004.351 Ilse Lichtenstein Meyer collection (translated from Hebrew).

2: From Emigration to Flight

Attempting to Get Out

Document 2–1: An Eye Witness, "Purgatory: The Fate of the Jews in Germany and Austria," no date (ca. late 1938), USHMMA RG 11.001M.36, reel 107 (SAM 1190-1-334).

Document 2–2: Henrietta Szold speaks to a group of Youth Aliyah immigrants from Austria at Kiryat Anavim, Palestine, October 1938, USHMMPA WS# 07146.

Document 2–3: "Jewish Youth to Palestine. New Registrants for *Hakhsharah*," *Jüdisches Nachrichtenblatt Wien*, August 18, 1939, 1 (translated from German).

Document 2–4: Letter by Samuel Gerson, Hamburg, Germany, to the senior finance president, Hamburg Currency Office, August 14, 1939, in *"Wo Wurzeln waren . . . ": Juden in Hamburg-Eimsbüttel, 1933 bis 1945*, ed. Sybille Baumbach et al. (Hamburg: Dölling und Galitz, 1993), 106 (translated from German).

Document 2–5: Flowchart and map depicting "Jewish migration" from Germany, Austria, and the Protectorate, October 31, 1940, USHMMA RG 17.017M, IKG Vienna 447, film 1259, 58128 (A/W 2557,2).

Document 2–6: Letter by Amalie Malsch, Düsseldorf, Germany, to her son Willy, United States, April 4 through 7, 1939, USHMMA RG 10.086 Malsch family papers (translated from German).

Document 2–7: Letters by Susanne (Suse) Behr, Hamburg, Germany, to Lilo Rieder, Philadelphia, February 27, 1939, and unspecified date (probably March 1939), USHMMA Acc. 2000.51 Liselotte Feinschil family papers (translated from German).

Document 2–8: *Kindertransport* identity document for Inge Engelhard issued by British authorities, spring 1939, USHMMPA WS# 99687.

Document 2–9: Martha Wertheimer, "Children Are Dispatched. Snapshots from a Jewish Orphanage," *Jüdisches Nachrichtenblatt Berlin*, January 5, 1939, 2 (translated from German).

Document 2–10: Document signed by the widow Miriam Goldfarb, Berlin, Germany, April 24, 1939, giving custody of her thirteen-year-old son, Eryk, to the Comité Israélite pour les enfants venant d'Allemagne et de l'Europe Centrale (Jewish Committee for Children from Germany and Central Europe) USHMMA Acc. 2004.362 Eric and Fee Goldfarb collection (translated from French).

Trying to Settle In

Document 2–11: Arnold Stein, Prague, diary entries for February 18 and March 14, 1939, LBINY MM132 (translated from German).

Document 2–12: Letter by Gina Castelnuovo, Copenhagen, Denmark, to Emergency Committee in Aid of Displaced Foreign Scholars, New York City, April 8, 1939, NYPL MssCol 922, box 49, file 1.

Document 2–13: The family of a Chinese translator who worked with Walter Jacobsberg, Shanghai, China, ca. 1940, USHMMPA WS# 25771.

Document 2–14: Letter by Tobias Farb, Shanghai, China, to an unnamed recipient in the United States, April 28, 1939, facsimile reprinted in *Archives of the Holocaust*, ed. Henry Friedlander and Sybil Milton (New York: Garland Publishing, 1995), 10/1:316–18.

Document 2–15: Jewish refugee women preparing vegetables in the refugee colony, Shanghai, China, undated (between 1939 and 1948), USHMMPA WS# 23569.

Document 2–16: "While You Are in England: Helpful Information and Guidance for Every Refugee," pamphlet distributed in England by the German Jewish Aid Committee, 1939, USHMMA Acc. 2003.58.1 Joseph family papers.

Document 2–17: Austrian Jewish refugees and local workers, La Paz, Bolivia, ca. 1940, USHMMPA WS# 33977.

Document 2–18: Letter by Eduard Cohn, Asunción, Paraguay, to AJJDC, New York, June 4, 1939, LBINY MF 488 (AJJDC case file).

Document 2–19: Letter by Leon Gattegno, president of the Jewish community of Salonika, to the World Jewish Congress, Paris, June 7, 1939, USHMMA RG 11.001 M36, reel 107 (SAM 1190-1-299) (translated from French).

Document 2–20: Letter by Lici Dzialowski, aboard the MS *St. Louis*, to Hella Slagter, June 12, 1939, USHMMA Acc. 1997.36 Betty Troper Jaeger papers (translated from German).

Document 2–21: Letter by Morris Troper, Paris, to Joseph C. Hyman, New York City, July 1, 1939, facsimile reprinted in *Archives of the Holocaust*, ed. Henry Friedlander and Sybil Milton (New York: Garland Publishing, 1995), 10/1:633–34.

3: Facing New Fear and Violence

Seeking Dignity in Culture and Religion

Document 3–1: Leo Israel Hirsch, "What Matters Now! What You Need besides a Permit and a Ticket," *Jüdisches Nachrichtenblatt Berlin*, August 11, 1939, 10 (translated from German).

Document 3–2: Willy Cohn, diary entry for May 10, 1939, translated from *Kein Recht, Nirgends: Tagebuch vom Untergang des Breslauer Judentums, 1933–1941*, ed. Norbert Conrads (Cologne: Böhlau Verlag, 2007), 2:642).

Document 3–3: Willy Cohn, diary entry for April 29, 1939, translated from *Kein Recht, Nirgends: Tagebuch vom Untergang des Breslauer Judentums, 1933–1941*, ed. Norbert Conrads (Cologne: Böhlau Verlag, 2007), 2:637.

Document 3–4: Responsum by Rabbi Menahem Mendel Kirschbaum, Kraków, Poland, 1939, recorded in *Tsiyun le-Menahem*, ed. Jehuda Rubinstein (New York: Research Institute of Religious Jewry, 1965), 361–65; translated from Hebrew and published in *Rabbinic Responsa of the Holocaust Era*, ed. Robert Kirschner (New York: Schocken, 1985), 56–61.

Document 3–5: Dr. Karl Rosenthal, poem titled "Holiday Happiness," no date (ca. 1939), USHMMA RG 10.087 Karl Rosenthal family papers (translated from German).

Czechoslovak Jews Confront Nazi Occupation

Document 3–6: Daily Information Bulletin issued by the Jewish Telegraphic Agency, April 4, 1939, USHMMA RG 11.001.M25, reel 106 (SAM 674-1-114) (translated from French).

Document 3–7: Speech by Rabbi Abraham Abba-Armin Frieder to the Jewish community in Nové Mesto, Slovakia, on laying the foundation stone to the Ohel David House, June 9, 1939, YVA RG M5.192.46–47 (translated from German and Hebrew).

Document 3–8: Letter by Walter Schwartz, a WJC official in Brünn (Brno), Czechoslovakia, to the WJC, Paris office, December 18, 1938, USHMMA RG 11.001.M36, reel 107 (SAM 1190-1-288) (translated from German).

The Limits of Jewish Identity and Future Expectations

Document 3–9: Memorandum by the Reichsvereinigung on a meeting held July 20, 1939, USHMMA RG 14.003M.01, BAB R 8150, 214–17 (translated from German).

Document 3–10: Letter by Jakob Sieskind, Leipzig, Germany, to Rabbi Gustav Cohn, Leipzig, November 27, 1938, USHMMA RG 14.035M, reel 1 (translated from German).

Document 3–11: Luise Solmitz, Hamburg, Germany, diary entries for July 8 and 9, 1939, FZGH 11 S 11 (translated from German).

Document 3–12: Letter by Jenny Marx, Mannheim, Germany, to Max Marx, Jerusalem, Palestine, April 21, 1939, private collection (translated from German).

Document 3–13: Itshele, "After the Speech (a Political Letter)," *Haynt* (Warsaw), February 3, 1939, 3 (translated from Yiddish).

PART II: INVASION AND EARLY OCCUPATION OF POLAND

4: Initial Reactions

The Invasion of Poland

Document 4–1: Dawid Sierakowiak, Łódź, Poland, diary entries for late August 1939, USHMMA RG 10.247 Dawid Sierakowiak diary collection (translated from Polish).

Document 4–2: Jewish Poles dig trenches in the city around the time of the German invasion, Warsaw, Poland, late August or early September 1939, USHMMPA WS# 41033.

Document 4–3: Miriam Wattenberg, Warsaw, diary-memoir entry for October 10, 1939, in *The Diary of Mary Berg: Growing Up in the Warsaw Ghetto* (Oxford: Oneworld Publications, 2006), 1–2, 7–8.

Document 4–4: Testimony of an anonymous woman from Kutno, no date (ca. 1940), USHMMA RG 15.079M (ŻIH Ring. I/839), reel 39 (translated from Polish).

Document 4–5: Jews move their belongings to the Kutno ghetto, no date (ca. June 1940), USHMMPA WS# 18609.

Document 4–6: Testimony by unknown woman from Lipno, recorded ca. 1940 in the Warsaw ghetto, USHMMA RG 15.079M (ŻIH Ring. I/854), reel 39 (translated from Polish).

The Assault on Jewish Life

Document 4–7: Rabbi David Lifszyc (later Lifshitz) in front of Torah scrolls smuggled from German-occupied Suwałki to Kalvarija, Lithuania, 1940, USHMMPA WS# 35460.

Document 4–8: Rosh Hashanah sermon of Rabbi Kalonymus Kalmish Shapira, September 14–15, 1939 (1 tishrei 5700), USHMMA RG 15.079M (ŻIH Ring. II/370), reel 58 (translated from Hebrew).

Document 4–9: Testimony by unknown woman from Lipno, recorded after 1939 in the Warsaw ghetto, USHMMA RG 15.079M (ŻIH Ring. I/974), reel 43 (translated from Polish).

Document 4–10: Shimon Huberband, Warsaw, "The Destruction of Synagogues, Study Halls, and Cemeteries," ca. 1941, USHMMA RG 15.079M (ŻIH Ring. I/108), reel 7 (translated from Yiddish).

Document 4–11: Registration card for Shimon Huberband issued by the Warsaw Labor Office, ca. 1941, USHMMA RG 15.079M (ŻIH Ring. II/385), reel 58 (translated from German).

Document 4–12: Testimony on persecution in Włocławek/Leslau, recorded in Jerusalem, Palestine, June 7, 1940, translated from Benjamin Mintz and Joseph Klausner, eds., in *Sefer ha-Zeva'ot. Eduyot ve-dinim ve-heshbonot al sho'ot ha-yehudim be-milhemet ha-olam ha-sheniya* (Jerusalem: R. Mass, 1945), 86.

Witnessing the Collapse of Poland

Document 4–13: Adam Czerniaków, Warsaw, diary entries for September and October 1939, in *Adama Czerniakowa dziennik getta warszawskiego: 6 IX 1939–23 VII 1942*, ed. Marian Fuks (Warsaw: Państwowe Wydawn. Naukowe, 1983), 48–51 (translated from Polish).

Document 4–14: Samuel Zeldman, "To Berlin, for a Military Parade," no date (ca. mid-1940), USHMMA RG 15.079M (ŻIH Ring. I/458), reel 17 (translated from Yiddish).

Document 4–15: Emanuel Ringelblum, "Polish-Jewish Relations in Occupied Warsaw," October 1939, USHMMA RG 15.079M (ŻIH Ring. I/91), reel 7 (translated from Yiddish).

5: Jewish Flight

Flight Routes

Document 5–1: Herman Kruk, Vilna, diary entries for September 19 to October 6, 1939 (written in January 1940), translated from Yiddish and published in Herman Kruk, *The Last Days of the Jerusalem of Lithuania: Chronicles from the Vilna Ghetto and the Camps, 1939–1944*, ed. Benjamin Harshav (New Haven, CT: YIVO Institute for Jewish Research and Yale University Press, 2002), 21–22.

Document 5–2: Alfred Tisch, Bacău, Romania, to WJC, Geneva office, "Report on the Establishment and Work of the Local Refugee Self-Help Committee in Bacău, Romania," December 1939, USHMMA RG 68.045M (WJC Geneva), reel 2, folder 9 (translated from German).

Document 5–3: Letter from Rudolf Katz, director of the Aliyah Committee in Bucharest, Romania, to Simon Mirelmann, Buenos Aires, Argentina, April 20, 1940, USHMMA RG 68.045M (WJC Geneva), reel 140, file 1290 (translated from German).

Document 5–4: Two pages from the certificate of Polish nationality issued to Samuel Soltz by the Polish consul in Kovno, Lithuania, 1939, USHMMPA WS# 86548A, 86548E.

Refugees in Vilna

Document 5–5: Jewish refugees waiting for aid distribution, Vilna, Lithuania, no date (ca. 1940), USHMMPA WS# 20707.

Document 5–6: Letter from Moshe Kleinbaum, Geneva, Switzerland, to Nahum Goldmann, chairman of the Administrative Committee of the WJC, March 12, 1940, facsimile reprinted in *Archives of the Holocaust*, ed. Henry Friedlander and Sybil Milton (New York: Garland Publishing, 1990), 8:119, 122–27.

Document 5–7: Dr. Garfunkelis, "Report of the Lithuanian Committee on Behalf of Polish Jewish Refugees," November 22, 1939, American Jewish Archives, WJC records, series A, box A2, file 2, *Day Book of the WJC II*, 37–38.

Occupied Poland: Leaders, Communities, Choices

Document 5–8: Excerpt from a memoir by Mieczysław Garfinkiel, written in 1946, USHMMA RG 02.208M (ŻIH 302/122) (translated from Polish).

Document 5–9: Testimony provided by unidentified female author regarding the German/Russian occupation of Zamość, no date (ca. 1941), USHMMA RG 15.079M (ŻIH Ring. I/935), reel 42 (translated from Yiddish).

Document 5–10: Letter from Moshe Kleinbaum, Geneva, Switzerland, to Nahum Goldmann, chairman of the Administrative Committee of the WJC, March 12, 1940, facsimile reprinted in *Archives of the Holocaust*, ed. Henry Friedlander and Sybil Milton (New York: Garland Publishing, 1990), 8:112–13.

Document 5–11: Excerpt from a memoir by Calel Perechodnik, written in 1943, USHMMA RG 02.208M (ŻIH 302/55) (translated from Polish).

Document 5–12: Excerpt from a memoir by Zofia Dulman, written in 1945, USHMMA RG 02.208M (ŻIH 302/261) (translated from Polish).

6: The Organization of Relief for Polish Jews

Organizing Help, Confronting Obstacles

Document 6–1: Report by AJJDC Warsaw about its work during the thirteen war months from September 1939 to October 1940, USHMMA Acc. 1999.A.0154 (ŻIH 210/6), 10–12 (translated from Yiddish).

Document 6–2: At the Warsaw office of the AJJDC, April 1940, USHMMPA WS# 48208.

Document 6–3: Morris Troper, "On the European Relief Front," *Contemporary Jewish Record* 3 (May–June 1940), 233–35.

Document 6–4: Excerpts from a letter by Dr. Abraham Silberschein, WJC Committee for Polish Relief, Geneva, Switzerland, to Stephen S. Wise, October 11, 1939, American Jewish Archives, WJC records, series A, box A2, file 2, *Day Book of the WJC I*, 26–28.

Coordinating More Efficient Relief

Document 6–5: Letter from Dr. Abraham Silberschein, WJC Geneva, to Morris Troper, director of AJJDC work in Europe, November 9, 1939, American Jewish Archives, WJC records, series A, box A2, file 2, *Day Book of the WJC II*, 23–26.

Document 6–6: Letter from Käthe Knöpfmacher, WJC, Geneva office, to Lillie Schultz, American Jewish Congress, New York City, December 8, 1939, USHMMA RG 68.059M (WJC London), reel 146, folder 1515.

Document 6–7: RELICO report about the Vilna committee's organizational efforts to assist Polish Jewish refugees in Lithuania, Romania, and Hungary, February 25, 1940, USHMMA RG 68.059M (WJC London), reel 142, folder 1477.

Document 6–8: Activity report of Chaim Barlas and the regional office of the Jewish Agency for Palestine in Geneva, Switzerland, between September 1, 1939, and January 25, 1940, USHMMA RG 68.045M (WJC Geneva), reel 20, file 147 (translated from German).

"The Situation of Polish Jewry"

Document 6–9: Excerpt from letter of Dr. Nahum Goldmann, chairman of the Administrative Committee of the WJC, Geneva, Switzerland, to Dr. Stephen S. Wise, New York, November 4, 1939, American Jewish Archives, WJC records, series A, box A2, file 2, *Day Book of the WJC I*, 48–52.

Document 6–10: Author unknown, Trieste, Italy, "The Situation of Polish Jewry: A Letter to the World Jewish Congress," November 16, 1939, American Jewish Archives, WJC records, series A, box A2, file 2, *Day Book of the WJC II*, 31–33.

PART III: WAR AND ITS REPERCUSSIONS IN THE REST OF EUROPE: SEPTEMBER 1939 TO DECEMBER 1940

7: Outside Poland: War and Its Repercussions

War in Poland Viewed from Afar

Document 7–1: Willy Cohn, diary entry for September 2, 1939, translated from *Kein Recht, Nirgends: Tagebuch vom Untergang des Breslauer Judentums, 1933–1941*, ed. Norbert Conrads (Cologne: Böhlau Verlag, 2007), 2:683–84.

Document 7–2: Mihail Sebastian, Bucharest, Romania, diary entry for September 21, 1939, in *Journal, 1935–1944* (Chicago: Ivan R. Dee in association with the USHMM, 2000), 239–40.

Document 7–3: Grete Steiner, Scheveningen, Netherlands, diary entries for September 1, 3, and 6, 1939, Ghetto Fighters' House Archives (Beit lohamei ha-getaot), Israel, 1064 (translated from German).

Document 7–4: Alfred Berl, Paris, France, "The Frenzy of Barbarism and the Jews of Central Europe," *Paix et Droit*, October 1, 1939, 1ff. (translated from French).

Document 7–5: Robert Weltsch, Jerusalem, Palestine, "Changed World," *Jüdische Welt-Rundschau* (special issue), October 27, 1939, 2 (translated from German).

Document 7–6: Letter by Dr. Nahum Goldmann, Geneva, Switzerland, to Dr. Stephen S. Wise, New York City, November 17, 1939, facsimile reprinted in *Archives of the Holocaust*, ed. Henry Friedlander and Sybil Milton (New York: Garland Publishing, 1990), 8:88–89.

Document 7–7: Gertrude van Tijn, Amsterdam, Netherlands, "The Refugee Problem in Connection with the General Situation in Holland. Confidential Report for the Joint Distribution Committee," February 29, 1940, USHMMA Acc. 1997.A.0117 (NIOD 217a), reel 448, 1, 3–4, 7–9.

Expansion of the War

Document 7–8: Willem Friedman, a soldier in the Belgian army, poses next to a piece of artillery, winter 1939–1940, USHMMPA WS# 20481.

Document 7–9: Leo Krell, a soldier in the Dutch army, poses on a motorcycle, ca. 1940, USHMMPA WS# 73215.

Document 7–10: Salomon Van den Berg, May 1940 diary entry, WL PIIIi (Belgium) no. 275 (translated from French).

Document 7–11: Albert Magsamen, from Brussels, Belgium, to the Belgian-French border, diary entries for May 10 through 13, 1940, YVA RG 09, no. 267 (translated from German).

Document 7–12: Jacob (Köbes) Müller, memoir entry written ca. late spring or early summer 1942, LBINY ME 1028 (translated from German).

Document 7–13: Daily Information Bulletin issued by the Jewish Telegraphic Agency, Paris, June 4, 1940, USHMMA RG 11.001M.25, reel 106 (SAM 674-1-130) (translated from French).

Document 7–14: Eugen Tillinger, "The Bridge of Hendaye: Eyewitness Account of the Mass Flight to Spain," *Aufbau* (New York), August 30, 1940, 2 (translated from German).

Document 7–15: Eugen Tillinger, "You've come from Lisbon? . . . Do tell! . . . ," *Aufbau* (New York), December 20, 1940, 2 (translated from German).

Document 7–16: Letter from an unnamed Jewish correspondent in Casablanca, Morocco, August 28, 1940, USHMMA RG 68.045M (WJC Geneva), reel 1, 203–20 (translated from German).

Document 7–17: Egon Weiss, en route to Palestine, diary entries written in 1940 and 1946, USHMMPA, private collection (translated from German).

Document 7–18: Telegram sent by the Israelite Community of Spanish Rite, Bucharest, Romania, to King Carol II, July 2, 1940, USHMMA RG 25.021 (CSHJR file III:2), reel 1, 51 (translated from Romanian).

Document 7–19: Emil Dorian, Bucharest, Romania, diary entry for July 16, 1940, in *The Quality of Witness: A Romanian Diary, 1937–1944*, ed. Marguerite Dorian (Philadelphia: Jewish Publication Society of America, 1982), 107–8.

8: Jewish Daily Life in Wartime

Direct Appeals to Authorities

Document 8–1: Letter by Luciano Morpurgo, Rome, Italy, to Benito Mussolini, September 9, 1939, in Luciano Morpurgo, *Caccia all'uomo! Vita sofferenze e beffe: Pagine di diario, 1938–1944* (Rome: Casa Editrice Dalmatia S.A., 1946), 42–45 (translated from Italian).

Document 8–2: Letter from the chief rabbi of France, Isaïe Schwartz, Vichy, France, to Marshal Pétain, French head of state, October 10, 1940, USHMMA RG 43.069M (Consistoire Central collection BCC-19a), reel 4 (translated from French).

Document 8–3: Letter from Wilhelm Filderman and Dr. I. Brucăr, Federation of Jewish Communities of Romania, Bucharest, to Ion Antonescu, Romanian prime minister, September 30, 1940, in *Documents Concerning the Fate of Romanian Jewry during the Holocaust*, ed. Jean Ancel (New York: Beate Klarsfeld Foundation, 1986), 1:528–30 (translated from Romanian).

Document 8–4: Memorandum from Wilhelm Filderman and Matatias Carp to the minister of the interior, November 25, 1940, in Matatias Carp, *Cartea neagră: Suferințele evreilor din*

Romania in timpul dictaturei fasciste, 1940–1944 (Bucharest: Atelierele grafice Socec, 1946), 1b:340 (translated from Romanian).

Document 8–5: Letter from Albert Koppenheim, Leipzig, Germany, to the Leipzig mayor/ City Office for Facilitation of Residential Construction, June 24, 1940, USHMMA RG 14.035M (Leipzig Jewish Community), reel 9 (translated from German).

Communal Survival, Communal Solidarity

Document 8–6: Géza Ribáry, Pest, Hungary, "The Most Important Present Tasks and Duties of Hungarian Jewry," 1941, translated from Hungarian and published in *The Holocaust in Hungary: An Anthology of Jewish Response*, ed. Andrew Handler (University: University of Alabama Press, 1982), 43–44.

Document 8–7: The Council of Representatives of the Israelite Community of Spanish Rite, Bucharest, Romania, "Bulletin of the Council of Representatives," no. 33, report on January 1 to December 31, 1940, USHMMA RG 25.021 (CSHJR, file III:2), reel 1 (translated from Romanian).

Document 8–8: W. Sch., "Schooling, Retraining," *Jüdisches Nachrichtenblatt Prag/Židovské listy*, December 15, 1939, 4 (translated from German).

Document 8–9: "The Meaning of Jewish Sacrifices," *Jüdisches Nachrichtenblatt Prag/Židovské listy*, December 28, 1939, 1 (translated from German).

Document 8–10: Letter from Joseph Pradelski, Luxembourg, to the Jewish community of Luxembourg, October 7, 1940, USHMMA Acc. 1999.A.0013 Consistoire Israelite Luxembourg, reel 5, folder 37 (translated from German).

Document 8–11: Marriage ads, *Jüdisches Nachrichtenblatt Prag/Židovské listy*, January 12, 1940, 10 (translated from German).

Document 8–12: Report by Nina Gourfinkel, Unoccupied Zone, France, "First Attempts at the Organization of Professional Restructuring," to Arieh Tartakower, Committee for Relief of the WJC, New York City, October 15, 1940, USHMMA RG 68.045M (WJC Geneva), reel 1 (translated from French).

Document 8–13: Song titled "Benei-Midbar," La Guette, France, USHMMA Acc. 2004.435 Naomi Elath papers (translated from French).

Individual Coping Strategies

Document 8–14: Letters by Lotte Meissner, Triesch, Protectorate of Bohemia and Moravia, to her son, Frank ("Mokele"), Denmark, March 21, 1940, and June 8, 1940, USHMMA Acc. 2007.228 Frank Meissner collection (translated from German).

Document 8–15: Letter by Jenny Marx, Mannheim, Germany, to Max Marx and family, Jerusalem, Palestine, January 14, 1940, private collection (translated from German).

Document 8–16: Mignon Langnas, Vienna, diary entries for February 11 and March 24, 1940, private collection (copy at USHMM Collections Division, translated from German).

Document 8–17: Gabriel Italie, The Hague, Netherlands, diary entries from October 27, November 28 and 29, and December 5, 1940, in *Het oorlogsdagboek van dr. G. Italie. Den Haag, Barneveld, Westerbork, Theresienstadt, Den Haag, 1940–1945* (Amsterdam: Contact, 2009), 88–89, 101–3, 104–5 (translated from Dutch).

Document 8–18: Jiří Orten, Prague, Protectorate of Bohemia and Moravia, diary entry for October 26, 1940, translated from Czech and published in *The Jews of Bohemia and Moravia: A Historical Reader*, ed. Wilma Abeles Iggers (Detroit, MI: Wayne State University Press, 1986), 361–62.

9: Deportations from the Reich

Early "Resettlements" to the East

Document 9–1: Letter from the Central Bureau of the World Jewish Congress, Geneva, to Dr. Stephen S. Wise, New York, November 10, 1939, American Jewish Archives, WJC records, series A, box A2, file 2, American Jewish Conference, *Day Book of the WJC II*, 27–30.

Document 9–2: S. Moldawer, "The Road to Lublin," *Contemporary Jewish Record* 3 (March–April 1940): 119.

Document 9–3: "Nazis Establish More Ghettos in Poland," *Canadian Jewish Chronicle*, January 12, 1940, 5.

Document 9–4: "The Central Consistory of Israelites of France and Algeria Protests against the Creation of the Lublin 'Reserve,'" JTA bulletin, January 6, 1940, USHMMA RG 11.001M.63, reel 218 (SAM 186-1-8), 68 (translated from French).

Another Wave of Deportations from the Reich to the East

Document 9–5: Letters by Martha Bauchwitz, Piaski, Lublin district, Generalgouvernement, to Luise-Lotte Hoyer-Bauchwitz, Stettin, Germany, February 27 and March 1940, translated from Else Behrend-Rosenfeld and Gertrud Luckner, eds., *Lebenszeichen aus Piaski: Briefe Deportierter aus dem Distrikt Lublin 1940–1943*, unabr. ed. (Munich: Deutscher Taschenbuch Verlag, 1970), 32–33 (emphases and ellipses in the original).

Document 9–6: Letter by Walter Steinbach, Tonden, Netherlands, to Hans Steinbach, Cairo, Egypt, February–March 1940, USHMMA RG 10.074 Steinbach family letters (translated from German).

Document 9–7: Protocol of board meeting of the Reichsvereinigung held February 29, 1940, Berlin, March 4, 1940, USHMMA RG 14.003M, folder 4 (BAB R 8150), 187 (translated from German).

The Persistent Threat of Deportations

Document 9–8: Letter by Else Demang of the Reichsvereinigung, Hannover, to the Wunstorf mental institution, September 21, 1940, translated from Asmus Finzen, *Massenmord ohne*

PART IV: PRECARIOUS SHELTER: LIFE IN THE EMERGING POLISH GHETTOS

10: Settling into Confined Spaces

Uprooting and Relocation

Ghetto Economies and Forced Labor

Document 10–8: Emanuel Ringelblum, Warsaw, diary entries for January 1940, translated from Emanuel Ringelblum, *Ksovim fun geto: Togbukh, 1939–1942* (Tel Aviv: I. L. Peretz, 1985), 65–69.

Document 10–9: Letter from Hanns Winter, Jewish Agency for Palestine, Youth Aliyah Section, Geneva, Switzerland, to Henrietta Szold, Jewish Agency, Youth Aliyah Division, Jerusalem, Palestine, February 6, 1940, USHMMA RG 68.045M (WJC Geneva), reel 20, file 147.

Document 10–10: Szmul Zygielbojm, "Kidnapping for Labor," no date (ca. December 1939), translated from *Zygielbojm-bukh* (New York: Farlag "Unzer tsayt," 1947), 142–50.

Document 10–11: Report on the labor camp at Józefów, Generalgouvernement, November 1940, USHMMA RG 15.079M (ŻIH Ring I/3), reel 1 (translated from Polish).

Document 10–12: Draft memo by JDC (Warsaw or Kraków office) on the state of Jewish affairs in the Generalgouvernement, no date (probably early fall 1940), USHMMA Acc. 1999.0154 (ŻIH 210/5) (translated from German).

11: Formal and Informal Leadership

Interceding with German Authorities

Document 11–1: Warsaw Jewish Council, "Memorandum on the Causes of Typhus in Warsaw and Proposals for Combating It," May 1940, USHMMA RG 15.079M (ŻIH Ring I/85), reel 7 (translated from German).

Document 11–2: Letter by Leo Schönker, chairman of the Jewish Council in Auschwitz, to Berlin Gestapo office, November 30, 1939, facsimile reprinted in *Archives of the Holocaust*, ed. Henry Friedlander and Sybil Milton (New York: Garland Publishing, 1995), 10/2:652–53.

Document 11–3: Letter by the administration of the old-age home Ezra in Falenica near Warsaw to the AJJDC office in Warsaw, March 5, 1940, USHMMA Acc. 1999.A.0154 (ŻIH 210/34), 28 (translated from German).

Document 11–4: Report of a conference in the Generalgouvernement in Kraków, February 29, 1940, USHMMA RG 15.079M (ŻIH Ring II 1/28), reel 48 (translated from Polish).

Centralized Authority and the Plight of the Jews in Łódź

Document 11–5: Letter by Łódź ghetto Council of Elders of the Jews to Zalomon Mojżesz regarding his horse and buggy, February 28, 1940, USHMMA RG 15.083M (PSAŁ, file 6), reel 2 (translated from German).

Document 11–6: Protocol of meeting of Łódź ghetto Council of Elders of the Jews, April 30, 1940, USHMMA RG 15.083M (PSAŁ, file 1), reel 1 (translated from German).

Document 11–7: Announcement of summer colony for children ages four to seven in the Łódź [Litzmannstadt] ghetto, summer 1940, USHMMA RG 15.083M (PSAŁ, file 1627), reel 380 (translated from German).

Document 11–8: Report of the chairman of the Council of Elders of the Łódź ghetto, May 15, 1941, USHMMA RG 15.079M (ŻIH Ring I/856), reel 39 (translated from Polish).

Document 11–9: Author unknown, diary entry from the Łódź ghetto, December 15, 1940, USHMMA RG 02.208M (ŻIH 302/191) (translated from Polish).

Document 11–10: Pola Mordkowicz, "On Lustig," poem written in the Sowliny refugee camp, April 15, 1940, USHMMA RG 15.079M (ŻIH Ring I/2), reel 1 (translated from Polish).

Relief Networks across Poland

Document 11–11: Letter from the Skawina *Judenrat* to the AJJDC office in Kraków, Generalgouvernement, requesting *lulav* and *esrog*, October 16, 1940, USHMMA Acc. 1999.A.0154 (ŻIH 210/79), folder 12 (translated from German).

Document 11–12: "Save the Jewish Child!" JSS poster, Warsaw, no date (ca. 1940), USHMMA Acc. 1999.A.0154 (ŻIH 210/46), folder 40 (translated from Yiddish).

Document 11–13: "A Visit to Unfortunate Children," Warsaw, no date (ca. August 1940), USHMMA RG 15.079M (ŻIH Ring II/107), reel 49 (translated from Yiddish).

Document 11–14: Letter from the Center for Refugees in Kraków to Wilhelm Goldblatt, vice president of the Jewish Council in Kraków, April 19, 1940, USHMMA RG 15.072M (ŻIH 218/17), reel 1 (translated from Polish).

Document 11–15: Letter from the Jewish Council in Hinterberg (formerly Zagórów) to the AJJDC office in Warsaw, December 12, 1940, USHMMA Acc. 1999.0154 (ŻIH 210/738), 8–9 (translated from German).

Document 11–16: Letter from the Presidium of Jewish Social Self-Help in Kraków, to the Jewish Council of Lublin, December 21, 1940, USHMMA Acc. 1997.A.0124 (ŻIH 211/644) (translated from Polish).

Document 11–17: Aleksander Fargel, "Account of the Social Welfare Measures Taken by the Aid Committee for Refugees and the Poor of the Jewish Council of Włoszczowa in 1940," no date (ca. January 1941), USHMMA RG 15.073M (ŻIH 223/1), reel 1 (translated from Polish).

12: Beyond Bread: Faith, Friendship, and the Future

Preserving the Spirit

Document 12–1: Kalman Huberband, Warsaw, "The 'march' into the *mikveh*," October 1940, USHMMA RG 15.079M (ŻIH Ring I/218), reel 11 (translated from Yiddish).

Document 12–2: Chaim Kaplan, Warsaw, diary entry for October 14, 1940, USHMMA RG 02.208M (ŻIH 302/218), 148–52 (translated from Hebrew).

Document 12–3: "Molotov in Berlin, and What Next?" *Yugnt shtime* (Warsaw), October 1940, 3–4, USHMMA RG 15.079M (ŻIH Ring I/685), reel 29 (translated from Yiddish).

Document 12–4: "Plan of Educational Work in the Food Supply Points at Karmelicka 29, Nowolipki 68, Krochmalna 36," Warsaw, no date (ca. 1940), USHMMA RG 15.079M (ŻIH Ring I/204), reel 10 (translated from Yiddish).

The Space of Correspondence

Document 12–5: Letter from Szlomo Czigelnik, Bratislava, Slovakia, to Nathan Schwalb, Geneva, Switzerland, December 23, 1940, USHMMA RG 68.045M (WJC Geneva), reel 25, file 169 (translated from German).

Document 12–6: Letters by Lutek Orenbach, Tomaszów Mazowiecki, Generalgouvernement, to Edith Blau, Minden, Germany, September 15 and October 18 and 19, 1940, USHMMA RG 10.250 Edith Brandon collection, folder 7 (translated from Polish).

Document 12–7: Letter by Ruth Goldbarth, Warsaw, to Edith Blau, Minden, Germany, September 22, 1940, USHMMA RG 10.250 Edith Brandon collection, folder 2 (translated from German).

Document 12–8: Letter and caricatures by Lutek Orenbach, Tomaszów Mazowiecki, Generalgouvernement, November 26, 1940, USHMMA RG 10.250 Edith Brandon collection, folders 7, 12 (translated from Polish).

Document 12–9: Letter by Lutek Orenbach, Tomaszów Mazowiecki, Generalgouvernement, to Edith Blau, Minden, Germany, December 9 and 10, 1940, USHMMA RG 10.250 Edith Brandon collection, folder 7 (translated from Polish).

Document 12–10: Letters by Ruth Goldbarth, Warsaw, to Edith Blau and Hermann Bradtmüller, Minden, Germany, December 17, 1940, USHMMA RG 10.250 Edith Brandon collection, folder 2 (translated from German).

Document 12–11: Letter by Ruth Goldbarth, Warsaw, to Edith Blau, Minden, Germany, December 25–26, 1940, USHMMA RG 10.250 Edith Brandon collection, folder 2 (translated from German).

Into the Second Year of the War

Document 12–12: Report No. 4 by Ignacy Schwarzbart, member of the Polish National Council, London, United Kingdom, November 20, 1940, facsimile reprinted in *Archives of the Holocaust*, ed. Henry Friedlander and Sybil Milton (New York: Garland Publishing, 1990), 8:141–44.

Document 12–13: Raymond-Raoul Lambert, Unoccupied Zone, France, diary entry for December 20, 1940, translated from French and published in *Diary of a Witness, 1940–1943*, ed. Richard I. Cohen (Chicago: Ivan R. Dee in association with the USHMM, 2007), 25–26.

Document 12–14: WJC Geneva, appeal to Jews, fall 1940, USHMMA RG 68.045M (WJC Geneva), reel 1.

Document 12–15: Letter by Richard Lichtheim, Geneva, Switzerland, to Dr. Leo Lauterbach, Jerusalem, Palestine, December 11, 1940, facsimile reprinted in *Archives of the Holocaust*, ed. Henry Friedlander and Sybil Milton (New York: Garland Publishing, 1990), 4:24–25.

Document 12–16: Franz Werfel, "Our Path Continues," *Aufbau* (New York), December 27, 1940, 1–2 (translated from German).

BIBLIOGRAPHY

THIS SELECTION from a vast and continuously growing number of publications complements the footnote references in the chapters and serves as an orientation for further study. It is not a compilation of all relevant literature. For more comprehensive listings of recent publications, check the bibliographic sections of *H&GS*, *LBIYB*, *YVS*, and other journals.

MEMORIAL BOOKS, REFERENCE WORKS, AND LISTINGS OF HOLOCAUST VICTIMS AND SURVIVORS

Brocke, Michael, and Julius Carlebach, eds. *Biographisches Handbuch der Rabbiner.* Vol. 2, *Die Rabbiner im Deutschen Reich 1871–1945.* Munich: K. G. Saur, 2009.

Czech, Danuta. *Auschwitz Chronicle, 1939–1945.* New York: Henry Holt, 1990.

Dean, Martin, ed. *The United States Holocaust Memorial Museum Encyclopedia of Camps and Ghettos, 1933–1945.* Vol. 2, *Ghettos in German-Occupied Eastern Europe.* Bloomington: Indiana University Press in association with the USHMM, 2011.

Digital Monument to the Jewish Community in the Netherlands. Available online at www.joodsmonument.nl.

Gedenkbuch, Bundesarchiv memorial book of Jewish victims from Germany, 1933–1945. Available online at www.bundesarchiv.de/gedenkbuch.

Gutman, Israel, ed. *Encyclopedia of the Holocaust.* 4 vols. New York: Macmillan, 1990.

Hundert, Gershon David, ed. *The YIVO Encyclopedia of Jews in Eastern Europe.* 2 vols. New Haven, CT: Yale University Press, 2008.

Laqueur, Walter, ed. *The Holocaust Encyclopedia.* New Haven, CT: Yale University Press, 2001.

Megargee, Geoffrey P., ed. *The United States Holocaust Memorial Museum Encyclopedia of Camps and Ghettos, 1933–1945*. Vol. 1, *Early Camps, Youth Camps, and Concentration Camps and Subcamps under the SS-Business Administration Main Office (WVHA)*. Bloomington: Indiana University Press in association with the USHMM, 2009.

Miron, Guy, and Shlomit Shulhani, eds. *The Yad Vashem Encyclopedia of the Ghettos during the Holocaust*. 2 vols. Jerusalem: Yad Vashem, 2009.

Pinkas ha-kehilot. Polin: entsiklopedyah shel ha-yishuvim ha-yehudiyim le-min hivasdam ve-ad le-ahar Shoat Milhemet ha-olam ha-sheniyah. 8 vols. Jerusalem: Yad Vashem, 1999.

Shapiro, Robert Moses, and Tadeusz Epsztein, eds. *The Warsaw Ghetto Oyneg Shabes–Ringelblum Archive: Catalog and Guide*. Bloomington: Indiana University Press in association with the USHMM and the Jewish Historical Institute, Warsaw, 2009.

Skolnik, Fred, and Michael Berenbaum, eds. *Encyclopaedia Judaica*. 2nd ed. Detroit, MI: Thomson Gale, 2007.

USHMM ITS Collection Data Base Central Name Index.

Yad Vashem Central Database of Shoah Victims' Names. Online at www.yadvashem.org.

PUBLISHED PRIMARY SOURCES AND MEMOIRS

Ancel, Jean, ed. *Documents Concerning the Fate of Romanian Jewry during the Holocaust*. 12 vols. New York: Beate Klarsfeld Foundation, 1986.

Arad, Yitzhak, Israel Gutman, and Abraham Margaliot, eds. *Documents on the Holocaust: Selected Sources on the Destruction of the Jews of Germany and Austria, Poland, and the Soviet Union*. Lincoln and Jerusalem: University of Nebraska Press and Yad Vashem, 1999.

Berg, Mary. *The Diary of Mary Berg: Growing up in the Warsaw Ghetto: A Diary*. Edited by S. L. Shneiderman [Sh. L. Shnayderman] and Susan Lee Pentlin. Oxford: Oneworld, 2006 (originally published in 1945 as *Warsaw Ghetto: A Diary by Mary Berg*).

Boas, Jacob, ed. *We Are Witnesses: Five Diaries of Teenagers Who Died in the Holocaust*. New York: Henry Holt, 1995.

Brandon, Edith. *Letters from Tomaszov*. London: self-published, 1994.

Cohn, Willy. *Kein Recht, Nirgends: Tagebuch vom Untergang des Breslauer Judentums, 1933–1941*. Edited by Norbert Conrads. 2 vols. Cologne: Böhlau, 2007.

Cytryn, Abraham. *A Youth Writing between the Walls: Notebooks from the Lodz Ghetto*. Jerusalem: Yad Vashem, 2005.

Czösz, Lászlo, and Gábor Kádár. *The Holocaust in Hungary*. Lanham, MD: AltaMira Press in association with the USHMM, forthcoming in 2012.

Dobroszycki, Lucjan, ed. *The Chronicle of the Łódź Ghetto: 1941–1944*. New Haven, CT: Yale University Press, 1984.

Feuchert, Sascha, Erwin Leibfried, and Jörg Riecke, eds. *Die Chronik des Gettos Lodz/Litzmannstadt* 5 vols. Göttingen: Wallstein, 2007.

Flinker, Moshe. *Young Moshe's Diary: The Spiritual Torment of a Jewish Boy in Nazi Europe*. Jerusalem: Yad Vashem, 1971.

Frank, Anne. *The Diary of Anne Frank*, rev. crit. ed. Edited by David Barnouw and Gerrold van der Stroom, New York: Doubleday, 2003.

Freier, Recha. *Let the Children Come: The Early History of Youth Aliyah*. London: Weidenfeld and Nicolson, 1961.

Friedlander, Henry, and Sybil Milton, eds. *Archives of the Holocaust: An International Collection of Selected Documents*. 21 vols. New York: Garland Publishing, 1990–1995.

Fry, Varian. *Assignment Rescue: An Autobiography*. New York: Scholastic, 1992 (originally published in 1945 as *Surrender on Demand*).

Gillis-Carlebach, Miriam. *Jewish Everyday Life as Human Resistance, 1939–1941: Chief Rabbi Dr. Joseph Zvi Carlebach and the Hamburg-Altona Jewish Communities*. New York: Peter Lang, 2009.

Gruner, Wolf, ed. *Die Verfolgung und Ermordung der europäischen Juden durch das nationalsozialistische Deutschland 1933–1945*. Vol. 2, *Deutsches Reich, 1938–August 1939*. Munich: Oldenbourg, 2008.

Grynberg, Michał, ed. *Words to Outlive Us: Voices from the Warsaw Ghetto*. New York: Metropolitan Books, 2002.

Handler, Andrew, ed. *The Holocaust in Hungary: An Anthology of Jewish Response*. University: University of Alabama Press, 1982.

Heberer, Patricia. *Children during the Holocaust*. Lanham, MD: AltaMira Press in association with the USHMM, 2011.

Hilberg, Raul, Stanislaw Staron, and Josef Kermisz, eds. *The Warsaw Diary of Adam Czerniakow: Prelude to Doom*. Chicago: Ivan R. Dee in association with the USHMM, 1999 (originally published in 1979).

Huberband, Shimon. *Kiddush Hashem: Jewish Religious and Cultural Life in Poland during the Holocaust*. Edited by Jeffrey S. Gurock and Robert S. Hirt. Hoboken, NJ: KTAV Publishing House, 1987.

Kaplan, Chaim A. *Scroll of Agony: The Warsaw Diary of Chaim A. Kaplan*. Edited by Abraham I. Katsh. Bloomington: Indiana University Press in association with the USHMM, 1999 (originally published in 1965).

Kermish, Joseph, ed. *To Live with Honor and Die with Honor! Selected Documents from the Warsaw Ghetto Underground Archives "O.S." ("Oneg Shabbath")*. Jerusalem: Yad Vashem, 1986.

Kirschner, Robert, ed. *Rabbinic Responsa of the Holocaust Era*. New York: Schocken, 1985.

Klemperer, Victor. *I Will Bear Witness: A Diary of the Nazi Years, 1933–1941*. New York: Random House, 1998.

Klüger, Ruth. *Still Alive: A Holocaust Girlhood Remembered*. New York: Feminist Press at the City University of New York, 2001.

Kohn, Jerome, and Ron H. Feldman, eds. *The Jewish Writings: Hannah Arendt*. New York: Schocken Books, 2007.

Kohner, Nancy. *My Father's Roses: A Family's Journey from World War I to Treblinka*. New York: Pegasus Books, 2009.

Kolmar, Gertrud. *My Gaze Is Turned Inward: Letters, 1934–1943*. Edited by Johanna Woltmann. Evanston, IL: Northwestern University Press, 2004.

Korczak, Janusz. *Ghetto Diary*. New Haven, CT: Yale University Press, 2003 (originally published in 1978).

Kruk, Herman. *The Last Days of the Jerusalem of Lithuania: Chronicles from the Vilna Ghetto and the Camps, 1939–1944*. Edited by Benjamin Harshav. New Haven, CT: Yale University Press, 2002.

Les enfants de la guette: Souvenirs et documents (1938–1945). Paris: Centre de documentation juive contemporaine, 1999.

Lieblich, Ruthka. *Ruthka: A Diary of War*. Brooklyn, NY: Remember, 1993.

Maier, Ruth. *Ruth Maier's Diary: A Young Girl's Life under Nazism*. Edited by Jan Erik Vold. London: Harvill Secker, 2009.

Mallmann, Klaus-Michael, Jochen Böhler, and Jürgen Matthäus, eds. *Einsatzgruppen in Polen: Darstellung und Dokumentation*. Darmstadt: Wissenschaftliche Buchgesellschaft, 2008.

Marum-Lunau, Elisabeth. *Auf der Flucht in Frankreich. "Boches ici, juifs là-bas": Der Briefwechsel einer deutschen Familie im Exil, 1939–1942*. Edited by Jacques Grandjonc and Doris Obschernitzki. Teetz, Germany: Hentrich & Hentrich, 2000.

McDonald, James G. *Refugees and Rescue: The Diaries and Papers of James G. McDonald, 1935–1945*. Edited by Richard Breitman, Barbara McDonald Stewart, and Severin Hochberg. Bloomington: Indiana University Press in association with the USHMM, 2009.

Moß, Christoph, ed. *A Thousand Kisses: The Letters of Georg and Frieda Lindemeyer to their Children, 1937–1941*. London: Bloomsbury Publishing, 2006.

Perechodnik, Calel. *Am I a Murderer? Testament of a Jewish Ghetto Policeman*. Edited by Frank Fox. Boulder, CO: Westview Press, 1996.

Riegner, Gerhart M. *Never Despair: Sixty Years in the Service of the Jewish People and the Cause of Human Rights*. Chicago: Ivan R. Dee, 2006.

Rosenfeld, Oskar. *In the Beginning Was the Ghetto: Notebooks from Łódź*. Evanston, IL: Northwestern University Press, 2002.

Rubinowicz, Dawid. *The Diary of Dawid Rubinowicz*. Edmonds, WA: Creative Options, 1982.

Sebastian, Mihail. *Journal, 1935–1944*. Chicago: Ivan R. Dee in association with the USHMM, 2000.

Seidler, Harry. *Internment: The Diaries of Harry Seidler, May 1940–October 1941*. Edited by Janis Wilton. Sydney: Allen and Unwin, 1986.

Shapira, Kalonymus Kalmish. *Sacred Fire: Torah from the Years of Fury, 1939–1942*. Edited by Deborah Miller. Northvale, NJ: J. Aronson, 2000.

Sierakowiak, Dawid. *The Diary of Dawid Sierakowiak: Five Notebooks from the Łódź Ghetto*. Edited by Alan Adelson. New York: Oxford University Press, 1996.

Stern, Kurt. *Was wird mit uns geschehen? Tagebücher der Internierung 1939 und 1940*. Berlin: Aufbau Verlag, 2006.

Weichherz, Béla. *In Her Father's Eyes: A Childhood Extinguished by the Holocaust*. Edited by Daniel H. Magilow. New Brunswick, NJ: Rutgers University Press, 2008.

Zelkowicz, Josef. *In Those Terrible Days: Writings from the Lodz Ghetto*. Edited by Michal Unger. Jerusalem: Yad Vashem, 2002.

MONOGRAPH STUDIES, EDITED VOLUMES, AND ARTICLES

Abitbol, Michel. *The Jews of North Africa during the Second World War*. Detroit, MI: Wayne State University Press, 1989.

Aly, Götz. *"Final Solution": Nazi Population Policy and the Murder of the European Jews*. London: Arnold, 1999.

————. *Hitler's Beneficiaries: Plunder, Racial War, and the Nazi Welfare State.* New York: Metropolitan, 2007.

Ambrosewicz-Jacobs, Jolanta, ed. *The Holocaust: Voices of Scholars.* Kraków: Austeria, 2009.

Amkraut, Brian. *Between Home and Homeland: Youth Aliyah from Nazi Germany.* Tuscaloosa: University of Alabama Press, 2006.

Arad, Yitzhak. *Ghetto in Flames: The Struggle and Destruction of the Jews in Vilna in the Holocaust.* New York: Holocaust Library, 1982.

Bajohr, Frank. *"Aryanisation" in Hamburg: The Economic Exclusion of Jews and the Confiscation of Their Property in Nazi Germany.* New York: Berghahn Books, 2002.

Bankier, David, and Israel Gutman, eds. *Nazi Europe and the Final Solution.* Jerusalem: Yad Vashem, 2003.

Bankier, David, and Dan Michman, eds. *Holocaust Historiography in Context: Emergence, Challenges, Polemics and Achievements.* Jerusalem and New York: Yad Vashem and Berghahn Books, 2008.

Barkai, Avraham. *From Boycott to Annihilation: The Economic Struggle of German Jews, 1933–1943.* Hanover, NH: University Press of New England, 1989.

Bartov, Omer. *The Holocaust: Origins, Implementation, Aftermath.* London: Routledge, 2000.

Bauer, Yehuda. *American Jewry and the Holocaust: The American Jewish Joint Distribution Committee, 1939–1945.* Detroit, MI: Wayne State University Press, 1981.

————. *The Death of the Shtetl.* New Haven, CT: Yale University Press, 2009.

————. *Jews for Sale? Nazi-Jewish Negotiations, 1933–1945.* New Haven, CT: Yale University Press, 1994.

————. *My Brother's Keeper: A History of the American Jewish Joint Distribution Committee, 1929–1939.* Philadelphia: Jewish Publication Society of America, 1974.

Bergen, Doris L. *War and Genocide: A Concise History of the Holocaust.* Lanham, MD: Rowman & Littlefield, 2009 (originally published in 2003).

Berghahn, Marion. *Continental Britons: German-Jewish Refugees from Nazi Germany.* Oxford: Berghahn Books, 2007.

Blatman, Daniel. *For Our Freedom and Yours: The Jewish Labour Bund in Poland, 1939–1949.* London: Vallentine Mitchell, 2003.

Bloxham, Donald. *The Final Solution: A Genocide.* Oxford: Oxford University Press, 2009.

————. *Genocide, the World Wars and the Unweaving of Europe.* London: Vallentine Mitchell, 2008.

Bondy, Ruth. *Trapped: Essays on the History of the Czech Jews, 1939–1945.* Jerusalem: Yad Vashem, 2008.

Bowman, Steven B. *The Agony of Greek Jews, 1940–1945.* Stanford, CA: Stanford University Press, 2009.

Braham, Randolph L. *The Politics of Genocide: The Holocaust in Hungary.* Condensed ed. Detroit, MI: Wayne State University Press, 2000 (originally published in 1981).

Breitman, Richard, and Alan M. Kraut. *American Refugee Policy and European Jewry, 1933–1945.* Bloomington: Indiana University Press, 1987.

Browning, Christopher R. *The Path to Genocide: Essays on Launching the Final Solution.* New York: Cambridge University Press, 1992.

Browning, Christopher R., with contributions by Jürgen Matthäus. *The Origins of the Final Solution: The Evolution of Nazi Jewish Policy, September 1939–March 1942.* Lincoln and Jerusalem: University of Nebraska Press and Yad Vashem, 2004.

Burleigh, Michael. *Death and Deliverance: "Euthanasia" in Germany, 1900–1945.* Cambridge: Cambridge University Press, 1994.

———. *The Third Reich: A New History.* New York: Hill and Wang, 2000.

Burleigh, Michael, and Wolfgang Wippermann. *The Racial State: Germany, 1933–1945.* New York: Cambridge University Press, 1991.

Burrin, Philippe. *Hitler and the Jews: The Genesis of the Holocaust.* London: Edward Arnold, 1994.

Caestecker, Frank, and Bob Moore, eds. *Refugees from Nazi Germany and the Liberal European States.* New York: Berghahn Books, 2010.

Caplan, Jane, and Nikolaus Wachsmann, eds. *Concentration Camps in Nazi Germany: The New Histories.* New York: Routledge, 2010.

Caron, Vicki. *Uneasy Asylum: France and the Jewish Refugee Crisis, 1933–1942.* Stanford, CA: Stanford University Press, 1999.

Carpi, Daniel. *Between Mussolini and Hitler: The Jews and the Italian Authorities in France and Tunisia.* Hanover, NH: Brandeis University Press in association with the University Press of New England, 1994.

Case, Holly. *Between States: The Transylvanian Question and the European Idea during World War II.* Stanford, CA: Stanford University Press, 2009.

Cesarani, David. *The Jewish Chronicle and Anglo-Jewry, 1841–1991.* New York: Cambridge University Press, 1994.

———, ed. *Holocaust. Critical Concepts in Historical Studies.* 6 vols. London: Routledge, 2004.

Cochavi, Yehoyakim. "'The Hostile Alliance': The Relationship between the Reichsvereinigung of Jews in Germany and the Regime." *YVS* 22 (1992): 237–72.

Cohen, Asher, and Yehoyakim Cochavi, eds. *Zionist Youth Movements during the Shoah.* New York: Peter Lang, 1995.

Davies, Norman, and Antony Polonsky. *Jews in Eastern Poland and the USSR, 1939–46.* New York: St. Martin's Press, 1991.

Dean, Martin. *Robbing the Jews: The Confiscation of Jewish Property in the Holocaust, 1933–1945.* New York: Cambridge University Press in association with the USHMM, 2008.

Dean, Martin, Constantin Goschler, and Philipp Ther, eds. *Robbery and Restitution: The Conflict over Jewish Property in Europe.* New York: Berghahn Books, 2007.

Dekel-Chen, Jonathan, David Gaunt, Natan M. Meir, and Israel Bartal, eds. *Anti-Jewish Violence: Rethinking the Pogrom in East European History.* Bloomington: Indiana University Press, 2010.

Diamond, Hanna. *Fleeing Hitler: France 1940.* New York: Oxford University Press, 2007.

Dwork, Debórah, and Robert Jan van Pelt. *Flight from the Reich: Refugee Jews, 1933–1946.* New York: W. W. Norton, 2009.

———. *Holocaust: A History.* New York, 2002.

Eber, Irene. *Chinese and Jews: Encounters Between Cultures.* London: Vallentine Mitchell, 2008.

Engel, David. *The Holocaust: The Third Reich and the Jews.* New York: Longman, 2000.

———. *In the Shadow of Auschwitz: The Polish Government-in-Exile and the Jews, 1939–1942.* Chapel Hill: University of North Carolina Press, 1987.

Engelking, Barbara, and Jacek Leociak. *The Warsaw Ghetto: A Guide to the Perished City.* New Haven, CT: Yale University Press, 2009.

Farbstein, Esther. *Hidden in Thunder: Perspectives on Faith, Halachah and Leadership during the Holocaust.* 2 vols. Jerusalem: Mossad Harav Kook, 2007.

Fink, Carole. *Defending the Rights of Others: The Great Powers, the Jews, and International Minority Protection, 1878–1938.* New York: Cambridge University Press, 2004.

Fleming, Katherine E. *Greece: A Jewish History.* Princeton, NJ: Princeton University Press, 2008.

Friedlander, Henry. *The Origins of Nazi Genocide: From Euthanasia to the Final Solution.* Chapel Hill: University of North Carolina Press, 1995.

Friedländer, Saul. *Nazi Germany and the Jews:* (vol. 1) *The Years of Persecution, 1933–1939.* New York: HarperCollins, 1997.

———. *Nazi Germany and the Jews:* (vol. 2) *The Years of Extermination, 1939–1945.* New York: HarperCollins, 2007.

Friedman, Philip. *Roads to Extinction: Essays on the Holocaust.* Edited by Ada June Friedman. New York: Conference on Jewish Social Studies and the Jewish Publication Society of America, 1980.

Friling, Tuvia. *Arrows in the Dark: David Ben-Gurion, the Yishuv Leadership, and Rescue Attempts during the Holocaust.* 2 vols. Madison: University of Wisconsin Press, 2005.

Garbarini, Alexandra. *Numbered Days: Diaries and the Holocaust.* New Haven, CT: Yale University Press, 2006.

Gerlach, Wolfgang, and Victoria J. Barnett, eds. *And the Witnesses Were Silent: The Confessing Church and the Persecution of the Jews.* Lincoln: University of Nebraska Press, 2000.

Goeschel, Christian. *Suicide in Nazi Germany.* New York: Oxford University Press, 2009.

Gottlieb, Amy Zahl. *Men of Vision: Anglo-Jewry's Aid to Victims of the Nazi Regime, 1933–1945.* London: Weidenfeld and Nicholson, 1998.

Gross, Jan T. *Polish Society under German Occupation: The Generalgouvernement, 1939–1944.* Princeton, NJ: Princeton University Press, 1979.

———. *Revolution from Abroad: The Soviet Conquest of Poland's Western Ukraine and Western Belorussia.* Exp. ed. Princeton, NJ: Princeton University Press, 2002.

Gruner, Wolf. *Jewish Forced Labor under the Nazis: Economic Needs and Racial Aims, 1938–1944.* New York: Cambridge University Press in association with the USHMM, 2006.

Gutman, Yisrael. *The Jews of Warsaw, 1939–1943: Ghetto, Underground, Revolt.* Bloomington: Indiana University Press, 1982.

Gutman, Yisrael, and Cynthia J. Haft, eds. *Patterns of Jewish Leadership in Nazi Europe, 1933–1945: Proceedings of the Third Yad Vashem International Historical Conference, Jerusalem, April 4–7, 1977.* Jerusalem: Yad Vashem, 1979.

Heim, Susanne, Beate Meyer, and Francis R. Nicosia, eds. *"Wer bleibt, opfert seine Jahre, vielleicht sein Leben": Deutsche Juden, 1938–1941.* Göttingen: Wallstein, 2010.

Hilberg, Raul. *The Destruction of the European Jews.* 3 vols. 3rd ed. New Haven, CT: Yale University Press, 2003.

Horwitz, Gordon J. *Ghettostadt: Łódź and the Making of a Nazi City.* Cambridge, MA: Belknap Press, 2008.

Institute of Jewish Affairs of the World Jewish Congress. *Unity in Dispersion: A History of the World Jewish Congress.* 2nd rev. ed. New York: Institute of Jewish Affairs of the World Jewish Congress, 1948.

Ioanid, Radu. *The Holocaust in Romania: The Destruction of Jews and Gypsies under the Antonescu Regime, 1940–1944.* Chicago: Ivan R. Dee, 2000.

Jackson, Julian. *France: The Dark Years, 1940–1944.* Oxford: Oxford University Press, 2001.

Kamenec, Ivan. *On the Trail of Tragedy: The Holocaust in Slovakia.* Bratislava: Hajko & Hajková, 2007.

Kaplan, Marion A. *Between Dignity and Despair: Jewish Life in Nazi Germany.* New York: Oxford University Press, 1998.

———. *Dominican Haven: The Jewish Refugee Settlement in Sosúa, 1940–1945.* New York: Museum of Jewish Heritage, 2008.

Kaplan, Thomas Pegelow. *The Language of Nazi Genocide: Linguistic Violence and the Struggle of Germans of Jewish Ancestry.* New York: Cambridge University Press, 2009.

Kassow, Samuel D. *Who Will Write Our History? Emanuel Ringelblum, the Warsaw Ghetto, and the Oyneg Shabes Archive.* Bloomington: Indiana University Press, 2007.

Katz, Steven T., Shlomo Biderman, and Gershon Greenberg, eds. *Wrestling with God: Jewish Theological Responses during and after the Holocaust.* New York: Oxford University Press, 2007.

Kranzler, David. *Japanese, Nazis & Jews: The Jewish Refugee Community of Shanghai, 1938–1945.* Hoboken, NJ: KTAV Publishing House, 1988.

Laqueur, Walter. *The Changing Face of Antisemitism: From Ancient Times to the Present Day.* New York: Oxford University Press, 2006.

Leighton-Langer, Peter. *The King's Own Loyal Enemy Aliens: German and Austrian Refugees in Britain's Armed Forces, 1939–45.* London: Vallentine Mitchell, 2006.

Levene, Mark. *Genocide in the Age of the Nation State.* 2 vols. London: I. B. Tauris, 2005.

Levy, James P. *Appeasement and Rearmament: Britain, 1936–1939.* Lanham, MD: Rowman & Littlefield, 2006.

London, Louise. *Whitehall and the Jews, 1933–1948: British Immigration Policy, Jewish Refugees and the Holocaust.* Cambridge: Cambridge University Press, 2000.

Lukas, Richard C. *The Forgotten Holocaust: The Poles under German Occupation, 1939–1944.* 2nd rev. ed. New York: Hippocrene, 1997.

Lumans, Valdis O. *Himmler's Auxiliaries: The Volksdeutsche Mittelstelle and the German National Minorities of Europe, 1933–1945.* Chapel Hill: University of North Carolina Press, 1993.

Maierhof, Gudrun. *Selbstbehauptung im Chaos: Frauen in der jüdischen Selbsthilfe, 1933–1943.* Frankfurt am Main: Campus, 2002.

Marcus, Joseph. *Social and Political History of the Jews in Poland, 1919–1939.* Berlin: Mouton, 1983.

Marrus, Michael R. *The Holocaust in History.* New York: New American Library, 1989 (originally published in 1987).

———. *The Unwanted: European Refugees from the First World War Through the Cold War.* Philadelphia: Temple University Press, 2002 (originally published in 1985).

Matthäus, Jürgen, and Mark Roseman. *Jewish Responses to Persecution.* Vol. 1, *1933–1938.* Lanham, MD: AltaMira Press in association with the USHMM, 2010.

Mazower, Mark. *Hitler's Empire: Nazi Rule in Occupied Europe.* London: Allen Lane, 2008.

Mazzenga, Maria, ed. *American Religious Responses to Kristallnacht.* New York: Palgrave Macmillan, 2009.

Mendelsohn, Ezra. *The Jews of East Central Europe between the World Wars.* Bloomington: Indiana University Press, 1987.

Meyer, Beate. *"Jüdische Mischlinge": Rassenpolitik und Verfolgungserfahrung, 1933–1945.* Hamburg: Dölling und Galitz, 1999.

Meyer, Beate, Hermann Simon, and Chana Schütz, eds. *Jews in Nazi Berlin: From Kristallnacht to Liberation*. Chicago: University of Chicago Press, 2009.

Michaelis, Meir. *Mussolini and the Jews: German-Italian Relations and the Jewish Question in Italy, 1922–1945*. Oxford: Clarendon Press, 1978.

Michlic, Joanna B. *Poland's Threatening Other: The Image of the Jew from 1880 to the Present*. Lincoln: University of Nebraska Press, 2006.

Michman, Dan. *The Emergence of Jewish Ghettos during the Holocaust*. Cambridge: Cambridge University Press, 2010.

———. *Holocaust Historiography, A Jewish Perspective: Conceptualizations, Terminology, Approaches, and Fundamental Issues*. London: Vallentine Mitchell, 2003.

Młynarczyk, Jacek Andrzej, and Jochen Böhler, eds. *Der Judenmord in den eingegliederten polnischen Gebieten 1939–1945*. Osnabrück: Fibre, 2010.

Moore, Bob. *Survivors: Jewish Self-Help and Rescue in Nazi-Occupied Western Europe*. New York: Oxford University Press, 2010.

———. *Victims and Survivors: The Nazi Persecution of the Jews in the Netherlands, 1940–1945*. London: Arnold, 1997.

Nicosia, Francis R. *Zionism and Anti-Semitism in Nazi Germany*. New York: Cambridge University Press, 2008.

Nicosia, Francis R., and David Scrase, eds. *Jewish Life in Nazi Germany: Dilemmas and Responses*. New York: Berghahn Books, 2010.

Ofer, Dalia. *Escaping the Holocaust: Illegal Immigration to the Land of Israel, 1939–1944*. New York: Oxford University Press, 1990.

Ofer, Dalia, and Lenore J. Weitzman, eds. *Women in the Holocaust*. New Haven, CT: Yale University Press, 1998.

Ogilvie, Sara A., and Scott Miller. *Refuge Denied: The St. Louis Passengers and the Holocaust*. Madison: University of Wisconsin Press, 2006.

Oppenheim, Israel. *The Struggle of Jewish Youth for Productivization: The Zionist Youth Movement in Poland*. Boulder, CO: East European Monographs, 1989.

Paucker, Arnold, ed., with Sylvia Gilchrist and Barbara Suchy. *Die Juden im nationalsozialistischen Deutschland / The Jews in Nazi Germany, 1933–1943*. Tübingen: J. C. B. Mohr, 1986.

Paulsson, Gunnar S. *Secret City: The Hidden Jews of Warsaw, 1940–1945*. New Haven, CT: Yale University Press, 2002.

Poliakov, Leon, and Jacques Sabille. *Jews under the Italian Occupation*. New York: Howard Fertig, 1983 (originally published in 1955).

Porat, Dina. *The Blue and the Yellow Stars of David: The Zionist Leadership in Palestine and the Holocaust, 1939–1945*. Cambridge, MA: Harvard University Press, 1990.

Poznanski, Renée. *Jews in France during World War II*. Hanover, NH: University Press of New England in association with the USHMM, 2001.

Quack, Sibylle, ed. *Between Sorrow and Strength: Women Refugees of the Nazi Period*. New York: Cambridge University Press, 1995.

Raider, Mark A., ed. *Nahum Goldmann: Statesman Without a State*. Albany: State University of New York Press, 2009.

Rayski, Adam. *The Choice of the Jews under Vichy: Between Submission and Resistance*. Notre Dame, IN: University of Notre Dame Press in association with the USHMM, 2005.

Röhm, Eberhard, and Jörg Thierfelder. *Juden, Christen, Deutsche, 1933–1945*. 4 vols. Stuttgart: Calwer, 1992–1995.

Rose, Norman. *Chaim Weizmann: A Biography.* New York: Penguin, 1986.

Roskies, David G. *Against the Apocalypse: Responses to Catastrophe in Modern Jewish Culture.* Cambridge, MA: Harvard University Press, 1984.

Rossino, Alexander B. *Hitler Strikes Poland: Blitzkrieg, Ideology, and Atrocity.* Lawrence: University Press of Kansas, 2003.

Roth, John K., and Elisabeth Maxwell, eds. *Remembering for the Future: The Holocaust in an Age of Genocide.* 3 vols. New York: Palgrave Macmillan, 2001.

Rothkirchen, Livia. *The Jews of Bohemia and Moravia: Facing the Holocaust.* Lincoln and Jerusalem: University of Nebraska Press and Yad Vashem, 2005.

Rutherford, Phillip T. *Prelude to the Final Solution: The Nazi Program for Deporting Ethnic Poles, 1939–1941.* Lawrence: University Press of Kansas, 2007.

Saint-Geours, Jean. *Témoignage sur la spoliation des Français juifs (1940–1944): Histoire et mémoire (1940–2000).* Paris: Éditions Le Manuscrit, 2008.

Sarfatti, Michele. *The Jews in Mussolini's Italy: From Equality to Persecution.* Madison: University of Wisconsin Press, 2006.

Segev, Tom. *One Palestine, Complete: Jews and Arabs under the British Mandate.* New York: Metropolitan Books, 2000.

Snyder, Timothy. *Bloodlands: Europe between Hitler and Stalin.* New York: Basic Books, 2010.

Solonari, Vladimir. *Purifying the Nation: Population Exchange and Ethnic Cleansing in Nazi-Allied Romania.* Baltimore: Johns Hopkins University Press, 2009.

Steinbacher, Sybille. *Auschwitz: A History.* New York: Ecco, 2005.

Steinweis, Alan E. *Kristallnacht 1938.* Cambridge, MA: Belknap Press, 2009.

Stone, Dan, ed. *The Historiography of the Holocaust.* New York: Palgrave Macmillan, 2004.

Tec, Nechama. *Resilience and Courage: Women, Men, and the Holocaust.* New Haven, CT: Yale University Press, 2003.

Tendyra, Bernadeta. *The Polish Government in Exile, 1939–45.* London: Routledge, 2011.

Trunk, Isaiah. *Judenrat: The Jewish Councils in Eastern Europe under Nazi Occupation.* Lincoln: University of Nebraska Press, 1996 (originally published in 1972).

———. *Łódź Ghetto: A History.* Edited by Robert Moses Shapiro. Bloomington: Indiana University Press, 2006.

Unger, Michal, ed. *The Last Ghetto: Life in the Lodz Ghetto, 1940–1944.* Jerusalem: Yad Vashem, 1995.

Weinberg, Gerhard L. *A World at Arms: A Global History of World War II.* Cambridge: Cambridge University Press, 1994.

Weiss, Aharon. "Jewish Leadership in Occupied Poland—Postures and Attitudes." *YVS* 12 (1977): 335–65.

Westermann, Edward B. *Hitler's Police Battalions: Enforcing Racial War in the East.* Lawrence: University Press of Kansas, 2005.

Wildt, Michael. *An Uncompromising Generation: The Nazi Leadership of the Reich Security Main Office.* Madison: University of Wisconsin Press, 2009.

Zapruder, Alexandra, ed. *Salvaged Pages: Young Writers' Diaries of the Holocaust.* New Haven, CT: Yale University Press, 2002.

Zimmerman, Joshua D., ed. *Jews in Italy under Fascist and Nazi Rule, 1922–1945.* New York: Cambridge University Press, 2005.

Zuccotti, Susan. *The Italians and the Holocaust: Persecution, Rescue, and Survival.* Lincoln: University of Nebraska Press, 1996 (originally published in 1987).

GLOSSARY

Aleynhilf (Yiddish: literally, self-help) This refers to the Jewish relief movement that emerged in the wake of the Nazi invasion of Poland in September 1939. Initially growing out of the Warsaw-based Coordinating Commission of Jewish Aid and Civic Societies in the first days of the war, the movement split into two major branches, both of which attempted to fill the vacuum in Jewish relief work created by the murderous escalation of Nazi anti-Jewish policies, as well as the flight of many prewar Jewish leaders. The Warsaw Aleynhilf, in which Emanuel Ringelblum played an important role, was a loose network of grassroots Jewish relief efforts, operating primarily in the Warsaw ghetto, often against the guidelines and policies set by the *Judenrat*. The Kraków-based office of Jewish Social Self-Help, led by Michał (Michael) Weichert, sought to provide aid to Jewish communities in the Generalgouvernement "legally," that is, by submitting to Nazi control.

See Samuel D. Kassow, *Who Will Write Our History? Emanuel Ringelblum, the Warsaw Ghetto, and the Oyneg Shabes Archive* (Bloomington: Indiana University Press, 2007).

aliyah (Hebrew: ascent) In the context of the Zionist movement, this term describes the mass settlement of Diaspora Jews in Palestine to establish a Jewish homeland. After 1933, *aliyah*, organized by the Palästina-Amt (the office of the Jewish Agency in Germany), became a prominent feature of Jewish emigration from Nazi Germany. In the period from 1933 to 1941, a total of more than fifty thousand Jews left the German Reich for Palestine; the Youth Aliyah organized by Recha Freier and others helped thousands of young Jews emigrate in the period up to Setpember 1939. With British restrictions on Jewish settlement in Palestine increasing from the mid-1930s, the illegal *aliyah* (*Aliyah Bet*)—that is, emigration to Palestine without permission of the British authorities—became steadily more significant and continued up to the founding of the state of Israel in 1948.

515

See Hagit Lavsky, "German Jewish Interwar Migration in a Comparative Perspective: Mandatory Palenstine, the United States, and Great Britain," in *Ethnicity and Beyond: Theories and Dilemmas of Jewish Group Demarcation*, ed. Eli Lederhendler (New York: Oxford University Press, 2011), 115–44.

Aliyah Bet see *aliyah*

American Jewish Joint Distribution Committee (AJJDC, also AJDC, JDC, and the Joint) Founded in 1914, the AJJDC provided assistance to Jews around the world, particularly in eastern Europe. From the Nazi seizure of power in 1933 until 1939, this umbrella for aid organizations in the United States was involved in emigration planning and relief work in Germany; during the war, the Joint extended its relief efforts into countries occupied or controlled by the Reich. In Poland following the German invasion, several employees in the AJJDC's Warsaw office, including Yitzhak Giterman and Emanuel Ringelblum, led the AJJDC's efforts to assemble a network of local organizations, such as Centrala Związku Towarzystw Opieki nad Sierotami i Dziećmi Opuszczonymi (CENTOS), Towarzystwo Ochrony Zdrowia Ludności Żydowskiej w Polsce (TOZ), Organization for Rehabilitation and Training (ORT), and others. After the end of the war, the organization also led important reconstruction efforts.

See Yehuda Bauer, *American Jewry and the Holocaust: The American Jewish Joint Distribution Committee, 1939–1945* (Detroit, MI: Wayne State University Press, 1981).

Anschluss (German: joining, connection) This word is euphemistic shorthand for the German annexation of Austria in March 1938. Although it constituted an act of aggression on the part of Germany against its independent neighbor that went hand in hand with mass arrests and anti-Jewish violence, the *Anschluss* met with widespread popular support, both in Austria and in Germany. Austria remained part of the German Reich until the end of World War II.

Antonescu, Ion (1882–1946) A right-wing Romanian politician and leader of Romania during most of World War II, Antonescu gained political power in 1940 by forming a partnership with the **Iron Guard**, an indigenous Romanian fascist movement, and establishing a one-party dictatorship under his rule. After Romania entered World War II on the side of the Axis powers, Antonescu purged his government of the Iron Guard and ran the country unchallenged. Following an unsuccessful attempt to negotiate with the Allies, he was deposed in 1944. Despite his unwillingness to bow to German demands regarding the implementation of the "Final Solution," Antonescu was responsible for the deportation and deaths of hundreds of thousands of Jews and Roma. After the war, he was put on trial in Bucharest and executed in 1946.

See Radu Ioanid, *The Holocaust in Romania: The Destruction of Jews and Gypsies under the Antonescu Regime, 1940–1944* (Chicago: Ivan R. Dee, 2000).

appeasement This pre–World War II policy, primarily adopted by Great Britain vis-à-vis Nazi Germany, aimed at avoiding military conflict in Europe by conceding to Hitler's demands, some of which were perceived in the West as legitimate expressions of German discontent with the post–World War I peace treaty. This applied to the remilitarization of the Rhineland in 1936 and the *Anschluss* of Austria in March 1938, as well as to German territorial claims against Czechoslovakia that led to the signing of the Munich agreement in September 1938. Appeasement was widely condemned after 1939 as a shameful and ultimately unsuccessful attempt to placate Hitler.

See David Faber, *Munich, 1938: Appeasement and World War II* (New York: Simon and Schuster, 2008).

"Aryan" (ant.: "non-Aryan"; German: *Arier, Nicht-Arier*) Originally a linguistic category in nineteenth-century ethnology, the term became firmly integrated into racial and eugenic discourse. Ideologues used this key, but not clearly defined, concept to support the thesis of the inequality of human races and the superiority of "Aryans" over other ethnic groups. The term often appeared to be synonymous with the equally amorphous word "Nordic" (*nordisch*), taking western European whites of a Christian background as its core. Nazi ideology used the construct of an "Aryan" ideal type to denigrate "non-Aryans," particularly Jews, in an attempt to prevent miscegenation and the birth of "mixed-breeds" ("*Mischlinge*") for the purpose of creating a racially homogenous "people's community" (*Volksgemeinschaft*). Racial segregation became legally codified in the Third Reich with the Civil Service Law, enacted in April 1933, and was developed further in the Nuremberg Laws and subsequent regulations. In countries allied to Germany—such as Italy, Slovakia, and Hungary—similar notions of racial homogeneity often played a direct or indirect role in the adoption of anti-Jewish laws and other measures.

See Michael Burleigh and Wolfgang Wippermann, *The Racial State: Germany, 1933–1945* (New York: Cambridge University Press, 1991); Claudia Koonz, *The Nazi Conscience* (Cambridge, MA: Harvard University Press, 2003).

Aufbau The newspaper *Aufbau* first appeared in New York in December 1934 under the auspices of the German-Jewish Club, Inc., formed in New York in 1924. During the next decades, the paper gave the German Jewish exile and emigrant community a mix of world news, cultural and political commentary, and announcements on New York–area social activities. The Berlin-born refugee journalist Manfred George took over the editorial reins in 1939, greatly improving the weekly's circulation figures (fifty thousand by 1944) and offering a platform for a range of prominent German- and English-language commentators, including Albert Einstein, Thomas Mann and his daughter Erika Mann, Stefan Zweig, and Hannah Arendt. During the war, *Aufbau* provided a vital source of information on developments in Europe, particularly on anti-Jewish measures as they unfolded. After the defeat of the Nazis, it would also help in reconnecting families and friends who had been separated by the war, publishing long lists of "missing persons."

See Hannah Arendt, *Vor Antisemitismus ist man nur noch auf dem Monde sicher: Beiträge für die deutsch-jüdischen Emigrantenzeitung "Aufbau," 1941–1945*, ed. Marie Luise Knott (Munich: Piper, 2000).

Baeck, Leo (1873–1956) A rabbi and scholar, Baeck held a number of prominent positions within German Jewish organizations during the interwar era. After the Nazis' rise to power, Baeck served as president of the central German Jewish body, which was replaced in early 1939 with the Gestapo-controlled Reichsvereinigung der Juden in Deutschland. Baeck intervened repeatedly with the Gestapo for the release or emigration of Jews and was deported to Theresienstadt in late January 1943, where he played an important, though largely informal role in the ghetto community. He survived the war, emigrated to London, and continued his political, religious, and educational endeavors until his death. In 1955, an institute for the study of German Jewish history was created in his name, with branches in London, New York, and Jerusalem.

See Beate Meyer, "Between Self-Assertion and Forced Collaboration: The Reich Association of Jews in Germany, 1939–1945," in *Jewish Life in Nazi Germany: Dilemmas and Responses*, ed. Francis R. Nicosia and David Scrase (New York: Berghahn Books, 2010), 149–69.

Barlas, Chaim (1898–1957) Born in Lithuania, Barlas was director of the Palestine office of the Jewish Agency in Warsaw from 1919 to 1925, director of the agency's Immigration Department from 1926 to 1948, and its representative in Geneva (1939–1940) and Istanbul (1940–1945). After the establishment of Israel, he became a high official in the Ministry of Immigration (1948–1949). He died in Israel.

See Dina Porat, *The Blue and the Yellow Stars of David: The Zionist Leadership in Palestine and the Holocaust, 1939–1945* (Cambridge, MA: Harvard University Press, 1990).

Blum, Léon (1872–1950) Blum served as leader of the French Section of the Workers' International and prime minister of France (1936–1937 and in 1938) in the government led by the Popular Front, a left-wing coalition. As the first Jewish prime minister of France, and in a time of domestic and international turmoil to boot, Blum was the object of considerable controversy. In 1942 the Vichy regime charged him with treason, but the trial was soon dropped, and Blum was deported to a concentration camp in Germany, where he was liberated in 1945. After the end of the war, he returned to France and resumed his political activities.

See Joel Colton, *Léon Blum: Humanist in Politics* (Cambridge, MA: Massachusetts Institute of Technology Press, 1974).

Bohemia and Moravia see Protectorate of Bohemia and Moravia

Bund, Bundism, the Bund (General Jewish Workers' Alliance; Yiddish: Algemeyner yiddisher arbeter bund) The Bund was founded in the last decade of the nineteenth century as a Jewish Socialist movement in the Russian Empire. Combining many strains of Jewish secular and progressive thought, the Bund advocated Marxist-inflected socialism and stood for Jewish secular society in eastern Europe, a society encompassed not by any particular territory but, rather, based on Yiddish culture with Yiddish as the Jewish national tongue. In the interwar period, the Bolsheviks suppressed the Bund, but the organization continued to operate in newly independent Poland. As Yiddish-speaking Jewish society was annihilated in the Holocaust, the Bund receded to the political margins after World War II.

See Zvi Gitelman, ed., *The Emergence of Modern Jewish Politics: Bundism and Zionism in Eastern Europe* (Pittsburgh, PA: University of Pittsburgh Press, 2003).

CENTOS (Central Office of the Union of Societies for Care of Orphans and Abandoned Children; Polish: Centrala Związku Towarzystw Opieki nad Sierotami i Dziećmi Opuszczonymi) Founded in 1924, CENTOS was the central Jewish organization in Poland for the care of children and orphans. After the Nazi invasion in 1939, CENTOS incorporated into its structure many previously independent Jewish care institutions and was one of several organizations to implement AJJDC-financed relief efforts in occupied Poland. CENTOS ran a network of boarding houses and orphanages, the best known of which was Janusz Korczak's orphanage in the Warsaw ghetto.

See Barbara Engelking and Jacek Leociak, *The Warsaw Ghetto: A Guide to the Perished City* (New Haven, CT: Yale University Press, 2009).

Central Consistory, Consistoire Central (Central Consistory of French Jews; French: Consistoire Central Israélite de France) Founded by Napoleon in 1808, the Consistory was the central council of Jewish congregations throughout France, as well as the official representative body of French Jewry as a whole. Responsible for managing religious infrastructure and serving as a conduit between state officials and the Jewish community, the Consistory played a prominent role in public life both before and after the German invasion of 1940. Following the installation of the Vichy regime, the Consistory transferred its base of operations to Lyon. It decried Vichy's introduction of discriminatory measures in October 1940 and June 1941, focusing its efforts on assisting French-born Jews.

See Renée Poznanski, *Jews in France during World War II* (Hanover, NH: University Press of New England in association with the USHMM, 2001).

Cohn, Willy (1888–1941) Born in Breslau, Lower Silesia, Cohn was a historian, educator, and veteran of World War I. After losing his teaching position in Breslau in April 1933, Cohn undertook numerous research projects on German Jewish history while maintaining his extensive diary commentaries. On November 21, 1941, Cohn, his wife, Trudi, and two of their daughters were deported to Kovno in German-occupied Lithuania and murdered upon arrival.

See Willy Cohn, *Kein Recht, Nirgends. Tagebuch vom Untergang des Breslauer Judentums, 1933–1941*, ed. Norbert Conrads. Vol. 1 (Cologne: Böhlau Verlag, 2007).

Coordinating Commission of Jewish Aid and Civic Societies (Coordinating Commission, or KK; Yiddish: Koordinir komisiye fun yidishe hilf- un sotsiale gezel-shaftn) This ad hoc body was formed by Jewish relief organizations in Warsaw in the first days of the German invasion of Poland in September 1939, with a goal of coordinating Jewish relief efforts in the new circumstances. The body was led by Michał Weichert and Emanuel Ringelblum, two men with a central role in the network of Jewish self-help initiatives that included Aleynhilf and Jewish Social Self-Help.

See Samuel D. Kassow, *Who Will Write Our History? Emanuel Ringelblum, the Warsaw Ghetto, and the Oyneg Shabes Archive* (Bloomington: Indiana University Press, 2007).

Czerniaków, Adam (1880–1942) An engineer from Warsaw and member of the Polish National Assembly in the interwar period, Czerniaków was appointed head of the Warsaw *Judenrat* by the Nazis in October 1939. As leader of the Jewish institution whose task was to assist the Nazis in their ultimately murderous anti-Jewish policies, Czerniaków did his best to prevent, delay, or assuage Nazi orders pertaining to the Jews in the Warsaw ghetto. When he finally realized that the imminent large-scale deportations to Treblinka in July 1942 meant death, he committed suicide rather than assist the Nazis. The diary Czerniaków kept until his death remains one of the best-known accounts of life in the Warsaw ghetto.

See Raul Hilberg, Stanislaw Staron, and Josef Kermisz, eds., *The Warsaw Diary of Adam Czerniakow: Prelude to Doom* (Chicago: Ivan R. Dee in association with the USHMM, 1999).

Eichmann, Adolf (1906–1962) Raised in the Austrian city of Linz, Eichmann joined the Nazi Party and the SS in Austria in 1932 before he moved to Germany, where he also joined Reinhard Heydrich's SD. Following the *Anschluss* of Austria, Eichmann assumed a key role as an expert for "Jewish affairs"; after the beginning of the war, he became the chief agent of Nazi anti-Jewish policies organized by the Reichssicherheitshauptamt (RSHA) that led to the deportation and systematic murder of the European Jews. Long in hiding after the war, he was finally abducted by the Israeli secret service in Argentina in May 1960 and put on trial in Jerusalem. Sentenced to death by the court, he was hanged in June 1962.

See Hans Safrian, *Eichmann's Men* (New York: Cambridge University Press in association with USHMM, 2010).

Einsatzgruppen Following the German invasion of Poland in 1939, these mobile units of the Security Police and SD headed by Reinhard Heydrich played a key role in the murder of civilians deemed inimical to the interests of the Reich. The *Einsatzgruppen* became most notorious during the German war against the Soviet Union, killing more than half a million civilians—mostly Jews—between late June and December 1941 alone.

See Jochen Böhler, Klaus-Michael Mallmann, and Jürgen Matthäus, eds., *Mass Murder in Poland, 1939: The Reports of the Einsatzgruppen* (Lanham, MD: AltaMira Press in association with the USHMM, forthcoming).

Eppstein, Paul (1901–1944) Born in Ludwigshafen, Eppstein studied sociology in Mannheim, where he was appointed lecturer in 1929. With Hitler's seizure of power in 1933, the college where he taught was shut down and Eppstein moved to Berlin. He joined the Reichsvertretung created by German Jewish representatives in 1933, which was reorganized by the Nazis into the Reichsvereinigung der Juden in Deutschland in 1939. After the arrest of its leader, Otto Hirsch, in 1940, Eppstein became de facto head of the organization. In 1943, he was deported to Theresienstadt, where he was murdered in 1944.

See Beate Meyer, "Between Self-Assertion and Forced Collaboration: The Reich Association of Jews in Germany, 1939–1945," in *Jewish Life in Nazi Germany: Dilemmas and Responses*, ed. Francis R. Nicosia and David Scrase (New York: Berghahn Books, 2010), 149–69.

Eretz Israel (Hebrew: Land of Israel) This term has scriptural and historical connotations. The Zionist movement began using it in the early twentieth century when referring to Palestine and the Jewish national home they sought to establish there; the term was also widely used by Zionist and non-Zionist Jews as synonymous with the English word "Palestine" during the British mandate. Since Israeli independence, the term *medinat Israel* (state of Israel) has been used to distinguish the state from a broader *Eretz*.

Évian Conference On President Franklin D. Roosevelt's proposal, representatives of thirty-two nations met in the French spa town of Évian between July 6 and 14, 1938, to discuss the issue of "political refugees" created by Germany's anti-Jewish policies. Because none of the participating governments was willing to accept an increased number of immigrants and subsequent attempts to negotiate the mass emigration of Jews with Germany failed, the conference failed to alleviate the plight of refugees aggravated by the *Anschluss* and subsequent German expansion.

See Richard Breitman and Alan M. Kraut, *American Refugee Policy and European Jewry, 1933–1945* (Bloomington: Indiana University Press, 1987).

Forverts A Yiddish daily, *Forverts* (known in English as *Jewish Daily Forward*) was established in 1897 in New York City and subsequently became the American Yiddish daily with the largest circulation, which in its heyday reached more than 275,000.

See the *Forverts* website at www.forward.com/about/history (accessed October 7, 2010).

Frank, Hans (1900–1946) An early member of the Nazi Party in Germany and legal advisor to Hitler, Frank rose through the party hierarchy, becoming "Reichsminister without portfolio" in 1934. After the German invasion of Poland in 1939, Frank became governor-general of the Generalgouvernement, overseeing the exploitation of that country and the persecution of "enemies of the Reich," including Jews. He was captured in 1945, tried for war crimes at the International Military Tribunal at Nuremberg, and hanged in 1946.

See Christopher R. Browning with contributions by Jürgen Matthäus, *The Origins of the Final Solution: The Evolution of Nazi Jewish Policy, September 1939–March 1942* (Lincoln and Jerusalem: University of Nebraska Press and Yad Vashem, 2004).

Fürst, Paula (1894–1942) Head of the education department of the Reichsvereinigung, Fürst was in charge of maintaining schools for thousands of Jewish students who were left without state support. After the remaining schools were shut down in June 1942, Fürst was deported to the Minsk ghetto, where she was murdered.

See Martin-Heinz Ehlert, *Paula Fürst: Aus dem Leben einer jüdischen Pädagogin* (Berlin: Text Verlag, 2005).

Generalgouvernement The German Reich annexed parts of western Poland after the Nazi invasion of that country in September 1939. The remaining territory—except for eastern Poland, which the Soviet Union occupied—remained under German occupation and was known from October 1939 as the *Generalgouvernement für die besetzten polnischen Gebiete* (General Government for the Occupied Polish Territories). Hitler appointed Hans Frank as governor-general of this region, to which large numbers of Poles and Jews were subsequently expelled from the newly annexed territories. Four of the six Nazi extermination camps would be located in this area as well. After the Nazi invasion of the Soviet Union in the summer of 1941, the formerly Soviet-occupied Polish eastern Galicia was added to the Generalgouvernement.

See Jan T. Gross, *Polish Society under German Occupation: The Generalgouvernement, 1939–1944* (Princeton, NJ: Princeton University Press, 1979).

Gestapo (Secret State Police; German: Geheime Staatspolizei) As the chief executive agency charged with fighting internal "enemies of the state," the Gestapo functioned—in many respects parallel to and in competition with the SD (see Reinhard Heydrich)—as the Third Reich's main surveillance and terror instrument, first within Germany and later in the occupied territories. After 1933, the Gestapo became part of a complex apparatus of state and party police agencies and maintained special administrative offices to supervise anti-Jewish policies. The Prussian Gestapo figured most prominently among its regional branches. In 1934 the Gestapo was placed under SS chief Heinrich Himmler, in mid-1936 it became part of Reinhard Heydrich's Security Police, and in September 1939 it was merged with the SD into the Reichssicherheits-Hauptamt (RSHA), which played a key role in the persecution and murder of European Jews.

See George C. Browder, *Foundations of the Nazi Police State: The Formation of Sipo and SD* (Lexington: Kentucky University Press, 1990).

Giterman, Yitzhak (1889–1943) Giterman was director of the AJJDC in Poland on the eve of World War II and a dedicated worker for Jewish relief during the occupation of the country. Since the early 1920s, he had supported Yiddish cultural work and eventually became director of the Joint's relief in Warsaw and a mentor to Emanuel Ringelblum. In September 1939, Giterman fled to Vilna, in Lithuania, where he resumed his relief work on behalf of embattled Polish Jews. In 1940, the Nazis seized the ship to Sweden on which Giterman was traveling; he ended up back in Warsaw, where he took active part in Aleynhilf efforts. The Nazis murdered him in January 1943.

See Samuel D. Kassow, *Who Will Write Our History? Emanuel Ringelblum, the Warsaw Ghetto, and the Oyneg Shabes Archive* (Bloomington: Indiana University Press, 2007).

Goldmann, Nahum (1895–1982) Goldmann was one of the founders and a longtime president of the WJC, as well as an ardent Zionist. Born in the Russian Pale of Settlement (today's Belarus), Goldmann lived in Frankfurt from the age of six. After fleeing the Nazis, Goldmann settled in New York in 1936, where he worked with Stephen Wise on organizing the WJC. He also represented the Jewish Agency for several years. During World War II, Goldmann lived in New York, where he worked on rescuing Jews from Nazi-occupied Europe. After the war he held several important positions in international Jewish organizations, including president of the World Zionist Organization.

See Mark A. Raider, ed., *Nahum Goldmann: Statesman without a State* (Albany: State University of New York Press, 2009).

hakhsharah (pl. *hakhsharot*: Hebrew: preparation) This was a center for training and education of young Jews prior to their planned move to Palestine (*aliyah*), especially as part of the Hehalutz movement. Several German Jewish organizations within and beyond the Zionist spectrum established training farms and other facilities for the purpose of preparing youth for emigration to Palestine.

Hehalutz (Hebrew: pioneer) This association of Jewish youth aimed to train its members to settle in Palestine. Founded in 1918, it became an umbrella organization for the pioneering Zionist youth groups across Europe. At its peak between 1930 and 1935, the movement counted one hundred thousand adherents, with sixteen thousand members on *hakhsharot*. During the war, Hehalutz worked to continue its activities from its new base in Geneva.

See Hava (Wagman) Eshkoli, "The Founding and Activity of the Hehalutz-Histradrut Rescue Center in Geneva, 1939–1942," *YVS* 20 (1990): 161–210.

Heydrich, Reinhard (1904–1942) Involved with *völkisch* circles since the early 1920s, in 1931 Heydrich received a commission from SS chief Heinrich Himmler to create a secret service (Sicherheitsdienst, or SD) for the Nazi Party, which he headed until his death. In the fall of 1939, Heydrich merged the SD with the Security Police to form the Reichssicherheitshauptamt (RSHA), the single most important agency overseeing Nazi anti-Jewish policies in Germany and the occupied territories, from ghettoization to deportation to mass murder. Heydrich died of his injuries a week after being attacked by Czech partisans in Prague.

See Mark Roseman, *The Wannsee Conference and the Final Solution: A Reconsideration* (New York: Metropolitan Books, 2002).

HICEM This Jewish aid organization was established in 1927 by a merger of three Jewish immigrant aid organizations: the U.S.-based Hebrew Sheltering and Immigrant Aid Society (HIAS), the British-based Jewish Colonization Organization (ICA or JCA), and the United Committee for Jewish Emigration. Initially based in Paris, HICEM aimed to help Jews in Nazi Germany and Nazi-controlled territories by arranging visas and passage to countries willing to accept the refugees. Following the German attack on France in 1940, HICEM relocated to New York.

See Valery Bazarov, "HIAS and HICEM in the System of Jewish Relief Organisations in Europe, 1933–41," *East European Jewish Affairs* 39, no. 1 (April 2009): 69–78.

Hilfsverein der deutschen Juden (Hilfsverein; Relief Association of German Jews) The Hilfsverein was established in 1901 to provide financial assistance and educational opportunities primarily for Jews living in eastern Europe. As the plight of German Jews worsened after Hitler's coming to power, the organization's main focus shifted toward fostering emigration. While the Jewish Agency catered to Jews trying to escape to Palestine, the Hilfsverein assisted those heading to other countries (roughly 120,000 emigrés through the end of 1938). The Gestapo-controlled Reichsvereinigung der Juden in Deutschland absorbed the organization in 1939.

See Salomon Adler-Rudel, *Jüdische Selbsthilfe unter dem Nazi-Regime 1933–1939 im Spiegel der Berichte der Reichsvertretung der Juden in Deutschland* (Tübingen: J. C. B. Mohr, 1974).

Himmler, Heinrich (1900–1945) A member of the *völkisch* movement and participant in the November 1923 Nazi putsch in Munich, Himmler was appointed by Hitler in early 1929 to become the leader (*Reichsführer*) of the SS (which until 1934 remained subordinate to the SA). After 1933 Himmler advanced rapidly from his initially small power base in Bavaria (he was police president in Munich in 1933) to become head of the Gestapo in Prussia (April 1934) and chief of the entire German police in mid-1936. During the war, Himmler further expanded his SS and police apparatus to uphold Nazi control in the Reich and in German-controlled countries and to play a key role in implementing the genocide of European Jewry.

See Richard Breitman, *The Architect of Genocide: Himmler and the Final Solution* (New York: Alfred A. Knopf, 1991).

Hirsch, Otto (1885–1941) A lawyer and former government official in the German state of Württemberg, Hirsch had long been active in German Jewish organizational life. He served as executive director of the Reichsvertretung der Deutschen Juden and later the Reichsvereinigung der Juden in Deutschland. Arrested several times (once in the summer of 1935, another time during the "*Kristallnacht*" pogroms in November 1938), Hirsch was eventually deported to the Mauthausen camp in 1941, where he died.

See Beate Meyer, "Between Self-Assertion and Forced Collaboration: The Reich Association of Jews in Germany, 1939–1945," in *Jewish Life in Nazi Germany: Dilemmas and Responses*, ed. Francis R. Nicosia and David Scrase (New York: Berghahn Books, 2010), 149–69.

Huberband, Rabbi Shimon (1909–1942) Born in Chęciny near Kielce, Huberband was a rabbi in Piotrków Trybunalski. His wife and child were killed in a German air raid in September 1939 during the Nazi invasion of Poland. Huberband returned to Piotrków Trybunalski but subsequently moved to Warsaw and eventually remarried. In Warsaw, Huberband began working with Aleynhilf, heading the organization's religious section; he also collaborated with Emanuel Ringelblum on the Oyneg Shabes archive. In August 1942, he was sent with his second wife to Treblinka, where both were murdered.

See Shimon Huberband, *Kiddush Hashem: Jewish Religious and Cultural Life in Poland during the Holocaust*, ed. Jeffrey S. Gurock and Robert S. Hirt (Hoboken, NJ: KTAV Publishing House, 1987).

Hyman, Joseph C. (1889–1949) Born in Syracuse, New York, Hyman worked for the Jewish Welfare Board during World War I. In 1922 he began his long association with the AJJDC, initially serving as an assistant to Herbert Lehman on reconstruction projects for Jews in Europe. Hyman soon rose to become secretary of the organization and was active in promoting economic development in Palestine and Jewish farm settlements in the Soviet Union, as well as in forging ties to other Jewish philanthropic projects. Beginning in the 1930s, he devoted considerable energy to developing refugee aid services and, later, relief and rescue work, first as executive director of the AJJDC and then as its executive vice chairman.

See Yehuda Bauer, *American Jewry and the Holocaust: The American Jewish Joint Distribution Committee, 1939–1945* (Detroit, MI: Wayne State University Press, 1981).

Intergovernmental Committee on [Political] Refugees An international body emerging as the only tangible result of the Évian Conference, the committee was created to negotiate for the emigration of Jews from Germany with the Nazi government. George Rublee of the United States was the first chair of the committee, succeeded in mid-February 1939 by British diplomat Sir Herbert Emerson. In February 1939, the committee discussed a plan with the Nazis aimed at the emigration of 125,000 Jews from the Reich. The plan hinged on German willingness to reach an agreement, international loans to finance the emigration, and the readiness of western countries to allow refugees in; it fell through on all three counts.

See Debórah Dwork and Robert Jan van Pelt, *Flight from the Reich: Refugee Jews, 1933–1946* (New York: W. W. Norton, 2009), 98–102; Saul Friedländer, *The Years of Persecution: Nazi Germany and the Jews, 1933–1939* (New York: HarperCollins, 1997), 314–16.

Iron Guard Founded in 1927 by Romanian nationalist Corneliu Zelea Codreanu, the well-organized, ultranationalist, and strongly antisemitic movement combined the founder's brand of Christian mysticism and revolutionary fascist ideology. The movement became strong enough to challenge the dominance of the conservative regime embodied by King Carol II. In 1938, apparently on the king's orders, Codreanu was assassinated and the state all but eliminated the Iron Guard leadership. However, in 1940, the ever-closer ties between the Romanian regime and Nazi Germany brought a joint government of Ion Antonescu (1882–1946) and the Iron Guard to power. Under the leadership of Horia Sima (1907–1993), who became deputy prime minister, the Iron Guard instigated waves of further antisemitic legislation and perpetrated pogroms and political assassinations of Jews and political opponents. In January 1941, during an unsuccessful coup, the Iron Guard went on a murderous anti-Jewish rampage in Bucharest in which more than a hundred Jews were killed. Subsequently, Antonescu successfully eliminated the organization from the government and forced its leaders into exile.

See Constantin Iordachi, "Charisma, Religion, and Ideology: Romania's Interwar Legion of the Archangel Michael," in *Ideologies and National Identities: The Case of Twentieth-Century Southeastern Europe*, ed. John R. Lampe and Mark Mazower (Budapest: Central European University Press, 2004), 19–53.

Jewish Agency for Palestine Established by the World Zionist Organization in 1921 as the Palestine Zionist Executive, this Zionist body was recognized by British authorities in Palestine as representing the Jewish community in the Mandate. In 1929, the Jewish Agency expanded to encompass non-Zionist Jewish organizations and later became a de facto Jewish self-government in Palestine. It established offices in Jerusalem, London, and Geneva to facilitate emigration to Palestine (*aliyah*) and provide representation to those Jews already there. It continued to do so until the founding of Israel in 1948. David Ben-Gurion served as head of the Jewish Agency from 1935 to 1948.

See Walter Laqueur, *A History of Zionism: From the French Revolution to the Establishment of the State of Israel* (New York: Schocken Books, 2003).

Jewish Chronicle Founded in 1841, the *Jewish Chronicle* is the oldest continuously published Jewish newspaper and has come to be regarded as the authoritative voice of British Jewry. During the Nazi period, its editorials and international news coverage documented the persecution of Germany's Jews. The newspaper continued to record the fate of the Jews abroad after war broke out—especially the plight of Polish Jewry in the first two years of the war—but the tone of editorials and news reports was muted in comparison to those following "*Kristallnacht.*"

See David Cesarani, *The Jewish Chronicle and Anglo-Jewry, 1841–1991* (New York: Cambridge University Press, 1994).

Jewish Social Self-Help (German: Jüdische Soziale Selbsthilfe, JSS) A Jewish humanitarian relief organization, JSS grew out of the Coordinating Commission, the initial gathering of Jewish humanitarian aid societies in Warsaw in the immediate wake of the Nazi invasion. Led by Michał Weichert, the organization was part of the larger Polish Jewish relief network and dedicated its work to aiding the populations of Nazi-occupied areas. In contrast to Emanuel Ringelblum's efforts in the Aleynhilf, another Jewish self-help effort confined to Warsaw that aspired to alleviate Jewish suffering in ways often at odds with official *Judenrat* policies, Weichert's JSS pursued the path of "legality" by strictly observing German regulations. Weichert moved to the Nazi "capital" of the Generalgouvernement, Kraków. From there the JSS worked to help embattled Jewish communities suffering ever more brutal Nazi occupation. The AJJDC continued to channel funds to JSS until late 1941, when the United States declared war against Germany.

See Yehuda Bauer, *American Jewry and the Holocaust: The American Jewish Joint Distribution Committee, 1939–1945* (Detroit, MI: Wayne State University Press, 1981).

Jewish Telegraphic Agency (JTA) Founded in 1914 as the Jewish Correspondence Bureau, in 1922 the JTA relocated from London to New York City and maintained news bureaus in Paris, Prague, Berlin, and Warsaw. The JTA sought from its very beginning to be a worldwide Jewish news service and since 1924 had published a daily bulletin of world news pertaining to Jewish interests. During the war and despite the closing of its offices in German-dominated countries, the JTA reported regularly on German anti-Jewish measures.

See the organization's website at www.jta.org/about/history (accessed October 15, 2010).

Judenrat (pl. *Judenräte*; German: Jewish Council) Partly triggered by Heydrich's September 21, 1939, order and partly based on initiatives by local German administrators, the aftermath of the German attack on Poland saw the establishment of Nazi-appointed Jewish administrative councils, or *Judenräte*. The councils were designed to execute the policies of Nazi occupation authorities (in German-occupied Poland and, later, in the Soviet Union) vis-à-vis the Jewish communities. As many Jewish leaders had fled the Nazi invasion of Poland, the Nazis appointed people (almost exclusively men) to the councils whom they expected to act authoritatively. *Judenrat* leaders were faced with the impossible task of attempting to alleviate Jewish suffering while fulfilling murderous Nazi demands: for example, calculating exact numbers of Jews available for forced labor, raising enormous amounts of money as "contributions" (in effect, ransoms) to the Nazis, and delivering people to be "resettled." The dilemma confronting the *Judenräte* became more irresolvable with the increasing severity of German measures; the range of responses by Jewish leaders varied widely, as exemplified by Chaim Rumkowski in Łódź and Adam Czerniaków in Warsaw.

See Isaiah Trunk, *Judenrat: The Jewish Councils in Eastern Europe under Nazi Occupation* (1972; Lincoln: University of Nebraska Press, 1996).

Jüdischer Kulturbund (Jewish Cultural Association) Formed in June 1933 as the Kulturbund deutscher Juden (Cultural Federation of German Jews), the organization quickly became the main building block for the performing arts in the Jewish sector and a venue for Jewish artists and audiences excluded from the nazified culture of the Third Reich. Under the close supervision of Joseph Goebbels's Propaganda Ministry, the Kulturbund conducted a host of theater and film performances, concerts, lectures, and other events open to members only. The Kulturbund published the only remaining Jewish periodical in Germany (*Jüdisches Nachrichtenblatt*) and was merged into the Reichsvereinigung in September 1941.

See Alan E. Steinweis, "Hans Hinkel and German Jewry, 1933–1941," *LBIYB* 38 (1993): 209–20.

Jüdisches Nachrichtenblatt After "*Kristallnacht*" the Jewish press in Nazi Germany was in effect outlawed. In its place, the Propaganda Ministry ordered the publishing of the *Jüdisches Nachrichtenblatt* in Berlin, thenceforth the only Jewish periodical allowed in Nazi Germany. Editorship and distribution were assigned to the Jüdischer Kulturbund; the editors and other staff were later subsumed by the Reichsvereinigung structure. After the *Anschluss*, the dismemberment of Czechoslovakia, and the establishment of the Protectorate of Bohemia and Moravia, similar regime-controlled newspapers were also published in Vienna and in Prague.

See Herbert Freeden, *The Jewish Press in the Third Reich* (Providence, RI: Berg, 1993).

Kaplan, Chaim A. (1880–1942?) Born in Horodyszcze in today's eastern Poland, Kaplan moved to Warsaw in 1902 and opened a Hebrew elementary school; until the end of his life, he remained a proponent of Hebrew as a modern spoken language, both through his teaching and his writings. He started keeping a diary in Hebrew in 1933; his chronicle of the outbreak of the war, the occupation, and the life and death of Warsaw's Jews is among the most insightful and poignant contemporary eyewitness accounts of the Holocaust. Kaplan and his wife probably perished in the Treblinka camp in late 1942 or early 1943.

See Chaim A. Kaplan, *Scroll of Agony: The Warsaw Diary of Chaim A. Kaplan*, ed. Abraham I. Katsh (Bloomington: Indiana University Press in association with the USHMM, 1999).

khurbn (or *churban*; Yiddish: great destruction) This word refers to the actions of the Nazis. Jews traditionally used *khurbn* to refer to the destruction of the First and Second Temples in Jerusalem in 586 BCE and 70 CE.

kibbutz (pl. kibbutzim; Hebrew: gathering) In the early twentieth century, the kibbutz was a form of collective settlement instigated by the Zionist movement in Palestine, based on ideas about shared forms of production, education, and ownership popular among reformist circles since the late nineteenth century. From that time onward, Zionist groups from the Russian Empire and central Europe had founded kibbutzim in Palestine. With increased numbers of youth making *aliyah* from Germany, the proportion of German Jews among the settlers grew in the 1930s.

See Michael Brenner, *Zionism: A Brief History* (Princeton, NJ: Markus Wiener, 2003).

Kindertransport (pl. *Kindertransporte*: children's transport) This term describes negotiations between Jewish relief organizations and the British government aimed at transporting Jewish children to Britain in the wake of *"Kristallnacht."* The first train with children left Berlin on December 1, 1938; the first transport from Vienna left nine days later. Transports from Prague were organized after the Nazi dissolution of Czechoslovakia in 1939. At their destinations, the children were placed in foster families or hostels. With the beginning of the war, the *Kindertransport* system collapsed; the last ship reached Britain from Holland in 1940. It is estimated that roughly ten thousand Jewish children found refuge in Britain and several thousand elsewhere.

See Mark J. Harris and Deborah Oppenheimer, *Into the Arms of Strangers: Stories of the Kindertransport* (London: Bloomsbury, 2000).

Kleinbaum, Moshe (1909–1972) Originally from Radzyń in Poland, Kleinbaum worked as an editor of the Yiddish daily *Haynt*. After escaping to Palestine in 1940, he soon became chief of staff of the Haganah, a post he left in 1945 for membership of the executive board of the Jewish Agency. After the establishment of Israel (where he was known as Moshe Sneh), he joined the Communist United Workers' Party and served in the Israeli assembly from its first session in 1949 through 1965.

See the Knesset website at www.knesset.gov.il/lexicon/eng/sneh_m_eng.htm (accessed September 14, 2010).

Klemperer, Victor (1881–1960) Son of a rabbi, Klemperer was a convert to Protestantism, a literary scholar, and a devoted diarist. From 1920 until 1935, he was a professor of Romance languages and literature at the Dresden Technical University. He survived Gestapo harassment and the war with his non-Jewish wife, eventually becoming a literature professor at the University of Dresden. His acclaimed study of language in the Third Reich, *LTI—Lingua Tertii Imperii*, first appeared in the late 1940s, and his insightful diaries of daily life under the Nazis appeared in print in the 1990s.

See Victor Klemperer, *I Will Bear Witness: A Diary of the Nazi Years, 1933–1941* (New York: Random House, 1998).

"*Kristallnacht*" (also "*Reichskristallnacht*," "Crystal Night," or "Night of Broken Glass") This is a euphemistic reference to the pogroms, arrests, and destruction of Jewish property that swept through Germany on the night of November 9 to 10, 1938. Acts of anti-Jewish violence had preceded that date, but now they escalated. The Nazi leadership staged Reich-wide pogroms to express "the German people's outrage" at the assassination of a German diplomat, Ernst vom Rath, in Paris by seventeen-year-old Herschel Grynszpan, whose parents had been deported from Germany across the Polish border in late October, together with thousands of other Jews of Polish origin. During "*Kristallnacht*," synagogues, shops, and apartments owned or occupied by Jews were destroyed; at least twenty-six thousand Jewish men were arrested and incarcerated in the Dachau, Sachsenhausen, and Buchenwald concentration camps. The official death total of ninety-one people represents only a fraction of the actual casualties. After this event, a wave of anti-Jewish regulations swept Germany and forced more German Jews to emigrate.

See Alan E. Steinweis, *Kristallnacht 1938* (Cambridge, MA: Belknap Press, 2009).

League of Nations Formed in the aftermath of World War I, the League represented an international project to prevent military confrontations and to ensure international stability through collective security. As part of the League's issuance of mandates to member countries for the purpose of administering territories ceded by Germany and Turkey, in 1920 Britain became the mandate power over Palestine. The League took an active interest in the protection of minority rights, including the civil rights of Jews, but failed to override the sovereign powers claimed by its member states. Attempts to negotiate disarmament agreements failed in the face of aggressive territorial expansion projects staged by Japan, Italy, and later Germany, all of which left the League.

See Carole Fink, *Defending the Rights of Others: The Great Powers, the Jews, and International Minority Protection, 1878–1938* (New York: Cambridge University Press, 2004).

Left Poalei Zion At the turn of the twentieth century, the ideological bridging of the gap between Zionism and Marxist socialism as exhibited in the work of Ber Borochov (1881–1917) gave birth to the Poalei Zion (Hebrew: workers of Zion) party. Founded in Kraków in 1904, it quickly spread across the Jewish communities in Austria-Hungary, the Russian Empire, and eastern European Jewish communities in the United States, Britain, and Palestine. Although a global Jewish movement, it was dominated by Polish and Russian wings: the Russian wing of the party emphasized class struggle and revolution over Zionist objectives; the Polish organization was more Zionist. In 1920, at the Vienna conference of the Second International, Poalei Zion split into right and left wings. The left wing, subsequently known as Left Poalei Zion, advocated Jewish class struggle in the Diaspora and embraced Yiddish as a vernacular of the Polish Jewish proletariat.

See Samuel D. Kassow, "The Left Poalei Zion in Inter-War Poland," in *Yiddish and the Left: Papers of the Third Mendel Friedman International Conference on Yiddish*, ed. Gennady Estraikh and Mikhail Krutikov (Oxford: European Humanities Research Centre, 2001).

Lichtheim, Richard (1885–1963) Born in Berlin, Lichtheim was active in German and international Zionist circles and settled in Palestine with his family in 1934. During World War II, he headed the World Zionist Organization's Geneva office, also serving as the Jewish Agency's Geneva representative. Lichtheim returned to Jerusalem in 1946 and penned a number of autobiographical and historical works.

See Werner Röder and Herbert A. Strauss, eds., *Biographisches Handbuch der deutschsprachigen Emigration nach 1933*. Vol. 1 (Munich: K. G. Saur, 1999).

Lilienthal, Arthur (1899–1942?) A lawyer and Berlin judge who had long been active in Jewish affairs in Prussia, Lilienthal became a leader in the Reichsvereinigung (having played an important role in its predecessor organization, the Reichsvertretung, as well). He was deported to his death in 1942.

See Beate Meyer, "Between Self-Assertion and Forced Collaboration: The Reich Association of Jews in Germany, 1939–1945," in *Jewish Life in Nazi Germany: Dilemmas and Responses*, ed. Francis R. Nicosia and David Scrase (New York: Berghahn Books, 2010), 149–69.

Marx, Jenny (1906–1942?) Born in Mannheim, Germany, Jenny Marx was interned in the Gurs camp and eventually deported to Drancy and then Auschwitz, where she was murdered. Her mother, Ernestine (née Hess), was also sent to Gurs and died in early 1944 in Mâcon, France. Siegmund Mayer (1907–1942?), Jenny's fiancé, was deported to Gurs the same day as the Marx women and killed in Auschwitz. Max Marx, Jenny's younger brother who had emigrated to Palestine in 1933, emigrated to the United States along with his wife and two-year-old son in December 1947.

See Klemens Holz and Leonore Köhler, eds., *"Auf einmal da waren sie weg": Jüdische Spuren in Mannheim* (Mannheim: Ed. Quadrat in cooperation with the Stadtjugendamt Mannheim, 1995).

Mayer, Saly (1882–1950) Mayer was a retired lace manufacturer and head of the Union of Swiss Jewish Communities (SIG) from 1936. During his tenure, SIG joined the World Jewish Congress; in the late 1930s, Mayer was increasingly involved in negotiations with the Swiss government over its policy for admitting refugees from Nazi Germany. Mayer also volunteered as the AJJDC representative in Geneva beginning in 1940; this post became increasingly important when the United States entered the war in December 1941. Later in the war, Mayer became involved in secret negotiations to bring Jews out of Nazi-occupied countries. After the war, he continued to work for the AJJDC in Europe, providing aid to liberated concentration camp inmates.

See Hanna Zweig-Strauss, *Saly Mayer (1882–1950): Ein Retter jüdischen Lebens während des Holocaust* (Cologne: Böhlau, 2007).

Merin, Moshe (also Mojżesz or Moses; 1906–1943) In late 1939, German authorities appointed Moshe Merin, before the war a commercial broker and since early September

1939 the head of the *Judenrat* in Sosnowiec, to head the *Zentrale der Ältestenräte der jüdischen Kultusgemeinden in Ostoberschlesien* (Central Office of Jewish Councils in East Upper Silesia), a kind of a supra-*Judenrat* in the formerly Polish district of East Upper Silesia, annexed by the Reich after the beginning of the war. Merin's central office oversaw thirty-four Jewish communities in the region, encompassing roughly one hundred thousand Jews. Merin could appoint and dismiss local *Judenräte* and even represent individual communities. He believed that making the local Jewish communities an essential source of labor for the Nazis was the way to save as many Jews as possible; he opposed underground activities for this reason. While food rations and living conditions for Jews in East Upper Silesia generally were better than in the Generalgouvernement and tens of thousands of Jews in the larger ghettos were not deported until the summer of 1943, Merin's subservient compliance with German demands for forced laborers and ultimately for the sacrifice of Jewish lives earned him the bitter hostility of many Jews. Merin was himself deported to his death in Auschwitz in the summer of 1943, when the region's ghettos were liquidated.

See Philip Friedman, "The Messianic Complex of a Nazi Collaborator in a Ghetto: Moses Merin of Sosnowiec," in *Roads to Extinction: Essays on the Holocaust*, ed. Ada June Friedman (New York: Conference on Jewish Social Studies and the Jewish Publication Society of America, 1980), 353–64.

"*Mischling*" (pl. "*Mischlinge*": mixed breed) This racial category rooted in nineteenth-century biological thinking was formally introduced into the Third Reich's anti-Jewish politics with the issuing of the Nuremberg Laws. "*Mischling*" designated an individual of both non-Jewish—that is, "Aryan"—and Jewish descent; if that person's parents were married, their union would be considered a "mixed marriage" ("*Mischehe*"). The Nuremberg Laws divided "*Mischlinge*" into distinct categories and criminalized sexual contacts between "Aryans" and Jews (*Rassenschande*) in order to prevent the birth of "*Mischlinge*." In 1939, there were ninety-seven thousand "*Mischlinge*" of the first and second degrees in the Reich; there were probably about thirty thousand in the Protectorate of Bohemia and Moravia. The fate of the "*Mischlinge*" was the subject of intense yet inconclusive debate within and between Nazi Party and state agencies until the end of the war. During the war and especially in German-occupied eastern Europe, "*Mischlinge*" were to a large degree treated like Jews and targeted for murder as part of the "Final Solution."

See Beate Meyer, *"Jüdische Mischlinge": Rassenpolitik und Verfolgungserfahrung, 1933–1945* (Hamburg: Dölling und Galitz, 1999); Raul Hilberg, *The Destruction of the European Jews*, 3rd ed. Vol. 2 (New Haven, CT: Yale University Press, 2003).

Molotov-Ribbentrop Pact Named for the foreign ministers of the Soviet Union and Nazi Germany, this agreement (also called the Hitler-Stalin or Nazi-Soviet Pact), signed on August 23, 1939, was on its face a nonaggression treaty between the two countries, with each pledging neutrality if the other went to war with a third. Beyond the nonaggression pledges, a secret protocol and further revisions of the treaty outlined the Nazi and Soviet "spheres of influence" in northern and eastern Europe, allowing for the subsequent separation of Poland and the Baltic States into German- and Soviet-dominated zones. Until the Nazi invasion of the Soviet Union in June 1941, the two countries divided the areas between them in accordance with the secret protocol, with some minor corrections. The Molotov-Ribbentrop Pact allowed Hitler to invade Poland a week after its signing, the event that brought Nazi Germany into war with Britain and France and sparked the beginning of World War II.

See Gerhard L. Weinberg, *A World at Arms: A Global History of World War II* (Cambridge: Cambridge University Press, 1994).

Munich agreement This agreement signed in Munich on September 29, 1938, by Nazi Germany, Italy, Britain, and France handed over the Sudetenland to Nazi Germany in return for Hitler's guarantees of "peace" in Europe. Although the agreement directly determined the fate of Czechoslovakia, the negotiations and final agreement were conducted without its representatives. By bowing to Hitler's territorial demands in central Europe (the *Anschluss* in March 1938 and the Munich agreement in September 1938) in hopes of forestalling a European war, Britain and France followed a policy of appeasement, acquiescing to Hitler's aggression. In violation of the Munich agreement, Nazi Germany occupied the remainder of the Czech lands on March 15, 1939, and incorporated them as the Protectorate of Bohemia and Moravia; Slovakia proclaimed its independence one day previously.

See David Faber, *Munich, 1938: Appeasement and World War II* (New York: Simon and Schuster, 2008).

Nisko This town in the western part of the Lublin district in Poland was, during World War II, part of the Generalgouvernement on the San River. In October 1939, Adolf Eichmann organized transports of Jews from the newly annexed East Upper Silesia, the Protectorate of Bohemia and Moravia, and Vienna to Nisko, where the deportees were to build barracks for a large camp. The Nisko scheme was part of a larger discussion among the Nazi leadership about how to "solve" the "Jewish problem" through expulsion, effectively by creating a Jewish reservation in the far eastern reaches of the Reich. Due to problems emanating from overall Nazi plans to Germanize Poland, Heinrich Himmler stopped the transports to Nisko in early November, and the camp itself was closed in April 1940, when the surviving Jews were returned to Austria and the Protectorate.

See Christopher Browning with contributions by Jürgen Matthäus, *The Origins of the Final Solution: The Evolution of Nazi Jewish Policy, September 1939–March 1942* (Lincoln and Jerusalem: University of Nebraska Press and Yad Vashem, 2004).

Nuremberg Laws This shorthand expression is frequently used to refer to the two basic pillars of Nazi antisemitic legislation—the Reich Citizenship Law (Reichsbürgergesetz) and the Law for the Protection of German Blood and German Honor (Gesetz zum

Schutze des deutschen Blutes und der deutschen Ehre)—promulgated, together with the Reich Flag Law (Reichsflaggengesetz), on September 15, 1935, during the annual Nazi Party rally and a specially convened session of the Reichstag in Nuremberg. The first law restricted citizenship (and thus full protection under the law) to those of "German or related blood," while the second measure proscribed marriage and sexual contact between this group and Jews. Subsequent regulations defined a "Jew" as someone with at least three Jewish grandparents (according to their religious affiliation) or someone descended from two Jewish grandparents who him- or herself practiced the Jewish religion or was married to a Jew. People with two Jewish grandparents but without Jewish religious affiliations and not married to Jews came to be defined as "*Mischlinge* of the first degree" (*Mischlinge ersten Grades*); people with one Jewish grandparent were labeled "*Mischlinge* of the second degree" (*Mischlinge zweiten Grades*). As the Reich expanded, so did the scope and geographic reach of the Nuremberg Laws. In the Protectorate of Bohemia and Moravia, the Nuremberg Laws came into effect in late April 1940, while anti-Jewish regulations had been in place following the German annexation. With later clauses added to facilitate the marking, deportation, murder, and expropriation of Jews, the Nuremberg Laws formed one of the basic laws of the Third Reich until its defeat in May 1945.

See Raul Hilberg, *The Destruction of the European Jews*, 3rd ed. (New Haven, CT: Yale University Press, 2003), 1:61–78.

ORT (Organization for Rehabilitation and Training; French: Organisation Reconstruction Travail) ORT was founded as the Society for the Promotion of Trades and Agriculture among the Jews in Russia in Saint Petersburg in 1880 to assist the mass of Jews in the Pale of Settlement to acquire the skills necessary to enter the sectors of the Russian economy. In 1921, ORT became the World ORT Union, an international organization that subsequently opened branches in Europe and the Americas. Together with other Jewish organizations during World War II, ORT in France organized vocational training for Jewish children and adults to help them adjust to the new, restrictive policies of the Vichy regime as well as to forge a new morale. Apart from its work in France, ORT played an important part in the daily life of Jews living in ghettos in Nazi-occupied eastern Europe.

See Sarah Kavanaugh, *ORT, the Second World War and the Rehabilitation of Jewish Survivors* (London: Valentine Mitchell, 2008).

OSE (Children's Relief Organization; French: Œuvre de secours aux enfants) Originally a Jewish aid organization founded in 1912 in Russia to provide medical care for embattled Jewish populations, the OSE relocated to Berlin and ultimately Paris in 1933, where it focused on aiding children and otherwise helping Jews with medical care. After the fall of France in 1940, its main office moved to Montpellier in the Vichy zone, where it provided medical and social care and created a network of Jewish homes aimed at helping refugees from central Europe, as well as the growing numbers of Jewish children from the Occupied Zone—orphans and children whose parents were destitute or had been incarcerated. By late 1941, the OSE was taking care of about twelve hundred children.

See Renée Poznanski, *Jews in France during World War II* (Hanover, NH: University Press of New England in association with the USHMM, 2001).

Oyneg Shabes (Yiddish: pleasure of the Sabbath) This secret archive was started in 1940 in Warsaw by Emanuel Ringelblum and a group of his associates. The name of the archive came from the group's weekly meetings on Saturdays. A historian by training and a fervent community organizer, Ringelblum conceptualized the archive as both a vital source for future historians interested in exploring Jewish society under unprecedented persecution and a way to strengthen the community in peril, an integral part of Aleynhilf and unarmed resistance efforts in the Warsaw ghetto. Ringelblum's collection project was sweeping: a network of his associates brought together documents and artifacts, recorded testimonies and eyewitness accounts, and wrote diaries, essays, poetry, and other texts, creating a collection that ranged from restaurant menus and tram tickets to eyewitness accounts of mass murder and essays on the Nazi annihilation assault. As it became clear that the ghetto was going to be liquidated, the activists of Oyneg Shabes buried their archival collections in metal containers. After the war, ten metal containers and two milk cans containing about twenty-five thousand documents were dug out of the ruins of Warsaw; a third cache of documents was never found. Of the dozens of Oyneg Shabes activists, only three survived the war.

See Samuel D. Kassow, *Who Will Write Our History? Emanuel Ringelblum, the Warsaw Ghetto, and the Oyneg Shabes Archive* (Bloomington: Indiana University Press, 2007).

Pétain, Marshal Henri-Philippe (1856–1951) Following the German occupation of the northern part of France and the Atlantic coastline in the west, in June 1940 the eighty-four-year-old World War I hero Pétain was appointed head of the *État français*, a collaborationist government in the resort town of Vichy, in the southern part of the country, which Nazi Germany did not occupy. While formally maintaining neutrality, Pétain ordered French forces in the colonies to fight on the side of the Axis and accommodated the economic demands of Nazi Germany. A staunchly collaborationist armed militia was also established on his watch, which hunted down Communists, Jews, and other "undesirables." Pétain's government strove to restore what it perceived as French honor in the face of national defeat; it also denaturalized foreign-born Jews and instituted anti-Jewish legislation and internment camps for Jews, many of whom German agencies deported to their death. In November 1942, in response to the Allied landing in North Africa, Nazi Germany occupied the French southern zone; thenceforth, Pétain played a largely ceremonial role. After the war, he was put on trial and sentenced to death, but his sentence was commuted to life in prison.

See Robert O. Paxton, *Vichy France: Old Guard and New Order, 1940–1944* (New York: Columbia University Press, 2001).

Protectorate of Bohemia and Moravia Hitler proclaimed this Czechoslovakian territory, mostly encompassing the historically Czech lands of Bohemia and Moravia, a German "protectorate" on March 16, 1939. Following the Munich agreement, which allowed the Reich to annex the Sudetenland, German policy further destabilized Czechoslovakia by encouraging Slovak secessionism. After Slovakia proclaimed independence under the aegis of the Nazis on March 14, 1939, Hitler pressured Czechoslovak president Emil Hácha into accepting the Nazi occupation and the proclamation of the Protectorate. Hácha nominally remained president, but Hitler appointed a German *Reichsprotektor* to administer the Protectorate. The Czech economy was forced into the service of the German war machine; antisemitic agitation and anti-Jewish measures, including confiscation of property and deportations to Nisko, followed.

See Livia Rothkirchen, *The Jews of Bohemia and Moravia: Facing the Holocaust* (Lincoln and Jerusalem: University of Nebraska Press and Yad Vashem, 2005).

Reichskommissar für die Festigung deutschen Volkstums (RKFDV; Reich commissioner for the strengthening of Germandom) On October 7, 1939, Hitler appointed Heinrich Himmler Reich commissioner for the strengthening of Germandom with the remit to resettle ethnic Germans from abroad in the newly annexed territories and to eradicate the "inimical influence" of non-German groups threatening the Reich. Subsequently, RKFDV agencies played an important role in the redrawing of the ethnographic map of German-dominated Europe. Through April 1941, in addition to the resettlement of ethnic Germans from the east in the newly annexed Polish territories, about half a million people—mostly Poles (among them, at least sixty-three thousand Jews)—were pushed out of these areas.

See Robert Koehl, *RKFDV: German Resettlement and Population Policy, 1939–1945: A History of the Reich Commission for the Strengthening of Germandom* (Cambridge, MA: Harvard University Press, 1957).

Reichssicherheitshauptamt (RSHA; Reich Security Main Office) Established by Heinrich Himmler on September 27, 1939, the Reich Security Main Office merged the SS intelligence service (Sicherheitsdienst, or SD) and the Security Police (comprising the Gestapo and the Criminal Police) into one office, creating a powerful Nazi intelligence and police structure. Under the leadership of Reinhard Heydrich, the RSHA was in charge of a wide range of tasks crucial to the Third Reich's criminal policies and assumed a critical role in the planning and implementation of the mass murder of the Jews.

See Michael Wildt, *An Uncompromising Generation: The Nazi Leadership of the Reich Security Main Office* (Madison: University of Wisconsin Press, 2009).

Reichsvereinigung der Juden in Deutschland (Reichsvereinigung; Reich Association of Jews in Germany) Formally installed in July 1939 and overseen by the Gestapo, the Reichsvereinigung succeeded the German Jewish umbrella organization, the Reichsvertretung der Deutschen Juden (Reich Representation of German Jews). While the new body intensified the Reichsvertretung's search for organized mass emigration and inherited many of its key officials—including Leo Baeck and Otto Hirsch—who could not or would not leave the country for a safe haven, the Reichsvereinigung over time became a tool for the administration, control, and ultimate deportation of Jews in Germany. Large-scale deportations of German Jews "to the East" began in November 1941; once the Reichsvereinigung had served the purpose set by the regime, it was dissolved in 1943 and its staff deported.

See Beate Meyer, "The Inevitable Dilemma: The Reich Association (Reichsvereinigung) of Jews in Germany, the Deportations, and the Jews Who Went Underground," in *On Germans and Jews under the Nazi Regime: Essays by Three Generations of Historians*, ed. Moshe Zimmermann (Jerusalem: Hebrew University Magnes Press, 2006), 297–312.

Reichszentrale für jüdische Auswanderung (Reich Central Office for Jewish Emigration) This Gestapo-run central agency for Jewish emigration was established on January 24, 1939, in Berlin for the purpose of streamlining and expediting Jewish emigration from the Reich. Modeled on the office created by Adolf Eichmann in Vienna after the *Anschluss*, the Reichszentrale simplified Jewish emigration by bringing together the various state agencies involved in the process. Subsequently, similar offices were opened in Prague, in the Protectorate of Bohemia and Moravia, and following the German occupation of the Netherlands in 1940, in Amsterdam.

See Raul Hilberg, *The Destruction of the European Jews*, 3rd ed. Vol. 2 (New Haven, CT: Yale University Press, 2003).

RELICO (Relief Committee for the War Stricken Jewish Population) This Jewish relief organization was established in Geneva in the fall of 1939 by Abraham Silberschein as part of the WJC. Originally, the primary functions of the committee were to assist in the search for missing persons and to provide material aid to Jewish refugees. In December 1939 RELICO received permission to send parcels of food, medicine, and clothing to Jewish communities in occupied Poland. As Nazi anti-Jewish policies intensified in scope and level of persecution, RELICO increasingly became involved with rescue, working to obtain temporary residence permits for refugees and helping them to leave Europe. Because of the committee's large network of contacts, RELICO officials had access to a wide spectrum of information about the development of the Nazi genocide and were involved in breaking the news about the German death camps.

See Raya Cohen, "The Lost Honour of the Bystanders? The Case of Jewish Emissaries in Switzerland," in *"Bystanders" to the Holocaust: A Re-evaluation*, ed. David Cesarani and Paul Levine (London: Frank Cass, 2002), 146–70.

Riegner, Gerhart (1911–2002) A lawyer born in Berlin, Riegner left Germany after Hitler's rise to power and began a long association with the WJC, serving first as a legal officer for the organization, then from 1939 as director of its office in Geneva. In that crucial location, he could obtain extensive information about the plight of Jews in occupied Europe and publicize their persecution. In an August 8, 1942, telegram directed to Jewish leaders—Stephen Wise in the United States and Sidney Silverman, a British MP—he famously spelled out the Nazi plan for killing millions of Jews in eastern Europe. After the war, Riegner worked for human rights under the auspices of various initiatives associated with the United Nations, and he continued his work for the WJC, rising to the post of secretary-general (1965–1983).

See Walter Laqueur and Richard Breitman, *Breaking the Silence: The German Who Exposed the Final Solution* (Hanover, NH: University Press of New England, 1994); Gerhart M. Riegner, *Never Despair: Sixty Years in the Service of the Jewish People and the Cause of Human Rights* (Chicago: Ivan R. Dee in association with USHMM, 2006).

Ringelblum, Emanuel (1900–1944) A Polish Jewish historian born in Buczacz in Galicia, Ringelblum arrived in Warsaw in 1919, where he became active in leftist Jewish politics, while simultaneously pursuing his interest in Jewish history. In the same period, he also became involved with the AJJDC's relief work in Poland, a position that allowed him to gain community-organizing experience. In October 1938, when Nazis expelled thousands of Polish Jews across the German border, Ringelblum and Yitzhak Giterman, both working on behalf of AJJDC's Warsaw office, were the first to organize humanitarian aid for the refugees stranded near the town of Zbąszyń. With the outbreak of the war and the German occupation of Poland, Ringelblum used his organizing experience and his connections at the Joint to coordinate a loose network of social organizations in Warsaw to help Polish Jewry both materially and spiritually. This effort became known as Aleynhilf (self-help); Ringelblum headed its influential Public Sector. As the Nazi persecution of the Jews assumed ever-worse proportions, Ringelblum organized a ghettowide effort in Warsaw, code-named Oyneg Shabes, to document Jewish life and society under the Nazi genocidal onslaught. Ringelblum was killed in 1944, along with his family.

See Samuel D. Kassow, *Who Will Write Our History? Emanuel Ringelblum, the Warsaw Ghetto, and the Oyneg Shabes Archive* (Bloomington: Indiana University Press, 2007).

Rumkowski, Mordechai Chaim (1877–1944) A businessman and an orphanage director from Łódź, Rumkowski was appointed *Judenältester* (eldest of the Jews) by the Nazis on October 13, 1939. Rumkowski was one of the most controversial *Judenrat* heads; in a dictatorial style, he controlled every sphere of organized life in the Łódź ghetto. He believed that as long as the ghetto economy was useful to the German war effort, most Jews from Łódź would be safe from deportation. Indeed, the majority of Łódź inhabitants were spared a worse fate in the period from the spring of 1942 through the spring of 1943, when most ghettos in eastern Europe were liquidated. In the summer of 1944, together with the remaining ghetto population, Rumkowski and his family were deported to Auschwitz, where they perished.

See Isaiah Trunk, *Łódź Ghetto: A History*, ed. Robert Moses Shapiro (Bloomington: Indiana University Press in association with the USHMM, 2006).

Sephardim (adj. Sephardi; from Hebrew *sefarad*, Spain, literally, Spaniards) This term refers to Jews who identify with the traditions and customs that originated in the medieval Jewish society of the Iberian Peninsula, in Spain and Portugal. Until the end of the fifteenth century, when they were expelled from the Iberian Peninsula by royal decrees (entailing expulsion from Spain in 1492 and mass conversion in Portugal in 1497), Iberian Jewry—prominent and well-established in mainstream society—had represented the center of the Jewish social, economic, political, and cultural world. Most expellees and their descendants settled in the Balkans and other parts of the Ottoman Empire, as well as in North Africa, where they came to constitute the core of Jewish society. They also created prosperous communities in the emerging trading centers in western Europe in the early modern period (most notably in Amsterdam, London, Hamburg, and Bordeaux), as well as in the Americas and other colonies of the European imperial powers. Subsequently, however, through the long processes of mass migration, American and European Jewries have become dominated by the customs and traditions of Jews from eastern Europe, and only in the lands of the former Ottoman Empire do the Sephardim constitute the majority of the Jewish populations.

See Esther Benbassa and Aron Rodrigue, *Sephardi Jewry: A History of the Judeo-Spanish Community, 14th–20th Centuries* (Berkeley: University of California Press, 2000).

Shapira, Kalonymus Kalmish (1889–1943) A Hasidic teacher and a rabbi of Piaseczno, near Warsaw, Shapira founded one of the largest Hasidic yeshivot in Warsaw and was a traditional Hasidic leader, encouraging individual and personal spiritual experiences among his followers. At the beginning of World War II, Shapira's son was killed in the bombing of Warsaw; his daughter was later deported. He nevertheless continued ministering to the needs of the Jews in Warsaw and became one of the most important spiritual presences in the Warsaw ghetto. His teachings written in the ghetto were discovered after the war and published as *Esh kodesh* (holy fire), presenting a poignant testament to faith and courage.

See Nehemia Polen, *The Holy Fire: The Teachings of Rabbi Kalonymus Kalman Shapira, the Rebbe of the Warsaw Ghetto* (Northvale, NJ: Aronson, 1994).

Silberschein, Abraham (1882–1951) Born in Lwów (German: Lemberg, then part of the Austro-Hungarian empire; Ukrainian: Lviv), Silberschein became a Zionist during his studies at the universities in Lwów and Vienna. In interwar Poland, Silberschein was involved in leftist Zionist projects like Jewish productivization efforts and the cooperative movement; he was one of the founders of the network of Jewish credit cooperatives in Galicia. The outbreak of World War II found Silberschein in Geneva. He remained in Switzerland during the war and from there organized relief efforts for the embattled Jews of Poland.

See Raya Cohen, "The Lost Honour of the Bystanders? The Case of Jewish Emissaries in Switzerland," in *"Bystanders" to the Holocaust: A Re-evaluation*, ed. David Cesarani and Paul Levine (London: Frank Cass, 2002), 146–70.

Solmitz, Luise (née Stephan; 1889–1973) A native of Hamburg, Solmitz worked as a high school teacher and later married Friedrich Wilhelm (Fredy) Solmitz (1877–1961), an engineer and flight officer in the German army during World War I. Because Fredy was Jewish and Luise was not, the Nazi regime regarded theirs as a "mixed marriage" (*"Mischehe"*); accordingly, their daughter, Gisela (b. 1920), became labeled first as a "non-Aryan" and then, after passage of the Nuremberg Laws, as a *"Mischling* of the first degree." As a partner in a "mixed marriage" with a child who had not been brought up as a Jew, Fredy was not deported during the war. The family lived in a small villa in Hamburg's Kippingstrasse 12, where after 1939 other Hamburg Jews were forced to move in order to concentrate the remaining German Jews in "Jew houses" (*Judenhäuser*). In 1943 Gisela married a Belgian and moved to German-occupied Belgium, where she remained at the end of the war.

See Richard J. Evans, "The Diaries of Luise Solmitz," in *Sisters of Subversion: Histories of Women, Tales of Gender*, ed. Willem de Blécourt (Amsterdam: AMB Press, 2008), 207–19.

Sudetenland This area of interwar Czechoslovakia with a large ethnic German population was annexed by Nazi Germany under the stipulations of the Munich agreement in September 1938. The Sudetenland remained an integral part of the German Reich until the end of the war. After Germany's defeat, the region was returned to Czechoslovakia and its ethnic German population subsequently expelled.

See Livia Rothkirchen, *The Jews of Bohemia and Moravia: Facing the Holocaust* (Lincoln and Jerusalem: University of Nebraska Press and Yad Vashem, 2005).

Szold, Henrietta (1860–1945) A Baltimore-born teacher and journalist, Szold was a Zionist and a social activist. In 1912, she founded Hadassah, the Women's Zionist Organization of America. After World War I, Szold conducted aid and health work in Palestine, where she eventually settled. She became director of the Youth Aliyah in Palestine in the early 1930s, a program instigated by the Jewish Agency along with a German Jewish youth organization.

See Erica B. Simmons, *Hadassah and the Zionist Project* (Lanham, MD: Rowman & Littlefield, 2006).

Tarbut (Hebrew: culture, civilization) The Zionist Tarbut association in Poland was founded in 1922; its leaders organized a network of secular Jewish schools and other educational institutions—from kindergartens to teachers' seminaries—in which the language of instruction was Hebrew. In the 1934–1935 school year, the Tarbut schools enrolled 43,258 students, more than any other network of Jewish schools.

See Joseph Marcus, *Social and Political History of the Jews in Poland, 1919–1939* (Berlin: Mouton, 1983).

TOZ (Society for the Protection of the Health of the Jewish Population in Poland; Polish: Towarzystwo Ochrony Zdrowia Ludności Żydowskiej w Polsce) Founded by

Jewish doctors and philanthropists in 1922, TOZ was the central organization providing health services to Jews in need in interwar Poland. It was affiliated with OSE but in reality ran an independent network of hospitals, medical stations, and maternity and child-care clinics. It also provided sanitary supervision for Jewish schools and organized summer trips for students. In the first years of the Nazi occupation of Poland, TOZ was one of the local partner organizations of the AJJDC.

See Yehuda Bauer, *American Jewry and the Holocaust: The American Jewish Joint Distribution Committee, 1939–1945* (Detroit, MI: Wayne State University Press, 1981); Ignacy Einhorn, *Towarzystwo Ochrony Zdrowia Ludności Żydowskiej w Polsce w latach, 1921–1950* (Toruń: Wydawnictwo Adam Marszałek, 2008).

Troper, Morris C. (1892–1962) A Brooklyn-born accountant and lawyer, Troper had been active in Jewish refugee aid since 1920. From 1938 to 1942, he served as chairman of AJJDC's European Executive Council. He strove to save Jewish refugees, including passengers on the ill-fated *St. Louis* voyage to Cuba in 1939. He closed the AJJDC's Paris office in June 1940, just hours before the Germans entered the city, and moved the organization's European headquarters to Lisbon. From 1942 to 1948 he worked on fiscal policy in the U.S. Army, rising from colonel to brigadier general in the Finance Reserve Corps.

See Henry Friedlander and Sybil Milton, eds., *Archives of the Holocaust: An International Collection of Selected Documents* (New York: Garland Publishing, 1995), 10/1:xx.

Twenty-First Zionist Congress Held in Geneva from August 16 to 26, 1939, on the eve of the Nazi invasion of Poland, this congress of the Zionist movement was characterized by a somber tone and debates about possible changes of policy in light of the British White Paper issued several months earlier. Although British policy was condemned officially and despite passionate speeches arguing for illegal immigration and confrontation with Britain, participants decided that the movement's leadership headed by Chaim Weizmann should stay in power, given the impending war.

See Walter Laqueur, *A History of Zionism: From the French Revolution to the Establishment of the State of Israel* (New York: Schocken Books, 2003).

Vichy (also Vichy regime or Vichy France; official name in French: *État français*, the "French state") This refers to the French government between the collapse of the Third Republic in July 1940 and the country's liberation from German occupation in August 1944. After France's defeat by Nazi Germany in 1940, a new government was created, which organized its seat in the French spa town of Vichy, in the Unoccupied Zone in southern France. Although it formally had jurisdiction over the entire French territory, in reality its laws were applicable in the Occupied Zone only to the extent that they did not contradict the German occupation administration. Led by Marshal Pétain, the Vichy regime rejected the progressive ideals of the French Revolution and the French republican tradition and anchored its values in the motto "Travail, Famille,

Patrie" (work, family, fatherland), rather than the "Liberté, Égalité, Fraternité" (freedom, equality, brotherhood) of the French Revolution. The Vichy regime was defeated along with its Nazi protector; its leaders fled in front of Allied forces liberating France in the summer of 1944 and organized a "government-in-exile" in Germany, until that country's final defeat in the spring of 1945.

See Robert O. Paxton, *Vichy France: Old Guard and New Order, 1940–1944* (New York: Columbia University Press, 2001)

Warthegau (also Reichsgau Wartheland) A Nazi German administrative unit in the Polish territory annexed after the invasion of Poland in 1939, Warthegau was a crucial territory in the initial Nazi population policy, when hundreds of thousands of people, mostly Poles, were expelled to the Generalgouvernement to make room for ethnic Germans resettled there from the east.

See Christopher R. Browning with contributions by Jürgen Matthäus, *The Origins of the Final Solution: The Evolution of Nazi Jewish Policy, September 1939–March 1942* (Lincoln and Jerusalem: University of Nebraska Press and Yad Vashem, 2004); Martin Dean, ed., *The United States Holocaust Memorial Museum Encyclopedia of Camps and Ghettos, 1933–1945*, vol. 2: *Ghettos in German-Occupied Eastern Europe* (Bloomington: Indiana University Press in association with the USHMM, 2011).

Wehrmacht This refers to the armed forces of Nazi Germany, consisting of the army, navy, and air force, subordinated to Hitler as commander in chief. The Wehrmacht had already committed grave crimes in the war against Poland in the fall of 1939, but in the German campaign against the Soviet Union starting in June 1941, it participated in the mass murder of Jews, Soviet civilians, and Soviet prisoners of war.

See Wolfram Wette, *The Wehrmacht: History, Myth, Reality* (Cambridge, MA: Harvard University Press, 2006).

Weichert, Michał (Michael) (1890–1967) Born in Podhajce, in eastern Galicia, Weichert gained renown in the interwar period as director of the Yiddish Experimental Young Theater in Warsaw. During the war, he headed the Nazi-controlled, Kraków-based Jewish Social Self-Help, the "official" Jewish aid organization in the Generalgouvernement. Having survived the war, he was put on trial in Poland for collaboration with the Nazis, was acquitted, and settled in Israel in 1958.

See David Engel, "Who Is a Collaborator? The Trials of Michał Weichert," in *The Jews in Poland*, ed. Sławomir Kapralski. Vol. 2 (Kraków: Judaica Foundation and the Center for Jewish Culture, 1999), 339–70.

Weizmann, Chaim (1874–1952) Born in what is today Belarus, Weizmann studied chemistry in Germany and Switzerland. He eventually settled in Britain, where he taught at the University of Manchester. He became important in the Zionist movement and later played a key role in the negotiations around the Balfour Declaration issued in

1917, in which Britain pledged its support for a Jewish "national home" in Palestine. He presided over the World Zionist Organization during the 1920s, then again from 1935 to 1946, and went on to become the first president of Israel.

See Walter Laqueur, *A History of Zionism: From the French Revolution to the Establishment of the State of Israel* (New York: Schocken Books, 2003).

Weltsch, Robert (1891–1982) A leading German Zionist, Weltsch became chief editor of the *Jüdische Rundschau*, the official newspaper of the Zionistische Vereinigung für Deutschland, after World War I until its dissolution in the wake of "*Kristallnacht*." A prolific writer and journalist, he published his best-known editorial in early 1933, "Tragt ihn mit Stolz, den Gelben Fleck" (wear the yellow badge with pride), in response to the Nazi anti-Jewish call for a boycott on April 1. Weltsch emigrated first to Palestine, where he started a new German-language newspaper (*Jüdische Welt-Rundschau*). After the war, Weltsch went to England and helped found the Leo Baeck Institute in 1955, for which he edited the *Leo Baeck Institute Yearbook*, as well as numerous anthologies. He spent his final years in Israel.

See Christian Wiese, "The Janus Face of Nationalism: The Ambivalence of Robert Weltsch and Hans Kohn," *LBIYB* 51 (2006): 103–30.

White Paper On May 17, 1939, the British government issued the so-called White Paper outlining its new policy on Palestine. Effectively reversing its commitment to a "national home for the Jewish people" there, as stipulated in the 1917 Balfour Declaration, the British now envisioned limiting Jewish immigration and land-purchasing rights and establishing a state with majority (Palestinian Arab) rule in the near future.

See Benny Morris, *Righteous Victims: A History of the Zionist-Arab Conflict, 1881–2001* (New York: Vintage, 2001); Walter Laqueur and Barry Rubin, eds., *The Israel-Arab Reader: A Documentary History of the Middle East Conflict* (New York: Penguin, 2008), 44–50.

Wise, Stephen Samuel (1874–1949) A Hungarian-born Reform rabbi in New York City, an American Zionist leader, and a delegate at the Second Zionist Congress in Basel, Switzerland, in 1898, Wise was also the founder and long-time leader of the American Jewish Congress and in 1936 became founding president of World Jewish Congress. Wise forged a number of relationships with key American policy makers, particularly within the Franklin Delano Roosevelt administration. Beyond Jewish politics, Wise took an active role in a wide range of progressive projects: he was one of the founders of the National Association for the Advancement of Colored People (1909) and the American Civil Liberties Union (1920). In the 1930s, Wise orchestrated efforts to boycott Nazi Germany and alert the general American public about Nazi crimes. During World War II, Wise lobbied for an increase in the number of Jewish refugees allowed into the United States and helped publicize the mass murder of the Jews taking place in Europe; his efforts have nevertheless drawn criticism from postwar generations as timid and insufficient.

See Gulie Ne'eman Arad, *America, Its Jews, and the Rise of Nazism* (Bloomington: Indiana University Press, 2000); Richard Breitman and Alan M. Kraut, *American Refugee Policy and European Jewry, 1933–1945* (Bloomington: Indiana University Press, 1987).

World Jewish Congress (WJC) The WJC was founded in 1936 by Stephen Wise and Nahum Goldmann with the aim of representing Jewish interests internationally. WJC headquarters were located in Paris; the organization's efforts in the 1930s focused on the deteriorating situation of German and, with the outbreak of World War II, European Jews. WJC staff worked to fight antisemitism and to organize economic aid and other relief for Jewish populations, as well as rescue and advocacy efforts. With the outbreak of the war, WJC moved its central office to Geneva, then in 1940 to New York City. After the war, WJC became very active in efforts to rebuild European Jewish communities: it assisted Holocaust survivors and advocated for substantial restitution and reparation payments from West Germany in particular.

See Institute of Jewish Affairs of the World Jewish Congress, *Unity in Dispersion: A History of the World Jewish Congress*, 2nd rev. ed. (New York: Institute of Jewish Affairs of the World Jewish Congress, 1948); Richard Breitman and Alan M. Kraut, *American Refugee Policy and European Jewry, 1933–1945* (Bloomington: Indiana University Press, 1987).

Yishuv (Hebrew: settlement) Originally used by Zionist settlers in Palestine in the late nineteenth century, the term refers to Jewish society in Palestine before Israeli statehood in 1948.

YIVO (Jewish Scientific Institute; Yiddish: Yidisher Visnshaftlekher Institut) Founded in 1925 in Vilna (then Poland; after 1939, Lithuania) with an office in Berlin, YIVO has maintained its status as one of the most important Jewish academic institutions up to the present day. YIVO was originally structured like the national academy of a European country with research divisions for philology, history, economics, statistics, and psychology. Its main goal was the study of eastern European Jewish culture and the establishment of Yiddish as a legitimate language of Jewish scholarship. In addition to its immense publishing activity—over twenty-five hundred items appeared between 1925 and 1941—YIVO gathered significant library and archival collections documenting the history of eastern European Jewry. In 1933, after the Nazi seizure of power, the Berlin office moved to Paris; in 1940, the Vilna headquarters under the leadership of Max Weinreich, one of its founders, moved to New York, where it has continued its work until today.

See David Fishman, *The Rise of Modern Yiddish Culture* (Pittsburgh, PA: University of Pittsburgh Press, 2005).

Youth Aliyah This organization, founded in 1933 by Recha Freier, promoted the idea of German youths attending training camps in Palestine after receiving their primary school education. Despite the increase in Nazi persecution of the Jews in Germany,

Freier tried to maintain the program while Henrietta Szold undertook similar activities aimed at the emigration of Jewish youngsters from Germany and their settlement in kibbutzim in Palestine.

See Brian Amkraut, *Between Home and Homeland: Youth Aliyah from Nazi Germany* (Tuscaloosa: University of Alabama Press, 2006); Recha Freier, *Let the Children Come: The Early History of Youth Aliyah* (London: Weidenfeld and Nicolson, 1961).

Żydokomuna (Polish: literally, Jew communism) This antisemitic stereotype, which emerged in interwar Poland, perceived Communist threats as part of a larger, global Jewish conspiracy to seize power.

See Joanna B. Michlic, *Poland's Threatening Other: The Image of the Jew from 1880 to the Present* (Lincoln: University of Nebraska Press, 2006).

CHRONOLOGY

THIS CHRONOLOGY is meant to provide additional context for the sources presented in this volume. More comprehensive discussions of anti-Jewish measures in Germany and German-dominated Europe between November 1938 and the end of 1940 can be found in specialized studies of the period, such as those referenced in this volume's chapters and bibliography.[1]

LATE 1938

November 9–10, 1938: "*Kristallnacht*" The Nazi Party–instigated pogrom in Germany (including Austria, annexed to the Reich in March 1938) results in the murder of more than one hundred Jews, the mass arrest of at least twenty-six thousand Jewish men and their incarceration in prisons or concentration camps, the massive destruction of buildings and other property owned by Jews, and a wave of discriminatory measures aimed at the expropriation, emigration, and stigmatization of Jews.

November 11–13, 1938: A meeting of German government representatives chaired by **Hermann Göring**, resulting in a series of new anti-Jewish regulations calling for payment by German Jews of 1 billion Reichsmark as "compensation for damages" during "*Kristallnacht*." In addition to closing all Jewish businesses and workshops, and banning

---

1. For prior events, starting with Hitler's coming to power in 1933, see the Chronology in Jürgen Matthäus and Mark Roseman, *Jewish Responses to Persecution,* vol. 1: *1933–1938* (Lanham, MD: AltaMira Press in association with the USHMM, 2010).

Jews from public theaters, cinemas, and exhibitions, Jewish students are barred from attending universities and non-Jewish schools.

Late November 1938–February 1939: Negotiations take place between George Rublee, head of the **Intergovernmental Committee on (Political) Refugees** established at the **Évian Conference**, and German government officials to facilitate large-scale Jewish emigration from Germany (150,000 to 400,000 persons over the age of three to five years) to destinations yet to be determined.

December 2, 1938: The first *Kindertransport* from Berlin arrives in Harwich, England, with two hundred children from a Jewish orphanage destroyed during "*Kristallnacht*." The British cabinet eventually grants asylum to approximately eleven thousand Jewish children from Germany, Austria, and Czechoslovakia, without allowing their parents into Britain as well.

December 22, 1938: The Hungarian government submits a bill to parliament designed to further restrict economic and other activities by Jews in the country.

December 27, 1938: The **Nuremberg Laws** take effect in the **Sudetenland**, ceded to Germany by Czechoslovakia following the **Munich agreement** of September 29–30, 1938.

1939

January 1, 1939: German Jews who do not already have first names perceived as "Jewish" by the Nazis are formally required to adopt the middle names "Israel" or "Sarah" in all written and oral transactions on the basis of a law enacted on August 17, 1938.

January 2, 1939: The Romanian government adopts a policy of pressuring Jews in Romania to emigrate as a step toward finding a "solution to the Jewish question on an International basis."

January 24, 1939: Hermann Göring authorizes **Reinhard Heydrich** to coordinate Jewish emigration from all Reich territory by all possible means, according to procedures already established by **Adolf Eichmann** in Vienna and making use of a newly created Reich Central Office for Jewish Emigration (**Reichszentrale für jüdische Auswanderung**). That same day, a confidential German-Polish agreement takes effect by which Poland accepts five to six thousand of the women and children pushed across the border by Germany in October 1938; no agreement can be reached regarding the seven to eight thousand Jews holding Polish passports but still living in Germany.

January 30, 1939: On the sixth anniversary of his appointment as chancellor, Adolf Hitler states in a speech to the Reichstag, "Today I will once more be a prophet: if the international Jewish financiers in and outside Europe should succeed in plunging the nations once more into a world war, then the result will not be the Bolshevizing of the earth, and thus the victory of Jewry, but the annihilation of the Jewish race in Europe [*Vernichtung der jüdischen Rasse in Europa*]!"

February 7, 1939: In a speech to diplomats and members of the diplomatic corps in Germany, leading Nazi Party official Alfred Rosenberg declares that the "Jewish question" will only be solved for Germany "once the last Jew has left the territory of the Third Reich" and that "the question of a decisive emigration" has become "a world-political problem of the most acute order."

February 9, 1939: Italian Royal Law Decree No. 126 establishes a corporation for the purpose of taking over, managing, and selling "that part of the property exceeding the limits permitted to Italian nationals belonging to the Jewish race." Further limitations on Jewish ownership of property and industrial and commercial activity in Italy are subsequently enacted. On the same day, Bulgaria enacts anti-Jewish regulations that include the forced removal of six thousand Jews with foreign citizenship.

February 17, 1939: The Jewish public in Germany is informed of the replacement of its former central organization with the Reich Association of Jews in Germany (**Reichsvereinigung der Juden in Deutschland**), which is closely controlled by the regime; on July 4, 1939, the authorities officially recognize the Reichsvereinigung as the sole body responsible for "the promotion of Jewish emigration" and supervising the Jewish school and welfare system in Germany. All persons defined as Jewish under the Nuremberg Laws (with the exception of foreign nationals and Jewish female spouses in "mixed marriages" with children) are required to join the Reichsvereinigung, which until its dissolution in 1943 remains under the control of Heydrich's Security Police and SD apparatus.

February 20, 1939: The Italian Fascist Party excludes persons of "Jewish race" from membership.

February 1939: Senator Robert F. Wagner (D-NY) and Rep. Edith Nourse Rogers (R-MA) jointly propose a bill in the U.S. Congress that, in a major liberalization of the 1924 Immigration Act, would effectively permit twenty thousand German Jewish children into the United States over a two-year period. Although the hearings create widespread public attention, the bill is rejected in June due to insufficient congressional support and public opinion polls indicating a negative attitude toward increased immigration.

March 14–15, 1939: Following the Slovak government's declaration of independence from Czechoslovakia, German troops occupy the Czech lands (including the capital Prague, with more than thirty-one thousand Jewish residents and a further twenty-five thousand refugees) and establish the **Protectorate of Bohemia and Moravia**. Both Hungary and Poland benefit from the German landgrab by acquiring their own parts of Czech territory. Hitler proclaims, "Czechoslovakia has ceased to exist."

March 22, 1939: German troops occupy the region of Klaipėda (German: Memel) in Lithuania, lost by Germany after World War I.

April 1, 1939: The Spanish Civil War officially ends following the victory of Gen. Francisco Franco's Nationalist forces, heavily aided by military support from Nazi Germany and Fascist Italy, over the last Republican forces. The civil war claims an estimated 250,000 dead and forces tens of thousands of Spaniards into exile, many of whom end up in French internment camps.

April 18, 1939: The Slovak state enacts its first anti-Jewish law, defining who is a "Jew" and introducing restrictions on access to professions. More than eighty-five thousand Jews live in Slovakia.

April 27–28, 1939: Germany cancels its nonaggression pact with Poland (concluded in January 1934) and its naval agreement with Britain (concluded in June 1935).

April 30, 1939: A new German law restricts the rights of Jewish tenants (*Gesetz über die Mietverhältnisse der Juden*), providing the legal basis for the concentration of German Jews into so-called Jew houses (*Judenhäuser*).

May 4, 1939: Hungary adopts a Second Jewish Law, more radical than the first passed in May 1938; it details who is a "Jew" and spells out further restrictions on employment, civil rights, and educational opportunities for Jews in Hungary.

May 13, 1939: The German ship MS *St. Louis* sails from Hamburg bound for Havana, Cuba, with 937 people on board (most of them German Jewish refugees). After being denied admission to Cuba and the United States, the ship is forced to return to Europe on June 17, with the refugees finding haven in Belgium, the Netherlands, Britain, and France.

May 17, 1939: Great Britain issues a **White Paper** limiting Jewish migration to Palestine to fifteen thousand people per year for the next five years. Simultaneously, the British government offers to accept ten thousand Jewish children from the Reich and Czechoslovakia, while a government commission suggests the settlement of up to five thousand Jewish immigrants in British Guiana (Guyana).

July 4, 1939: The Reichsvereinigung der Juden in Deutschland is officially recognized (see entry for February 17, 1939).

July 26, 1939: Replicating the Viennese and Berlin models, Eichmann's office establishes a Central Office for Jewish Emigration in Prague for Jews living in the Protectorate of Bohemia and Moravia.

August 19, 1939: The Italian government bars entry to Italy for Jews from Germany, Poland, Hungary, and Romania (and later Slovakia). At the same time, the government begins preparations for interning all foreign Jews found in Italy or confining them to small towns, with arrests beginning in June 1940.

August 23, 1939: The governments of Germany and the Soviet Union sign a nonaggression pact, also called the **Molotov-Ribbentrop Pact**, which includes a secret protocol regarding the division of eastern Europe into German and Soviet "spheres of interest."

August 26, 1939: Due to heightened international tensions, the Twenty-First Zionist Congress closes in Geneva, Switzerland, earlier than planned.

September 1, 1939: German troops invade Poland; the Polish army is defeated within weeks. The Luftwaffe's shelling and bombing of Polish cities cause heavy casualties among the civilian population. Warsaw surrenders to the Germans on September 27–28, 1939. Subsequently, Poland is taken off the political map, with some parts of German-controlled Poland annexed to the Reich (e.g., as Reichsgau Wartheland or **Warthegau**; see Map 3, p. xiv), while others are incorporated into the **Generalgouvernement** established in October under **Hans Frank** (see entry for October 10, 1939). Among the roughly four hundred thousand Polish POWs, an estimated sixty thousand are Jews of whom twenty to twenty-five thousand perish in German captivity. In the course of the military campaign, units of the German army and the SS, particularly the *Einsatzgruppen*, commit atrocities against civilians. Of the sixteen thousand Poles executed by German units in September 1939, at least five thousand are Jewish.

September 8, 1939: Following an order by Heydrich targeting all male Jews with Polish citizenship living in Germany, police arrest roughly two thousand Jewish men for transfer to concentration camps.

September 17, 1939: The Soviet Union invades eastern Poland, with the Bug River becoming the new demarcation line for the partition of German- and Soviet-occupied Poland. After Germany and the Soviet Union agree to the final boundaries of their "spheres of interest" in Poland on September 28, 1939, approximately 2 million Polish Jews are trapped in German-occupied Poland, with the remaining 1.3 to 1.5 million under Soviet rule.

September 21, 1939: Heydrich instructs the *Einsatzgruppen* chiefs on how to deal with the Jewish population, including the establishment of Jewish Councils (*Judenräte*; sing. *Judenrat*) in Polish towns and cities.

September 23, 1939: Radios owned by Jews in Germany are confiscated.

September 27, 1939: The **Reichssicherheitshauptamt** (RSHA) is formed in Berlin, integrating the Security Police and SD under Heydrich into one bureaucratic apparatus within which Eichmann and his office coordinate anti-Jewish policies.

October 4, 1939: The German military administration of Warsaw (replaced in late October by civil administrators of the Generalgouvernement) establishes a *Judenrat* in the city. **Adam Czerniaków** is made head of the twenty-four-member Jewish Council responsible for implementing German orders for the city's roughly 360,000 Jews.

October 7, 1939: Hitler appoints Heinrich Himmler as Reich commissioner for the strengthening of Germandom (Reichskommissar für die Festigung deutschen Volkstums) in charge of the Germanization of the newly occupied areas, including the expulsion of unwanted elements among the population and the resettlement of ethnic Germans (*Volksdeutsche*) into the Reich.

October 8, 1939: Orders are issued by the German mayor of Piotrków Trybunalski (German: Petrikau), a town located in the Radom district of what will become the Generalgouvernement, to establish a Jewish ghetto, the first in German-controlled Poland. All of the roughly fifteen thousand Jews (of the fifty thousand total inhabitants) are forced to move into a dilapidated part of town by October 31.

October 10, 1939: Replacing the German military administration, the General-gouvernement under Hans Frank is officially established with Kraków (German: Krakau) as its capital.

October 13–14, 1939: **Mordechai Chaim Rumkowski** is appointed *Judenältester* (eldest of the Jews) by the German administration of the city of Łódź. The city has some 233,000 Jewish residents on the eve of the war, tens of thousands of whom flee or are deported to the Generalgouvernement in late 1939.

October 18–27, 1939: As part of the plans for a "Jewish reservation" developed by Eichmann's office, deportation transports with almost five thousand Jews from Vienna, Ostrava (in the Protectorate), and Katowice (in German-annexed East Upper Silesia) leave for **Nisko** in the Lublin district of the Generalgouvernement.

October 25, 1939: The German city administration in Włocławek (German: Leslau) in the Warthegau orders Jews to wear a yellow cloth triangle on the back of their clothes. In the following months, German local and regional administrations issue similar regulations requiring the marking of Jews.

October 26, 1939: Hans Frank introduces forced labor for all Jews between the ages of fourteen and sixty in the Generalgouvernement, forming the basis for subsequent regulations and running parallel with the ongoing expropriation and theft of Jewish property.

November 9, 1939: The city of Łódź (renamed Litzmannstadt) is incorporated into the Reich as part of the Warthegau and subsequently gets drawn into Himmler's large-scale, though mostly unsuccessful plans to force resettlement of six hundred thousand Jews and four hundred thousand Poles. In the middle of November, German authorities destroy the main synagogues in Łódź.

November 12, 1939: Based on guidelines issued by Himmler and in anticipation of the resettlement of ethnic Germans from Soviet-controlled areas, German authorities begin the deportation of Jews from the incorporated Polish territories. During the first half of December 1939, almost ninety thousand Jews are forced out of the Warthegau into the Generalgouvernement.

November 23, 1939: A decree issued by Hans Frank standardizes the marking of Jews in the Generalgouvernement. By December 1, 1939, all Jews over the age of ten residing in the Generalgouvernement must wear white armbands bearing a Star of David on their right sleeve.

November 28, 1939: Frank decrees the establishment of Jewish Councils in towns and cities of the Generalgouvernement, with details to be determined by the local and regional German authorities.

December 7, 1939: In the Dziekanka asylum in the formerly Polish province of Posen, an SS unit murders 1,172 inmates. The murder is part of a wider pattern of killings of mentally ill patients in German-dominated Poland. These massacres are conducted independently of the clandestine murder of hospital inmates in the Reich organized since the beginning of the war ("Aktion T4"), which by the summer of 1941 will have claimed the lives of an estimated seventy thousand men, women, and children.

1940

February 8, 1940: German authorities in Łódź decree the forced resettlement of the remaining 160,000 Jews into a ghetto in a small section of the city without proper sanitation or running water.

February 12, 1940: In a meeting presided over by Hermann Göring, leading members of the German regime discuss "eastern questions" (*Ostfragen*). Göring favors an "orderly emigration of Jews," as opposed to an unsystematic Jewish expulsion into the Generalgouvernement without the consent of Frank or his administrators.

February 15, 1940: More than eleven hundred Jews are deported from the east German city of Stettin into the Lublin region of the Generalgouvernement. This is the first deportation of Jews from Germany proper (*Altreich*), followed by the forced removal of roughly one hundred sixty Jews from the city of Schneidemühl in the German province of Pomerania on March 12, 1940. These deportations largely stem from local Nazi officials' initiatives, though they are also carried out against the backdrop of Himmler's plans to remove unwanted minorities from German territories. The miserable and subhuman conditions in the Lublin district led to the death of approximately 30 percent of those transported within the first six months of their arrival.

March 8, 1940: German administrators in Warsaw shelve the idea of creating a ghetto in the city, the official argument being its negative economic repercussions. While Jewish leaders around Czerniaków are successful in petitioning the Germans in this instance, the ghetto is established later that year (October 12, 1940).

March 13–14, 1940: The King-Havenner bill, designed to facilitate refugee settlement in Alaska and supported by U.S. Secretary of the Interior Harold L. Ickes, is introduced in the U.S. Congress. Facing strong opposition from nativist groups, the State Department, and Alaskans themselves, the bill ultimately dies in subcommittee.

March 23, 1940: Göring prohibits further deportations into the Generalgouvernement without his or Frank's prior approval, effectively ending the deportations to the Lublin district that had begun in October 1939.

March 26, 1940: The Warsaw American Jewish Joint Distribution Committee (AJJDC) office announces that it has been granted permission to import matzos to Warsaw for the upcoming Passover holiday. An estimated 250,000 Jews in Warsaw receive some form of Passover relief from the AJJDC in 1940.

March 27, 1940: The Warsaw Jewish Council receives German orders to begin the construction of walls around a "plague-infected area" in the Jewish residential section of Warsaw. By the beginning of June, a large part of the wall is erected.

April 8, 1940: The Wehrmacht High Command orders the exclusion of "*Mischlinge* of the first degree" from the German army, as well as husbands of Jewish or "first-degree *Mischling*" women.

April 8–11, 1940: Soviet units execute over twenty thousand Polish army officers and other prisoners, burying them in mass graves in the Katyn Forest near Smolensk in the Soviet Union.

April 9, 1940: German troops invade Denmark and Norway. At that time, roughly six thousand Danish Jews and fifteen hundred Jewish refugees reside in Denmark, and about eighteen hundred Jews live in Norway, including three hundred refugees.

April 24, 1940: Racial laws defining who is or is not a Jew or a person of "mixed blood" are officially issued in the Protectorate of Bohemia and Moravia, affecting more than ninety thousand people.

April 27, 1940: Heydrich orders the deportation of twenty-five hundred German Sinti ("Gypsies") into the Generalgouvernement. That same day, Himmler orders the creation of a concentration camp in Auschwitz in German-annexed East Upper Silesia; on April 30, SS Capt. Rudolf Höss is appointed camp commander. The first 728 Polish prisoners arrive on June 14, 1940.

May 7, 1940: Mordechai Chaim Rumkowski, head of the Łódź Jewish Council, receives the final ordinance from German authorities sealing off the Łódź ghetto. This completes a process that commenced in February 1940, confining over 160,000 people into a severely overcrowded residential area.

May 10, 1940: German troops invade the Netherlands, Belgium, Luxembourg, and France. British Prime Minister Neville Chamberlain resigns, and Winston Churchill succeeds him. The Wehrmacht overruns Luxembourg in one day; the Netherlands capitulate on May 15, and Belgium fights for eighteen days before surrendering. In Belgium, roughly 90,000 Jews fall into German hands, of which only 10 percent are Belgian citizens; 140,000 Jews live in the Netherlands, including 14,000 refugees from the Reich, while many of the 3,500 Jews in Luxembourg have fled to Belgium and France prior to the German advance.

May 26, 1940: The Allies begin evacuating over three hundred thousand British and French forces at Dunkirk in the face of the German invasion of France, ending the process by June 6. With the subsequent German advance on Paris, Chief Rabbi of France Isaïe Schwartz, the main leaders of the **Consistoire Central**, and the heads of Jewish immigrant organizations follow the departure of the French government from the capital. Nearly one hundred thousand French Jews and German Jewish refugees stream to the south of the country, many seeking to cross the frontier into Spain. Of the approximately three hundred thousand Jews in France, almost 50 percent were born outside that country.

June 6, 1940: A memorandum created in the German Foreign Office proposes several options for solving the "Jewish question," including mass deportations to Madagascar, a French colony.

June 10, 1940: Italy declares war on Great Britain and France. One month later the Italian air force launches bombing raids on targets in Tel Aviv and Haifa, killing and wounding hundreds.

June 14, 1940: German forces enter Paris.

June 15–17, 1940: In accordance with the Molotov-Ribbentrop Pact and its demarcation of German-Soviet "spheres of interest," Soviet troops occupy Estonia, Latvia, and Lithuania. These Baltic states are formally incorporated into the Soviet Union.

June 22, 1940: France signs an armistice with Germany, which provides for the German military occupation of the northern half of the country and permits the establishment of a collaborationist regime in the unoccupied south.

June 24, 1940: In a letter to Reich Foreign Minister Joachim von Ribbentrop, Heydrich requests involvement in German Foreign Office plans regarding the "solution of the Jewish question" and states that the scope of the "overall problem," with 3.25 million Jews under German rule, calls for replacing emigration with an unspecified "territorial final solution" (*territoriale Endlösung*).

June 27, 1940: Under German pressure, Romania cedes Bessarabia and northern Bukovina to the Soviet Union. The forced Romanian withdrawal triggers numerous acts of anti-Jewish violence by Romanian forces and leads thousands of Jews to flee across the border into the Soviet Union.

July 3, 1940: Eichmann summons representatives of the Reichsvereinigung as well as the Vienna and Prague Jewish communities to inform them about an "overall solution to the European Jewish question" (*Gesamtlösung der europäischen Judenfrage*) planned for after the war and affecting 4 million Jews. Eichmann demands a memo within forty-eight hours outlining how the "removal" of all Jews from the Reich can be achieved. That same day, a more concrete plan for the resettlement of all European Jews after the war to the French island of Madagascar is drafted in the German Foreign Office.

July 4, 1940: The Berlin police president reduces the time during which Jews in the city can purchase food each day to between 4:00 p.m. and 5:00 p.m.

July 10, 1940: After the fall of France in June, Marshal **Henri-Philippe Pétain**, a World War I hero, becomes head of a new French government. The government establishes its seat in the spa town of Vichy in the southern, unoccupied part of the country and adopts a reactionary program of "national renovation," replacing the republican ideals of liberty, equality, and fraternity.

July 12, 1940: Hans Frank reports to Generalgouvernement officials about plans to "transport" all Jews from the Reich, the Protectorate, and the Generalgouvernement to Madagascar immediately after the war.

July 16, 1940: Following the annexation of Alsace-Lorraine by Germany, Jews in the city of Colmar are pushed across the border into France.

July 22, 1940: The **Vichy** regime passes a law that allows the denaturalization of all persons who acquired French citizenship after 1927.

July 28, 1940: Hitler urges the Slovak leadership to adopt a more radical anti-Jewish policy. In August, the Reich appoints an "advisor on Jewish affairs" for the purpose of putting additional pressure on the Slovak government. Starting in September, a range of measures targeting Slovak Jews is enacted.

August 1940: The German air force begins its massive attacks on Britain in preparation for a ground invasion. Despite falling short of its goal of achieving air supremacy, the Blitz continues. More than forty thousand civilians are killed by the German bombing of British cities up to May 1941.

August 9, 1940: The Romanian regime passes a "Jewish statute" that revokes the citizenship of Jews, prohibits "mixed marriages," and massively restricts Jews' economic and social status; among the exceptions are World War I veterans and their wives and children.

August 16, 1940: The deadline for the sixty to eighty thousand Jews living in Kraków to leave the capital of Frank's Generalgouvernement "voluntarily" passes; after this date, with the exception of roughly fifteen thousand people holding jobs, all Jews are gradually expelled.

August 30, 1940: As part of the Second Vienna Award enforced by Germany, Romania cedes Northern Transylvania to Hungary, putting 150,000 more Jews under Hungarian control. Taking into account the prior loss of northern Bukovina and Bessarabia to the Soviet Union, Romania's Jewish population drops from 728,000 to 302,000.

September 6, 1940: Following the resignation of King Carol II of Romania, the extreme right-wing **Iron Guard** Legionnaires join **Ion Antonescu**'s military government. Anti-Jewish measures continue even after Antonescu has forced the Iron Guard into illegality in January 1941.

September 9, 1940: In Luxembourg, where roughly two thousand Jews remain, German administrators introduce anti-Jewish regulations similar to the ones existing in the Reich.

September 27, 1940: The German military administration in the occupied part of France orders the registration of Jews. That same day, Germany, Italy, and Japan sign the Tripartite Pact (Axis Berlin-Rome-Tokyo), joined in November by Slovakia, Romania, and Hungary.

October 2, 1940: German city officials in Warsaw decide to concentrate the city's Jews in a ghetto. All Jews in the city are ordered to move into the ghetto by the end of the month.

October 3, 1940: Coinciding with Rosh Hashanah, the Jewish New Year, the Vichy regime, on its own initiative, enacts the Statut des juifs (Jewish Statute), which excludes Jews from public functions and duties and defines a "Jew" as a person with three grandparents "of the Jewish race" or with two Jewish grandparents if his or her spouse is also Jewish. The law provides the basis for the subsequent marginalization of Jews in French society and the economy. Similar measures are thereafter introduced in Algeria, Morocco, and Tunisia.

October 4, 1940: The Vichy regime authorizes internment of foreign Jews in "special camps" or assigns them to reside in remote locations under police surveillance.

October 6, 1940: The German administration of the Netherlands restricts the employment and membership of Jews in public institutions.

October 7, 1940: The Bulgarian government decides to introduce a law for the "protection of the nation," which includes anti-Jewish regulations and takes effect in January 1941.

October 22, 1940: Registration of Jewish businesses in the Netherlands begins, accompanied by a more detailed definition of who is "Jewish."

October 22–23, 1940: Following orders by regional Nazi Party leaders (Gauleiter), more than sixty-five hundred Jews from southwestern Germany (Baden, Saar-Palatinate) are deported to unoccupied southern France despite protests by Vichy authorities, who intern the deportees in the Gurs camp. From October 22 until the end of January 1941, roughly 650 Luxembourg Jews are pushed over the border into Vichy-controlled territory.

October 27, 1940: In the Warthegau, 290 Jewish inmates of the Kalisz asylum are murdered using carbon monoxide.

October 28, 1940: The German military administration for Belgium and northern France orders the registration of all Jews and Jewish businesses, as well as the exclusion of Jews from public office. Forty-two thousand Jews are affected; an estimated ten thousand avoid being registered.

October 29, 1940: Following the Italian attack on Greece, British forces land in the country. Greece is only defeated by the Axis in the spring of 1941, after Germany joins its ally Italy in the military campaign.

November 15, 1940: According to a report by Heydrich, almost three hundred thousand Poles are forced out of the annexed Polish territories into the Generalgouvernement up to November 1940; in addition, Frank's fiefdom becomes the destination of six thousand Jews "resettled" from Prague, Vienna, Ostrava, and Stettin, as well as twenty-eight hundred "Gypsies." More than fifty thousand French citizens and Jews are pushed out of the annexed provinces of Alsace and Lorraine into France.

November 15–16, 1940: German authorities seal off the Warsaw ghetto, with its roughly 380,000 residents, thereby confining approximately 30 percent of the city's population to about 2.4 percent of Warsaw's total area. Tens of thousands of additional refugees are later sent to the ghetto.

December 18, 1940: Hitler signs the order for Operation Barbarossa, the German attack on the Soviet Union to be initiated by May 15, 1941. Due to the German military campaign in the Balkans, however, the attack is delayed until June 22, 1941.

INDEX

Entries that appear in boldface can be found in the Glossary. Cities and countries are listed according to the borders of 1933.

ABOUT THE AUTHORS

Alexandra Garbarini, historian, associate professor in the Department of History and chair of the Program in Jewish Studies at Williams College. She is the author of *Numbered Days: Diaries and the Holocaust* (2006).

Emil Kerenji, historian, applied research scholar at the Center for Advanced Holocaust Studies of the USHMM. His most recent publication is "Yugoslav Worlds of Hanna Lévy-Hass," in Hanna Lévy-Hass's *Diary of Bergen-Belsen* (2009).

Jan Lambertz, historian, contributing editor for the *Documenting Life and Destruction* book series at the Center for Advanced Holocaust Studies of the USHMM. Most recently she also served on the research team of the Independent Historians Commission on the Role of the German Foreign Office during National Socialism and after 1945.

Avinoam J. Patt, historian, Philip D. Feltman Professor of Modern Jewish History at the Maurice Greenberg Center for Judaic Studies at the University of Hartford. He is the author of *Finding Home and Homeland: Jewish Youth and Zionism in the Aftermath of the Holocaust* (2009).